EF

3

# THE UNKNOWN MAYHEW

# The
# UNKNOWN MAYHEW

by

EILEEN YEO and E. P. THOMPSON

PANTHEON BOOKS
A Division of Random House
New York

First American Edition

# CONTENTS

205546

5

# ILLUSTRATIONS

7

# PREFACE

Henry Mayhew published eighty-two letters in the *Morning Chronicle* between October 19th, 1849 and December 12th, 1850. These letters often occupied six full columns of the newspaper, and averaged 10,500 words each. This book can offer a selection only from this prodigious total of nearly one million words. Our task of selection was made easier by the fact that Mayhew himself drew upon a part of his material when he compiled *London Labour and the London Poor*, as we have shown in Appendix One. As a general rule we have selected material which was not reprinted by Mayhew himself in his book, although we have broken the rule on several occasions where evidence or testimonies seemed especially important to the view of a whole trade (as with some material included on the shoemakers and wood-workers) or to the development of Mayhew's own thought.

In cutting down the remaining material to manageable size, we have attempted to follow a middle road between the needs of the specialist historian or sociologist and those of Mayhew's wider reading-publics. We cut a number of statistical tables (many of which were derived from standard sources, readily available to the specialist), and, where Mayhew cited the testimonies of two or three workers in the same branch of a trade, we have chosen the most representative or most interesting. Cuts have always been indicated and when whole sections or testimonies have been cut we show this in a footnote. In addition to these cuts within sections of the work, we found it necessary to omit several entire letters or groups of letters : on the Ragged Schools, on the seamen's life on shore and in his lodging-houses, on the volume of trade in wood, and on the wood-turners. The paragraphing and the sub-titles are our own.

We wish to thank the Librarians of the British Museum, the Goldsmith's Library (London University), Guildhall Library, and the Victoria and Albert Museum, for permission to use material from their collections; Mr. Ben Weinreb for permission to reproduce an unpublished letter of Mayhew's in his possession; Professor John Bradley and Mr. Stephen Yeo for reading and criticising the text, in part or whole; Mrs. Pamela James and Mrs. Joan Robson who helped to prepare the manuscript for the Press; and the score or more of our friends and colleagues who have patiently answered enquiries and given us information.

Early reports on our research, some parts of which have been incorporated into the two introductory essays, first appeared in *The Victorian Poor* (Victorian Society, London, 1967); "The Political Education of Henry Mayhew", *Victorian Studies*, XI, September 1967; and the *Bulletin of the Society for the Study of Labour History*, XVI, Spring 1968. Our thanks are due to the editors of these publications.

E.P.T.
E.Y.

# MAYHEW AND THE
## *MORNING CHRONICLE*

E. P. THOMPSON

"Do you read the *Morning Chronicle*?" Douglas Jerrold asked Mrs. Cowden Clarke in February 1850 :

> Do you devour those marvellous revelations of the inferno of misery, of wretchedness, that is smouldering under our feet? We live in a mockery of Christianity that, with the thought of its hypocrisy, makes me sick. We know nothing of this terrible life that is about us—us, in our smug respectability. To read of the sufferings of one class, and the avarice, the tyranny, the pocket cannibalism of the other, makes one almost wonder that the world should go on, that the misery and wretchedness of the earth are not, by an Almighty fiat, ended. And when we see the spires of pleasant churches pointing to Heaven, and are told—paying thousands to Bishops for the glad intelligence—that we are Christians! the cant of this country is enough to poison the atmosphere.

"I send you the *Chronicle* of yesterday", he continued :

> You will therein read what I think you will agree to be one of the most beautiful records of the nobility of the poor; of those whom our jaunty legislators know nothing; of the things made in the statesman's mind to be taxed—not venerated.[1] I am very proud to say that these papers of Labour and the Poor were projected by Henry Mayhew, who married my girl. For comprehensiveness of purpose and minuteness of detail they have never been approached. He will cut his name deep.[2]

This should not be read only as the tribute of a fond father-in-law. From December 1849 until February 1850, the months at which public interest in the series was at its peak, the *Morning Chronicle* survey of "Labour and the Poor" seized public interest in a way which has scarcely ever been equalled in British journalism. It was claimed at the time, by one of its participants, to be "unquestionably

[1] Jerrold sent Mrs. Clarke Letter 37 (the first letter on the toymakers), see below p. 280.
[2] Charles and Mary Cowden Clarke, *Recollections of Writers* (1878), pp. 290–1 : Walter Jerrold, *Douglas Jerrold* (1914), pp. 529–30.

11

the greatest, most original, and expensive project ever attempted
by one single newspaper"[3] and it is difficult to know where to turn
for a comparison. Nor could any newspaper (or television producer) of the present time contemplate initiating so extensive a
survey.

Mayhew did, in some sense, "cut his name deep". Those parts
of his London letters which he later re-arranged and (with fresh
material) published as *London Labour and the London Poor* (1861-2)
have been quoted, selected, and re-printed ever since. But he out-
lived his fame by a quarter of a century, and only the most taciturn
obituaries signalled his death in 1887. He was the subject of no
biography and there is something like a conspiracy of silence about
him in some of the reminiscences and biographies of his contemporaries. His marriage with Jane Jerrold seems to have been an
uneasy one, which may explain the scanty references to him by
members of that family. He was ousted, early on, from his co-
editorship of *Punch*, and members of the increasingly-conservative
*Punch* table, under Mark Lemon and Shirley Brooks, made a
deliberate and malicious attempt to excise him from the official
history. In writing about Mayhew one is always conscious that—
apart from the brightly-illuminated years 1849–51—the greater
part of the man is in shadow.[4]

Born in 1812, the son of Joshua, a substantial London solicitor,
he was sent to Westminster School (a school-fellow was Thomas
Arnold), and ran away at the age of fifteen, in indignation at the
headmaster's intention of flogging him for revising his Greek
grammar in the Abbey service. (His revision had been to such effect
that it had brought him, in one week-end, from the bottom to the
top of his form's examinations—an anecdote which illustrates both
his indolence and his capacity for concentration.)[5] His father sent
him to sea for a year, on the India line, as a midshipman in the
"tea-service" to Calcutta, and then took him into his legal chambers.
The apprenticeship was brief and stormy; and Henry's subsequent
breach with his father was of an emotional intensity which continued
for many years, and which underlay his later rejection of "respect-

[3] Angus Bethune Reach in the "London Letter" of the *Inverness Courier*,
5 December 1850.
[4] We are not the first to have been baffled in this way. We have found
useful, for Mayhew's literary career, Angela M. Hookham's unpublished
thesis, "The Literary Career of Henry Mayhew, 1812–1817" (Birmingham
University, 1962). John L. Bradley's introduction to the World's Classics
*Selections from London Labour and the London Poor* (Oxford, 1965) is
based upon research whose thoroughness can only be appreciated by those
who have attempted to follow up the same slender biographic clues.
[5] F. H. Forsall, *Westminster School, Past and Present* (1884), pp. 329–30.

able" bourgeois property values. In 1848 he published in
Cruikshank's *Comic Almanack* a poem, "The Respectable Man",
which friends recognised as containing a portrait of Joshua :[6]

> It is said he's a tyrant at home,
> That the jewels his Wife has for show,
> Were all of them salves for some wound—
> That each diamond's heal'd up a blow;
> That his Children, on hearing his knock,
> To the top of the house always ran—
> But with ten thousand pounds at his Banker's
> He's *of course* a respectable Man.

Although Joshua granted Henry, and his brothers, an allowance
of £1 per week, this was accompanied by so much tugging at the
strings and will-shaking that it was always in hazard :

> Then he makes a fresh will ev'ry quarter—
> Or when he's a fit of "the blues"—
> Or his Wife has offended him somehow—
> Or some Son will not follow his views;
> And he threatens to leave them all beggars,
> Whene'er they come under his ban—
> He'll bequeath all his wealth to an Hospital,
> Like a highly respectable Man.

But it should be remembered that Mayhew remained, through his
twenties and perhaps his thirties, a rebel on an allowance : and the
old man's power over him was such that, even in his forties, the
unexpected presence of his father in an audience reduced him to
stage-struck confusion.[7]

There were seventeen children in the Mayhew family, and four
of his brothers found their way into some literary profession. His
elder brother, Thomas, designed also for the law, broke into radical
journalism at the time of the Reform Bill crisis. He was editor of
Henry Hetherington's *Penny Papers* and of the first months of the
*Poor Man's Guardian* (July–December 1831?) and was credited by
a critic with having begun "the property warfare", being one of the
first "to mix up such a subject with radical politics".[8] From 1832

---

[6] G. Cruikshank, *The Comic Almanack*, 2nd series, 1848, pp. 204–5; H.
Sutherland Edwards, *Personal Recollections* (1900), pp. 57–8.
[7] Willert Beale, *The Light of Other Days* (1890), I, pp. 274–5; this refers
to a performance of "Punch on the Platform" at Brighton, circa 1857. Joshua
died in 1858, leaving a complicated will with legacies to his children graded
according to his notions of respectability.
[8] *Scourge*, 31 December 1834.

to 1834 he was engaged in various ventures in cheap popular publishing, including the "Penny National Library", whose failure may have been one cause of his suicide in October 1834.[9] His brother Edward succeeded in veterinary authorship, writing standard textbooks on the care of the dog and the horse, at the same time as he served as Fine Arts critic on the *Morning Post*. His brothers Horace and Augustus—or "Gus"—were associates for many years in Henry's own easy-going literary Bohemia. Horace outlasted Henry for many years at the *Punch* table; he wrote nothing of the least significance (even, it would seem, for *Punch*), and although he liked to be teased as a "Red Republican",[10] he liked it to remain *as* a tease; reminiscences show him as a good-natured Victorian "gay dog", drinking, womanising, and exchanging self-conscious chaff which passed for wit. Gus was Henry's close friend and literary associate, joining with him ("The Brothers Mayhew") in several novels and money-spinning ventures, and sharing some of the honours of *London Labour and the London Poor*.[11]

Through the 1830s and into the 1840s Henry Mayhew's movements are not easy to chart. He was in London most of the time, engaging in various literary and dramatic ventures; but he was also in Paris for a time (where he first met Douglas Jerrold), and he was also for a year or two in retirement on the banks of the Wye.[12] It is perhaps more helpful to indicate the kinds of world that Mayhew touched upon than his exact location within them. He was connected in the 1830s with the light satirical weekly, *Figaro in London*, which had been founded by his Westminster school-fellow, Gilbert à Beckett; in the late 1830s, in partnership again with à Beckett, he took a lease on the Queen's Theatre. Some light is thrown upon à Beckett's interests when he was presented, in 1834, in the insolvent debtors' court as proprietor and editor of *Figaro in London* and

[9] For Thomas Mayhew, see Patricia Hollis, *The Pauper Press* (1970), p. 313; and her introduction to *Poor Man's Guardian* (Merlin Press reprint, 1968). Also C. H. Timperley, *Encyclopaedia of Literary and Typographical Anecdote* (1842); C. Scott and C. Howard, *Edward Leman Blanchard* (1891), I, p. 171; *Men of the Time* (1856 edition), entry on Henry Mayhew.

[10] F. C. Burnand, *Records and Reminiscences* (1917 edn.), p. 182.

[11] See below p. 60. There are pleasant reminiscences of Gus and of Edward in G. Hodder, *Memories of My Time* (1870); Gus and Horace swim in and out of Gustav L. M. Strauss, *Reminiscences of an Old Bohemian* (1883); Horace is summarized in M. H. Spielmann, *The History of "Punch"* (1895), pp. 327–9.

[12] The best sources are Athol Mayhew, *A Jorum of "Punch", with those who helped to brew it* (1895); *Men of the Time* (1856 edition); and for Paris (1835?) Walter Jerrold, *Douglas Jerrold*, Chapter VIII. Professor Bradley's introduction to the World's Classics Mayhew includes the most helpful discussion of the literary output of these years.

*The Wag;* lately joint proprietor with Thomas Lyttelton Holt of *The Evangelical Penny Magazine,* Dibdin's *Penny Trumpet, The Thief, Poor Richard's Journal,* and *The People's Penny Pictures,* and formerly proprietor of *The Terrific Penny Magazine, The Ghost, The Lover, The Gallery of Terrors,* and two auxiliary journals of *Figaro.*[13] There is a sense of *dejà vu* when Mayhew himself petitioned for bankruptcy in 1846, and was found to be involved with the same Thomas Lyttelton Holt in a short-lived railway mania sheet, the *Iron Times* (from which he had anticipated an income of £1,000 p.a. but had in fact received only £50 and four £30 bills of exchange). Mayhew was at the same time claiming that he was owed moneys by the periodicals *Era* and *Gulliver,* from *Punch,* the *Punch Almanack,* the *Prince of Wales's Primer,* the *Pocket Book,* and various ephemeral publications which (he claimed) were the joint work of himself and Mark Lemon (his former co-editor of *Punch*) but for which Lemon alone had been paid.[14]

This literary world of à Beckett and Holt, Mark Lemon and Mayhew should not be taken too seriously. The farces and burlettas are as light as thistledown, although Professor Bradley can find some merit in Mayhew's first farce, *The Wandering Minstrel* (1834). The fly-by-night journals and almanacks had little intention beyond the removal of pennies from the pockets of an expanding easily-entertained reading-public. *Figaro in London* (which Mayhew probably edited in 1836–8) was the most reputable and long-lasting of these before the birth of *Punch;* but it has very little of the attack of the Hone-Cruikshank tradition of 1815–20 (from which it is partly derived), and its social criticism is insubstantial beside a score of radical or Owenite journals of the same years, commencing with Thomas's *Poor Man's Guardian.*

Mayhew took his place in a literary bohemia, whose radical anti-establishment values were assumed. Several of his associates were, like him, literary adventurers who had dropped out of the reputable professions.[15] They dramatised their rather humdrum lives and bolstered their self-confidence by combining in various dining clubs, where eccentric display was fostered, heavy drinking reached competitive proportions (George Cruikshank, one of the

[13] Alfred Bunn, *A Word with "Punch"* (n.d.), p. 6.

[14] *The Times,* 12 February 1847; for some confirmation of Mayhew's claim against Lemon, see J. L. Bradley, op. cit. p. xxiii.

[15] Thus Shirley Brooks, the son of an architect, was articled to a solicitor, but "took to literature", serving his apprenticeship as parliamentary reporter to the *Morning Chronicle*; Percival Leigh, John Leech, and Albert Smith were all medical students before they found their way to *Punch.* And compare Charles Dickens.

most genuinely gifted and entertaining members of the circle, had still not suffered his conversion to teetotalism), and the members cultivated with painful self-esteem an aggressive verbal "wit" at which Douglas Jerrold alone excelled.[16]

It was a radical bohemia, but the character of this radicalism is not easy to define. After 1832 there is a sense of ways that are dividing—one leading through political Owenism to Chartism, the other to *Punch*. But for at least a decade metropolitan journalists of both tendencies could find common cause in hostility to orthodox political economy and to the dogmas of Poor Law Commissioners, and in ridicule of aristocracy and of the dignitaries of the Church. Some part of the radicalism of the *Punch* circle was, like some of the radicalism of the 1960s, more a matter of gesture and of style than of practice. And, as in the 1960s, satire became a means of disguising a general ambivalence of political and social stance. Hostility to the aristocracy and to bourgeois property-values, hostility to humbug, bumbledom and snobbery, the general appeal to goodness of heart : these may be taken as given in the men of the disestablished press and the popular theatre : to define these attitudes (and to recognize their strengths) we need think only of Dickens. But the stance of these writers was, nevertheless, firmly with the metropolitan professional men and lower middle-class : one reason why reform was necessary was to silence the hubbub and "fustian oratory" of the Chartist demagogues; their noise served only to distract men of goodwill from finding practical solutions to particular social evils.

The fragility of this radicalism is easy to demonstrate; it can be seen as one follows the career, in the 1840s and into the 1850s, of *Punch* or of William Makepeace Thackeray.[17] The strength of this radicalism may be seen in the work of Douglas Jerrold, who was the continuer, in a somewhat softened and sentimentalised form, of a democratic and anti-clerical tradition which was consciously derived from the radicalism of John and Leigh Hunt of the *Examiner*. It was Jerrold who gave to *Punch* both its radical attack and its "occasional gravities" in its first five years (1841–6), and who, in a famous letter to Dickens in 1846, lamented what Thackeray and Lemon were making of the journal :

---

[16] See David Massen, *Memories of London in the 'Forties* (1908), p. 218, for a comment on "Our Club" off Covent Garden, of which both Jerrold and Mayhew were members: "Its special characteristics were a perpetual brilliant chaff and repartee, a wit, a banter, a certain habit of mutual fooling. . . ."

[17] See Gordon N. Ray, *Thackeray, The Uses of Adversity* (1955), pp. 362–373, for the contest for the political direction of *Punch* between Jerrold and Thackeray, which was, of course, won by the latter by 1846.

I am convinced that the world will get tired (at least I hope so) of this eternal guffaw at all things. After all, life has something serious in it. It cannot all be a comic history of humanity. Some men would, I believe, write the Comic Sermon on the Mount.[18]

Jerrold's wit had a rasping edge, but the edge was directed always towards the "Right"—towards pomp and ceremony, towards capital punishment and militarism, towards politicians (Whig or Tory) and political economists; whereas towards the "Left" of Chartists and populist Radicals he was always able to keep up some openness of dialogue, as he did between 1846 and 1848 in *Douglas Jerrold's Weekly Newspaper*.[19] If there was a parting of the ways in radical Bohemia in the 1840s, Henry Mayhew without doubt belonged to Jerrold's graver and more deeply-committed camp : it was to Jerrold ("whom, knowing most intimately, the author has learnt to love and honour most profoundly") that Mayhew dedicated, in 1851, the first volume of *London Labour and the London Poor*.

*Punch*, during the year of Mayhew's editorship, was the journal which MacReady described as "a poor pleasantry by a set of low-mannered, ignorant, and ill-conditioned men, who rejoice in the miserable Jerrold as their captain".[20] It was only one of a dozen similar ventures with which Mayhew was associated in a decade : but it was the only one to find the right formula. Despite subsequent attempts to obscure the facts, that formula undoubtedly owed more to Mayhew than to any other man.[21] It would seem that he was ousted after a year from his editorial role not (as was sometimes later suggested) because of general indolence and incapacity, but

---

[18] Walter Jerrold, *Douglas Jerrold and "Punch"* (1910), p. 67.

[19] Harney described its politics to Engels: "Contains a good deal of 'Free Trade', and glorification of the 'League'. He is for the 'Sovereignty of the people', not defined. He is for National Education as a benefit to Universal Suffrage. He is 'not for the impracticable', and therefore dismisses as a *mischievous delusion* the doctrine of *perfect equality*. Instead he is for various 'Social improvements', 'shorter hours', 'sanitary reforms', 'small farms', 'perpetual leases', etc." *The Harney Papers* ed. F. G. Black and R. M. Black, (Assen 1969), p. 247.

[20] *The Diaries of William Charles MacReady*, ed. W. Toynbee (1912), II, p. 183; entry for 6 September 1842.

[21] Edmund Yates suggested that 95 per cent of the original formula was due to Mayhew: see Joseph Hatton, "The True Story of 'Punch' ", *London Society*, vol. 28, p. 237. M. H. Spielmann's careful examination tends to confirm this suggestion : see pp. 13, 19, 28. Mayhew himself published his own claim to have been the first editor and founder of *Punch* as early as 1849 (The Brothers Mayhew, *The Magic of Kindness* (1849), Preface); to its shame *Punch* denied this claim (apparently on the authority of Shirley Brooks) immediately after Mayhew's death, and again in its Jubilee number.

because of an erratic alternation between intense application and inattention to necessary business.[22] Whatever virtues Mayhew possessed, they were not those of an anchor man.

As *Punch* drifted away from him, so he drifted, in the mid-1840s towards both marriage and insolvency. He married Jane Matilda Jerrold in 1844,[23] moved from his lodgings in Clement's Inn to The Shrubbery, Parson's Green where he "contracted large debts for furnishing and ornamenting the premises",[24] and found himself by the end of 1846 in the Court of Bankruptcy, where Mr. Commissioner Goulburn told him that he was fortunate that his improvidence had not landed him in prison, and offered him only the temporary protection of the Court.[25] He had contracted between 1843 and 1846 debts amounting to some £2,000 and his average annual income from his multifarious literary efforts did not seem to amount to more than £400. Some of his claims against Mark Lemon, for his share in their joint productions, dated back over ten years; Mayhew had not (his counsel pleaded) "pressed the claim before, being in the habit of meeting Mr. M. Lemon daily, and not liking to raise a question of money, which might cause a rupture."

This is Henry Mayhew, then, two or three years before the *Morning Chronicle* series commenced. He was in a hole, and was trying to write himself out of it. He and his brother Gus threw several pot-boilers on the market, the best of which was something more than a pot-boiler : *The Greatest Plague of Life: or the Adventures of a Lady in Search of a Good Servant* (1847). This well-observed and deservedly successful comic novel rang the changes upon the theme of a spoilt and insensitive genteel housewife searching for impossible qualities of obsequious industry in successive truculent maids-of-all work.[26] In some respects he seems to fit perfectly a Victorian bohemian stereotype, with his counsel in the Court

[22] Thus *Punch*'s first printer described how Mayhew would often work alongside the compositor, and testified that most of the cuts in the first few volumes were worked up by artists from Mayhew's rough sketches: Spielmann, op. cit., pp. 269–70. See also R. G. G. Price, *A History of Punch* (1957), pp. 44–45, for the letter of another old printing-worker, testifying to Mayhew's activity. But Athol Mayhew (who supports these general claims) shows his father attempting at one time to co-edit *Punch* from the distance of Herne Bay: Athol Mayhew, op. cit., p. 124.

[23] J. L. Bradley, op. cit., p. xxi, discusses the slender evidence which suggests that the marriage was an uneasy one.

[24] *The Times*, 12 February 1847.

[25] Ibid., and Public Record Office, Court of Bankruptcy records, B 6/76 and B. 6/84 (July 1846), B 7/57 (November 1846).

[26] The idea seems to have been suggested by Jerrold: see "Letter I", *Punch's Complete Letter Writer, The Works of Douglas Jerrold* (1864), III, p. 454.

of Bankruptcy admitting him to be "too sanguine in his hopes, and somewhat irregular in his accounts, but those failings were almost universal among men of genius. . . ." And, in the taverns and clubs around theatre-land we catch glimpses of him "with an extraordinary mop of dark hair that sadly wanted trimming"[27] quaffing, quipping, his pockets filled with unfinished copy. There are even accounts of him, in his cheap pre-1841 lodgings in Hemming's Row (a district off Leicester Square inhabited mainly by ivory-turners and carvers) remorselessly pursuing the philosopher's stone : or, more strictly, attempting to make artificial diamonds in his landlady's best copper pans, and nearly blowing up the house in the process.[28]

There are, however, occasional jarring notes, anecdotes which do not accord with this bohemian identikit. Even in the flow of trivial comedy he could sometimes strike a more disturbing note :

"One for the pot!" he exclaimed; "What do you mean by that? How can the pot want a spoonful? . . ."

"Lord! how foolish you are, Edward! Why, of course, it's only an extra spoonful, to make it better for ourselves. . . ."

"Ah!" he returned—"I see! It's the old story over again : doing something for ourselves, and making it out as if for another. And I'm very much afraid that, in these days of excessive philanthropy, more than one-half of what is termed charity is, after all, nothing more than 'one for the pot'."[29]

He puzzled even his close associates, who sensed in him a brilliance and depth of mind at odds with his avocations. He was capable of writing with one hand a burletta and with the other a learned and philosophically cogent essay in associationist psychology.[30] It appeared to more than one of his acquaintances that, with some turn of fate, Mayhew might become a formidable philosopher or sociologist, a John Stuart Mill or a Herbert Spencer.

His remains a puzzling character and some final clue seems to be missing. He was, until 1849, less a man of accomplishment than a kind of literary and intellectual projector, whose irregularly organ-

[27] Athol Mayhew, op. cit., p. 94.

[28] Ibid., pp. 49–51; H. B. Clayton, *Notes and Queries*, 11th Series (1912), V, p. 433.

[29] *The Greatest Plague of Life*, p. 137.

[30] Henry Mayhew, "What is the Cause of Surprise? and What Connection has it with the Laws of Suggestion?", *Douglas Jerrold's Shilling Magazine*, VI (1847), pp. 547–66. This essay develops ideas in an ambitious but short-lived forray into educational philosophy: Henry Mayhew, *What to Teach, and How to Teach it; so that the child may become a good and wise man* (1842).

ized life meant that he was continually running off columns of trivia in order to catch up with his debts. His counsel's word "sanguine" is, perhaps, helpful. "A more sanguine man than my father never breathed," confirmed his son.[31] He was insufficiently aggressive, remarked another observer, and too easily put upon;[32] although Mark Lemon and other associates appear to have treated him badly, he never answered back in print. Mayhew and Dickens were well-known to each other;[33] cne wonders whether Mayhew reminded Dickens of his own father, and whether there was in his character some dash of Mr. Micawber?

In 1849 something did at length turn up. By the summer of that year it is clear that he was writing, at least occasionally, for the *Morning Chronicle*. The *Chronicle*'s Whig proprietor, Sir John Easthope, had sold it in February 1848 to a liberal-conservative or Peelite group of proprietors who included the Duke of Newcastle, the Earl of Lincoln, Sidney Herbert and A. J. Beresford Hope. The editor, John Douglas Cook, was to move on later to edit the *Saturday Review*; in 1849 he appears as an earnest Peelite, suspicious of the full orthodoxy of political economy, but moving steadily along the Gladstonian current towards Liberalism and Free Trade.[34]

The paper had, decidedly, a philanthropic and evangelical conscience; and its columns, in the summer and autumn of 1849, do not make pleasant reading. Column after column deals in detail with the causes of sanitary reform : sewerage, water supplies, the choked burial grounds of the metropolis. Even its own reporters became somewhat jaded with the fare. "We are quite bewildered", wrote Angus Reach,

> by the number and variety of the schemes propounded for model lodging-houses, for the consumption of smoke, for the extirpation of cess-pools, for the avoidance of all deleterious gases . . . for removal of intramural grave-yards, and all nauseating slaughter-houses and unwholesome manufactories.[35]

[31] Athol Mayhew, op. cit., p. 56.

[32] *Notes and Queries*, 11th Series (1912), V, pp. 317–8.

[33] They had many common friends, and in particular Jerrold. In 1845 Mayhew and Dickens took part together in a *Punch* amateur performance of *Every Man in his Humour*, Mayhew as Knowell, Dickens as Captain Bobadil: J. Hatton, "The True Story of 'Punch'," *London Society*, Vol. 29 (1876), p. 259. Harland S. Nelson has demonstrated Mayhew's influence in "Dickens's *Our Mutual Friend* and Henry Mayhew's *London Labour and the London Poor*", *Nineteenth-Century Fiction*, XX (1965), pp. 207–222.

[34] Charles Mitchell, *The Newspaper Press Directory* (3rd edn., 1851), p. 74; H. R. Fox Bourne, *English Newspapers* (1887), II, 154–5.

[35] "London Letter", *Inverness Courier*, 29 November 1849.

The summer of 1849 saw the conjunction of two events : relief at the recession of Chartism, and horror at the incidence of cholera. Within three months deaths from cholera were estimated at thirteen thousand in London, twenty thousand in the rest of the country. The tide in London reached its peak on 10 September with 432 victims recorded; on the 11th it receded to 316. In the correspondence columns of the *Chronicle* doctors and laymen debated the still-unknown means of propagation of the disease : was it zymotic, or caused by noxious miasmas, or by water? Although John Snow's classic study in epidemology arose from this debate, it was still unknown. But the district registrars' reports—published in full in the paper—seemed to lead on to inescapable conclusions. On 24 September there was published an unsigned article by Mayhew—"A Visit to the Cholera Districts of Bermondsey". "So well-known are the localities of fever and disease, that London would almost admit of being mapped out pathologically, and divided into its morbid districts and deadly cantons." Mayhew went on to describe Jacob's Island in a famous passage :

We then journeyed on to London-street, down which the tidal ditch continues its course. In No. 1 of this street the cholera first appeared seventeen years ago, and spread up it with fearful virulence; but this year it appeared at the opposite end, and ran down it with like severity. As we passed along the reeking banks of the sewer the sun shone upon a narrow slip of the water. In the bright light it appeared the colour of strong green tea, and positively looked as solid as black marble in the shadow—indeed it was more like watery mud than muddy water; and yet we were assured this was the only water the wretched inhabitants had to drink. As we gazed in horror at it, we saw drains and sewers emptying their filthy contents into it; we saw a whole tier of doorless privies in the open road, common to men and women, built over it; we heard bucket after bucket of filth splash into it, and the limbs of the vagrant boys bathing in it seemed by pure force of contrast, white as Parian marble. . . .

In this wretched place we were taken to a house where an infant lay dead of the cholera. We asked if they *really did* drink the water? The answer was, "They were obliged to drink the ditch, without they could beg a pailful or thieve a pailful of water." But have you spoken to your landlord about having it laid on for you? "Yes, sir; and he says he will do it, and do it, but we know him better than to believe him."[36]

[36] This article was later reprinted in Viscount Ingestre (ed.), *Meliora* (1852).

On 9 October 1849, the *Morning Chronicle* commented in an editorial : "The pestilence has ravaged, not our parks, squares and terraces, but the narrow courts and pent-up alleys of the metropolis." "The *primary* cause of the pestilence is to be found in the filth and squalor of the poor. . . . We, the richest nation on the face of the earth, have allowed our fellow-creatures to 'fust' in styes, reeking with filth, such as farmers, now-a-days, know that swine would pine and dwindle in. We have allowed them . . . to quench their thirst and cook their food with water poisoned with their own excretions."[37]

Historians have in recent years drawn attention to the very powerful social emotions aroused by plague, accentuating, sometimes to the point of hysteria, what is latent in class relations. The cholera epidemic in Paris in 1832 brought with it, Professor Louis Chevalier has shown, an accession of class hatred. But the social context of London in 1849 was somewhat different. England had lived through 1848 virtually unscathed : several of the Chartist leadership were in prison (where two died during the epidemic); the movement was in virtual collapse. On 18 October the *Morning Chronicle* announced the commencement of a series of articles, which would present "a full and detailed description of the moral, intellectual, material, and physical condition of the industrial poor throughout England". The first article, which appeared from Manchester on that day, commenced with a long homily : "Wonderful has been our recent escape from the fever of convulsion which fixed upon almost all Europe." But the fever referred to was, not cholera, but revolution. We should, the writer continued, show our gratitude to the people. "Because no labourer here called out 'A bas les riches', are we to persevere in calling, 'A bas les pauvres' ?"

Thus the series commenced as an effort at social reconciliation, in the aftermath of Chartism and under the impulse of an acute, temporary, and almost hysteric wave of social conscience provoked by plague. The series had been proposed by Mayhew.[38] It comprised

[37] *Morning Chronicle*, 24 September, 9 October 1849.

[38] This claim, made by both Mayhew and Jerrold, was (like the origin of *Punch*) disputed. The *Morning Chronicle* editorialized (31 October 1850) that "he was in no sense the originator of the undertaking", and Angus Reach declared (*Inverness Courier*, 14 November 1850) that "he had nothing whatever to do with the original conception of the matter". Perhaps. It is true that *The Times* pioneered the idea with its "Commissioner" in Ireland during the famine, while other foretastes of the project may be seen in Thomas Cooper's provincial surveys for *Douglas Jerrold's Weekly Newspaper* and in the "London Penetralia Series" in G. Cruikshank's short-lived *Our Own Times* (April–July 1846), a series in which Reach (and Mayhew?) took part. But the *full* scheme of the metropolitan survey very clearly was Mayhew's own.

at first three series, one article appearing daily: two each week from Mayhew, the "Special Correspondent for the Metropolis" (or, sometimes, "Metropolitan Commissioner"), two from a provincial correspondent, who toured the manufacturing and mining districts, and two from a correspondent in the rural districts. Angus Bethune Reach reported from some of the northern centres of industry, including Sheffield, and Charles Mackay covered Liverpool and Birmingham. Alexander Mackay commenced as rural correspondent, and was succeeded by Shirley Brooks, who covered the Midlands.[39] In London, Henry Mayhew was assisted by his brother Augustus among others.[40] All three series continued (although appearing somewhat less frequently) throughout 1850, and were supplemented by a series of reports on Western Europe and Russia.[41] Mayhew broke abruptly his connection with the *Morning Chronicle* in October 1850, and thereafter commenced *London Labour and the London Poor* in part-publication from his own office.[42]

Altogether it is the most impressive survey of labour and of poverty at the mid-century which exists. The surveys of provincial England are inferior to Mayhew's London, not only because the reporters lacked Mayhew's genius, but also because they were itinerant reporters whereas Mayhew was able to work systematically and to build up a cumulative picture. Nevertheless, the provincial series includes much very observant work which has for too long been neglected. Wherever the correspondents visited, their articles were the subject of earnest local discussion.[43] No doubt circulation

---

[39] See H. R. Fox Bourne, *English Newspapers* (1887), II, pp. 154–5; Charles Mackay, *Forty Years' Recollections* (1877), I. p. 154; II, pp. 151–6; Charles Mackay, *Through the Long Day* (1887), II, p. 11; Edmund Yates, *Recollections and Experiences* (1884), II, pp. 144–5, 334; William Simpson, "Two Famous Correspondents: the Reachs, Father and Son", *Inverness Courier*, 24, 27 and 31 January and 3 February 1905. Charles Mackay's investigation of the Mormon emigration through the Port of Liverpool was expanded into a book, *The Mormons* (1851).

[40] See below p. 60.

[41] Shirley Brooks was the correspondent in South Russia, Syria and Egypt, his reports being reprinted as *Russians of the South* (1854) and Angus Reach (whose reports were republished as *Claret and Olives, from the Garonne to Rhone* (1852) was the correspondent in Denmark and Southern France: see G. A. Sala, *Life and Adventures* (1895), I, p. 199; Charles Mackay, *Forty Years' Recollections*, II, pp. 152–6; E. Yates, op. cit., II, p. 145; G. S. Layard, *A Great "Punch" Editor, Being the Life . . . of Shirley Brooks* (1907); Joseph Hatton in *London Society XXX* (1877), p. 60.

[42] See below, pp. 41–44.

[43] "I have visited the penny news-rooms, the Temperance-hall, and the public tap-room," wrote a Manchester reader, "and found the subject of the letter the principal topic of criticism!", "One who has Wrought at the Loom", *Morning Chronicle*, 29 October 1849.

of the paper was also boosted, and competitors were of course ready to dismiss the entire project as a "stunt".[44] The series received editorial attention in scores of provincial newspapers, extracts were re-printed not only in the conventional press, but also in the *Northern Star*, the *Red Republican* and the *Democratic Review*, while Ledru Rollin gutted both the metropolitan and provincial series for his polemical jeremiad, *The Decline of England* (1850).[45]

Mayhew's articles moved rapidly towards their first climax—the examination of the needlewomen and (after turning aside for four letters on costermongers) the tailoring workers: both groups of workers had been investigated before Christmas, 1849.[46] The revelations about prostitution among the needlewomen were perhaps the most sensational moment of the series. It was a sensation which even the Editor of the *Morning Chronicle* may have been somewhat concerned about. When Mayhew convened a meeting of about one thousand female slop workers on 3 December (to whom he issued a mass public questionnaire)[47] there walked onto the platform—unannounced beforehand to Mayhew or to anyone else—Lord Ashley and Mr. Sidney Herbert. Mr. Mayhew might disclose, but Philanthropy would dispose. Lord Ashley announced at once and without preliminaries that "he had come to the conclusion that the only remedy for their distress was emigration". There were (as Herbert purported to show subsequently)[48] 500,000 surplus females in England and Wales and (could the hand of Providence be seen in this?) exactly 500,000 too few females in the colonies. Lord Ashley then bowed out to applause : he had to attend another meeting. The cause became known henceforth as "Mr. Sidney Herbert's Emigration Plan", and his philanthropy was applauded in successive editorials in the *Morning Chronicle* (although it was suggested that the surplus females should be "filtered" through some Magdalen institution before being sent to Australia—an image which reveals the continu-

---

[44] The *Atlas* dismissed the articles as "a mere mercantile speculation. They were simply designed to attract notice to a paper, rather put to its shifts. . . . The Commissioners were instructed to peer into the holes and corners of poverty, and to fetch from thence the most marketable facts": quoted in *Ragged School Union Magazine*, II, May 1850.

[45] The series also spurred provincial newspapers and correspondents to undertake their own investigations: among those we have noted are John Glyde, *The Moral, Social and Religious Condition of Ispwich* (Ipswich, 1850); *Inquiry into the Condition of the Poor of Newcastle-Upon-Tyne (Newcastle Chronicle*, Newcastle, 1850); "The Condition of the Working Classes of Edinburgh and Leith", the *Edinburgh News*, appearing at intervals between 25 September 1852 and 29 July 1854. See below, p. 65.

[46] See Appendix I.

[47] See *Morning Chronicle*, 4 December 1849, p. 6.

[48] Letter to the *Morning Chronicle*, 5 December 1849.

ing preoccupation with cholera). The important, often-stressed, point was that Philanthropy and Political Economy were in equation : the slop workers were poor because they were in excess of demand.[49] And with the thought that they might soon leave these shores, the half-open shutters of the middle-class conscience could again begin to close. Her Majesty the Queen and Prince Albert headed the subscription-list for the shipments—a notable scoop for the *Morning Chronicle*.[50]

At this point, in mid-December 1849, we are at an interesting point of tension. On the one hand, the *Chronicle* editorially was rolling upon its tongue such phrases as "sound political economy", "redundant labour market", and "the harvest is relatively small and the labourers are too many". "We must send them forth to a field where the harvest is more abundant".[51] But political economy (it argued) might properly be qualified by philanthropy and meliorative public reform. It called upon its readers, editorially, "to lay to heart the revelations we have made; and to perform this duty too long left unperformed—taking up the cause of the poor as that one, above all, which is divinely ordained as the noblest sacrifice of humanity. . . . We are no Christians in deed while these things go unremedied."[52]

These dangerous capitulations to sentiment were challenged in a savage series of articles in the *Economist*. The "lugubrious accounts" published in the *Chronicle* were "unthinkingly increasing the enormous funds already profusely destined to charitable purposes, adding to the number of virtual paupers, and encouraging a reliance on public sympathy for help instead of on self-exertion". The articles in the *Chronicle* :

> have given occasion to throw discredit on free trade, to cast a slur on commercial greatness, to beget doubts of the advantages of civilisation, to bring reproach upon cheapness, and excite a strong communist feeling against competition.[53]

Money subscribed to pay for the passage of emigrant slop workers would be capital withdrawn from more useful employment. Anyway, the needlewomen "deported" to Sydney or Van Diemen's Land

---

[49] "The truth is, our wealth and our population have both outgrown the narrow area of our country. We want more room." Herbert in *Morning Chronicle*, 5 December 1849.

[50] The committee of the Fund for Promoting Female Emigration included Lord John Russell, the Marquess of Westminster, four earls, two bishops, Baron Lionel de Rothschild, M.P., and Lord Ashley.

[51] *Morning Chronicle*, editorial, 11 December 1849.

[52] Ibid., editorial, 5 December 1849.

[53] *Economist*, 15 December 1849.

would be totally unfitted for the hardship of life in the outback, and would find there even less employment for their needles. The remedy? This was known to all who knew their Malthus :

The people can only help themselves. Only they can put restrictions on the increase of their numbers, and keep population on a level with capital. . . . Their fate is given into their own hands; they are responsible for their own conditions; the rich are no more responsible for their condition than they are responsible for the condition of the rich; and if they cannot help themselves, all experience demonstrates that the rich cannot help them.[54]

The *Morning Chronicle* replied editorially to the attacks of the *Economist*, hurling some insults at the purist dogmas of political economy. The editor of the *Economist* was accused of shrinking from looking poverty and misery in the face :

It is precisely this sort of moral cowardice and laziness on the part of the ruling classes, that has shaken European society and Government to its centre. If Englishmen would keep the "Communist" plague from their own shores, it is not to be done by a timid avoidance of everything like an honest inquiry into social maladies.[55]

To this there was added the ultimate utilitarian argument in defence of philanthropy :

A State provision for the poor does more to undermine the spirit of self-reliance than all our charitable institutions and benevolent schemes put together. But would the most ultra-Malthusian risk the total and immediate repeal of our Poor-law? And if not, why not? Because it would bring about a revolution.[56]

A consensus of the provincial press appeared to favour "Mr. Sidney Herbert's Emigration Plan", turning out many columns of editorial humbug from which a sample from the *Birmingham Mercury* will suffice :

Dwelling upon the notorious fact that women preponderate in England, and men in Australia, (Mr. Herbert) proposes emigration as the exact and obvious remedy for this terrible state of things, recommends the smiling shores and plentiful labour of our southern colonies as the refuge from the hard life at home, and fatal

---

[54] Ibid., 22 December 1849. *The Economist* returned to the attack in two articles on "Female Emigration" on 9th and 23rd February 1850, exposing the moral dangers to which the emigrants were subjected on ship-board.
[55] *Morning Chronicle*, editorial, 18 December 1849.
[56] Ibid., editorial, 24 December 1849.

necessity of the brothel; and urges the wealthy classes to a liberal subscription for the purpose of converting, as soon as possible, the famishing English needlewoman into the comfortable Australian matron.

The case of the needlewomen serves, indeed, as a useful litmus-paper for testing social attitudes. Gladstone, of course, gave the emigration scheme wholehearted support : the saving of falling women was a cause after his heart, and he received from Sidney Herbert detailed bulletins on progress :

> I have some difficulty in restraining the clerical members of the Committee, who are impatient, not unnaturally, to send off at once some of these poor creatures who are exposed to so much want and temptation. . . . We do not preclude ourselves from taking male emigrants when the presence of the male would keep up the family tie—a husband, a brother, or a father, for example. I think the preservation of the family tie of the first importance.[57]

Peel on the other hand, refused his support and had clearly been impressed by the arguments of the *Economist* : "I fear the consequences of the additional stimulus to the seeking of employment in London, and therefore, to the overstocking of the labour market, which vague aspirations after the lot of an emigrant, as a last or perhaps as a first resource, may administer."[58] Disraeli's comment was less ceremonious : "Sidney Herbert is in a pretty scrape," he wrote to Lord Malmesbury, "35,000 needlewomen to be deported at £15 a-piece . . . would take upwards of £600,000. He should have subscribed at least one year's income as an example, and if he succeeds in his object, which is impossible, he will do no good."[59] Carlyle, with his customary perversity, discovered a line of argument of his own :

> Shirts by the thirty-thousand are made at twopence-halfpenny each; and in the meanwhile no needlewoman, distressed or other, can be procured in London by any housewife to give, for fair wages, fair help in sewing. Ask any thrifty house-mother, high or low, and she will answer . . . No *real* needlewoman, "distressed" or other, has been found attainable in any of the houses I frequent. Imaginary needlewomen, who demand considerable wages, and have a deepish appetite for beer and viands, I hear of everywhere; but their sewing proves too often a distracted

[57] Lord Stanmore, *Sidney Herbert, a Memoir* (1906), I, p. 114.
[58] Ibid., I, p. 118.
[59] Ibid., p. 119.

puckering and botching; not sewing, only the fallacious hope of it, a fond imagination of the mind.[60]

The popular Radicals and Chartists, for whom the whole scheme was reminiscent of Botany Bay, were generally contemptuous of Herbert's scheme. George Reynolds saw it as a plan "concocted by certain aristocrats and parsons for inducing poor women to become voluntary candidates for transportation". After humiliating scrutiny of their personal and moral affairs, and medical inspection, they were to be sent off to a land of snakes and cannibals, and offered as wives to transported felons : "The doctrine of surplus population is a base, wicked, wilful lie; and it is only preached to divert men's minds from the . . . investigation into the real causes of the wide-spread pauperism, distress, and misery apparent in this country."[61] George Julian Harney, at a rally of London Chartists, declared that "he had no objection to emigration, provided the right persons were sent away—the idlers and the plunderers (Cheers). But he strongly objected to the transportation of the industrious classes."[62] The younger Christian Socialists had some sympathy with this standpoint, and proposed schemes of Home Colonization instead. But they were rebuked by their master, F. D. Maurice. "Colonization," he wrote to J. M. Ludlow (in defence of Herbert's scheme), "is not transportation; it is a brave, hearty, Saxon, Christian work."[63]

The "Metropolitan Commissioner" of the *Morning Chronicle* took no open part in this argument. But it is clear from subsequent comments that he was radically critical of Sidney Herbert's intervention, finding the cause of the degradation of the needlewomen, not in the doctrine of surplus labour, but in the conditions of slop-work and unregulated competition.[64] And it is possible to detect, from this

[60] T. Carlyle, *Latter-Day Pamphlets* (1898 edn.) pp. 27–8. Carlyle's indignation was directed, not against the needlewomen nor against the *Morning Chronicle* which he thanked ("for a service such as newspapers have seldom done") but against "the leave-alone principle" in "the universal stygian quagmire" of British industrial life—a point which the *Economist* overlooked when pressing him into service against Mayhew (16 November 1850).

[61] *Reynold's Political Instructor*, 5 January 1850: see also 12 January.

[62] *Northern Star*, 19 January 1850.

[63] F. Maurice, *Life of F. D. Maurice* (1884), II, p. 28; see also Torben Christensen, *Origin and History of Christian Socialism 1848–54* (Aarhus, 1962), pp. 125–6. Both Mansfield and Ludlow expressed publicly their reservations about Herbert's scheme.

[64] See his comment cited on p. 40 below. See also "Answers to Correspondents", No. 39, 6 September 1851; and *1851: or the Adventures of Mr. and Mrs. Sandboys* (1851), p. 78, where he ridicules Herbert and the commercial editor of the *Economist* who attribute "the extreme depression of our

time, a dissociation between the editorial columns of the paper and Mayhew's Letters. These moved on from the female slop-workers to the situation of the male piece-workers in the "dishonourable" tailoring trade. While the *Chronicle*, editorially, continued to stress an overstocked labour market, Mayhew concentrated his attention upon the evils of unregulated competition, and brought into his reports evidence from the tailoring workers such as this : "These evils, I am convinced, do not arise from over-population, but rather from over-competition."[65] Sweated conditions Mayhew now began to see as a *systematic* exploitation, a system :

> unheard of and unparalleled in the history of any country; so deep laid a scheme for the introduction and supply of underpaid labour to the market, that it is impossible for the working man not to sink and be degraded by it into the lowest depths of wretchedness and infamy.[66]

On 14 December 1849 Mayhew convened a public meeting of tailoring workers, who were to remain some of his staunchest friends. These men were understandably alarmed lest the calm eye of Philanthropy might next fall on *them*.[67] These reports and this meeting, following, upon the exposure of the conditions of the female slop-workers, finally activated the Christian Socialists, who had been from the first among Mayhew's most attentive readers.[68] "People cannot sit still under the sting of this glorious Chronicle : and they *will* do *something*," Mansfield wrote to Ludlow.[69] "Have you, or have you not, read the letters in the Morning Chronicle?" Ludlow ricocheted to Kingsley, referring in particular to Letter XVII, "describing the slavery of the journeymen tailors to the great slop-sellers :"

> If you have not, read them forthwith. If you have, tell me whether I am not right in saying that operative associations or

matrimonial markets" to "an over-production of spinsters"; also *Cruikshank's Comic Almanack*, second series (1851), pp. 330–1.
[65] See below, p. 188.
[66] See below, p. 196.
[67] For the report of the meeting, see Letter XVII below.
[68] F. J. Furnivall recalled that at the regular meeting of the group at Maurice's "the letters on 'Labour and the Poor' . . . were the subject of frequent and earnest talk. Few of us had any idea of the wide-spread misery in the workmen's homes around us, and fewer still knew how the slop-system had been at work. . . ." Ludlow insisted week after week that "we must no longer be accomplices in this state of things. We *must* get an honest middleman between us, and some working-men. . . ." *The Working-Men's College Magazine* I, (September 1860).
[69] 5 December 1849, cited in Christensen, op. cit., p. 125.

partnerships as they have in Paris *must* be set up forthwith, whilst the subject is yet fresh in people's minds. . . .[70]

Ludlow had himself already drawn extensively upon Mayhew's earlier articles for his essay, "Labour and the Poor", which, appearing in *Fraser's Magazine* in January 1850, was to set the keynote for the next three years of Christian Socialist agitation. The letters on the needlewomen and the tailors were to be central territory to which all the spokesmen of the group returned again and again. Kingsley drew upon them not only for his tract, *Cheap Clothes and Nasty*, but also for *Alton Locke*. Thomas Hughes wrote (with the habitual sonorous naiveté of the group) that Mayhew's articles revealed "a power (the slop system) all but invincible", which "seemed to have arisen before them in an instant", and "which was treading the life and soul out of the seemingly helpless carcass of English society".[71] Kingsley drew a moral even more apocalyptic :

> The continual struggle of competition . . . will depress the workmen to a point at which life will become utterly intolerable . . . the boiler will be strained to bursting pitch, till some jar, some slight crisis, suddenly directs the imprisoned forces to one point, and then—What then?
> Look at France, and see.[72]

Even Maurice was jogged out of his high-toned inertia by the zeal of his younger disciples : "Those *Morning Chronicle* letters," he wrote, "have set us all grieving, thinking, and I hope with some measure acting."[73]

The action to which Maurice referred was the establishment, early in February 1850, under the direction of the Christian Socialist brotherhood and under the superintendence of Walter Cooper, a London tailor and former Chartist, of the Working Tailor's Association—the first of a small group of experiments in co-operative production, involving tailors, needlewomen, bakers, printers, shoe-

---

[70] 17 December 1849, in ibid., p. 130.

[71] Thomas Hughes, "History of the Working Tailor's Association", *Tracts on Christian Socialism*, II (April, 1850), p. 4. Hughes also drew heavily upon Mayhew in *A Lecture on the Slop System . . . delivered at the Literary and Mechanic's Institute at Reading, on February 3rd, 1852* (Exeter, 1852).

[72] "Parson Lot", *Cheap Clothes and Nasty* (1850), p. 19. This was reprinted as No. II of *Tracts by Christian Socialists*, and also as Preface to *Alton Locke*.

[73] F. Maurice, op. cit. II, p. 35 ; see also Archdeacon Manning to Ludlow : "Mayhew's letters open up a terrific depth on which we are unconsciously reposing." N. C. Masterman, *John Malcolm Ludlow* (Cambridge, 1963), p. 126.

[74] See the accounts in C. E. Raven, *Christian Socialism, 1848–54* (1920), Ch. VI, and Christensen, op. cit, Chs. III and IV.

makers, and even pianoforte-makers.[74] Few were involved in these ventures[75] and they were of greater ideological than practical significance,[76] although they occasioned Ludlow's lively journal, *The Christian Socialist*, brought him into contact with co-operators in the North of England, and were an index of the relaxation of the intense class hostilities of Chartist years.[77] Although Walter Cooper himself clearly felt that the *Morning Chronicle* articles served as a major impulse in originating the movement,[78] Mayhew appears not to have been consulted by its projectors, nor taken into their confidence. This may have been a deliberate omission by the Christian Socialists—Maurice, in particular, was determined to maintain complete control over his little movement and to allow no outsiders into its counsels—or it may have been an expression of scepticism or antipathy on Mayhew's part. He absented himself from a very large meeting of journeymen tailors in Exeter Hall (17 January 1850), which called in general terms for Government intervention against the slop-system.[79] Two or three months later Mayhew was soliciting support for a Tailor's Guild, whose functions would be those of an ambitious friendly society, with club-house and library, saving's bank and loan office, "an office for the insurance of an uniform rate of income to the workmen throughout the 'brisk' and 'slack' seasons of the year", and a poor fund.[80] Although the Guild was declared to be, "unequivocally, neither political nor communistic", this did not prevent the *Economist* from directing more thunder at Mayhew's head, accusing him, together with the Christian Socialists, of "attempts to inoculate English society with a French disease".[81] The *British Quarterly Review* (May 1850) also saw him as part of the phenomenon of a revived British Socialism, and as "invested . . . by the popular appreciation of his services,

[75] Thus the Working Printers' Association had a nucleus of four members: J. B. Leno, *The Aftermath* (1892), pp. 44–7; C. E. Raven, op. cit., p. 208.

[76] See John Saville, "The Christian Socialists of 1848", in *Democracy and the Labour Movement* (1954).

[77] See N. Backstrom, "The Practical Side of Christian Socialism in Victorian England", *Victorian Studies*, VI, No. 4 (June 1963).

[78] W. Cooper, "History of the Working Tailors' Association", *Christian Socialist*, 19 July 1851; and Cooper's evidence before the Select Committee on Investments for the Savings of the Middle and Working Classes, *P.P* 1850 XIX, pp. 52–3, Q. 580.

[79] Mayhew was to have taken the chair, but had an "unexpected engagement"; he was also absent, in the following week, from a meeting of East End tailors. There is some suggestion that the meeting had been called by the more "honourable" employers: *Morning Chronicle*, 18 and 22 January 1850.

[80] "Recent Aspects of Socialism", *British Quarterly Review*, II, May 1850, pp. 492–.3

[81] *Economist*, 4 May 1850.

with a kind of unofficial authority or chiefship in the metropolis".

The Letters on the needlewomen and the tailors (November 1849 to January 1850) represent the peak moment of the series' impact. Mayhew's exposures, following upon the cholera, provoked a spasm of guilt and concern among the wealthy, reaching from the most August (the Queen's patronage of Female Emigration) through the most serious and alert (Ludlow in *Fraser's Magazine*)[82] to the most banal. This was provided by Martin Tupper, the poet laureate of the *lumpen-bourgeoisie*;

> O! there is much to be done, and that soon :
> Classes are standing asunder, aloof :
> Hasten, Benevolence, with the free boon,
> Falling as sunshine on Misery's roof.[83]

Yet in all this susurration of class guilt, this parade of exposed manly consciences, the thoughts of the prime actor, Henry Mayhew, remain enigmatic. It is true that his own passing references to orthodox political economy were becoming both increasingly well-informed and increasingly caustic. But, equally, his tone was becoming curt with the sentimentalists and do-gooders of the upper classes.

The row between the *Morning Chronicle* and the *Economist* had scarcely died down before Mayhew was involved in a row on his own account, but this time with Benevolence itself. The occasion lay in three letters on the Ragged Schools (of which Lord Ashley was patron and president) which appeared in March 1850. After setting forward fairly Ashley's own statements of principles and purposes, and the claims of the Ragged School Union that their philanthropy was, among other things, reforming the vagrants and delinquents of the streets and reducing crime, Mayhew quoted testimony of police officers and employers to show that no such results were being effected. He constructed close statistical tables which suggested that delinquency did not decrease through the proximity of ragged schools; if anything, it increased; and, in the one or two

[82] The distance travelled between November 1849 and January 1850 can be seen in the contrast between Ludlow's intelligent and well-written piece (J. T., "Labour and the Poor", *Fraser's Magazine*, January 1850) and a commonplace piece in *Fraser's* of November 1849 on "Work and Wages", which is a tissue of bourgeois class prejudice: married women are driven into needlework by "the misconduct and reckless extravagance of their husbands"; the working men of England are "a ragged class", "the greatest slovens in Europe", wasting their earnings "on the low indulgence of the gin-shop and the pot-house"; and their only salvation must come from "practising the unpretending virtues of cleanliness, sobriety, order, and economy, and displaying in the management of their own small affairs the same careful and anxious foresight which renders the majority of the middle class secure against destitution".

[83] Viscount Ingestre (ed.), *Meliora*, pp. 286-7.

PLATE I.  Henry Mayhew

A. Satirical—by Cruikshank, 1842

B. Sympathetic—Boys from the Field Lane School now in the Navy, 1863

PLATE II. Two Views of Ragged School Boys

cases where a decrease in the incidence of juvenile crime could be shown, it could be correlated with greater probability with slum-clearance (and the pushing of the criminal population into rookeries in other districts) than with the influence of the schools. As for the smattering of education some of the lads received, he quoted a police officer : "We are teaching the thieves to prig the articles marked at the highest figures." (Mayhew compiled other statistics to suggest that there was no direct correlation between illiteracy and delin-quency.) The industrial training offered to the children was scanty and imperfect. The most serious complaint against the schools was that the delinquents inducted the other children of the poor into their own ways, so that the schools became actual nurseries of delin-quency. Proceedings at several of the schools were ungovernable and hilarious. The boys went for a "lark" and to get warm : on a "hanging-day" the schools were nearly empty. The children terror-ized the teachers, who in certain classes dared only to give them magic lantern shows; when the hymns were announced, they sang their own ribald verses or broke out into the pop numbers of the time— "Oh Susannah . . . I'm off to Alabama, With a banjo on my knee."[84]

Mayhew may not have been as disinterested an observer as he pretended. The satirist and founder of *Punch* was likely to have formed a distaste for evangelical reformers in his twenties; and he is likely to have been rankling under the way in which Ashley and Herbert, without consultation, took over the slop workers' agitation. But his criticisms were substantially based and were made in the name of emergent social science (for in his later work Mayhew emerges as a serious criminologist.)[85] From the start of his investiga-tion, moreover, he had watched philanthropy within a severe per-spective. "I need not dilate," he wrote in his first Letter on the ragged schools, "upon the fact of the far superior charity (in pro-portion to their means) not seldom extended by the industrious poor to their utterly destitute friends and neighbours, compared with that of even the most benevolent of the wealthy classes."

The ragged school Letters drew from Ashley pained and heavy reproof. He declared that Mayhew had "asserted things which he dared not repeat at the bar of his God".[86] And it would be surpris-

[84] Letters XLIII, XLIV, XLV and XLIX, 19, 25 and 29 March and 25 April 1850; and letter in reply from the Secretary of the Ragged School Union, *Morning Chronicle*, 22 April 1850. See also below, p. 61.

[85] Henry Mayhew and John Binny, *The Criminal Prisons of London* (1862).

[86] See the attempts to undo Mayhew's damage in the *Ragged School Union Magazine*, II (May and June 1850). It would seem that Dickens, when he wrote *Our Mutual Friend*, had come to share many of Mayhew's criticisms: see Philip Collins, "Dickens and the Ragged Schools", *Dickensian*, LV, May 1959.

B

ing if Sidney Herbert, among the proprietors of the *Morning Chronicle*, did not make his displeasure known. We are justified in taking this passage from *London Labour and the London Poor* as an accurate reflection of Mayhew's view of Ashley and his friends :

> Philanthropists always seek to do too much, and in this is to be found the main cause of their repeated failures. The poor are expected to become angels in an instant, and the consequence is, they are merely made hypocrites. . . . It would seem, too, that this overweening disposition to play the part of pedagogues (I use the word in its literal sense) to the poor, proceeds rather from a love of power than from a sincere regard for the people. Let the rich become the advisers and assistants of the poor, giving them the benefit of their superior education and means—but leaving the people to act for themselves—and they will do a great good, developing in them a higher standard of comfort and moral excellence, and so, by improving their tastes, inducing a necessary change in their habits. But such as seem merely to lord it over those whom distress has placed in their power, and strive to bring about the villeinage of benevolence, making the people the philanthropic, instead of the feudal, serfs of our nobles, should be denounced as the archenemies of the country.[87]

And, in a critical account of another of Lord Ashley's pet schemes, the "model" lodging-houses, he pointed the same moral in another way :

> There is after all but one way to help the Poor, that is to teach the Poor to help themselves; and so long as committees of noblemen have the conduct of their household affairs, so long as my Lord This or That is left to say at what time they shall go to bed and when they shall get up, there can be no main improvement in their condition. The Curfew Bell, even though instituted by the most zealous benevolence, is still as irksome as that enjoined by the most arrogant despotism.[88]

It was not on this issue, however, that relations between Mayhew and the *Morning Chronicle* came finally to breaking-point. The story is unclear, and must be teased out of a few hints and Mayhew's retrospective account. There was without doubt running friction between Mayhew and the Editor from at least as early as February 1850, although the break did not come until October. A leading issue was that of free trade and protection. In investigations of the clothing trades, the docks, and the boot and shoe trades,

---

[87] Loc. cit. (1861), II, p. 264.
[88] "Answers to Correspondents", No. 21, 3 May 1851;

Mayhew (by predisposition a free trader) became impressed with evidence that (as he later put it) while free trade suited the capitalist, protection often served the working man better.[89] At the least he insisted that the workmen's own statements on this side of the question be inserted. But (he complained) the Editor resorted increasingly to petty censorship : "if he put any statement in his letters which clashed with the Editor's ideas of free trade, the pen was immediately drawn through it".[90]

The first major cuts were made in a letter on the boot and shoe trades, when the following passage was struck out of a bootmaker's testimony :

> The trade, I know, generally consider that free trade is of advantage to the moneyed man, and not to the working classes. A man who has a regular income can get more for his money when things are cheap. The working classes of this country are unable to compete with foreigners. . . . With dear Governments and dear rents it is useless talking of cheap prices in this country, unless they are obtained at the ruin of the working classes. Let *us* be free, I say, and then people may talk of free labour as much as they like. But we have no means of saying our say. If we hold public meetings, Government calls it conspiracy. I take it, though, we are as much an element of the State as either the landlords or the capitalists; and I look upon it as a dead robbery that I should be forced to pay taxes that I have not the least voice in imposing.

Mayhew's comment that such opinions were widespread among the working classes was also cut. He protested formally in a private letter to the Editor, and received assurances that his copy would not be interfered with. But within a few weeks "the same dishonest tampering" commenced again.[91] In his letter on the timber docks he claimed subsequently, the italicised passages below had been "studiously withheld from the public by the Editor of that *Free-Trade* Journal" :

[89] Ibid., No. 34, 2 August 1851.

[90] The fullest report of differences with the *Morning Chronicle*, from Mayhew's side, was given by him at a public meeting on 28 October 1850, convened by a committee of the tailors (secretary, Robert Essery) and published by them: *Labour and the Poor: Report of the Speech of Henry Mayhew, Esquire, and the evidence adduced at a Public Meeting held at St. Martin's Hall, Long Acre, on Monday evening, October 28, 1850. Convened by the Committee of the Tailors of London for the purpose of exposing the falsehoods contained in an article that appeared in the Morning Chronicle of Friday October 4th, 1850 on the Sweating or Domestic System. . . .* (Printed for the Committee, 1850). (Cited hereafter as *Report of the Speech*).

[91] Ibid., *passim*.

*"I don't know what is the cause of the reduction of the wages,"
said a 'rafter', but the men thinks it is generally owing to the
cheapness of provisions. They say, what's the use of provisions
being cheap if they lowers our wages."
"The men are dissatisfied," observed a deal porter. "They say
they would sooner have it as it was, because they say, if provisions
comes up again, they won't get no higher price for their labour."*
The wages of the casual dock labourers have been reduced a great
deal more than those of the constant men. Three months ago they
had 18s. a week, and now the highest wages paid to the casual
labourers is 15s. a week. *This again the men say is all owing to
the cheapness of provisions.*[92]

The *Chronicle*, Mayhew commented on another wrapper, "Had
long been theorizing in the contrary direction, and, consequently
could not be expected—even in an 'impartial' enquiry—to stultify
itself by publishing facts in opposition to its own preconceived
opinions. It had asserted that wages in no way depended on the
price of food, and it would, therefore, never have done for so
impartial a journal to have been the means of proving that they
did." The treatment of the facts by that "economical school to which
that journal belongs" would have been very different "had the
operatives . . . been steam-engines instead of mere human
machines".[93]
After this, Mayhew's "situation on the paper became one of a
not very amicable nature. He and the conductors were continually
disputing. . . ."

At last they proposed to him that he should describe the state of
the workers in metals, in two articles, but feeling that he could
not, in justice to the operatives or himself, do so as an honest
man, he replied "No; I have done with it;" and he then left.[94]

Two or three days later, on 4 October 1850, the paper published
an article describing, in the most complimentary terms, the tailoring
establishment of Messrs. H. J. & D. Nicoll, of Regent Street.
The article, which was not, of course, from Mayhew's pen, praised
piecework as against day-work, pointed to the advantages of family
work in the "domestic system" at home, and thereby controverted
the central arguments about unregulated casual labour with which

[92] "Answers to Correspondents", No. 34, 2 August 1851.
[93] Ibid., No. 15, 22 March 1851. In defence of the Editor it should be
noted that he allowed through a number of statements hostile to Free Trade,
some of which were copied by his Protectionist rivals.
[94] *Report of the Speech*, p. 6.

Mayhew was so notably identified : "it gave the lie," Mayhew declared, "to all that had been put forward" in his own metropolitan letters. He wrote immediately to the Editor, asking that it be stated that he was not the author : the Editor refused.[95]

Meanwhile, some of Mayhew's readers, including close supporters among the tailors, were thrown into consternation by his apparent change of front. He felt himself bound to make a public declaration repudiating the *Chronicle*. On 28 October he addressed a public meeting, convened by the London tailors, in St. Martin's Hall, Longacre, at which an attendance of 1,500 was claimed. Here he told the story of his differences with the Editor, returned to his attack on the out-work and slop system, tore apart his successor's article, and made a detailed and damaging assault on Messrs. Nicoll, which culminated in the cry :

Away with such hypocrisy! the sooner the mask of Philanthropy is torn from the faces of these social ghouls, these commercial cannibals, the better.

The fact that one of the Nicoll brothers was Sheriff of London, an advertiser in the *Morning Chronicle*, and a professed philanthropist, aroused his extreme anger :

Here are we, in this the nineteenth century, conferring civic honours and dignities upon a person whose mode of dealing is a disgrace and an abomination. . . . We should learn to look upon these men as the greatest enemies to the country—as the really "dangerous classes".

The attack was extended to a general onslaught against advertising, slop-work, and the dogmas of Free Trade. Of advertising :

Puffing . . . seemed always to be carried on at the expense of the poor. There was the puffery of plate-glass and gas-light . . . and was it not evident that all this glitter and blaze must either increase the price of the articles sold or decrease the wages of those producing them?

The country was infected by a veritable mania, "a *rabies*", for cheapness : but cheap goods could only be produced by ever cheaper labour. Mayhew revealed himself to be a convert to the protectionist views of the boot-maker, and he urged the meeting (to protracted cheers) "not to follow men like Mr. Cobden and Mr. Bright".[96]

---

[95] Ibid., p. 3.
[96] *Report of the Speech passim; Morning Herald*, 29 October 1850.

According to the report in the *Northern Star* he also strongly denounced "all the petty contrivances of amelioration proposed by Lord Ashley and other namby-pamby reformers". He was aware that the press would call him a Socialist or a Chartist; and, replying to the vote of thanks, he declared that—as far as he had gone so far—"the best remedy was a combination of working men in trades' unions".[97] His arguments were substantial and well-documented, although in pressing his attacks on Messrs. Nicoll and Messrs. Moses, and upon the importation of cheap foreign labour, his rhetoric became xenophobic and anti-semitic.[98]

Thereafter Mayhew was on his own. His breach with the *Morning Chronicle* was a seven days' wonder in the press, and provided some copy for protectionist journals which saw in it only another stick to beat the free traders with; when Mayhew refused to play their game they dropped him in favour of the larger quarry of Lord John Russell and the "no popery" agitation.[99] The *Chronicle*, editorially, dismissed Mayhew's charges as "preposterous". It testified to his zeal and ability, but commented : "He did not resign his engagement—although it has ceased . . . :"

> The plain matter of fact—and we dare him to deny it—is, that his engagement was terminated, because he wished to *prolong*, instead of shortening it—to write *more* articles (instead of fewer) than we had arranged to take from him.

As for Mayhew's complaints about editorial interference, the only passages struck out from his copy were "pointless repetitions, vague generalities, irrelevant expressions of mere opinion, and declamatory invectives against particular classes. . . ."[100] Mayhew's fellow correspondent, Angus Bethune Reach, commented upon the controversy with a waspishness which perhaps reveals his jealousy of Mayhew's

[97] *Northern Star*, 2 November 1850. The *Star* congratulated him editorially: his "actual experience of the working man's life" has "imbued his mind with the same philosophy" as among the industrial classes, expressed with a new freshness and force.

[98] According to one report, Mayhew declared: "the magistrates were too ready to listen to any paltry Jew who might come from Judas Jacobs, or any other Hebrew, to swear, by Barabbas, or Iscariot, or any of the brutal race that were thus festering upon us (cheers)" : *Bell's Weekly Messenger*, 2 November 1850.

[99] See editorials in *Morning Herald*, 9 and 30 October, 4 November 1850; in *Standard*, 9, 30 and 31 October, 1 and 2 November 1850; in *Bell's Weekly Messenger*, 2 November 1850.

[100] *Morning Chronicle*, 31 October and 5 November 1850. These comments appear to confirm Mayhew's statement (above, p. 36) that editorial limitation upon his treatment of the metal workers was the final occasion of the breach.

pre-eminence and national reputation. "It has been deemed advisable," he wrote, "to deprive him of the chance of resigning . . . :",

> I am disposed to think . . . that the editor of the *Chronicle* would have done well had he struck his pen through at least four of every eight columns of the disjointed lucubrations and melodramatic ravings of Mr. Mayhew's sentimental draymen and poor artizans. Ever since Mr. Mayhew's communications on the state of the poor attracted any attention, their author has kept summoning together public meetings, of the classes among whom he had been mingling, apparently for no other purpose than to puff his own benevolent spirit.[101]

Thus the recognition of his peers. A year of uninhibited enquiry in the pages of the *Chronicle* had brought into being a formidable alliance in his opposition : Philanthropy, Political Economy, and Free Trade : jealous fellow-journalists : and the nervous employers whom he had investigated or whom he might investigate in subsequent weeks. The actual executioners seem to have been the influential Nicoll brothers, who were London's major makers of the paletot coat, and who had been the subject of Mayhew's investigation in an early Letter.[102] The laudatory article on their establishment by Mayhew's anonymous successor (4 October) was paid for in full by lavish advertising revenue.[103] The Nicolls had for some months sought to counteract the effect of Mayhew's earlier revelations, announcing schemes for the development of their workshops, and publishing figures which purported to show that the earnings of their workmen averaged 30s. and of their needlewomen 20s. a week. (These figures were controverted by detailed evidence adduced by some of their own employees at the meeting of October 28th, and Mayhew later noted that the Nicoll brothers "are said to have amassed £80,000 each, in a few years, simply by reducing the wages of the 1,000 workmen they employ to one-third below that of the 'honourable' trade".)[104]

Now the *Economist* attempted to deliver the *coup de grace*. Attributing to Mayhew the statement that "a vast proportion" of London's 30,000 needlewomen and 23,000 journeymen tailors sub-

---

[101] "London Letter", *Inverness Courier*, 14 November 1850.

[102] See Letter XVIII, below pp. 221–3, 226.

[103] Throughout the second half of October H. J. & D. Nicoll carried daily 18 inches of advertising, in English, French, and German, on the front page of the *Morning Chronicle* (a full-length column measured 20½ inches).

[104] *Report of the Speech*, pp. 40ff (for the evidence of Nicoll's workers); "Answers to Correspondents", No. 16, 29 March 1851 (also Nos. 9 and 14, 8 February and 15 March 1851); H. S. Edwards, op. cit., p. 60.

sisted on 2½d. a day, the journal claimed that Mayhew's figures were wholly unreliable, being based, not upon the books of the employers but upon the workers' own statements—which anyone acquainted with industry should know to be of "utter untrustworthiness", "entirely false and irreconcilable with known, recorded, and public facts". The *Economist* accepted without hesitation Messrs. Nicoll's own statement of their employees' earnings ("a prosperous and admirably conducted establishment"), summoned to their aid Carlyle's "thrifty house-mother" unable to obtain the services of needlewomen for love or money,[105] cited portentously a recent case in the police-courts of a 7d.-a-day sempstress who had pawned linen given out to her for shirt-making (she turned out to be a bad lot and a *second* offender), commented that the conductors of the *Chronicle* were quite right not to insert "the tirades against Free Trade and absurd commentaries on Commercial Policy with which some ignorant boot-maker favoured him", and concluded that Mayhew has "a deplorable absence of those qualities of caution, candour, sobriety of mind, and soundness of judgement, without which a man's observations are worth almost as little as his reasonings".

Only a part of Mayhew's long letter of reply was inserted in the *Economist* five weeks later. In this, he denied having suggested that those subsisting on 2½d. a day constituted a substantial proportion of those working in the clothing trades :

> I never said nor gave the public reason to infer what you assert. Mr. Sidney Herbert, in his letters to the *Chronicle* concerning the needlewomen, certainly *did* make such a statement. . . . I was most anxious that this should be contradicted at the time, and requested the Editor of the *Chronicle* to allow me to disabuse the public mind upon the subject. But, for certain private reasons, he was indisposed to thwart the emigration crotchet of his friend Mr. Herbert. That gentleman was an inveterate economist, and so was the Editor of the *Chronicle*. Like yourself, their creed was that low wages—wages that required prostitution to be generally resorted to in order to subsist upon them—could only be the consequence of too many workers; hence, of course, their minds were prone to believe, and anxious to make out . . . that the needlewomen living on 2½d. per diem were twice and even thrice as many as I had literally given them any warrant for. Without this, it would have been difficult to have accounted *economically* for the fact, or to have made the public believe that emigration was the only remedy for the evil.

On the question of consulting the accounts of employers, he offered

---

[105] See above p. 27.

a direct rebuttal, citing his consultations with Cubitt, of the building-trade, Seddon, the upholsterer, and Box, the shoe manufacturer :

> Whenever an opportunity has been offered me by an employer to check the statement of the workpeople by his accounts, I have never failed to avail myself of it—and . . . these, when sifted, have proved the statements of the employed to be true and those of the employers to be false.

He had offered, publicly and without response, to examine the books of Messrs. Nicoll and to compare these with the statements of their workers. The *Economist* was not impressed with this reply : "we most utterly refuse accept with passive credence the statements of so easy a believer, so unsound a thinker, and so illogical a reasoner".[106]

Denounced by established authority, Mayhew had turned to the investigated themselves for his support. Addressing a meeting "of the working classes" in Tottenham Court Road on November 5th, he had moved a resolution as to the insecurity and misery of labour :

> that this state of things is caused by a misapprehension of the economical law of "demand and supply", which, as it is now understood, means the lawless and inhuman competition of the fraudulent and strong against the honest and weak; and that the best remedy for this is an equitable arbitration or mediation between demand and supply by the means of co-operation among the people.

The free traders he now declared to be "the greatest enemies of the working classes".[107] It was to this kind of audience that he now turned, for the continuation of his enquiry. By December he had established his own London office, and commenced issuing *London Labour and the London Poor* in twopenny weekly parts. Much of this was a re-working, expansion, and re-arrangement of material on the street-traders which had already appeared in the *Chronicle*. The parts were bound up in volume form before the end of 1851, and this material was reproduced, in its turn, for the first two volumes of the 1861 edition. From August 1851 the material on the street-traders was alternated each fortnight with a new enquiry into prostitution (material later used in Volume 4 of *London*

---

[106] *Economist*, 16 November and 21 December 1850.

[107] *Leader*, 9 November 1850. Both Walter Cooper and Lloyd Jones also addressed this meeting, and it may represent Mayhew's closest association with the Christian Socialists. In the previous week Mayhew had chaired a meeting of ballast heavers: *Northern Star* 2 November 1850.

*Labour*).[108] The parts continued to be published until February 1852, when Mayhew's evil genius struck once again, in the form of an injunction in Chancery restraining him and his publisher (John Howden) from selling or collecting any moneys on the parts, as a result of a dispute with his printers.[109] Litigation was protracted and, during its course, Mayhew's enthusiasm evidently died away. Although some parts of the work were taken up again in 1856, only a fragment of the vast scheme of enquiry which Mayhew once envisaged was ever completed.[110]

What is most interesting, in this new phase of publication, is the palpable sense of relationship between Mayhew and his audience— a relationship which, until then, had been mediated through the correspondence columns of the *Chronicle*. Each twopenny part was bound in a wrapper, on which Mayhew printed information and enquiries received from readers, together with his own replies. More and more he used the wrappers to develop his political and economic theories.[111] Eventually these arguments burst out into a separate publication, commencing in November 1851, and running for at least four numbers, entitled *Low Wages: their Causes, Consequences and Remedies*.[112]

Alongside the theoretical arguments, Mayhew maintained a more personal correspondence on the wrappers with some of his readers. From the time of the first articles in the *Morning Chronicle* readers had begun sending in donations for distribution to the subjects of his enquiry. Mayhew was sternly condemnatory of indiscriminate charity:

> Mr. Mayhew has, in his dealings with the poorer classes, seen too many instances of the evils of promiscuous charity, to consent to become the dispenser of alms. The most dangerous lesson that can possibly be taught to any body of people whatsoever is, that there are other means of obtaining money than by working for it.[113]

He was, however, willing to establish through his publisher a "Loan-Office for the Poor", through which deserving subjects might obtain

[108] See Appendix I.
[109] *Times*, 17 March 1852, p. 6; Public Record Office, C.33/1107.
[110] See Appendix I, p. 476.
[111] These theories are discussed by Eileen Yeo below.
[112] The only numbers which we have been able to trace are in the Goldsmith's Collection in the University of London Library.
[113] "Answers to Correspondents", 8 February 1851; cf. *1851: or the Adventures of Mr. and Mrs. Sandboys* (1851), p. 12: "Of all lessons there is none so dangerous as to teach people that they can live by other means than labour."

either small outright grants or loans on easy terms of repayment in order to obtain the necessary stock or equipment to carry on their trades. The sums advanced were petty, and the number receiving them amounted to only a few score. One of the more successful appeals came from "the poor half-witted and very persecuted harp-player, so well-known in the streets of London", who addressed to the public his own petition :

> Your humble Partitionar as been obtaining a lively hood the last 4 years by playing an harp in the streets and is desirous of doing so but from the delapedated condition of my present instrument I only produce ridicule instead of a living Trusting you will be kind anough to asist me in getting another I beg to remain your humble Partitionar, FOSTER.

Foster received £2 10s. for a new harp, by outright donations. The largest sum advanced on loan was to C. Alloway, the crippled seller of nutmeg-graters, whose portrait and harrowing story[114] brought sympathy and recognition in the streets : "I am gazed at in the street," he wrote, "and observations made within my hearing with respect to the Exact likeness of the portrait." More than £9 was advanced to him, to be repaid at 1s. a week, but he was beset at once with new disasters; he invested in a donkey, ordered a cart, and bought some hardware stock, but the donkey became ill, and the carpenter absconded with his money. The most ambitious effort of the "Loan-Office" appears to have ended in failure.[115]

It is difficult not to feel that Mayhew was over-extending his energies, and dissipating them, in 1851. The investigation of the street-traders continued throughout the year (the first volume of *London Labour and the London Poor* being published, from the parts, in July); the investigation of prostitution commenced in August. A new novel by Henry and Gus, *The Image of his Father,* was published at some time in 1851—a novel with an intricately-worked plot of mistaken identities, supplemented with lavish backgrounds of seedy solicitors, retired Anglo-Indians, and spiced with anti-semitism.

[114] See *London Labour and the London Poor* (1861), I, pp. 329–333.
[115] "Answers to Correspondents", No. 11, 22 February; No. 19, 19 April; No. 29, 28 June; No. 33, 26 July 1851. The wrappers also advertised certain other ventures for assisting the industrious artisan : a "Mutual Investment Society" (a building society) and "Mutual Pension Society", both of which were managed by Howden, Mayhew's publisher, and with both of which Horace (but not Henry) Mayhew was officially connected; a "London Coster-mongers Friendly Association"; and the Christian Socialists' "Central Co-operative Agency", established "to counteract the system of Adulteration and Fraud now prevailing in Trade, and to promote the principle of Co-operative Association".

In addition, he had in February commenced publishing in monthly parts a novel, 1851: *or the Adventures of Mr. and Mrs. Sandboys*, illustrated by George Cruikshank; yet another novel by Henry and Gus, *The Shabby Fammerley* (a sequel to *The Greatest Plague in Life*) commenced part publication in November. Meanwhile, Henry reported on the Great Exhibition in a series of sixteen articles for the *Edinburgh News* between May and September and commenced issuing *Low Wages* in parts at the end of November. Such an output is scarcely consistent with the character which Mayhew is customarily given, as "an indolent and irresponsible man who loved conversation as much as he hated writing", although it may be consistent with another part of that character—"his improvidence kept him almost always in debt".[116] Indeed, while Mayhew's most systematic thought belongs to the wrappers of 1851, his most profound experience of London poverty belongs, most probably, to the previous year. It is reasonable to suppose that he had at first undertaken the "metropolitan commision" in the normal course of journalistic vocation : a serious and worth-while job, but at the same time a good money-spinner, likely to last. But in a matter of weeks he had been totally seized by the problems and the needs of the people whom he was investigating. The discontents of the poor of the world's largest metropolis beat upon the door of his office. He heard and reported hundreds of life-histories, becoming the confessor and the vector for the despairing and the inarticulate. He walked through the alleys of the slums, entered the houses, attended meetings of the trades. The problems of urban demoralization became, for a time, focused upon his single consciousness.

In this way, a vocation had become a mission; and, as he bumped up against one vested interest after another, whether in hard economic life or in academic political economy, he was forced into greater commitment and leadership. (It was as Mr. Mayhew, "our able and distinguished advocate . . . the champion of the working classes", that he was introduced to the public meeting of the tailors in October 1850). At the same time, he had translated his old vocation of journalism for the new (and, to his mind, more lofty) vocation of the impartial social scientist :

I made up my mind to deal with human nature as a natural philosopher or a chemist deals with any material object; and, as a man who has devoted some little of his time to physical and metaphysical science, I must say I did most heartily rejoice that it should have been left to me to apply the laws of the inductive

[116] Gordon N. Ray, *Thackeray, the Uses of Adversity*, p. 357.

philosophy for the first time, I believe, in the world to the abstract question of political economy.[117]

He continued in this exalted state of mind into 1851 : *London Labour* was to be "the first real History of the People that has ever been attempted in any country whatsoever".[118] But as he comes to the end of 1851, one feels that he was forced increasingly to resume his older journalistic vocation, with its familiar working habits, dead-lines, and hashing-up of hasty material for a ready market. The novel, *1851*, was killed off with remarkable lack of ceremony, almost in mid-paragraph : evidently it was not paying enough to be worth the bother. The "Answers to Correspondents" on the wrappers reveal less and less contact with the working trades of London, the audience of October 1850. Possibly his decision to commence the investigation of prostitution rather than of the workers in textiles (his original intention) was influenced by a change in his readership and a need to promote his sales. Whatever the reasons, the Mayhew of the *Morning Chronicle* was already beginning to recede, and the somewhat quainter—but also more dramatic and more readable—Mayhew of the London street folk was taking his place. After another decade or two, this was the only Mayhew that was remembered—even perhaps, by himself.

In this century, Mayhew, the systematic empirical sociologist, has been almost lost sight of, and has been replaced by a Mayhew who was a gifted impressionist with an eye for "character". The present book may redress the balance too far. For both Mayhews of course lived in a single skin and were necessary to each other. The glorious irreverent statements of the patterers, street sellers, and Irish, which are his best-known writings, are material which only a man at odds with the usual moralisms and hypocrisies could have gathered. He had the insatiable appetite for individuality of the "low life" journalists with whom he served his apprenticeship. The satirist and the social investigator were necessary to each other. His matchless ear for the stress of feeling within colloquial speech (a Fantoccini man told him : "it looked quite fearful-like to have every word as he uttered written down") his ability to identify during interview, to break down the vast distance between gentlefolk and poor—these things could not have been possible unless the poor had detected in him, and perhaps in his brother Gus, an irreverence which matched their own. Perhaps Mayhew was the more able to bridge the social distances because he was not (in the obscure accounts which are left to us) a pillar of the Victorian virtues himself.

It may be unfair to select from one of the provincial correspondents of the *Morning Chronicle* an unusually insensitive passage. But it is of service because it illustrates, in a single passage, all the kinds of Victorian social commentary which Mayhew *never* in his great period perpetrated. In this example, the "Rural Commissioner" was commenting censoriously upon the prevalence in the countryside of the pilfering of wood for fuel : "What is the consequence? The child who becomes adept in stealing wood is soon qualified for robbing a hen-roost. From that again to stealing a sheep there is but another step; and, in the words of a clergyman with whom I was conversing on this subject, 'when a man goes out to steal a sheep he is ready for anything'." While pursuing this topic, the vicar and correspondent were strolling down a lane alongside the vicar's glebeland, when they suddenly encountered an eight-year-old boy, caught red-handed dragging some "timber" down the lane :

"Where did you get that piece of timber?" asked the vicar. "I found it on the road," said the boy. . . . This was a falsehood, for he had taken it out of the neighbouring copse. The vicar sent for the mother of the child. Her plea was that she sent him for wood, but did not enjoin him to steal it. She well knew, however, that he could not get it without stealing it. . . . What an education is this for a child ! . . . the evil is, teaching the child deliberately to do that which he knows and feels to be wrong. He does it *animo furandi*, and thus it is that the line between right and wrong is so early erased from his mind.[119]

The poor trusted Mayhew because it was plain that he never suffered from this kind of middle-class moral halitosis. The common factor which unites the Mayhew of the *Comic Almanac* and of the *Morning Chronicle* investigation is contempt for the values of the "highly respectable man".[120] At his public meeting with the tailors in October 1850 he burst out :

It is easy enough to be moral after a good dinner beside a snug sea-coal fire, and with our hearts well warmed with fine old port. It is easy enough for those that can enjoy these things daily to pay their poor's rates, rent their pew, and love their neighbours as themselves : but place the self-same "highly respectable"

[119] *Morning Chronicle*, 1 December 1849.
[120] See above, p. 13, c.f. *1851: or the Adventures of Mr. and Mrs. Sandboys*, p. 84: "Major Oldschool . . . had that 'highly respectable' appearance which invariably accompanies the white hair so peculiar to Bankers, Capitalists, and Pomeranian dogs."

people on a raft without sup or bite on the high seas, *and they would toss up who should eat their fellows.* Morality on £5,000 a year in Belgrave Square is a very different thing to morality on slop-wages in Bethnal Green.[121]

At the same time he rejected the disposition to "varnish matters over with a sickly sentimentality, angelizing or canonising the whole body of operatives of this country, instead of speaking of them as possessing the ordinary vices and virtues of human nature".[122] He was concerned with the "moral acclimatization" of a common human nature :

> Might not the "finest gentleman in Europe" have been the greatest blackguard in Billingsgate had he been born to carry a fish-basket on his head instead of a crown? and by a parity of reasoning let the roughest "rough" outside the London fish-market have had his lot in life cast "by the Grace of God, King, Defender of the Faith", and surely his shoulders would have glittered with diamond epaulettes instead of fish scales.[123]

Exactly what happened to Mayhew after 1852 has eluded our research. There is a consensus of silence in the reminiscences of contemporaries which must, one feels, arise from deliberate evasion. He seems to have been beset with financial and legal difficulties, and there is a suggestion also of marital difficulties, which resulted in an estrangement from his father-in-law, Douglas Jerrold, which lasted until the latter's death-bed.[124] The industry which marked the years 1849–51 appears to have declined, and Mayhew reverted to bohemian ways—and yet, one feels, without the easy *bonhomie* which enabled his equally bohemian brother, Horace, to endear himself to his companions. Some of his journalistic acquaintance, like the republican W. J. Linton, dismissed him curtly.[125] Others were more generous, but rarely specific. Sutherland Edwards said he had more brains than all the rest of the family "but less conduct".[126] Vizetelly, who knew him in later years, described him as a man of "multi-

[121] *Report of the Speech*, p. 36.
[122] *1851: or the Adventures of Mr. and Mrs. Sandboys*, p. 154.
[123] *London Labour and the London Poor* (1861), I, p. 320.
[124] See Walter Jerrold, op. cit. p. 654. We have no information as to the cause of the estrangement. Mayhew and his wife were clearly together in 1864 when Mayhew prefaced his *German Life and Manners* with a two-page dedication to her: "literally my *right hand*, scribbling to my dictation often night and day". Professor J. W. Bradley informs us that he shares our view that the marriage was under strain, and he has evidence which suggests that the Mayhews were separated at the time of her death (in 1880).
[125] See W. J. Linton, *Memories* (1895), p. 58.
[126] H. S. Edwards, op. cit., p. 59.

farious schemes and singularly original ideas, but of torpid energy";[127] and, in another account, he returned to this theme of unrealized abilities :

> Mayhew . . . was constantly planning some new publication or broaching novel ideas on the most out-of-the-way subject. He would scheme and ponder all the day long, but he abominated the labour of putting his ideas into tangible shape. He would talk like a book on any subject for hours together if he could only find listeners, but could with difficulty be brought to put pen to paper. . . .[128]

Another friend described him as "lovable, jolly, charming, bright, coaxing, and unprincipled. He rarely wrote himself, but would dictate, as he walked to and fro, to his wife, whom he would also leave to confront his creditors."[129]

In 1856, with litigation in Chancery drawing to its leisurely conclusion, he showed a burst of his old energies and intellectual command. Not only did he take up and complete some of his work on the street-traders[130] but he commenced an even more ambitious venture, in *The Great World of London*, running in monthly part-publication from March to November 1856. The prospectus for this envisaged a life's work, in which the massive (and only partly completed) examination of labour and the poor was to take its place as only one part of a total survey of London life, commencing with Legal London, Medical London, Religious London, etc.[131] After some pages of introduction, Mayhew plunged into a systematic, fully-documented, and at times brilliantly-observed survey of the prisons of London, ending abruptly in mid-sentence with Part IX; evidently, shortly after the publication folded, Mayhew left the country, and his publishers later commissioned John Binny to complete the volume, under the title *The Criminal Prisons of London and Scenes of Prison Life* (1862).[132] In 1856, also, he had tried his hand again

[127] H. Vizetelly, *Glances Back Through Seventy Years* (1893), I, p. 408.

[128] M. H. Spielmann, *The History of "Punch"*, p. 268.

[129] Ibid., p. 268.

[130] An announcement on the wrapper of Part VIII of *The Great World of London*, dated 23 September 1856, stated that "so large a portion of the manuscript of Volume III" of *London Labour and the London Poor* was in the printer's hands, that publication could be expected at a very early date. In fact publication did not take place until 1861, but there is evidence of material in Volume III (e.g. p. 65) collected in 1856.

[131] Mayhew may possibly have farmed out some of the investigation in *The Great World*, as he did the greater part of *London Labour and the London Poor*, Volume IV, in which Hemyng, Binny, and Halliday did all the interviewing.

[132] The publishers, Griffin, Bohn & Co., may have commissioned Binny

as a playwright and a dramatization of *London Labour* was performed, under the title *How We Live in the World of London*. Like others of his circle—Mark Lemon or Charles Dickens—he was attracted to the stage himself; and, perhaps in the same year, he attempted to recoup his fortunes by a tour of personal performances in "Punch on the Platform"—a venture which ended in disaster.[133] Thereafter he spent more and more time in Germany, (perhaps in part to avoid his creditors?) where he was in the late 1850s,[134] in the early 1860s, and again in 1870, when he and his son Athol served as war correspondents in the Franco-Prussian War. His German experiences provided him with material for a substantial study of *German Life and Manners*, which includes much interesting information and close observation, marred by extraordinary chauvinist feeling, and tirades against the dirtiness, stupidity, meanness, miserliness, uncouth eating-habits, obscenity, and duplicity of the Thuringian people of all classes.[135] He was in England again, for at least some time in the mid-1860s, when he promoted and wrote some part of another venture in part-publication, *The Shops and Companies of London and the Trades and Manufactories of Great Britain* (1865). This shows flashes of his old vigour and observation, but in general the decline is sad from *The Great World of London*, a decline which was accompanied by the now-familiar story of insolvency and unpaid contributors.[136] As late as 1874 he was still warming up the entrée of 1849–51, producing in *London Characters* a series of sketches, a part of which were drawn from the *Morning Chronicle* investigation.[137] One last flash of characteristic Mayhew was left—a survey, in 1871, of working-men's clubs, in which, for a few pages, he saw and wrote as he had been able to do twenty years before.[138]

without Mayhew's permission: their note at the front of the book reads—"the publishers think it right to state that, in consequence of Mr. Mayhew's absence from England, they placed the completion of the volume in the hands of Mr. Binney, who has supplied all after page 498".

[133] Willert Beale, *The Light of Other Days* (1890), I, pp. 271–5.

[134] See Henry Mayhew, *The Rhine and the Picturesque Scenery* (1856), and *The Upper Rhine: the Scenery of its Banks and the Manners of its People* (1858).

[135] See also the Podsnappery: "There is an inner life pervading the heart of England, graced with home feelings and affections, which makes our national character, in a measure, a sealed book to foreigners": *German Life and Manners as Seen in Saxony at the Present Day* (1864), I, p. xi.

[136] See A. W. à Beckett, *The á Becketts of "Punch"* (1900), pp. 24–7.

[137] See Appendix I.

[138] Henry Mayhew, *Report Concerning the Trade and Hours of Closing Usual among the Unlicensed Victualling Establishments Now Open for the Unrestricted Sale of Beer, Wine, and Spirits, at Certain So-Called "Working Men's Clubs", Distributed Throughout the Metropolis* (1871).

Such life-histories are, perhaps, not uncommon : men or women whose genius coincides with social demands and beneficent circumstances once only in their lives—flaring briefly before dying down to smoke and embers once again. The *Morning Chronicle* enquiry is at the heart of this brief burst of illumination, when Mayhew's prodigious but undisciplined talents and his bohemian irreverence combined in a unique human investigation.

# MAYHEW AS A
# SOCIAL INVESTIGATOR

EILEEN YEO

Henry Mayhew has never received serious consideration as a systematic empirical investigator. Historians and sociologists, who appreciate the rich social evidence in his work, see him as no more than a gifted journalist, with an undisciplined zest for collecting facts about the poor and picturesque characters among the poor. This image derives from a reading of *London Labour and the London Poor* in the 1861 edition which contained only a part of the London investigations and a puzzling sample of interpretive writing.[1] To assess Mayhew as an investigator, it is more useful to follow him chronologically, examining the London survey as it developed. His starting point, the letters to the *Morning Chronicle* between 1849 and 1850, which are reprinted in this book for the first time, and the "Answers to Correspondents" column, a feature of the weekly parts of *London Labour* in 1851, reveal his anxiety about the methods of social investigation and an eagerness to analyze his findings. These were the years, as E. P. Thompson has shown, when Mayhew was capable of his best work. Freed temporarily from financial worries and able to stretch his mind in ways not immediately designed to make quick money, his intense commitment to the project was continually sharpened by public interest and controversy. On the basis of this earlier and largely unstudied material, Mayhew emerges as a self-conscious investigator whose survey of industrial conditions in London and attempts at economic and sociological analysis entitle him to an important place in the history of social investigation.

[1] In a review of the 1861 edition of *London Labour and the London Poor*, Brian Harrison called it "a very ill-constructed work whose defects amply justify Ruth Glass's complaint that 'there is no theme; by and large there is description without selection or analysis'". Similar opinions from T. S. Simey and C. A. Moser are recorded here. "London's Lower Depths", in *New Society*, 2 November 1967, pp. 638–9. On the other hand, F. Bédarida, though he didn't explore the claim, wrote that Mayhew's work was done "selon un methode scientifique qui annonce la sociologie urbaine"; "Londres au Milieu du XIX[e] Siecle: Une Analyse de Structure Sociale", in *Annales-Economies, Sociétés, Civilisations*, March-April 1968, p. 269. For the relation of Mayhew's earlier work to the 1861 edition of *London Labour and the London Poor*, see Appendix I below.

I

The *Morning Chronicle* project appeared at the end of two decades which had produced a rich crop of investigations into the condition of the working class. In the face of dramatic industrial and urban change, frightening developments like cholera and radical protest movements, middle class investigators saw systematic fact collecting at once as true scientific empiricism and as the necessary first step to formulating social policy and programmes of action. The increasing use of government investigatory bodies was a feature of these years; the Royal Commissions and Select Committees which took evidence on the administration of the Poor Laws, on the Health of Towns and on conditions in selected industries are well known. Not surprisingly the prejudices of the investigators coloured the scope and terms of the inquiries as well as the conclusions. Few of these inquiries were centrally concerned with the extent and causes of poverty or with the relation between employment conditions and poverty. Blinkered by the political economy maxim that the adult male worker must be left free from legislative "interference" to the mercies of the free market and disturbed that the factory system might tend to destroy the family, the major industrial studies of factories (1833), mines (1842) and agriculture (1843 focused on the physical and moral condition of children (and women) at work. The outstanding exception, the inquiry into the condition of the hand-loom weavers (1838–41), did consider the economic position of the whole family. Its sensitive questionnaire gave clear instructions to calculate net wages, taking into account expenses necessary to work and the amount of unemployment during the year, and to find the economic causes of hardship—albeit with a built-in bias against trade unions and strikes which were automatically assumed to be causes of low wages.[2] But the Commission's brief was not imitated during this period.

Less familiar, though directly helping to create the climate for government survey work, voluntary statistical societies existed in nearly every major city and carried out rigorous and systematic investigations into the condition of the local poor in places like Manchester, Bristol and London.[3] The members of the provincial societies were mainly prosperous, powerful and philanthropic local

[2] For the full questionnaire see Hand-loom Weavers, "Report of the Commissioners", in *Parliamentary Sessional Papers*, 1841, X, Appendix No. 1.

[3] The British Association added a statistical section in 1833 and local groups were founded in Manchester and London in 1834, in Birmingham (1835), in Bristol and two in Glasgow (1836), in Ulster (1837), in Liverpool and Leeds (1838), and in Dublin (1847).

businessmen while London's largest contingent was professional and academic. The Manchester Statistical Society, with a membership limit of fifty, was the most remarkably close-knit; its leading members, often related by marriage, were either owners of spinning mills or bankers, who worshipped together at the Cross Street and Moseley Street Unitarian chapels and underwrote philanthropic agencies like the Manchester and Salford District Provident Society. Although basically satisfied with the new manufacturing system and the rapid expansion of port cities, the statisticians were deeply worried by the concentration of the poor in the centre of large towns away from contact with the upper classes, who had been the traditional force for social guidance and control. They regarded their societies not only as the pioneers of "statistical science" but as the most relevant agencies in the new urban setting to collect information which would serve as the preliminary to effective philanthropic action. The Rev. Lant Carpenter of the Bristol Society observed that in country places

> it was not so difficult for benevolent individuals to discriminate and to bestow their claims so as to benefit society; but in large cities and towns statistical enquiries were of the greatest moment.[4]

Their inquiries into the "condition of the working classes" examined the extent to which social *discipline* prevailed among the poor. It was "moral and intellectual condition" they were concerned with, to be measured by a stock questionnaire about overcrowding, domestic management, religious affiliation, church going, literacy and school attendance. Making pioneer use of the door-to-door survey, they visited all working class families (those below the rank of shopkeeper plus small shopkeepers selling to the poor in a designated area (usually a parish or police district) and published their findings in statistical tables preceded by a brief report.[5] But innovations in the technique of making an inquiry should not obscure the fact that these were social discipline surveys not poverty surveys. Indeed the early inquiries seemed to be based on the assumption that the broader social and economic environment had little bearing on respectable behaviour.[6] No questions were asked about

---

[4] *Journal of the Statistical Society of London*, I, 1839, p. 551.

[5] See *Report of a Committee of the Manchester Statistical Society on the Condition of the Working Classes in an Extensive Manufacturing District* in 1834, 1835, and 1836 (London, 1838); C. B. Fripp, "Report of an Inquiry into the Condition of the Working Classes of the City of Bristol", in Bristol Statistical Society, *Proceedings of the Third Annual Meeting* (Bristol, 1839).

[6] It is true that the London society's surveys consistently pointed to high rents and consequent overcrowding as a cause of lax moral conduct, but the Bristol society smugly ascribed bad housing to bad morals and saw the cure

wages, hours or regularity of employment, although occupations were listed. After the depression of 1841 more attention was paid to wages and the London society's survey of St. George's in the East (Stepney) even tried to correlate wages with the usual moral indices concluding that "the excess of inferior habits in the inferior occupations will be traced generally".[7] But the report gave no indication of how the average weekly wage was arrived at, whether expenses necessary to the job had been deducted or seasonal unemployment had been allowed for. And no deeper questions were asked about why certain occupations provided only low wages.

It was Henry Mayhew, as metropolitan commissioner for the *Morning Chronicle,* who set out to conduct the first empirical survey into poverty *as such.* A comparison between Mayhew's opening letter and those of the industrial and rural commissioners highlights what a new and, for a journalist, what a remarkable role he set himself. They poured out highly emotive paragraphs about the late revolutions in Europe and the startling social contrasts between rich and poor in England before announcing their intention vaguely to explore the condition of the working classes. Mayhew, by contrast, tried for the first time in the history of English social investigation to define a poverty line :

> Under the term "poor" I shall include all those persons whose incomings are insufficient for the satisfaction of their wants—a want being, according to my idea, contra-distinguished from a mere desire by a positive physical pain, instead of mental uneasiness, accompanying it. The large and comparatively unknown body of people included in this definition I shall contemplate in two distinct classes, viz., the *honest* and *dishonest* poor; and the first of these I purpose subdividing into the striving and the disabled—or, in other words, I shall consider the whole of the metropolitan poor under three separate phases, according as they *will* work, they *can't* work, and they *won't* work.[8]

in a "reasonable sense of decency and cleanliness engendered in their minds". London Statistical Society, "Report . . . on the State of the Working Classes in the Parishes of St. Margaret and St. John, Westminster", in *JSSL,* III, 1840, pp. 17–18; Bristol, *Third Annual Meeting,* p. 8. Other London remarks on rents in C. R. Weld, "On the Condition of the Working Classes in the Inner Ward of St. George's Parish, Hanover Square", in *JSSL,* VI, 1843, pp. 117–118; "Report of a Committee . . . to investigate the State of Inhabitants and their Dwellings in Church Lane, St. Giles", in Ibid., XI, 1848, p. 17.

[7] "Report . . . of . . . an Investigation into the State of the Poorer Classes in St. George's in the East", in *JSSL,* XI, 1848, p. 215. The survey was actually begun in 1844.

[8] Mayhew's interest in defining a poverty line waned as he became more

Mayhew left his poverty line in embryonic form, defining it with no more precision than Booth and with much less than Rowntree. The survey began with an exploration of "those who *will* work". At no point, unlike Booth or Rowntree, did he intend to take a door-to-door poverty census or count the heads of the poor. Rather, to "methodize" the work, he posited a relationship between poverty and low wages,[9] which quickly proved a promising line of inquiry after pilot visits to the Spitafields weavers, casual labourers at the docks and the many kinds of needlewomen. He was not content to do quick impressionistic sketches of industry like the peripatetic provincial commissioners. Nor was he satisfied to follow in the footsteps of the earlier statisticians and calculate wages for workers from a miscellany of occupations located by means of a door-to-door survey. He wished systematically to establish conditions of employment, especially wage levels, in the metropolitan trades, relate these to the life style of the poor and, at the same time, explore the industrial causes of low wages and poverty. Later questionnaires reflect his continued and maturing pre-occupation with the task of documenting conditions of employment while seeking for their causes. For example, replying to a keen draper's assistant who wanted to send evidence, Mayhew wrote,

> The information required upon this and, indeed every other trade is, (1) The division of labour in the trade, citing the nature of the work performed by the different classes of workmen; (2) the hours of labour; (3) the labour market, or the mode of obtaining employment; (4) the tools employed and who finds them; (5) the rate and mode of pay to each different class of workmen, dividing the wages or salaries into two classes, the "fair" and the "unfair"; (6) the deductions from the pay in the form of fines, "rents", or stoppages of any kind; (7) the additions to wages in

preoccupied with the industrial causes of low wages. There is some hint that he later toyed with a dietary criterion when he solicited "accounts as to the individual expenditure of operatives. These would be of the greatest service as the means of arriving at the number of ounces of solid food consumed by working men in particular trades, so that the quantity may be contrasted with other trades, as well as with the dietaries of paupers and prisoners". "Answers to Correspondents", *London Labour and the London Poor,* Cover No. 7, 1851. His definition of a "point of sufficiency" of wages is the only other form in which a minimum appears and this is a poverty line from the working man's point of view, see below p. 463.

[9] See Letter II below, p. 104. His determination to concentrate on wages was further hardened when he discovered that information about wages was not to be found in any of the standard statistical sources and a "primary object" became "to obtain, for the first time in this country, a list of prices paid to the workpeople of London for their labour"; see Letter X below, p. 159.

the shape of perquisites, premiums, allowances, etc.; (8) a history
of the wages of the trade, with the dates of increase or decrease
in the pay, and the causes thereof; (9) the brisk and slack season of
the trade, with statement of the causes on which they depend, as
well as the number of extra hands required in the brisk season
as compared with the slack; (10) the rate of pay to those who are
"taken on" only during the brisk season; (11) the amount of surplus labour in the trade and the cause of it, whether from (a)
overwork, (b) undue increase of the people in the trade, (c) change
from yearly to weekly hirings, (d) excessive economy of labour, as
"large system" of business, (e) introduction of women; (12) the
badly-paid trade—(a) the history and causes of it, (b) what is the
cheap labour employed, or how do the cheap workers differ from
those who are better paid : are they less skilful, less trustworthy,
or can they *afford* to take less, deriving their subsistence from other
sources? (c) is the badly-paid trade maintained chiefly by the
labour of apprentices, women, etc, etc.? (d) is it upheld by middlemen, "sweaters", or the like? (e) are the men injured by *driving*
(that is, by being made to do more work for the same money) or
by *grinding* (that is, by being made to do the same or more work
for less money), or are they injured from a combination of both
systems? (f) who are the employers paying the worse wages?—
are they "cutting men", that is to say, men who are reducing the
men's wages as a means of selling cheap; or are they "grasping
men", who do it merely to increase their profits; or small capitalists, who do it in order to live? Proofs should be given of all stated.
Accounts of earnings and expenditure are of the greatest importance; also descriptions of modes of life and habits, politics, religion,
literature, and amusements of the trade. . . .[10]

An industrial survey had another advantage. "I am unable to
generalize", he apologized in letter III, "not being acquainted with
the particulars, for each day's investigation brings me into contact
with a means of living utterly unknown among the well-fed portion
of society".[11] Astounded at his own ignorance, a subsidiary aim of the
survey became to compile a "cyclopaedia of industry", to make the
working life of the poor known to the rich. The study of the London poor in an industrial context, first occupation by occupation
and then trade by trade, became the large organizing principle of
the first part of the survey. He "digressed" only occasionally, to
make immediate use of contacts who would otherwise be lost to him,
and so began a study of other groups like vagrants (a section of those

[10] "Answers to Correspondents", No. 48, 8 November 1851.
[11] *Morning Chronicle*, 26 October 1849.

who *won't* work). Or he personally examined what conventional philanthropic wisdom called causes of poverty, like low lodging houses or remedies, like ragged schools. The study of employment conditions was the continuous thread giving coherence of purpose to the majority of the *Morning Chronicle* letters.

But how to study employment conditions and poverty was problematic, especially as the legacy of technique bequeathed by earlier investigators like the statisticians was not very useful. Moreover Mayhew was an anthropologist, though not a relativist. With a sensitivity and tolerance almost unique among his contemporary investigators, or later "social scientists", he had a sure sense that the opinions of the poor, their aspirations and expectations, their evaluation of their lot and life in general were as important to the inquiry as facts about wages. "My vocation", he announced, "is to collect facts and register opinions".[12] Of course, Mayhew was also a journalist who had to supply copy that was good to read but, as the reader can judge, this was secondary. The metropolitan letters were packed with a surprisingly large amount of statistics and very laborious wage calculations. Besides, the other commissioners did not automatically feel that the opinions of the poor would make a lively text for they made only sparing use of them. Mayhew the anthropologist and journalist complemented and strengthened each other. For both, an entirely statistical method of presenting fact was not appropriate, just as a door-to-door inquiry was not adequate to explore a trade.

The early *Morning Chronicle* letters show how Mayhew painstakingly evolved a method of investigation, which may not have been totally successful, but was relevant to the kinds of factors he wished to explore. To determine the history, structure and wages of any trade, Mayhew had hoped to compose a counterpoint between the testimony of employers and working men,[13] accompanied by information from government reports. But government statistics for wages were unavailable and Mayhew attributed this to the secretiveness of employers, another stumbling block in his investigations :

> The chief difficulty which besets an undertaking of this character lies in the indisposition of the tradesmen—and especially those who are notorious for selling cheap, and consequently giving a less price to their workpeople—to make known the sums that they pay for the labour employed upon the different arts of manufacture in which they deal. I believe, this, is the main reason why

[12] See Letter II below, p. 605.
[13] See Letter VI below, p. 117.

such information remains to be acquired. To obtain it, the work-people themselves must be sought out, and seen privately in their own homes. Another obstacle to the attainment of the information, is that the workpeople are in general but poor accountants. They are unused to keep any account, either of their income or expenditure. Hence they have generally to trust to their memories for a statement of their earnings; and it is only with considerable difficulty and cross-questioning that one is able to obtain from them an account of the expenses necessarily attendant upon their labour, and so, by deducting these from the prices paid to them, to arrive at the amount of their clear earnings. Moreover, though I must confess I have met with far more truthfulness on the part of the operative than on that of the employer, still, I believe the workpeople are naturally disposed to imagine that they get less than they really do, even as the employer is inclined to fancy his workmen make more than their real gains.[14]

In most cases, Mayhew had to rely almost entirely upon work-people for evidence, which led to constant concern about his sample and the credibility of the information that was offered. He finally settled on a technique of interviews with a representative cross-section of workers in a trade about their conditions of employment and life style. The selection of informants was always made in con-sultation with a "gentleman" acquainted with the trade, workpeople well known by other workpeople to have a comprehensive view of the trade and, increasingly and preferably, with trade societies where they existed.[15] The letters on the tailors give a clear picture of how, in the best of the industrial profiles, he sliced through a trade in several ways to get representative types. Quite explicitly readers were informed,

I consulted several of the most experienced and intelligent work-men, as to the best means of arriving at a correct opinion respect-ing the state of the trade. It was agreed among us that, first, with regard to an estimate as to the amount of wages, I should see a hand employed at each of the different branches of the trade. After this I was to be taken to a person who was the captain or leading man of a shop; then to one who, in the technicality of the trade, had a "good chance" of work and finally to one who was only casually employed. It was considered that these classes taken

[14] See Letters IX and X below, pp. 152–3, 159ff.
[15] For the use of "gentlemen", see Letter VII on slopworkers and needle-women, and for trade unions, Letter XXXII on the shoemakers, below, pp. 127, 236.

in connection with others, would give the public a correct view of the condition, earnings and opinions of the trade.[16]

As with every trade, the division of labour was one crucial cutting edge and a representative worker doing each job was contacted, in this case, trousers, coat and waistcoat hands. But great care was always taken to establish the wage range and different terms of hire within particular jobs. Supplementary interviews were conducted with the highest paid "captain" of a shop, with a fully employed tailor and with a hand who worked only during the "brisk season". Moving from the unionized to the cheap branch of the trade, the interviews continued with men who worked on the premises of a slop-shop, men who took work direct from the slop-house to make up at home and finally those who received their outwork through the hands of middlemen. Constantly on the look-out for the *causes* of low wages, whenever Mayhew found systems or practices which maintained the cheap trade, extra interviews were collected to probe them. The sweating system was subjected to multiple scrutiny, through interviews with an actual sweater, a journeyman lodging with a sweater and an outdoor worker for a show-shop (this was Nicoll of Regent Street) which had discharged all its tailors to carry on working through sweaters. The same was done with the "kidnapping system" to recruit Irish and country lads and with the immigration of foreign labour.

Yet Mayhew still worried lest this technique of locating representative individuals be confused with an attempt to tell extreme sob stories. "I seek for no extreme cases", he assured his readers, "if anything is to come of this hereafter, I am well aware that the end can be gained only by laying bare the sufferings of a *class*, and not of any particular individuals belonging thereto".[17] He worked out a system of multiple and usually statistical checks on individual testimonies. In keeping with his original intention, he presented any information from government reports or standard statistical manuals which might test allegations about the causes of economic change.[18] But he also went to great trouble to pursue original inquiries—which yielded information available nowhere else—collecting facts from employers, increasingly from tradesmen and merchants, from local authorities and voluntary societies and even from the metropolitan

[16] Letter XVI. The following discussion is also based on XVII and XVIII, below.

[17] Letter VII below, p. 127.

[18] Thus after shoemakers complained that they were injured by the reduction of tariff duties on foreign shoes, statistics were published in Letter XXXIII showing the movement of import duties and the volume of foreign imports.

and provincial police.[19] He kept inventing new ways to use working class informants for cross-checking purposes. He solicited account books for written evidence of wages especially over a "series" of years. He called meetings of operatives in order to get a larger number of informants and "arrive at a correct average as to the earnings of the class". He availed himself eagerly of any trade union surveys about wages and conditions, covering a large sample of members.[20]

Apart from invaluable evidence in the letters themselves, it is hard to catch a glimpse of Mayhew actually at work in the field or composing the articles since none of the original notebooks seem to have survived. There is only one breezy account written by a catty acquaintance, Sutherland Edwards, fifty years later :

> He was in his glory at the time. He was largely paid, and the greatest joy of all, had an army of assistant writers, stenographers, and hansom cabmen constantly at his call. London labourers . . . were brought to the *Chronicle* office, where they told their tales to Mayhew, who redictated them, with an added colour of his own, to the shorthand writer . . . Augustus helped him in his vivid descriptions, and an authority on political economy controlled his gay statistics.[21]

This club-man's view, though misleading, does contain some significant half-truths. The investigations were the work of a team, several of whose members can be identified. "Gus" Mayhew, Henry's younger brother who had collaborated with him on several novels and pot-boilers, probably helped fairly often both in collecting material and in writing it up.[22] Two other important assistants came

---

[19] In Letters VII and VIII, he juxtaposed tables of prices collected from contractors in military clothing to the testimonies of operatives, concluding "the agreement between the two speaks highly for the honesty of both parties"; see also *London Labour and the London Poor* (1851), preface, p. iv. For his inquiries into prostitution, he circulated a questionnaire which was completed by the metropolitan police and more than 60 provincial police authorities, as well as voluntary societies, hospitals and workhouses: "Answers to Correspondents", No. 41, 20 September, No. 43, 4 October, No. 45, 18 October; No. 49, 15 November 1851, etc.

[20] See Letter XI for his discussion and use of the first two checks, below 162ff. For use of trade union surveys made by the shoemakers and cabinet-makers, see Letters XXXII and LXIII, below, pp. 229, 360.

[21] H. Sutherland Edwards, *Personal Recollections* (London, 1900), p. 60.

[22] W. Tinsley, *Random Recollections of an Old Publisher* (London, 1900), II, pp. 73–4 suggest that Gus "did a good share of the rough work in interviewing", a view shared by H. Vizetelly, *Glances Back Through Seventy Years* (London, 1893), I, p. 408. Gus's novel *Paved with Gold, or the Romance and the Reality of the London Streets* (London, 1858), showed that

to light during the controversy with the Ragged School Union, when they leapt to Mayhew's defence after his whole method had been impugned by the Union Secretary. Both Richard "late of the City Mission" Knight and Henry Wood stayed with Mayhew when he left the *Chronicle* and Mayhew paid Wood the compliment of having contributed so much material to *London Labour and the London Poor* that he might be "fairly considered as one of its authors". We have not been able to find out anything more about Wood. He may possibly have been the back-room boy who worked through and prepared the standard national and metropolitan statistics which Mayhew drew upon so lavishly.[23] But Knight had impeccable credentials. In the two years before he joined Mayhew, he had been a salaried missionary of the London City Mission, serving the district of New Court in the City.[24] His work there included routine visits to the poor in their own homes and would have given him valuable contacts and experience. The selection process for agents was stiff; a candidate had to produce testimonials from his pastor and "two or three other approved Christian persons" and outlast a series of interviews and a three month probation period.

The team had been working together for "several months" before the ragged schools inquiry, and had probably established a fairly constant division of labour. It would seem that Mayhew defined the framework of the investigation and then gave to Knight the job of finding some of the addresses of credible and representative informants. "I beg to be permitted to state", Knight wrote of Mayhew,

that, having been engaged for these several months past, it never has been his practice either to select his cases or to publish the statements of individuals without previously obtaining some voucher for their credibility. I can conscientiously declare that I have never received instruction from him to furnish him with the addresses of such parties as might not be justly considered fair types of the class into whose condition he has been inquiring at the time.[25]

he had investigated juvenile delinquency and vagrancy; the Preface explained that the sections on crossing sweepers and a rat match were first undertaken at his brother's request to form part of *London Labour*.

[23] The statistical member of the team continued in Mayhew's service after he left the *Chronicle*: see the reference to "the gentleman to whom the calculation of the statistics of this periodical is confided" in "Answers to Correspondents", No. 39, 6 September 1851.

[24] London City Mission, *12th Annual Report* (1847), *13th Annual Report* (1848). For the selection of missionaries see the *2nd Annual Report* (1836).

[25] *Morning Chronicle*, Letter XLIX, 25 April 1850.

From Henry Wood's testimonial, it is clear that some of the less important interviews were farmed out to him, and his notes were then passed on to Mayhew. The more important interviews were conducted jointly, with Mayhew interrogating the witness and Wood performing the role of stenographer. Wood also insisted that Mayhew did not "lead" the witnesses with any bias, or suppress evidence which he disliked, and confirmed that "your Correspondent's instructions to me have invariably been, to take average cases and to test their truthfulness by all possible means".[26]

It is not, in these latter days of sociology, surprising that Mayhew employed interviewers; what is surprising is the care with which he supervised the work, and his own personal presence in the work at every stage, with a scrupulousness which might well put some incomparably better financed and equipped investigators of the present day to shame. Throughout the first twelve months of the inquiry the columns of the *Morning Chronicle* were open to critics who wished to challenge his evidence in any form, and thereafter he made the wrappers of the parts available for critical correspondence. What is remarkable is that he came under searching attack, on grounds of selection and misrepresentation of evidence, on only one occasion (the Ragged Schools case), and, in our view, the honours of this contest were emphatically his. Other critics who challenged the statements of some of his informants were usually willing to give credit to the general authenticity of his reports. Thus the managers of a Sailors' Home, defending themselves against criticism, added that "your Correspondent, with his companion, had during the last two or three weeks paid several visits" to the Home, consulted its cash-books, ledgers and accounts, and conversed with the boarders privately, and acknowledged that all had been done in "a spirit of truth and justice".[27]

Mayhew was clearly in control of the operation and beyond devising the ways to get information, his remarkable gifts as an interviewer, his rare ability to inspire confidence and establish

[26] Ibid.
[27] *Morning Chronicle*, 2 May 1850. However, in the haste of weekly publication, the standard of proof-reading was not always high and after 1852 Mayhew's attention appears to have relaxed so that errors which were drawn to his attention during the course of part-publication went uncorrected or unqueried in the edition of 1861. Thus in "Answers to Correspondents", No. 21, 3 May 1851, the landlord of several model lodging houses, and a group of residents in one lodging house off Drury Lane challenged the statements of an informant. Mayhew apologized for reporting erroneous information but in this case (as in others) the parts already printed were bound up without correction for volume one of *London Labour* (1851) and republished without alteration in 1861.

quick rapport, made these techniques produce their best results. Far from causing embarrassment, in Mayhew's hands, the meetings of operatives helped to create a strong sense of shared experience which encouraged rather than inhibited the most intimate personal statements. The needlewomen, who had turned to prostitution to supplement their meagre earnings, laughed together and cried together and one by one gave very frank accounts of their life stories.[28] His visits to working men and women in their homes, where he must have appeared a most unusual upper-class caller, treating them with obvious respect and actually eager to hear their opinions, were not considered intrusions. If it wasn't for his sympathetic presence, tricks like fingering a utensil or looking pointedly at an object in the room to force a comment on it would not have been sufficient to draw out people like the proud upholsteress who insisted, "I don't tell my affairs to everybody. It's quite enough for me to struggle by myself. I may feel a great many privations that I do not wish to be known", or the distressed gentlewoman who refused to say anything which might reveal her identity but ended up by giving such a detailed life history that her friends could not help but recognize her.[29]

By means of the interviews with representative operatives, the core of his method, Mayhew was able to elicit the range of information he wanted. When possible, the informants were seen in their own homes where they could talk most freely. Of course, Mayhew

[28] Letter XI, below, p. 168. Mayhew's skill was never more obvious than at a meeting for young thieves, part of the inquiry into those who *won't* work. Here group identity was no problem, for the boys showed such rowdy solidarity that the meeting almost didn't begin. The turning point came when Mayhew touched on the subject of low lodging houses and the boys refused to talk, afraid that they would have no place to go if lodging houses were closed down. Mayhew played ruthlessly on their fears, but ended with such an inspired gesture of confidence in his audience that he managed to gain their trust. Stating that no thief had ever cheated him, Mayhew singled out a boy who had gone to prison twenty-six times, gave him a sovereign and asked him to return with the change, promising that there would be no punishment if he did not come back. The effect on the meeting was electric: "They mounted the forms in their eagerness to obtain the first glimpse of his return. It was clear that their honour was at stake; and several said they would kill the lad in the morning if he made off with the money. Many minutes elapsed in almost painful suspense, and some of his companions began to fear that so large a sum of money had proved too great a temptation for the boy. At last, however, a tremendous burst of cheering announced the lad's return. The delight of his companions broke forth again and again, in long and loud peals of applause, and the youth advanced amidst triumphant shouts to the platform, and gave up the money in full." After this episode, the meeting became "more rational and manageable", and several boys spontaneously gave their life stories. *Morning Chronicle*, Letter XXXI, 31 January 1850.

[22] Letter IX; the distressed gentlewoman appears below, p. 153.

led his witnesses, as any interviewer must, but it is easy to recon-
struct the more-or-less standard questionnaire which was evidently
rehearsed. The interviews nearly always began with questions about
wages and conditions of employment—job held, length of time in
the trade, payment for quantity of work performed, expenses necessarily attached to the job, hours of work, regularity of employment
throughout the year, net weekly wage in the "brisk" and "slack"
seasons, average weekly wage over the year. Then the informant
was usually asked to contrast wages and conditions at present with
the past (most workmen had at least twenty years of experience to
draw on) and to account for changes which had taken place in the
trade or to discuss features of the work situation which particularly
pleased or disturbed him. Frequently, though less consistently, consumption patterns were assessed by questions about household
expenditure and pawning. Mayhew did not paraphrase the interviews but compressed (and no doubt edited) the informant's own
words into a continuous monologue which enabled readers to see
the world through the eyes of the poor and were often very reveal-
ing about language and values. However, this should not be confused
with a journalistic desire to create picturesque and colourful "characters" for their own sake. The largest part of the testimony was
always devoted to the often tedious business of calculating wage
figures and to the informants' views on economic change.

One way to test the truth of the assertion that "Mayhew's work
was essentially a form of higher journalism, not of social analysis",[30]
is to compare his *Morning Chronicle* letters with the various genres
of social reporting which burgeoned between 1840 and 1860. While
the statisticians were boasting that "the spirit of the present age has
an evident tendency to confront the figures of speech with the figures
of arithmetic", their claims were being undercut by the fashion
among newspapers and periodicals for sponsoring investigations of
the working class, often out of a grandiose sense of professional
mission. "The extraordinary influence of the Newspaper Press in
this country", the *Newcastle Chronicle* editorialized,

> has been exercised in a manner alike remarkable and praise-
> worthy. In addition to the formation and guidance of public
> opinion, some of its more influential organs have taken upon

<hr>

[30] H. J. Dyos, "The Slums of Victorian London", in *Victorian Studies*,
September 1967, p. 13. His full verdict was that Mayhew's "findings, made
in the first place for the *Morning Chronicle* inquiries of 1849–50, provided
little more than a panorama of the poverty—and of the itinerant employment—to be seen on the streets. It is possible to say that they suffered from
his under-disciplined curiosity and his spontaneous desire to make the poor
known to the rich."

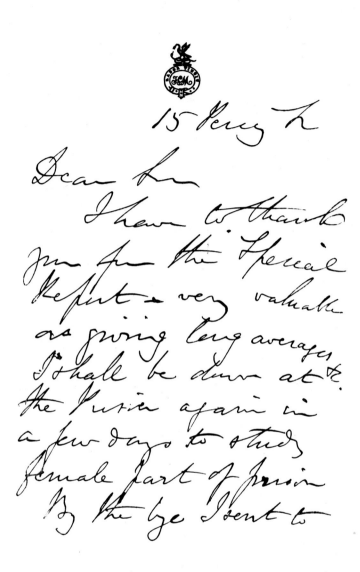

PLATE III

Part of a Letter from Mayhew to an Official of Tothill
Fields Prison. He asked permission to photograph dinner
in the boys' oakum room giving assurances that in the
finished engravings the identity of the prisoners would be
unrecognizable.

PLATE IV. The serving of Dinner in the Oakum-Room of the Boys' Prison at Tothill Fields from *The Criminal*

themselves an important function, rightly belonging to the Government; they have ascertained, by minute investigation, the real condition of the masses, and have thus revealed to the astonished public, facts . . . imperatively needful to be known and pondered, not only by the legislature, but by all who feel an interest in the mitigation of evil, and the elevation of humanity.[31]

The higher journalism can be divided into area studies and industrial studies. Where the correspondent was itinerant, whether the Eyewitness (ex-Chartist Thomas Cooper) or the *Morning Chronicle* provincial commissioners and could stay in each place for only a short time, the area studies tended to give only a quick sketch of the economic situation, usually focussing on the major industry in the locality, and then moved on to the moral and intellectual condition of the operatives much in the tradition of the statistical investigators, though working through word pictures instead of numbers; the *Newcastle Chronicle* inquiry hardly touched on employment at all. The industrial studies, superficially closer to Mayhew's format, suffer from being more concerned to describe than to collect material for analytical purposes. George Dodd's work for the *Penny Magazine* was a species of industrial tourism, which gave clear pictures of how the workshop looked and how the product was made, but said little about social relationships of production or wages and hours of work, while James Devlin's articles on the "Industrial Interests" quickly abandoned the present to explore the remote history of trades "till the time of the conquest". Only the survey of "The Condition of the Working Classes of Edinburgh and Leith", appearing in the *Edinburgh News* approached Mayhew's standard, but then it was directly modelled on Mayhew's work, and yet while more tidy and compact, it lacked much of Mayhew's sociological fascination.[32] In all these journalistic studies, there was little of Mayhew's scrupulous attention to making clear what methods of investigation were to be followed or how the credibility of evidence

---

[31] *Inquiry into the Condition of the Poor of Newcastle-upon-Tyne from the Newcastle Chronicle* (Newcastle, 1850), p. 5.
[32] The Eyewitness reports on "The Condition of the People of England", appeared in *Douglas Jerrold's Weekly Newspaper* at weekly or fortnightly intervals between 25 July 1846 and 26 December 1846. James Devlin's articles for the same newspaper began on 5 September 1846. George Dodd's articles were subsequently collected into *Days at the Factories or the Manufacturing Industry of Great Britain Described,* Series I, London (1843). The *Edinburgh News* series appeared at weekly and fortnightly intervals between 25 September 1852 and 29 July 1854 : this survey was not concerned at all with poverty but with the industrial condition of the true working class— artisans and labourers—emphatically omitting the street folk.

# 66 THE UNKNOWN MAYHEW

was to be established. Nor were the working people allowed to speak for themselves.

What people often have in mind, when they lump Mayhew with other journalists, is a type of low life reporting about the "scenes and characters of London", which did suffer from under-disciplined curiosity and over-developed theatricality. This genre of literary rambles had much earlier roots in light-hearted and thrilling tours of quasi-criminal London, exhibiting its "cheats and villanies", still very much the subject of Tom and Jerry's camera obscura in 1821.[33] By the 1840's and especially after 1850 (boosted by Mayhew's work on the street folk), a steady stream of books and periodicals poured out to quench the thirst of the rich for information, preferably lively and entertaining, about the poor. Much of this journalism, particularly from the Mayhew circle, was a thinly disguised bid to capitalize on a public appetite, using the poor as more grist for the literary mill. But there was sometimes an undertone of serious purpose, as in J. E. Ritchie's tours of London pubs and clubs to expose areas of moral degradation and to chart the field for philanthropic work. (Despite himself Ritchie obviously enjoyed the vitality of the scenes he too insistently denounced.) The magazines and books were always collections of a staggering number of vignettes, characterized by the lack of any consistent theme or problem for investigation apart from the spectacle of low London and its "ever-changing kaleidoscopes of form and feature"[34]—utterly different from Mayhew's dogged preoccupation with employment and poverty in the *Morning Chronicle*.

Their main concern was to create dramatic word pictures; C. M. Smith assured his readers that though he never knowingly overstepped the limits of fact, he had "endeavoured, however trivial the topics to clothe each one in something resembling at least a literary garb".[35] Favourite themes were fairs, pubs or markets which lent

[33] See Pierce Egan, *Life in London; or the Day and Night Scenes of Jerry Hawthorn, Esq. and his Elegant Friend Corinthian Tom Accompanied by Bob Logic, the Oxonian, in their Rambles and Sprees through the Metropolis* (London, 1821).

[34] See, for example, Charles Knight (ed.), *London*, 6 volumes (1841–1843); "London Penetralia" series in *Our Own Times*, April-July 1846; Albert Smith (ed.), *Gavarni in London: Sketches of Life and Character* (London, 1849); G. M. Smith, *Curiosities of London Life: or Phases Physiological and Social of the Great Metropolis* (London, 1853), also his *Little World of London or Pictures in Little of London Life* (London, 1867); J. E. Ritchie, *The Night Side of London* (London, 1857), his *Here and There in London* (1859) and *About London* (1860); G. A. Sala, *Gaslight and Daylight, with Some London Scenes they Shine Upon* (London, 1872). For other books in this genre, see H. J. Dyos' excellent bibliographical footnotes in "The Slums of Victorian London".

[35] Smith, *Curiosities of London Life*, pp. VI-VII.

themselves to description in language like "the bustle and variety of the spectacle" and "the nature of each particular scene and the character of the actors therein". Individuals were inflated into theatrical characters so that a beggar became "a *tableau vivant* of unmerited poverty", a coal heaver "the next who figures upon our picturesque stage—the knight of the fan-tail and shovel".[36] In his industrial studies, Mayhew kept such purple passages and theatricalizing of work people down to the minimum. Although Mayhew's idea of taking testimonies from the poor is seen as a journalistic device, it is interesting how little direct quotation figured in this characters and scenes genre. If the author used speech at all, he invented dialogue for his characters for literary purposes; C. M. Smith wrote in the first person as a bus conductor, using his working class character only as a literary vehicle to tell a story about the affairs of a family who used the bus.[37]

Artisans or labourers did not often appear among the London characters, the street folk were more "picturesque", but when occasionally they were dealt with, the treatment was so inferior to Mayhew's that comparison almost becomes a nonsense. Thus C. M. Smith managed to cover the ethnic character of more occupational groups in a piece called "Genesis of the Workers", than Mayhew studied in the whole of the *Morning Chronicle*, linking his piece in a casual stream of consciousness way.[38] Why his subjects should have come to London or what effect they have on the trades they enter was not of much interest to him—though of consuming concern to Mayhew. In C. M. Smith's voluminous output there was also a profile of the "Garret Master" which ended with a visit to a garret master at home, and turned into a nasty little drama about the wages of gin, with no dialogue at all :

[36] C. Kenney "Covent Garden", p. 28; Angus Reach (later a *Morning Chronicle* provincial correspondent) "Beggars", p. 11; T. Miller "Car Men and Coal-Heavers", p. 40, all in *Gavarni in London*.

[37] "Views of Life from a Fixed Stand-Point", in *Little World of London*, pp. 13–18.

[38] Having said that "an immensely disproportionate" number of bakers are Scotsmen, he changed the subject by cosily informing us that "next door to our baker lives a barber who tells us that half the barbers in London are London born, but that a good many of the fashionable hairdressers are from the watering-places and genteel towns. Our communicative barber, who is not perpetually shaving, ekes out his time by breeding, and teaching, and doctoring canary-birds; upon all which matters he has something to say that may be worth hearing. The tobacco trade he says is in the hands of Londoners, but the best tobacco decidedly comes from Bristol. The Jews have a good deal to do with cheap cigars, which are manufactured both by men and women; and some of them, he avers, may be made to smell uncommonly like a dish of cabbage by simply boiling them for an hour." *Little World of London*, p. 300.

I heard a light foot on the stairs; and the door opening, a little girl of about six, almost decently clad in comparison with the others, entered the room, clasping a black bottle carefully in both hands. The mother, apparently unwilling that a stranger should be aware of the nature of the burden brought by the child, was about concealing it in a cupboard; but the father, who, I now for the first time perceived, was on the high road to intoxication, swore at her angrily for pretending to be ashamed of what he proclaimed she liked as well as anybody, and loudly demanded the gin-bottle. With a sigh and a look of shame she complied with his desire, when he immediately applied himself to the contents with an air of dogged satisfaction . . . here want was not the destroyer; a fiend of more hideous aspect and deadlier purpose held undisputed sway in this wretched abode of perverted industry and precocious intemperance . . . the hateful vice of intoxication. . . .[39]

Although Mayhew sometimes, and with scrupulous brevity, set the scene of the interior where he was to do an interview, the primary job was the interview establishing wages and employment conditions. In matters like his task and methods of social investigation, Mayhew completely transcended the London low life genre.

Of course, Mayhew could not be as systematic in the presentation of material as he wished. The relentless schedule of weekly or more frequent deadlines virtually forced him to publish his notebooks as he went. In these circumstances, his various techniques of investigation (interviews and multiple checks) became the contents of the letters, introduced by a general picture of the division of labour, work-processes, history and union organization of each trade. No one was more aware than Mayhew of how unsystematically he moved from trade to trade and he continually apologized that,

this unsystematic mode of treating the subject is almost a necessary evil attendant upon the nature of the investigation. In the course of my inquiries into the earnings and condition of one class of people, sources of information respecting the habits and incomings of another are opened up to me, of which, for several reasons, I am glad to avail myself at the immediate moment, rather than defer making use of them at a more fitting and orderly occasion.[40]

But lack of system of this kind should not obscure the more basic

[39] *Curiosities of London Life*, pp. 36–37. The vignette of the Garret-Master was sandwiched between profiles of "The Mushroom Hunter" and "The Label Printer".

[40] *Morning Chronicle*, Letter XII, 27 November 1849.

consistency and continuity of the major questions he asked and techniques of investigation he used.

## II

Mayhew, in fact, worked constantly to develop a coherent framework for the survey and here revealed a curious and characteristic habit of mind. Mayhew was a relentless classifier. Like Booth and other nineteenth century investigators, he borrowed an idea of scientific procedure from biology and thought one of the "most important" ways to order a body of information was through "a correct grouping of objects into genera, and species, orders and varieties".[41] A fondness for making categories and sub-categories stamped all his interpretive writing, but his biological imagination was most fertile in a search for a "scientific" classification of the working class to establish the order in which to study and present different occupational groups. First dividing "those who *will* work" into artisans, labourers and costers, he further refined his classification in letter LII, where he grouped the artisans more specifically around the raw material they worked upon. When he next returned to his hobby horse, at the beginning of the prostitution volume, the classification had mushroomed far beyond the needs of the survey to include the whole of the British population arranged according to function in the economy.[42] Mayhew began to use his classification in the letters on the workers in wood (LIX–LXIX) and aimed eventually to rearrange all his industrial material on the new principles in *London Labour and the London Poor* but did not reach his target.[43] However, there was never any suggestion that this search for static "natural systems" would shed much light on the causal connections between employment and poverty. Rather, the classification was a way to give order to the "cyclopaedia of industry", the volumes of evidence in the bluebook. Even in the most

[41] *L.L. & L.P.* (1851), III, p.4.

[42] By this time, Mayhew had deliberately made the classification a project in itself, no longer a subsidiary part of the survey, because he felt the systems already in use were so inadequate. He reviewed and criticized the systems used in the census and the various industrial exhibitions (making rude remarks about the classification graciously bestowed by Prince Albert on the Great Exhibition), and then elaborated his own. This time he divided those who will work into the Enrichers—under which he included collectors, extractors, growers, artificers, auxiliaries (placing both capitalists and unskilled labour here)—Distributors, Benefactors, Servitors, and then went on to itemize those who cannot work, will not work and need not work. *L.L. & L.P.* (1851), III, (1861) IV, pp. 4–27. Earlier versions of the classification in Letters III and LII, 26 October 1849, 16 May 1850.

[43] See Appendix I, below.

abstract discussions of scientific procedure, Mayhew also spoke of the "imaginative quality of mind", which was "synthetic or combinative, in its operation, and so invents . . . generalizes".[44]

Mayhew's attempts to interpret his raw material and generalize about the industrial causes of low wages and poverty more than counterbalance his biological inclinations. In this connection, the *Chronicle* letters and "Answers to Correspondents" columns provide a unique and fascinating record of a mind in action. Mayhew was a sophisticated empiricist who had no mystical faith that all the facts when collected would automatically suggest their relation to each other but interpreted his material as he went along. His hypotheses (he would call them "speculations") developed continually as he discovered new facts and he was led to refine his questions and solicit new information in turn. It is worth noting that Mayhew saw himself as an empiricist with

> the right of changing or modifying his sentiments as often as a more enlarged series of facts, may present new views to his mind. It is in this light that he wishes his speculations to be received— for speculations they are, though perhaps based on a greater number of phenomena than any economist has as yet personally obtained. For the present he can only declare his determination to follow the facts, whithersoever they may lead (for he has no object but the truth), and if he be open to the charge of generalizing, before he has made himself acquainted with all the particulars, he at least has a greater right to do so than any economist of the present day—seeing that he is perhaps the first who has sought to evolve the truths of the Labour Question by personal investigation.[45]

From week to week it is possible to trace the subtle interplay between facts and hypotheses in Mayhew's mind.

The survey began with a cluster of hypotheses about "those who *will* work". Attributing their poverty to low wages, high prices or improvident habits, Mayhew decided to focus on occupations which were notorious for paying low wages.[46] His first call, on Spitalfields, immediately threw into question another preliminary hypothesis, that low wages were to be found among the unskilled while artisans because of their training and skills were well paid, for the skilled silk weavers appeared "to constitute a striking exception to the rule, from what cause I do not even venture to conjecture" (although

---

[44] *Low Wages, Their Causes, Consequences and Remedies* (London, 1851), p. 1.

[45] "Answers to Correspondents", No. 16, 29 March 1851.

[46] Letter II, below, p. 104.

later in the survey he felt quite confident that he could explain their position).[47] Moving next to unskilled labour in the docks, he then returned to the periphery of the artisan world when he studied slop workers in tailoring, military clothing and needlewomen generally. He quickly came to feel that the artisans would have to come within his scope; for to examine the causes of low wages, dynamic factors had to be considered and these could not be adequately probed in a study of slop workers in isolation. "If we wish to obtain a knowledge of the history and progress of the slop trade", Mayhew wrote in Letter XVI,

> we must first inquire into the nature and characteristics of that art of which it is an inferior variety; and it is with this view that, before investigating the condition of the male slop-worker, I have made it my business to examine into the state of the Operative Tailors of London.

The trade now became his characteristic unit of study. Painstaking work on the tailors, shoemakers, carpenters and cabinetmakers (in this writer's opinion his best industrial profiles), clearly revealed the recent development of a slop branch which was a jungle of rampant competition inhabited by a new competitive type of employer and untamed by trades union organization or legislative regulation. An ill-omen for the future, as well-paid artisans and respectable masters repeatedly testified, competition from the slop branch tended to depress conditions within the honourable section. More relevant than the earlier distinction between skilled and unskilled, were the workmen's own categories of "honourable" and "dishonourable" labour to which Mayhew also gave a less emotive definition, calling honourable labour unionized men, who could exert some control over wages, and dishonourable labour "non-society men", whose wages were determined "solely by competition".[48]

The interviews with representative individuals revealed a wage range which descended rapidly once the border between honourable and dishonourable labour had been crossed. However provident a workman might try to be, poverty stubbornly accompanied the low wages and irregularity of work in the slop branch of a trade. Indeed Mayhew began to feel that a more subtle process was at work where poverty itself was creating improvident habits.[49] Although he continued to document the incidence of poverty in the various trades, he became increasingly concerned to explore how the cheap trade was maintained and how low wages and casuality were created.

[47] *Morning Chronicle*, Letter III, 26 October 1849.
[48] Letter LXIV, below, p. 373.
[49] See below, p. 82.

It had been a matter of routine procedure to expose the particular system for organizing labour in each cheap trade, introduced or exploited by competitive employers. But in Letters LXV and LXVI on the slop cabinet-makers, Mayhew began to speculate about whether all the specific patterns had a more general effect. The cheap cabinet trade seemed especially to stimulate his generalizing imagination because it provided an example so contrary to received political economy and a challenge to facile pronouncements about over-population and repugnant nostrums like emigration. Here was a trade where the supply or number of workmen had dropped by a third, where the work had increased (what Mayhew called demand) and yet where wages had plummeted 300–400 per cent between 1831 and 1841.

Mayhew began to speculate more generally that exploitation could create an unnecessary excess of hands. He insisted that the supply of labour was not simply the number of workmen in any trade but that their "productiveness" also had to be considered. The main characteristic of any slop branch was that employers ruthlessly forced the productivity of labour, trying to get more work done by the same or fewer men at the same or lower wages. This increase in productivity resulted in an *artificial* surplus of hands, the reduction of wages and, Mayhew later added, increasing irregularity or casuality of work. In Mayhew's words,

> any system of labour which tends to make the members of a craft produce a greater quantity of work than usual, tends at the same time to overpopulate the trade as certainly as an increase of workmen. This law may be summed up briefly in the expression that *over-work makes under-pay.*[50]

The reverse of the proposition, "under-pay makes over-work" was also true. With shrewd insight, Mayhew observed that when wages fell, the workman "seldom or never thinks of reducing his expenditure to his income, but rather increasing his labour, so as still to bring his income, by extra production, up to his expenditure". Overwork again leading to under-pay, a vicious downward spiral was set in motion.

Under the general concept of forced productivity, or what he later called "economy of labour", Mayhew was eventually able to

[50] Letter LXVI, below p. 385. Mayhew later wrote, "a surplusage of hands in a trade tends to change the employment of the great majority from a state of constancy and regularity into one of casuality and precariousness", and estimated that "in the generality of trades . . . one-third of the hands are fully employed, one-third partially, and one-third unemployed throughout the year". *L.L. & L.P.* (1851), II, pp. 300–301.

group the seemingly endless variety of patterns for organizing labour which he discovered in the London slop trades.[51] In Letter LXVI, he highlighted the anomalous fact that the means used to force productivity in London were not always new and sophisticated, not always the division of labour or the large system of production cited by the political economists, but involved employers and slop-sellers exploiting older economic patterns for new purposes.

Primarily the mechanisms tended to connect the workman's interest directly to his labour either 1. through piece work— the case in the tailoring trade after the strike of 1834 had failed or 2. by the transformation of the journeyman into a small master, at once capitalist and labourer, like the chamber master among the shoemakers and the garret master in slop cabinet making. The small masters, although capitalists, were in a very vulnerable position because they did not raise their own food and thus had to bring their wares to market immediately, where they quickly became the prey of slop-sellers. Small masters and domestic piece-workers tended to employ a variety of secondary means to increase their output; these included scamping their work (omitting details to get through it faster), and extending their hours to include even the Sunday. Worst of all, domestic workers tended to become middlemen, employing cheap labour like apprentices or members of the family who need not have come into the labour market at all if the pressure to produce more had been eased. To Mayhew the middle man operative was the tragic victim and villain of the system : "all my investigations go to prove that it is . . . this contractor—this trading operative—who is invariably the prime mover in the reduction of the wages of his fellow workmen".[52]

By the time Mayhew started publishing *London Labour* on his own, he was a very angry man. What was intended as an impartial and straightforward examination of poverty and industry had turned into a vicious dogfight with powerful ideological and vested interests. His break with the *Morning Chronicle* over free-trade and Mr. Nicoll of Regent Street, constant hounding from the *Economist* and his growing dossier of exploitation in the London trades all

[51] Mayhew later grouped many "systems" under the heading of economy of labour in the section "Of the Scurf Trade Among the Rubbish-Carters", *L.L. & L.P.* (1851), II, pp. 328ff. In the same volume, where he discussed "Casual Labour in General", he put the means used to economize labour under three heads—"causing men to work quicker" (here he added machinery and gave the example of the sawyers trade), "causing men to work longer", and changes in the mode of work or hiring (where he included dock labour hired casually for the duration only of the specific job), pp. 301ff.

[52] *L.L. & L.P.* (1851), II, p. 329.

combined to bring his fury, muzzled until now, to the boiling point. At last in the new "Answers to Correspondents" column, he had a platform to make crystal clear his own point of view and openly speculate on his findings. Not unexpectedly the political economists, seen as the custodians of the dominant ideology, came in for near libellous abuse. Not only were their writings inadequate to explain the facts—"economists . . . have shown the same aversion to collect facts as mad dogs have to touch water. It is so much easier to ensconce themselves in some smug corner and there remain all day, like big-bottomed spiders, spinning cobweb theories amid heaps of *rubbish.*" Their prescriptions buttressed only the capitalist's interest— "That which is said by the economists to be the greatest possible benefit to the community is a gain only to the small portion of it termed the moneyed classes,"—and were grossly immoral, though masquerading as amoral :

> dogmas . . . which are enunciated with the same confidence as if they were matters of Revelation, constituting as it were the Bible of selfishness—the Gospel preached by Mammon giving unto us the last new commandment. "*Do* your neighbour *as* your neighbour would *do* you", in contradistinction to that higher code of kindness and charity which Edinburgh Reviewers and Manchester Men do not hesitate now to rank as morbid sentimentalism.[53]

Mayhew used his anger to intellectual advantage. Further provoked by correspondents who defended political economy, though often in a bowdlerized popular form, stimulated by simple requests to explain how wages were regulated and how they should be regulated, he broadened his scope still further to include the national economy. He came to see the London trades not in isolation but as an integral part of the capitalist industrial system, sharing its rhythms but intensifying them in a more exploitative way. The question of low wages was linked with wages in general. On the weekly covers, Mayhew presented a closely reasoned set of "lectures" to undermine the Ricardian economists' version of supply and demand.[54]

[53] "Answers to Correspondents", No. 34, 2 August; No. 44, 11 October; No. 20, 26 April 1851.
[54] The most important "lectures" appeared in "Answers to Correspondents" No. 16, 29 March; Nos. 18–22, 12 April–10 May; No. 42, 27 September; No. 50, 22 November; No. 54, 20 December 1851; No. 56, 3 January; No. 58, 17 January 1852. All are available in the British Museum copy of the 1851 edition. Mayhew said he would consider how the "profit fund" influenced the "wage fund" and if this discussion ever appeared it was probably in No. 26, 7 June 1851. Exhaustive inquiries have failed to locate this lecture which might shed further light on crucial points like capitalist motivation and the movement of profits.

In the end (and not surprisingly) Mayhew did not destroy and re-make the world of economic orthodoxy in which he lived. The lectures reveal that he did not have the colossal intellectual equipment of a Marx, necessary to mount a successful attack. He had to make his forays sporadically in weekly instalments and this could not lead to thoroughness, profundity or even consistency. Perhaps the serialized book *Low Wages,* which was meant to be a reworking and expansion of the theories first presented on the covers of *London Labour,* might have corrected some of this defect, but it seems to have reached only four numbers, dying in mid-sentence.[55] One is left with the feeling that the lectures are the work of a massive autodidact who had the naïve habit of going the long way round to prove a point and cited evidence and authorities of vastly unequal quality side by side. Often hypothetical situations, cited for argument's sake, are then assumed to be the fact without proof. To some extent this was the result of Mayhew not having enough empirical information, even about the London trades, for the kinds of factors,

---

[55] The prospectus for *Low Wages* began with a declaration that "Mr. Mayhew from the commencement of his investigations has found the received doctrines of Political Economy are insufficient either to explain or remedy the evils of unregulated labour, and he has been long engaged in generalizing the facts he has collected in the course of his inquiries, and in making deductions therefrom, with a view to the better understanding of the 'perils of the nation'.

"Some of the articles on the 'Labour Question' which have been printed on the wrappers of London Labour will be inserted in the present volume, which, being of a special character, it is thought advisable to issue in a distinct form, so that the facts collected by the Author may exist separately from the opinions engendered by them in his mind". The Table of Contents for the 25 projected numbers then read:

"1st   High and Low Wages, Fair and Unfair Wages; Good and Bad Wages; What is meant by them; and is there a uniform set of circumstances regulating the sum paid as remuneration for labour.

2nd   What *should* regulate wages. (This was as far as he got.)

3rd   What *does not* regulate wages. Here will be discussed the Wage Law of Supply and Demand as propounded by Political Economists.

4th   What *does* regulate wages.

5th   Of a minimum wage and of the difference of wages.

6th   Of the causes of Low Wages in connection with large and small capitalists and the different grades of employers and labourers.

7th   Of the means by which Low Wages are carried out. Here will be given details of the several tricks resorted to by employers to lower the ordinary rate of remuneration.

8th   Of the consequences of Low Wages. Here will be considered the causes of Crime and Pauperism.

9th   Of the remedies for Low Wages. Here the several plans for the alleviation of the distress of the country will be dispassionately reviewed and discussed."

*L.L. & L.P.,* No. 49, 15 November 1851, back cover.

like the material, wage and profit funds, which he now wanted to explore. There is some evidence that he saw his theories as working hypotheses which could explain what he knew was happening in London and a few mechanized industries but which now had to be tested by the collection of more facts.[56] But Mayhew posed any number of awkward questions of the orthodoxy and his treatment of the way wages were regulated within the capitalist system did amount to a refinement of the supply and demand apparatus though not, as he thought, a total destruction of it. In providing an alternative way to fix wages, basing them on equity instead of a scramble, Mayhew did strike out on a different, if not an entirely smooth, path.

Despite shifting positions of attack, the fixed target was the economists' law, in the words of J. S. Mill, that "wages depend upon the demand and supply of labour; or, as it is often expressed, on the proportion between population and capital", population referring to the number of workmen for hire, and capital to the part of the circulating capital set aside for wages.[57] The bulk of the lectures examined the constraints that operated on the wage fund and, tied up with this, the movement of wage rates in the present economic system. Mayhew was very irked by the Ricardian formulation in terms of population and wage fund which simply gave the average amount of income earmarked for the labourer, "without telling us how much he will be required to do for such an income".[58] To Mayhew, wages always meant the *rate* of wages, "the relation between

[56] Information about the cotton trade from statistical manuals like Banfield and Weld's *Statistical Companion* and Salt's *Facts and Figures* were "the only facts that Mr. Mayhew has been able as yet to obtain respecting the relative quantity of materials made up and the prices paid to the operative for so doing, in a given trade in England". In the midst of his lectures, he invited readers to send information which would help fill the blanks about wage, material and profit funds in particular industries: "all that will be necessary for working-men to detail will be (1) the sum paid to them for the making of a particular article, (2) the wholesale cost of the materials entering into that article, and (3) the wholesale (and, if possible, retail) price of such article when finished. . . ." "Answers to Correspondents", No. 21, 3 May; No. 34, 2 August, 1851. This information was also needed to provide the factual groundwork for an alternative wage structure; see below, p. 81.

[57] "Answers to Correspondents", No. 16, 29 March 1851.

[58] "Answers to Correspondents", No. 22, 10 May; No. 20, 26 April 1851. Mayhew also said that the Ricardian law had another form, namely that wages depended on supply of labour and demand, or quantity of work to be done, which gave only an account of the amount of work for each man to do but included nothing about pay. In fact, the Ricardians did not see demand in terms of work to be done and Mayhew's putting formulae into their mouths betrays not so much a lack of familiarity with their work as his own urgent need to consider both work and pay in any discussion of wages.

the remuneration and the work, that is to say, the quantity of
money received in exchange for a definite quantity of labour".[59]
The amount of labour was of central importance in the London investigations where the terrible twins over-work and under-pay had always
appeared hand in hand. But the economists did not take into
account wage rate and so could not expose the actual wage trends
in industry or express how increases in productivity correlated with
wages. Mayhew thought it his contribution to reveal that under
the present system the wage fund was in conflict with the working
capital which governed the amount of work to be done. It was this
conflict which "affords the sole explanation for the growing tendency
to overwork and underpay", not only in the London sweated trades
but throughout the industrial world.[60]

Jumping to the same level of generality as the economists, Mayhew used his most abstract and mathematical reasoning with the
ebullient zeal of a new convert. He assumed a total operating
capital in the national economy and each industry which had been
saved out of the previous year's income after the profits had been
extracted (a year's income was the "produce fund"). This operating
capital might be divided into a "distributive fund" to cover costs
of distribution, a "sinking fund" for capital investment in buildings
and machinery and the "circulating capital" which paid both for
raw materials and wages. Mayhew assumed that the total capital
was fixed in any given year so that an increase in any of its components during that year would involve a decrease in others and
especially the "wage fund". But the most important relationship was
between the two components of the circulating capital, for the
"material fund" expressed the value of materials to be made up or
the gross quantity of work to be done. Thus, if the "material fund"
increased, then the "wage fund" decreased and the wage rate fell.
In simple language, the wage law now became, *"the more work
there is to do, the less the workpeople will get for it"*.[61]

[59] "Answers to Correspondents", No. 22, 10 May; No. 50, 22 November
1851.
[60] "Answers to Correspondents", No. 19, 19 April 1851.
[61] Put in a more complicated way, Mayhew said that "the Wage-Law has
two distinct forms: 1st, the *particular* amount of remuneration for a particular amount of work (wage rate) is *inversely* proportional to the quantity of
the circulating capital expended in the purchase of materials. 2nd, the aggregate amount of remuneration or annual income of each labourer is inversely
proportional; (a) to the number of labourers, the hours of labour, or the rate
of labouring; and (b) to the relative amount of the Material-Fund." He tried
to put the wage law into mathematical form supplying a set of equations
which culminated in one designed to calculate wage rate:
"let C. represent the Circulating Capital; M. the Material-Fund; W. the

Mayhew felt that this model of a juggling act at the expense of the wage fund described the actual trend in industry. In the London sweated trades, a transfer of resources from the wage to the material fund had created the unrelenting pressure toward increased productivity, while the distributive fund had also increased to cover the costs of a large distributive network of slop-sellers with their lavish advertising practices.[62] Not only did wage rates fall here, but weekly

Wage-Fund; L. the number of Labourers; I. the average Income obtained by each labourer; Q. the average quantity of work performed by each; and P. the Pay for making up a certain amount of materials (wage rate); then we have the following results:

(1) $C - M = W$

(2) $C - W = M$

(3) $\dfrac{C - W}{L} = Q$

(4) $\dfrac{C - M}{L} = I$

(5) $\dfrac{C - M}{L} \div \dfrac{C - W}{L} = P$"

"Answers to Correspondents", No. 22, 10 May 1851. He felt that these equations expressed the crucial fact that the number of workers in the labour market did not affect wage rate but only "annual income". However, this held true only when Mayhew made the same assumption as the political economists that the amount of the wage fund would not be affected by the number of workers in the labour market; in reality, the wage fund would not remain static if the number of workers were increased above the number minimally needed to do the work, or if the productivity of workers was so dramatically increased that fewer men were needed to do the same or more work. In both cases the employer would tend to exploit the competition between labourers for the available jobs by simply decreasing the wage fund. No. 16, 29 March 1851; No. 56, 3 January 1852.

In No. 22, Mayhew provided a clear table to illustrate the effect on wage rate and average income where the variables, circulating capital, wage fund, material fund and number of labourers, were altered. However, he ran into trouble trying to express the quantity of work by the amount of the material fund. This worked so long as the price of materials remained constant. But if the price of materials fell, then the same amount of the material fund would purchase more and create more work. He tried to correct for this situation by insisting that "a decrease in the price of materials is the same as an increase in the amount of the material fund".

[62] "Answers to Correspondents", No. 22, 10 May 1851. Mayhew was especially sensitive to rocketing costs because of the use of new techniques like advertising: "trade is forced in every way, and every kind of expedient put in practice, so as to dispose of a great quantity of commodities, and thus enhance the aggregate amount of profits. Prices are cut down to the very quick—Capital is lavished either on advertisement, circulars, or the decoration of premises—gas-lights, plate-glass, and architectural embellishments are used as snares to catch customers—'tremendous failures', 'awful sacrifices', 'bankrupt stocks', mock 'auctions', 'selling off', pretended 'fires'

wages plunged beneath subsistence level. In the advanced industrial sector, the sinking fund, paying for machinery and factory buildings, was being increased at the expense of the circulating capital, a possibility already admitted by Ricardo and J. S. Mill.[63] Within the circulating capital, according to Mayhew, it was the wage fund which was being squeezed most, for the most profitable way to use a machine was to keep it as fully occupied as possible which "must necessitate a vast increase in the quantity of materials and so give rise to an equally vast decrease in the remuneration of the work-people".[64] Mayhew documented falling wage rates in the cotton trade, although he did not remark that this had led to starvation weekly wages for those actually in work. Instead he insisted that the logic of economy of labour in a mechanized industry was to use the machine to get increased productivity with fewer men, as evidenced by the displaced hand-loom weavers in the cotton trade and the unemployed London sawyers. Redundancy was the fertile source of poverty in the mechanized industries.[65] The same transfer of resources which injured the workman fattened the profits of the capitalist who could make up more goods at the same cost.[66]

Yet this industrial system would produce its own chronic instability. While not predicting a time when capitalism would be unable to contain its contradictions, Mayhew felt that declining wages and unemployment meant reduced purchasing power which would lead to endemic crises of overproduction and underconsumption—"when the manufacturers of a country are brought to a stand-still because, from the increase of the Material-Fund, and decrease of the Wage-Fund, we have made up more commodities than the mass of the people have the means of purchasing, and thus produced, at one and the same time, more and more clothing, and more and more naked-ness—too many shoes, and too many bare feet—too many shirts and too many shirtless".[67]

---

and 'custom house seizures', and a thousand other tricks, are resorted to, merely to push off an extra number of commodities; while the extra number of commodities so to be pushed off necessitates of course the manufacture of a greater quantity of materials". "Answers to Correspondents", No. 20, 26 April 1851.

[63] "Answers to Correspondents", No. 19, 19 April 1851. See J. S. Mill, *Principles of Political Economy with Some of their Applications to Social Philosophy*, 3rd ed. (London, 1852), I, pp. 114–5, 117. Mill, however refused to conceive of the wage fund being depleted by the material fund, p. 122.

[64] "Answers to Correspondents", No. 19, 19 April 1851.

[65] "Answers to Correspondents", No. 28, 21 June 1851. For falling wage rates see No. 21, 3 May 1851.

[66] "Answers to Correspondents", No. 22, 10 May, 1851; No. 56, 3 January, No. 58, 17 January 1852.

[67] "Answers to Correspondents", No. 20, 26 April 1851.

The shifting equilibrium between funds was no self-acting mechanical system. The system was based on social relationships and power struggles in the industrial world. In any given year the amount of capital available for wages was variable and depended upon the power of the capitalist in a struggle with workers who had power only when protected by legislation or when unionized—"were it not for the trades societies, the country would have been destroyed by the greed of the capitalists long ago".[68] How, Mayhew asked, did his form of the wage law (overwork leads to underpay),

> differ *essentially* from the economical dogma? The answer is—it differs most essentially, in not being a natural and necessary law consequent upon the ordained succession of events, and in being comparatively an *arbitrary* result, dependent upon the mere will, the greed, ambition, or what you please of the trader, who, being able to alter, in a great measure, as he thinks fit, the proportion between the sum devoted to the purchase of materials and the sum devoted to the payment of the labourers, has it in his power to vary the rate of wages almost at pleasure.[69]

Indeed the real ceiling on wages, far from being the capital saved out of last year's produce, was the coming year's selling price :

> Here then is the true criteria which determines the value of all labour—*what it will bring*. This is the test which guides the employer himself in the wages he pays for the work; that is to say it regulates the maximum price which he will consent, or, indeed, can afford to give; though of course he will purchase the labour as much lower as the necessities of the workmen will allow him.[70]

The capitalists' behaviour was exploitative not only because it led to the impoverishment of the workers, but because it robbed the worker of the value his labour had created which belonged to him "by the most cogent of all rights to individual possession—*the right of creation*".[71] Like his contemporaries the Owenites, whose ideas were in the air though he hadn't read their works, and like

---

[68] "Answers to Correspondents", No. 44, 11 October 1851.
[69] "Answers to Correspondents", No. 50, 22 November; No. 34, 2 August; No. 39, 6 September 1851.
[70] *Low Wages*, p. 55. It is curious that while Mayhew painted the jungle of competition in lurid colours in his actual studies of trades, showing how employers also struggled competitively for survival, in his theoretical writings, he often used terms of moral disapprobation connoting that it was the arbitrary decision of the capitalist, not the pressure of a system, that brought him to reduce wages.
[71] "Answers to Correspondents", No. 42, 27 September 1851.

Marx, Mayhew saw exploitation in terms of the appropriation by the capitalist of the surplus value created by the worker :

> Mr. Mayhew himself believes that the working men of England are grossly wronged by capitalists. All production is according to the very first principles of political economy—a partnership between the man of money and the man of muscles, in which the monied man agrees to advance the working man his share of the produce in the form of wages. . . . In place of the original compact a new law has been instituted, by which the *necessities* of the working man—instead of equity—are made to determine the value of his labour. This is what is called the law of supply and demand, which taking no heed of the result (that is to say, whether the value of the materials on which the workman has exercised his skill has been doubled or increased even a hundred fold by the operation), says that the proportion of the wealth which is to come to the labourer is to be regulated by no other principle than what the capitalist can induce or force him (by starvation or chicanery) to accept.[72]

Throughout the weekly covers and in *Low Wages*, Mayhew tried to develop an "equitable wage principle" following his own dictum that "a new Political Economy, one that will take *some little notice* of the claims of labour, doing justice as well to the workmen as to the employer, stands foremost among the desiderata, or things wanted in the present age".[73] Mayhew was no socialist. He wanted to retain private ownership but make wages reflect the actual value created by the workmen. To achieve an equitable share-out, he felt it necessary to abolish the wage fund altogether and pay both the capitalist and labourer from the future produce fund since,

> the Wage-Fund has nothing to do with the real *worth* of the labour but is simply the sum set aside for the maintenance of the workmen during the performance of their work, and the Produce-Fund alone is that out of which they should be remunerated, receiving, after the payment of all dues, in proportion to the amount which they have contributed towards it.[74]

His plan amounted to a more radical version of profit sharing experiments being discussed at the time which would allow the workman only a fixed proportion of the profits in addition to his wage. In Mayhew's scheme, the capitalist was entitled to an ordinary

[72] "Answers to Correspondents", No. 10, 15 February 1851.
[73] "Answers to Correspondents", No. 40, 13 September 1851.
[74] *Low Wages*, p. 46.

rate of interest on capital invested in the business, an extra return
for the risk of capital to cover the possibility of loss (he never hinted
how this problematic sum was to be calculated) and finally a salary
for the management of the business "as is commensurate with the
value of his services". The workers were entitled to the rest.[75]
Mayhew never suggested how the capitalist could be made to accept
this profit sharing arrangement, a crucial omission, since the capitalist in his economic model was a particularly greedy animal. In his
*Morning Chronicle* Letters, on the *London Labour* covers, Mayhew
showed sympathy for an almost bewildering variety of agencies and
reforms, ranging from trades unions to co-operative production to
legislation abolishing payment in public houses. But in the absence
of any clear programmatic suggestions linked specifically to his new
economic guidelines, Mayhew's attempts to be constructive remain
weak. He knew what existed better than anyone else—and he hated
it. He knew in general terms, both theoretically and practically,
what was needed, but he could not fully supply it.


## III

Mayhew never treated the poor simply as economic men or considered them only at work. His interviews brought him into contact
with men and women who thought of themselves in a social situation, whose hopes and fears revolved around their homes, their
families and their friends, as well as their jobs. Mayhew's mind
never stood still. Like his economic thought, his understanding of
the social life of the poor developed and deepened. Although he
was less addicted to building abstract conceptual models and more
often revealed a shift of emphasis in the sociological material he
presented, he was able to make a number of conceptual break-
throughs.

Early in the survey, before he had matured his analysis of
the causes of casual labour, Mayhew was already examining the
social and moral impact of a casual rhythm of work. As he studied
unskilled labour in the docks, Mayhew developed a general concept
of how irregular work and fluctuating wages tended to lead to un-
stable and "improvident" habits and turned the favourite Victorian
shibboleth that bad morals cause poverty upside down. He noted
that the dock labourer's wage plunged from fifteen shillings one
week to nought the next and he offered a psychological explanation

[75] *Low Wages*, p. 13. Mayhew hinted that the workman might be paid in
instalments receiving interim wages to cover subsistence need and his part
of the profits when the produce was sold, p. 50.

for the improbability that such a workman could develop a routinized and respectable way of life :

> Regularity of habits are incompatible with irregularity of income; indeed, the very conditions necessary for the formation of any habit whatsoever are, that the act or thing to which we are to become habituated should be repeated at frequent and regular intervals. It is a moral impossibility that the class of labourers who are only occasionally employed should be either generally industrious or temperate—both industry and temperance being habits produced by constancy of employment and uniformity of income. Hence, where the greatest fluctuation occurs in the labour, there, of course, will be the greatest idleness and improvidence; where the greatest want generally is, there we shall find the greatest occasional excess; where from the uncertainty of the occupation prudence is most needed, there, strange to say, we shall meet with the highest improvidence of all.[76]

Here, clearly laid out, was the insight supposedly pioneered by Booth and Rowntree and especially by Beveridge in his work on chronic underemployment some sixty years later.

Mayhew soon became aware that different groups of workers reacted in very different ways to the fact or threat of casualization, as reflected in their differing attitudes to protest movements. Thus, in Letter XIX, when Mayhew moved from the tailors, his first study of a trade, to the coalwhippers in the docks (not as is usually supposed at the very end of the survey), he observed :

> it seems as if we were in a new land, and among another race. The artisans are almost to a man red-hot politicians. They are sufficiently educated and thoughtful to have a sense of their importance in the state. . . . They begin to view their class, not as a mere isolated body of workmen, but as an integral portion of the nation, contributing their quota to the general welfare. If property has its duties as well as its rights; labour, on the other hand, they say, has its rights as well as its duties. . . .
>
> The unskilled labourers are a different class of people. As yet they are as unpolitical as footmen, and instead of entertaining violent democratic opinions, they appear to have no political opinions whatever; or, if they do possess any, they rather lead towards the maintenance of "things as they are", than towards the ascendancy of the working people. I have lately been investigating the state of the coalwhippers and these reflections are

---

[76] *Morning Chronicle*, Letter IV, 30 October 1849.

forced upon me by the marked difference in the character and sentiments of these people from those of the operative tailors. Among the latter class there appeared to be a general bias towards the six points of the Charter; but the former were extremely proud of their having turned out to a man on the 10th of April, 1848 and become special constables for the maintenance of law and order on the day of the great Chartist demonstration.[77]

Through his evidence Mayhew came to use the crucial idea that economic change was refracted through a cultural lens. Though he never came up with Booth's succinct statement about the kinds of factors which would help to account for feelings of content and discontent (see page 94), when Mayhew asked informants to react to changes in their jobs, he guided them to give testimony which always contained the raw material for such explanations. The traditions and memories of groups of workers were highlighted to establish whether their present position contrasted favourably or unfavourably with the past. Mayhew carefully recorded the terms in which satisfactions and discontent were expressed and where, in their total social lives, working people felt that precious expectations were violated and intolerable strains created.

His interviews with representative journeymen in the London trades revealed privileged groups of artisans who had suffered a sharp decline in wages within living memory but who also felt that their dignity and independence were being undermined as their relationship with employers deteriorated into one of crude cash-nexus. Their sense of grievance did not concern the workshop alone, for as often, they expressed anxiety about the repercussions of economic change on a healthy family life and a secure old age. Thus the tailors and shoemakers complained bitterly about being forced to put their wives to work. But nowhere was the comprehensive nature of worry and discontent made more clear than in the interview with the two old sawyers, members of a group that had been displaced by machinery during the previous twenty years.[78] They gave vivid accounts of the period before 1830, when wages were good and corporate solidarity and pride so vigorous that,

> we used to have a trade dinner every year, somewhere out of town, and to go up to the tavern—wherever it was—in grand purcession, with bands of music and flags flying (we had a union jack that cost forty odd pound then).

[77] *Morning Chronicle*, Letter XIX, 21 December 1849; *L.L. & L.P.* (1861) III, p. 233.

[78] Letter LIX, below, p. 331.

Collapse of their trade not only violated the most fundamental right, the right to work, but jeopardized their plans for old age and their customary way of providing for their children's futures—"It was a rule in our trade that the eldest son was entitled to his father's business. Now I don't see a sawyer in London who has an apprentice".

Among the artisan groups who had traditionally thought themselves useful members of the state, whose status had deteriorated dramatically and whose family patterns had been painfully disrupted, Mayhew found the most responsiveness to the arguments of the main protest movements. The tailors and shoemakers were keen Chartists and the sawyers, as was evident from their testimony about machinery, were well acquainted with Owenism.

By contrast, the coalwhippers, in a casual job averaging even lower wages than the two sawyers, were politically conservative. Mayhew pointed to the fact that they *felt* their condition had recently improved, when the system of paying wages in public houses was abolished by legislative act in 1843. "Now the thing is materially altered, thank God", one whipper reflected, again emphasizing the impact of economic change on family life,

> my wife and (six) children can go to chapel at certain times, when work is pretty good, and our things are not in pawn. By the strictest economy, I can do middling well—very well when compared with what things were. When the new system first came into operation, I felt almost in a new world. I felt myself a free man; I wasn't compelled to drink; my home assumed a better aspect, and keeps it still.[79]

It was in the case of the costermongers that Mayhew made most clear how a sub-culture coloured political attitudes. The costers had the most irregular work and wage of all. But one fact was certain—they hated the police. The police harried them at work, pushing them off the streets when they tried to sell their wares; the police continually interfered with their favourite amusements, gambling games and trials of strength. In the coster code, "to serve out (beat up) a policeman is the bravest act by which a costermonger can distinguish himself". Mayhew observed that the costers were "nearly all Chartists". But far from demanding their rights in the corporate body of the nation like the artisans, Chartism meant to them first and foremost fighting the police, since they equated the police with "the governing power". What little sense they had of

[79] *Morning Chronicle*, Letter XIX, 21 December 1849. Mayhew eventually incorporated the working man's view of wages in relation to family life into his own conceptual framework, see below, p. 465.

any wider community was based on their most immediate experience. "Their notions of an aristocracy of birth or wealth", Mayhew
wrote, "seem to be formed on their opinions of the rich, or reputed
rich salesmen with whom they deal; and the result is anything but
favourable to the nobility".[80]

Mayhew's work on the costermongers enabled him to grope toward the concept of a sub-culture which he could not, in the end,
successfully formulate. For some time he had become more aware
of varying cultural patterns and, from his letters on the workers
in wood (LIX–LXIX), gave noticeably more space to corporate
social characteristics, at the beginning of his study of a trade. But
the costermongers presented a group whose lives were based on a
code of shared meanings as different from that of other London
workmen as from respectable middle class Englishmen. Yet the
system of values seemed coherent and consistent in itself. When
Mayhew returned to the costers for the second time, at the beginning
of the weekly numbers of *London Labour*, he produced a full-
blown cultural study, treating them at length as a group with dis-
tinctive social habits. He discussed the conditions of the trade, their
amusements, politics, sex habits, religious attitudes, education,
language and dress.

He tried to inform and generalize his discovery of a sub-culture
by developing current ethnological notions into a category of wandering tribes in civilized society. By the mid-century, ethnology had
retreated from the earlier cultural studies of the Scottish Enlighten-
ment and had abandoned the exploration of systems of social,
economic and political relationships characterizing social stages from
savagery to civil society.[81] Instead, the emphasis was now on tracing
the history of the various races of mankind largely through linguistic
and physiological evidence. As often happens, such a shift in scope
has to do with social factors outside the "discipline", and many of
the anthropological luminaries of the 1840's and 1850's were
Quakers active in the anti-slavery movement who saw in their
studies a way of proving the essential unity, despite superficial differences, of the origin of all mankind. Mayhew was a keen dabbler in
the anthropology of his day—he entered with great relish into
learned discussions about the linguistic derivation of coster slang

---

[80] "The Politics of the Costermongers—Policemen," in *L.L. & L.P.* (1851),
I, pp. 20, 16.
[81] See A. Ferguson, *An Essay on the History of Civil Society* (1767) and
J. Millar, *The Origin of the Distinction of Ranks*, 3rd ed. (1779). For a
fuller picture of mid-nineteenth century ethnology and its learned societies, see
J. W. Burrow, *Evolution and Society, A Study in Victorian Social Theory*
(Cambridge, 1966).

with correspondents[82]—but we can find no evidence that he took his
interest any further by joining the Ethnological or Anthropological
Society; nor did these august bodies take any notice of his work.

From Dr. J. C. Prichard,[83] Mayhew picked up the idea that men
in different social stages (hunting, herding and civil society) had
different skull formations; and in Dr. A. Smith's work on South
Africa,[84] he noticed that more settled tribes were often surrounded
by wandering tribes. Mayhew borrowed the idea of social stages
but said that they could co-exist in one society and even more boldly
that they could exist side by side in a civilized society. Though the
concept of wandering tribes in civilized society was an ingenious
creation, as anthropology, it was not so sensitive as the actual account
of coster life. The main characteristics of "wandering tribes"
throbbed with disapproval. They were the opposite of middle class
values and behaviour and stressed such disruptive tendencies that
they suggested complete social disorganization. The members of
wandering tribes in England, Mayhew alleged,

> are all more or less distinguished for their high cheekbones and
> protruding jaws—for their use of a slang language—for their lax
> ideas of property—for their general improvidence—their repug-
> nance to continuous labour—their disregard of female honour—
> their love of cruelty—their pugnacity—and their utter want of
> religion.[85]

Mayhew was no relativist. But in his actual account of the costers,
he showed that their life was organized, although around different
values. When he treated sex habits and family organization, for so
many of the Victorian middle class the bedrock of social stability,
he showed that different patterns of behaviour, which he did not
approve, did not inevitably lead to social chaos. The costers
cohabited and hardly ever married, yet family and community life

[82] See among many examples, "Answers to Correspondents", No. 53, 13
December 1851.
[83] J. C. Prichard (1786–1848), the leading anthropologist of his day and
second president of the Ethnological Society was especially known for his
work *The Natural History of Mankind*, which went through numerous
editions. A Quaker and early advocate of the Aborigines Protection Society,
he was an active medical man in Bristol where he was also vice-president
of the local Statistical Society.
[84] Sir Andrew Smith, M.D., Deputy Inspector General of Hospitals, was
sent by the government to investigate Bushman unrest in 1828 and later led
a zoological expedition into the interior of South Africa (1834–36). He wrote
a paper on the "Origin and History of the Bushmen", *Philosophical Magazine*, IX, 1831, but his projected comprehensive work on the Ethnology of
Africa was never published.
[85] *L.L. & L.P.* (1851), I, p. 3.

continued. "The married women", Mayhew observed, "associate
with the unmarried mothers of families without the slightest scruple.
There is no honour attached to the marriage state and no shame
to concubinage. Neither are the unmarried women less faithful to
their 'partners' than the married; but I understand that, of the
two classes, the unmarried betray the most jealousy". As for the
children, Mayhew said " 'chance children', as they are called, or
children unrecognized by any father are rare among the young
women of the costermongers".[86] It was quite an achievement to
locate sub-cultures among the poor in fact, if not successfully in
theory. The early statisticians assumed any divergence from middle
class behaviour to equal bestiality. Mid-century investigators habitu-
ally used wooden models of "respectable" working men and the
"perishing and dangerous classes".

## IV

Mayhew's ability to see poverty in the round, as the product of
an economic system, with devastating moral and social consequences
and yet varied cultural manifestations, amounted to a unique and
short lived moment in middle-class consciousness. During the mid-
century years, investigators fragmented the study of the poor just
as they dismembered Mayhew's study of poverty when they took
notice of it.[87] New fields for the diagnosis and treatment of social
problems had emerged during the "hungry forties"—most important
among them were public health or sanitary science and juvenile
delinquency or reformatory science—which dealt with partial aspects
of poverty and the poor. The development of these fields was related
to the professionalization of certain groups, especially doctors and
lawyers, who saw a public service image as one way to establish

[86] Ibid., pp. 20–21.
[87] Thus the Rev. T. Beames, the spiritual force behind the Society for
Improving the Dwellings of the Working and Poorer Classes and the author
of the first analytic study of urban slums, greatly admired Mayhew's work,
but picked out only those parts which related to housing: *The Rookeries of
London: Past, Present and Prospective* (London, 1852), pp. 39, 79ff.
Similarly, John Garwood, making a plea for support of the London City
Mission, raided Mayhew's work for facts about the London cabdrivers,
omnibus men and Irish, groups which the Mission thought especially in need
of its services: *The Million Peopled City; Or, One-Half of the people of
London Made Known to the Other Half* (London, 1853). Mary Carpenter,
*the* acknowledged authority on the treatment of the perishing and dangerous
classes during the mid-century, took quick and angry notice only of Mayhew's work on ragged schools: *Reformatory Schools for the Children of
the Perishing and Dangerous Classes, and for Juvenile Offenders* (London,
1851), p. 126.

their legitimacy. The *British Medical Journal* in a typical mood of self-congratulation welcomed the first meeting of the National Association for the Promotion of Social Science with the words :

> We rejoice that an occasion is about to arise in which medicine will be enabled to assert its position in the face of the world as one of the most philanthropic professions. The science of Public Health has been built up and maintained by the leading men of our own body, and it behoves us to keep the lead we have so worthily obtained.[88]

Helping to shape the interests of the Social Science Association (the most useful mirror of fashions in mid-century social study), doctors like Edwin Lankester and architects like George Godwin concentrated on how public health and housing affected the life of the poor, bringing conditions of employment into the causal picture only when these had a bearing on health.[89] Lawyers like M. D. Hill and newly organized charity workers like Mary Carpenter saw the social causes of crime largely in terms of the troubled family environ-ments of the perishing and dangerous classes but paid little attention to the economic constraints working on problem families.[90] It was not, perhaps, until 1868 and a London depression that a group of London lawyers again asked how patterns of urban employment affected poverty and rediscovered the problem of casual labour.[91] But all these various environmental causes, each the province of different specialists, were not seen together as they operated compre-hensively on a group of people in a trade or in a neighbourhood. The "Great Depression" of the seventies and eighties, which shook middle class confidence in an unprecedented way, the reawakening

[88] 12 September 1857.

[89] The National Association for the Promotion of Social Science, which ran from 1857 to 1886, published annual *Transactions* and a *Journal* in 1866 which then became its *Sessional Proceedings*; all of these are a verit-able goldmine for information and attitudes. Besides papers read to the Public Health Department (especially the discussion of "The Effects of Occupation on Health" in 1862), see George Godwin, *London Shadows, A Glance at the Homes of the Thousands* (London, 1854) and *Town Swamps and Social Bridges* (London, 1859).

[90] See papers read to the Punishment and Reformation Department and Mary Carpenter, *Reformatory Schools*.

[91] See, e.g., A. H. Hill, *Our Unemployed: an Attempt to Point out Some of the Best Means of Providing Occupation for Distressed Labourers, etc.* (London, 1868), pp. 7–8, published by the Social Science Association. C. P. B. Bosanquet, *London: Some Account of Its Growth, Charitable Agencies and Wants* (London, 1868), pp. 133–136. E. Denison, "Some Remedies for Metropolitan Pauperism", in *Letters and Other Writings*, ed. Baldwin Leighton (London, 1872), pp. 199–200.

of working class militancy and the intensification of all the problems investigated by Mayhew helped to set the stage for Booth and Rowntree to treat poverty as a whole once again.

If Mayhew was the most perceptive investigator of his day, the question remains, how does he compare with Booth and Rowntree, usually regarded as the better investigators, the pioneers of the social survey and the first to study poverty in an empirical way?[92]

Booth and Rowntree had different initial aims from Mayhew. Both wished first to identify the actual number of poor in a locality—Booth partly to refute Hyndman's contention that 25 per cent of people in the East End were living in extreme poverty and Rowntree to test Booth's metropolitan findings in a provincial town during a year of unusual prosperity. As a result both were more preoccupied with the definition of a poverty line. Yet Booth's poverty line remained nearly as impressionistic as Mayhew's and as saturated with middle class prejudices. Booth described the poor "as living under a struggle to obtain the necessaries of life and make both ends meet" while the "very poor live in a state of chronic want", and set the poverty line at an arbitrary wage figure of 18–21 shillings per week.[93] Only the more rigorous Rowntree, making use of the new science of nutrition, calculated the lowest budget which would be necessary to keep a family in a bare state of "physical efficiency" before he expressed his poverty line in terms of an average weekly wage.[94] Booth was really more interested in his classes A, B, C and D than the poverty line and these were not firm income categories but had much to do with external appearance and respectability. The crucial Class A, one of the two classes who were very poor, was not an income category at all but a receptacle for morally obnoxious types.[95]

Beyond a simple poverty census, Booth and Rowntree wished to examine the immediate causes of poverty and Booth to test how much poverty might be related to "questions of habit" (the immoral causes), "questions of circumstance" (illness and large families) and "questions of employment". But Mayhew developed a more successful method for collecting information to relate poverty to employ-

[92] T. S. and M. B. Simey, *Charles Booth, Social Scientist* (London, 1960) pp. 4, 247, C. A. Moser, *Survey Methods in Social Investigation* (London, 1958), pp. 18–20, M. Abrams, *Social Surveys and Social Action* (London, 1951), pp. 33, 34.

[93] Charles Booth, *Life and Labour of the People in London* (London, 1904), Poverty Series, I, p. 33.

[94] Seebohm Rowntree, *Poverty, A Study of Town Life* (London, 1901), pp. 87ff.

[95] Booth, *Life and Labour*, Poverty, I, pp. 37–8. Also see pp. 39–53 for descriptions of the other classes.

ment than Booth. Booth's team did not do a first hand door-to-door survey but relied on the books of the school board visitors : "with the insides of the houses and their inmates", Booth wrote, "there was no attempt to meddle", as this would have amounted to an abuse of the school visitors' help.[96] Thus all the information about wages and regularity of work on which his calculation of those poor through questions of employment would hinge came second hand from the school visitors who probably did not go into these matters with the indefatigable care of Mayhew. Nor at any point did Booth detail just how wages and regularity of work were assessed.

Rowntree came much closer to Mayhew, for his agent was instructed to collect wage figures and correct them, making allowances for unpaid short time and public holidays, overtime and cost of tools. But when information was not available from the workman (and the reasons for unavailability were never discussed), Rowntree based his estimates on wages paid in his own factory plus information from "other large employers of labour in the city".[97] Many years earlier, Mayhew had warned that this was dangerous procedure, for without "wilful dishonesty" an employer would tend to give the nominal wage for the best paid workman, whereas it was necessary to distinguish between nominal and actual wages and to discover the range of wages earned within the same occupational group as well as the flat numerical average.[98] Whatever the weaknesses of their methods, both concluded that the largest amount of the poverty they discovered might be ascribed to questions of employment. Booth's figures were 55 per cent in Classes A and B, 68 per cent in C and D; Rowntree insisted that more than half of primary poverty was caused by low wages.[99]

Rowntree felt that it was outside the scope of his inquiry to examine the ultimate causes of low wages, or, what he called, "the whole social question".[100] But Booth, keen to pursue the subject further, never ultimately devised a method to investigate what conditions within industry might cause poverty, the problem which Mayhew tackled from the beginning with some success. Booth made a promising start in the Poverty section of his inquiry when he sent some of his team to study a few sweated industries which were the subject of controversial debate, notably Beatrice Webb, who made her debut as a social investigator examining the docks and tailoring. Her work, the best in volume IV, stressed the organization

[96] Ibid., p. 25.
[97] Rowntree, *Poverty*, pp. 26–27.
[98] "Answers to Correspondents", No. 40, 13 September 1851.
[99] Booth, *Life and Labour*, Poverty, I, p. 147; Rowntree, *Poverty*, p. 130.
[100] Rowntree, *Poverty*, pp. 119, 145.

of labour which led to low wages and casuality, and made general remarks about the effect of casuality on social habits. But she never calculated wage figures as carefully as did Mayhew and, since she remained in the workplace, she did not show how selected families were concretely affected by the forces she described.[101]

Booth's Industry Series, which was meant to interlock with the Poverty investigations, failed completely. Instead of relating conditions of labour in the industries he studied to the life style of typical families, he got sidetracked by a facile statistical correllation, the overcrowding index, which led nowhere. Booth found that the percentage of the population living in overcrowded houses coincided neatly, too neatly with the percentage in all his classes under E. In each trade profile, the proportion of workmen earning a certain weekly wage was set against the proportion in overcrowded conditions, which sometimes produced rather startling discrepancies.[102] It would seem that setting up the overcrowding index sapped much of Booth's inventive energy. Even when the index revealed industries where the incidence of poverty was high, he did not or could not conceive that a further structural analysis was needed to determine why this should be so.[103] Mayhew's method of interviews with representive workers in a trade enabled him to establish which industries produced poverty at the same time that he could explore the structural mechanisms which caused low wages and casuality. Indeed Booth's industrial profiles read more like aimless descriptions than studies harnessed to an inquiry about poverty. But Booth himself admitted that he had failed to make the two sections of his massive project interconnect.[104]

Although Booth did not develop a method for analysing an industry so as to be able to relate employment and poverty, he did attempt to interpret the empirical evidence about the sweated trades amassed in the Poverty section of the inquiry. Here again the contrast with Mayhew is interesting. For while Mayhew was able to emancipate himself from a tendency to classify and searched for valid generalizations about the dishonourable trades, Booth retreated further into his biological shell, stressing the particular rather than

[101] Beatrice Potter (Webb), "The Docks", and "The Tailoring Trade", chaps. II and III in *Life and Labour*, Poverty, IV.

[102] As in the case of the woodworkers, *Life and Labour* (London, 1903), Industry I, p. 231 where "exceptional circumstances", had to be invoked—the wage returns had been too high and rentals in the inner ring of London were also high—to explain away the discrepancy. See the Simeys, *Charles Booth*, p. 205 for other instances. Booth relied heavily on information from employers for his wage figures.

[103] Simeys, *Charles Booth*, pp. 200, 205.

[104] Booth, *Life and Labour*, Poverty, I, p. 151, footnote.

the general. Thus in his article entitled "Sweating", Booth ended
up by saying there was no such thing as sweating, but particular
evils in particular trades which he carefully itemized. He felt

> able to assert without hesitation that there is no industrial
> system co-extensive with the evils complained of, although there is
> unfortunately no doubt at all that very serious evils exist. It is not
> one but many systems with which we have to deal, each having
> its special faults.[105]

It would be a mistake to think that Booth did not have more
general ideas about how the economy worked, but these were by
and large *a priori* judgments, brought in to interpret facts which
did not warrant their use. It would almost seem that Booth was
unable to generalize where such an exercise might tend to undermine his basic prejudice that capitalism was fundamentally a healthy
system. Thus in Poverty volume I, he made sweeping generalizations
about how Class B because of their general inadequacy, from illness,
lack of intelligence or quickness, swamped the labour market, took
work away from C and D and put these more respectable workmen
into a precarious position.[106] Basically, the personal deficiencies of
Class B accounted for poverty, which was not far from restating
the old moral argument for poverty. On the basis of this proposition,
Booth then made his most radical policy recommendation, that Class
B be removed from the labour market altogether and placed in industrial colonies to leave breathing space for C and D.[107] Mayhew
may have come to somewhat the same conclusion about the effect of
competitive on honourable labour, but it was not the personal short-
comings of casual labourers which made them economic threats.
Rather, the system of forced productivity at lower wages exploited
the use of "B" and also forced many perfectly good working men
to go casual.

In his use of qualitative evidence and in his sensitivity to sub-
cultures among the poor, Mayhew far surpassed both Booth and
Rowntree. Rowntree was aware that cultural evidence qualified
his criteria for secondary poverty and used it sparingly but percep-
tively in this context.[108] However, his cultural portraits of each class
in the chapter on "the Standard of Life" were too brief and
riddled with Nonconformist prejudices to let a picture of life

---

[105] Ibid., Poverty, IV, p. 330.

[106] Ibid., Poverty, I, pp. 154, 162, 176.

[107] Ibid., pp. 167ff. It will be remembered that Booth wrote of C and D,
"they are my clients. To their service especially I dedicate my work." Ibid.,
p. 177.

[108] For example, Rowntree, *Poverty*, p. 116, footnote 2.

in the subjective terms of the class unwittingly emerge. Booth never put himself into a position where he could explore social attitudes and stumble on to sub-cultures. From the beginning, he crudely equated qualitative evidence with sensationalism, insisting that he would "make use of no fact to which I cannot give a quantitive value".[109] It is all the more curious that he was so resistant to subjective evidence because in volume I of the Poverty Series, he made one of the most perceptive observations about the need for qualitative evidence to assess a standard of living. He wrote :

> Seen from without, the same habits of life, amount of income, method of expenditure, difficulties, occupations, amusements, will strike the mind of the on-looker with an entirely different meaning according as they are viewed as part of a progress towards a better and higher life, or of a descent towards a more miserable and debased existence. Felt from within, a position will be acceptable and even happy on the upward road, which on the downward path may be hardly endurable. The contrast with that to which men have been accustomed is doubtless the principle factor in sensations of well or ill being, content or discontent. . . . In all this what is true of the individual is no less true of the class. To interpret aright the life of either we need to lay open its memories and understand its hopes.[110]

Mayhew, not Booth, actually practised what Booth preached.

Basically Booth was a middle class moralist who saw any departure from middle class norms as social disorganization and immorality. What little feeling he had for the culture of the poor he gained from living with three East End families who belonged to his classes C, D and E, and whose standards approximated closely to middle class values. Yet even in his chapter on "Class Relations" where he tried "to breathe life into the dry bones of statistics", he gave a sadly unilluminating account of the people with whom he lodged, using such language as

> wholesome pleasant family life, very simple food, very regular habits, healthy bodies and healthy minds; affectionate relations of husbands and wives, mothers and sons, of elders with children, or friend with friend.[111]

When it came to Class A, which was not an economic but a moral category, without any attempt to study their habits, Booth dismissed them *a priori* as a "savage, semi-criminal class of people" to be

---

[109] Booth, *Life and Labour*, Poverty, I, p. 6.
[110] Ibid., pp. 172–3.
[111] Ibid., p. 158.

"harried out of existence". Composed of occasional labourers, street-sellers, loafers, criminals and semi-criminals, they "render no useful service, they create no wealth : more often they destroy it. They degrade whatever they touch, and as individuals are perhaps incapable of improvement".[112]

Mayhew's imaginative leaps into the minds and hearts of the poor are not just texts to be fitted into a version of the history of "social science". He made a rare contribution to human understanding. He knew what we still have to learn—that people are not to be treated as averages according to whether they fall above or below some quantified poverty line. The communal traditions and memories of groups of people, their aspirations and fears have to be understood before policy makers draw up their plans for others. At the least, Mayhew's industrial survey offers the social and economic historian a veritable storehouse of riches. He was at work in London at a crucial time of transition between two phases of capitalism, when a more regulated and humane economy was giving way to a stage of intense and savage competition. Because he was a sociological economist by instinct, he was able to capture the meaning of this change in terms of social relationships of production; nowhere in nineteenth-century literature is there such a meticulous probing of the man metamorphoses of the relationship between capitalist and labourer nor such a careful documentation of wages and working conditions. It is true that Mayhew the investigator in action was often better than Mayhew the conceptualizer of his own findings; he had the weaknesses of his great strengths. It is time to rescue Mayhew from the endless search after romantic vignettes of the poor. The writings in this book are selected to achieve this end and present him for what he was during his best years—a seeker after "the better understanding of the 'perils of the nation' ".

[112] Ibid., pp. 174, 169, 37–38.

*Selections from*

# THE MORNING CHRONICLE,

## LABOUR AND THE POOR.

### THE METROPOLITAN DISTRICTS.
[FROM OUR SPECIAL CORRESPONDENT.]

# Henry Mayhew

# INTRODUCTION

*A View from St. Paul's*[1]

The city of London, within the walls, occupies a space of only 370 acres, and is but the hundred and fortieth part of the extent covered by the whole metropolis. Nevertheless, it is the parent of a mass of united and far spreading tenements, stretching from Hammersmith to Blackwall, from Holloway to Camberwell. A century ago, according to Maitland, the metropolis had drawn into its vortex one city, one borough, and forty-three villages. Despite its vast extent, still its increase continues to be so rapid, that every year further house room has to be provided for twenty thousand persons—so that London increases annually by the addition of a town of considerable size. At all times there are 4,000 extra houses in the course of erection. By the last return the metropolis covered an extent of nearly 45,000 acres, and contained upwards of two hundred and sixty thousand houses, occupied by one million eight hundred and twenty thousand souls, constituting not only the densest, but the busiest hive, the most wondrous workshop, and the richest bank in the world. The mere name of London awakens a thousand trains of varied reflections. Perhaps the first thought that it excites in the mind, paints it as the focus of modern civilization, of the hottest, the most restless activity of the social elements. Some, turning to the west, see it as a city of palaces, adorned with parks, ennobled with triumphal arches, grand statues, and stately monuments; others, looking at the east, see only narrow lanes and musty counting-houses, with tall chimneys vomiting black clouds and huge masses of warehouses with doors and cranes ranged one above another. Yet all think of it as a vast bricken multitude, a strange incongruous chaos of wealth and want—of ambition and despair—of the brightest charity and the darkest crime, where there is more feasting and more starvation, than on any other spot on earth—and all grouped round the one giant centre, the huge black dome, with its ball of gold looming through the smoke (apt emblem of the source of its riches!) and marking out the capital, no matter from what quarter the traveller may come.

In the hope of obtaining a bird's-eye view of the port, I went up to the Golden Gallery that is immediately below the ball of St.

---

[1] This view is assembled from Letters I and LVII.

Paul's. It was noon, and an exquisitely bright and clear spring day; but the view was smudgy and smeared with smoke. And yet the haze which hung like a curtain of shadow before and over everything, increased rather than diminished the giant sublimity of the city that lay stretched out beneath. It was utterly unlike London as seen every day below, in all its bricken and hard-featured reality; it was rather the phantasm—the spectral illusion, as it were, of the great metropolis—such as one might see it in a dream, with here and there stately churches and palatial hospitals, shimmering like white marble, their windows glittering in the sunshine like plates of burnished gold—while the rest of the scene was all hazy and indefinite. Even the outlines of the neighbouring streets, steeples, and towers were blurred in misty indistinctness. Clumps of buildings and snatches of parks looked through the clouds like dim islands rising out of the sea of smoke. It was impossible to tell where the sky ended and the city began; and as you peered into the thick haze you could, after a time, make out the dusky figures of tall factory chimneys plumed with black smoke; while spires and turrets seemed to hang midway between you and the earth, as if poised in the thick grey air. In the distance the faint hills, with the sun shining upon them, appeared like some far-off shore, or a mirage seen in the sky—indeed, the whole scene was more like the view of some imaginary and romantic Cloudland, than that of the most matter-of-fact and prosaic city in the world. As you peeped down into the thoroughfares you could see streams of busy little men, like ants, continually hurrying along in opposite directions; while, what with carts, cabs, and omnibuses, the earth seemed all alive with tiny creeping things, as when one looks into the grass on a summer's day. As you listened you caught the roar of the restless human tide of enterprise and competition at work below; and as you turned to contemplate the river at your back, you saw the sunlight shining upon the grey water beneath you like a sheet of golden tissue, while far away in the distance it sparkled again as the stream went twisting through the monster town. Beyond London-bridge nothing was visible; a thick veil of haze and fog hung before the shipping, so that not one solitary mast was to be seen marking the far-famed port of London. And yet one would hardly have had it otherwise! To behold the metropolis without its smoke—with its thousand steeples standing out against the clear blue sky sharp and definite in their outlines— is to see London as it is not—without its native element. But as the vast city lay there beneath me, half hid in mist and with only glimpses of its greatness visible, it had a much more sublime and ideal effect from the very inability to grasp the whole of its literal reality.

From St. Paul's I made my way to the Custom house, where, by the courtesy of the authorities, I was allowed to view the port of London from the roof of the "Long Room". A noble sight it was! The river before me bristled with a thousand masts, and the city behind me with a thousand steeples. On the opposite side of the shore, chimneys as tall and straight as the masts in front of them, poured forth their clouds of black smoke, while over the tops of the warehouses might be seen the trail of white steam from the railway engine cutting through the roofs. The sun shone bright upon the river, and as its broken beams played upon the surface, it fluttered and sparkled like a swarm of fire-flies. Down "the silent highway" barges tide-borne floated sideways, with their long thin idle oars projecting from their sides, like fins. Others went along with their windlass clicking, as they raised the mast and sail that they had lowered to pass under the bridge. Then would come a raft of timber, towed by a small boat, and the boatman leaning far back in it as he laboured at the sculls; and presently a rapid river steamer, stuck all over with passengers, would flit past, and you would catch a whiff of music from on board as it hurried by. The large square blocks of warehouses on the opposite shore were almost hidden in their shadow, which came slanting down far out into the river, covering as with a dark veil the sloops, schooners, and bilanders lying in the dusk beside them.

Further down the river stood a clump of Irish vessels, with the light peeping through the tangled rigging, and their masts thick together as their native pine trees, some with their sails hanging loose and flaccid, and others with them looped in rude festoons to the yards. Beside them lay barges filled with barrels of beer and sacks of flour; and a few yards beyond was a huge foreign steamer, with its short, thick, black funnel, and blue paddle-boxes. Then came hoys laden with straw and coasting goods, so deep in the water that, as the steamers dashed by, you could see the white spray beat against the tarpaulins that covered their heaped-up cargoes. Next to these, black-looking colliers, and Russian brigs from Memel and Petersburg, lay in a dense mass together. Behind them stood the old "suffrance wharfs" with their peaked roofs, and unwieldly cranes; while far at the back might be seen one solitary tree. Further down by the river side was a huge old-fashioned brewery, with its jet of white steam shooting through the roof; and in the haze of the extreme distance the steeple of St. Mary's, Rotherhithe, looked, grey, dim, and spectral-like. Then, as you turned again to look at the bridge, you caught glimpses of barges in the light seen through the arches below, and the tops of carts, omnibuses, and high loaded waggons moving to and fro above. Looking down towards the wharfs

next the bridge, you could see the cranes projecting from "Nichol-
son's", with bales of goods hanging from them and dangling in the
air. Alongside here lay a schooner and a brig, both from Spain, and
laden with fruit, and, as you cast your eye below, you behold men
with cases of oranges on their backs, bending beneath their load as
they passed from the ship across the dumb lighter to the wharf. In
front of the schooner were lug-boats and empty lighters, standing
high above the water as they waited to be laden.

Next to this was Billingsgate, with the white bellies of the fish
just visible in the market beneath, and streams of men passing backwards and forwards to the riverside. Immediately beneath me was
the gravelled walk of the Custom-house Quay, where children
strolled with their nursemaids, and hatless yellow-legged, blue-coat
boys, and youths fresh from school, had come either to look at the
shipping, or to skip and play among the barges. Here boats went
by with men standing up in the stern and working a scull behind,
like a fish's tail. Some yards off, were Dutch eel boats, of polished
oak, with round bluff bows and unwieldly green-tipped rudders.
Then came a tier of huge steamers with gilt sterns and mahogany
wheels, and their bright brass binnacles glittering in the sun; at the
foremost head of one, the blue-peter was flying as a summons to
the hands ashore to come on board previously to starting, while the
clouds of smoke that poured from the thick red funnel told that the
fires were ready lighted. Behind these lay the Old Persius—the
receiving ship of the Navy—with her top-masts down, her tall
black sides towering high out of the water, and her white ventilators
hanging above the hatchways. After her came other schooners, brigs,
and sloops—with their yards aslant and their sails looped up. Beside
the wharf in front of these lay lug-boats and sloops, filled with square
cases of wine, while bales of hemp, barrels of porter, and crates of
hardware, swung from the cranes, and were lowered into the boats
or lifted out of the sloops and "foreign brigs" below. Further on
you could just make out the Tower-wharf, with its gravelled walk
and the red-coated and high-capped sentry pacing to and fro.
Beyond this again you saw the huge, massive warehouses of St.
Katharine's Docks, with their big signet letters on their sides, their
many prison-like windows, and their cranes to every floor. At the
back stood the square old Tower, with its four turrets, and its grey,
buttressed walls peering over the waterside.

As I stood looking down upon the river the hundred clocks of the
churches around me—with the golden figures on their black dials
twinkling in the sunshine—chimed the hour of two in a hundred
different tones, while, solemnly above all, boomed forth the monster
bell of St. Paul's, filling the air for minutes afterwards with a deep,

melodious moan; and scarcely had it died away before there rose
from the river the sharp tinkle of "four bells' from the multitude of
ships and steamers below. Indeed, there was an exquisite charm in
the different sounds that smote the ear from the busy port of
London. Now you would hear the tinkling of the distant purl-man's
bell, as in his boat he flitted in and out among the several tiers of
colliers. Then would come the rattle of some chain suddenly let go;
after this, the chorus of many seamen heaving at the ropes; while,
high above all, would be heard the hoarse voice of some one from
the shore, bawling through his hands to his mate aboard the craft
in the river. Anon you would catch the clicking of the capstan palls,
as they hove some neighbouring anchor, and, mingled with all this,
would be heard the rumbling of the waggons and carts in the streets
behind, and the panting and quick pulsation of the steamers on the
river in front of you. Look or listen which way you would, the many
sights and sounds that filled the eye and ear told each its different
tale of busy trade and boundless capital. In the many bright-
coloured flags that fluttered over the port, you read how all corners
of the earth had been ransacked, each for it peculiar produce. The
massive warehouses at the water-side looked like the storehouses of
the wealth of the world, while, in the tall mast-like chimneys, with
their black flags of smoke streaming from them, you saw how all
around were at work, fashioning the far-fetched produce into new
fabrics. As you beheld the white clouds of the railway engine scud-
ding above the roofs opposite, and heard the clatter of the carts and
waggons behind, and looked down the endless vista of masts that
crowded each side of the river, you could not help feeling how every
power known to man was used to bring and diffuse the riches of
every part of the world over this little island.

Those who have only seen London in the day-time, with its flood
of life pouring through its arteries to its restless heart, know it not in
its grandest aspect. It is not in the noise and roar of the cataract of
commerce pouring through its streets, nor in its forest of ships, nor
in its vast docks and warehouses, that its true solemnity is to be seen.
To behold it in its greatest sublimity, it must be contemplated by
night, afar off, from an eminence. The noblest prospect in the world,
it has been well said, is London viewed from the suburbs on a clear
winter's evening. The stars are shining in the heavens, but there is
another firmament spread out below, with its millions of bright
lights glittering at our feet. Line after line sparkles, like the trails
left by meteors, cutting and crossing one another till they are lost
in the haze of the distance. Over the whole there hangs a lurid cloud,
bright as if the monster city were in flames, and looking afar off like
the sea by night, made phosphorescent by the million creatures dwell-

ing within it. At night it is that the strange anomalies of London are best seen. Then, as the hum of life ceases and the shops darken, and the gaudy gin palaces thrust out their ragged and squalid crowds, to pace the streets, London puts on its most solemn look of all. On the benches of the parks, in the nitches of the bridges, and in the litter of the markets, are huddled together the homeless and the destitute. The only living things that haunt the streets are the poor wretches who stand shivering in their finery, waiting to catch the drunkard as he goes shouting homewards. Here on a doorstep crouches some shoeless child, whose day's begging has not brought it enough to purchase even the twopenny bed that its young companions in beggary have gone to. There, where the stones are taken up and piled high in the road, and the gas streams from a tall pipe in the centre of the street in a flag of flame—there, round the red glowing coke fire, are grouped a ragged crowd smoking or dozing through the night beside it. Then as the streets grow blue with the coming light, and the church spires and chimney tops stand out against the sky with a sharpness of outline that is seen only in London before its million fires cover the town with their pall of smoke—then come sauntering forth the unwashed poor, some with greasy wallets on their back, to hunt over each dirt heap, and eke out life by seeking refuse bones or stray rags and pieces of old iron. Others, on their way to their work, gathered at the corner of the street round the breakfast stall, and blowing saucers of steaming coffee drawn from tall tin cans, with the fire shining crimson through the holes beneath; whilst already the little slattern girl, with her basket slung before her, screams watercresses through the sleeping streets.

*The task: Letter I— 19 October 1849*

To me has been confided the office of examining into the condition of the poor of London; and I shall now proceed to state the view I purpose taking of the subject.

Under the term poor I shall include all those persons whose incomings are insufficient for the satisfaction of their wants—a want being, according to my idea, contra-distinguished from a mere desire by a positive physical pain, instead of a mental uneasiness, accompanying it. The large and comparatively unknown body of people included in this definition I shall contemplate in two distinct classes, viz., the *honest* and *dishonest* poor; and the first of these I purpose sub-dividing into the *striving* and the *disabled*—or in other words, I shall consider the whole of the metropolitan poor under three separate phases, according as they *will* work, they *can't* work, and they *won't* work. Of those that will work, and yet are unable to

obtain sufficient for their bodily necessities, I shall devote my attention first to such as receive no relief from the parish; and under
this head will be included the poorly-paid—the unfortunate—and
the improvident. While treating of the poorly-paid, I shall endeavour to lay before the reader a catalogue of such occupations in London as yield a bare subsistence to the parties engaged in them. At
the same time I purpose, when possible, giving the weekly amount
of income derived from each, together with the cause—if discover-
able—of the inadequate return, After this, it is my intention to visit
the dwellings of the unrelieved poor—to ascertain, by positive inspection, the condition of their homes—to learn, by close communion
with them, the real or fancied wrongs of their lot—to discover, not
only on how little they subsist, but how large a rate of profit they
have to pay for the little upon which they do subsist—to ascertain
what weekly rent they are charged for their waterless, drainless,
floorless, and almost roofless tenements; to calculate the interest
that the petty capitalist reaps from their necessities. Nor shall I fail
to point out how, when the poor are driven to raise a meal on their
clothes or their bedding, he who makes the advance is licensed by
law to receive as much as 20 per cent for the petty loan upon the
land. But, however alive I may be to the wrongs of the poor, I shall
not be misled by a morbid sympathy to see them only as suffering
from the selfishness of others. Their want of prudence, want of
temperance, want of energy, want of cleanliness, want of knowledge,
and want of morality, will each be honestly set forth. This done, I
shall proceed to treat of the poor receiving parish relief, outside and
inside the union; after which, the habits, haunts, and tricks of the
beggars of London will be duly set forth; and finally, those of the
thieves and prostitutes.[2]

[2] In the remainder of this letter, Mayhew gave "a general idea of the
wealth and poverty, the power and weakness, the knowledge and ignorance,
the luxury and want, the crime and charity, which all lie muddled together
in London".

# THE SPITALFIELDS SILK-WEAVERS

## LETTER II—23 OCTOBER 1849

*Causes of poverty and selection of the weavers*

In my first letter I stated that I purposed considering the whole of the metropolitan poor under three distinct phases—according as they *will* work, as they *can't* work, and as they *won't* work. The causes of poverty among such as are willing to work, appeared to me to be two : 1. The workman might receive for his labour less than sufficient to satisfy his wants. 2. He might receive a sufficiency, and yet be in want, either from having to pay an exorbitant price for the commodities he requires in exchange for his wages, or else from a deficiency of economy and prudence in the regulation of his desires by his means and chances of subsistence. Or, to say the same thing in a more concise manner, the privations of the industrious classes admit of being referred either to (1) low wages, (2) high prices, or (3) improvident habits.

In opening the subject which has been entrusted to me, and setting forth the plan I purpose pursuing, so as to methodize and consequently simplify the investigation of it, I stated it to be my intention to devote myself primarily to the consideration of that class of poor whose privations seemed to be due to the insufficiency of their wages. In accordance with this object, I directed my steps first towards Bethnal-green, with the view of inquiring into the rate of wages received by the Spitalfields weavers. My motive for making this selection was, principally, because the manufacture of silk is one of the few arts that continue localized—that is restricted to a particular quarter—in London. The tanners of Bermondsey—the watchmakers of Clerkenwell—the coachmakers of Long-acre—the marine-store dealers of Saffron-hill—the old clothes-men of Holywell-street and Rosemary-lane—the potters of Lambeth—the hatters of the Borough, are among the few handicrafts and trades that, as in the bazaars of the East, are confined to particular parts of the town. Moreover, the weavers of Spitalfields have always been notorious for their privations, and being all grouped together within a comparatively small space, they could be more easily visited, and a greater mass of information obtained in a less space of time, than in the case of any other ill-paid metropolitan handicraft with which I am acquainted.

In my inquiry I have sought to obtain information from the artisans of Spitalfields upon two points in particular. I was desirous to ascertain from the workmen themselves, not only the average rate of wages received by them, but also to hear their opinions as to the cause of the depreciation in the value of their labour. The result of my inquiries on these two points I purpose setting forth in my present communications; but, before entering upon the subject, I wish the reader distinctly to understand that the sentiments here recorded are those wholly and solely of the weavers themselves. My vocation is to collect facts, and to register opinions. I have undertaken the subject with a rigid determination neither to be biased nor prejudiced by my own individual notions, whatever they may be, upon the matter. I know that as in science the love of theorizing warps the mind, and causes it to see only those natural phenomena that it wishes to see—so in politics, party-feeling is the coloured spectacles through which too many invariably look at the social events of this and other countries. The truth will be given in its stark nakedness. Indeed, hardly a line will be written but what a note of the matter recorded has been taken upon the spot, so that, no matter how startling or incredible the circumstances may seem, the reader may rest assured that it is his experience rather than the reporter's veracity that is at fault.[1]

## Cultural habits of the weavers

The history of weaving in Spitalfields is interesting, and tends to elucidate several of the habits existing to this day among the class. Upon the revocation of the edict of Nantes in 1685, numerous French artisans left their native country, and took refuge in the neighbouring states. King James II encouraged these settlers, and William III published a proclamation, dated 25 April 1689, for the encouraging the French Protestants to transport themselves into this kingdom, promising them his royal protection, and to render their living here comfortable and easy to them. For a considerable time the population of Spitalfields might be considered as exclusively French; that language was universally spoken, and even within the memory of persons now living their religious rites were performed in French in chapels erected for that purpose. The weavers were, formerly, almost the only botanists in the metropolis, and their love of flowers to this day is a strongly marked characteristic of the class. Some years back, we are told, they passed their leisure hours, and generally the whole family dined on Sundays, at the

[1] Here the high density and bad condition of housing in Bethnal Green were discussed, with information from Gavin's *Sanitary Ramblings*.

little gardens in the environs of London, now mostly built upon. Not very long ago there was an Entomological Society, and they were among the most diligent entomologists, in the kingdom. This taste, though far less general than formerly, still continues to be a type of the class. There was at one time a Floricultural Society, an Historical Society, and a Mathematical Society, all maintained by the operative silk-weavers; and the celebrated Dollond, the inventor of the achromatic telescope, was a weaver; so too were Simpson and Edwards, the mathematicians, before they were taken from the loom into the employ of Government, to teach mathematics to the cadets at Woolwich and Chatham. Such *were* the Spitalfields weavers at the beginning of the present century; possessing tastes and following pursuits the refinement and intelligence of which would be an honour and a grace to the artisan even of the present day, but which shone out with a double lustre at a time when the amusements of society were almost all of a gross and brutalizing kind. The weaver of our own time, however, though still far above the ordinary artisan, both in refinement and intellect, falls far short of the weaver of former years.

## Economic position of the weavers

Of the importance of the silk trade, as a branch of manufacture, to the country, we may obtain some idea from the estimate of the total value of the produce, drawn up by Mr. McCulloch, with great care, as he tells us, from the statements of intelligent, practical men in all parts of the country, conversant with the trade, and well able to form an opinion upon it. The total amount of wages paid in the year 1836 (since when, he says, the circumstances have changed but little) was upwards of £3,700,000, the total number of hands employed, 200,000; the interest on capital, wear, tear, profit, etc., £2,600,000; and the estimated total value of the silk manufacture of Great Britain, £10,480,000. Now, according to the census of the weavers of the Spitalfields district, taken at the time of the Government inquiry in 1838, and which appears to be considered by the weavers themselves of a generally accurate character, the number of looms at work was 9,302, and those unemployed, 894.[2] But every two of the looms employed would occupy five hands; so that the total number of hands engaged in the silk manufacture in Spitalfields, in 1838, must have been more than double that number—say 20,000. This would show about one-tenth of the silk goods that were pro-

[2] This census and T. Heath's testimony (cited later) come from the report of J. Mitchell on "The East of England" for the Royal Commission on the Hand-loom Weavers, *Parliamentary Sessional Papers*, 1840, vol. xxiii.

duced in Great Britain in that year to have been manufactured in Spitalfields, and hence the total value of the produce of that district must have been upwards of one million of money, and the amount paid in wages about £370,000.

Now, from inquiries made among the operatives, I find that there has been a depreciation in the value of their labour of from 15 to 20 per cent, since the year 1839; so that, according to the above calculation, the total amount of wages now paid to the weavers is £60,000 less than what it was ten years back. By the preceding estimate it will be seen that the average amount of wages in the trade would have been in 1839 about 7s. a week per hand, and that now the wages would be about 5s. 6d. for each of the parties employed. This appears to agree with a printed statement put forward by the men themselves, wherein it is affirmed that "the average weekly earnings of the operative silk weaver in 1824, under the act then repealed, taking the whole body of operatives employed, partially employed, and unemployed, was 14s. 6d. Deprived of legislative protection," they say, "there is now no means of readily ascertaining the average weekly earnings of the whole body of the employed and unemployed operative silk weavers; but, according to the best approximation to an average which can be made in Spitalfields, the average of the weekly earnings of the operative silk weaver is now, taking the unemployed and the partially employed, with the employed of those remaining attached to the occupation of weaver, only 4s. 9d. But this weekly average would be much less if it included those who have gone to other trades, or who have become perpetual paupers." Hence, it would appear that the estimate before given of 5s. 6d. for the weekly average wages of the employed is not very far from the truth. It may therefore be safely asserted that the operative silk weavers as a body, obtain £50,000 worth less of food, clothing, and comfort per annum now than in the year 1839.

Now let us see what was the state of the weaver in that year, as detailed by the Government report, so that we may be the better able to comprehend what his state must be at present : "Mr. Thomas Heath, of No. 8 Pedley-street," says the Blue Book of 1839, "has been represented by many persons as one of the most skilful workmen in Spitalfields. He handed in about 40 samples of figured silk done by him and they appear exceedingly beautiful. This weaver also gave a minute and detailed account of all his earnings for 430 weeks, being upwards of eight years, with the names of the manufacturer and the fabrics at which he worked. The sum of the gross earnings for 430 weeks is £322 3s. 4d., being about 14s. 11¾d.— say 15s. a week. He estimates his expenses (for quill-winding, picking, etc.) at 4s., which would leave 11s. net wages; but take the expenses

at 3s. 6d.—it is still only 11s. 6d. He states his wife's earnings at
about 3s. a week. He gives the following remarkable evidence :
Have you any children? No; I had two, but they are both dead,
thanks be to God! Do you express satisfaction at the death of your
children? do! I thank God for it. I am relieved from the burden
of maintaining them, and they, poor dear creatures, are relieved
from the troubles of this mortal life." If this, then, was the condition
and feeling of one of the most skilful workmen ten years ago, earning 11s. 6d. a week, and when it was proved in evidence by Mr.
Cole that 8s. 6d. per week was the average net earnings of twenty
plain weavers—what must be the condition and feeling of the weaver
now that wages have fallen from 15 to 20 per cent since that period !

*Interviews with weavers in their homes*

I will now proceed to give the result of my inquiries into the subject; though, before doing so, it will be as well to make the reader
acquainted with the precautions adopted to arrive at a fair and
unbiased estimate as to the feelings and condition of the workmen in
the trade. In the first place, having put myself in communication
with the surgeon of the district, and one of the principal and most
intelligent of the operatives, it was agreed among us that we should
go into a particular street, and visit the first six weavers' houses that
we came to. Accordingly, we made the best of our way to the nearest
street. The houses were far above the average abodes of the weavers,
the street being wide and airy, and the houses open at the back,
with gardens filled with many-coloured dahlias. The "long lights"
at top, as the attic window stretching the whole length of the house
is technically called, showed that almost the whole line of houses
were occupied by weavers. As we entered the street, a coal cart,
with a chime of bells above the horse's collar, went jingling past us.
Another circumstance peculiar to the place was the absence of children. In such a street, had the labour of the young been less valuable,
the gutters and door-steps would have swarmed with juveniles.

We knocked at the door of the first house, and, requesting permission to speak with the workman on the subject of his trade, were
all three ushered up a steep staircase, and through a trap in the
floor into the "shop". This was a long, narrow apartment, with a
window back and front, extending the entire length of the house—
running from one end of the room to the other. The man was the
ideal of his class—a short, spare figure, with a thin face and sunken
cheeks. In the room were three looms and some spinning wheels, at
one of which sat a boy winding "quills". Working at the loom was a
plump, pleasant-looking girl, busy making "plain goods". Along

the windows, on each side, were ranged small pots of fuchsias, with their long scarlet drops swinging gently backwards and forwards, as the room shook with the clatter of the looms. The man was a velvet weaver. He was making a drab velvet for coat collars. We sat down on a wooden chair beside him, and talked as he worked. He told us he was to have 3s. 6d. per yard for the fabric he was engaged upon, and that he could make half of a yard a day. They were six in family, he said, and he had three looms at work. He got from 20s. to 25s. for the labour of five of them, and that only when they all are employed. But one loom is generally out of work waiting for fresh "cane". Up to 1824, the price for the same work as he is now doing was 6s. The reduction, he was convinced, arose from the competition in the trade, and one master cutting under the other. "The workmen are obliged to take the low prices, because they have not the means to hold out, and they know that if they don't take the work others will. There are always plenty of weavers unemployed, and the cause of that is owing to the lowness of prices, and the people being compelled to do double the quantity of work that they used to do, in order to live. I have made a stand against the lowness of prices, and have lost my work through refusing to take the price. Circumstances compel us to take it at last. The cupboard gets low, and the landlord comes for his weekly rent. The masters are all trying to undersell one another. They never will advance wages. Go get my neighbour to do it, each says, and then *I'll* advance. It's been a continuation of reduction for the last six-and-twenty years, and a continuation of suffering for just as long. Never a month passes but what you hear of something being lowered. Manufacturers may be divided into two classes—those who care for their men's comforts and welfare, and those who care for none but themselves. In the work of reduction certain houses take the lead, taking advantage of the least depression to offer the workmen less wages. It's useless talking about French goods. Why, we've driven the French out of the market in umbrellas and parasols—but the people are a-starving while they're a-driving of 'em out." A little time back he'd only one loom at work for eight persons, and lived by making away with his clothes. Labour is so low he can't afford to send his children to school. He only sends them of a Sunday—can't afford it of a work-a-day.

At the next house the man took rather a more gloomy view of his calling. He was at work at brown silk for umbrellas. "His wife worked when she was able, but she was nursing a sick child. He had made the same work he was then engaged upon at 1s. a yard not six months ago. He was to have 10d. for it, and he didn't know that there might not be another penny taken off next time. Weavers were all a-getting poorer, and masters all a-getting country houses. His master had been a-losing terrible, he said, and yet he'd just taken a country mansion. They only give you work just to oblige you, as an act of charity, and not to do themselves any good—oh, no! Works fifteen hours, and often more. When he knocks off at ten at night, leaves lights up all round him—many go on till eleven. All he knows is, he can't! They are possessed of greater strength than he is, he imagines. In the dead of night he can always see one light some-where—some man "on the finish". Wakes at five, and then he can hear the looms going. Low prices arise entirely from competition among the masters. The umbrella silk he was making would most likely be charged a guinea; what would sixpence extra on that be to the purchaser, and yet that extra sixpence would be three or four shillings per week to him, and go a long way towards the rent? Isn't able to tell exactly what is the cause of the depression—"I only know I suffers from it—aye, that I do! I do! and have severely for some time," said the man, striking the silk before him with his clenched fist. "The man that used to make this here is dead and buried; he died of the cholera. I went to see him buried. He had 11d. for what I get 10d. What it will be next God only knows, and I'm sure I don't care—it can't be much worse. Mary," said he to his wife, as she sat blowing the fire, with the dying infant on her lap, "how much leg of beef do we use?—4 lb., ain't it, in the week, and 3 lb. of flank on Sunday—lucky to get that, too, eh?—and that's among half a dizen of us. Now, I should like a piece of roast beef, with the potatoes done under it, but I shall never taste that again. And yet," he said, with a savage chuckle, "that there six-pence on this umbrella would just do it. But what's that to people! What's it to them if we starve?—and there is many at that game just now, I can tell you. If we could depend upon a constancy of work, and get a good price, why we should be happy men; but I'm sure I don't know whether I shall get any more work when my cane's' out. My children I'm quite disheartened about. They must turn out in the world somewhere, but where Heaven only knows. I often bother myself over that—more than my father bothered him-self over me. What's to become of us all? What's to become of us all—nine thousand of us here—besides wives and children—I can't say."

These two specimens will give the reader a conception of the feelings and state of the rest of the weavers in the same street. In all there was the same want of hope—the same doggedness and half-indifference as to their fate. All agreed in referring their misery to the spirit of competition on the part of the masters, the same desire to "cut under". They all spoke most bitterly of one manu-

facturer in particular, and attributed to him the ruin of the trade.
One weaver said he was anxious to get to America, and not stop "in
this infernal country", for he could see the object of the Government was the starvation of the labouring classes. "If you was to
come round here of a Sunday," said he, addressing himself to us,
"you'd hear the looms going all about; they're obliged to do it or
starve. There's no rest for us now. Formerly I lived in a house
worth £40 a year, and now I'm obliged to put up with this damned
dog-hole. Every year bad is getting worse in our trade, and in others
as well. What's life to me? Labour—labour—labour—and for what?
Why for less and less food every month. Ah, but the people can't
bear it much longer; flesh, and blood, and bones must rise against it
before long."

*Opinion of Chartist weavers*

Having, then, seen and heard the opinions of six of the operatives
taken promiscuously, I was desirous of being placed in a position
to see different classes of the same trade. I wished to be placed in
communication with some of the workmen who were known to
entertain violent political opinions. I was anxious also to be allowed
to see weavers who were characterized by the possession of such
tastes as formerly distinguished the class. Unfortunately, however,
though I was kindly taken to the houses of two or three individuals
of known scientific tastes and acquirements, the parties were all
absent from their homes. I was conducted, however, in the evening
to a tavern, where several of the weavers who advocate the principles
of the People's Charter were in the habit of assembling. I found the
room half full, and immediately proceded to explain to them the
object of my visit, telling them that I intended to make notes of
whatever they might communicate to me, with a view to publication in the *Morning Chronicle*.

After a short consultation among themselves, they told me that,
in their opinion, the primary cause of the depression of the prices
among the weavers was the want of the suffrage. "We consider that
labour is unrepresented in the House of Commons, and being unrepresented, that the capitalist and the landlord have it all their
own way. Prices have gone down among the weavers since 1824
more than one half. The hours of labour have decidedly increased
among us, so that we may live. The weavers now generally work
one-third longer than formerly, and for much less." "I know two
instances," said one person, "where the weavers have to work from
ten in the morning to twelve at night, and then they only get meat
once a week. The average time for labour before 1824 was ten hours

a day, now it is fourteen. In 1824 there were about 14,000 hands employed, getting at an average 14s. 6d. a week, and now there are 9,000 hands employed, getting at an average only 4s. 9d. a week, at increased hours of labour. This depreciation we attribute, not to any decrease in the demand for silk goods, but to foreign and home competition. We believe that the foreign competition brings us into competition with the foreign workmen; and it is impossible for us to compete with him at the present rate of English taxation. As regards home competition, we are of opinion that, from the continued desire on the part of each trade to undersell the other, the workman has ultimately to suffer. We think there is a desire on the part of every manufacturer to undersell the other, and so get an extra amount of trade into his own hands, and make a large and rapid fortune thereby. The public, we are satisfied, do not derive any benefit from this extreme competition. It is only a few individuals who are termed by the trade slaughterhouse-men—they alone derive benefit from the system, and the public gain no advantage whatever by the depreciation in our rate of wages. It is our firm conviction that if affairs continue as at present, the fate of the working man must be pauperism, crime, or death."

*An average case of destitution in the trade*

It was now getting late, and as I was anxious to see some case of destitution in the trade, which might be taken as a fair average of the state of the second or third-rate workman, I requested my guide, before I quitted the district, to conduct me to some such individual if it were not too late. He took me towards Shoreditch, and on reaching a narrow back street he stood opposite a three-storied house to see whether there was still a light shining through the long window in the attic. By the flickering shadows the lamp seemed to be dying out. He thought, however, that we might venture to knock. We did so, and in the silent street the noise echoed from house to house. But no one came. We knocked again still louder A third time, and louder still, we clattered at the door. A voice from the cellar demanded to know whom we wanted. He told us to lift the latch of the street door. We did so—and it opened. The passage looked almost solid in the darkness. My guide groped his way by the wall to the staircase, bidding me follow him. I did so, and reached the stairs. "Keep away from the banisters," said my companion, "as they are rather rotten and might give way." I clung close to the wall, and we groped our way to the second floor, where a light shone through the closed door in a long luminous line. At last we gained the top room, and knocking, were told to enter. "Oh, Billy, is that you," said an old man sitting up, and looking out from between the curtains of a turn-up bedstead. "Here, Tilly," he continued to a girl who was still dressed, "get another lamp, and hang it up again the loom and give the gentleman a chair." A backless seat was placed at the foot of the old weaver's bed-stead; and when the fresh lamp was lighted, I never beheld so strange a scene. In the room were three large looms. From the head of the old weaver's bed a clothes line ran to a loom opposite, and on it were a few old ragged shirts and petticoats hanging to dry. Under the "porry" of another loom was stretched a second clothes line, and more linen drying. Behind me on the floor was spread a bed, on which lay four for the more convenient stowage of the number. They were covered boys, two with their heads in one direction and two in another, with old sacks and coats. Beside the bed of the old man was a mattress on the ground without any covering, and the tick positively chocolate-coloured with dirt.

"Oh, Billy, I am so glad to see you," said the old weaver to my companion; "I've been dreadful bad, nearly dead with the cholera. I was took dreadful about one o'clock in the morning; just the time the good 'ooman down below were taken. What agony I suffered to be sure! I hope to God you may never have it. I've known four hundred die about here in fourteen days. I couldn't work! Oh, no! It took all the use of my strength from me, as if I'd been on a sick bed for months. And how I lived I can't tell. To tell you the real truth, I wanted such as I never ought to want—why, I wanted for common necessaries. I got round as well as I could; but how I did it I don't know—God knows; I don't, that's true enough. I hadn't got any money to buy anything. Why, there's seven on us here—yes, seven on us—all dependent on the weaving here, nothing else. What was four shilling a yard is paid one and nine now, so I leaves you to judge, sir—an't it Billy? My work stopped for seven days, and I was larning my boy, so his stopped too, and we had nothing to live upon. God knows how we lived. I pawned my things—and shall never get 'em again—to buy some bread, tea, and sugar, for my young ones there. Oh! it's like a famine in these parts just now among the people, now they're getting well. It's no use talking about the parish; you might as well talk to a wall. There was hardly anybody well just round about here, from the back of Shoreditch Church, you may say to Swan-street. The prices of weaving is so low, that we're ashamed to say what it is, because it's the means of pulling down other poor men's wages and other trades. Why, to tell you the truth, you must need suppose that 1s. 9d. a yard ain't much and some of the masters is so cruel, that they gives no more than 1s. 3d.—that it. But it's the competitive system; that's what the Government ought to put a stop to. I knows persons who makes the same work as mine—scores of 'em—at 1s. 3d. a yard. Wretched is their condition! The people is a being brought to that state of destitution, that many say it's a blessing from the Almighty that takes 'em from the world. They lose all love of country—yes, and all hopes; and they prays to be tortured no longer. Why want is common to a hundred of families close here to-morrow morning; and this it is to have cheap silks. I should like to ask a question here, as I sees you a-writing, sir. When is the people of England to see that there big loaf they was promised—that's it—the people wants to know when they're to have it. I am sure if the ladies who wears what we makes, or the Queen of England was to see our state, she'd never let her subjects suffer such privations in a land of plenty.

"Yes, I was comfortable in '24. I kept a good little house, and I thought as my young ones growed up—why I thought as I should be comfortable in my old age, and 'stead of that, I've got no wages. I could live by my labour then, but now, why it's wretched in the extreme. Then I'd a nice little garden and some nice tulips for my hobby, when my work was done. There they lay, up in my old hat now. As for animal food, why it's a stranger to us. Once a week, may be, we gets a taste of it, but that's a hard struggle, and many a family don't have it once a month—a jint we never sees. Oh, it's too bad! There's seven on us here in this room—but it's a very large room to some weavers'—their's a'n't above half the size of this here. The weavers is in general five or six all living and working in the same room. There's four on us here in this bed. One head to foot—one at our back along the bolster; and me and my wife side by side. And there's four on 'em over there. My brother Tom makes up the other one. There's a nice state in a Christian land! How many do you think lives in this house! Why 23 living souls. Oh! a'n't it too bad! But the people is frightened to say how bad they're off, for fear of their masters and losing their work, so they keeps it to themselves—poor creatures. But oh, there's many worse than me. Many's gone to the docks, and some turned coster-mongers. But none goes a stealing nor a sojering, that I hears on. They goes out to get a loaf of bread—oh, it's a shocking scene! I can't say what I thinks about the young uns. Why you loses your nat'ral affection for 'em. The people in general is ashamed to say how they thinks on their children. It's wretched in the extreme to see one's children, and not be able to do to 'em as a parent ought; and I'll say this here after all you've heerd me state—that the Government of my native land ought to interpose their powerful arm to put a stop to such things. Unless they do, civil society with us all is at an end. Everybody is becoming brutal—unnatural. Billy, just turn up that shell now, and let the gentlemen see what beautiful fabrics we're in the habit of producing—and then he shall say whether we ought to be in the filthy state we are. Just show the light, Tilly! That's for ladies to wear and adorn them, and make them handsome." (It was an exquisite piece of moroon coloured velvet, that, amidst all the squalor of the place, seemed marvellously beautiful, and it was a wonder to see it unsoiled amid all the filth that surrounded it). "I say, just turn it up Billy, and show the gentleman the back. That's cotton partly, you see, sir, just for the manufacturers to cheat the public, and get a cheap article, and have all the gold out of the poor working creatures they can, and don't care nothing about them. But death, Billy—death gets all the gold out of them. They're playing a deep game, but Death wins after all. Oh, when this here's made known, won't the manufacturers be in a way to find the public aware on their tricks. They've lowered the wages so low, that one would hardly believe the people would take the work. But what's one to do!— the children can't *quite* starve. Oh no!—oh no!"

Fig. 1.   Penny card sold on behalf of the
Spitalfields weavers, 1829.

# THE SLOPWORKERS AND
# NEEDLEWOMEN

## LETTER VI—6 NOVEMBER 1849[1]

Let me pass to the subject of this communication—viz., the in-comings and the conditions of the "slopworkers" of London. . . . I had seen so much want since I began my investigation into the condition of the labouring poor of London that my feelings were almost blunted to sights of ordinary misery. Still I was unprepared for the amount of suffering that I have lately witnessed. I could not have believed that there were human beings toiling so long and gaining so little, and starving so silently and heroically, round about our very homes. It is true, one or two instances of the kind had forced themselves into the police reports, and songs and plays had been written upon the privations of the class; still it was impossible to believe that the romance of the song-writer and the fable of the playwright were plain, unvarnished, every-day matters of fact—or, even admitting their stories to be individually true, we could hardly credit them to be universally so. But the reader shall judge for himself.

I will endeavour to reproduce the scenes I have lately looked upon—and I will strive to do so in all their stark literality. It is difficult, I know, for those who are unacquainted with the misery hiding itself in the bye-lanes and alleys of the metropolis to have perfect faith in the tales that it is my duty to tell them. Let me therefore once more assure the sceptical reader, that hardly a line is written here but a note was taken upon the matter upon the spot. The descriptions of the dwellings and the individuals I allude to have all been written with the very places and parties before me; and the story of the people's sufferings is repeated to the public in the self-same words in which they were told to me. Still it may be said that I myself may have been imposed upon—that I may have been taken to extreme cases and given to understand that they are the ordinary types of the class. This, I am ready to grant, is a common source of error; I will therefore now explain the means that I adopted, in this instance in particular, to prevent myself being deluded into any such fallacy.

[1] This letter began with a passage on low-lodging houses which ended the study of casual labour at the docks in letters III–V.

116

*No co-operation from "slop-sellers"*

My first step was to introduce myself to one of the largest "slop-sellers" at the East-end of the town; and having informed the firm that I was about to examine into the condition and incomings of the slop-workers of London, I requested to know whether they would have any objection to furnish me with the list of prices that they were in the habit of paying to their workpeople, so that on my visiting the parties themselves—as I frankly gave them to understand I proposed doing—I might be able to compare the operatives' statements as to the prices with theirs, and thus be able to check the one with the other. Indeed, I said I thought it but fair that the employer should have an opportunity of having his say as well as the employed. I regret to say that I was not met with the candour that I had been led to expect. One of the firm wished to know why I singled their house out from the rest of the trade. I told him I did so merely because it was one of the largest in the business, and assured him that, so far from my having any personal object in my visit, I made it a point never to allude by name to any employer or workman to whom I might have occasion to refer. My desire, I said, was to deal with principles rather than persons; whereupon I was informed that the firm would have no objection to acquaint me with the prices paid by *other* houses in the trade. "If you merely wish to arrive at the principle of the slop business, this," said one of the partners, "will be quite sufficient for your purpose." Though I pressed for some more definite and particular information from the firm, I could obtain nothing from them but an assurance that a statement should be written out for me immediately as to the general custom of the trade, and that if I would call at any time after sunset on Saturday evening, it should be at my disposal.

I soon saw that it was useless seeking to obtain any other information from the parties in question—so, taking my departure, I made the best of my way to the workmen in the neighbourhood. My time being limited, I consulted with a gentleman who is thoroughly conversant with the character of several of the operatives, as to the best and fairest means of taking an unprejudiced view of the state of the slop-workers of London; and it was agreed between us that as the work was performed by both males and females, it would be better first to direct my attention to the state of the male "hands" employed by the trades; while, in order to arrive at an accurate estimate as to the incomings and condition of the class generally, it was deemed better to visit some place where several of the operatives were in the habit of working together, so that the opinions of a number of individuals might be taken simultaneously upon the subject.

*Interviews with male slop-workers*

Accordingly I was led, by the gentleman whose advice I had sought, to a narrow court, the entrance to which was blocked up by stalls of fresh herrings. We had to pass sideways between the baskets with our coat-tails under our arms. At the end of the passage we entered a dirty-looking house by a side entrance. Though it was noonday, the staircase was so dark that we were forced to grope our way by the wall up to the first floor. Here in a small back room, about eight feet square, we found no fewer than seven workmen, with their coats and shoes off, seated cross-legged on the floor, busy stitching the different parts of different garments. The floor was strewn with sleeve-boards, irons, and snips of various coloured cloths. In one corner of the room was a turn-up bedstead, with the washed-out chintz curtains drawn partly in front of it. Across a line which ran from one side of the apartment to the other were thrown coats, jackets, and cravats of the workmen. Inside the rusty grate was a hat, and on one of the hobs rested a pair of old cloth boots; while leaning against the bars in front there stood a sack full of cuttings. Beside the workmen on the floor sat two good-looking girls—one crosslegged like the men—engaged in tailoring.

My companion having acquainted the workmen with the object of my visit, they one and all expressed themselves ready to answer any questions that I might put to them. They made dress and frock coats, they told me, Chesterfields, fishing coats, paletots, Buller's monkey jackets, beavers, shooting coats, trowsers, vests, sacks, Codringtons, Trinity cloaks and coats, and indeed every other kind of woollen garment.[2] They worked for the ready-made houses, or "slop-sellers". "One of us," said they, "gets work from the warehouse, and gives it out to others. The houses pay different prices. Dress coats, from 5s. 6d. to 6s. 9d.; frock coats the same; shooting coats, from 2s. 6d. to 2s. 9d. In summer time, when trade is busy, they pay 3s. Chesterfields, from 2s. 6d. to 3s., some are made for 2s.; paletots, from 2s. 6d. to 3s." "Aye, and two days work for any man," cried one of the tailors with a withered leg, "and buy his own trimmings, white and black cotton, gimp, and pipeclay." "Yes," exclaimed another, "and we have to buy wadding for dress coats; and soon, I suppose, we shall have to buy our own cloth and all

[2] For a helpful description of the styles and fabrics mentioned here and later in the chapter on the tailors, see C. W. and P. Cunnington, *Handbook of English Costume in the Nineteenth Century* (London, 1959).

together." Trowsers from 1s. 6d. to 3s.; waistcoats, from 1s. 6d. to 1s. 9d. Dress and frock coats will take two days and a half to make each, calculating the day from six in the morning to seven at night; but three days is the regular time. Shooting coats will take two days; Chesterfields take the same time as dress and frock coats; paletots, two days; trowsers, one day.

"The master here" (said one of them scarcely distinguishable from the rest) "gets work from the warehouse at the before-mentioned prices; he gives it out to us at the same price, paying us when he receives the money. We are never seen at the shop. Out of the prices the master here deducts 4s. per week per head for our cup of tea or coffee in the morning, and tea in the evening, and our bed. We sleep two in a bed here, and some of us three. In most places the workmen eat, drink, and sleep in one room; as many as ever the room will contain. They'd put twenty in one room if they could."

"I should like to see the paper this'll be printed in," cried the man with the withered leg. "Oh, it'll be a good job, it should be known. We should be glad if the whole world heard it, so that the people should know our situation. I've worked very hard this week, as hard as any man. I've worked from seven in the morning till eleven at night, and my earnings will be 13s. this week; and deducting my 4s. out of that, and my trimmings besides—the trimmings comes to about 1s. 9d. per week—which takes 5s. 9d. altogether, and that will leave me 7s. 3d. for my earning all the week, Sunday included. It's very seldom we has a Sunday walking out. We're obliged to work on Sunday all the same. We should lose our shop if we didn't. 8s. is the average wages take the year all through. Out of this 8s. we have to deduct expenses of lodging, trimming, washing, and light, which comes to 5s. 9d. We can't get a coat to our backs.". . .

"We're called under-the-bed workers, or workers for the 'sweaters'. All the persons who work for wholesale houses are 'sweaters'. Single workmen cannot get the work from them, because they cannot give security—£5 in money, or a shopkeeper must be responsible to that amount. Those who cannot give security are obliged to work for 'sweaters'. The reason for the warehouses requiring this security is, because they pay so badly for the work they are afraid to trust the journeyman with it. But in the regular trade, such as at the West-end, they require no security whatever. In the slop trade the journeymen do not keep Monday—they can't do it, Sunday nor Monday either—if they do they must want for food. Since we've been working at slop trade we find ourselves far worse off than when we were working at the regular trade. The journeymen of the slop trade are unable to earn 13s. where the regular journeyman can earn 30s., and then we have to find our own trimmings and candlelight. I'd sooner be transported than at this work. Why, then, at least, I'd have regular hours for work and for sleep; but now I'm harder worked and worse fed than a cab-horse."

During my stay in this quarter an incident occurred, which may be cited as illustrative of the poverty of the class of slop-workers. The friend who had conducted me to the spot, and who knew the workmen well, had long been striving to induce one of the men— a Dutchman—to marry one of the females working with him in the room, and with whom he had been living for many months. That the man might raise no objection on the score of poverty, my friend requested me to bear with him half the expense of publishing the banns. To this I readily consented, but the man still urged that he was unable to wed the girl just yet. On inquiring the reason we were taken outside the door by the Dutchman, and there told that he had been forced to pawn his coat for 6s., and as yet he had saved only half the amount towards the redemption of it. It would take him upwards of a month to lay by the remainder. This was literally the fact, and the poor fellow said, with a shrug of his shoulders, he could not go to be married in his shirt sleeves. He was told to make himself easy about the wedding garment, and our kind-hearted friend left delighted with the day's work.

### Interview with a female operative

I now wished to learn from some of the female operatives what prices they were paid, and requested my friend to introduce me to some work-woman who might be considered as one of the most provident, industrious, and best-conducted in the trade. The woman bears, I understand, an excellent character, and she gave the following melancholy account of her calling. . . .

"Upon the average," she says, "at all kinds of work, excepting the shirts, that I make, I cannot earn more than 4s. 6d. to 5s. per week—let me sit from eight in the morning till ten every night; and out of that I shall have to pay 1s. 6d. for trimmings, and 6d. candles every week; so that altogether I earn about 3s. in the six days. But I don't earn that, for there's the firing that you must have to press the work, and that will be 9d. a week, for you'll have to use half a hundred weight of coals. So that my clear earnings are a little bit more than 2s., say 2s. 3d. to 2s. 6d. every week. I consider the trowsers the best work. At the highest price, which is 10s. a dozen, I should make no more than eight of them in a week; that would give me 6s. 8d. The trimmings of that eight pair would cost me 1s., the candle 6d., and the coals 9d., for pressing, leaving 4s. 5d. clear— and that is the very best kind of work that can be got in the slop trade. Shirt work is the worst work, the very worst, that can be got. You cannot make more of those at 6s. a dozen than one a day, yielding 3s. a week. The trimmings would be about 3d. for the shirts, and the candle 6d., as before, making 9d. to be deducted, and so leaving 2s. 3d. per week clear. I have known the prices much better when I first began to work at the business, some nineteen years ago. The shirts that they now give 6d. for were then 1s.; and those now at 2d., were 8d. The trowsers were 1s. 4d. and 1s. 6d. a pair, the best— now they give only 10d. for the best. The other articles are now equally low."

"I cannot say," she added, "what the cause may be. I think there are so many to work at it that one will underwork the other. I have seen it so at the shop. The sweaters screw the people down as low as they possibly can, and the masters hear how little they can get their work done for, and cut down the sweaters, and so the workpeople have to suffer again. Every shop has a great number of sweaters. Sometimes the sweaters will get as much as 2d. or 3d.; indeed, I've known 'em take as much as 4d. out of each garment. I should suppose one that has a good many people to work for her— say about a dozen—I suppose that she'll clear from £1 to £1 5s. per week out of their labour.

"The work people are very dissatisfied, and very poor indeed— yes, very poor. There is a great deal of want, and there is a great deal of suffering amongst them. I hear it at the shop when I go in with my work. They have generally been brought up regularly to the trade. It requires an apprenticeship. In about three months a person may learn it, if they're quick; and persons pay from 10s. to £1 to be taught it, bad as the trade is. A mother has got two or three daughters, and she don't wish them to go to service, and she puts them to this poor needlework; and that, in my opinion, is the cause of the destitution and the prostitution about the streets in these parts. So that in a great measure I think the slop trade is the ruin of the young girls that take to it—the prices are not sufficient to keep them—and the consequence is, they fly to the streets to make their living. Most of the workers are young girls who have nothing else to depend upon, and there is scarcely one of them virtuous. . . .

"My daughter is a most excellent waistcoat hand. I can give you an account of her work, and then, of course, you can form an idea of what everybody else gets. The lowest price waistcoat is 3s. per dozen, and the highest 9s. They are satin ones. She can make one satin one per day, and three of the 3s. ones. She earns, upon an average, about 4s. per week; deduct from this, trimmings about 6d. for the lowest, and 1s. per week for the highest price. As we both sit to work together, one candle does for the two of us, so that she earns about 3s. per week clear, which is not sufficient to keep her even in food. My husband is a seafaring man, or I don't know what I should do. He is a particularly steady man, a teetotaller, and so indeed are the whole family, or else we could not live. Recently my daughter has resigned the work and gone to service, as the prices are not sufficient for food and clothing. I never knew a rise, but continual reductions. I know a woman who has six children, and she has to support them wholly on slop work. Her husband drinks, and does a day's work only now and then, spending more than he brings home. None of her children are able to work. I don't know how on earth she lives, or her little ones either. Poor creature, she looked the picture of distress and poverty when I last saw her."

## Statement of a lady shirt worker

This woman I had seen away from her home, so I requested my friend to lead me to the dwelling of one of the shirt workers, one that he knew to be a hard-working, sober person, so that I might judge of the condition of the class.

The woman lived over a coal and potato shed, occupying a small close room on the "second floor back". It did not require a second glance either at the room or the occupant to tell that the poor creature was steeped in poverty to the very lips. In one corner of the apartment was rolled up the bed on the floor. Beside the window was an oyster tub set upon a chair. At this she was busy washing, while on the table a small brown pan was filled with the newly washed clothes; beside it were the remains of the dinner, a piece of dry coarse bread, and half a cup of coffee.

In answer to my inquiries, she made the following statement: "I make the 'rowers', that is the rowing shirts. I'm only in the shirt line. Do nothing else. The rowers is my own work. These (she said, taking a cloth off a bundle of checked shirts on a side table) is 2d. a piece. I have had some at 2½d., and even 3d., but them has full linen fronts and linen wristbands. These are full-fronted shirts—the collars, wristbands, and shoulder-straps are all stitched, and there are seven buttonholes in each shirt. It takes full five hours to do one. I have to find my own cotton and thread. I gets two skeins of cotton for 1d., because I am obliged to have it fine for them; and two skeins will make about three to four shirts. Two skeins won't quite make three-and-a-half, so that it don't leave above seven farthings for making each of the shirts. If I was to begin very early here, about six in the morning, and work till nine at night, I can't make above three in the day at them hours. I often work in the summer time from four in the morning to nine or ten at night—as long as

I can see. My usual time of work is from five in the morning till nine at night—winter and summer; that is about the average time throughout the year. But when there's a press of business, I work earlier and later. I often gets up at two and three in the morning, and carries on till the evening of the following day, merely lying down in my clothes to take a nap of five or ten minutes. The agitation of mind never lets one lie longer. At the rowers work I don't reckon I makes 5s. a week at the best of times, even working at the early and late hours; and working at the other hours I won't make above 3s. 6d. Average all the year round I can't make more than 4s. a week, and then there's cotton and candles to buy out of that. Why, the candles will cost about 10d. or 1s. a week in the depth of winter, and the cotton about 3d. or 4d. a week, so that I clears about 2s. 6d. a week—yes I reckon that's about it! I know it's so little I can't get a rag to my back. I reckon nobody in the trade can make more than I do—they can't—and there's very few makes so much, I'm sure.

"It's only lately that I found a friend to be security for the rowing shirts, or else before that I only received 1½d. for the same shirts as I now have 2d. for, because I was forced to work for a sweater. These prices are not so good as those usually paid in the trade; some houses pay 3s. a dozen for what I have 2s. for. A few weeks—that is, about six week's ago—the price was 2s. 6d. a dozen; but they always lowers the prices towards winter. Never knew them to raise the prices. I have worked at the business about eight years, and when I first began the 'rowers' were at 3s. 6d. a dozen—the very same article that I am now making for 2s. They in general keep the sweaters employed in winter—some call them the 'double hands', and they turn off the single hands first, because it's the least trouble to them. The sweaters, you see, take out a great quantity of work at a time. The sweaters, many of them, give security to £20. I've known some of them take out as much as a chaise-cart full of various sorts of work, according to the hands they've got employed. One that I know keeps a horse and cart, and does nothing himself—that he don't. I suppose he's got near upon a hundred hands, and gives about £50 security. He was a pot-boy at a public-house, and married a shirt maker. The foremen at the large shops generally marry a shirt maker, or some one in the line of business, and then take a quantity of work home to their wives, who give it out to poor people. They take one-fourth part out of the price, let it be what it will."

She produced an account-book, of which the following is a copy:

| 1849. | | | s. | d. |
|---|---|---|---|---|
| July | 2. | Nine at 2d. | 1 | 6 |
| July | 4. | Nine at 2d. | 1 | 6 |
| July | 7. | Three at 2d. | | 6 |
| July | 10. | Nine at 2d. | 1 | 6 |
| July | 12. | Seven at 2½d. | 1 | 5½ |
| July | 17. | Nine at 2½d. | 1 | 10½ |
| July | 19. | Nine at 2½d. | 1 | 10½ |
| July | 21. | Six at 2d. | 1 | |
| July | 24. | Twelve at 2¼d. | 2 | 3 |
| July | 26. | Six at 2¼d. | 1 | 1½ |
| July | 27. | Six at 2½d. | 1 | 3 |
| July | 28. | Six at 2½d. | 1 | 3 |
| July | 31. | Six at 2½d. | 1 | 3 |
| Aug. | 2. | Three at 3d. | | |
| | | (bespoke) | | 9 |
| Aug. | 2. | Nine at 2½d. | 1 | 10½ |
| Aug. | 6. | Nine at 2½d. | 1 | 10½ |
| Aug. | 11. | Six at 2½d. | 1 | 3 |
| Aug. | 14. | Twelve at 2½d. | 2 | 6 |
| Aug. | 16. | Four at 2d. | | 8 |
| Aug. | 17. | Six at 2½d. | 1 | 3 |
| Aug. | 21. | Eight at 2½d. | 1 | 8 |
| Aug. | 23. | Eight at 2d. | 1 | 4 |
| Aug. | 25. | Eighteen at 2d. | 3 | 0 |
| Aug. | 31. | Seventeen at 2d. | 2 | 10 |
| Sept. | 11. | Nine at 2d. | 1 | 6 |
| Sept. | 13. | Nine at 2d. | 1 | 6 |
| Sept. | 17. | Twelve at 2d. | 2 | |
| Sept. | 25. | Eight at 2¾d. | 1 | 10 |
| Sept. | 27. | Eight at 2½d. | 1 | 8 |
| Sept. | 29. | Twelve at 2d. | 2 | |
| Oct. | 6. | Twelve at 2d. | 2 | |

To be in by 12 Tuesday, or not to be paid for:

| | | | | |
|---|---|---|---|---|
| Oct. | 9. | Nine at 2d. | 1 | 6 |
| Oct. | 16. | Twelve at 2d. | 2 | |
| Oct. | 29. | Nine at 2d. | 1 | 6 |

£2 12 4

Hence it will be seen that the average earnings were 2s. 10¼d. per week, from which are to be deducted cotton and candle, costing say, 10¼d. a week, and so leaving 2s. per week clear for 17 weeks. These prices are all "first-handed.'. . .

*Visit to a destitute waistcoat maker*

The next party I visited was one who worked at waistcoats, and here I found the keenest misery of all. The house was unlike any that I had seen in the same trade; all was scrupulously clean and neat. The old brass fender was as bright as gold, and worn with continued rubbing. The grate, in which there was barely a handful of coals, had been newly black-leaded, and there was not a cinder littering the hearth. Indeed, everything in the place evinced the greatest order and cleanliness. Nor was the suffering self-evident. On the contrary, a stranger, at first sight, would have believed the occupant to have been rather well-to-do in the world. A few minutes' conversation with the poor creature, however, soon told you that the neatness was partly the effect of habits acquired in domestic service, and partly the result of a struggle to hide her extreme poverty from the world. Her story was the most pathetic of all I had yet heard :

"I work for a slop-house—waistcoat work." She said—"I don't make sleeve waistcoats, but body waistcoats, and the lowest price I get is 4d.; I have had 'em as high as 1s. 3d. I take the run, such as they have got to give me—sometimes one thing and sometimes another in the waistcoat way. Some have better work than others, but my eyesight won't admit of my doing the best work. Some waistcoats are as much as 1s. 9d., some 2s. I have worked twenty-six years at the same warehouse. The general price for the waistcoats I have now is 6d., 8d., and 10d. I can make one a-day sometimes, and sometimes three in two days, just as it happens, for my health is very bad. . . . I must work very close from about nine in the morning to eleven at night, to earn that.

"Prices have come down very much indeed since I first worked for the warehouse—*very much*. The prices when I was first employed there were as much as 1s. 9d. for what I get now 1s. 1d. for. Every week they have reduced something within these last few years. Work's falling very much. The work has not riz, no! never since I worked at it. It's lower'd but it's not riz. The masters seem to say that the work is lowered to them—that they can't afford to pay a better price, or else they would. The parties for whom I work lay it to the large slop-houses. They say it's through them that the work has lowered so. I find it very difficult to get sufficient to nourish me out of my work. I can't have what I ought to have. I think my illness at present is from over-exertion. I want more air than I can get. . . . My greatest earnings are 2s. 6d., and I generally average about 3s. Many weeks, I have been wholly without working—not able to do it. Young people that have got good health and good work might, perhaps earn more than I do; but at the common work I should think they can't make more than I can.

"I never was married. I went out to service when I was younger, and to waistcoating after quitting service; so that I might be at home with mother and father, and take care of them in their old age. I rent the house. It's where I buried mother and father from;

and as such I have kept it on since they've been dead. I let the two rooms, but I don't gain anything by it. I stand at about tenpence a week rent when I live in the top room and let the others; but sometimes it's empty, and I lose by it. Some time ago, too, a party ran away, and left £3 10s., in my debt. That nearly ruined me. I've not got the better of it yet.

"I've been very short—very short indeed, sir; in want of common necessaries to keep my strength and life together. I don't find what I get by my labour sufficient to keep me. I've no money anywhere, not a farthing in the house; yes, I tell a story, I've got a penny. If I were to be taken ill I don't know what I should do. But I should be obliged to do as I've often done before. The Almighty is my only support. For my old age there is nothing but the workhouse. . . . I've sold several things to make up, when I've come short. The things here belonged to father and mother. I've sold a great many that they left me. Many people who follow the same business I think are worse off, if anything, than I am; because I've got a home, and I strive to keep it together, and they've not."[3]

### Return to the slop warehouse

On my way home from these saddening scenes, I called at the wholesale slop warehouse, for the promised statement as to the prices paid by the generality of the trade. After waiting a considerable time, at length one of the principals and foremen came to communicate to me the desired information.

The usual sum earned by a person working at the slop trade is, they told me, *three pence per hour!*

Women working at moleskin trowsers, they said, would earn, upon an average, 1s. 10d. every day of ten hours' labour.

At waistcoats females would earn generally at the rate of 2s. per day of ten hours' labour.

The foreman and the principal then wished to know in what state I had found the workpeople generally. I told them I had never seen or heard of such destitution. "Destitution!" was the exclamation. "God bless my soul, you surprise me." "And I think it but right, gentlemen," I added, "to apprise you that your statement as to prices differs most materially from that of the workpeople;" and so saying, I took my departure.

[3] An interview with a lady-like and even more destitute waistcoat maker has been cut.

## LETTER VII—9 NOVEMBER 1849

*Condition of the workers in contract clothing*

From the slop-workers of the eastern parts of London I now come to consider the condition of the male and female operatives employed in making the clothes of the army, navy, police, railway, customs, and post-office servants, convicts, and such other articles of wearing apparel as are made either by contract or in large quantities. Small as are the earnings of those who depend for their living upon the manufacture of the ready-made clothes for the wholesale warehouses of the Minories and the adjoining places, still the incomings of those who manufacture the clothes of our soldiers and sailors, Government, railway-police, and custom-house officers, are even less calculated to support life. I thought the force of misery could no further go than with the waistcoat and shirt hands that I had visited last week. And yet, since then, I have seen people so overwhelmed in suffering, and so used to privations of the keenest kind, that they had almost forgotten to complain of them. The cause of these things, as I said before, I do not pretend to deal with. I have taken the matter up merely with the view of laying before the public a true and un-biased statement of the incomings and condition of the workpeople of the metropolis; and I can assure the reader I am at no little pains in order to arrive at a fair average estimate of the state of those persons to whom I direct my attention. I seek for no extreme cases. If anything is to come of this hereafter, I am well aware that the end can be gained only by laying bare the sufferings of the *class*, and not of any particular individuals belonging thereto. Moreover, I wish it to be known, that in the course of my investigations I make a point of placing myself under the guidance of those gentlemen who have long known the character of the workpeople whom I visit, so that I may be led to those who are suffering from insufficient remuneration for their labour rather than from an improvident expenditure of their gains. Further still, whenever an extraordinary case presents itself to me, I generally make a point of inquiring in the immediate neighbourhood as to the character of the individual, so that I may trust to no *one* man's opinion for what I assert.

*The contract system and competitive bidding*

With this preamble, let me now set forth as briefly as possible the manner in which the clothing for the army is regulated. I deal with the army in particular, because it may be taken as a fair type of all the other classes of Government or contract work that appear to be considerably underpaid. For this purpose, I cannot do better than avail myself of the Government Report from the Select Committee on Army and Navy Appointments [1833] : . . .

"Sir R. Donkin, in his examination, made the following observations :

"We have 105 battalions of infantry; the clothing of these costs 255,000*l* a-year by the army estimates, of which 63,000*l* a-year go to the colonels as their emoluments; that is to say, the public pay these 105 colonels 63,000*l* a-year more than the clothing costs, for purposes which are perfectly understood and admitted; that is, to increase the colonel's income; it amounts to 600*l* a-year each, that is the 63,000*l* gives 600*l* a-year for each of the 105 colonels; I am taking the greatest amount."

It appears, then, that the army clothing in the year above alluded to cost, for 105 battalions of infantry, £255,000. The supply of this was intrusted to 105 colonels, and they paid £192,000 for the goods, taking to themselves £63,000 profit out of the transaction. The evidence of Mr. Pearse, one of the army clothiers, before the same committee, was as follows :

"In what manner are your contracts made with the colonels of the regiments you clothe?—In point of fact we make no contract with them, it being well known that amongst the variety of clothiers there prevails a competition amongst them to provide clothing as cheap as it is possible to be effectually done; this competition brings the prices to a point at which all the respectable clothiers from time to time make their charges to the colonels. I request to observe, that if the competition was not so very severe, and no competition prevailed, a higher price would be assuredly charged than at present, as, in point of fact, the price which the clothiers charge is not adequate as compared to the profits of other branches of business, but there is no risk or adventure in it; therefore I am the more satisfied that the profit may not exceed the ordinary interest of money, 5 per cent, or from 5 to 8 per cent for commercial profit; it is to be observed, that this is a transaction which returns capital only in about sixteen months, as shown by statements delivered."

Of the evils of this competitive system, the following extract from the same gentleman's evidence may be taken as an apt illustration. Its influence upon the workpeople will be afterwards exposed :

"When the contract was opened, Mr. Maberly took it at the same price in December, 1808; this statement shows the effect of wild competition. In February following, Esdailes' house, who were accoutrement makers, and not clothiers, got knowledge of what was Mr. Maberley's price, and they tendered at 12s. 6½d. a month afterwards; it was evidently then a struggle for the price, and how the

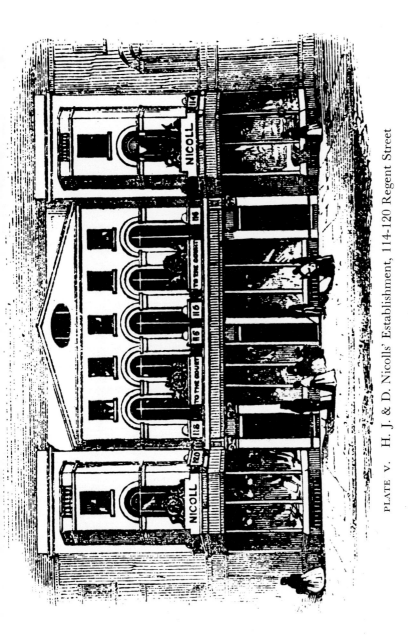

PLATE V.   H. J. & D. Nicolls' Establishment, 114-120 Regent Street

quality the least good (if we may use such a term) could pass. Mr. Maberly did not like to be outbidden by Esdailes; Esdailes stopped subsequently and Mr. Maberly bid 12s. 6d. three months after, and Mr. Dixon bid again, and got the contract for 11s. 3d. in October, and in December of that year another public tender took place, and Messrs. A. and D. Cook took it at 11s. 5½d., and they subsequently broke. It went on in this sort of way of changing hands every two or every three months, by bidding against each other. Presently, though it was calculated that the great coat was to wear four years, it was found that those great coats were so inferior in quality, that they wore only two years, and representations were accordingly made to the Commander-in-Chief, when it was found necessary that great care should be taken to go back to the original good quality that had been established by the Duke of York, by which the colonels of regiments were governed, and which, when supplied by the colonels' clothiers, was very strictly attended to."

This leads me to the army clothiers themselves. Of the profits of these gentlemen, I am in no way disposed to complain. Indeed, as a body of men, they appear to have no very exorbitant gains. . . .

*Prices that are and ought to be paid*

I will now proceed to set forth the prices paid for the different articles of Army, Navy, Marine, Police, and Convict clothing, distinguishing between those that *are* paid, and those that *ought to be* paid to afford workmen even a bare subsistence. These have been furnished to me by an old-established firm, and the statement of the gentleman supplying them to me is this—"The work is to be considered as even with the best workmen and workwomen uncertain. I have not found one that has not been at times without work. Therefore, if they are paid barely sufficient to keep body and soul together when labouring hard, think of their situation when they are without work. Many are obliged to work on the Sabbath, and many have told me," adds my informant, "that they are in the constant habit of rising at four or five in the morning and working till ten, eleven, or twelve at night." (The prices appear on pp. 130–2.)

I shall now in due order proceed to set before the public the "plain unvarnished tales" of the operatives themselves. The slight discrepancies in price that the intelligent reader may discover, he will easily understand to arise from the fact of the different workpeople working for different houses, and of the sums paid by the clothiers being so various, that the gentleman alluded to above (Mr. Shaw) pays as much as 5d. more on the coat than any of the other clothiers.

E

*Statement of prices as they are and as they should be at the lowest living prices:*

|  | Price now paid | Lowest price that should be paid |
|---|---|---|
| **NAVY** | | |
| Navy jackets take 18 hours to make. Fine blue cloth jackets, paid for each .................................... If made from a shop, 10s. would be paid. A man making one of these jackets had a large family, or he said he would rather walk the streets until he dropped, before he would take the work at such a price. | 2s. 6d. to 2s. 8d. | 5s. and 6s. |
| **ROYAL MARINE CLOTHING** | | |
| Private's coat and epaulettes take 13 or 15 hours to make each. Under former contractors, 1s. 1d., 1s. 2d., 1s. 4d. Now about ...................... | 1s. 9d. | 3s. to 3s. 6d. |
| Private's trowsers, 4 to 5 hours, were paid, 2½d. and 3d. Now .............. | 4d. and 4½d. | 8d. and 9d. |
| Waistcoat ................................. | 4d. and 4½d. | 10d. |
| Great coats ............................. | 3½d. and 4d. | 1s. and 1s. 2d. |
| The work-people find thread out of these prices, and have to work very long to get any food. | | |
| Duck trowsers paid .................... | 2½d. | |
| Shirts ....................................... | 3¼d. | |
| **ARMY** | | |
| Great coat for the army and artillery, contracted for, first for the materials, and then for making up, under 1s. each, including cutting, &c., take 7 hours to make one coat; some women can only make one in the day, say three in two days paid at 5d. each; per week, 3s. 9d. It will cost for thread, 9d. For lodging, fire, candles, living and clothes leaves, 3s. .............................. | | 1s. 6d. and 2s. |
| **SECOND AND THIRD REGIMENT GUARDS** | | |
| Private's coat (without looping) takes 15 to 16 hours making ............... | 2s. 2d. to 2s. | 3s. 4d. to 3s. |
| Private's trowsers take 6 hours ......... | 8d. to 6½d. | 10d. |
| White jacket, 5¼ to 6 hours making... | 6½d. to 6d. | 10d. |

|  | Price now paid | Lowest price that should be paid |
|---|---|---|

### INFANTRY PRIVATES' CLOTHING

| | | |
|---|---|---|
| Coats 10 to 12 hours making without the pocket .............................. | 1s. 2d. | 1s. 9d. to 2s. |
| Pair of trowsers, 4½ to 5 hours' work .. | 7d. to 6d. | 9d. |
| East India jacket ........................ | 9d. to 11d. | 1s. 4d. |

### RIFLE BRIGADE

| | | |
|---|---|---|
| Coat ...................................... | 1s. 9d. | 2s. 6d. |
| Trowsers ................................. | 6½d. | 9d. |

### ARMY NECESSARIES

| | | |
|---|---|---|
| Cotton shirts take about seven hours each to make .......................... | 4½d. | 10d. to 1s. |
| Summer trowsers ....................... | 7d. | 10d. |
| Undress jacket .......................... | 10d. | 1s. 4d. |

### ROYAL ARTILLERY

| | | |
|---|---|---|
| Private's coat, 18 to 20 hours' work, nearly two days' work, at each ...... | 1s. 7d. and 1s. 8d. | 3s. 6d. to 4s. |
| Private's trowsers, with scarlet stripes, take 7 hours, per pair .............. | 6½d. | 1s. 2d. to 1s. 4d. |

The poor people who work at this clothing are compelled to work almost all night to get food, and very frequently on the Sabbath— the day of rest!

### MILITARY PENSIONERS

| | | |
|---|---|---|
| Blue cloth coat, takes 1½ to 2 days to make, at each .......................... | 2s. 2d. | 4s. 6d. to 5s. |

### CLOTHING FOR CONVICTS

| | | |
|---|---|---|
| Jacket, double stitched, takes 5 hours to make each garment; thread, ½d. | 3d. | 9d. to 1s. |
| Trowsers, ditto, 4 hours .............. | 3d. | 9d. to 1s. |
| Waistcoat, ditto, 2 hours .............. | 1¼d. | 4d. to 6d. |
| Partly coloured overalls, two pairs in 10 or 11 hours ....................... | 5d. | 9d. to 1s. |

Some of the people work from 5 o'clock in the morning until 10 at night.

### CONVICTS' SHOES

| | | |
|---|---|---|
| Mr. Gotch, one of the most respectable manufactures, gave for making, per pair ...................................... | | 1s. 6d. |
| Was given under the contract ........ | 1s. 2d. | |

|  | Price now paid | Lowest price that should be paid |
|---|---|---|
| CONVICTS' SHIRTS | | |
| Mr. Pigott, contractor, gave for the making 2s. 3d. per dozen or 1½d. to 2d. each, to workwomen ......... | 1½d. to 2d. | |
| POLICE | | |
| Blue coat, price paid for making, when first supplied by Messrs. Hebbert & Co., 4s. 6d. Reduced by them 6d. at a time, to 3s. Messrs. Dolans in 1844 gave 3s. Messrs. Gilpin & Co. .. The coat takes 15 to 17 hours to make. Some can only make one in two days. I am informed that the prices calculated to be paid when it was first provided was 7s. | 2s. 10d. | 5s. to 6s. |
| Great coat paid for and reduced in the same manner ...................... | 2s. 10d. | 5s. to 6s. |
| Dress trowsers, 9 or 10 hours, 1s. 6d. Reduced to .......................... | 1s. 2d. | 2s. 6d. to 3s. |
| Undress trowsers, 8 or 9 hours, 1s. 2d. | 10d. | 2s. to 2s. 6d. |
| Making the leather top and sides of the hat used to be paid 5d. Now... | 2¼d. | |
| Boots. Mr. Gotch, one of the best manufacturers, calculated 3½d. per pair more for the workmen than is paid now. | | |

Again, I wish the reader to understand that the following are the ordinary cases of the trade; they have, most assuredly, *not* been selected for the purpose.

### *Testimony of a man making soldiers' trowsers*

The first person whom I visited was a male hand, and on entering his house I certainly found more comforts about it than I had been led to expect. He lived in a back room built over a yard. It was nicely carpetted, and on one side, to my astonishment, stood a grand piano. There were several pictures hanging against the walls, and a glass full of dahlias on the mantelpiece. I could tell, however, by the "wells" beneath the two large sofas that they were occasionally used as bedsteads, and the easy-chair in which I was requested to take a seat was of so extravagant a size that it was evident it was occasionally put to the same purpose. I had been given to understand that the man was in the habit of taking lodgers, and this in a measure accounted for the double duty assigned to the different articles of furniture in the room.

"I make the soldiers' trowsers, the Foot Guards principally," said the man in answer to my questions, "gets 6d. a pair, and have to find thread. . . . I can make a pair in five hours, but there isn't one in a hundred can do this, and it will take a middling worker eight hours to finish one pair. But then I put the seams out, and if I did them at home it would take me six hours to do all myself. Without the seams I can do three pair a day. In summer I can do four, working very hard, and not being taken off for anything. I cannot get work always. Now I'm sitting still—have had nothing to do this five weeks of any consequence.

"At the best of times, when work is very brisk, and in the summer time too, I never earn more than 8s. a week. This is the money I have for my work, and from this there is to be deducted thread for the sixteen pair, and cotton for the felling of the same, and this comes to about 16d., and the cost of fire may, with the wood and altogether, be taken at 1s. Over and above all this, I have to pay 1d. per pair for the stitching of the seams, and 9d. a week for a woman to fetch and take my work to and from the warehouse. So that altogether there is 4s. 5d. to be deducted from the 8s., and so leaving only 3s. 9d. as my earnings per week at the very best of times. For weeks and weeks I don't get anything. The work isn't to be had. The year before last I was standing still full twenty weeks— couldn't get work at all at no warehouse. Last year I had full eight weeks and nothing to do all the time; and this year I have been unemployed a full month at least. During the last five weeks I have only had fifteen pair to make. It is now sealing time—that is the period when the different estimates are given in—and we are always slack then. I never keep any account of my earnings. All I know is, when the money comes in it's as much as I can do to pay my way. Taking one week with another, I'm sure I do not average, throughout the year, more than 5s. a week at the very outside; and out of this there is a full half to be paid for expenses.

"I get them from a person who gets them from the warehouse. These intermediate persons are called piece-masters, and they get a penny profit upon each garment, whether it be trowsers, coats, or great coats, and the prices I have stated are those the piece-master pays to me. They won't give them to such little hands as me. They give out a great quantity at a time, and must have them all in at a particular day—very often the next taking-in day. I fancy at one time they used to keep a stock by them; but of late years there have been so many alterations that they're afraid to do it. The piece-masters have to give security—£50 I think it is—very often; and the single hands, before they can be taken on, must be recommended to the piece-master. . . . I have got my security down at the warehouse, but it takes so much time taking and fetching, and waiting while examined, that I prefer to work for a piece-master rather than the warehousemen. If they're not properly done, the foreman will cut the seam right up, and send them back, and there'll be no money till they're finished. The foremen, generally have no feeling about the poor—that's true. I'm sure they haven't. If the workpeople can treat them with what they like, and that's liquor, they'll pass the things quicker.

"The low prices I believe to arise from the very low prices the contracts are taken at. Well, sir, look here, the soldiers, I hear, give 8s. a pair for what we get 6d. for the making of. The cloth cannot cost them more than half-a-crown. If I was to get it, I could have it for that; but they must get it considerably less from taking large quantities, which their money empowers them to do. The trimmings, including buttons and pockets, would cost about 6d., and the red stripes 3d. more, so that 6d. making, 9d. trimming and stripes, and cloth 2s. 6d., altogether 3s. 9d., and the other 4s. 3d. is profit. The piece-master, out of this, gets 2d. a pair; this is their gains for taking them in and running the risk of the people stealing the materials. The remaining 4s. 1d. is the profit of the warehouseman and the other parties connected with the trade, so that I'm sure if Government would take it into their hands, and give the clothes out themselves, the poor workpeople might have prices that would keep them from starving. . . .

"We had better go to bed and starve at once, and that's what most all are doing who are at this kind of work. The general class of people who work at it are old persons who have seen better days, and have nothing left but their needle to keep them and who *won't* apply for relief—their pride won't let them—their feelings objects to it—they have a dread of becoming troublesome. The other parties are wives of labourers and those who leave off shirt making to come to this. There are many widows with young children, and they give them the seams to do, and so manage to prolong life, because they're afeard to die, and too honest to steal. The pressing part, which is half the work, is not fit for any female to do. I don't know but very few young girls—they're most of them women with families as I've seen—poor, struggling widows a many of 'em."

If, as you say, your clear earnings throughout the year, taking one week with another, are only 2s. 6d. a week, how do you manage to support life upon that sum?—"I couldn't do it—oh, dear no; I couldn't have held till now, nor even one month upon it. But the fact is, I let a part of my place to young men at 2s. a week, and for that I find them bed, candles, soap, towels, sheets, and the use of the sitting-room and the fire, and that's my dependence. But one thing I must tell you, I can't go on with that much longer unless things alter, because I can't get my sheets out of pledge to change them, and my feather-bed I've been obliged to pawn.

"I'll tell you, sir, I was a draper's assistant formerly; lived in the first situations in London, Bath, and other places; but, of course, their salaries are small, and one is obliged to dress well on it. Well, I got a situation in the country, so that I might save something, which I could not do in town. I remained in my country situation nearly two years, and saved close upon £50 in that time. This I allowed to remain in my master's hands, thinking it would be safe, so that I might not spend it. He broke, and I lost my whole. There was not money enough to pay the law expenses, or of course I should have had my money first as a servant.

"Then I came back to London, I tried to get a situation, and found, as I was getting advanced in years, they preferred young men. Well, I couldn't starve, but I knew nothing that I could get a living at but as a draper's assistant, and that I couldn't get on account of my age. I can't tell you the distress of mind I was in of course, for I was very anxious lest in my old age I should be left to want. We don't think of old age when we're young, I'm sorry to say. Where I was lodging then, a woman made soldiers' trowsers, and as my hands were lissome, and I had occasion to use the needle frequently in the drapery trade, to tack the tickets on cloth and such like, why I thought I might get a crust by them. It was only living, that I tried for, unless I'd tailor. I couldn't have done this, if it hadn't been from being accustomed to the needle. Well, I tried; and the man I did a few for was very pleased with 'em, and gave me some more. They was 3½d. a pair convicts' trowsers. I soon found that, at that price, I couldn't stop in the lodgings I had and pay my way. I was paying 2s. 6d. a week. So I takes a cellar at 1s. 6d., buys a little bit of canvass, and some straw; sleeps on the floor, had a chair and table—that was all. Then the man I had done the trowsers for took me to the City, and got me some better work. He said I could do finer things. Then the warehouse gave me as many as fifty pair of artillery trowsers to make.

"Then I found I was living too far from my work; so I sells off my things for 4s. 6d., comes to Holborn; there was two rooms to let at 3s. 6d., and I thought I could take a lodger at 2s.; a relation of mine promised kindly to lend me the beds, which they did, and I've paid for 'em little by little, since then. After this I scraped together somehow or other—how I did it I don't know, but it come from God's goodness, I suppose—I got enough to buy another bed, and take another lodger at the same price. The only thing that we can make a little money of is beds; but at that you lose a good deal, as well as get. And so I went, and I am where I am now. I've four lodgers at present, but two of those I get nothing from, as they're out of situations, and they owe me a goodish sum now; but may be I shall have it all, or a good part, when they gets into work again. My two other lodgers pay me very well indeed; they bring me in my 4s. a week and that pays my rent; and thank God I only owe one week. But if the work don't come in, I don't know what I shall do.

"A little while ago I had two brothers with me, ill during the time of the cholera. I tried all I could to get them into the hospitals, but they was ill three weeks before I could. During that time I had to provide them with everything. One was obliged to have two clean shirts a day, and I was forced to pledge my feather-bed, and sheets, and blankets, to keep them. I couldn't see them lost, and let them starve under my own roof. I got them at last out of the hospital, and they've gone into the country, and I've never even heard of them. They owe me altogether, for washing, living, lodging, and food, £2 13s. 9d. I think they're honest young men and would pay me if they could. Maybe they're ashamed to write to me—yes, I dare say they are, for they were good young men—though I never had their money, I'll say that of them. They was gentlemen's servants, and can't do much now. All this I shouldn't mind so much about if it wasn't for my bedding. I could get round if it wasn't for that. If I can't get my bedding back I must lose my lodgers. Their sheets has been on now nearly three months, and I'm sure they can't stand it much longer, and they won't. To my own bed I've none at all. As for myself, I ain't had a clean shirt for this month. I really can't afford to pay for the washing. I've never been able to get any new clothes since I've been at the trade. Fourpence I gave for the very coat I've got on from a gentleman's servant, and the other things has been gave to me by asking, which is very painful.

"The greater part of the things you see about here don't belong to me. This piano, now, belonged to a young man, a lodger of mine. His father was a musician. The young man bought it for £3 15s. He got married, and wanted a chest of drawers for his wife (oh, good gracious, if he was to hear of this he'd kill me). Well, I passed my word for the drawers, and he left this piano with me as security. That cat you see there now you'll say as I have no business to have, if I'm so poor. She costs me 3½d. a week, as much as half a quartern, and I grudge it, but a poor maiden lady, who's starving, brought her to me, and begged me, with almost tears in her eyes, to take care of it for her, for she couldn't afford to give it a meal—she hadn't one for herself. She's a teacher of music, and I'm sure she's dying for want of food. She's just out of the hospital, and, oh, dear, much too proud to go into the house—I wouldn't even say such a thing to her, it would break her heart. I know she's never had anything but tea—tea, tea, for months. She's a relation of the Pitt family, and the composer of several pieces of sacred music, but the plates are in pawn for 4s., and she can't even do anything with that. She's lost all her teaching, and is now in want of even the commonest food. I think the poor are not in such distress as persons in her circumstances of life. If she's ashamed to apply to the parish, you may depend she's ashamed to let any one else know how badly she's off.

"The only extravagance I have that I know of is my bird, and he costs me a farthing a week. Poor dickey! I shouldn't like to part with him. It's the only company I have. The cat I'm not very fond of. As for meat, I haven't had a taste of it for the last month."

The statement of the man was of so extraordinary a nature, that, on leaving the house, I took the trouble to inquire into his character. His landlord informed me that he was one of the most worthy, benevolent, and eccentric men that he had ever known. He was punctual in the payments of his rent, and, indeed, a most sober, industrious, and exemplary person. The duplicates of the bedding the man himself showed me, and the person who directed me to his house spoke even more highly of him than did his landlord.

## Statement of a piece-mistress

I was now desirous to see a piece-master, in order that I might find out whether they really did make the amount of money that they were believed to do out of the workpeoples' labour, and found the family in the lowest state of destitution. The party lived in a back-kitchen, in a house over Waterloo-bridge. It was mid-day when I got there, and the woman and her boy were dining off potatoes and some "rind" of bacon that her daughter, who was "in place" had given to her rather than it should be thrown away.

"Poor people," said she, "you know is glad to get anything." Then, observing me noticing the crockery, which was arranged on a shelf in one corner, she added :

"Ah, sir, you needn't look at my crockery ware—I'll show it to you," she said, taking down several basins and jugs. They were all broken on one side but turned the best side outwards. "There isn't a whole vessel in the place; only nobody would know but they were sound, you see, to look at 'em. I get some of the army work—some of the common trowsers. I has a penny a pair out of them—that's the only way of living I have, sir. I get a meal of victuals now and then from my landlady. I'm a piece-mistress. I get the work out of warehouse, and give it to the work people. I has a penny a pair out of them. I has twopence out of some—they are the sergeants. Perhaps I'd get 40 pair out in a week, perhaps 30 pair, and may be 10—when they has them I get them. Before my husband died I've had 100 pair out in a week. God bless thee, man, many people has more—they has them out by wholesale, these large hands. I've had none this fortnight, and more—only one ten pair. Some of them takes them away in cart-loads. The piece-makers have such bundles of hands they can get a good lot done. Oh, Lord, we never had £2 a week by it, nor £1 either.

"The pay's very bad, sir. The most my husband ever had one week by it was about £1. He had work out of four warehouses. Those that has plenty of work, and gets the best, will make more by it— a good deal more. Where the piece-master draws £18 to £20 a week they must have a good profit out of that, and some of them draws more; but it's not all their own; they has their workpeople to pay out of that. So that the piece-master might draw £3 to £4 a week at the very best time—that's when the police-clothing is out. They gets more out of that than anything else, there isn't much by these pensioners at all. They get 1d. upon a pair of trowsers, some 2d., but that's for the police trowsers, the dress ones. Upon the police coats they get 2d. some, and some 4d. out of the price, but now I believe its only 2d. out of them. What they gets out of the soldiers' jackets I'm sure I can't say. We never had none of them. Out of the tide-waiters' coats we ought to have 6d.; the warehouse paid 7s. 6d. for them. Out of the trowsers we used to have 2d.; the price the warehouse paid was 1s. The waistcoat price was 10d. from the warehouse; we had nothing out of that. He used to have 8s. 6d. for the suit, and he used to pay 7s. 6d. for it; so he got 1s. out of them. Used to get nothing else. Used to have the pensioners' sometimes. Paid 1s. 9d., and we had 3d. out of them.

"At the time my husband lived we did pretty well. Was never out of work. If we hadn't it from one warehouse we had it from the others we worked for. He has been three years buried next Easter Sunday, and there's many a night since I've went to bed without my supper, myself and my children. Since then I've had nothing, only just a few odd trowsers now and then. I had to go to the workhouse last winter, myself and my children; I couldn't get a meal of victuals for them, and this winter I suppose I shall have to go into it again. If I haven't work I can't pay my rent. Three weeks ago I had only twenty pair to make, and that's 1s. 8d. for myself and boy to live upon (my other's out in the Marine

School), and my rent out of that is 1s. 6d. My boy gets 1s. 6d. a week besides this, and only for that I couldn't live at all. And that's drawed before it's earned. I'm obliged to go on credit for my things and pay with my boy's money, and glad to have it to pay. I call it a good week if I get 40 pair of trowsers to give out. This is 3s. 4d. to me, and upon that me and my boy must both live; and there was my other boy to do the same too when I had him. I occasionally get a bit of broken victuals from those that know me round about. I little thought I should be so miserable as I am. That fender is not mine. I borrowed it off my landlady; nor that saucepan neither; I got it to boil my potatoes in. Indeed you may say I very often want. We should be starved entirely if it was not for my landlady, and that's the blessed truth. I belongs to Lambeth parish, and they don't even give me a ha'p'orth out of it, not even a loaf of bread. It's often we're a day and two nights without food, me and my boys together.

"I never did treat a foreman with rum to get any work, nor did the man ever want it from me, I'll give every one his due. He has come to see himself and his wife, and lent me 2s.—I shall not belie any-one—and often gave me a few pence when I came into the ware-house. It is not generally believed by us that foremen are obliged to be treated in order to get the work. I never heard of such a thing and I'm sure I never did it. The reason why I've had so little lately is because I can't get it so well done as the others. The workpeople won't do as I tell 'em. Some makes them well, and more don't. My husband's security is at the warehouses yet. I can't tell you how much they're for, 'cause I never seed them. He was an honest, up-right man. They often trusted him as much as £100. The work people misses him now, but nobody misses him so much as I do. Then I could go clean and respectable, but now I don't know where to turn my head for a meal of victuals this blessed night. . . ."[4]

*Interview with a woman doing the worst paid convict work*

As I had been informed that the convict work was the worst paid of all labour, I was anxious to obtain an interview with one who got her living by it. She lived in a small back room on the first floor. I knocked at the door, but no one answered, though I had been told the woman was within. I knocked again and again, and, hearing no one stirring, I looked through the keyhole and observed the key was inside the door. Fearing that some accident might have hap-pened to the poor old soul, I knocked once more, louder than ever.

[4] There followed an interview with a 62 year old widow making marine uniforms.

At last the door was opened, and a thin aged woman stood trembling nervously as she looked at me. She stammered out with a gasp, "oh! I beg pardon, but I thought it was the woman come for the shilling I owed her." I told her my errand, and she welcomed me in. There was no table in the room; but on a chair without a back there was an old tin tray, in which stood a cup of hot, milkless tea, and a broken saucer, with some half dozen small potatoes in it. It was the poor soul's dinner. Some tea-leaves had been given her, and she had boiled them up again to make something like a meal. She had not even a morsel of bread. In one corner of the room was a hay mattress, rolled up. With this she slept on the floor. She said,

"I work at convict work, 'the greys'; some are half yellow and half brown, but they're all paid the same price. I makes the whole suit. Gets 7¾d. for all of it—3d. the jacket, 3d. the trowsers, and 1¼d. the waistcoat, and finds my own thread out of that. . . . There's full a day and a half's work in a suit. I works from nine in the morning till eleven at night. (Here a sharp-featured woman entered and said she wished to speak with the "convict worker" when she was alone. "She came," said the poor old thing when the woman had left, "because I owes her a shilling. I'm sure she can't have it, for I haven't got it. I borrowed it last week off her.") "In a day and a half," she continued, with a deep sigh, "deducting the cost of thread and candles for the suit (to say nothing of firing), I earns 3¾d.—not 2d. a day. The other day I had to sell a cup and saucer for a half-penny, 'cause crockeryware's so cheap—there was no handle to it, it's true—in order to get me a candle to work with. . . .

"I can't tell what I average, for sometimes I have work and sometimes I an't. I could earn 3s. a week if I had as much as I could do, but I don't have it very often. I'm very often very idle. I can assure you I've been trotting about today to see after a shilling job and couldn't get it. (The same woman again made her appearance at the door and seeing me still there did not stop to say a word. "What a bother there is," said the convict-clothes-maker, "if a person owes a few halfpence. That's what made me keep the door locked"). I suppose her mother has sent for the old shawl she lent me. I havn't no shawl to my back—no, as true as God I haven't; I haven't indeed! I'm two months idle in the course of the year." She went on again, "Oh yes, more than that; I've been three months at one time, and didn't earn a halfpenny. That was when I lived up at the other house. There was no work at all. We was starving one against the other. I'm generally about a quarter part of my time standing still; yes, that I am, I can assure you. About three shillings a week, I tell you, is what I generally earn at convict work when I'm fully employed; but then there's the expenses to be taken out of that.

"I've worked at the convict work for about fourteen or fifteen years—ever since my husband's been dead. He died fourteen year ago last February. I've nobody else dependent upon me. I hadn't need to have, I'm sure. I hadn't a bit of work all last Friday and all last Saturday—no, not till Monday. I work for a piece-master. I don't know what profit the piece-master gets. The convicts' great coats are 5d., and I can do about three of them in two days, and they will take about 1½ oz. of thread, that's 3d.; so that in two days, at that work, I can earn one shilling clear, saying nothing of candles. That's much better work than the other." (The cat, almost as thin as its mistress, here came scratching for some of the potatoes.)

"Yes, there's people much worse off than me, but they gets relief from the parish. They tell me at the union I am young enough to work, and yet I am turned of 70. I find it very hard—very hard, indeed; oh, that I do, I can assure you. I very often want. I wanted all last Sunday, for I had nothing at all then. I was a-bed till twelve o'clock—lay a-bed 'cause I hadn't nothing to eat. There's more young girls work at the trade now. A great quantity works at it 'cause they can see better than us. They couldn't get the dresses they wears if they was virtuous.

"My husband was a file-cutter; he did pretty fairly. While he was alive, I didn't want for anything, and since his death I've wanted very often; I've wanted so as I haven't had a home to put my head into. Then I slept along with different friends, and they gave me a little bit, but they were nigh as bad off as myself, and couldn't spare much. Trade is very bad now; there are a many of us starving; yes, indeed there is—the old people in particular; the young'uns make it out other ways. I pays 1s. 6d. rent. The things are my own, such as there is. I've no table; I was obliged to sell it; I've sold 'most everything I've got; I can't sell no more, for there's none now that will fetch anything. I only wish I could get a shawl, to keep the cold off me when I takes my work home—that's all."[5]


## LETTER VIII—13 NOVEMBER 1849

The facts that I have to set before the public in my present communication are of so awful and tragic a character that I shall not even attempt to comment upon them. The miseries they reveal are so intense and overwhelming that, as with all deep emotions, they are beyond words.

[5] Finally, Mayhew interviewed the widow of a shoemaker, evicted for non-payment of rent, and her neighbour who was housing her, a woman with four children abandoned by her engineer husband.

*Colonels' profits*

Let me, however, before proceeding to the more immediate subject of this letter, state as concisely as possible the sums allowed to the colonels of the different regiments for the clothing of the army, together with the sums paid by them for the same. I am anxious, from the unpleasant aspect of the transaction, to do this in as matter-of-fact a manner as I can. The information here given, be it observed, is all derived from the Government Report upon the appointments of the army and navy.

First, of the sums allowed to the colonels. The clothing allowances, says the Report are fixed annual rates borne on the establishment of the regiment, as thus detailed :

|  | *Cavalry* | | | *Infantry* | | |
|---|---|---|---|---|---|---|
|  | £ | s. | d. | £ | s. | d. |
| Sergeant | 5 | 19 | 0 | 7 | 9 | 2 |
| Corporal | 6 | 10 | 3 | 4 | 19 | 6 |
| Private | 4 | 0 | 3 | 2 | 6 | 0 |
| Drummer or Trumpeter | 6 | 10 | 3 | 4 | 19 | 6 |

These rates are fixed by warrants of 22nd and 30th July, 1830

I shall now append to the above the following statement as to the sums paid to, and profits taken by, the colonels, for the clothing of the men in their respective regiments :

ESTIMATE OF THE ANNUAL COST OF CLOTHING, CAPS, AND ACCOUTREMENTS FOR A REGIMENT OF INFANTRY, FOR 1832; VIZ., CLOTHING DELIVERED TO THE SOLDIER 1ST JANUARY, 1832, TO BE WORN TILL 1ST JANUARY, 1833.

|  | *Sergeants* | | | *Corporals* | | | *Drummers* | | | *Privates* | | |
|---|---|---|---|---|---|---|---|---|---|---|---|---|
|  | £ | s. | d. | £ | s. | d. | £ | s. | d. | £ | s. | d. |
| Off-reckonings *(or sums allowed to the colonels for clothing, caps, and accoutrements per man)* | 7 | 9 | 2 | 4 | 19 | 6 | 4 | 19 | 6 | 2 | 6 | 0 |
| Annual cost *(or sums paid by the colonels for clothing, caps, and accoutrements per man)* | 3 | 4 | 9 | 1 | 17 | 4 | 2 | 14 | 4 | 1 | 16 | 10 |
| *Profit per man to colonel* | 4 | 4 | 5 | 3 | 2 | 2 | 2 | 5 | 2 | 0 | 9 | 2 |
| At £4 4s. 5d. for 43 sergeants |  |  |  |  |  |  |  |  |  | 181 | 9 | 11 |
| At £3 2s. 2d. for 36 corporals |  |  |  |  |  |  |  |  |  | 111 | 18 | 0 |

|  | Sergeants | Corporals | Drummers | Privates |
|---|---|---|---|---|
|  | £ s. d. | £ s. d. | £ s. d. | £ s. d. |
|  |  |  |  | Prices paid to maker |
| At £2 5s. 2d. for 14 drummers |  |  |  | 31 12 4 |
| At £0 9s. 2d. for 713 privates |  |  |  | 326 15 10 |
|  |  |  |  | 651 16 1 |
| Deduct, extra for Staff and Band |  |  |  | 37 0 0 |
| Total annual Profit to the Colonel |  |  |  | £614 16 1 |

Here, then, we perceive that £614 16s. 1d. is the annual profit or "emolument" derived by each colonel of infantry. There are 105 infantry colonels, making in all upwards of £64,000, or 25 per cent, out of the £255,000 allowed for the clothing of the infantry.

After this the following answers of Sir R. Donkin, when before the Government committee, will be perfectly intelligible :

"Do you think the colonels of regiments would, in consideration of being exonerated from their present risk and responsibility with respect to the clothing, be content to receive 400l a year as a compensation for their profit upon it?—I think certainly not.

"Would they accept of 500l a year?—No, nor 600l; whether viewed in a pecuniary way, or as connected with that feeling which we all have towards our corps.". . .

### List of Prices

It now only remains for me to add a list of the prices paid to the workpeople for making up such articles of clothing for the army as were omitted in my last letter. . . . To the following statement of the prices paid for making up the army clothing, I have added those given for the making of the uniforms of the police . . . for though the wages given for them are not quite so iniquitous as those paid for the army, still they are so much below subsistence point that they may be fairly brought under the same head.

*List of prices paid to the workpeople by the Army clothiers and Contractors, etc.*

|  | Prices paid to maker |
|---|---|
| **ARMY** |  |
| Calico shirts take 7 or 8 hours each (some take a day). can make two in a day of from 16 to 18 hours long. |  |
| Price for each ..................................................... | 4½d. |
| For 18 hours' work the maker gets 9d., and six days at |  |

9d., gives 4s. 6d. for weekly earnings; out of this she pays 1s. 6d. per week for a room, for candles 1d. per night, or 6d. per week; for coal 1d. per day, or 6d. per week; and for thread for shirts, 4d. per week, in all 2s. 10d.; so that she earns 1s. 8d. clear per week, and that after working from 16 to 18 hours each day.

| | |
|---|---:|
| Party-coloured overalls ................................................ | 5d. |

Say 10 or 11 hours to make 2 pair.

| | |
|---|---:|
| Blue cloth cape ....................................................... | 2s. 3d. |

Takes a man from 13 to 14 hours to make.
Man with assistance of wife can make one in 11½ hours.

| | |
|---|---:|
| Soldiers' summer trowsers ........................................... | 6d. |

Must work from four in the morning to ten at night to make two pair; in 18 hours these will yield 1s. Deduct, thread 1½d. and candle 1d., and we have 9½d. for the day's work of 18 hours' long.

| | |
|---|---:|
| Haversacks, coarse duck, from ..................................... | 1¼d. to 1½d. |

Those at 1½d. have more work in them than the others.
A woman can make 4 a day of the first and 9 a day of the latter, if she works from 15 to 16 hours each day.

| | |
|---|---:|
| Great coats (each) .................................................... | 5d. |
| Ditto for Artillery with strap behind .......................... | 5½d. |
| Ditto for Marines .................................................... | 5d. |

## 17TH LANCERS

| | |
|---|---:|
| Cloak ................................................................... | 2s. 0d. |

Cannot be made under 13 hours; the cloak used to be 2s. 6d., and not so well made formerly

## GUARDS

| | |
|---|---:|
| Private's coat ......................................................... | 2s. 2d. |

Takes 15 or 16 hours to make.

| | |
|---|---:|
| Private's trowsers ................................................... | 8d. |

Takes 6 hours to make.

| | |
|---|---:|
| 2nd Guards ............................................................ | 7½d. |
| 3rd Ditto ............................................................... | 6½d. |
| White jacket, kersey 2d Regiment ............................... | 6d. |
| Ditto Ditto　　　　　3d Ditto, with pocket ..................... | 6½d. |

Can earn at these from 5s. to 6s. per week.

## EAST INDIA SERVICE

| | |
|---|---:|
| Jackets ................................................................. | 9d. |

## POLICE

| | |
|---|---:|
| Great coat ............................................................. | 3s. 0d. |

Takes two days and a half in winter, working 8 hours per day.

## PROVINCIAL POLICE

| | |
|---|---:|
| Coat .................................................................... | 3s. 6d. |

Takes two days to make, hard work.

Prices paid
to maker

PENSIONERS (For *Board of Ordnance*)

Blue cloth coat, double-breasted, skirt sewn on, sleeves lined
with brown holland, scarlet collar and cuffs, slash on
sleeves, and two button-holes on each, pockets, three
hooks and eyes on collar .......................................    2s. 2d.
Takes one day and a half to make.

### CONVICTS

Jacket, double stitched .............................................    4d.
Trowsers ..............................................................    2½d.
Waistcoat  ............................................................    1½d.

The whole suit .......................................................    8d
From which thread and candles have to be deducted.

. . .

The above list of prices has been furnished to me by an eminent
army clothier and contractor, and it is here given so that the public
may be able to compare the employers' statement with that of the
workpeople. I shall now in due order lay before the reader the
operatives' version of the business, so that he may have an opportunity of checking the one account by the other. The agreement
between the two speaks highly for the honesty of both parties.

*A woman making army and police uniforms*

I was conducted by one who knew the trade well to a hard working woman living in one of the close foetid courts running out of
Gray's-inn-lane. Her statement was as follows :

"I make the soldiers' trowsers and jackets, and the undress white
ones; also the police trowsers, the railroad cord trowsers and jackets,
and the pensioners' trowsers. For the police I get 10d. the undress—
and 1s. 1d. the dress ones. The one is a finer cloth than the other.
They take one day each to make, from six in the morning to eight
or nine at night. There's thread to find and cotton, about 1d. per
pair. The soldiers' trowsers are 6½d. per pair. I can make two pair
in a day, but it must be a very long day. I sew the seams myself.
I don't put them out, like some. The undress white jackets are 5d.
each, and they take two of those in a day. We don't like them.
They're harder work than the trowsers; then they must be kept
so very clean; if we soil them, we're made to pay for 'em. . . . The
soldiers have to pay 8s. for their trowsers, and 8s. for their jackets—
so I hears. The police dress trowsers used to be 1s. 3d., now they
are 1s. 1d. The pensioners' trowsers are 6d. a pair, but there's more
work in them than in the regulation, owing to the broad stripe.
One seam does with the double stripe, but the broad stripe requires
two, and the price is the same. These take rather longer than the

other trowsers. The white duck trowsers are 5d. a pair. They take about the same time making, or a little longer this cold weather, they're so hard. The soldiers' great coats are 5d. They take much longer to make than the trowsers. Two hands must work hard to make three coats in a day. The expenses for trimmings is quite as much as for trowsers. The soldiers' lavender summer trowsers are 6½d., and, if anything, more trouble; they're all double seams, and the same expense for thread. The overalls for the horse soldiers are the worst of all; they take two hours longer to make than the others. Why, there's twelve times round the crutch piece. Oh, that's the most scandalousest work that ever was done. The seams has all to be felled down the same as a flannel would have to be. Them are the worst work of all.

"Upon an average, at all kinds of work, I suppose I could earn 1s. a day, if I had it to do, but I can't get it. It's three weeks today since I had any work at all, and I very often stand still quite as long. It's not a farthing more than 3s. a week that I earn, take it all the year round; and out of that there's thread, candle, and firing to be taken away, and that comes to 1s. a week for coal, candle, and wood, and 6d. for thread, leaving about 1s. 6d. for my clear earnings, after working the whole week through. But that's better than nothing.

"My husband's lately been in the hospital. I was in first a month with the same complaint—inflammation of the lungs and fever. I thought it came on from this close room. My husband wanted things to strengthen him after he came out of the hospital (he'd been there four weeks), and I couldn't give them to him out of my small earnings, and he was obliged to go into the workhouse. It was only six o'clock tonight that he came out. They gave him a shilling and a loaf of bread to bring home. I don't know that any person can be much worse off than we are. I am sure I haven't anything that I could pledge. I've been obliged to pawn his tools and if he was to go to work tomorrow he hasn't a tool that he could use. He can get a very good character. I may perhaps chance to get a bit of meat once a week—but that's a godsend."

She then took down a box, and opening it, said : "There, sir; there is the things we have been obliged to make away with in the last twelve-month, merely to live. The last thing I pledged was his trowel—he's a mason, sir—to get some tea and sugar to take to him to the hospital. I got 9d. upon it. If he had employment, we should get on very comfortable. If it hadn't been for this illness we should have done very well, him and me together."[6]

[6] Statements appeared here from a married man who worked at postman's coats and a woman with two sons who did looping.

*Prostitution among needlewomen*

During the course of my investigation into the condition of those who are dependent upon their needle for their support, I had been so repeatedly assured that the young girls were mostly compelled to resort to prostitution to eke out their subsistence, that I was anxious to test the truth of the statement. I had seen much want, but I had no idea of the intensity of the privations suffered by the needlewomen of London until I came to inquire into this part of the subject. But the poor creatures shall speak for themselves. I should inform the reader, however, that I have made inquiries into the truth of the almost incredible statements here given, and I can in most of the particulars at least vouch for the truth of the statement. Indeed, in one instance—that of the last case here recorded—I travelled nearly ten miles in order to obtain the character of the young woman. The first case is that of a good-looking girl. Her story is as follows :

"I make moleskin trowsers. I get 7d. and 8d. per pair. I can do two pairs in a day, and twelve when there is full employment, in a week. But some weeks I have no work at all. I work from six in the morning to ten at night; that is what I call my day's work. When I am fully employed I get from 7s. to 8s. a week. My expenses out of that for twist, thread, and candles are about 1s. 6d. a week, leaving me about 6s. per week clear. But there's coals to pay for out of this, and that's at the least 6d. more; so 5s. 6d. is the very outside of what I earn when I'm in full work. Lately I have been dreadfully slack; so we are every winter, all of us 'sloppers', and that's the time when we wants the most money. The week before last I had but two pair to make all the week; so that I only earnt 1s. clear. For this last month I'm sure I haven't done any more than that each week. Taking one week with another, all the year round I don't make above 3s. clear money each week. I don't work at any other kind of slop-work. The trowsers work is held to be the best paid of all. I give 1s. a week rent.

"My father died when I was five years of age. My mother is a widow, upwards of 66 years of age, and seldom has a day's work. Generally once in the week she is employed pot-scouring—that is, cleaning publicans' pots. She is paid 4d. a dozen for that, and does about four dozen and a half, so that she gets about 1s. 6d. in the day by it. For the rest she is dependent upon me. I am 20 years of age the 25th of this month. We earn together, to keep the two of us, from 4s. 6d. to 5s. each week. Out of this we have to pay 1s. rent, and there remains 3s. 6d. to 4s. to find us both in food and clothing. It is of course impossible for us to live upon it, and the consequence is I am obligated to go a bad way. I have been three years working at slop-work.

"I was virtuous when I first went to work, and I remained so till this last twelvemonth. I struggled very hard to keep myself chaste, but I found that I couldn't get food and clothing for myself and mother, so I took to live with a young man. He is turned 20. He is a tinman. He did promise to marry me, but his sister made mischief between me and him, so that parted us. I have not seen him now for about six months, and I can't say whether he will keep his promise or not. I am now pregnant by him, and expect to be confined in two months' time. He knows of my situation, and so does my mother. My mother believed me to be married to him. She knows otherwise now. I was very fond of him, and had known him for two years before he seduced me. He could make 14s. a week. He told me if I came to live with him he'd take care I shouldn't want, and both mother and me had been very bad off before. He said, too, he'd make me his lawful wife, but I hardly cared so long as I could get food for myself and mother.

"Many young girls at the shop advised me to go wrong. They told me how comfortable they was off; they said they could get plenty to eat and drink, and good clothes. There isn't one young girl as can get her living by slop work. The masters all know this, but they wouldn't own to it of course. It stands to reason that no one can live and pay rent, and find clothes, upon 3s. a week, which is the most they can make clear, even the best hands, at the mole-skin and cord trowsers work. There's poor people moved out of our house that was making ¾d. shirts. I am satisfied there is not one young girl that works at slop work that is virtuous, and there are some thousands in the trade. They may do very well if they have got mothers and fathers to find them a home and food, and to let them have what they earn for clothes; then they may be virtuous, but not without. I've heard of numbers who have gone from slop work to the streets altogether for a living, and I shall be obligated to do the same thing myself unless something better turns up for me.

"If I was never allowed to speak no more, it was the little money I got by my labour that led me to go wrong. Could I have honestly earnt enough to have subsisted upon, to find me in proper food and clothing, such as is necessary, I should not have gone astray; no, never—As it was I fought against it as long as I could—that I did—to the last. I hope to be able to get a ticket for a midwife; a party has promised me as much, and, he says, if possible, he'll get me an order for a box of linen. My child will only increase my burdens, and if my young man won't support my child I must go on the streets altogether. I know how horrible all this is. It would have been

much better for me to have subsisted upon a dry crust and water
rather than be as I am now. But no one knows the temptations of
us poor girls in want. Gentlefolks can never understand it. If I had
been born a lady it wouldn't have been very hard to have acted
like one. To be poor and to be honest, especially with young girls,
is the hardest struggle of all. There isn't one in a thousand that can
get the better of it. I am ready to say again, that it was want, and
nothing more, that made me transgress. If I had been better paid I
should have done better. Young as I am, my life is a curse to me.
If the Almighty would please to take me before my child is born,
I should die happy."[7]

*A tragic and touching romance*

The story which follows is perhaps one of the most tragic and
touching romances ever read. I must confess that to myself the
mental and bodily agony of the poor Magdalen who related it was
quite overpowering. She was a tall, fine-grown girl, with remarkably regular features. She told her tale with her face hidden in her
hands, and sobbing so loud that it was with difficulty I could catch
her words. As she held her hands before her eyes I could see the
tears oozing between her fingers. Indeed I never remember to have
witnessed such intense grief. Her statement was of so startling a
nature, that I felt it due to the public to inquire into the character
of the girl. Though it was late at night, and the gentleman who had
brought the case to me assured me that he himself was able to
corroborate almost every word of the girl's story, still I felt that I
should not be doing my duty to the office that had been entrusted
to me if I allowed so pathetic and romantic a statement to go forth
without using every means to test the truth of what I had heard.
Accordingly, being informed that the girl was in service, I made
the best of my way not only to her present master, but also to the
one she had left but a few months previous. The gentleman who had
brought her to me, willingly accompanied me thither. One of the
parties lived at the East end of London, the other in the extreme
suburbs of London. The result was well worth the journey. Both
persons spoke in the highest terms of the girl's honesty, sobriety,
industry, and of her virtue in particular.

With this preamble let me proceed to tell her story in her own
touching words:

"I used to work at slop-work—at the shirt work—the fine full-
fronted white shirts; I got 2¼d. each for 'em. There were six button-

[7] Here Mayhew interviewed 2 widows, occasional prostitutes, whose piece-
mistress said that they were "hardworking and sober individuals".

holes, four rows of stitching in the front, and the collars and wrist-bands stitched as well. By working from five o'clock in the morning till midnight each night I might be able to do seven in the week. These would bring me in 17½d. for my whole week's labour. Out of this the cotton must be taken, and that came to 2d. every week, and so left me 15½d. to pay rent and living and buy candles with. I was single, and received some little help from my friends; still it was impossible for me to live. I was forced to go out of a night to make out my living. I had a child, and it used to cry for food. So, as I could not get a living for him myself by my needle, I went into the streets and made out a living that way. Sometimes there was no work for me, and then I was forced to depend entirely upon the streets for my food. On my soul I went to the streets solely to get a living for myself and child. If I had been able to get it otherwise I would have done so.

"I am the daughter of a minister of the gospel. My father was an Independent preacher, and I pledge my word, solemnly and sacredly, that it was the low price paid for my labour that drove me to prostitution. I often struggled against it, and many times have I taken my child into the streets to beg rather than I would bring shame upon myself and it any longer. I have made pincushions and fancy articles—such as I could manage to scrape together—and taken them to the streets to sell, so that I might get an honest living, but I couldn't. Sometimes I should be out all night in the rain, and sell nothing at all, me and my child together; and when we didn't get anything that way we used to sit in a shed, for I was too fatigued with my baby to stand, and I was so poor I couldn't have even a night's lodging upon credit. One night in the depth of winter his legs froze to my side. We sat down on the step of a door. I was trying to make my way to the workhouse, but was so weak I couldn't get on any farther. The snow was over my shoes. It had been snowing all day, and me and my boy out in it. We hadn't tasted any food since the morning before, and that I got in another person's name. I was driven by positive starvation to say that they sent me when they did no such thing. All this time I was struggling to give up prostitution, I had many offers, but I refused them all. I had sworn to myself that I would keep from that mode of life for my boy's sake. A lady saw me sitting on the door-step, and took me into her house, and rubbed my child's legs with brandy. She gave us some food, both my child and me, but I was so far gone I couldn't eat.

"I got to the workhouse that night. I told them we were starving, but they refused to admit us without an order; so I went back to prostitution again for another month. I couldn't get any work. I had no security. I couldn't even get a reference to find me work at second hand. My character was quite gone. I was at length so disgusted with my life that I got an order for the workhouse, and went in there for two years. The very minute we got inside the gate they took my child away from me, and allowed me to see it only once a month. At last I and another left the 'house' to work at umbrella covering, so that we might have our children with us. For this work we had 1s. a dozen covers, and we used to do between us from six to eight dozen a week. We could have done more, but the work wasn't to be had. I then made from 3s. to 4s. a week, and from that time I gave up prostitution.

"For the sake of my child I should not like my name to be known, but for the sake of other young girls I can and will solemnly state that it was the smallness of the price I got for my labour that drove me to prostitution as a means of living. In my heart I hated it; my whole nature rebelled at it, and nobody but God knows how I struggled to give it up. I was only able to do so by getting work at something that was better paid. Had I remained at shirt-making, I must have been a prostitute to this day. I have taken my gown off my back and pledged it, and gone in my petticoat—I had but one—rather than take to the streets again; but it was all in vain. We were starving still; and I robbed the young woman who lodged in the next room to me of a gown, in order to go out in the streets once more and get a crust. I left my child at home wrapped in a bit of old blanket while I went out. I brought home half-a-crown by my shame, and stopped its cries for food for two days.

"My sufferings have been such that three days before I first tried to get into the workhouse I made up my mind to commit suicide. I wrote the name of my boy and the address of his aunts and pinned them to his little shift, and left him in bed—for ever as I thought—and went into the Regent's-park to drown myself in the water near the road leading to St. John's-wood. I went there because I thought I was more sure of death. It was farther to jump. The policeman watched me, and asked me what I was doing. He thought I looked suspicious, and drove me from the Park. That saved my life. My father died, thank God, when I was eight years old. My sisters are waistcoat hands, and both starving. I hardly know whether one is dead or not now. She is suffering from cancers brought on by poor living. I am now living in service. I have been so for the last year and a half. I obtained a character from a Christian gentleman to whom I owe my salvation. I can solemnly assert since I have been able to earn a sufficient living, I have never once resorted to prostitution. My boy is still in the workhouse. I have been unable to save any money since I have been in service. My wages are low, and I had scarcely any clothes when I went there. If I had a girl of my own I should believe I should be making a prostitute of her to put to slop work. I am sure no girl can get a living at it without, and I say as much after thirteen years' experience of the business. I never knew one girl in the trade who was virtuous; most of them wished to be so, but were compelled to be otherwise for mere life."

## LETTER IX—16 NOVEMBER 1849

*Difficulty of obtaining information about wages*

I have lately devoted myself to investigating the incomings and condition of the Needlewomen of London generally. My object is, in the first place, to obtain an authentic list of the prices paid to the different artisans and labourers throughout the metropolis. It is curious that this should remain undone, and even untried, to the present day. But so it is. Mr. Porter, in his *Progress of the Nation,* tells us :

"The most extensive register, in point of time, that we have of the rate of wages is found in returns made to Parliament by Greenwich Hospital. Unfortunately, however, the descriptions of artisans employed in the establishment are few, and their occupations come altogether under the description of skilled labour. Besides this, the returns made up to 1805 are given only at intervals of five years, while the rates published are those paid to masters, who contract for the performance of the work, and are not the sums received by the workmen.

"No one, unless he have made the attempt to obtain information of this kind, can be aware of the difficulty opposed to his success. After many and long-continued efforts to that end, it is not possible here to bring forward many authentic or continuous statements of the rates of wages in this country."

The chief difficulty which besets an undertaking of this character lies in the indisposition of the tradesmen—and especially of those who are notorious for selling cheap, and, consequently, giving a less price to their workpeople—to make known the sums that they pay for the labour employed upon the different articles of manufacture in which they deal. I believe, this, is the main reason why such information remains to be acquired. To obtain it, the workpeople themselves must be sought out, and seen privately in their own homes. Another obstacle to the attainment of the information, is that workpeople are in general but poor accountants. They are unused to keep any account, either of their income or expenditure. Hence they have generally to trust to their memories for a statement of their earnings; and it is only with considerable difficulty and cross-questioning that one is able to obtain from them an account of the expenses necessarily attendant upon their labour, and so, by deducting these from the prices paid to them, to arrive at the amount of their clear earnings. Moreover, though I must confess I have met with far more truthfulness on the part of the operative than on that of the employer, still I believe the workpeople are naturally disposed to imagine that they get less than they really do, even as the employer is inclined to fancy his workmen make more than their real gains.

I should, however, while speaking of the objection of employers generally to make known the prices paid to their workpeople, make honourable exception of Mr. Shaw, the army clothier. I have no doubt that there are many more actuated, like that gentleman, with a desire both to bring under the notice of the public the small sum of money paid for the labour of those they employ, as well as to increase—even at the expense of their own profits—rather than to lower the wages of their workpeople. But as yet I have not met with them. Wherever the labourer is worse paid, and there is consequently the greater necessity for the amount earned to be made public, *there*, as with  . . .  the large slop-seller alluded to in a former letter, do I find the greatest indisposition on the part of the employers to afford me the least assistance; as yet I must in truth say I have only found a disposition to mis-state and mislead. However, the subject, I am well aware, is of far too great importance in a national point of view to be thwarted by individuals whose interest it is to keep the price of the labour market secret. The Proprietors of the *Morning Chronicle* have undertaken to obtain, for the first time in this country, an account of the earnings of the workpeople of the metropolis; and if they fail, why it shall not be for want of energy or zeal.[8]

## A distressed gentlewoman doing needlework

I had seen all classes of needlewoman but one. I had listened to the sufferings of the widow, the married woman, and the young unmarried girl, who strove to obtain an honest living by their needle. I had also heard, from their own lips, the history of the trials and fall of those who had been reduced to literal beggary and occasional prostitution by the low price given for their labour. Still it struck me that there was one other class of needlewoman whose misery and privations must be more acute than all. It was the distressed gentlewomen—persons who, having been brought up in ease and

[8] Interviews with female staystitchers, shoebinders, a stockmaker, a cloak-maker, an upholstress and a second distressed gentlewoman have been cut from this letter.

luxury, must feel their present privations doubly as acute as those who, in a measure, had been used to poverty from their very cradle.

I was directed to one of this class who was taking care of a large empty house at the west end of the town. I was no sooner in the presence of the poor family than I saw, by the manner of all present, how differently they had once been situated. The lady herself was the type of distressed gentlewoman. I could tell by the regularity of her features that her family for many generations past had been unused to labour for their living, and there was that neatness and cleanliness about her costume and appearance which invariably distinguished the lady from the labouring woman. Again, there was a gentleness and a plaintiveness in the tone of her voice that above all things mark the refinement of a woman's nature. The room in which the family lived, though more destitute of every article of furniture and comfort than any I had yet visited, was at least untainted by the *atmosphere* of poverty. I was no longer sickened with that overpowering smell that always hangs about the dwellings of the very poor. The home of the distressed gentlewoman consisted literally of four bare walls. There was no table, and only two chairs in the place. At the foot of the lady was an old travelling trunk, on which lay a few of the nightcaps that she and her daughters were occupied in making. One of the girls stood hemming by the window, and the other was seated in a corner of the room upon another trunk, busily engaged in the same manner. Before the fender was a piece of old carpeting about the size of a napkin. On the mantelpiece were a few balls of cotton, a small tin box of papers, and a Bible and Prayer Book. This was literally all the property in the place. It was not difficult to tell, by the full black eyes, olive complexions, and sharp Murillo-like features of the daughters, that their father, at least, had been of Spanish extraction. The mother herself, too, had somewhat of a foreign look, though this I afterwards discovered arose from long residence with her husband abroad.

It was not till now that I had found my duty in any way irksome to me; but I must confess, when I began to stammer out the object of my visit to the distressed lady, I could not help feeling that my mission seemed like an impertinence, and to betray a desire to pry into the miseries of the poor that was wholly foreign to my intention.[9] I could see by the proud expression of the gentlewoman's

[9] Later, this deference for distressed gentlewomen completely disappeared: "it has been invariably found by Mr. Mayhew that 'those who have seen better days' constitute the worst class of the poor. The experience of the *Morning Chronicle*, where £800 was dispensed, went to show that the least faith of all was to be placed in the 'broken-down gentlefolk' "; "Answers to Correspondents," No. 29, 28 June 1851.

features that she felt the privacy of her poverty had been violated by my presence, and I was some little while endeavouring to impress upon her that I had not come to her with the mean object of publishing to the world the distress of *individuals*, which I was well aware was made doubly bitter from the fear of its becoming known, even to their friends, much more to the public in general. At length I informed her that whatever she might communicate to me would be given to the public in such general terms that it would be impossible to recognize that she was the person alluded to. Upon this assurance she told me as follows :

"I work at needlework generally—I profess to do that, indeed that is what I have done ever since I have been a widow. But it is shocking payment. What I am engaged upon now is from a private lady. I haven't,as yet, made any charge. I don't know what the price will be; I did intend to ask 3d. each. The lady has been a great friend to me. I can't say exactly how long it will take me. Persons call to look at the house, and I have interruptions. They are plain nightcaps that I am making, and are for a lady of rank. Such persons generally, I think, give the least trouble for their work. I can't say how long they take me each to make. I've been very ill, and I've had the children to help me. I shouldn't like to say what I could not exactly count upon—it would be saying what wouldn't be true. I never made any before. There will be five when I have finished them all. There are three done, and this one I have in my hand is about half done. When was it we had them, my dear?" said the lady to her daughter, who stood sewing at the window. The young lady returned no answer, and the mother continued, "I can't recollect when we had them, for we have been so much worried. Two or three times the thieves have attempted to get into the house. On last Wednesday someone tried to open the street door, thinking the house was empty. The fright has made me almost forget everything, I can assure you. Since Wednesday myself and my eldest daughter (the other goes to school) have done very nearly four of the nightcaps. But that is not by sitting to work at them continually. During that time we have made a flannel jacket as well. My daughter, indeed, made it, for I haven't been able, though of course I attended to it. The flannel jacket was for a shop. They would not have given me more than 8d., though it was lined inside with calico, and indeed was more like a coat. I found some part of the lining, though not the whole; there was a great deal of work in it—fourteen buttonholes, and I charged them 1s. They demurred at the charge, and said, if they sent me another they would only give 10d. for 8d. was their usual price. I made one of the sleeves and my daughter made the rest. We were engaged on it all day. There were a great many seams in it, and they must have been neatly put out of hand or else the people at the shop wouldn't have given me the price; nor, indeed, would they give me any other work.

"Since Wednesday myself and my daughter have made one flannel jacket and just upon four nightcaps; that's all, and they will come altogether to 2s. The lady won't put the price herself upon the nightcaps, and I feel timid in asking a price of a lady that's been a friend to me. Latterly I've had no work at all, only that which I got from an institution for distressed needlewomen. They were children's chemises. I think I made seven. Didn't I?" she inquired of one of her daughters—"Yes mamma," was the young lady's answer. "I ought to keep a book myself," the mother went on to say—"I used to do so of all the prices. I did the seven chemises in a fortnight, and got 7s. for them. I have also made within this time one dozen white cravats for a shop; they are the white corded-muslin cut across, and the very largest. I have 6d. a dozen for hemming them, and had to find the cotton of course. I have often said I would never do any more of them; I thought they would never have been done, there was so much work in them. Myself and daughter hemmed the dozen in a day. It was a day's very hard work. It was really such very hard work that I cried over it. I was so ill, and we were wanting food so badly. That is all that myself and daughter have done for this last month. During that time the two of us (my daughter is eighteen) have earned 6d., and 7s., and 2s., making in all 9s. 6d. for four weeks, or 2s. 4½d. per week, to keep three of us. I have not been constantly employed all the month; I should say I have been half the time occupied. The nine and six-pence may be fairly considered as the earnings of the two of us, supposing we had been fully occupied for a fortnight. My daughter and I have earned at plain needlework a good deal more than that. But to get more we have scarcely time to eat. I have, with my daughter's labour and my own earned as much as 10s.; but then such hard work injures the health. I should say an industrious quick hand might earn at plain needlework, taking one thing with another, 3s. 6d. a week, if she were fully employed. But there is a great difficulty in getting work—oh, yes, very great. The schools injure the trade greatly. Ladies give their work to the National Schools, and thus needlewomen who have families to support are left without employment. That I, think, is the principal cause of the deficiency of work—and many others I know consider so with me. I think that is also the cause of the prices being so low. Yes, I know it is, because ladies will tell you plainly, I can have the work done cheaper at the school. Generally, the ladies are much harder as to their terms than the tradespeople; oh, yes, the tradespeople usually show more lenity towards the needlewomen than the ladies. I know the mistress of an institution who refused some chemises of a lady who wanted to have them made at 9d. She said she would not impose upon the poor workpeople so much as to get them made at that price.

"Of course we could not have subsisted upon the 2s. 4½d. a week, which we have earned for the last four weeks. I have got many duplicates in the house to show how we *did* live. I was obliged to take the blankets off the bed, and sleep with only a sheet to cover us. I sold my bedstead for 3s. 6d. to a person, who came herself and valued it. That very bedstead, not a month ago, I gave 8s. 6d. for. It was what they call a cross-bedstead. Our bolster we were obliged to pledge. That was quite new; it cost 2s. 6d., and I pledged it for a shilling. Our blankets, too, we pledged for 1s. each; they cost me 6s. the pair; but I've taken one out since. Of course now we sleep upon the floor. Our inside clothing we have also disposed of. Indeed, I will tell you, we are still without our clothing, both my daughter and myself; and I have chewed camphor and drank warm water to stay my hunger. My pains from flatulence have been dreadful. We have often had no breakfast, and remained without food till night, all of us; and at last I have made up my mind to pledge my flannel petticoat, and get 6d. on that. Once we were so badly off that I sent for a person to come and pledge my bed. She pledged it for half-a-crown. This person told a lady in the neighbourhood what I had done, and the lady came in the evening and brought me 5s., and with that the bed was redeemed. We all like to preserve life, sir. Life is sweet when we have a family, however much we may want. . . .

"What I want is a situation for my eldest daughter. She can speak Spanish, and she works well at her needle. I myself speak Spanish and French. You won't put that in the newspaper, will you?" she asked me. I told her I would insert nothing that she wished to keep secret. She said, "I am afraid they will guess it is I. I would rather starve than it should be known who I am. I do not wish to be made a public spectacle of. I am not ashamed to be poor, understand— for I am so through no fault of my own—but my friends would be ashamed to have my poverty known." I told her I would do as she wished, and I assured her that I had come there to alleviate rather than to aggravate her distress. After a little hesitation she consented to the publication of what she might communicate to me, and continued as follows :—"You may say my father was an officer in the English army, and my grandfather was an officer in the English army too. I have a brother-in-law a clergyman. It's not in his power to assist me. My husband was an officer in the army as well, but he was in foreign service. He has been dead five years. He left me penniless, with three children. My son is in the West Indies. He is doing well there : he is but young—he is only 17. He has £36 a year and his board. He assisted me last year. I was in hopes to have some assistance this year, according to the last letter I had from him. I do feel it very hard that I—whose father and grandfather have served the country—should be left to suffer as I do. I don't consider, if you understand me, sir, that we have any merit or claim upon the Government; still I cannot but think it hard that the children of those who have served their country so many years should be so destitute as we are.

"All we want is employment, and that we cannot get. Charity, indeed, is most irksome to us—we may well say that. My husband's family were all very wealthy, but they've lost nearly all in the revolutions abroad. I would not object to travel with a lady, but I could never say farewell for ever to my own country—that is what I think and feel. Before I came here I paid 4s. a week. I did not pay it all myself. (Here I was shown the letter of a lady of high rank, promising to be answerable for her rent). Now I pay no rent, and have not done so since the 19th September. The same good lady recommended me to the house-agent, and he gave me this house to take care of. I do think it most cruel that in the midst of all our distresses and poverty persons must try to enter the house. I am sure they must come to take our lives—it cannot be for what we have ! We are all alone, here, without anyone to protect us, and we are very timid. Last night I was afraid to go to church, for I thought they would get into the premises in our absence. Several times late at night I have heard them put a false key into the door. Nobody knows what I suffer. Last Friday night—it must have been past midnight—I heard them knocking at the wash-house window, as if to take out the pane of glass, and I had the presence of mind to throw up the window of this room. We sleep here on the floor. I called out, saying, Who is there? Such was my fright that I trembled all day Saturday. I would rather go to the workhouse than stop here. But, of course, after all my struggles, I would not go there, no ! though I *am* a destitute widow. Thank God, I'm not in debt—that is a great consolation to me. I don't owe any person a penny."

I hardly knew how to ask one whose narrative and manner bore so plainly the impress of truth, for proofs of the authenticity of her statements; still I felt that it would not be right, without making some such inquiries, to allow the story of her sufferings to go forth to the world. I explained to her my wishes, and she very readily showed me such papers and official documents as put her statement as to birth and the position of her husband utterly beyond a doubt. She was afterwards kind enough, for the sake of others situated like herself, to let me see the duplicates of the different articles that her poverty had compelled her to raise a meal upon. They told so awful a tale of want, that I begged permission to copy them. The articles pledged, and the sums lent upon them, were as follows : Gown, 1s.; bed, 1s.; petticoat and nightgown, 1s.; gown, 1d.; gown skirt, 1s.; umbrella, 1s.; petticoat and shawl, 1s.; bolster, 1s.; petti- coat and shift, 1s.; ditto, 6d.; counterpane, 2s.; cloak, 3s.; a whittle, 3s.; gown, 1s.; petticoat and piece of flannel, 9d.; wedding-ring, 2s. 6d. The lady also took me into the garden to show me the window by which the thieves had sought to enter the house at midnight. On the flagstones immediately beneath it, and which were green with damp and desolation, were the marks of men's hobnailed boots.

It is but right, for the poor gentlewoman's sake, that I should add that her statement has been fully investigated and corroborated. She seems a lady in every way worthy of our deepest commiseration.


## LETTER X—20 NOVEMBER 1849

*Method of figuring wages*

In my last letter, it may be remembered, I stated that my primary object was to obtain, for the first time in this country, a list of the prices paid to the workpeople of London for their labour. I then described a few of the difficulties besetting such a task. Of these there are two more important than all besides. One of these is the objection of the employer generally to allow his profits to be known; for, of course, if he revealed the amount that he pays in wages for the manufacture of the articles in which he deals, the price at which he sells these articles would easily enable others to ascertain his gains. The same desire for secrecy is exhibited by all classes of "middlemen"—whether known by the name of chamber- masters, piece-masters, or sweaters. The second difficulty which I mentioned, arises not from any indisposition on the part of the workpeople to make known the sums they are paid for their labour— indeed they are generally as willing as their employers are unwilling to do so—but rather from their incapability to enter into the neces- sary calculations. It should be borne in mind, that it is not an account of the earnings of any one week that is required—the *average* weekly income of a particular class of operatives throughout the year is what I seek to ascertain. To arrive at this, however, demands so long a series of accounts and reckonings, that the generality of work- people are unable, without considerable assistance, to go through them. Hence it is impossible to come to any satisfactory result without a personal visitation and cross-questioning of the operatives themselves. Upon the character of these questions the soundness of the conclusion of course depends, and I am, therefore, anxious that the public should know how I proceed in the matter.

My first inquiries are into the particular branch of the trade under investigation upon which the workman is engaged. I then request to be informed whether the individual has his or her work first or second-handed; that is to say, whether he or she obtains it direct from the employer, or through the intervention of some chamber or piece-master. If the work comes to the operative in question second-handed, I then endeavour to find out the prices paid for the work itself to the first hand, as well as the number of workpeople that the first hand generally employs. This done, I seek to be informed whether the work of the individual I am visiting is piece or day-work. If day-work, I learn the usual hours of labour per day, and the rate of wages per week. If it be piece-work, I request to be made acquainted with the prices paid for each description of work *seriatim*—the time that each particular article takes to make— and the number of hours that the party usually works per day. By these means I arrive at the gross daily earnings. I then ascertain the cost of trimmings, candles, and such other expenses as are necessary to the completion of each particular article; and, deducting these from the gross gains per day, I find what are the clear daily earnings of the individual in question. I then check this account by obtaining from the workman a statement as to the number of such articles that he can make in a week—and, deducting expenses, I see whether the clear weekly earnings agree with those of the clear daily ones. After this I request to know the amount of the earnings for the last week—then those for the week before—and then those for the week before that. Beyond this point I find that memory generally fails. Out of the scores of operatives that I have now visited, I have found *only one* instance in which the workman keeps a regular account of his weekly gains.

By the means above detailed I am enabled both to check and counter-check the statement furnished to me in the first instance. To avoid, however, the possibility of error, I seek for a further proof—and that is the account of the quantity of work given out to the workpeople by the employer. This is generally in the master's own handwriting; and, it forms, when obtainable, the most conclusive evidence as to the amount of work done in the week by the workmen—while, if extending many weeks back, it enables me with ease to arrive at an average result. I regret to say, however, that such books are far from being invariably kept by employers. Some workpeople are paid immediately that the work is taken in,

PLATE VII. A View of Ludgate Hill by Gustave Doré, 1872

PLATE VIII.   Spitalfields Weavers at Work, 1854

ABROAD.

AT HOME.

PLATE IX.   The Needlewoman. A *Punch* Cartoon, 1850

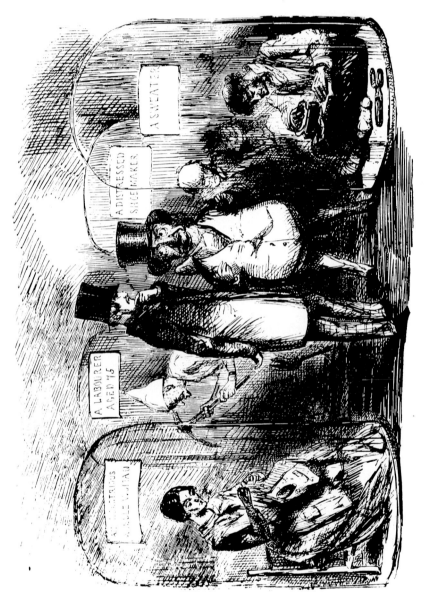

SPECIMENS FROM MR. PUNCH'S INDUSTRIAL EXHIBITION OF 1850.

PLATE X

and no such account is required. However, it is but due to the character of the workpeople to say, that in no one instance have I yet
discovered the least wilful mis-statement as to the prices paid, or
the total amount of their weekly earnings. It is true that sometimes
the statements of the day's earnings do not immediately tally with
those of the week; but this I frequently find, on investigation, to arise
from the fact of their not having made any allowance for the time
lost in taking their work in, and getting a fresh supply out of the
warehouse.

As a class, I must say the workpeople that I have seen appear
remarkably truthful, patient, and generous; indeed, every day teaches
me that their virtues are wholly unknown to the world. Their intemperance, their improvidence, their want of cleanliness, and their
occasional want of honesty, are all that come to our ears. As I said
before, however, I doubt very much whether *we* should not be as
improvident and intemperate if our incomes and comforts were as
precarious as theirs. The vices of the poor appear to be the evils
naturally fostered by poverty—even as their virtues are such as want
and suffering alone can beget. Their patience is positively marvellous.
Indeed, I have seen this last week such contentment, under miseries
and privations of the most appalling nature, as has made me look
with absolute reverence upon the poor afflicted things. I have beheld
a stalwart man, with one half of his body dead—his whole side
paralyzed, so that the means of subsistence by labour were denied
him—and his wife toiling day and night with her needle, and getting
at the week's end but one shilling for her many hours' labour. I
have sat with them in their wretched hovel shivering without a
spark of fire in the grate—and the bleak air rushing in through
every chink and crevice. I have been with them and their shoeless
children at their Sunday dinner of boiled tealeaves and dry bread,
and I have heard the woman, with smiling lips, not only tell me,
but show me, how contented she was with her lot, bearing the heavy
burden with a meek and uncomplaining spirit, such as philosophy
may dream of, but can never compass. The man and his wife were
satisfied that it was the will of God they should be afflicted as they
were, and they bowed their heads in reverent submission to the
law. "It may be hard to say why we are so sorely troubled as we
are," said the heroic old dame, "but we are satisfied it is all for the
best.". . .

When I have obtained an account of the clear earnings of the
workpeople during such times as they are fully employed, I seek
to procure from them a statement of what they imagine to be their
weekly earnings—taking one week with another—throughout the
year. Having got this—I then set about to discover how often in

F

the course of the year they are "standing still" as they term it. I inquire into the number and duration of "the slacks". This done, I strive to obtain from the operative an average of the weekly earnings during such times.

I then make a calculation of the total of the workpeople's gains when fully employed for so many months, and when partially occupied for the remainder of the year. By this means I am enabled to arrive at an average of their weekly earnings throughout the whole year; and I then compare this with the statement which I have previously received from them on the subject. It is seldom that I find much discrepancy. I finally check the whole account of their earnings by a statement of their expenditure. I generally see their rent-book, and so learn the sum that they pay for rent, and I likewise get a detail of their mode and cost of living. Hence the reader will perceive that every means are adopted to insure an accurate result. Moreover, the character of the informant is invariably inquired into, especially with regard to the truthfulness, industry, and sobriety of the individual.[10]

## LETTER XI—23 NOVEMBER 1849

In my last letter I described the means I had adopted in order to arrive at a fair and correct estimate as to the average earnings of those who depend on their needle for their subsistence. All classes of workpeople have been visited—male and female—old and young—the married, the single, and the widowed—the distressed gentlewoman and the struggling Magdalen—those who had husbands to help them, and those who were alone and unassisted in their toil—those who had the work direct from the warehouse, and those who received it from a piece-mistress, mulcted of its fair proportion. . . .

### Two further tests for wages

Nevertheless, in the course of my investigations I have felt the difficulty of dealing with individuals. I was therefore anxious, before quitting the present subject, to test the *particular* conclusions at which I had arrived by two different modes—first, by an account of the earnings *for a number of years* of some sober and hardworking individual who might be taken as a fair type of the class, so that my deductions might be drawn not from any one *year*, but from a

[10] The rest of the letter consisted of interviews with sisters who worked on furs, a married woman who embroidered police clothing, a garter maker and a bracemaker with her crippled husband.

*series.* The other test to which I was desirous of putting the statements that I had made public was that of assembling a large body of people and taking the general statistics of the meeting. By both of these ordeals has the subject been tried, and I now proceed to lay the result before the public.

### Numbers engaged in slopwork and needlework

Let me, however, first endeavour, by means of The Occupation Abstract of the Government Report on the Population of Great Britain, to come to some rough notion as to the number of individuals engaged in slopwork and needlework throughout the metropolis.

According to this report, then, there were of :

| | | | | |
|---|---|---|---|---|
| Seamstresses and Seamsters | 6,269, | of whom | 5,602 | were females under 20 |
| Ditto (shirt) | 382 | of whom | 332 | were females under 20 |
| Slopworkers | 254 | of whom | 196 | were females under 20 |
| Stay and corset makers | 1,753 | of whom | 1,329 | were females under 20 |
| Stock (men's) makers | 356 | of whom | 230 | were females under 20 |
| Straw Bonnet and straw hat makers | 1,319 | of whom | 1,049 | were females under 20 |
| Glovers | 677 | of whom | 331 | were females under 20 |
| Furriers | 1,236 | of whom | 464 | were females under 20 |
| Embroiderers | 692 | of whom | 499 | were females under 20 |
| Cap makers and dealers | 549 | of whom | 272 | were females under 20 |
| Bonnet makers | 1,417 | of whom | 1,090 | were females under 20 |
| | 14,904 | | 11,394 | |

If we add to these the dressmakers and milliners

| | | |
|---|---|---|
| | 20,780 | 17,183 |
| We have the total number | 35,684 | 28,577 |

From the above 35,684 we must deduct those who are in business for themselves, and these, according to the "London Post-Office Directory" for 1850, are :

| | |
|---|---|
| Shirtmakers | 58 |
| Stay and corset makers | 265 |
| Stock makers | 25 |
| Straw bonnet and straw hat makers | 356 |
| Glovers | 67 |
| Furriers | 144 |
| Embroiderers | 33 |
| Cap makers | 47 |
| Bonnet makers, milliners, and dressmakers | 1,060 |
| | 2,055 |

And 2,055 deducted from 35,584 leaves 33,529 as the gross number of individuals engaged in needlework and slopwork throughout

London, of whom considerably more than three-fourths, or no less than 28,577, are females under twenty years of age.

The earnings of all the above classes have been investigated, with the exception of the Milliners and Dressmakers. These being somewhat better paid than the generality of other needlewomen, I have purposely deferred all inquiry into the prices given to them till another and more fitting occasion. So that, deducting these, we may safely say there are 13,900 engaged in slopwork and the lower grades of needlework, of whom 11,394 are females under twenty years of age.

*Testing by accounts especially for a series of years*

And as regards the average earnings of this large body of individuals, according to the accounts that have been furnished to me by the workpeople, the average *clear* income of the shirtmakers, blouse, trowsers, waistcoat, and other hands appears to be from 2s. 6d. to 3s. 6d., exclusive of trimmings. As I said before, these accounts had been tested whenever it was possible, by the books of the employers themselves, in which the earnings of the operatives are set down by the master; and recently four more books have been placed in my hands, from which the following results have been obtained :

Account No. 1 extends over a period of 31 weeks. In the course of this time £7 11s. 3½d. has been earned at the best kind of shirt-work. This gives an average of 4s. 10½d. per week. From this the expense of cotton at the least has to be deducted, which leaves 4s. 4½d. as the clear weekly gains for upwards of half a year. Account No. 2 is for the making of Flushing coats, and for this work 15s. has been earned in four weeks, which gives an average of 3s. 9d. a week, or deducting trimmings about 3s. as the clear weekly income. Account No. 3 is for shirts, like No. 1, and runs over five months. During this time £2 17s. 7d. has been received, which gives 2s. 10½d., or, deducting cotton, 2s. 4½d., as the clear earnings per week. The last of these accounts, extending over a period of less than a year, amounts to 17s. 9d., which has been gained at trowsers work in fifteen weeks, and so gives 1s. 2d. per week as the average earnings. But deducting trimmings, the clear gains would be only 8d. per week for the whole of that time.

The defect, however of all the above accounts is, that they are not of a sufficient duration to admit of our arriving at a fair average. The particulars are too few to allow us to generalize with safety on the subject. I sought, therefore, for some other statement, which, extending over many years, would enable me to draw conclusions with something like certainty, both as to the customary earnings and the periods at which the business was brisk and slack throughout each year. Such a statement was most difficult to be found; but at length, after an infinity of fruitless inquiries, I was able to obtain an account of the earnings of *two* females, working together for a period of four years. The very fact of keeping such an account shows a habit of prudence which stamps the individuals as being far above the ordinary run of needlewomen; and, moreover, they were generally employed at a class of work (drawn-bonnet making) which is much better paid than either the trowsers or shirt work; indeed, it was possible for each of them, by sitting up as many as three nights in the week, to earn 10s. by such means; and it was only when this better-class work was not to be obtained, that they resorted to "trowsers work" as a means of living. Hence it will be seen that the result of the subjoined statement—low as it is—must still be above the income of the ordinary needlewomen. . . .

SUMMARY OF THE ACCOUNT

| | *1846* £ *s.* *d.* | *1847* £ *s.* *d.* | *1848* £ *s.* *d.* | *1849* £ *s.* *d.* | *Average for four Years* £ *s.* *d.* |
|---|---|---|---|---|---|
| FIRST QUARTER | | | | | |
| arnings of 1st quarter | 5 8 6½ | 4 14 0 | 1 19 1½ | 3 10 6 | 3 18 0½ |
| verage earnings per week | 0 8 4 | 0 7 2¾ | 0 3 0 | 0 5 5 | 0 6 0 |
| educt trimmings* | 0 1 4½ | 0 1 2½ | 0 0 6 | 0 0 10¾ | 0 1 0 |
| ear earnings per week | 0 6 11½ | 0 6 0¼ | 0 2 6 | 0 4 6¼ | 0 5 0 |
| SECOND QUARTER | | | | | |
| arnings of 2d quarter | 10 10 9 | 9 5 8 | 10 4 7 | 9 7 3 | 9 17 0¾ |
| verage earnings per week | 0 16 2½ | 0 14 3¼ | 0 15 8¾ | 0 14 4¾ | 0 15 1¾ |
| educt trimmings | 0 2 8¼ | 0 2 4½ | 0 2 7¼ | 0 2 4¾ | 0 2 6¼ |
| ear earnings per week | 0 13 6¼ | 0 11 10¾ | 0 13 1½ | 0 12 0 | 0 12 7½ |
| THIRD QUARTER | | | | | |
| rnings of 3d quarter | 4 6 5½ | 3 12 5 | 2 16 1 | 2 9 10 | 3 6 2¼ |
| erage earnings per week | 0 6 7¾ | 0 5 6¾ | 0 4 3¾ | 0 3 10 | 0 5 1 |
| educt trimmings | 0 1 1¼ | 0 0 11 | 0 0 8½ | 0 0 7½ | 0 0 10 |
| ear earnings per week | 0 5 6½ | 0 4 7¾ | 0 3 7¼ | 0 3 2½ | 0 4 3 |

* The trimmings are taken at 2d in the shilling, or ⅙th of the gross earnings. This, I have the word of the woman furnishing the account, is rather under than above the actual cost.

| | 1846 £ s. d. | 1847 £ s. d. | 1848 £ s. d. | 1849 £ s. d. | Average for four Years £ s. d |
|---|---|---|---|---|---|
| | | FOURTH QUARTER | | | |
| Earnings of 4th quarter | 2 19 7½ | 3 5 5 | 2 9 5 | 2 1 7¾ | 2 14 0 |
| Average earnings per week | 0 4 7 | 0 5 0¼ | 0 3 9½ | 0 3 3¾ | 0 4 1 |
| Deduct trimmings | 0 0 9 | 0 0 10 | 0 0 7½ | 0 0 6½ | 0 0 8 |
| Clear earnings per week | 0 3 10 | 0 4 2¼ | 0 3 2 | 0 2 9¼ | 0 3 5 |
| | | FOR THE YEAR | | | |
| Earnings for the whole year | 23 5 4½ | 20 17 6 | 17 9 2½ | 17 9 2¾ | 19 15 3 |
| Average earnings per week | 0 8 11¼ | 0 8 0¼ | 0 6 8½ | 0 6 8½ | 0 7 7 |
| Deduct trimmings | 0 1 5¾ | 0 1 4 | 0 1 1¼ | 0 1 1¼ | 0 1 3 |
| Weekly earnings of 2 for the year | 0 7 5½ | 0 6 8¼ | 0 5 7¼ | 0 5 7¼ | 0 6 4 |
| Weekly earnings of each for ditto | 0 3 8¾ | 0 3 4 | 0 2 9½ | 0 2 9½ | 0 3 2 |
| Deduct rent of each | 0 1 3 | 0 1 3 | 0 1 3 | 0 1 3 | 0 1 3 |
| To pay for food and clothes per week, each | 0 2 5¾ | 0 2 1 | 0 1 6½ | 0 1 6½ | 0 1 11 |
| Ditto per day, each | 0 0 4¼ | 0 0 3½ | 0 0 2½ | 0 0 2½ | 0 0 3 |

From the above it will be seen that, after paying their rent, all these two work women had left to purchase food and clothing was, throughout the year 1846, *fourpence farthing* each per day—throughout the year 1848, *twopence halfpenny*—and throughout the present year, *twopence halfpenny* also. To get this amount each, it should be remembered that they had to work from eighteen to twenty hours every day, including Sundays.

In every year, they told me, there are generally seven months, and at the very least six, that they cannot pay rent, and during the other six months they have to work night and day in order to clear off the back rent. They can't go into a better lodging, because they can't get credit for the winter months. The room is taken furnished. It is a small attic, seven feet square, without any fireplace and several panes are gone from the windows. There is scarcely any furniture; only one chair. The other party has to sit on the bed. They pay 2s. 6d. a week. The first winter they came the landlady insisted on having her rent every week, and that winter they were three months and never had a bit of bread, not a crumb, to eat. They used to live on oatmeal altogether. Frequently they had a pennyworth between them for the whole day. After the first year the landlady, having had experience of their honesty, allowed them to go on credit during the winter. In fact, they were obliged to allow their rent to go to 12s. 6d., in arrear the first winter of all. But they paid it directly they had work, and since then the landlady never troubles them during the winter for the rent—never, indeed, asks for it. She is satisfied that they will pay it directly they can. They are convinced that no one else would do the same thing, for their landlady is very kind to them, and allows them the occasional use of her fire.

They never go in debt for anything but their rent. If they haven't got money they go without—never run credit for anything to eat. If they have anything to pledge, they get their food that way; and if they are quite "up", and have nothing to pledge, "why then," said one of the poor old creatures, smiling to me, "we starve : yes, we're obliged to it. We'd rather do that than go in debt. We should always be thinking about it. I'm sure, last winter the rent we owed was always in my head. When I went to bed and when I got up, I was afraid we should never rub it off." One of the parties is an old maiden woman, and the other a widow. The one is 43 years, and the widow 54. They have been working together seven years. The widow was in better circumstances. Her husband was a farmer in Yorkshire, and her father was a very large farmer in the same county. The maiden woman was formerly in service; now she is afflicted with the lumbago, and is able only to work at her needle. Today she is washing, and she will be ill for two or three days afterwards. . . .

*Second Test—meeting of needlewomen forced to take to the streets*

I now come to the second test that was adopted in order to verify my conclusions. This was the convening of such a number of needle-women and slop-workers as would enable me to arrive at a correct *average* as to the earnings of the class. I was particularly anxious to do this, not only with regard to the more respectable portion of the operatives, but also with reference to those who, I had been given to understand, resorted to prostitution in order to eke out their subsistence. I consulted a friend who is well acquainted with the habits and feelings of the slop-workers as to the possibility of gathering together a number of women who would be willing to state that they had been forced to take to the streets on account of the low prices for their work. He told me he was afraid from shame of their mode of life becoming known, it would be almost impossible to collect together a *number* of females who would be ready to say as much *publicly*. However, it was decided that at least the experiment should be made, and that everything should be done to assure the parties of the strict privacy of the assembly. It was arranged that the gentleman and myself should be the only male persons visible on the occasion, and that the place of meeting should be as dimly lighted as possible, so that they could scarcely see or be seen by one another or by us. Cards of admission were issued and distributed as privately as possible, and to my friend's astonishment, as many as twenty-five came, on the evening named, to the appointed place—intent upon making known the sorrows and sufferings that had driven them to fly to the streets in order to get the bread which the wretched prices paid for their labour would not permit them to obtain.

Never in all history was such a sight seen or such tales heard. There, in the dim haze of the large bare room in which they met, sat women and girls, some with babies suckling at their breasts—others in rags—and even these borrowed, in order that they might come and tell their misery to the world. I have witnessed many a scene of sorrow lately; I have heard stories that have unmanned me; but never till last Wednesday had I heard or seen anything so solemn, so terrible, as this. If ever eloquence was listened to, it was in the outpourings of those poor lorn mothers' hearts for their base-born little ones, as each told her woes and struggles, and published her shame amid the convulsive sobs of the others—nay, of all present. Behind a screen, removed from sight, so at not to wound the modesty of the women—who were nevertheless aware of their presence—sat two reporters from this Journal, to take down *verbatim* the confessions and declarations of those assembled, and to them I am indebted for the following report of the statements made at the meeting:

A gentleman who has for many years taken a deep interest in the subject, and myself, severally addressed those present, and urged them to speak without fear, and to tell the whole truth with regard to their situations, assuring them that the only way to obtain their deliverance from their present condition was, that they should speak for themselves, tell their own tale, simply, and without exaggeration, with the most scrupulous regard to truth.

Thus admonished, the following statements were made by the parties:

The first speaker was a middle-aged woman, who stood up and said:

"I am a slop-worker, and sometimes make about 3s. 6d. a week, and sometimes less. I have been drove to prostitution sometimes, not always, through the bad prices. For the sake of my lodgings and a bit of bread I've been obligated to do what I am very sorry to do, and look upon with disgust. I can't live by what I get by work. The woman who employs me, and several more besides, gets 11d. and 1s. a pair for the trowsers we make, and we get only 4d. or 5d. We can't do more than a pair a day, and sometimes a pair and a half. It's starving. I can't get a cup of tea and a bit of bread. I was married, and am left a widow, and have been forced to live in this distressed manner for the last four years. I've been to several different people to get work, but they are all alike in taking advantage of our unfortunate situation.". . .

The next speaker was one with scarcely any clothing upon her back. She said :

"I'm a slop-worker, and have got a little boy eighteen months old, and I'm not able to do much work. I work with another woman, and get 7d. and 6d. a pair for doing trowsers. I'm often out of work, and the last fortnight or three weeks I've had nothing to do. I've got no husband, but am compelled to live with a man to support me, for the sake of my child. The father of the child is a labouring man in the docks. He helps to support the child when he can, but he is sometimes employed only two or three days in the week, and at other times not that. He hasn't left me. He gets 2s. 4d. a day when he has work. He has work today, and last Friday was the first he had for a fortnight. He applies daily at the docks, and can't get it; but when they're busy he gets his turn. I can state solemnly in the presence of my Maker, that I live with him only to get a living and save myself from doing worse. But if I could get a living otherwise, I can't say I would leave him. At my own work, I sometimes make 2s., and at others only 1s. 6d. a week. He's willing to marry me the first day that he can afford; but he hasn't the money to pay the fees. Sometimes he is a fortnight or three weeks, and even a month without any work at all, and last week we were forced to go to the Refuge for the Destitute."

The next was a good-looking girl. Her father had driven her from home, and she could not live by shoe-binding. She said :

"Five years ago my father turned me out of doors. The shoe-binding is so low that I wasn't able to pay 1s. a week for my lodging, and that caused me to turn out into the street. Then it was three weeks before I ever was in a bed. I sat on London-bridge a fortnight before Christmas five years ago. My father took me home again three years ago, but he turned me out again, and I was forced to go back to the street. He says he can't keep us at home. He is a soap-boiler. My mother died about twelve years ago. There were nine of us when she died, and we're all living still. My father said he could not keep us any longer. I work whenever I can get it at trowsers work; but can't get it always. I used to get it first-hand till lately; but latterly I've worked for a woman who takes it in. I do a pair a day, and sometimes more. I sometimes used to make 1s. 6d., and at others 2s. a week; and when I have the best employment I can generally earn about half-a-crown.". . .

The next speaker made the following statement:

"I am a shirt-maker, and make about three shirts a day, at 2½d. a piece, every one of them having seven button-holes. I have to get up at six in the morning, and work till twelve at night to do that. I buy thread out of the price; and I cannot always get work. I sometimes make trowsers; but I have not constant work with both put together. I sometimes make 2s. 6d. a week; 3s. is the most I ever made, and I have to buy thread out of that. Three shirts a day takes ¾d. for thread; that will be 18 farthings a week, or 4½., say 6d. altogether. So that my regular wages are not more than 2s. 6d. or 2s., sometimes not more than 1s. 6d. I am now living with a young man. I am compelled to do so, because I could not support myself. I know he would marry me if he could. He is a looking-glass frame maker. He works for himself, and hawks them about. Sometimes he has not money enough to buy wood. He used to make more when I first lived with him than he does now. Sometimes he earns nothing. He has earned nothing for the last three weeks. If he had money I know he would marry me. Sometimes he is out all day, and does not get a farthing—not a bit to eat. Sometimes we have been for two days with a bit of dry bread and cold water. We both strive hard for work, that we do. I don't believe anybody can try harder to get work than we do.". . .

This one had scarcely sat down before a woman with an infant in her arms stood up, and spoke as follows:

"I was left a widow with two children, and I could get no work to keep me. I picked up with this child's father, and thought with the little help that he could give me I might be able to keep my children; but after all I was forced by want and distress and the trouble of child-bed to sell all I had to get a bit of victuals. I was forced to go into the house at Wapping to be delivered of this child. This woman (pointing to a neighbour) took care of my other children. He (the father) came to me, gave me 5s., and told me that if I could take a room he would do all he could for me. I took a room at 1s. 6d. a week, and bought half a truss of straw; and he told me he would marry me if ever it was in his power. I could not go out into the world again; but this woman will tell you that all I have got under me and over me you may buy for 6d. I live with that man still, and sometimes I have not a bit to eat. I thought more of my little boy having a bit to eat than myself. He had been stealing some coals, and he is now imprisoned. I was forced to let him go to try to get a bit of victuals, for I had nothing more to make away with.

My boy was taken up for stealing 3 lbs. of coals. He did not bring the coals to me; he was taken before he could get home. I believe he stole them for my sake; not to spend in any other way but to get a bit of bread and a bit of fire for his mother."

Another orphan then got up :

"I was left an orphan ten years ago," said she, "and took to needle-work. I took to slop-shirts, but could not get a living by that, and so I took to the seaming of trowsers. Still I could not get a living, and by that means I lost what bit of furniture I had left. I could not pay my rent, and was in arrears three weeks. My landlord turned me out, and I had nowhere to go, till I was taken to a brothel by a person that I met, but I don't know who it was. I remained in that condition till such time as I fell in the family way, and the young man I fell in that state by went away and left me destitute. I was 14 days and 14 nights and never saw a bed. It froze hard and snowed very fast, and I was left exposed till it pleased God Almighty to send the person I live with now to help me. I am advanced in the family way at present. I am living with a man now, but not in the married state. It's not in his power to marry me, his work won't allow it; and he's not able to support me in the manner he wishes, and keep himself. He has never but two meals a day—breakfast and supper. I think he would marry me if he had the marriage fees, willingly. It's not in my power to afford better clothing than I've got on. I hadn't a dinner today. I don't consider that I've tasted a Sunday's dinner for six months. I can't earn myself 4d. a-day, taking one day with another. I've 1s. 6d. a week rent to pay out of that, and firing and food to find. Unless I was to go to other means, it wouldn't be in my power to do anything to support myself. I don't do it from inclination. I would leave it as soon as I could. I've been forced occasionally to resort to prostitution; but now I'm trying, by living on the small pittance I can get, to avoid it. I detest it : I was never reared to it. I was brought up to the church and to attend to my God. I was always shown a different pattern; but misfortune over-took me. If I could get a living without it I would leave it."

The next speaker was the most eloquent of all. I never before listened to such a gush of words and emotion, and perhaps never shall again. She spoke without the least effort, in one continued strain, for upwards of half an hour, crying half hysterically herself, while those around her sobbed in sympathy :

"Between ten and eleven years ago I was left a widow with two young children, and far advanced in pregnancy with another. I had no means of getting a living, and therefore I thought I would take up slop-work. I got work at slop-shirts—what they call second-hand. I had no security, and therefore could not get the work myself from the warehouse. Two months before I was confined, I seemed to do middling well. I could manage three or four shirts—what they call "rowers"—at 3d. each, by sitting closely at work from five or six in the morning till about nine or ten at night; but of course, when I was confined I was unable to do anything. As soon as I was able to sit up I undertook slop-shirts again; but my child being sickly, I was not able to earn so much as before. Perhaps I could earn 9d. a day by hard work, when I get 3d. each shirt; but sometimes I only get 2½d., and I have been obliged to do them at 1½d. each, and, with my child sickly, could only earn 4d., or at most 6d. a day. At other times I hadn't work. On the average I calculate that I have earnt 9d. a day when the prices were better.

"1s. 9d. a week went for rent; and as to a living, I don't call it that; I was so reduced with it, and my child being so bad, it couldn't be considered a living. I was obliged to live on potatoes and salt; and for nine weeks together I lived on potatoes, and never knew what it was to have a half-quartern loaf—for the loaf was 9d. then. By that means my health was declining, and I wasn't able to do hard work. My child's health, too, was declining, and I was obliged to pawn the sheets of my bed and my blankets to procure a shilling. At last I found it impossible to pay my rent. I owed 7s. arrears, and my landlady plagued me much to pay her. She advised me to raffle away a large chest that I had. I did so, and gained 12s., and then paid her the 7s. I owed her; but I became so reduced again, that I was obliged to get an order to get into the 'house'.

"I didn't wish to go in, but I wanted relief and knew I couldn't get it without doing so. I felt it a hard trial to have my children taken from my bosom : we had never been parted before, and I can't help remembering what were my feelings then as a mother who always loved her children. I thought rather than we should be parted that I would make away with myself. But still I applied to the parish, and never shall forget the day that I did so. I was told to go, and I would get a loaf by applying. I went in, and my heart was full at the thought of taking home a quartern loaf to my starving children. But I was disappointed; and seeing a loaf given out to other parties, I can say that I should have felt glad even of the crumbs to take home to my poor children if I could have got near enough. Christmas came round, and I thought, poor things, they will be without a Christmas dinner, and so I got an order to go into the Wapping workhouse. Yet my feelings were such that it was impossible I could enter, and I remained out five weeks after I had got the order, and pledged, as far as I could, anything that would fetch 2d., obtaining also a little assistance from slop-work. But I got so little that I found it impossible to live. The time came to get another order, and I went with my clothes patched from top to bottom, yet I trust they were clean. And never shall I forget that Saturday afternoon as I travelled along Gravel-lane to the 'house', with feelings that it was impossible for me to enter, for I thought, 'How can I bear to have my dear children taken away from me—they have never been taken away from me before?' I reflected, 'What can I do but go there,' so I mustered courage at all events to get to the gate; and, oh! it is impossible to describe what my feelings were as I passed through.

"I was admitted to a room where they were toasting the bread for the mistress's tea. A little girl was there, and she said, 'Look at these dear little children, I will give them a bit of the toast.' The children took it, and thought it very nice, but they little thought that we were so soon to be parted. The first was seven years old, the second three, and the infant was in my arms. A mother's feelings are better felt than described. The children were taken and separated, and then, oh my God! what I felt no tongue can tell. (Here the woman's emotions overcame her, and she could not proceed with her narrative for weeping. At length recovering she continued): I was in hopes of getting my children back within a week or two, but my business could not be settled so soon. My babe took the measles; they went inwardly, and it took a deep decline. I knew it was very bad, and asked leave to go and see him. The mistress was very kind, and gave me leave. I found my child very bad, and the infant in my arms seemed declining every day. My feelings then were such as I can't tell you. I thought—'Oh! if I could only get out and have my children with myself, how much better it would be.' I hurried them to settle my business for me; it originated in a dispute between St. George's and Wapping about our parish, my husband being at the sugar-house at work.

"At last the dispute was settled, but the one child died, whilst the other—the youngest—was dying. I was so anxious to get out that I could not wait till my child was buried. I asked relief to be settled on me out of doors, and it was granted. I was allowed 1s. a week and two loaves. The acting master asked me if I had any place to go to. I said I would take a room. 'Have you any bed?' he asked. I said 'yes, but no bedding.' I was obliged to pledge it before I entered the house. He was a kind man, and said no doubt the overseers would get my blankets and bedding for me. 'My dear woman,' he said (for he saw I was an affectionate mother, and that I had nothing to begin with) 'here is a shilling for you.' He took it out of his own pocket, and I thought it was very kind. The children were brought from Limehouse, and one of them was dead at the time. I went with an anxious heart to see its corpse, but I felt 'I cannot stay with

you till you are buried.' Well, I found my poor boy but a shadow—
a mere skeleton of what he had been. I was overcome with my
feelings, and I thought, 'Here is one dead, and another near death!'
But I got up, and before even I went to my room in Whitechapel
I went to a doctor; but he said the boy was too far gone—that he
wanted no medicine, but nourishing, for he was in a decline. I took
him home, and said, 'One shilling a-week and two loaves will not
support us; there are three of us, and we can't be supported by that,
with this sickness. Well, I must take to slop-shirts again.' I did so.
But I was not able to earn so much as I used to do. I sometimes did
three a-day at 2½d., sometimes three at 1½d., having needles and
thread to find out of that. Half an ounce of coffee went us three
times, and it had to be boiled up again, which made but a scanty
meal with a few potatoes. However, I was very glad to put up with it.

"And then at last I found it impossible to get on; when a man
lodging in the house was anxious to get a partner, and made offers
to me. I thought it better to accept them than to do worse; and by
his promising to be good to me, I did comply. Soon after, it pleased
God to take my other boy from me; till at last I was in trouble
again, and the result was that I was in the family way, and thought,
'Now, what shall I do? My character is gone; it was good before,
but now it is blemished.' The man did his part as well as he could,
but the work he got was so little that he was not able to support us
in a proper manner. We took a room together, and I am sorry to say
some days he brought home nothing—other days perhaps, no more
than 2½d. or 3d., or a few half-pence, that he might pick up for
carrying a letter to the Post-Office, or the like, for a gentleman.
Some days, perhaps, he would earn 1s., and for the next three days
again not a farthing. And I earned so little myself, that the times
going on so bad, I did not know what to do. I told the man that he
and I must part; for I had seen nothing but starvation with him.

"My time was up, and it pleased the Lord that I was delivered
of twins (here the poor creatures seemed visibly affected with the
multiplied distresses of the speaker), and then my hands were full
again. I looked at my babies, and there being two of them, felt that
I could never support them, and I became delirious for hours. The
doctor, a kind-hearted man, said many a lady would be glad to
have two such children as these. I said, God bless them, I shall have
matches to sell with them to get them a bit of bread. Before I was
able I was obliged to turn out. It was winter time, and I tried slop-
shirts again to get a living, and was unable to earn 6d. a day.

"I got 10s. behind in my rent, my landlord threatened to take my
sticks if I did not pay; and at last I went into the streets with
matches. It was on a Saturday night, and I went to Shoreditch,

thinking I would not be known, and fixed my position opposite the church, before a large china warehouse, kept by a man who, it was said, would not allow any one to stand before his door. I was determined to persevere till turned away, as nothing could be done without it, and my children must have bread. I was not turned away, because I think the man sympathized with me, and I stood that night till my own and my child's pockets were full with the pence we received. At eleven o'clock, my child said her pocket string had broke, and she would lose her money if she did not go away. We therefore went home, and on counting our money, we had got no less than 6s. 3d., which we considered a good day's work. I said we would stop the lion's mouth with 3s., and so I paid 3s. of my rent that night. We had a meat dinner on Sunday. It was ox's cheek, with a few potatoes, and that we considered a glorious dinner. Next Saturday night I went out again to Shoreditch, expecting as good success as before, but holding my head down like a bulrush, for fear that somebody would pass that knew me. I had not stood long before a female companion of my early days came up and observed me; she looked at me and said, 'Susan, in the name of goodness, is that you— and what has brought you here?' I said, Oh, Mary Ann, don't ask me, for I can't answer you—shame has brought me here. She offered me 1s., which I at first refused to take, as she was a poor woman herself; but she made me comply, saying she wished she could afford more. Well, I did not succeed so well as I had done before, because I only got 4s. altogether, including my friend's 1s., but I felt very well satisfied, as it was much better than slop-work. Well, one of my twins soon after died, and was buried by the parish. I had no parish relief then, for what I had done would make me be treated like a common prostitute, and I could not bear that. At last, one cold, snowy Saturday night, I only obtained 9d., and after that resolved to go out no more. At last I consented, as the man wished me, to live with him again. But he earned very little, and I only got 2d. for what I had got 2½d. for before at slop-work, and five farthings for what used to be 1½d.

"Utterly distressed, I thought again of making away with my children. I locked the door, with the intention of taking their lives first and then my own, but God touched my conscience, and I could not do it. I kneeled down at the bed-side and prayed God to hold my hand. I got up with a grateful heart, determined to trust in Providence. But I owed my landlord 12s., and he threatened to take my things. He owed £12 of rent himself, however; and when the broker took my landlord's things he took mine. I was turned into the street on New-Year's-eve—that was five years ago—in a state of pregnancy, with my little twin and my little girl along with me. I stood there till eleven, and I thought of an old lady I knew who kept a kitchen at King-street, and sent the man I was living with to ask her to give me a night's shelter. She said, 'Yes, as long as I have a roof above my head I will give you refuge.' I was very thankful; but could not expect them to turn out of their bed to give it to us, so we lay upon the floor without taking off our clothes.

"At last the man and I got a garret for ourselves, and, through the kindness of my friends and one of the gentlemen now present, I got a little furniture for it. I determined to separate from the man, being deeply impressed of the sin in which I was living. I was 8s. in debt at that time. I took to the trowsers again. My girl learned, and we got a warehouse. I was not very quick myself, and we could not earn enough to support us. I am confident we did not earn 3s. 6d. each on the average. We earnt 5s. and 6s. between us, and if we earnt 7s. by sitting up two nights a week, we felt that we had done a good week's work. A niece of mine came to me from Sheffield, about this time, and set to work with us. The three of us could earn 10s. or 11s. a week between us by sitting up three nights a week. Coal, candle, and twist had to be found out of our earnings. My niece left us, being dissatisfied with her lot. I continued in that way, away from the man, for two years, and at last found it would not do.

"I got married two years ago, and have given up slop-work, and go out charring and washing. My daughter still continues at slop-work, however; but I am sure she could not live by it if she had nothing done for her, and depended on that alone. My firm belief, before God and man, is, that three out of every four of the young women of London who do slop-work are obliged to resort to private or public prostitution to enable them to live. But I hope better things are coming at last; and God bless the gentlemen, I say, who have set this inquiry a-going to help the poor slop-workers, and I hope that public attention being now called to these matters, the oppressed will be oppressed no longer, and that the Parliament House even will interpose to protect them. But I am sorry to say the good are not always the powerful, nor the powerful always the good."

For a few minutes no one spoke. All were evidently pondering upon the tale they had just heard. . . .

After this the following pathetic statement was made :

"I am a tailoress, and I was brought to ruin by the foreman of the work, by whom I had a child. Whilst I could make an appearance I had to work, but as soon as I was unable to do so I lost it. I had an afflicted mother to support, who was entirely dependent upon me. She had the tic-douloureux for three months, and was unable to do anything for herself. I went on so for some months, and we were half starved, by means of my having so little work. I could only earn from 5s. to 6s. a week to support three of us, and out of that I had 1s. 6d. to pay for rent, and the trimmings to buy, which cost me 1s. a week full. I went on till I could go on no longer, and we were turned out into the street because we could not pay the rent—me and my child; but a friend took my mother. Everyone turned their back upon me—not a friend stretched out a hand to save me. For six weeks I never lay down in a bed; my child and me passed all that time in the streets.

"At last of all I met a young man, a tailor, and he offered to get me work for his own base purposes. I worked for him—worked for him till I was in the family way again. I worked till I was within two months of my confinement. I had 1s. a day, and I took a wretched kitchen at 1s. a week, and 2s. I had to pay to have my child minded when I went to work. My mother left her friend's and went into the house, but I took her out again, she was so wretched, and she thought she could mind the child. In this condition we were all starving together. No one would come near us who knew my disgrace. and so I resolved I would not be my mother's death, and I left her. She went to her friend's, but she was so excited at going that it caused her death, and she died an hour after she got into her friend's house. An inquest was held upon her, and the jury returned a verdict that she died through a horror of going into the workhouse. I was without a home. I worked till I was within two months of my confinement, and then I walked the streets for six weeks, with my child in my arms.

"At last I went into Wapping Union; my child was taken from me, and there (bursting into tears) he was murdered. I mean he was torn from me, and when I next saw him he was a mere shadow. I took my discharge, and took him out, dying as he was. I took one in my arms, and my boy, dying as he was, and we wandered the streets for two or three days and nights. I then went back to the house. The matron said she would not take my child from me. She said he was dying, and he should die beside me. He died eleven days after we went in. I took my discharge again. I tried again to get a living, but I found it impossible, for I had no home, no friends, no means to get work. I then went in again, and the Lord took my second child.

"I came out again and went into a situation. I remained in that situation fourteen months, when I was offered some work by a friend, and I have been at that work ever since. I have a hard living, and I earn from 4s. 6d. to 5s. a week. My children and mother are both dead. The tailor never did anything for me. I worked for him and had 1s. a day. I never had one to stretch out a hand to save me, or I never should have had a second fall. From seven in the morning till one or two o'clock I work at making waistcoats and coats. I have 5d. a piece for double-breasted waistcoats and coats, and 10d. and 11d. a piece for slop coats. I can assure you I can't get clothes or things to keep me in health. I never resorted to the streets since I had the second child.". . .

After having made these statements, they were asked what were their lowest earnings last week, when it appeared that four had earned under 1s., four under 1s. 6d., four under 2s., one under 2s. 6d. One woman said 3s. 6d. had been earned between two of them, another said she had earned 3s. 6d., while a third declared she had not earned anything. Three said they had parted with their work for food. It was the unanimous declaration of the whole present, that if the meeting had been more generally known several hundreds would have attended, who would conscientiously have made the same declaration they had done—that they were forced into a wrong course of life by the lowness of their wage.

In answer to a question whether any had other clothes than what they appeared in, the very idea of a change of garments appeared to excite a smile. One and all declared they had not, and most asserted that even those they wore were not their own. One said, "This bonnet belongs to another woman;" another said, "This shawl belongs to my neighbour;" another said, "I have no frock, because I had to leave it in pawn for 6d.;" another said, "I have been forced to sit up this afternoon and put many a patch on this old frock, for the purpose of making my appearance here this evening;" another said, "The gown I have got on does not belong to myself;" while still another added, "I had to take the petticoat off my child, for 6d. to get victuals last Sunday morning."

### Statistics of the meeting below

Whilst the meeting above reported was taking place, a large number, hearing that the female slopworkers had been requested to assemble, had congregated in the room below, and we immediately descended to take the statistics of the earnings and conditions of those who had collected there. At this meeting there were 62 females present. Of these, 3 were under the age of 20; 13 were between 20 and 30, 19 were between 30 and 40, 13 were between 40 and 50, ten were between 50 and 60, and 3 between 70 and 80. Of these, 30 were married, 23 were widows, 9 were single. There were 8 widows with one child, 4 with 2 children and 2 with 3. There were 5 married women with 1 child, 4 with 2, 6 with 3, 1 with 4, 3 with 5, and 1 with 7 children. 22 worked first handed, and 32 second, none appeared to work at third-hand. 4 were living at the houses of "sweaters", having tea and lodgings found them. The earnings of last week were—21 below 1s.; 7 below 1s. 6d.; 6 below 2s.; 5 below 2s. 6d.; 10 below 3s.; 1 below 3s. 6d.; 1 below 4s.; 2 below 5s.—below 6s., none; and the inquiry as to whether there were any who earned 7s. present was thought so absurd, that it was received with shouts of laughter.

They all agreed that they must work hard, and sit up till twelve or one at night, to make from 6d. to 9d. a day clear; and that, taking one week's earnings with another, 1s. 6d. a week might be the average earnings throughout the year.

That they were several months in the year without work was the unanimous declaration. Opinions seemed to be equally divided whether for four or six months.

There were present twenty-three shirt-makers, one of whom made shirts at three farthings a piece and found cotton. The other prices and number of individuals present were—at 1d., 4; 1¼d., 10; 1½d., 10; 2d., 13; 2½d., 9; 3d., 6; 3½d., 6; 4d., 2; 4½d., 2; 5d., none; 6d., answered by great laughter.

Of trowsers makers there were 11. The prices at which they worked were—2 for 1½d. a pair, 7 at 2d., 5 at 3d., 3 at 4d., 4 at 5d., 7 at 6d., 1 at 8d., and 1 at 10d.—all finding trimmings, at 1d. per pair.

There were a few makers of waistcoats, who said the prices averaged from 2½d. to 7d., the latter price being paid for satin ones (laughter). It was also stated that blouses were made from 2½d. to 5d., finding trimmings. Jackets, of which a woman produced one as a pattern, were 2¾d.; two could be made in a day, and the trimmings would cost ¼d. This woman worked first-hand.

There were 17 coat hands. The prices and number of hands present were—3 for 5d. a coat, some at 6d. and 8d. One woman said she got as high as 1s. 9d.; but the ordinary price was from 10d. to 1s., and these lined all through. Tweeds, fustians, moleskins, and pilots were from 1s. to 1s. 3d., heavy lined work. A 1s. coat would cost from 1½d. to 2d. for trimmings.

An attempt was made to ascertain from those present how many might be engaged in slop working. One shop, it was stated, employed from 500 to 600 hands, another about 150, another from 300 to 400, another 1,000, another 40 to 50, another 500, another 300, another 600, another 50, another 30, another 50, another 1,000, another 600, another 250, another 40, another 100, another 300, another 25; being altogether, on a rough estimate, from 6,000 to 7,000 persons employed in this wretched mode of subsistence.

The question how many had meat every day for dinner seemed to these poor creatures an exquisite joke, and they laughed heartily on its being put. Four had meat three days a week, and 29 on Sundays, the parties stating, at the same time, that they were indebted for this to their husbands, none got it by their own labour; they could hardly get a cup of tea.

Another question that greatly excited their merriment was how many had been obliged to go to the pawnshop, as it was found that nearly every one of them was familiar with that refuge for the unfortunate. Four of them had goods pledged to the extent of £4, two to the value of £3, eleven of £2, thirteen of £1, seven of 10s., four of 5s., and fourteen had goods in pawn under 5s. value; thirteen widows and single women had parted with their beds, and twenty-six had parted with their under-clothing. These facts were received with such signs of astonishment that it was evident even those assembled were not aware of the destitution of the workwomen.

Of the earnings of the husbands of the married women, it appeared that one earned under 15s. last week; nineteen earned under 10s.; six earned under 5s.; three under 4s.; one under 2s.; three under 1s.; while six had earned nothing whatever. Of these last, the women told piteous tales. One had been paralyzed seven months; two were dock labourers, but had earned nothing for weeks; another, a plasterer, had been out of work for twelve weeks; while another could get no work since February last.

There were three who paid under 1s. for their lodgings; nineteen who paid under 1s. 6d.; eighteen under 2s.; ten under 2s. 6d.; one under 3s.; three under 3s. 6d.

Ten had been forced to go into the workhouse; nineteen had been forced to pawn their work; thirty-one had been without food for a whole day through; five had fasted for a day and a half; while no fewer than seven had been obliged to go without food for the period of two days. Yet, with one single exception, none of these women would admit that they had ever had recourse to prostitution. Three had been driven to beg in the streets; one said she had often been very near taking to prostitution, but never did. They were, however, unanimous in declaring that a large number in the trade—probably one-fourth of the whole, or one-half of those who had no husband or parent to support them—resorted to the streets to eke out a living. Accordingly, assuming the Government returns to be correct, and that there are upwards of eleven thousand females under twenty living by needle and slop-work, the numerical amount of prostitution becomes awful to contemplate. One woman stated that all those who appeared with good clothes might be taken to resort to that mode of life; but she added, certainly with great truth, "you see there are none of that kind here."

This closed the meeting.

# THE TAILORS

## LETTER XVI—11 DECEMBER 1849[1]

If we wish to obtain a knowledge of the history and progress of the slop-trade, we must first inquire into the nature and characteristics of that art of which it is an inferior variety; and it is with this view that, before investigating the condition of the male slop-worker, I have made it my business to examine into the state of the Operative Tailors of London.

### Number of tailors

The Tailors, as a body, form a very large proportion of the population of London. Arranging the occupations of the people in the metropolis in the order of the number of individuals belonging to them, we shall find that the tailors stand fourth upon the list. First come the Domestic Servants of London, numbering as many as 168,000 individuals, and constituting about one-twelfth of the whole population of the metropolis. The second in the order of their numbers are the Labourers, who are 50,000 strong. Third in numerical rank stand the Boot and Shoe Makers, mustering upwards of 28,000; and fourth, the Tailors, amounting to 23,517. After them come the milliners and dressmakers, and then follow the commercial clerks—both of which classes comprised, at the time of taking the last census for London, upwards of 20,000 individuals.

Of the above 23,517 tailors, there are, according to the Post-office Directory, 2,748 in business for themselves. This leaves a total of 20,769 operatives. But several of those whose names are entered in the Directory are also, I am told, working men—that is to say, they act as journeymen as well as work upon their own account. We may, therefore, fairly estimate the number of operative tailors in the metropolis at not less than 21,000 individuals.[2]

[1] The letter began with a section on the costermongers, the subject of letters XII–XV.
[2] Using statistics for the inmates of workhouses and gaols (England and Wales), Mayhew here compared the poverty and criminality of the tailors with occupational groups already studied. His economic analysis of poverty was apparent when he gave the reader the chance to decide "how much of the pauperism arises from deficient wages, and how much from those habits of improvidence, which are the necessary consequence of uncertainty of employment."

*"Honourable" and "dishonourable" trades—trades societies*

The tailoring trade is divided by the workmen into "honourable" and "dishonourable". The honourable trade consists of that class who have the garments made on their own premises, at the supposed rate of 6d. per hour—the dishonourable, of those who give the work out to "sweaters", to be done at less than the standard price. The dishonourable part of the trade is again subdivided into the classes belonging to show-shops—that is such as do a cheap bespoke business—and those belonging to slop-shops, or, in plainer terms, to such as do a cheap ready-made business.

Of the 21,000 working tailors above specified as resident in London, I should add that there are not above 3,000 belonging to what is called the honourable portion of the trade. The remaining 18,000 are those who are engaged in the cheap, slop, or dishonourable trade. . . .

The journeymen tailors working for the "honourable" part of the trade are in "Union". This "Union" consists of six distinct societies, which meet at certain taverns or public-houses at the west end of the town. The number of journeymen at present in union is 3,000. In the year 1821 there were between 5,000 and 6,000. It is supposed that from two to three thousand have left the "honourable" trade and become "sweaters".

Besides the above-mentioned six societies, there are four "out-standing houses", as they are termed, which, though not acting in union with the six others, still are regulated by the same laws and conducted upon the same principles. Two of these are foreign societies, and two supply Stultz only with workmen. The number in connection with the four outstanding houses is 400.

The different societies are likewise used as houses of call for the masters. The men belonging to a particular society, who are out of employ, attend the house at the appointed call-times (there are three in the day). A master requiring extra hands directs the captain of the workshop to engage the requisite number. He generally sends to the society of which he is a member, and there the workmen who stand next upon the books are taken on.

*Legislation in connection with the trade*

The date and purport of the various enactments in connection with the trade I find stated as follows, in a memorial of the Operative Tailors of London, to the "Right Hon. the Lords of the Privy Council for Trade", in the year 1845 :

"So far back as the 33d Edward I, the 6th Henry VI and the 2nd and third Edward VI, the law directed that master tailors residing within the weekly bills of mortality should, under severe penalty, provide on their own premises healthful and commodious apartments wherein to execute to completion the materials entrusted to their skill and honour. From the 7th George I to the 8th George III chief magistrates were empowered to regulate the place of work, the hours and wages of journeymen tailors, within the weekly bills of mortality."

"Within these last twelve or fifteen years, however," says a subsequent memorial from the same parties, "the corrupt middle-man system has sprung up amongst us, which is the cause of leaving so many first-rate operatives unemployed the greater part of the year; for when two home workers, by working over-hours and Sabbath days, perform the work of three men employed on the premises of the master tailor, as intended by the Legislature, it must prove a great grievance to the numerous unemployed, who are compelled in hundreds of instances to make application for parochial relief, as well as the other private charities, for themselves and numerous families; a circumstance unknown until the corrupt middle-man system crept in amongst us.

"Many of our unemployed (continues the memorial) are compelled by necessity to make application to this class of middle-men for employment, who practise the most grievous impositions upon the persons employed by them, by reducing their wages and enforcing the truck system, by compelling the men to take their diet with them at whatever price they think proper to charge, though many of those men have large families of their own to support; and frequently by obliging their men to lodge with them."

Up to the year 1834, the 8th of George III ("which," I am told "regulated the time of labour for tailors at twelve hours per day, with the intent of compelling the masters to get their work done on the premises, as well as of equalising employment, and giving to each operative tailor the opportunity of earning a decent maintenance for himself and his family") was tolerably well adhered to; but at that period the masters gradually infringed the provisions of the act. Sweaters became numerous, and a general strike was the consequence. The strike acted antagonistically to the view of the journeymen tailors, and from that time up to the present, sweaters and underpaid workmen have increased, until the state of trade, as regards the operative tailors, appears to be approaching desperation.

*How to inquire*

Before entering upon my investigations, I consulted several of the most experienced and intelligent workmen, as to the best means of arriving at a correct opinion, respecting the state of the trade. It was agreed among us that, first, with regard to an estimate as to the amount of wages, I should see a hand employed at each of the different branches of the trade. After this I was to be taken to a person who was the captain or leading man of a shop; then to one who, in the technicality of the trade, had a "good chance" of work; and, finally, to one who was only casually employed. It was considered that these classes, taken in connection with the others, would give the public a correct view of the condition, earnings, and opinions of the trade. To prevent the chance of error, however, I begged to be favoured with such accounts of earnings as could be procured from the operatives. This, I thought, would place me in a fair condition to judge of the incomings and physical condition of the class; but still I was anxious to arrive at something like a criterion of the intellectual, political, and moral character of the people, and I asked to be allowed an interview with such persons as the parties whom I consulted might consider would fairly represent these peculiar features of their class to the world. The results of my inquiry I shall now proceed to lay before the public. Let me, however, first acknowledge the courtesy and consideration with which I was everywhere received; indeed, the operatives generally seemed especially grateful that their "cause" had at length been espoused by the press, and wherever I went I found all ready to give or obtain for me any information I might desire.

## A trowsers hand

The first I saw was a trowsers hand.

There are three classes of workmen, said my informant—coat, waistcoat, and trowsers hands. The trowsers hands are a class by themselves. Occasionally the persons who make the trowsers make waistcoats also, and these are called "small workers". But in some shops there are different hands for each different garment. For all garments there is what is termed a "log"; that log is the standard of prices in the trade. Formerly the rate of payment was by the day—6s. for twelve hours' work; but at the time of the general strike (about 16 or 18 years ago) the masters made out another scale of prices, and changed the mode of payment from day work to piece work. The prices of each garment, as determined by them, were regulated according to the quantity of work in it, and the time that such work would take to do. The workman by this log is still paid at the rate of 6d. per hour, but the time required to make each garment is estimated, and the workmen are paid by the garment rather than by the time. An ordinary pair of gentlemen's trowsers without pockets (such as are known in the trade as plain trowsers), are estimated at ten hours' work, and consequently are paid 5s. for. . . . Trowsers are generally very good jobs, because I am told the time they take in doing is reckoned "pretty fairly". By the change from day-work to piece-work the regular trowsers hands suffered scarcely any loss upon the prices of the garment. The time of making was justly reckoned, and the price paid in the regular and "honourable" trade remains about the same. The trowsers hands have not suffered so much by the change of payment from day-work to piecework as by the prevalence of the system of sweating, which has increased considerably since the alteration in the rate of payment.

*Visit to a coat hand*

Next I visited a coat hand. He lived in a comfortable, first-floor, and had invited several fellow-workmen to meet me. . . . There are generally three hands, he told me, engaged upon a coat. One makes the collar and sleeves, and the two others are engaged each upon one of the fore parts, or right or left side of the coat. The prices paid for making each of these parts of the coat depend upon the quantity of the work. These prices are regulated by the log of the shop. There is no general log for the West-end, but each particular house fixes its own price for the different garments to be made— or rather each particular house estimates the time required, for making each garment as it thinks fit, and pays at the rate of 6d. an hour for the work. . . .

A person who was present at the house of my informant, assured me that the shop for which he worked paid only 15s. 3d. for precisely the same quantity of work as that for which my informant's shop paid 16s.—the amount of work in the coat being estimated by the one master at two days six-and-a-half hours, and at two days eight hours by the other. All agreed that there are many houses in the "honourable" trade who estimate the time even much lower than the above; so that the log, instead of being a general standard, appears to be merely an arbitrary measure as to time. It is generally understood among the workmen who "belong to society" that they are not to work for less than sixpence per hour. The masters are well aware of this, and consequently never offer to pay less, but avail themselves of their privilege of reducing the estimate as to the time of making. If they wish to have a coat at a lower price than is usually paid, they declare that it takes so many hours less to make. The workmen often object to this, and the consequence is, the master seeks out other hands, who are willing to accept the work at the time stated.

In the year 1834 the system of payment was changed from day work to piece work. Before that time, each man employed received 6d. per hour for every hour that he was upon the establishment; it mattered not whether the master found him in work or not, he was paid all the same. Since the piece-work system. however, men are kept for days upon the establishment without receiving a penny. It is a general rule now throughout the trade for masters to keep more hands than they have employment for, especially in the slack or "vacation", as it is called. The effect of the piece-work system has been this, I am told—that the workman has to work now a day and a half for a day's wages, and that system alone has been instrumental to the reduction of prices. Men have more work to do now to get the same amount of money; and the consequence is, fewer hands are employed, and the surplus workmen offer their labour at a lower price.

Again, under the piece-work system, work is given out to be done. Hence, the journeyman who takes it home, and gets other hands to do it for him at a lower price than he himself receives, thus becomes changed into a sweater, or middleman, trading upon the labour of others. Finding that he can get the work done as low as he pleases, by employing women and children upon it, he goes to the master, and offers to do it at a lower price than is usually paid for it. Again, the price paid to each particular person is unknown to the other; so that the master, finding that the sweaters can get work done at almost any price, keeps continually cutting down the sum paid for making up the different garments, and then tries to force the regular hands to take the same price. Indeed, this is so frequently the case now in the shops, that I am told it is the common practice to take off the price paid for some "extra" upon a garment, and to threaten the workmen if they refuse to give it out to the sweaters. One master whom I have been told of, offered a journeyman certain work to do at a certain price. This the journeyman objected to do, whereupon the master stated "That others did it at a much lower figure." The workman replied, "That to do it and live they were obliged to make up their subsistence-money by prostitution." The answer of the master was, "That he cared nothing how they did it, he had to compete with others." The master, I am informed, bears the character of being a highly religious man.[3]

[3] The next informant, a waistcoat hand, also said that time was underestimated in his shop and attributed the fall in wages to competition from sweaters who employed cheap female labour. (For the impact of the wife's work on family life, see L.L. & L.P., 1861, II, 314–15.) Mayhew then printed several tabulated accounts of wages.

## Classes of workmen

I was desirous of seeing certain hands whose earnings might be taken as the type of the different classes of workmen in the trade. These, I had been informed, consisted of three distinct varieties : —First, those who are in constant employment at a particular shop as captains. Secondly, those who are tolerably well employed during the year, and have the preference for work as leading men in particular shops. Thirdly, those who are only casually employed either in the brisk season or when there is an extra amount of work to be done. The captains have continual employment, and receive from three shillings to six shillings per week over and above their own earnings, for the superintendence of the workmen. The leading men are generally employed. They are always connected with the shop, and remain there whether there is work to be done or not. The casual men are such as are taken on from the house of call when there is an extra amount of work to be done. The casual hand is engaged sometimes for two or three days, and sometimes for only two or three hours—to the great accommodation of masters, who are certain of having their work not only done to time, but paid for by the society to which the hands belong, if damaged or spoiled by the workmen.

## The captain of a shop

I consulted several gentlemen connected with the trade as to a person who might be taken as a fair type of the first class, and was directed to one who gave me the following information :

"I am a captain at an old-established house—indeed, one of the first and best at the West-end. I receive £1 19s. per week—that is, £1 16s. for my work, and 3s. extra for my duties as captain. My wages never amount to less. I have been twenty years employed at the same house, in the same capacity, and for the whole of those twenty years my earnings have remained the same. I have brought up a large family, and am landlord of the house in which I live. I pay £55 a year for it, and let off nearly sufficient to pay the rent. Four or five of my shopmates are housekeepers, and they have been in our establishment as many years as myself. It is one of the few honourable houses remaining in the trade, and may be cited as an instance of what the trade formerly was. The workmen in our establishment are all, without any exception, honest, sober, industrious, moral men; the majority of them are married, and maintain their wives and families in decency and comfort. The workmen there employed may be taken as a fair average of the condition, habits, and principles of the journeyman tailor throughout the trade before the puffing and sweating system became general.

"Ever since the alteration from day work to piece work the condition of the working tailor has materially declined. Under the day-working system a master, taking on a man from a house of call, was obliged to find him work or pay him his wages during the time he remained in his workshops; but now, under the piece-working system, a master will often keep and send for more men than he requires, knowing that he has only to pay for the quantity of work done, and being desirous to make as great a display of 'hands' as possible. Further than this, under the piece-working system, the workman has the opportunity of taking garments home to be made; and the consequence is, being out of the master's sight, he puts on inexperienced hands to the different parts of the garment —and then, finding that by the assistance of women and girls he can get through a greater amount of work than he possibly could by his own unaided labour, he seeks employment from other masters at a lower price than the regular standard, and so subsides into a sweater, and underbids the regular workman.

"The masters have now learned that tailoring work, under the sweating system, can be done at almost any price; and hence those who are anxious to force their trade by underselling their more honourable neighbours advertise cheap garments, and give the articles out to sweaters to be made by women and girls. By such means the regular tailor is being destroyed; indeed a man's own children are being brought into competition against himself, and the price of his labour is being gradually reduced to theirs. These evils, I am convinced, do not arise from over-population, but rather from over-competition. Women and children, who before were unemployed in the tailoring trade, now form a large proportion of the operative part of it. I know myself that, owing to the reduction of prices, many wives who formerly attended solely to their domestic duties and their family are now obliged to labour with the husband, and still the earnings of the two are less than he alone formerly obtained. The captains of shops in the honourable trade generally make as much as I do. By the sweating system I am satisfied the public are no gainers—the price of the workmen is reduced, but still the garment is no cheaper. The only parties profiting are the sweater and the dishonourable tradesman. In fact another profit has now to be paid; so that, though the party doing the work is paid less, still the sweater's profit, which has to be added, makes little or no difference in the price of the garment to the public. I know myself that it is so."

*A fair average of the fully employed tailor*

The next person I sought out was one who might be taken as a fair average of the industrious and fortunate workman. I was anxious to meet with a person whose earnings might be considered as a type, not of the *highest* wages received by the operatives, but of the earnings of those who are fully employed in a shop where the best prices are paid, and where the customers are of the highest rank. I consulted with a number of workmen as to a person of such a character, and I was sent to an individual who gave me the following statement :

"I have been fifteen years employed in the same house. It is one of the first-rate houses at the West-end. My master pays the best prices, and I consider him a very fair man. He gives the same price for the better class of garments as he did fifteen years ago. . . . It is now about five years ago since my master began to make any reduction upon the price paid for making any garment whatsoever. Before that every article was paid for at the rate of 6d. per hour; but between the years 1844 and 1845—I cannot call to mind the exact date—my master had a consultation with his captain as to making up the new cheap tweed wrappers, which were coming into general fashion at that time; and he decided upon paying for them at a rate which, considering the time they took to make, was less than the regular sixpence per hour. He said that the show-shops at the East-end were daily advertising tweed wrappers at such a low figure that his customers, seeing the prices in the news-papers, were continually telling him that if he could not do them they must go elsewhere. Since then cheap overcoats, or wrappers, have been generally made in our shop and I believe that my master would willingly give over making them, if it were not for the extreme competition which has been going on in the tailoring trade since their introduction. Amongst all the best and oldest houses in the trade at the West-end they are gradually introducing the making of the cheap paletots, Oxonians, Brighton coats, Chesterfields, &c., &c.; and even the first-rate houses are gradually subsiding into the cheap advertising slop tailors. If the principle goes on at the rate that it has been progressing for the last five years, the journeymen tailors must ultimately be reduced to the position of the lowest of the needlewomen.

"I have kept an account of my wages for the last 16 years; but I have destroyed several of the books, thinking them of no value. My wages have not declined since that period, because I am regularly employed, and my master's house has not yet become one of the cheap advertising shops—and I don't think it will in *his* time. In the year 1833, being the first I was in London, I remember well that my wages throughout the year averaged £1 6s. per week. I can say so positively, for I have long been in the habit of estimating them. I never did so before that time (because I was not out of my apprenticeship till then), and I recollect the first year particularly. Indeed, as it happens, I have the account here. I thought I had burnt it."

He then showed me an account of his earnings for the year above-mentioned. It began 6 April 1833, and ended 29 March 1834. The gross earnings were £69 3s. 6d., which gave an average of £1 6s. 7¼d. per week. The lowest sum received in any one week during that year was 4s. 6d., and the next week he had no employment whatso-ever. This occurred in the month of September. The highest sum earned was £1 16s., and this occurred for seven weeks in succession during the months of May and June. At the latter period the business, I am told, is always brisk, and lasts generally three months. The slack usually begins in August and lasts till the middle of October, or two months and a half. The average weekly earnings for three months during "the brisk" of the year 1833 were £1 14s. 8¼d. The average weekly earnings for ten weeks during the slack of the same year were 17s. 1d.

He has no account-books from the year 1833 to 1844 at present with him. In the year 1844 his gross earnings were £76 15s. 9d., which gives an average of £1 9s. 5¾d. The average weekly earnings during "the brisk" season were £1 13s. 3½d., and the average earnings per week during the slack were £1 9s. 9½d. He tells me that the cause of the difference between these two years was, that in the year 1844 he had got the best chance of work in his shop; and this is shown by the difference between his earnings during the slack of those two years. In 1844 he made 12s. 8d. per week *more* than he did in 1833; whereas during the brisk season, he made 1s. 4½d. *less* per week in 1844 than he did in 1833. He tells me that the cause of this last difference is, that the men are now paid by the piece instead of by the day, and their masters' shops are consequently not opened so early in the morning as they were formerly.

During 1848 his gross earnings were £76 17s. 3d., which gives an average per week of £1 9s. 6¾d. During the brisk of last year he made £1 10s. 0¾d. The cause of the difference between the brisk of this year and that of 1844 was that my informant was partially engaged for six weeks of the time upon a jury at Westminster. In the slack of the year the average weekly earnings were 19s. 9d. During the brisk months of the present year his weekly earnings have been £1 12s. 2¾d. During the slack of the present year he has earned £1 3s. 8½d.; so that the decline in the earnings of this person since 1844 has been 1s. 0¾d. during the brisk, and 6s. 1d. per week during the slack. The gross earnings during the present year have been £82 4s., which gives an average per week of £1 12s. 4½d. Hence, upon the whole, he has earned 2s. 10¾d. per week more than he did in 1844, and 2s. 9¼d. per week more than he did in 1848.

The cause of his wages not having declined is, he tells me, that he has the first chance of work at his shop; but his earnings constitute no average of the earnings of the workmen generally. He estimates the weekly income of those who have the second best chance of work, and are employed in the same shop all the year round, at £1 2s. During the slack he considers their average weekly earnings to be about 10s., and during the brisk about £1 5s. . . . .

*Statement of a casual hand*

The statement of the casual hand is far different from either of the above. He says: "I am not 'in the command of a shop'—that is, I have no regular work, but am employed principally at the brisk season of the year. The brisk season lasts for three months in the shop, and for two months outside of it—or in other words, the work at the commencement and the end of the brisk season is only sufficient to keep the hands, regularly employed in the shop, fully engaged, and between these two periods extra hands are taken on to do the work which then becomes more than the regular hands can accomplish. I am one of those extra hands, and May and June are the two months I am principally employed. During those months I earn £1 5s. per week, and I must be fully employed to get as much as that. The reason of this is, because the time required for making the garments is not fairly estimated.

"After the brisk season the casual hands are mostly off trade, and have little or no work at the honourable part of the business. From the month of July to the end of the month of April the journeymen tailors who have not the command of a shop are principally dependent upon what is termed 'sank work'. This consists of soldiers', police, Custom-house, post, and mail clothing. At this work I could earn about 6s. per week if I could get as much as I could do, but there is not enough to keep all the men in full employment. Some weeks I *do* make my 6s.—others I make only 4s.; then again I occasionally make only 6s. in a fortnight. I think I can safely say my weekly earnings at 'sank work' average about 4s.; but during the time I am engaged at 'sank work' I have the chance of the calls at my society. I attend at the house twice a day regularly. Since the brisk season I have not been employed at the honourable part of the trade more than one day per month, and I never missed attending a single call. Hence, I make upon an average about £10 by my work at the honourable part of the trade during the two months of the brisk season; then I get about £8 16s. by 'sank work', at 4s. per week, for the rest of the year; and besides this I earn by casual employment at the honourable part of the trade about £3; this altogether brings my yearly income to £21 16s., which gives an average of 8s. 4½d. per week. This I really believe to be exactly what I *do* get. Those casual hands that do not take to sank work, work under the sweaters, at whatever the sweater may be pleased to give them. At the sweaters' they make more than at the 'sank work', but then they have to work much longer hours.

"Such is the difference of prices in my trade, that during the months of May and June I make trowsers at 5s. per pair, and after that I make them at 6½d. per pair. The garments of course have not the same amount of work in them, but at those which are better paid I can earn in a day 5s., whilst I can only earn 1s. at the others in the same time. I believe the hands that cannot command a shop are similarly situated to myself. There are from 600 to 700 persons off work for ten months in the course of the year. I know this from having heard a gentleman who has paid great attention to the trade affirm that the unemployed were from 20 to 25 per cent of the whole number of the operatives 'in union'."

### A type of the intemperate tailor

The next party whom I saw was one to whom I had been referred as a type of the intemperate and improvident but skilful tailor. I was anxious, as intemperance is said to be one of the distinguishing characteristics of the working tailors, to hear from one who was notorious for his indulgence in this vice what were the main causes that induced the habit, so that by making them public the more intelligent workmen might be induced to take some steps to remedy the evil. As I before said, the necessary consequence of all uncertain labour is to produce intemperate habits among the labourers; and tailoring, it has been shown, has its periods of slack and brisk, as well as dock-labour. But it will be seen that there are other causes as well at work to demoralize, and occasionally to change, the operative tailor from the sober, industrious, and intelligent artisan, into the intemperate, erratic, and fatuous workman. I would not, however, have it inferred from the above remarks that intemperance is a vice for which the whole or even the majority of the class are distinguished. On the contrary, from all that I have lately seen and heard, it is my duty to state that I believe intemperance to be

PLATE XI. The Honourable Tailor

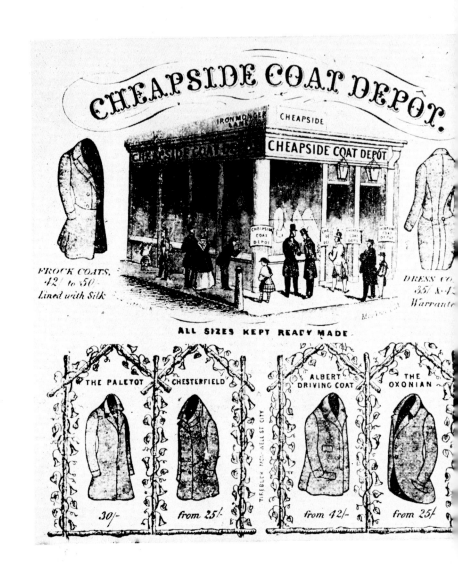

PLATE XII. Gentleman's Fashions

an exception rather than a rule with the body. I have found that
operative tailors, and especially those who have regular employment, enlightened, provident, and sober to a degree that I certainly
did not anticipate. Indeed, the change from the squalor, foetor,
and wretchedness of the homes of the poor people that I had lately
visited, to the comfort, cleanliness, and cheerfulness of the dwellings
of the operative tailors, has been as refreshing to my feelings as the
general sagacity of the workmen has been instrumental to the
lightening of my labours.

The person to whom I was referred gave me the following
extraordinary statement: "I work at coats generally, and for one
of the best houses. I am reckoned one of the most skilful hands in
the trade. I might be always in work if it were not for my love of
drink. Most of the foremen know me, and object to give me work
on account of my unsteadiness. If it were not for my skill I should
be out of work altogether, for I never would consent to work
under a sweater. I would rather starve than be instrumental to the
reduction of the price of my labour. As an instance of my skill I
may mention that I recently made a waistcoat of my own invention,
which was highly esteemed by my fellow workmen. I do not wish
to particularize the waistcoat more fully, lest it should be known
who it is that supplies you with this information. I am not a
leading hand in any shop, but one who is casually employed. I
might be a leading man if it were not for my love of drink, but,
owing to that, I am only taken on when the brisk season commences.

"It is to the casual hands that the intemperance of the tailors as
a class is mostly limited—those who have regular employment are
in general steady, decent, and intelligent people. The intemperance
for which the casual hands are distinguished arises chiefly from
their being 'called on' at public-houses. A master who wants an
extra number of workmen to complete his work, sends to a certain
house of call in the neighbourhood; this house of call is invariably
a public-house, and there the men who are out of work assemble
as early as a quarter before nine in the morning to hear whether
any call will be made. There are three of these calls in the course
of the day: one at a quarter before nine (as before mentioned), a
second at a quarter before one, and a third at a quarter before nine
at night. The men off trade and seeking for employment are kept
knocking about at the public-house all the day through. The
consequence of this is that the day is passed in drinking, and habits
of intemperance are produced which it is almost impossible to with-
stand. Those who have got money treat those who have none; and
indeed, such are the inducements to drink, that it is almost impossible
for the tailor who is not regularly and constantly employed to

G

remain sober. During the slack season or vacation, there are from 50 to 100 hanging about each of the houses of call; and there are five of these houses 'in society', and four foreign houses, or nine in all. In the vacation there must be from 500 to 1,000 people out of employ, who pass their days continually at the public-house. It astonishes me how some of them live. They cannot go home to their garrets, for they have no fire there, and if they absent themselves from the public-house they lose their chance of work. Some of those who are 'off trade' go into the country during the vacation, and others join the sweaters. But the majority remain about the public-house. They can't spend much, because they have it not to spend, but every penny they can get goes in drink, and many of the number pawn their coats and waistcoats in order to get liquor. I myself have duplicates enough to make a small pack of cards, for things that I have converted into gin. Ah! I like gin—you can see through it. Beer is like a fish-pond. What I hang on to is 'Old Tom'; a glass of that neat is my weakness—to mix it spoils it to my fancy—that's true. I drink a tremendous lot. I can drink twenty glasses in the course of the day easy. . . .

"Another cause of the intemperance of tailors is, that the operatives are usually paid at a tavern or beer-shop. There are generally three hands employed in making one coat, and these go partners—that is, they share among them the sum of money paid for making the entire garment. It is necessary, therefore, that change should be got in order to divide the proceeds into 'thirds'. This change the publican always undertakes to provide, and the consequence is, the men meet at his house to receive their weekly earnings. I have known the publican often keep the men an hour waiting for the change. The consequence of this system of paying at public-houses is, that the most intemperate and improvident of the workmen spend a large portion of their wages in drink. I myself generally spend half (unless my Missus catches me); and on several occasions I have squandered away in liquor all I had earned in the week. My Missus knows my infirmity, and watches me of a Saturday night regularly. She was waiting outside the public-house where you picked me up, and there were three or four more wives of journeymen tailors watching outside of the tavern, besides my old woman. These were mostly the wives of the men who are casually employed. The intemperate operative tailors seldom take half of their earnings home to their wives and families. Those who are employed by the sweaters are as intemperate as the casual hands in the honourable part of the trade. The cause of the drunkenness of the men working under sweaters is, that the workmen employed by them are the refuse hands of the regular trade. They mostly

consist of the men who have been scratched off the books of the
societies through spoiling or neglecting the work of their employers
from intemperate habits. I know the misery and evil of this love
of drink : it is the curse of my life, but I cannot keep from it.
I have taken the pledge four or five times, and broken it just as
often. . . ."

*Views of a chartist tailor*

I now give the views of an intelligent Chartist, in the same
calling, and in his own words : "I am a Chartist, and did belong
to the Chartist Association. My views as to the way in which
politics and Government influence the condition of journeymen
tailors are these—Government, by the system now adopted with
regard to army and police clothing, forces the honest labouring
man, struggling for a fair remuneration for his labour, into a false
position, and makes him pay extra taxes to those paid by other
branches of the community; they force him into this false position
by disposing of Government work at such contract prices that no
man can make a decent livelihood at it. One of the best workmen,
employed the whole week, cannot earn more than 12s. weekly on
soldiers' or policemen's clothing, out of which he must pay for all
the sewing trimmings, except twist; and having to make the articles
at his own place, of course he must find his own fire, candles, &c.
Tailors in prison are put to work by the Government at clothes
that come into the market to compete with the regular trader
employing the regular artisan. The public pays the taxes from
which prisons are supported, and the smallest amount, even a penny
a pair, is regarded by the authorities as a saving on the cost of
prisons; and, indeed, they keep the prisoner at work, if he earns
nothing, as the public pays all the expense of the prison. The
working tailor pays *his* quota of the taxes out of which the tailor
put to work in prison is maintained, and the prisoner so maintained
is made to undersell the very tax-payer who contributes to his
support. My opinion is, that if tailors in gaol were not employed
by Government, it would leave the market more open to the
honourable portion of the trade, and there would be no discreditable
employing of a felon—for felons *are* so employed, to diminish the
small earnings of an honest man. At Millbank, they teach men to
be tailors, who are always employed, while the honest operative is
frequently subjected to three months' compulsory idleness; six weeks,
towards the close of the year, is a very common period of the tailor's
non-employment. I think that if the Charter became law it would
tend to improve our (the journeymen tailors') condition, by giving

us a voice in the choice of our representatives, who might be so selected as thoroughly to understand the wants of the working man, and to sympathize with his endeavours for a better education and a better lot altogether."[4]

## LETTER XVII—14 DECEMBER 1849

### The East-end slop trade

I now proceed in due order to give an account of the cheap clothes trade in the East-end of London. I deal with the Eastern slop tailors first, because I am informed that the slop trade of the West is of more recent date.

I believe that the facts which I publish in my present communication will lay bare a system unheard of and unparalleled in the history of any country; indeed there appears to be so deep laid a scheme for the introduction and supply of underpaid labour to the market, that it is impossible for the working man not to sink and be degraded by it to the lowest depths of wretchedness and infamy. If we wish to see the effect of this system upon the physical, intellectual, and moral character of the workpeople, we should spend a week in visiting the homes of the operative tailors connected with the honourable part of the trade, and those working for the slop-trade. The very dwellings of the people are sufficient to tell you the wide difference between the two classes. In the one you occasionally find small statues of Shakespeare beneath glass shades; in the other all is dirt and fœtor. The working tailor's comfortable first-floor at the West-end is redolent with the perfume of the small bunch of violets that stand in a tumbler over the mantelpiece; the sweater's wretched garret is rank with the stench of filth and herrings. The honourable part of the trade are really intelligent artisans, while the slopworkers are generally almost brutified with their incessant toil, wretched pay, miserable food, and filthy homes.

Nor are the shops of the two classes of tradesmen less distinct one from the other. The quiet house of the honourable tailor, with the name inscribed on the window blinds, or on the brass-plate on the door, tells you that the proprietor has no wish to compete with or undersell his neighbour. But at the show and slop-shops every art and trick that scheming can devise or avarice suggest, is displayed to attract the notice of the passer-by, and filch the customer from another. The quiet, unobtrusive place of business of the old-fashioned

---

[4] The letter ended with a report on the decline of the trade from a tailor prominent in the union, who had made the trade his particular study.

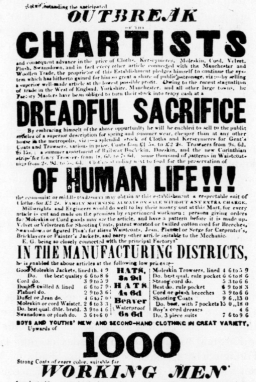

Fig. 2. Slop-shop Advertising on Political
Themes: "Chartism" Handbill.

tailor is transformed into the flashy palace of the grasping tradesman. Every article in the window is ticketed—the price cut down
*to the quick*—books of crude, bald verses are thrust in your hands,
or thrown into your carriage window—the panels of every omnibus
are plastered with showy placards, telling you how Messrs. —— defy
competition.

The principal show and slop-shop at the East-end is termed
the ——, and now occupies the ground of several houses. The
windows are of rich plate glass—one window, indeed, is nearly
thirty feet high—and it is said, that at the time of the attack upon
the house by the mob, the damage done by breaking two of the
windows amounted to £150. The business is not confined to tailor's
work. The proprietors are furriers, hatters, and bootmakers, hosiers,
cutlers, trunk-sellers, and milliners. They keep six horses and carts
constantly employed in their business, and, I am told, pay above
£1,000 a year for gas. The show-rooms are lighted by large ormolu
chandeliers, having thirty-six burners each.

## Meeting of East-end tailors

In pursuance of the system I have adopted, in order to arrive
at a correct estimate as to the earnings of the labouring classes,
whose condition I may be investigating, I invited the working
tailors of the East-end to meet me on Tuesday evening last, at the
British and Foreign School, Shakespeare's-walk, Shadwell. A reporter
was sent from the office of this journal to give an account of the
meeting, and the following is his report of the statement made on
the occasion :

The METROPOLITAN CORRESPONDENT of the *Morning Chronicle*
informed the meeting that he was now directing his attention
to the operative tailors of the metropolis, in connection both
with the honourable and the dishonourable part of the trade;
and that, consequently, he was anxious to arrive at certain facts in
relation to their earnings and their condition, in order to lay them
before the public. The objects of the meeting were the following :
1. To learn whether, and how, the slop trade influences the regular
and honourable tailoring trade. 2. To ascertain the amount of the
average weekly earnings of the hands engaged in the slop and
regular trade. 3. To hear an account of the sufferings and privations
endured by the work-people through the low price paid for their
labour. 4. To discover, if possible, whether the low prices arise from
competition among the masters or from competition among the
work-people. 5. To find out whether there is any practical remedy
for the evil. It was only facts that were required. Perhaps the most

# GREAT
# Demonstration of the People

has been fully, fairly, and justly exemplified to the Proprietors of the "Great Eastern Clothing and General Outfitting Establishment, Sixty-three, Shoreditch;" the System upon which this Immense Business has been established has been appreciated and responded to by a discriminating Public, far beyond the most sanguine expectations of the Proprietors, their aim being to provide no Materials but first-rate, trimmings of the highest quality, Cut and Workmanship second to no house in the United Kingdom, and not like those "that

# Three Days

Sun dries up their future prospects;" our standing as great Tailors of the East, "has become firm, immovable;" the grandest point's obtained—Confidence! Possessed of that, who can shake our standing? Deprived of that, we grasp at Nothing! If there had been

# Public Rejoicing!

at the Eastern End of our Great Metropolis for the formation of so vast an Emporium, filled as it were with Veins of Public Good, it would have been equally as consistent as the occasional revelling of modern times

# To Celebrate

"some great event perchance that's made us poor," What policy is there in it? But anon, to our subject, we will join hearts and hand for the

# Total Abolition of the

System of Monopoly in all its various forms, and to prove we are anxious in every particular to meet the Public's wants for the present season, we respectfully submit the following List of Prices:—

"Some thousands of Gents' Winter Coats in all their varied forms, commencing with stout Pilots, lined through, from nine "and sixpence to eighteen shillings; an immense variety of Beaver, Chesterfields, Codringtons, and other Over-coats, silk velvet "collars and cuffs, from twenty-one shillings to thirty-eight; Milled, Tweed, &c. &c., from twelve and six to eighteen shillings; "stout ditto ditto, suitable for business, from nine and six; gents. superior waterproof Beaver or Pilot, Kersing, Fishing, or "Driving Coats, from twelve to twenty-six shillings; Velvet and Doeskin ditto in great variety; some hundreds of superfine Frock "and Dress Coats in the most fashionable styles of the season, varying from twenty-one to thirty-eight shillings; an elegant "assortment of Cashmere, Toilinette, and Thibet Vestings, in rich and chaste designs; our Stock of Fancy and other Trousers will "be found magnificent, embracing every description of fabric, both English and Continental. The Repeal of the

# Tax on Bread!!

"no doubt will cause a great advance in the price of all Woollen, Cotton, and every other fabric of British Manufacture, "consequently the Proprietors of the Great Eastern Clothing Emporium, seeing what must inevitably follow ' the free trade in "Corn,' having at their command unlimited Capital, they have purchased to a great amount goods of every description, suitable "alike for the present and forthcoming season, and which they pledge themselves to retail to the public at prices lower than the "cheapest house in the trade.

"The largest Stock of Boys' and Youths' Trousers, Jackets, and Over-coats in the world; Children's Dresses in the admired "costumes of the day. The public are also informed that one part of the Premises is exclusively set apart for the Manufacture of "Mechanics' Clothing, to which every attention is paid to the getting up of every article in the best manner possible. Very stout "Cord Trousers, lined through, from four and six to seven shillings; Superfine ditto, best that can be made, eight and sixpence; "Moleskin ditto, lined, four and three; Superior ditto, patent finish, six and six; best Manufactured, seven and sixpence; prime "Cord and Moleskin Jackets, double breasted and rolling collar, from four and three to six and nine; superior ditto ditto, best "quality, seven and sixpence; Cord, Moleskin, and Cloth Vests, with or without sleeves, in great variety; an immense Stock of "Moleskin, Velvet, and Jean Coatees, suitable for all and every purpose; Jean, Flannel, and Tweed Jackets, from two and nine to "eight and sixpence.

"Family Mourning to any extent at five minutes' notice; in fact, persons of all classes, from the retired merchant to the daily labourer, will find the Stock of this Emporium unrivalled as regards Variety, Quality, and Lowness of Price; and in conclusion, the Proprietors wish to impress upon the minds of the public the exact position of this "Great Mart," viz.—

# CORSS & ROBERTS,
# Great Eastern Clothing Emporium,
# 63, SHOREDITCH,
# CORNER OF CHURCH STREET.

Fig. 3.   Slop-shop Handbill: Repeal of the Corn Laws.

important of these objects was the fourth; and he had called
together those who were present for the purpose of ascertaining
their opinions upon the question. Did the existing depression arise
from the struggle of the trading classes to live, or from the struggle
of the labouring classes to live? Were masters continually underselling one another, or were workmen continually underbidding
one another? This was what he wanted to learn from individuals
practically acquainted with the subject. He wished to know further,
whether it was acknowledged that the commencement of the
system of day-work, was the commencement of the declension in
the price of their labour?

Several men exclaimed that it was. One man added that the
decline began to be more rapid after that time; but piece-work as
well as day-work was carried on to a small extent in some shops
at the West-end. He was one who joined in the strike at that period,
and he remembered working in a shop where piece-work was carried
on at the same time with day-work, but at good and fair prices.
Another man said he remembered no piece-work in the best shops;
but there was extra work which was paid for at the rate of sixpence
the hour.

The meeting then expressed its conviction, by a show of hands,
that the cause of the declension of wages had been the change from
day-work to piece-work; that this change had led to great competition among workmen and to the introduction of female labour in
the craft. Before this period, the meeting further signified a journeyman tailor could support a wife and family by his own labour; and
a respectable-looking elderly man declared that it could be done
much better in those times, for the wages of a man then were
twenty-five per cent more than the wages now of a man and his
wife put together. The depresssion had not arisen from an excess
in the number of tailors, but from females and children, who
originally did no work, being brought into the trade, as well as
from the introduction of "sweaters". The depression was further
promoted by a certain amount of competition from the prisons and
the workhouses.

These principles having been distinctly enunciated by the meeting,
they were earnestly desired to mention nothing but facts in the
statements they might make, and to abstain from all personal or
offensive remarks.

A journeyman tailor then came forward, and spoke at some
length. He said the present system of labour wasted the physical
and mental energies of the class to which he belonged. Their
grievances were not imaginary, and he complained that the cause
of the labouring poor had been hitherto neglected. He had himself

just made a Wellington surtout, which took him twenty-six hours' hard work. He was paid 5s. for it, but out of this small amount he had 1s. 6d. to pay for trimmings, thread, candles, and fire, so that there was just 3s. 6d. left. His wife was ill, being in a consumption. A physician who had seen her, told him that if he did not apply for relief to the parochial officers he would be guilty of man-slaughter. But he would not so degrade himself. He further com-plained of the misery caused by the sweating system, and mentioned some establishments at the East-end where men were apparently employed upon the premises. They were, however, merely for a deception, being only finishers. In one large shop the middleman and sweater received 7s. 6d. for making a coat, but he only paid to the poor tailor 5s., who had to provide out of it thread, trimmings, and other materials. How, he asked, was it possible for men with families to live upon such wages?

Another tailor here stepped forward, and said that, though a great deal of distress and privation had been laid bare by the exertions of the *Morning Chronicle*, not one-half or one-quarter had yet been discovered. So it was with the wages of the poor. Much was known in relation to them, but not all. He attributed a large amount of distress among the London tailors to certain large establishments conducting their business through "sweaters". They were sweaters upon a large scale. These places did not work for the poor, but for the aristocracy. He was employed in making coats which were advertised at from five to twenty guineas. The aristocracy, not the poor, bought these coats, though the labour in making them was not half paid. Indeed, he knew that customers belonging to the aristocracy, though they were ashamed of being seen in certain large establishments at the East-end, sent written orders for the foreman to wait upon them. The great financial economist of the age, —— —— was also such a customer. Such, further, were some of the principal inhabitants of —— whose names could be furnished; and even clergymen of the Church of England. A tailor who had a family needed the aid of his wife to assist him in making a living. The woman, in some cases, was absolutely needed to make three-fourths of the garment; and he knew a man who worked for one of the cheap establishments, now in almost the last stage of a consumption, who had paid to the establishment out of his miserable earnings 30s. in less than three months, in the shape of fines. Another journeyman tailor, who was known to most present, had a wife and five children, several of whom were ill with fever. He had, further, to support an aged father. This man made a coat for 8s. for the house in question, but he was half an hour behind time in taking it in; he therefore got nothing for making it, though he had found thread, candle, and fire. This was a positive fact.

"And there are many others besides that," exclaimed a voice.

A person inquired whether it was meant that the man got nothing for making the coat?

"Not a farthing," replied the narrator.

"He was fined the 8s. for being behind time," observed a person in the crowd.

An inquiry was here made whether such a custom as this was likely to become general?

The TAILOR who made the statement, said that would depend upon others. He was speaking, however, of the establishment to which he belonged, and in which he was for the present permitted to be a "captain". The same establishment sometimes put out bills, "a thousand tailors wanted", and he had been caught by them. He had been working for a very good shop at the West-end, but happened to be idle for a few weeks, consequently he was "hard-up". A friend advised him to apply where the 1,000 tailors were wanted, and he got work. This was his first introduction to the slop system; and his earnings had been so small, with the assistance of a female —though he would not acknowledge himself a "sweater"—that, if he were fined as some had been, he should have to give the employer more money than he received himself. Distress among the operative tailors had been brought on to a greater extent than in other classes by female competition. He hoped public opinion would be elicited in their favour, and then he was sure the splendid palaces of beauty, erected out of the toils of the poor, would fade away.

A PALETOT MAKER said the party for whom he worked— and he made the best coats in the establishment—had two shops, and that there was a difference in the prices paid at the two places. Coats made neat, with capes, were charged 1s. more than a dress coat at one shop; and at the other 1s. less; and the prices were so calculated that the man who obtained it had to calculate upon his wife helping him. Drab coats with capes, stitched all round, were paid for at 12s., the man finding his own trimmings (hear, hear). He knew it for a fact, for he had done the work and received the money himself. At the commencement of winter, a Witney coat was sent out to be made, with double seams, but because the cloth was softer, he could only obtain 8s., although the work in it was the same as in the last. First one man refused it, and then another, and then a complaint went to the employer, who was told by the men that, as they had to pay 1s. for trimmings, they could not, at such a price, get a living by it. The price was raised to 10s., and at 10s. it now remained; but for the same description of coat, which he had made not in the house, but in the shop, he had received 24s. There would be no difference made in the price upon account of the softness of the cloth. At the same shop 8s. were paid for extra paletots to a Jew who contracted for the whole, and 7s. 6d. for others. For exactly the same garments he had received from a regular shop 16s. Another "novelty", as it was called, had just been introduced in a coat with eight or nine rows of stitching inside and out and round the cape, for making which 18s. was paid. The ordinary price for making such a coat was 36s.; consequently, the employer paid just one half the money he ought to do, solely from expecting women to take part in the work. In this case the workmen had to find their own trimmings and silk, which he estimated would cost 1s. 9d. He could scarcely make half of such a coat in two days even by working extra hours.

"You must work hard to do that," said a middle-aged man.

One of the previous speakers said the selling price of this kind of coat was four guineas. It was made of Tweed cloth at 6s. 6d. a yard, and it would take $2\frac{1}{2}$ yards. He went into the shop in question and asked what had been paid for the labour upon it, but they refused to tell him. But he should say that, taking twelve hours a day to be a fair day's labour, it could not be made under eight or nine days.

An OPERATIVE TAILOR declared that the great middleman in the establishment referred to got half-a-crown out of the making of every paletot.

"What is your opinion," it was asked, "as to the cause of depreciation in prices?"

The answer, prompt and ready, was—"Men of capital underselling each other."

"Do you know," it was further enquired, "of any place where sweaters seek out for female labourers" (hear)? . . .

At this stage a young man came forward and said he lived in the neighbourhood of New-buildings, Gravel-lane, Hounsditch. There was a place he said, kept by a well-known sweater in that vicinity, where each woman paid 3d. to have her name put down on a slate for work. The name being on the slate any foreign tailor could apply to see it, and the proprietor was thus enabled to supply either girls or women. In short, the house to which he referred was a house of call for women who were seeking for labour to compete with men. He worked for —— at what was called the up-stairs trade. Last week he made a coat, double stitched and braided, for 8s., out of which he had to find his own trimmings; but the coat was thrown back on his hands because the double stitches were not all sewn with silk. The making of the coat cost him three-and-a-half

days' labour; but he might possibly have made it in three days by
working sixteen or eighteeen hours (hear, hear). He had made a
coat of bear-skin, which took him four days' hard work, for about
eighteen hours each day, for 8s. The creasing alone was a day's
work for any man. He had also made shooting-coats with eight
pockets, laps, and seamed, for 7s., finding his own trimmings (hear).
But, further, if work was not delivered at the exact time, there was
a fine of 3d. for the first hour, and 6d. for every hour afterwards.
These rules were written up in the place where the work was given
out. Besides, if the garment was not in till four o-clock on Friday,
they would not take it in, and you were obliged to wait till the next
week for your money. He wished it to be known that only five
months ago he came out of his apprenticeship. He had served six
years at the business, and £7 premium was paid with him, and
such had been the sort of work he had since been occupied upon.
Let him work as hard as he could for eighteen hours every day he
could not make more than 12s., and out of that sum trimmings cost
him 2s., light 6d., and coals 1s. 6d., so that he only had 8s. for his
support.

"Lights, at this season, will cost you 3d. a night," exclaimed a
bystander, "if you burn it for ten hours, as you must, expressly for
your work."

It was here asked whether this was an extra expense upon the
ordinary cost of fire and lighting?

"Yes," resounded from the whole meeting. "And rent, too," said
one individual.

"If you were working in a shop, that expense would be saved?"
was the next inquiry.

"It would," replied a number of voices; "and we should be saved
the expense of irons, boards, and rent."

A WORKMAN at one of the most extensive-slop-sellers' said,
that, some years ago, the proprietors of that establishment were in
the habit of expressing their readiness to exhibit their book of wages.
This book was a deception, inasmuch as each £1 or £2 entered
against a name had to be divided between six or even more individuals; so that it could not be correct to ascribe these earnings to
one man.

The following statement was then read :

"Gentlemen—I have worked for the firm of —— about four years.
About three weeks ago, the foreman sent a sailor's jacket to me,
about six o-clock in the evening; it was to be made with slash
sleeves, double-breasted, sewed on lappel, and the price was 6s.;
and it was wanted at two o'clock the next day. I sent it back again,

and said I could not make it by that time. He said I must make it;
whereupon I sent it back again, and said I could not make it. Well,
then he sent the wife about, from place to place, to see if any one
else would make it, but no one else would make it in the time. So
then he said he would give me longer time to make it. I undertook
it; and when the job was opened, there were no sleeve linings in it.
I sent in for the sleeve linings, and got them. I sat up all night and
got another man to help me, and when I sent the jacket in, because
he said I was behind my time, he fined me 6d., and when I went
to receive my wages on the Saturday night 6d. was deducted for the
sleeve linings, which I never had. I stood there one Saturday, and
in about three hours I counted 19s. of fines, some 1s., some 2s., and
so on. The trimmer took it into his head one day to fine a woman
1s., because, he said, she was saucy. The husband went to know
what was the reason his wife was fined 1s. for. His answer was, 'I
shall fine you another, and then one cannot laugh at the other.'
The man, feeling himself badly treated, goes to the head of the
firm, and his answer is, 'If you do not like it, you may leave it.'
So the man was obliged to put up with the consequence or lose his
bread. If I had kept a proper account of all the fines that have
been levied on me since I have worked for the firm, it would have
amounted to not less than £3."

The person referred to in this communication here stood up, and
said he had asked for the money back, but it was refused, and he
was threatened. Having a wife and two children dependent upon
him, he was obliged to submit. He had a coat given him last
Thursday, to make by half-past three the next day. He sat up to
do it, but fell asleep at four, and did not awake till eight on the
Friday morning, so that he could not take in the coat till half-past
seven at night. The establishment was then closed, but he went to
the private door, where he was told the coat would do the next
morning. He sent it by his wife the next morning, but when he
came to receive his wages on Saturday night, he was fined 6d. out
of 8s., for its being late. His fines in four years, he believed, had
amounted to £4 15s., and he could hardly tell for what. . . .
A young man here stepped forward and told a striking tale. He
said he had been apprenticed to a tailor in Ipswich—that a premium
of £100 had been paid with him—and that, having finished his
servitude and being out of work, he resolved to come up to London.
In the first year of his apprenticeship he received 8s. a week; in the
second 10s., for which he toiled from seven in the morning till ten
at night. He had no friend, no home, at Ipswich, and he came to
London, where the first person he met was a sweater, who told

him he could produce more than 16s. a week. Well, he toiled from 7 in the morning till 12 at night. The sweater then asked whether he would work upon the Sunday? He objected; and upon the Saturday night, instead of having 2s. or 3s. in his pocket, *he was brought in 6d. in debt.* The sweater he found took coats from —— at 3s. 6d., but he paid the workpeople only 2s. 6d., out of which they had to find their own trimmings. When he complained, the sweater told him he must work on Sunday; but he said, "I'll go without my victuals first" (cheers).

"What did you give for your food?" asked a voice in the meeting.

"I took my teas and breakfasts with him," was the reply. "I was charged 4d. for each, 2d. for dinner, and 2d. for supper. I made five coats in the week, which came to 12s. 6d. My victuals cost 1s. a day; lodgings were 2s. 6d.; 1s. 6d. went for fire and candles; 1s. 3d. for trimmings; which makes 12s. 3d. I can't make up the remainder, and I suppose I was cheated out of it. Through my circumstances I have been obliged to sell my shirt to get lodgings. Yesterday I went to a Frenchman that takes out work in Colchester-street, and he offered me 5s. a week to work from seven in the morning till ten at night. I asked him to give me lodgings besides, but he would not, and I was obliged to walk about. I went to three unions, but none of them would let me in; and I am now without a shirt to my back, because I sold it to get shelter, after I had walked till two o'clock in the morning."

This statement excited great commiseration, and a spontaneous wish arose to make a subscription for the young man upon the spot. Other means, however, were found to relieve his immediate necessities.

Several other statements were afterwards made, all showing the oppressions to which the operative tailors are subjected.

The results of the meeting were as follows :

The average earnings of those engaged at the slop-trade were 9s. 7¼d., or 8s. clear. The aggregate earnings of 71 hands last week, amounted to £34 11s. 1d., or 9s. 4d. each—less than 8s. clear.

The average earnings of the honourable part of the trade were 15s. 5d. per week, clear of all deductions. 77 hands earned last week altogether £57 6s. 10d.

The amount in pawn was £110 5s. by the slop trade, and £121 1s. 6d. by the members of the honourable trade—in all £231 6s. 6d. by 148 people.

### Coat hands of the better class

An offer was made to introduce me privately into the workshop of a large show and slop-shop at the East-end of the town, where I might see and interrogate the men at work on the premises; but to this I objected, saying I did not think it fair that I should enter any man's premises with such an object, unknown to him. I was then told that several of the workmen would willingly meet me and state the price they received for their labour, and the unjust system upon which the establishment was conducted. This statement I said I should be very glad to listen and give publicity to. Accordingly, three of the better class of hands waited upon me, and gave me the following account :

"We work at the slop trade. We mean, by the slop trade the cheap ready-made trade. The dishonourable part of the tailoring trade consists of two classes—viz., those who are connected with show-shops and slop-shops. The show-shops belong to the cheap 'bespoke trade', and the slop-shops to the cheap 'ready-made trade'. Many of the large tailoring houses at the East-end of London are both show-shops and slop-shops. By a show-shop we mean one where the different styles of garments are exhibited in the window, ticketed as 'made to measure at a certain price'. By a slop-shop we mean one where the garments themselves are sold ready-made, and not a similar one made to measure at a certain price. In the cheap or ready-made trade a large number of one kind of garment is made up, either for home consumption or for exportation—whereas, in the show or cheap bespoke trade, only one of the same kind of garment is made up at one time.

"We all three of us work at coat-making. We are paid piece-work. The full price—that is, the highest amount paid for any coat made on the establishment—is 10s. The coat for which this price is given is a full-trimmed frock or dress coat. By 'full-trimmed' we mean lined throughout with silk and with quilted sides. The price for such a coat in the honourable trade is 18s., that is the very lowest price—the best houses would pay from 21s. to 24s. The time that such coats will take to make is four days, estimating twelve hours work to the day. . . . We have all worked in the honourable trade, so we know the regular prices from our own personal experience. Taking the bad work with the good work, we might earn 11s. a week upon an average. Sometimes we do earn as much as 15s.; but to do this, we are obliged to take part of our work home to our wives and daughters. We are not always fully employed. We are nearly half our time idle. Hence our earnings are, upon an average throughout the year, not more than 5s. 6d. a week."

"Very often I have made only 3s. 4d. in the week," said one. "That's common enough with us all, I can assure you," said

another. . . . "We all make for —— ——, 'the poor man's friend',"
said they satirically. "We used to have to make for him frequently,
but now he has shifted to another slop-shop near London-bridge,
where the same starvation prices are paid. We have also made garments for Sir —— ——, and Dr. ——. We make for several of the
aristocracy We cannot say whom, because the tickets frequently
come to us as Lord —— and the Marquis of ——. This could not
be a Jew's trick because the buttons on the liveries have coronets
upon them. And again, we know the house is patronized largely by
the aristocracy, clergy, and gentry, by the number of court-suits and
liveries, surplices, regimentals, and ladies, riding-habits that we continually have to make up. There are more clergymen among the
customers than any other class, and often we have to work at home
upon the Sunday at their clothes, in order to get a living. The customers are mostly ashamed of dealing at this house, for the men who
take the clothes to the customers' houses in the cart have directions
to pull up at the corner of the street. We had a good proof of the
dislike of gentlefolks to have it known that they dealt at that shop
for their clothes, for when the trowsers buttons were stamped with
the name of the firm, we used to have the garments returned, daily,
to have other buttons put on them; and now the buttons are
unstamped. . . ."[5]

*An out-door worker of the inferior description*

My next visit was to an out-door worker of the inferior description, from whom I received the following account :

"I work at the inferior work for the slop-trade. This kind of
work is never done 'in doors'—that is, on the premises of the
master. The inferior work consists of Shooting coats, Fishing coats,
Oxonion coats, Paletots, Reefing jackets, Pilot coats, Chesterfields,
Codringtons, Bullers, Sacks, Sailors' jackets, and Spanish cloaks.
The last mentioned garment is the worst paid of all the work I
have to do. For making a large Spanish cloak, with a hood to come
over the head, and with six holes on each side of the garment, and
three banyan plaits at the hips, I get 2s. The cloak has more work
in it than an ordinary great coat—indeed, it is similar in make to
an old-fashioned great coat, with a hood to it. It takes two
days—working 17 hours each day—or very nearly three ordinary
days—to make one of these cloaks. I could earn at this kind of
work from 4s. to 4s. 6d., and out of this, I should have to pay 7d.
for trimmings and about 1s. for lighting and firing. Hence my clear

[5] An interview with an out-door hand, employed on superior descriptions
of work appeared here.

weekly earnings would be from 2s. 6d. to 3s. These garments are given out only at a very slack time of the year, when they know that the men must do them at the employers' own price. . . .

"Taking the good with the bad work that I do, I should say that I make on an average about 5s. or 6s. a week clear. I do make more occasionally, but then I have to work longer time to get it. By working over hours and Sundays, I manage to make from 8s. to 9s. clear. To get this much, I must begin work at six in the morning, and sit close at it till eleven at night. This statement includes, of course, the necessary loss of time consequent on going backwards and forwards, taking work in, and getting fresh work out, and having to make alterations as well. I work first-handed—that is, I am not employed by any sweater. I originally belonged to the honourable part of the trade. I have made shooting coats for masters at the West-end, and had 14s. for making the very same garment as I now get 3s. for. When working at the honourable trade, my average weekly earnings were about £1, including vacation. Now I don't get half that amount. It is six or seven years ago since I worked for the West-end shops. My wife did no work then. I could maintain her in comfort by the produce of my labour. Now she slaves night and day, as I do : and very often she has less rest than myself, for she has to stop up after I have gone to bed to attend to her domestic duties. The two of us, working these long hours, and the Sundays as well, can only get 15s. . . . I attribute the decline in the wages of the operative tailor to the introduction of cheap Irish, foreign, and female labour. Before then we could live and keep our families by our own exertions; now our wives and children must work as well as ourselves to get less money than we alone could earn a few years back.

"My comforts have not in any way increased with the decrease in the price of provisions. Bread, tea, meat, sugar, are all much cheaper than they were five years ago. Bread three years since this winter, was 11d. and 11½d. the quartern, now it is 4½d. and 5d.— that is more than half as cheap, and yet I can safely say I am twice as badly off now as I was then; and so I know are all the people in my trade. Our wages have gone down more than provisions; that is to say, we and our wives work more than twice as hard, and we get less food and less comfort by our labour.

"Fifteen or twenty years ago such a thing as a journeyman tailor having to give security before he could get work was unknown; but now I and such as myself could not get a stitch to do first handed, if we did not either procure the security of some householder, or deposit £5 in the hands of the employer. The reason of this is, the journeymen are so badly paid that the employers know they can barely live on what they get, and consequently they are often driven to pawn the garments given out to them, in order to save themselves and their families from starving. . . . The journeymen who get the security of householders are enabled to do so by a system which is now in general practice at the East-end. Several bakers, publicans, chandler-shop keepers, and coal-shed keepers make a trade of becoming security for those seeking slop-work. They consent to be responsible for the workpeople upon the condition of the men dealing at their shops. The workpeople who require such security are generally very good customers, from the fact of their either having large families, all engaged in the same work, or else several females or males working under them, and living at their house. The parties becoming securities thus not only greatly increase their trade, but furnish a second-rate article at a first-rate price. It is useless to complain of the bad quality or high price of the articles supplied by the securities, for the shop-keepers know, as well as the workpeople, that it is impossible for the hands to leave them without losing their work. I know one baker whose security was refused at the slop-shop because he was already responsible for so many, and he begged the publican to be his deputy, so that by this means the workpeople were obliged to deal at both baker's and publican's too. I never heard of a butcher making a trade of becoming security, because the slop-work people cannot afford to consume much meat. The same system is also pursued by lodging-house keepers. They will become responsible if the workmen requiring security will undertake to lodge at their house.

"Concerning the system of fines adopted at the lower class of slop-houses, I know that within the last week a new practice has been introduced of stopping 1d. out of the wages for each garment that is brought in after eleven o'clock on the Saturday. By this means upwards of £1 was collected last Saturday night. This the proprietor of the shop pretends to distribute in charity; but if he does so, the charitable gift passes as his own money, and we have no means of knowing how much he collects and how much he distributes. There is also a fine of 4d. for each louse found on the garments brought in. The fine for vermin at other houses is sometimes as high as 6d., and at others as low as 3d. The poor people are obliged to live in the cheapest and filthiest places, and have, even if they feel inclined, little or no time to 'clean themselves'. If a louse is found on the garments brought in by any of the 'lady sweaters', who are generally much better dressed than the poor workpeople, it is wrapped up in a piece of clean paper, and presented to the 'lady' in an undertone, so that the other parties present may not be aware of the circumstance. If the vermin be found upon the garments brought in by the poor people, the foremen make no secret of it, and fine them 4d., in the presence of all in the shop. When the wife of a sweater returns home, and tells the hands working under her husband that 4d. has been stopped for a louse found upon the garments taken in, an angry discussion often arises among the workpeople as to whose it was."[6]

*Statement of a master in the City*

The following is the statement of a master in the City, to whom I was referred as a very intelligent man, and one greatly respected. "I have been in business fifteen years. When I commenced I used to get good prices, but now I am compelled to give as good an article at a lower price—fully twenty per cent lower—in order to compete with ready made and cheap clothes shops. I have not in consequence reduced the wages of the men in my employ, so that my profits are considerably reduced, while my exertions, and those of other tradesmen similarly circumstanced, to keep together a 'connection', which may yield fair prices and a fair remuneration, have to be more strenuous than ever. Year by year I have found the cheap establishments affect my business, and it seems to me that if the system pursued by the show and slop houses be not checked it will swamp all the honourable trade, which becomes every year smaller. Customers bargain now more than ever as to price, their constant remark being, 'I can get it for so much at —— —— ——'s.'

"When I began business the cheap system had not been started. Slop-sellers formerly were those who made inferior clothing, badly cut and badly made, and paid for accordingly. Now there must be—for these great cheap houses—good work for bad wages. Some years ago a great part of the slop-seller's business was to make clothes for the slaves in the West Indies, for East Indian regiments, jackets for sailors, and such like. When I began business the slop trade was a distinct thing from what is understood as the 'regular' trade of the tailor. Tailoring was then kept to itself. There were not half the good hands to be got then that there are now. A really first-rate hand was comparatively scarce. Now I can get any number of first-rate hands, as I give full wages. I could get twenty such hands, if I wanted them in a few hours.

"My business, to compete with the slop-sellers, requires the most incessant attention, or I am sure it would fall. I cannot now afford to give such a term of credit as formerly. My regular hands earn the same wages as they have earned all along; they perhaps average

[6] A brief account of "kidnapping" was followed by the narrative of a tailor forced to become a sweater and to put his wife and children to work.

### THE COBDEN TESTIMONIAL.

THE League's dissolv'd, and mark ! see Cobden stand
The pride and glory of his native land!
He met his foes, no matter time or place,
And, by his weapons, made the wealthy shake;
The great Monopolist he caus'd to tremble,
And to no purpose did he e'er dissemble,
But stood his ground, and manfully went on
Progressing, 'till his glorious cause was won ;
And now we hail with great sincere delight,
The purpos'd plan his labours to requite.
May those respond, who can, unto the sound.
And raise the cash—One Hundred Thousand Pound !
Now to another subject we move on,
And show that Grove and Cobden's aim was won.
One sought to crush the tax upon our food
(A thing much wanting for the country's good);
The other wish'd monopoly in dress to quell,
And best of clothes at lowest price to sell ;
He push'd his system. on his point intent,
To gain a place in public confidence.
His plan so simple, great impression made.
He found each day increase tenfold his trade.
Now view his premises, just look around,
His business so gigantic doth astound ;
And all the world no doubt, in turn, will go,
To view E. Groves's Grand, his Giant Dress Depôt.

Observe the addresses—
The Great Western Emporium, 114 and 115, Edgeware-road, Paddington ; the Great
Southern Clothes Exchange, 39, 40, and 41, Lower Marsh, Lambeth. Branches, 60,
New Cut, and 116, High-street, Shoreditch.

Proprietor—EDWARD GROVES.

Fig. 4.   Newspaper "Poems" using Political Themes.

A.   Cobden and Corn Law Repeal.

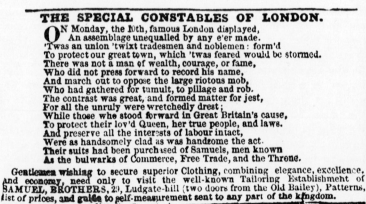

### THE SPECIAL CONSTABLES OF LONDON.

ON Monday, the 10th, famous London displayed,
An assemblage unequalled by any e'er made.
'Twas an union 'twixt tradesmen and noblemen : form'd
To protect our great town, which 'twas feared would be stormed.
There was not a man of wealth, courage, or fame,
Who did not press forward to record his name,
And march out to oppose the large riotous mob,
Who had gathered for tumult, to pillage and rob.
The contrast was great, and formed matter for jest,
For all the unruly were wretchedly drest ;
While those who stood forward in Great Britain's cause,
To protect their lov'd Queen, her true people, and laws.
And preserve all the interests of labour intact,
Were as handsomely clad as was handsome the act.
Their suits had been purchased of Samuels, men known
As the bulwarks of Commerce, Free Trade, and the Throne.

Gentlemen wishing to secure superior Clothing, combining elegance, excellence,
and economy, need only to visit the well-known Tailoring Establishment of
SAMUEL, BROTHERS, 29, Ludgate-hill (two doors from the Old Bailey), Patterns,
list of prices, and guide to self-measurement sent to any part of the kingdom.

B.   The Kennington Common Chartist Demonstration, 1848.

25s. to 30s. a week through the year. My trade is looked upon as an exception to the general lowering of price and wretched payment of the workmen round about here. I find the effects of the ready-made trade most at holiday times, Easter and Christmas, when business used to be the best. People at those times now run to the slop-shops. I have worked my business up in my own way, but I am convinced that if I had to begin it now, instead of fifteen years ago, I could not have established myself with a body of respectable and regular customers, at fair prices; not even with more capital at my command. I must have adopted the low-priced system. As businesses 'of the old school' fall off, the customers go to the slop-sellers. Such businesses as mine are becoming fewer; tailors' shops now must be on a very large scale, or they are not to be carried on profitably at all."

*Visit to a destitute tailor*

A card was put into my hands on my rounds : it ran as follows :

to be raffled
on Monday. the 17th. of December at the,
Angel & crown, ship alley, Wellclose sqre.

## A WAISTCOAT.

the property of W. W., who has had a Long fit of Sickness.
Chairman Mr. J. F. — Dep. Mr. P. C.

Tickets 6d. Each          Music provided.

I lost no time in seeking out the sick man and found him truly destitute. I was directed to one of the back streets of the Commercial-road; and there, in a small, close, and bare, unfurnished room, stretched on a bed scantily covered, I found the poor sick slop-worker. On the floor sat a man cross-legged at work, who had no place to carry on his trade. He had come to sit in the dying man's room, and to use the sleeve-boards and irons that the invalid had no use for. On the narrow wooden mantel-shelf stood a row of empty physic bottles and an old wine glass; beside the man's bed-side was a small deal table, on which was a mildewed orange, half peeled. The ceiling was browned in patches with the wet that had leaked through from the roof. The wife followed me upstairs. There was no chair in the room, and one was borrowed from below for my accommodation. She told me the house was "dreadful damp; it was never dry, winter or summer; the wet often streamed down the walls." I had seen many squalid, desolate homes, but this was more wretched than all.

I asked why the sick man was not taken to hospital. The man himself could not speak for coughing. The wife told me he could not go to the hospital, his clothes were all in pledge; they had been taken to the pawnshop for the subsistence of the family. "If it hadn't been for that we must all have starved," she said. "This last five weeks he has been confined to his bed, and we have been obliged to make away with all we had. I have pawned all my under-clothing. I have five children; the eldest fourteen, and the youngest two years and a half old. I have pledged almost all their clothes, and if I could have taken anything else off the poor little things, I should have done it to get victuals for them." The man himself now raised his head from below the bed-clothes. His long black hair was thrown off his forehead, and his face, which had once been handsome, was suffused with perspiration. His black unshorn beard made him look paler perhaps than he was. He breathed hard and quickly. He told me he could not go to the hospital, because he should lose his work if he did so. "I worked at the out-door work for a large slop-shop. I did the bespoke work," said he.

"Look here," cried one of his friends, dragging a coat from off the sick man's bed. "See here; the man has no covering, and so he throws this garment over him as a shelter." (It was a new pilot coat that was to be taken in that evening for the shop.) I expressed my surprise that the bed of the sick man should be covered with the new garment, and was informed that such in the winter time was a common practice among the workpeople. When the weather was very cold, and their blankets had gone to the pawnshop, the slop-workers often went to bed, I was told, with the sleeves of the coat they were making drawn over their arms, or else they would cover themselves with the trowsers or paletots, according to the description of garment they had in hand. The ladies' riding habits in particular, I was assured, were used as counterpanes to the poor people's beds, on account of the quantity of cloth in the skirts.

"He will get 3s. for making such a coat as this," continued the sick man's friend, still holding up the garment, and out of that he will have to pay 6d. for trimmings and expenses. It will take him two days to make such a coat, working 12 hours each day. But in the slop-trade we hardly understand 12 hours work in a day; our time for labour is mostly 18 hours every day. Doing 12 hours work a day he could make 7s. 6d. a week clear at such work, and out of that he has to keep himself, a wife, and five children, and pay rent. "I can earn upon an average," he said, "by my own labour, from 9s. to 10s. a week clear."

Here my attention was distracted by a loud voice below stairs. It was one of the servants of the slop-house, come to demand a certain garment that had been given out to the sick man to make, and which he had employed a party to finish for him. It had been pawned when completed to keep the sick man's family from starving, and when the poor fellow was told the cause of the noise below stairs, he trembled like a leaf, and the perspiration again started in large drops to his forehead. "Let me drink," he said. I asked to see the pawn tickets. They were shown me, and I was told by one of the parties present in the room, that the firm, having heard of my inquiry into the condition and earnings of the workpeople, were calling in all garments, so as to prevent my seeing the prices marked upon the tickets sent out with the clothes. The same person assured me that a servant of the house had called upon him that morning, and demanded a particular garment that he had to make for them. It was in pawn, he told me, and he had been obliged to pledge the work of another employer, in order to redeem the coat demanded. Indeed I was assured that such was the distress of the workpeople that there was scarcely one that had not work of their employers in pawn—that one coat was continually substituted for another to prevent inquiries, and that a month's interest was paid on each, though it was generally in pawn but a few days. The workpeople dreaded detection more than anything, because it was sure to be followed by the withdrawal of their security, and this was their ruin.

"I came over from Ireland several years back," continued the sick man, in answer to my questions. "I worked from a house of call for about ten years after I came to England, and then I came to this slop work, at which I have been about twelve years. When I was engaged at the honourable trade I could make three times as much as I do now. I was very comfortable then." "We are not so now, God knows," said the wife. "When I fell sick, I had 9s. a week from my society, now I have not a farthing from anybody, nor do I know where to get a farthing if I wanted it. Since I have been at the slop work I have neither been able to save anything nor to keep my children as I wanted to. I couldn't even send them to church of a Sunday for want of their clothes. I fell ill two years ago, with a pain in my chest and side, and a bad cough. It was working long hours that made me bad. My side is quite raw from blistering. There are many men who are working at this business, who have not been outside the doors and smelt the fresh air for months and months together. In some places the workmen have only one coat to put on between six, and many cannot spare the time. The wife goes to take the work in and get the work out. For two years I have fought against my complaint. I never was to stay well in this house. I slept down on the ground floor, and I think that was the cause of my illness. There are no drains at all to the house, and the stagnant water remains underneath the boards downstairs. In the yard the standing water is like a cesspool.

"I went on for two years working away, though I was barely able, and at last, five weeks ago, I was dead beat. I couldn't do a stitch more, and was obliged to take to my bed. Since then we have been living on what we pawned. There was nothing else to be done, and as a last resource we have got up a raffle. We generally do assist one another, if we can; but we are all so poor we have scarcely a penny for ourselves, any of us. I have come down to my very last now, and if I don't get better in health what will become of us all I don't know. We can't do without something to eat. My children cry for victuals as it is, and what we shall do in a little while is more than I can say. . . ."

## LETTER XVIII—18 DECEMBER 1849

*West-end and East-end: statistics*

Of the 21,000 journeymen tailors at work in the metropolis there were, in the year 1844, 3,697 employed on the premises of the masters in the "honourable" trade at the West-end of London, and 2,384 working out of doors at the "dishonourable" show and slop trade. Hence there were 6,081 journeymen tailors engaged at the West-end, and about 15,000 employed at the East-end of the metropolis. In the East there are upwards of 80 slop and show shops, many employing from 2,000 to 3,000 hands. There were in 1844 only 72 masters in the West, who had all the work made on their premises; besides these, there were 270 masters, who had only part of their work made in-doors, and 112 who had none at all done at home. Hence the West-end branch of the business consisted principally of 454 masters, of whom less than one-sixth belonged to what is called the "honourable" part of the trade. Since then, I am assured by one who has long made the business his peculiar study, that the 72 honourable masters have declined to at least 60, while the 172 dishonourable ones have been more than doubled. The men employed in-doors have decreased from 3,600 to less than 3,000, and those employed out of doors have increased from 2,300 to more than 4,000. Hence the honourable part of the trade is declining at the rate of 150 men per year; so that in 20 years at least the whole business will have merged in the show and slop shops; and the wages of the men have fallen from 18s. a week—which I find is the average of the honourable part of the trade—to 11s.—the average of the slop trade. . . .

In the year 1844 there were at the West-end 676 men, women

and children working under "sweaters", and occupying nine-two small rooms, measuring 8 feet by 10, which upon average was more than seven persons to each apartment. This number of individuals was composed of 179 men, 85 women, 45 boys, 78 girls, and 256 children—the latter being members of the sweater's family. I am assured that these numbers have at least been doubled in the last five years, and that the number of boys, girls, and women introduced into the trade by the sweaters since the year 1844 is certainly three times as many as it was then. The number of individuals who made a practice of working on the Sunday at the time the investigation was made, 852; this, I am informed, has considerably increased.[7] The better class of artisans denounce the system of Sunday working as the most iniquitous of all the impositions on the honourable part of the trade. They object to it, not only on moral and religious grounds, but economically also. "Every 600 men employed on the Sabbath," they say, "deprive 100 individuals of a week's work; every six men who labour seven days in the week must necessarily throw one other man out of employ for a whole week. The seventh man is deprived of his fair share of work by the overtoiling of the other six." This Sunday working, I am told, is a necessary consequence of the cheap slop trade. The workmen cannot keep their families by their six days' labour, and therefore they not only, under that system, get less wages and do more work, but by their extra labour throw so many more hands out of employ. . . .

## Meeting of West-end tailors

On last Friday evening a very numerous meeting was held at the Hanover-square rooms, in order to arrive at statistical results concerning the earnings of the working tailors of the West-end. As many as 2,000 attended, and the respectable appearance of the operatives formed a striking contrast to those who had been present at the meeting at Shadwell. . . .[8]

The statistical results of the meeting were as follows :

Returns of the earnings were obtained from 434 operative tailors. Of these 152 were coat hands, who could earn £298 0s. 9d. by working 1,029 days 8 hours, which is at the rate of 5¾d. per hour. According to the returns of those engaged at the dishonourable part of the trade, the coat hands for the slop-shops could earn only at the rate of 2d. per hour. 97 were trowsers hands, and they could earn

[7] This information came from a "Report of the Operative Tailors in 1844" based on "an inquiry instituted among the operative tailors by their own body."

[8] The proceedings of this meeting have been cut.

£14 0s. 9d. in 48 days and 10 hours, being at the rate of 5¾d. per hour. At the slop trade, according to the return of 12 hands, the average rate of earnings was 1¼d. per hour.

|  | £ | s. | d. |
|---|---|---|---|
| The aggregate earnings last week of the 434 hands working at the honourable trade were | 461 | 12 | 2½ |
| The amount that they had in pawn was | 310 | 13 | 6 |
| The average rate of earnings of each of the hands last week was | 1 | 1 | 3¼ |
| And the average rate of weekly earnings throughout the year |  | 18 | 9½ |

There were 104 hands who earned above £1 a week, 229 who got more than 15s., 79 who made above 10s., and 22 whose earnings exceed 5s. per week.

Since the above meeting I have devoted my attention to the investigation of the West-end show trade. I have also made further inquiries into the system adopted for the introduction of cheap Irish and foreign labour.

### The principle of sweating: a sweater speaks

I will first proceed to give the reader a more perfect idea than I have yet been able to do of the principle of sweating. I first sought out a sweater himself, from whom I obtained the following information. . . .

"I employ persons to work under me—that is, I get the work, and give it to them to do. I generally have two men working at home with me. I take a third of the coat, and I give them each a third to do. They board and lodge with me altogether—that is, they have their dinners, teas, breakfasts, and beds in my place. I give them at the rate of 15s. a coat—that is, I take 1s. off the price I receive, for the trimmings and my trouble. The trimmings come to 9d., and the extra 3d. is profit for my trouble. They pay me at the rate of 2s. 6d. per week for washing and lodging—the washing would be about 6d. out of the money. They both sleep in one bed. Their breakfasts I charge 4d. each for—if "with a relish", they are 5d. Their teas are 4d., and their dinners are 6d.—altogether I charge them for their food about 8s. 2d. a week, and this with lodging and washing comes to from 10s. 6d. to 11s. per week. The three of us working together can make six coats in the week, if fully employed—on an average we made from four to five coats—and never less than four. This would bring us in altogether, for four coats, £3 4s. Out of this the shares of each of my two men would be £1. The rest I should deduct for expenses. Then their living would be from about 10s. 6d., so that they would get clear 9s. 6d. per week over and above their living. I pay 7s. 6d. a week rent. I have two rooms, and the men sleep in the work room. I get every week for the four of us (that is for myself, my missus, and the two men—we live all together) about four or five ounces of tea, and this costs me 1s. 5d. I have 1s. worth of coffee, and about 1s. 6d. worth of sugar. The bread is 3s. 6d. per week, and butter 2s. 11d. The meat comes to about 8s., and the vegetables 2s. 4d. The lighting will be 1s. 9d., firing 1s. 6d. This will come to 30s. for the board and lodging of the four of us, or at the rate of 7s. 6d. per head. I should therefore clear out of the living of my men about 3s. a week each, and out of their work about 8d., so that altogether I get 3s. 8d. a week out of each man I employ. This, I believe, is a fair statement. I wish other people dealt with the men as decently as I do. . . .

The usual number of men working under each sweater is about six individuals : and the average rate of profit, about £2 10s., without the sweater doing any work himself. . . ."

### A tailor working under a sweater

After this I made the best of my way to one who was working under a sweater, and who was anxious, I was told, to expose the iniquities of the whole system. He said : . . .

"Four years come this winter was the last time that I had employment at the honourable part of the trade. But before that I used to work for the sweaters when the regular business was slack. I did this unknown to the society of which I was a member. If it had been known to them, I should have had to pay a certain penalty, or else my name would have been scratched off the books, and I should have no more chance of work at the honourable trade. When working for the honourable trade I was employed about one-third of my time, and I should say I earned about £30 in the year. I was out of work two-thirds of my time. I never saved anything out of my wages when I was fully employed. I generally got into debt in the slack time, and was obliged to work hard to pay it off in the brisk. It was during the vacation, eight years back, that I first went to a sweater. Sweaters were scarcely known 25 years back, and they increased enormously after the change from day work to piece work. I could get no employment at my regular trade, and a sweater came down to the house and proposed to me privately to go and work for him. It was a regular practice then for the sweaters to come to the house and look out for such as had no employment and would work under price. I kept on the four years secretly working for the

sweaters during vacation, and after that I got so reduced in circumstances that I could not appear respectable, and so get work amongst
the honourable trade.

"The pay that I received by working for the sweaters was so little
that I was forced to part with my clothes. When I first went to work
for the sweater, I used to get 4s. 6d. for making the third part of a
coat. It would take from 11 to 13 hours to make a third. I could
have done as many as six thirds, but could not get them to do. The
sweater where I worked employed more hands than he had work for,
so that he could get any job that was wanted in a hurry done as
quickly as possible. I should say upon an average I got two-thirds
of a coat to make each week, and earned about 7s. Some weeks of
course I did more; but some I had only one, and often none at all.
The sweater found me in trimmings. His system was the same as
others, and I have worked for many since in the last eight years.
The sweaters all employ more men than they want, and I am sure
that those who work for them do not get more than two-thirds of a
coat to make every week, taking one week with another.

"Another of the reasons for the sweaters keeping more hands
than they want is, the men generally have their meals with them.
The more men they have with them, the more profit they made. The
men usually have to pay 4d., and very often 5d. for their breakfast,
and the same for their tea. The tea or breakfast is mostly a pint of
tea or coffee, and three to four slices of bread and butter. I worked
for one sweater who almost starved the men; the smallest eater there
would not have had enough if he had got three times as much.
They had only three thin slices of bread and butter, not sufficient
for a child, and the tea was both weak and bad. The whole meal
could not have stood him in 2d. a head, and what made it worse
was, that the men who worked there couldn't afford to have dinners,
so that they were starved to the bone.

"The sweater's men generally lodge where they work. A sweater
usually keeps about six men. These occupy two small garrets; one
room is called the kitchen, and the other the workshop; and here
the whole of the six men, and the sweater, his wife, and family, live
and sleep. One sweater I worked with had four children, six men,
and they, together with his wife, sister-in-law, and himself, all lived
in two rooms, the largest of which was about 8 feet by 10. We worked
in the smallest room and slept there as well—all six of us. There were
two turn-up beds in it, and we slept three in a bed. There was no
chimney, and indeed no ventilation whatever. I was near losing my
life there—the foul air of so many people working all day in the
place and sleeping there at night was quite suffocating. Almost all
the men were consumptive, and I myself attended the dispensary

for disease of the lungs. The room in which we all slept was not more than six feet square. We were all sick and weak, and loath to work. Each of the six of us paid 2s. 6d. a week for our lodging, or 15s. altogether, and I am sure such a room as we slept and worked in might be had for 1s. a week; you can get a room with a fireplace for 1s. 6d.

"The usual sum that the men working for sweaters pay for their tea, breakfasts, and lodging is 6s. 6d. to 7s. a week, and they seldom earn more money in the week. Occasionally at the week's end they are in debt to the sweater. This is seldom for more than 6d., for the sweater will not give them victuals if he has no work for them to do. Many who live and work at the sweater's are married men, and are obliged to keep their wives and children in lodgings by themselves. Some send them to the workhouse, others to their friends in the country. Besides the profit of the board and lodging, the sweater takes 6d. out of the price paid for every garment under 10s.; some take 1s., and I do know of one who takes as much as 2s. This man works for a large show-shop at the West End. The usual profit of the sweater, over and above the board and lodging is 2s. out of every pound. Those who work for sweaters soon lose their clothes, and are unable to seek for other work, because they have not a coat to their back to go and seek it in. Last week I worked with another man at a coat for one of Her Majesty's Ministers, and my partner never broke his fast while he was making his half of it. The Minister dealt at the cheap West End show-shop. All the workman had the whole day-and-a-half he was making the coat was a little tea.

"But sweater's work is not as bad as Government work, after all. At that we cannot make more than 4s. or 5s. a week altogether, that is, counting the time we are running after it, of course. Government contract work is the worst work of all, and the starved-out and sweated-out tailor's last resource. But still Government does not do the regular trade so much harm as the cheap show and slop shops. These houses have ruined thousands. They have cut down the prices so that men cannot live at the work; and the masters who did and would pay better wages, are reducing the workmen's pay every day. They say they must either compete with the large show-shops or go into the *Gazette*."

## System by which sweaters are supported

Of the system by which the sweaters are supported, the following information will give the public some little notion :

"I do the superior out-of-door work for a large show shop at the

West-end," said the party from whom I had the information. . . . "In 1844 I belonged to the honourable part of the trade. Our house of call supplied the present show-shop with men to work on the premises. The prices then paid were at the rate of 6d. per hour. For the same driving capes that they paid 18s. then, they give only 12s. now. For the dress and frock coats they gave 15s. then, and now they are 14s. The paletots and shooting coats were 12s.; there was no coat made on the premises under that sum. At the end of the season, they wanted to reduce the paletots to 9s. The men refused to make them at that price, when other houses were paying as much as 15s. for them. The consequence of this was, the house discharged all the men, and got a Jew middleman from the neighbourhood of Petticoat-lane, to agree to do them all at 7s. 6d. a piece. The Jew employed all the poor people who were at work for the slop ware-houses in Hounsditch and its vicinity. This Jew makes on an average 500 paletots a week. The Jew gets 2s. 6d. profit out of each, and having no sewing trimmings allowed to him, he makes the work-people find them. The saving in trimmings alone to the firm, since the workmen left the premises, must have realized a small fortune to them. Calculating men, women, and children, I have heard it said that the cheap house at the West-end employs 1,000 hands. The trimmings for the work done by these, would be about 6d. a week per head, so that the saving to the house since the men worked on the premises has been no less than £1,300 a year, and all this taken out of the pockets of the poor. The Jew who contracts for making the paletots is no tailor at all. A few years ago he sold sponges in the street, and now he rides in his carriage. The Jew's profits are 500 half-crowns, or £60 odd, per week—that is upwards of £3,000 a year. Women are mostly engaged at the paletot work.

"When I came to work for the cheap show-shop I had £5 10s. in the saving bank; now I have not a halfpenny in it. All I had saved went little by little to keep me and my family. I have always made a point of putting some money by when I could afford it, but since I have been at this work it has been as much as I could do to *live*, much more to *save*. One of the firms for which I work has been heard publicly to declare that he employed 1,000 hands constantly. Now the earnings of these at the honourable part of the trade would be upon an average, taking the skilful with the unskilful, 15s. a week each, or £39,000 a year. But since they discharged the men from off their premises they have cut down the wages of the workmen one half—taking one garment with another—*though the selling prices remain the same to the public*, so that they have saved by the reduction of the workmen's wages no less than £19,500 per year. Every other quarter of a year something has been 'docked' off our earnings, until it is almost impossible for men with families to live decently by their labour; and now, for the first time, they pretend to feel for them. They even talk of erecting a school for the children of the workpeople; but where is the use of their erecting schools, when they know as well as we do that, at the wages they pay, the children must be working for their fathers at home? They had much better erect workshops, and employ the men on the premises at fair living wages, and then the men could educate their own children, without being indebted to their 'charity'."

## "Kidnapping" system

In my last I merely hinted at the system adopted by wily sweaters to entrap inexperienced country and Irish hands into their service. Since then I devoted considerable attention to the subject, and am now in a position to lay before the public the following facts in connection with this trade :

The system of inducing men by false pretences on the part of the *sweaters*, or, more commonly, of *sweaters' wives*, to work for them at wretched wages, I heard described in various terms. Such persons were most frequently called *kidnapped men*. The following narrative, given to me by one of the men concerned, and corroborated by one of his Irish fellow-victims, supplies an instance of the stratagems adopted. The second Irishman had but—as he said to me—"changed his house of bondage"; he had fallen into the hands of another sweater, his coat was in pawn, and he could not, in spite of all his struggles, lay by enough to redeem it. The wife of a sweater (an Irishman, long notorious for such practices), herself a native of Kerry, visited her friends in that town, and found out two poor journeymen tailors. One was the son of a poor tailor, the other of a small farmer. She induced these two young men to follow her to London, immediately after her return, and at their own expense. She told them of her husband's success in trade, and of the high wages to be got in London by those who had friends in the trade, and engaged the two for her husband. Their wages were to be 36s. a week *"to begin with"*.

When the Irishmen reached the sweater's place, near Hounsditch, they found him in a den of a place (I give the man's own words), anything but clean, and anything but sweet, and were at once set to work at trowser making, at 1s. a pair, finding their own trimmings. Instead of 36s. a week, they could not clear more than 5s. by constant labour and the sweater attributed this to their want of skill— they were not capable of working well enough for a London house. He then offered to teach them, if they would bind themselves apprentices to him for a year certain. During the year they were to have board and lodging, and £5 each, paid at intervals as they required it. The poor men having no friends in London, and no acquaintances even whom they might consult, consented to this arrangement, and a sort of document was signed.

They then went to work on this new agreement, their board being this—For breakfast—half a pint of poor cocoa each, with half a pound of dry bread cut into slices, *between the two*; no butter. Dinner was swallowed, a few minutes only being allowed for it, between four and five. It was generally a few potatoes and a bit of salt fish, as low priced as could be met with. At seven, each man had half a pint of tea and the same allowance of bread as for breakfast. No supper. They slept three in a bed, in a garret where there was no ventilation whatever.

The two men (apprenticed as I have described) soon found that the sweater was unable to teach them anything in their trade, he not being a superior workman to either of them. At three weeks' end they therefore seized an opportunity to escape. The sweater traced them to where they had got work again, took with him a policeman, and gave them in charge as runaway apprentices. He could not, however, substantiate the charge at the station-house, and the men were set at liberty. Even after that the sweater's wife was always hanging about the corners of the streets, trying to persuade these men to go back again. She promised one that she would give him a handsome daughter she had for his wife, and find the new married pair "a beautiful slop-shop" to work for, finding them security and all, and giving them some furniture, if he would only go back. The workman so solicited excused himself on the plea of illness. After this the father of this youth, in Kerry, received an anonymous letter, telling him that his son had run away from his employer, carrying with him a suit of clothes, and that he (the father) should have his son written to, and persuaded to return, and the robbery might be hushed up. This was every word false, and the anonymous letter was forwarded to the son in London, and when shown to the sweater he neither admitted nor denied it was his writing, but changed the conversation.

The third entrapped workman that I saw was a young man from the country, who was accosted in the street by the sweater's wife, put down to work under the same false pretences with the others, faring as they did until he effected his escape. The sweater had then but those three hands—he wanted more if his wife could have entrapped them. He had had six so entrapped or cheated in some similar way. Their hours of work were from seven in the morning to twelve at night.

PLATE XIII.    Cruikshank's Comment on Advertising Practices, "Alarming Sacrifice", 1851

PLATE XIV. The Honourable Shoemaker

Of this *street kidnapping system* I give another instance, and in the words of the kidnapped—"I am now twenty-one, and am a native of Kilfinnan, in the county Limerick, Ireland. My parents died when I was five. A brother, a poor labouring man, brought me up, and had me apprenticed to a tailor. I served seven years. After that, before I ever worked as a journeyman in Ireland, I thought I would come to London to better myself, and I did come; but didn't better myself—worse luck. I 'tramped' from Kilfinnan to Cork, starting with 18s., which I had saved, and with no clothes but the suit I had on. I started because London has such a name among the tailors in Ireland, but they soon find out the difference when they come here. A journeyman tailor in Kilfinnan works for 2s. 6d. a week, his lodging, and two meals a day. In the morning, bread and milk, and plenty of it; in the evening, potatoes and meat, but meat only twice or thrice a week; fish always on fast-days and sometimes on other days. I spent in tramping from Kilfinnan to Cork, 38 Irish miles, 6s. I took my passage from the Cove of Cork by a steamer to Bristol, paying 10s. for it. I landed at Bristol with 2s.; tramping it up to London; a waggoner once gave me a lift of eighteen miles for nothing. I had no help from the trade as I came alone. I begged my way, getting bits of bread and cheese at farmers' houses and such places.

"In five days I reached London, knowing no one but a labourer of the name of Wallace. I found he was dead. That's eighteen months ago. One of Wallace's friends said I should do best at the East-end, but bad's the best I did. I took his advice, and went on that way, and was in Bishopsgate-street, when I met ——, a sweater. He spoke to me, saying, 'Are you a tailor seeking work?' I answered, 'Yes, to be sure.' He then said he would give me plenty of good work, if I would go with him. I went with him to Brick-lane, where he lived, and he said I must first go a week on trial. I got nothing but my board for that week's work—working six days, long hours. After that he offered me 3s. 6d. a week, board and lodging, not washing. I had no friends, and thought I had better take it, as I did. For breakfast I had less than a pint of cocoa and four slices of thin bread and butter—bad bread from the 'security' baker's, the worst of bread—only the butter was worse. For dinner—but sometimes only was there dinner, perhaps two days a week, perhaps only one—we had potatoes and salt fish. I couldn't eat salt fish, *so* he had it regular. Sometimes I got a bite of a bull's cheek. Bad as I lived in Ireland, it was a great deal wholesomer than this—and I had plenty of it too. My master there gave me a belly-full, here he never did. I slept with another man in a small bed; there were three beds with six men in them in a middle-sized room, the room where the six

H

men worked. My employer, his wife and I worked downstairs. He boarded and lodged them all—they living as I did. Some of them, working fifteen hours a day, earned 5s. or 6s. a week. I worked and hungered this way for four months, and then we quarrelled, because I wouldn't work all Sunday for nothing, so I left. I'm badly off still."

*Foreign labour*

The continual immigration of foreign labour that I had discovered to be part of the system by which the miserable prices of the slop-trade were maintained, was the next subject to which I directed my inquiries, and I was able to obtain evidence which clearly proves how the honourable part of the trade are undersold by the "sloppers". The party who gave me the following valuable information on this head was a Hungarian Jew sweater. He said :

"I am a native of Pesth, having left Hungary about eight years ago. By the custom of the country I was compelled to travel three years in foreign parts before I could settle in my native place. I went to Paris after travelling about that time in the different countries of Germany. I stayed in Paris about two years. My father's wish was that I should visit England, and I came to London, in June, 1847. I first worked for a West-end show-shop—not directly for them, but through the person who is their 'middle-man', getting work done at

## THE "NATIONAL ANTHEM" IMITATED.

To be Sung in Commemoration of her Majesty's Visit to the City, on Tuesday, the 30th of October, 1849.

O AID our spacious Mart!
Support our noble Mart!
Do aid our Mart!
Make it victorious,
Widely notorious,
Mighty and glorious—
Long live the Mart!

When trading foes arise,
Scatter its enemies,
And make them fall ;
Frustrate their trading tricks,
To you our Warehouse sticks,
On you our hopes we fix,
On you we call.

We've choicest Dress in store,
With styles unknown before,
Cheap, strong, and smart ;
Our Dress, which daily draws,
Is form'd on Fashion's laws,
And ever gives you cause
To aid our Mart.

E. MOSES and SON, 154, 155, 156, 157, Minories; and 83, 84, 85, and 86, Aldgate. City.

Fig. 5. The "National Anthem".

what rates he could for the firm, and obtaining the prices they allowed for making the garments. I once worked four days and a half for him, finding my own trimmings, etc., for 9s. For this my employer would receive 12s. 6d. On each coat of the best quality he got 3s. and 3s. 6d. profit. He then employed 190 hands; he has employed 300; many of those so employed setting their wives, children, and others to work, some employing as many as five hands this way. The middleman keeps his carriage, and will give fifty guineas for a horse. I became unable to work, from a pain in my back, from long hours at my occupation. The doctor told me not to sit much, and so, as a countryman of mine was doing the same, I employed hands, making the best I could of their labour. I have now four young women (all Irish girls) so employed. Last week one of them received 4s., another 4s. 2d., the other two 5s. each. They find their own board and lodging, but I find them a place to work in—a small room, the rent of which I share with another tailor, who works on his own account. There are not so many Jews come over from Hungary or Germany as from Poland. The law of travelling three years brings over many, but not more than it did. The revolutions have brought numbers this year and last. They are Jew tailors flying from Russian and Prussian-Poland to avoid the conscription. I never knew any of those Jews go back again. There is a constant communication among the Jews, and when their friends in Poland and other places learn they're safe in England, and in work and out of trouble, they come over too, even if they can earn more at home. I worked as a journeyman in Pesth, and got 2s. 6d. a week, my board, washing, and lodging. We lived well, everything being so cheap. The Jews come in the greatest number about Easter. They try to work their way here, most of them. Some save money here, but they never go back; if they leave England, it is to go to America."[9]

[9] The letter ended with the testimony of a German Jew, an account of a House of Call for women and more information about fines.

# THE BOOT AND SHOE MAKERS

## LETTER XXXII—4 FEBRUARY 1850[1]

*Number of boot and shoe makers*[2]

The present letter will be the first of a short series upon the state of the Metropolitan Boot and Shoe Makers. . . .

First let me show the numerical relation of the London shoe makers to the other trades carried on in the metropolis :

### POPULATION OF THE PRINCIPAL OCCUPATIONS IN THE METROPOLIS

| | | | |
|---|---|---|---|
| Domestic servants | 168,701 | Army | 8,043 |
| Labourers | 50,279 | Cabinet-makers and | |
| Boots and shoe makers | 28,574 | upholsterers | 7,973 |
| Tailors and breeches | | Silk-manufacturers | 7,151 |
| makers | 23,517 | Schoolmasters, &c | 7,138 |
| Dressmakers and | | Seamen | 7,002 |
| milliners | 20,780 | Butchers | 6,450 |
| Clerks (commercial) | 20,417 | Bricklayers | 6,743 |
| Carpenters and joiners | 18,321 | Blacksmiths | 6,716 |
| Laundry-keepers | 16,220 | Printers | 6,618 |
| Porters, messengers and | | Seamsters and | |
| errand boys | 13,103 | seamstresses | 6,269 |
| Painters, plumbers and | | Booksellers &c. | 5,499 |
| glaziers | 11,517 | Coachmen and guards, &c. | 5,428 |
| Bakers | 9,110 | Weavers (all branches) | 5,065 |

Hence it will be seen that the class of whom I am treating are the most numerous of all the handicraftsmen, not only in Great Britain, but likewise in the metropolis. The London population of boot and shoe makers is composed as follows :

### BOOT AND SHOE MAKERS IN THE METROPOLIS IN 1841

| | | | |
|---|---|---|---|
| Males—Above 20 years of age | 22,400 | | |
| Males—Under 20 years of age | 2,457 | | |
| | | 24,857 | |
| Females—Above 20 years of age | 3,157 | | |
| Females—Under 20 years of age | 560 | | |
| | | 3,717 | |
| Total | | | 28,574 |

[1] After the tailors, Mayhew studied the dockworkers and vagrancy in letters XIX–XXXI.

[2] As with later trades, Mayhew also included information about the number of workers in Great Britain, broken down by county.

But the 28,574 individuals here given consist of both employers and employed, and in an inquiry like the present it is as necessary to distinguish the capitalist from the workpeople as to know the ages of the parties working. The Occupation Abstract of the Population Returns affords us no means of making this distinction. We may, however, collect from the "London Post-office Directory", the number of persons in business for themselves. These are as follows :

### MASTER BOOT AND SHOE MAKERS
(From the "London Post-office Directory, 1849")

| | |
|---|---:|
| Boot and shoe factors | 3 |
| Wholesale boot and shoe makers | 73 |
| Retail boot and shoe makers | 2,008 |
| | 2,084 |

Of this number there are 89 who are ladies' shoe makers; 2 belonging to the wholesale, and 87 to the retail trade. Besides the above, there are:

| | | |
|---|---:|---:|
| Wholesale stay and shoe makers | 7 | |
| Shoe and stay mercers | 5 | |
| Total number of master shoemakers in London | — | 2,096 |
| Deducting the masters from the entire number of boot and shoe makers in the metropolis, we have for the | | |
| total number of working men and women | | 26,478 |

There are then 2,096 master boot and shoe makers, and 26,478 workpeople. . . .

### Earnings: trade union survey

I am informed by one of the most intelligent of the workmen, that several years ago an average of the earnings of the entire metropolitan trade was taken, when the weekly income of each man was found to amount to 15s. Of the particulars from which this calculation was made, I have been unable to obtain any information. In March, 1838, however, a meeting of the London Eastern or City Society of Journeymen Boot and Shoe Makers of he men's branches was held at the Hall of Science, City-road, when t was resolved, "that, with a view to arrive at a true knowledge of heir actual condition, it be rendered obligatory upon each member )f the society to give in, by the next general meeting night, a full nd accurate statement of the wages which he has received weekly luring the term of four weeks, beginning on the 19th February nd ending on the 19th March, 1838, so that by a calculation of hose facts an average of the receipts of the journeymen boot and hoe makers of the eastern division of London might be arrived at."

For the better carrying out of this resolution the society was

230 THE UNKNOWN MAYHEW

divided into seven sectional parts. Each of these sections is given in the tables below, together with the numbers of married and unmarried persons included therein, and every other particular that was required to be stated; and the information then collected has been kindly placed at my disposal by Mr. Devlin, one of the most intelligent of the body. The bootclosers are placed first in the table, the bootmen second, and the shoemen (with whom are incorporated the pumpmen and the jobbers) in the third and last statement. *Ch.* means children; *Ass.*, such children as assisted their parents; and *App.*, apprentices. The total strength of the society at that time consisted of 588 members, of whom 511 furnished returns:

| Section | | Unmarried | Month's Receipts £ s. d. | | | Married | Month's Receipts £ s. d. | | | Ch. | Ass. | App. |
|---|---|---|---|---|---|---|---|---|---|---|---|---|
| Closers | 1 | 1 | 2 | 19 | 7 | 7 | 30 | 2 | 2 | 7 | 4 | 2 |
| | 2 | 2 | 4 | 10 | 9 | 7 | 35 | 10 | 9 | 19 | 0 | 2 |
| | 3 | 2 | 7 | 15 | 11 | 4 | 14 | 6 | 5 | 0 | 0 | 1 |
| | 4 | 7 | 18 | 17 | 4 | 8 | 38 | 13 | 8 | 26 | 2 | 5 |
| | 5 | 7 | 27 | 15 | 2 | 11 | 48 | 10 | 5 | 28 | 4 | 2 |
| | 6 | 5 | 16 | 5 | 9 | 1 | 6 | 6 | 3 | 6 | 2 | 0 |
| | 7 | 4 | 14 | 14 | 7 | 7 | 49 | 4 | 9 | 7 | 0 | 5 |
| | | 28 | £92 | 19 | 1 | 45 | £222 | 14 | 5 | 93 | 12 | 17 |
| Bootmen | 1 | 12 | 43 | 2 | 1 | 11 | 46 | 12 | 8 | 19 | 2 | 1 |
| | 2 | 20 | 68 | 12 | 3 | 24 | 91 | 11 | 2 | 58 | 1 | 1 |
| | 3 | 19 | 66 | 17 | 6 | 34 | 131 | 13 | 3 | 53 | 0 | 0 |
| | 4 | 12 | 38 | 5 | 2 | 46 | 146 | 11 | 6 | 64 | 0 | 2 |
| | 5 | 20 | 62 | 9 | 1 | 21 | 93 | 2 | 2 | 40 | 0 | 2 |
| | 6 | 23 | 65 | 18 | 8 | 18 | 71 | 13 | 9 | 41 | 0 | 2 |
| | 7 | 22 | 74 | 14 | 11 | 31 | 109 | 7 | 3 | 48 | 0 | 0 |
| | | 128 | £419 | 19 | 8 | 185 | £619 | 11 | 9 | 323 | 3 | 8 |
| Shoemen | 1 | 1 | 2 | 10 | 10 | 3 | 7 | 11 | 0 | 7 | 0 | 1 |
| | 2 | 3 | 5 | 6 | 6 | 10 | 27 | 1 | 4 | 9 | 0 | 1 |
| | 3 | 12 | 26 | 16 | 1 | 11 | 20 | 6 | 6 | 9 | 0 | 0 |
| | 4 | 9 | 21 | 13 | 10 | 7 | 18 | 5 | 3 | 8 | 0 | 0 |
| | 5 | 2 | 4 | 14 | 6 | 3 | 12 | 10 | 1 | 5 | 0 | 0 |
| | 6 | 0 | 0 | 0 | 0 | 3 | 7 | 16 | 10 | 0 | 1 | 1 |
| | 7 | 12 | 32 | 19 | 7 | 8 | 21 | 6 | 0 | 0 | 0 | 0 |
| | | 39 | £94 | 1 | 4 | 45 | £114 | 17 | 9 | 38 | 1 | 3 |

The following is an average of the earnings per week of the several hands engaged in the different departments of the trade above given:

|  | s. | d. |
|---|---|---|
| 73 boot closers, with 29 assistants, in all 102 hands, earning collectively £315 13s. 6d. per month, gives an average income to each hand per week | 15 | 5¾ |

|  | s. | d. |
|---|---|---|

313 bootmen, with 11 assistants, in all 324 hands, earning collectively £1,039 11s. 5d. per month, gives an average income to each hand per week ... 16 0½

84 shoemen, with 4 assistants, in all 88 hands, earning collectively £208 19s. 1d. per month, gives an average income to each hand per week ... 11 10¼

470 closers, bootmen, and shoemen, with 44 assistants, in all 514 hands, earning collectively £1,564 4s. per month, gives an average income to each hand per week ... 15 2¾

The differences of individual earnings were as follows, at their maximum and their minimum condition; the other receipts varying between the extremes :

### MINIMUM OF THE EARNINGS OF BOOTMAKERS
#### Least Earnings

| Class of Workman | In the Month Unassisted | Assisted | In the Week Unassisted | Assisted |
|---|---|---|---|---|
| Closer | 0 16 3 | 3 1 4 | — | 0 6 10 |
| Bootman | 1 15 0 | 3 2 9 | — | 0 13 0 |
| Shoeman | 1 18 0 | 2 3 0 | — | 0 7 0 |

### MAXIMUM OF THE EARNINGS OF BOOTMAKERS
#### Greatest Earnings

| Class of Workman | In the Month Unassisted | Assisted | In the Week Unassisted | Assisted |
|---|---|---|---|---|
| Closer | 17 15 0 | 10 3 5 | 2 4 0 | 3 1 9 |
| Bootman | 8 0 6 | 7 19 6 | 2 11 0 | 2 1 8 |
| Shoeman | 4 7 0 | 5 3 3 | 1 4 6 | 1 11 7 |

It is to be feared that since these returns were obtained the earnings of the journeymen have seriously declined; indeed, if the Population Returns of 1831 and 1841 are to be credited, the number of hands in the boot and shoemaking trade increased to so great an extent that this circumstance alone could not but tend necessarily to depreciate the journeyman's wages :

### RATE OF INCREASE IN THE BOOT AND SHOE MAKING TRADE

Boot and shoe makers and menders in Great Britain:

| | |
|---|---|
| Males—of 20 years and upwards, in 1831 | 133,248 |
| Males—of 20 years and upwards, in 1841 | 175,769 |
| Increase in ten years | 42,521 |

According to the regular increase of the population (at the rate of 10 per cent in ten years), the boot and shoe makers, above twenty years of age, should, from 1831 to 1841, have increased only 13,324; whereas, by reference to the above returns, it will be seen that the rate of increase during that period was more than three times that amount.

Of the average rate of wages now received by the journeyman of London generally, I am not at present in a position to speak with confidence.[3]

## Temperament of the shoemakers

The boot and shoe makers are certainly far from being an unintellectual body of men. They appear to be a stern, uncompromising and reflecting race. This, perhaps, is to be accounted for by the solitude of their employment developing their own internal resources, and producing that particular form of mental temperament which is generally accompanied with austerity of manner. The Spitalfields weavers I found to be distinguished for the tastefulness and gentleness of their pursuits. They were remarkable as flower and bird fanciers. This was perhaps due to their French extraction. They were not deep thinkers, but men of natural taste. The shoemakers are distinguished for the severity of their manners and habits of thought, and the suspicion that seems to pervade their character.

## Division of labour

I now proceed to give a description of the trade of boot and shoe making as it is conducted in the metropolis. In the first place, the workpeople are divided into two classes—the *"men's-men"* and the *"women's-men"*, or the makers of the men's and the makers of women's goods. In addition to these two departments, there is the *strong* and the *slop* trade. With each of these branches I purpose dealing separately. In the present letter it is my intention to treat solely of the men's business, and more particularly of that branch of it which is called the Western Division, as contradistinguished from the City or Eastern Division of the trade. The journeymen are divided into *closers* and *makers*—a distinction which, in all the better description of shops is rigidly observed, and a distinction moreover which is, I understand, peculiar to this country, and rigorously maintained in London more than elsewhere. . . . The *closer*—strictly—deals only with the upper part of the boot or shoe; the *maker* afterwards affixes "the bottom stuff"—the insoles, soles, and heels—and so completes it. The material is given to the closer at

---

[3] There followed a statistical section comparing the "moral and physical condition" of the shoemakers with tailors and labourers.

the shop of his employer, having first gone through the hands of the clicker, or cutter-out. The clicker's share of the work must be done with the greatest nicety, so as to adapt the proportions of the leather he cuts to the measurement of the foot, or else, as a work-man expressed it to me, "there can be no *success* in a boot." The closer's work is light compared to that of the maker, and a portion of it is done by women—indeed, the *closing* of the shoe is principally in the hands of females, many of them the wives and daughters of the workmen. The most "skilled" portion of the labour is, however, almost always done by the man; and invariably so, I understand, in *the closing of the top-boots* (called "Jockeys" by the trade). . . . The closer's work, called "the legs", is handed, when completed, to the *maker* (called *the boot or shoe man*), who finishes it, as I have stated.

All descriptions of workmen in that part of the trade which I now treat of (the West-end union trade) work at their own abodes, where some have the aid of apprentices.

The division of labour above detailed ensures the production of the highest degree of excellence in the workmanship of a boot. The only inconvenience that I heard complained of, as a consequence of this division, was that the maker had sometimes to be idle until the closer finished his (the first portion of the labour). Indeed, such remarks as "I'm fast for want of my legs", or "I'm sitting still, waiting for my legs", are common among the makers. . . .

*The Union and strikes*

I now come to speak of the union of "men's-men" working at the Western division of the trade. *The Union, or West-end body of Associated Shoemakers,* consists, at the present time, of seven divisions, each division having its own place of meeting, and each meeting being officered by a clerk or secretary, as well as a delegate; the seven delegates of the seven divisions forming a committee, to whom is "delegated" the duty of taking all "returns" at the times of the assembly of the members—and as these returns are cast up in the total, so the sense of the whole seven divisions is obtained "for" or "against" any particular measure which has become the subject of shoemaker legislation. The only other officer of the society, is a general secretary, who has a moderate permanent salary, sufficient to keep him without doing any other work—the present holder of the office being a functionary of long standing, and much esteemed by the body. This officer has furnished me with the following particulars in connection with the society :

Number of men in Union in the quarter ending April, 1849, 790;

in the July quarter of the same year, 890; and in the September quarter, 860; while in January of the present year there were 820 names on the trade-books. "I find," he adds, in giving these figures, "there has been but little alteration in our numbers during the last twenty years."

"Wages," he also states, "in the first-rate shops, remained stationary from 1812 to 1830, when, after a struggle of six months, a reduction on the making and closing combined of a pair of boots took place, and shoes and jobbing were reduced in proportion. In 1838 a sort of equalization on the payments made by a lower class of employers was attempted with considerable success, and since that time things have in general remained in the same state in regard to the first and second-rate shops, although those of an inferior order have reduced more and more, and are also becoming daily more numerous than ever."

The immediate object of these unions is to uphold the rate of wages paid to the journeymen. For this purpose it has generally been the custom to publish a statement of the wages or prices paid by the employers for the different kinds of work after any alteration has been agreed upon. Before giving the tables of wages which have been adopted by the trade, I should, however, explain that the workmen are divided into *flints*, *refractories*, and *scabs*. The "flint" is the man who will not work for one farthing less than the wages recognized by his union; the "refractory" is the man who shirks the regulations, but still professes to be a union man; and the "scab" is the man who works for a lower rate of wages, and will work for a shop on strike at a reduced rate of wages, or in violation of any other rule of the union. The trade is also divided into *legal* (or "wages") and *illegal* (or "scab") shops—respectively equivalent to what I described among the tailors as the *honourable* and *dishonourable* branches of the trade; and the legal shops are sub-divided into high, low, and middling, according to the prices. The "legal" shops are those giving any of the scales of wages allowed by the unions; the "illegal" are those who get their work done at the lowest rate of wages that they can. Among the staunch men of the trade, the words "He's nothing but a scab", expresses a high degree of contempt.

I must now allude to the measures that have been resorted to by the workmen in order to effect an increase, or to prevent a decrease, in the rate of their remuneration—viz., *the strikes*. Many of the older workmen make these their epochs. "It was before (or after) the great strike of 1812"—or, "It was before the change in 1830", are not uncommon phrases. The strike of 1812, I am informed by an intelligent bootman, was for a rise of 6d. a pair on the wages both for closing and making, "all round"—that is, on every description of work in boots and shoes, together with certain allowances for "extras". The masters, at that time, after holding out for thirteen weeks, gave way, yielding to all the demands of the men. "The *scabs* had no chance in those days," said my informant, "the wages-men had it all their own way; they could do anything, and there were no slop-shops then. Some scabs went to Mr. Hoby *'occasioning'* (that is, asking whether he 'had occasion for another hand'), but he said to them, 'I can do nothing; go to my masters (the journeymen) in the Parr's Head, Swallow-street' (the sign of the public-house used by the men that managed the strike)." This was the last general strike of the trade; for in 1830, though the shoemakers joined the grand union of all the trades, walking with them in procession with a petition on behalf of the Dorchester labourers—the procession, six deep, extending from Copenhagen-fields to Kennington-common—they did not "strike" for an advance, but only resisted the attempt of the masters to lower their wages.

*Anti-free-trade feeling*

Such, then, are the divisions, and the laws and customs of the craft. There is still one other important matter, in connection with the trade, that requires to be set forth before proceeding to give the statements of the men themselves. I refer to the alteration of the duties upon foreign boots which has taken place within the present century. To these the majority of the workmen attribute a considerable part of the decline of their wages. For, as regards the principles of free-trade, I found the shoemakers anything but ardent supporters of the new commercial policy—indeed they often enough expressed (as is natural) an opinion that in their own particular craft there should be some protection or legislative restriction as to wages. As a proof of the anti-free-trade feeling existing among the shoemakers, my attention was directed by one person to the following passage in a report issued by the Central Association of Metropolitan Trades in 1842 :

"Now, the only discernible object of the proposers of the new tariff, if any object can be discerned through the mist of obscurity which is involved, is to increase the amount of revenue on this and similar articles, by encouraging their importation at considerably reduced duties. For this purpose, then, the duty on :

| | |
|---|---|
| Women's leather boots and shoes is reduced | 1s. 6d. per pair |
| Men's boots | 2s. 5d. per pair |
| Men's shoes | 1s. 0d. per pair |

The consequence of this reduction of duty will unquestionably be a vast increase of revenue—for, when a similar reduction took place in 1826, the revenue, in the short space of two years, rose from £645 to £12,835. But what were the consequences of this increase of revenue in 1828, to the workmen engaged in this branch of trade? Why, it deprived hundreds and thousands of their means of subsistence, and reduced them to such a state of destitution that 120 shoemakers were in the workhouse of the parish of Westminster alone, where previous to the reduction there had been only three. And what will be the consequences of the present reduction of duty? Why, the recurrence of that destitution and misery experienced in 1828."

## *Statement from an intelligent member of the West-end trade*

In order to obtain a full statement from one of the most intelligent members of the West-end trade as to the causes which the journey-men shoemakers consider to have been instrumental in causing a reduction in their earnings, I consulted the Society upon the subject. Hearing that there was to be a meeting of twenty-one delegates from the various sections of the Western Division, concerning the interests of the trade, and having been informed that these delegates had been chosen, by the sections which they represented, as the most intelligent and experienced of the bodies to which they belonged, I requested that the twenty-one when assembled would select, from among them, one who could give me an account on the principal circumstances affecting the trade.

I was furnished with the address of an individual who certainly was a favourable specimen of his class. He was a fine sample of the English artisan. His children (there were three) were especially remarkable for their cleanliness, telling of the careful matron, and they played about the room, while the man sat at work, in a manner that showed little restraint in the presence of their father. Indeed it was easy to see, as well by the tidiness of the room as by the conduct of the children, that both the workman and his wife were very superior persons. The man had clearly the interests of his class deeply at heart, and spoke of such failings of his brother artisans as were alluded to in conversation with much concern and an evident anxiety for their welfare. He was tolerant, dispassionate, and almost philosophic in his tone of thought, and had a strong literary taste and a love of reflection. He talked as he worked.

"I am a *boot-closer*, working for the best shop," he said. "I am not fully employed. I have an equal share of work with my shop-mates, and try to fill up my spare time with what we call 'by-strokes' (that is by seeking for extra employment at other shops). I get the best prices. In the course of last season I have made, with an apprentice and my wife's assistance, and working Sunday and all the rest of the week, and sitting up for two entire nights in the course of that time—with all this I *have* made, I say, as much as £3. How much I myself earned of that sum I cannot say—I might have done half of it. I think I could earn 35s. for one week at a time in the season, but then I couldn't keep it up at that rate. I can myself, without any assistance, earn with comfort 27s. a week when I can get it. To do that much, however, I must sit at my work for 14 hours every day. Out of the 27s. I shall have to pay about 1s. 6d. for grindery, and 9d. for oil for my light. So that my clear week's earnings at the best would be between 24s. and 25s. When I was a single man my average earnings throughout the year came to £1 2s. 6d. per week, but I had a good seat of work all that time. I think my average wages during that time were, in the season (that is from April to July), about 26s. a week, and out of the season about £1 a week. Single-handed I think I earn about the same now.

"A great number of closers earn less than I do; some may earn a little more. I think that, to take the average of the closers generally, throughout the town, their income would be about £1 a week. In some individual instances the weekly earnings might be as low as 15s.; but I know that the accounts taken of the earnings of the whole trade, in and out of union, in 1837, gave an average of 17s. a week to each of the 13,000 individuals who then followed the business in London. Since that time wages have gone down about 15 per cent. At this rate I calculate the average wages of our body would be about 15s. per man—some, of course, getting more, and others less. But the hands generally have less to do than what they had in 1838, owing to the greater number of people working at the trade. I should say that all through the trade, taking one hand with another, each man has 10 per cent less work to do; so that I calculate, if an average was taken of our earnings now, the same as in 1837, it would be found that we should be earning generally 13s. 6d. a week each.

"In 1812 the boot-makers received their highest wages. If an average could have been taken then of the earnings of the trade, one with another, I think it would have been about 35s. per man. The great decrease (from 35s. to 13s. 6d. a week) that has taken place is not so much owing to the decrease of wages as to the increase of hands, and the consequent decrease of the work coming to each man. I know myself that my late master used to earn £2 per week on an average many years back, but of late years I am sure he has not made 15s. a week. I have, moreover, often heard it said that in former times three men (with two sons each to assist them) have drawn £21 as wages in one week from their employer. This gives very nearly £2 8s. per week per man, or 8s. each per day. And now a man must work hard to get 5s., even when fully employed. But he not only has less pay now but has less work to do.

"There are a great many causes, I think, for this great reduction in our wages and our earnings. These are chiefly—the importation of foreign goods, the increase of the Northampton goods, and the competition of the masters and the men themselves. Concerning the importation of French goods, I consider the effect they have in reducing our wages to be this : Boots and shoes are produced in France and introduced into this country at a lower cost. The English masters, therefore, in order to compete with foreigners, reduce our wages as a necessary result. The reason why we cannot produce boots so cheap as the French is owing to the difference of rents, and the mode of living in France and England. I myself lived for some time in Boulogne, and my rent there was one-half less than what I paid here. A man, if he is short of work may take it out of his stomach—he can eat a meal or two less; but he can't have it out of his rent—*that* must go on, either asleep or awake. Again, my living cost me much less in France than it does in this country, even now. I got only half the wages there that I did here, and yet I lived more happily and comfortably. The quantity of employment that I got there was much about the same as here. But these are not the only reasons why the French can produce cheaper than we can. The fact is, one workman there will have from six to seven boys (in a factory where I worked this was the case, and I knew it was generally so). I don't know what wages were given to the lads, but the workman himself used to draw from 70 to 80 francs weekly, and had full employment. Another reason why the French can produce cheaper than we can, you see, sir, is because the French have not our immense national debt to bear them down; and all these things considered, I maintain that it is impossible for an English workman to compete with a Frenchman. Again, there is a great rage for everything French, and so there is not the same employment for *us*. French goods is the fashion of the day. This is certainly not due to any superiority on the part of the workman, which is evident from the fact that an English workman readily obtains employment in France, and—in Boulogne certainly— gets half a franc more for making boots than a Frenchman. As to the injury that the introduction of French boots into England has done the English workman, I will mention this fact, that immediately the duty upon them was reduced, our wages were reduced likewise.

This, I think, was in 1842 (Sir Robert Peel's tariff). Our wages then fell 15 per cent, and have never got up since, and besides this, the quantity of employment among us has decreased most materially.

"The Northampton goods injure us to an equal, if not a greater extent. They produce even cheaper than the Frenchmen, but then it is done upon the factory system. The greatest part of the boots made there are produced, as in France, by a number of lads working under one master, and this is carried on even to a greater extent than in France. In fact, it is a common saying among us that every child in Northampton has a leather apron. The Northamptoners have nearly cut the French out of the market. Most of the French boots sold in London are Northampton made—for there, from the employment of a greater number of children than in France, they produce cheaper still. Again, the rents of the Northampton people are much lower than here; in fact it is the London rents that eat the people up.

"But a greater evil than all is the competition among the masters; almost every one, excepting the most respectable of them, is trying to force a trade by underselling the others. This, of course, masters may do in two ways—either by the reduction of their own profits or by cutting down the wages of the working-men. The cheap men may, perhaps, take a little off *their* profits, but in general they undersell their neighbours by means of taking as much as they can off *our* wages. These are always the first things they attack. Masters tell us that their customers can get boots elsewhere at a lower price, and they must either reduce their prices or lose their customers altogether. This competition among the masters is one of the chief causes of the competition among the working-men. A workman being paid less for his work is obliged to do more, in order to get a living at his trade. Let us say that he does half as much again as he used to do—then doesn't it stand to reason that there must be less work left for the others to do; and hence, on a reduction of wages, a number must be thrown out of employ. Again, in order to gain a competency at the low-price work, an operative employs his wife, and, in many cases, two or three lads to help him, and then he finds that he can produce a greater quantity as a less price than other workmen. He then, in order to keep all the boys in full employ, offers to the employers to do their work at a less price than the usual wages. So that you see the masters compete and the men compete, and between them the trade is being ruined as fast as it can. Yes, it ultimately must come to that. I often lie awake and think of the evils in our trade, but can't see how it's to be altered. I trace it in this way. The cheap French and Northampton goods deprive the employers of their regular customers, and that causes them to compete with the cheap shops, and consequently to cut down our wages. Then this in its turn causes the workmen to compete, and to underwork one another, in order to obtain employment. I tell you what it is, sir, we shall shortly have the same system in London as in France and Northampton, unless something is done to stop it.

"A man's own children will soon be the means of driving him from the market altogether, or compelling him to come down to their rate of wages; and if we are forced to put our children to work directly they are able, they cannot receive any education whatever, and then their minds and bodies will be both stunted. Of course, that must have a demoralizing effect upon the next generation. For my own part, as the trade is going down every day, I could not think of bringing my boys to it, considering their future welfare—and what else I am to do with them I can't say. My earnings are so small now and my income so much reduced, that I shouldn't have the means to apprentice them to any other trade. In the years '45, '46, and '47 I was in a much better condition than I am now. Then I was able to take my periodicals in. I used to have near a shilling's worth of them every week, sir. I took in *Chambers's Journal*. I took in 'Knight's Cyclopaedia' and others of the same kind. I used to have my weekly newspaper, too. But since '48 I have not had the most of them, and I now take in none at all—I can't afford it. In '45 and '46, I was able to live better than I do now. The cheap provisions have done me no good whatever." "My husband," interrupted the wife, "has been making less since food has been getting cheaper. In '46 his work was more regular than it is now. When we were first married the wages were 1s. 4d. a pair of boots more than they are at present, and more of them to do. Two years ago the meat was very dear, I recollect, and the potatoes and bread too; but there is no fault to be found with the present price of provisions. But since they have been getting cheaper, I am sure that our comforts have been decreasing rather than increasing. Why, sir, if it goes on this way, the workhouse stares us in the face. But the intention we have is to go into a club this winter, and raise funds to emigrate to America, unless the trade improves greatly, which we see no prospect of." "I don't see myself (said the man at work) how it is to be altered. I, like thousands of others of the working men, have been struggling hard for these many years, and yet I get no forwarder. Last year I went back in my rent £10, and how I am to fetch it up I can't say. I suppose I must go to the loan-office, and pay through the nose for the money. I should be the happiest mortal alive, and be contented, if I could be certain of a fair quantity of employment and a fair rate of wages for it, but it's vexatious in the extreme to an industriously inclined working man to go to seek work and be unable to get it. . . ."

## LETTER XXXIII—7 FEBRUARY 1850[4]

*Contrast between past and present*

To enable the reader to contrast the present rate of the workman's income with the past, and so to judge of the earnings of a *bootman* in the palmy days of the trade, I give the statement of a first-rate workman employed by the late Mr. Hoby. My informant is now a small master on his own account. He was what is called a *ready man*; that is, one who can work at his trade with more than average celerity.

"I got work at Mr. Hoby's," he said, "not long after the battle of Waterloo, in 1815, and was told by my fellow-workmen that I wasn't born soon enough to see good times; but I've lived long enough to see bad ones. Though I wasn't born soon enough, as they said, I could earn and did earn £150 a year, something short of £3 a week; and that for eight years, when trade became not so good. Mr. Hoby used to send out returned boots (misfits) to America, and in a slack time kept his regular hands going, making boots for the American market, and paying his bootmen 7s. 2d. a pair for them. I never sat still for want of work until he dropped this foreign trade. One week a shopmate of mine had twenty pairs to take pay for. The regular wages was 8s. 2d. for the ground-work of Wellingtons with three-quarter heels, and liberal extras. I could then play my £1 a corner at whist. I *wouldn't* play at that time for less than 5s. I could afford a glass of wine, but never was a drinker; and, for all that, I had my £100 in the Four per Cents for a long time (I lent it to a friend afterwards), and from £40 to £50 in the savings bank. Some made more than me, though I *must* work. I can't stand still. One journeyman, to my knowledge, saved £2,000; he once made 34 pairs of boots in three weeks. The bootmen then at Mr. Hoby's were all respectable men; they were like gentlemen—smoking their pipes, in their frilled shirts, like gentlemen—all but the drunkards. At the trade meetings, Hoby's best men used to have one corner of the room to themselves, and were called the House

[4] To enable "the reader to judge" the harm done by the import of foreign shoes, Mayhew provided tables here to show the changes in rates of import duty 1787–1849—and the quantities of footwear imported. Deleted too is a list of prices from official union publications for 1809, 1812 and 1838, illustrating the decline in wages.

of Lords. There was more than 100 of us when I became one; and before then there were even a greater number. Mr. Hoby has paid five hundred pounds a week in wages. It was easy to save money in those days; one could hardly help it. We shall never see the like again."

By way of contrast to the preceding statement, I subjoin the account of a first-class bootman of the present day, whom I saw at work in a room he devoted to the purposes of his labour. He gave me the following statement :

"I have been acquainted with the business for thirty-one years, fifteen years of it as a bootman in London. The wages I received fifteen years ago when I was first employed as a bootman in London, were the same as they are now—or nearly the same—in the shop I have worked for until lately. I had 6s. 6d. per pair for the ground-work of Wellington boots or top boots. There are no extras in the making of top boots; they are now seldom worn except by gentlemen when hunting, and among grooms when in full dress. The best week's work that ever I had in London was £2 0s. 2d. from my own labour, but I had to work late and early, with hardly leisure for meals. With the wages I have told you taking one week with another, I did not earn, as my book shows, more than 20s. a week on an average for the whole time I have been employed. I am now on work at 8s. a pair for the bottom work, but without any extras except sockets; take the work as it comes, so much a pair. At my present work I may average rather more than 21s. a week. I could make far more with constant work. The best workmen have often to sit idle compulsorily. I fear that wages will fall lower still. Many of the aristocracy get their boots from Paris or from a French tradesman in London; but that matters little, for the French masters in London generally give fair wages— some employing no French workmen at all; so that we can't, as reasonable men, complain of them. For every pair of boots ordered from Paris, there is a man the less employed for a day or two in London; so that the labour-market is overstocked. Through men being forced to be idle, the masters can dictate their own terms, and men must give way, or get no work at all; and so wages fall. Masters all tell us that the repeal of the corn-laws enables us to live cheaper, and so wages may properly be reduced—also that, owing to the lowness of provisions and to compete with French goods, they must either at once, or sooner or later, lower their prices. Wages always fall as fast as provisions, and where the present downward tendency will stop I cannot form a notion."

I was afterwards informed that the Bootman's statement was not a criterion as to the average earnings of the trade, he representing merely the very highest class. I therefore saw several others, and give the following extract from the communication made to me by an intelligent man, as embodying the statements of them all. All attributed the falling off in their earnings not to any reduction in prices, but to the slackness of employment :

"I have been more than twenty-five years in the trade," he said, "as boy and man, and have been familiar with the London trade for nine years. At that time (nine years ago) there was decidedly more employment. I then earned 21s. a week the year through on Wellington boots at 7s. a pair (with extras). Now my work is little different as regards the prices paid to me by the employer, but my average earnings do not exceed 14s."[5]

### The City division: two principal strikes

It now only remains for me to give the statements of the City or East-end division of the trade. As a means of connecting the one division with the other, I cannot do better than cite the following interesting narrative of two of the principal strikes in the trade, especially as that which occurred in 1812 was not only the means of separating the City from the West-end Society, but also the cause of the introductions of the cheap Northampton boots into the London market. It is only necessary that I should add, the following account is from the pen of one of the more intelligent of the working men :

"*Limebeer's strike*, which took place in 1806 or 7—I cannot say which—was a hard-fought battle, in which the workmen became eventually the victors. Limebeer was a master living near Bow Church, Cheapside—the shop in which he resided is a shoemaker's to this day. He wanted to reduce the wages of his workmen, and they 'struck the shop'. That there was not a general reduction attempted at that time, is proved by the strike having been limited principally to Limebeer's shop, as is evident from its being called by his name. If it had been otherwise, the strike would not have been so called. Limebeer took every advantage that his situation as a master gave him, backed by capital, and assisted by the strong arm of the law. He sent some of his men to Newgate, where they remained for a considerable time, but there they lived like fighting cocks, for the restrictions of the prison dietary had not then come into fashion. They eat and drank, and made the dark walls of

[5] Testimonies from two West-end boot-closers, a shoeman and a pump-man appeared here, followed by tabulated accounts of the earnings of several West-end journeymen.

Newgate ring with the praises of Crispin, while their wives and families were liberally supported. Cuflin, then a 'crack prizeman' and afterwards an eminent master in Spur-street, Leicester-square, and Willy, afterwards a celebrated master in the Strand, whose shop was about where Exeter-hall now stands, had the supplying them with their daily rations. I remember some doggerel verses written on the occasion, which run :

> 'Limebeer the matter will remember—
> Cuflin supplied the belly timber :
> Lean they went in, but by my troth, sirs,
> As fat as bears from winter's quarters
> They all came out; while Limebeer's purse
> For his mad struggling felt the worse.'

Limebeer, in revenge, swore he would ruin the trade *in toto*, and with that design he invented the system of making boots and shoes with nails and screws. The struggle to perfect this reduced him almost to beggary, and was eventually the cause of his death. Some people said he died from grief, others that he died by his own hand; however, be that as it may, neither masters nor men were gainers by the strike.

"The next, or *divisional strike*, was more disastrous; this took place in 1812, and through it the West-end and City separated, and became two distinct bodies. This took place as follows : the trade came to a resolution to get rid of what was considered a great grievance both by many masters as well as their men, viz. : that some shops in the neighbourhood of high-rated shops, paid a very inferior rate of wages. After several meetings of the trade, they came to the resolution of 'striking up the low-rated shops' to a more equal statement, by demanding an advance of 6d. on boots and 4d. on shoes from all shops that paid under a certain rate. At the same time, that the trade should not be generally disturbed, they levied a fine of a guinea a man that should strike for an advance from any shop of the fair statement. Everything seemed to be going on fairly, and many masters concurred in the scheme, until the men of Mr. Humby's shop, which was reckoned among the first-rates, struck for the 6d. advance. This set the whole trade in a flame. General meetings were called, and the unanimous voice of the trade came to the resolution of enforcing the guinea fine against each of Humby's men. They resisted, and the trade sent a deputation to the master, who hesitated, he not being in a condition to have his shop disturbed at the time. While matters were in this position, Hoby's men to screen Humby's men, with whom they were leagued, struck for the advance, and gained it, so that the whole trade was thrown into confusion. Meeting after meeting was called daily, and every resource of the trade drained to bear the expense of them. The society sent the men on strike into the country, and paid the families of the men who left home a fair subsistence money. The daily meetings were continued, and resolutions agreed to one day were rescinded the next. All was in confusion. The City men accused the West-end with being the cause, and the West-end men were glad to have a reason for quarrelling, and wished for separation.

"The masters formed themselves into a coalition, appointed an acting committee, and bound themselves by rules to support each other by undertaking that each shop should do the other's work in cases of emergency. Such masters as were found out, or even supposed to have done so, were immediately struck; so that there were but few shops but what were in confusion. The masters met at the Crown and Anchor. Other high-wages shops then struck, and the cry out for the division of the East and West end trade became more violent; and on a division at a general meeting called for the purpose, it was resolved by a large majority in their favour. The masters, too, were combined against the men, while they were thus broken up and divided. Several masters, not being able to get their work made in town, cut it out and sent it to Northampton and other parts of the country to be manufactured, resolving on a general reduction; while others had their export orders executed in the country, and the men left town and made the work at a far greater reduction of wages than were offered in the lowest-rated shops in town. Warehouses for the sale of country work were then opened in many parts of the metropolis, while merchants gave their export orders to Northampton, so that the trade was lost to both masters and men, and though nearly 45 years have passed since that period the trade has never recovered the blow it then struck against its own prosperity.

"Thus, through this foolish system and petty quarrelling, confidence has been lost, wages depressed, the trade scattered, and a slop article forced on the consumer, whose manufacture robs the purchaser of his money, while it starves the manufacturer and his family spreading misery and want, which spreads eventually from one branch of the community to another, for one cannot suffer without all bearing a part in the evil. Before the strike of 1812 no Northampton goods had been introduced into London, and all boots and shoes exported from London were made in the metropolis up to that time. But after that period the sale of Northampton goods became general, and they have done more harm to the trade than the reduction on the French work. *Wages have been on the decline ever since then.*"

*Developments in the East-end trade since 1825*

The number of members belonging to the City or Eastern Division of the Associated Boot and Shoe Makers fluctuates between 500 and 600; the number increasing in the spring of each year, according as the trade grows busier, and remaining high until the autumn, when the trade begins to fall away, and the men who had come to town for the season return to the country.[6]

As to the changes which have taken place in the City trade, I had the following statement from an intelligent man :

"From the strike in 1825, which was confined to the City, to 1838, there was but little change in the wages paid to the workmen, the change in the tariff in 1833 not affecting the wages, but we were obliged to change more to the French style of boot making, which involved much greater labour. In 1838 there was another strike, called the Coronation Strike, because taking place at the period of her Majesty was crowned. The object was this—to bring up the lower-paid shops, paying 5s. for new boots, to 6s. (with extras), so approaching the amount paid by the best employers, and the shoes from 3s. to 3s. 6d. The masters, after a very slight opposition, gave way, the best shops being benefited by the change, because one means of their being undersold was checked, however slightly. These masters combined to destroy the power and uses of the union, and partially succeeded. The more honourable part of these *combining* masters, however, did not reduce their wages to any extent, but some knocked off trifling extras. The other portion, whom we call dishonourable, endeavoured at this time to reduce the wages, as well as resist the very reasonable strike for an advance.

"The reduction then contemplated by such masters has been gradually effected since by taking off allowances for extras, and introducing what is called 'shop work', which, they said, was to compete with the French. This 'shop work', so to compete, they stated, could not be paid at the rate of 'bespoke' work; and they took care, at the same time, to insist upon even better work, and *all* the extras, and that on a reduction in the prices to the journeymen (closers and makers) of from 2s. 6d. to 3s. per pair. . . . All this, mind you, is greatly to the injury of our most honourable employers; and since the practice of 'shop work' has been adopted, the competition is so strong, that I fear, without an understanding between the best employers and the unions, the 'dishonourable' masters will effect the ruin of the others. . . .

"I will explain to you the advantages of the unions to masters as

[6] Information about wages in the East-end has been cut.

well as to men. When all masters agree to a society's statement of wages any attempt at a reduction makes us withdraw society men from a master making such an attempt. By that means we compel him to employ inferior workmen—the best workmen are in union—and so prevent the competition with the best made articles which are now, by some masters breaking through the system of the union, brought into ruinous competition with honourable tradesmen, at starvation wages to the men. I think this would be a remedy—to frame laws, for masters and men in union, to pay and receive fixed wages in certain districts—to be called first, second, and third class—each to guarantee that no one class should encroach on the rules regulating the others. That might stop all strikes and disagreements, and tend to a well-regulated system, keeping out the mere 'scab shops' that go for starvation wages, driving them into the hands of only the worst workmen; and so preventing the existent competition."

## LETTER XXXIV—11 FEBRUARY 1850

### Earnings of East-end men's-men

The following account of the earnings of the "men's-men" working for the best shops and the best prices, in the eastern division of the Boot and Shoe making trade, may be taken as a fair average of the wages of the men engaged at the different branches in that district. As far as individual statistics may be relied on, these particulars may be said to represent the income of the class to which the parties belonged from whom they have been obtained: (wages overleaf)

On reference to the table overleaf, it will be found that the earnings of the City men's-men scarcely differ from those of the men's-men at the West-end.[7]

### The women's trade

Having now dealt with the different branches of the *men's trade* in connection with the shops where the best wages are given, I proceed to give an account of the earnings of the operatives in connection with the *women's trade* in a similar position. Of the income and condition of the men "out of society", or working for the lower class of employers, I shall reserve my account until my next letter.

The business of women's shoemaking, like all businesses where a great degree of skill must be exercised to ensure excellence in the

---

[7] A table showing the percentage increase and decrease of numbers in various trades between 1831 and 1841 appeared here, testing the contention of women's men that their trade was overpopulated.

## EAST-END BOOTMAN (FIRST PRICE), No. 1

| | First Quarter | | | Second Quarter | | | Third Quarter | | | Fourth Quarter | | | Total for the Year | | |
|---|---|---|---|---|---|---|---|---|---|---|---|---|---|---|---|
| | £ | s. | d. | £ | s. | d. | £ | s. | d. | £ | s. | d. | £ | s. | d. |
| 1834 | 16 | 6 | 5 | 19 | 18 | 1 | 18 | 12 | 10 | 18 | 9 | 9 | 73 | 7 | 1 |
| Average pr week | 1 | 5 | 1¼ | 1 | 10 | 7¼ | 1 | 8 | 8 | 1 | 8 | 5¼ | 1 | 8 | 2 |
| 1835 | 18 | 5 | 8 | 17 | 19 | 4 | 18 | 10 | 7 | 20 | 15 | 7 | 75 | 11 | 2 |
| Average pr week | 1 | 8 | 1½ | 1 | 7 | 7½ | 1 | 8 | 6 | 1 | 11 | 11½ | 1 | 9 | 0 |
| 1836 | 19 | 6 | 0 | 18 | 17 | 9 | 20 | 3 | 2 | 20 | 2 | 5 | 78 | 9 | 4 |
| Average pr week | 1 | 9 | 8¼ | 1 | 9 | 0½ | 1 | 11 | 0 | 1 | 10 | 11¼ | 1 | 10 | 2 |
| 1837 | 19 | 11 | 1 | 19 | 3 | 7 | 20 | 7 | 11 | 18 | 12 | 0 | 77 | 14 | 7 |
| Average pr week | 1 | 10 | 1 | 1 | 9 | 6 | 1 | 11 | 4½ | 1 | 8 | 7¼ | 1 | 9 | 10 |
| 1845 | 16 | 5 | 11 | 18 | 13 | 9 | 17 | 18 | 2 | 18 | 16 | 0 | 17 | 13 | 10 |
| Average pr week | 1 | 5 | 0¾ | 1 | 8 | 9 | 1 | 7 | 6½ | 1 | 8 | 11 | 1 | 7 | 6 |
| 1846 | 17 | 7 | 3 | 17 | 13 | 9 | 17 | 8 | 11 | 16 | 14 | 9 | 69 | 4 | 8 |
| Average pr week | 1 | 6 | 8½ | 1 | 7 | 2½ | 1 | 6 | 10 | 1 | 5 | 9 | 1 | 6 | 7 |
| 1847 | 17 | 7 | 2 | 15 | 17 | 7 | 16 | 17 | 6 | 16 | 16 | 5 | 66 | 18 | 8 |
| Average pr week | 1 | 6 | 8¼ | 1 | 4 | 5 | 1 | 5 | 11½ | 1 | 5 | 10½ | 1 | 5 | 8 |

## EAST-END BOOTMAN (SECOND PRICE), No. 2

| | £ | s. | d. | £ | s. | d. | £ | s. | d. | £ | s. | d. | £ | s. | d. |
|---|---|---|---|---|---|---|---|---|---|---|---|---|---|---|---|
| 1845 | 15 | 15 | 9 | 15 | 0 | 9 | 16 | 16 | 6 | 17 | 1 | 0 | 64 | 14 | 0 |
| Average pr week | 1 | 4 | 3¼ | 1 | 3 | 1½ | 1 | 5 | 10½ | 1 | 6 | 2¾ | 1 | 4 | 10½ |
| 1846 | 19 | 6 | 0 | 19 | 10 | 2 | 18 | 14 | 9 | 18 | 6 | 9 | 75 | 17 | 8 |
| Average pr week | 1 | 9 | 8¼ | 1 | 10 | 1¾ | 1 | 8 | 9¾ | 1 | 8 | 2½ | 1 | 9 | 2 |
| 1847 | 15 | 15 | 7 | 14 | 10 | 0 | 15 | 17 | 3 | 14 | 13 | 6 | 60 | 16 | 4 |
| Average pr week | 1 | 4 | 3¼ | 1 | 2 | 3½ | 1 | 4 | 4¾ | 1 | 2 | 6¾ | 1 | 3 | 4½ |
| 1848 | 12 | 19 | 0 | 13 | 4 | 0 | 13 | 11 | 9 | 17 | 6 | 9 | 57 | 1 | 6 |
| Average pr week | 0 | 19 | 11 | 1 | 0 | 3½ | 1 | 0 | 10¾ | 1 | 6 | 8 | 1 | 1 | 11½ |

## EAST-END BOOT-CLOSER (FIRST PRICE), No. 3

| | £ | s. | d. | £ | s. | d. | £ | s. | d. | £ | s. | d. | £ | s. | d. |
|---|---|---|---|---|---|---|---|---|---|---|---|---|---|---|---|
| 1848 | 13 | 5 | 10½ | 16 | 10 | 2½ | 16 | 7 | 6 | 16 | 5 | 5 | 62 | 9 | 0 |
| Average pr week | 1 | 0 | 4½ | 1 | 5 | 4¾ | 1 | 5 | 2¼ | 1 | 5 | 0¼ | 1 | 4 | 0 |

## EAST-END BOOT-CLOSER (SECOND PRICE), No. 4

| | £ | s. | d. | £ | s. | d. | £ | s. | d. | £ | s. | d. | £ | s. | d. |
|---|---|---|---|---|---|---|---|---|---|---|---|---|---|---|---|
| 1847 | 13 | 10 | 3 | 13 | 6 | 5 | 11 | 16 | 11 | 12 | 4 | 11 | 50 | 18 | 6 |
| Average pr week | 1 | 0 | 9 | 1 | 0 | 5½ | 0 | 18 | 1¾ | 0 | 18 | 9 | 0 | 19 | 7 |

## EAST-END BOOT-CLOSER (FIRST PRICE), TWO HANDS, No. 5

| | £ | s. | d. | £ | s. | d. | £ | s. | d. | £ | s. | d. | £ | s. | d. |
|---|---|---|---|---|---|---|---|---|---|---|---|---|---|---|---|
| 1839 | 24 | 19 | 1 | 24 | 14 | 7½ | 21 | 17 | 9 | 26 | 11 | 11 | 98 | 3 | 4 |
| Average pr week | 1 | 18 | 4½ | 1 | 18 | 0½ | 1 | 13 | 8 | 2 | 0 | 11 | 1 | 17 | 9 |
| 1847 | 22 | 10 | 4 | 18 | 19 | 0 | 15 | 12 | 10 | 20 | 2 | 0 | 77 | 4 | 2 |
| Average pr week | 1 | 14 | 7½ | 1 | 9 | 2½ | 1 | 4 | 0¾ | 1 | 10 | 11 | 1 | 9 | 8 |

## EAST-END BOOT-CLOSER (SECOND PRICE), TWO HANDS, No. 6

| | £ | s. | d. | £ | s. | d. | £ | s. | d. | £ | s. | d. | £ | s. | d. |
|---|---|---|---|---|---|---|---|---|---|---|---|---|---|---|---|
| 1849 | 19 | 19 | 7 | 19 | 1 | 0 | 15 | 8 | 2 | 14 | 3 | 1½ | 68 | 11 | 10 |
| Average pr week | 1 | 10 | 8¾ | 1 | 9 | 3½ | 1 | 3 | 8¼ | 1 | 1 | 9¼ | 1 | 6 | 4½ |

manufacture, has its divisions and sub-divisions, but these are far less numerous than they were, and are even becoming less so still, one now blending with another. Some, however, are still employed, if not entirely, on *sew-rounds* (a pump sole sewn all round) and on the best descriptions of shoes—silk, satin, or morocco. Some few are employed as *weltmen*, that is, in making welted shoes (or boots), but the majority are what is known as *general men*—men who can make up any description of work that the tradesman has to give out. The sew-round, whose work is the most exact and delicate, can readily "turn his hand to welts", but the weltman, if long used to welts alone, cannot so easily make sew-rounds.

The Society of the Women's-men, or men working for the best rate of wages, consists of five distinct divisions, including the West-end—the Chelsea—the East-end—the Borough—and the Stepney districts.[8]

### A West-end sew-round of the first class

*A West-end sew-round of the first class* gave me the following statement :

"I have known the women's trade ever since I was nine—about twenty-seven years. When I worked as a journeyman on first-class sew-rounds, I could earn 32s. That's more than fourteen years ago. Take the year round, I now average 24s. a week; but my work (having a turn at corks in the winter) runs up more money than other men's. The first cause of the decline in earning is, I think, owing to the bringing in of cheap French goods, and to the number of 'slaughter shops' (slop shops) now open. There were not near so many slaughter shops open until French goods came in so cheap. Wages have fallen greatly at the bespoke shops within these twelve or fourteen years. About seven years ago, as well as I recollect the time, there was a reduction of wages paid by the best shops, amounting from 2s. to 3s. a week on the earnings of the men. I used to get 3s. where I now get 2s. 8d. for satin sew-rounds. On pump boots in my time there has been a reduction of 8d., and all other things in proportion. The cheapness of corn is certainly a great advantage to the working man; but the masters, it is generally feared, will take advantage of it, and offer to reduce wages further. When the in-come-tax was first put on several masters reduced the wages they paid from 10 to 15 per cent, and so more than paid it that way. It's the slackness of work in many good shops that is the injury. If men can't get regular employ there, they are forced to work, in the

[8] A statement of piece rates and weekly earnings in the women's branch, 1811–1840 has been cut.

way of by-strokes, for lower-priced shops—and so low-priced work, well made, gets its hold."[9]

### Earnings of West-end and Chelsea women's men

The earnings of the *West-end and Chelsea women's men*, calculated from accounts which have been supplied to me are as follows :

WEST-END WOMEN'S GENERAL MAN (FIRST PRICE), No. 1

|  | First Quarter | | | Second Quarter | | | Third Quarter | | | Fourth Quarter | | | Total for the Year | | |
|---|---|---|---|---|---|---|---|---|---|---|---|---|---|---|---|
|  | £ | s. | d. | £ | s. | d. | £ | s. | d. | £ | s. | d. | £ | s. | d. |
| 1849 | 13 | 4 | 3 | 12 | 7 | 4 | 13 | 10 | 5 | 13 | 10 | 10 | 52 | 12 | 10 |
| Average pr week | 1 | 0 | 4 |  | 19 | 0¼ | 1 | 0 | 9½ | 1 | 0 | 10½ | 1 | 0 | 2¾ |

WEST-END WOMEN'S GENERAL MAN (FIRST PRICE), No. 2

|  | £ | s. | d. | £ | s. | d. | £ | s. | d. | £ | s. | d. | £ | s. | d. |
|---|---|---|---|---|---|---|---|---|---|---|---|---|---|---|---|
| 1848 | 16 | 16 | 2 | 13 | 6 | 0 | 12 | 11 | 11 | 12 | 4 | 11 | 54 | 19 | 0 |
| Average pr week | 1 | 5 | 10¼ | 1 | 0 | 5½ |  | 19 | 3½ |  | 18 | 9 | 1 | 1 | 1½ |

WEST-END WOMEN'S GENERAL MAN (SECOND PRICE), No. 3

|  | £ | s. | d. | £ | s. | d. | £ | s. | d. | £ | s. | d. | £ | s. | d. |
|---|---|---|---|---|---|---|---|---|---|---|---|---|---|---|---|
| 1849 |  | 9 | 16 | 3 |  | 9 | 13 | 6 |  | 9 | 14 | 5 |  | 9 | 11 | 7 | 38 | 15 | 9 |
| Average pr week |  | 15 | 1 |  | 14 | 10½ |  | 14 | 11¼ |  | 14 | 8¾ |  | 14 | 11 |

WEST-END WOMEN'S GENERAL MAN (THIRD PRICE), No. 4

|  | £ | s. | d. | £ | s. | d. | £ | s. | d. | £ | s. | d. | £ | s. | d. |
|---|---|---|---|---|---|---|---|---|---|---|---|---|---|---|---|
| 1848 | 8 | 1 | 8 | 8 | 4 | 1 | 8 | 9 | 5 | 6 | 17 | 10 | 31 | 13 | 0 |
| Average pr week |  | 12 | 5 |  | 12 | 7¼ |  | 13 | 0¼ |  | 10 | 7 |  | 12 | 2 |

CHELSEA WOMEN'S GENERAL MAN (SECOND PRICE), No. 5

|  | £ | s. | d. | £ | s. | d. | £ | s. | d. | £ | s. | d. | £ | s. | d. |
|---|---|---|---|---|---|---|---|---|---|---|---|---|---|---|---|
| 1848 | 9 | 3 | 10 | 9 | 7 | 8 | 10 | 19 | 9 | 10 | 11 | 0 | 40 | 2 | 3 |
| Average pr week |  | 14 | 1½ |  | 14 | 5 |  | 16 | 10¾ |  | 16 | 2¾ |  | 15 | 5 |
| 1849 | 9 | 16 | 10 | 9 | 13 | 4 | 10 | 1 | 7 | 9 | 19 | 3 | 39 | 11 | 0 |
| Average pr week |  | 15 | 1¼ |  | 14 | 10¼ |  | 15 | 6 |  | 15 | 3¾ |  | 15 | 2½ |

### A City sew-round working for the best rate of wages

As to the earnings of the City *women's men* working for the best rate of wages, I obtained the subjoined statement :

"I belong to the *City* branch of the Society of Women's Shoemakers. I am a *sew-round man*. I make the lighter description worn by ladies, such as silk and satin shoes. The binder prepares 'the upper'—whether of silk, satin, kid, or any other material—and the upper, so prepared, is given out to the 'sew-round man' to be sewn to the sole. The term sew-round is given to distinguish the branch

---

[9] Interviews with a West-end sew-round of the third class and a general man doing the better class of work, to whom Mayhew had been directed by the Union secretaries, followed here.

from any other description of shoe worn by ladies, and consists in sewing the 'upper' once round to the sole. The sole is generally of one substance, being of the very lightest description. I work for the best wages that are given by the 'order warehouses' of the City. The parties who give out ladies' work in the City may be divided into the 'bespoke shops' and the warehouses. These warehouses supply the country shops and the export trade. They give the work out to each workman in large quantities. The workmen who take the work out generally do not belong to societies.

"The majority of the warehouses give very low wages, as low as they possibly can. I work for one of the most liberal of these warehouses. Before doing so I was working for the bespoke trade. . . . Deducting expenses, a 'women's-man's' earnings at bespoke work would be about 13s. a week throughout the whole year. At the best kind of warehouse work a women's-man may earn about the same per week on an average; but, to do that, as the work is worse paid, of course the man must work longer hours in the brisk season, and oftener in the slack. At the lowest price warehouses it is impossible to say how little a man may earn. To get a bare living he must work a greater number of hours, and very hard, or else he must employ a number of boys. This class of work belongs properly to slop-work, and is mostly carried on by the employment of boys.

"This boy labour is one of the chief evils of our trade. I will give you an instance. A deputation of women's-men waited upon some of the employers respecting the frequent reductions taking place in the wages of the men. The employers remarked that many of the men were enabled to make a very decent appearance, notwithstanding the reductions which were said to be so great an evil. Whereupon the deputation replied, that such an appearance was kept up solely by boy work. The masters made answer that they cared not whether boy or man was employed, so long as they got their work cheap. 'Let them all get boys,' was the reply. The deputation then wished to know what was to become of the men; but the employers again asserted that it mattered not to them so long as they got their work cheap. To such an extent has the system of employing boys increased in the trade that it's a saying among the men now, that it's impossible to do without a boy to help. These boys are not apprentice boys, but taken on from ten to sixteen years of age, and instructed in the trade. Thus, a sharp lad will be perfect in two years, and then his labour is brought into the market, to reduce the man to the boy's level. . . .

"I attribute the decline in wages (I'm speaking of my own particular shop and my own particular branch, so as to confine myself to facts that have come within my own knowledge), to the introduction of French goods and the superabundance of labour in the market, produced by the employment of boys. I will give you an example of the effect that the lowering the duty upon the French goods had upon our wages. Immediately after the reduction of the duty in 1842 my employer went to Paris, and bought over 20 gross of French silk and satin goods. He showed a sample of these to the workmen employed upon similar kind of work, and produced the invoice to prove how cheap he could purchase such an article upon the Continent. He did not state that he purposed making a reduction of the wages, but strongly insinuated as much; and from that time to the present he has steadily lowered our wages at every slack season of the year . . .

"It would make your blood boil to know how little is paid for the cheapest shoe work; and yet the masters confess that it is out of this badly paid work that they get the most profit. My employer himself told me as much. 'Trash,' said he, 'as it is, I get more out of it than I do out of the better work, and with less trouble to myself.' He was speaking of a large order to Canada, and comparing it with another for the better description of goods from a respectable house in town. So bad is the trash work which we send out to the colonies, that we are losing even the little export trade that is left us as fast as we can. All the capitalist thinks of is to obtain a sightly article at the lowest possible figure. The durability of the goods he never troubles his head about; indeed he never examines them for that : the present gain is his only object, and *we* are the main losers in the end. He tells us, if we complain, that the trade is overstocked with hands, when he himself has deprived us of the work through his own cupidity. The market being overstocked by the means I have before stated—that is, by the introduction of French goods throwing so many men out of employment, and the loss of the export trade— the more skilful hands alone can get work at the better price shops. The consequence is that the less skilful are left without any work to do; they then begin and manufacture on their own account. This is the trash-work previously described, and this they hawk round to the trade wherever they can get sale for it, and at any price. The trash-work is produced by what are called chamber-masters; and, in order that they may be able to undersell the regular trade, these chamber-masters employ boys of all ages, whom they obtain from the workhouses and prisons. By means of their labour, boots and shoes are got up and sold to the slaughter-houses at prices that must ultimately starve all the better workmen out of the trade. . . ."[10]

[10] A short account of wages and conditions in the Stepney and Borough districts has been deleted; here too "the principal evil is the chamber-masters, with the system of compound labour by boys, girls, and women".

*The "strong" trade*

I now give a short account of *the "strong" trade*, or rather of such portion of it as is recognized as "legal", owing to its being in union. The wares made by these men are described by a correspondent, whose letter I give. Strength, so as to ensure durability of wear, is the main thing aimed at. To effect this, heavy nails (both hammered and cast) are used to strengthen the sole, which, with the upper part, is of thick coarse leather, with nails or iron tips round the heels. The work was well described to me as "downright labour"; and my informant, a "strong" man, who made light of his labour, might have added, "of the hardest kind." The threads used to sew the sole to the welt are, as was described to me by another workman, "thick enough to frighten a West-end bootman". The hands of some of the men are callous, like horn, from the induration caused by the constant friction of the threads. One hard-working man, however, after he had been obliged to be idle for a while, when he got to work again, had his hands blistered and cut by the threads in a way to inspire an involuntary shudder, the cuts and blisters being black with wax. Even in the wares of these men, however, there was a proof of the excellence to which workmanship must be carried in London. I saw a "strong" man at work, and he expended some time in polishing the sole of a very strong cheap shoe, so as to make it sightly (*or* as they frequently call it, *viewly*); this was the more noticeable, as the work was for no window-show, and the sole, of course, would be dirtied by the first wear; but still, with the poorest, the eye must be pleased.

I give the statement of a man familiar with the strong trade for the last 11 years: "When I first knew the trade 11 years ago, work was good; any man who could put leather together in the shape of a shoe could get work as a strong man—with the proviso, however, that the work must be strong for wear; it must hold together firmly with wax and thread, so as not to fall to pieces. Nothing depended upon skill at the time, but on bone and sinew; a man of great physical strength might then earn his 24s. a week, by working very long hours; the average weekly earnings of the strong man at that time I reckon at 16s. My average earnings were that. . . . The average earnings of strong men now I reckon at 12s. a week, the cost of grindery not included; but that is only when men are in full work. Men casually employed will not average much more than half that sum; in fact, things have come to such a state, that we are now going on the co-operative system; we must take to that, or men may starve to death. I believe that the masters have next to nothing left from their competition one with another—I mean nothing left in the way of profit over and above all the cost of material, and fair wages, out of the price for which they sell the goods—and so they drive at profit by reducing the poor workman's wages still lower. We are heartily sick of strikes, which, as they have been conducted generally, have been, and can be, of no permanent benefit to the men.

"Had we £50 we could employ all our men next month, and pay at the rate of 5 per cent per annum interest. We could appeal to the better class of workmen, and I think could get better prices. I have no doubt of it. I know that former attempts of the kind have failed, but then they were managed by people who did not understand the business. Indeed, we are now in operation in the co-operative way, by way of a commencement, though not in so large a way as we wish and intend. There is, I consider, no class so adapted for co-operation as our class of strong men. We could appeal to the sympathies of the great body of labouring men. We have nothing to do with gentlemen's work, and don't want. France doesn't *interfere* with our trade, neither does Northampton; we are all in all among ourselves. The great impediment to our getting on has been our poverty, and the ignorance it carries along with it. As for what things tend to in the future, I'll tell you. I hate physical force and revolutions, but I went to Kennington-common on the 10th of April, knowing or caring nothing what might happen."

Of the "truck" and "lodging" system pursued among the "strong" men, I shall have something to say in my next.

## The slop trade

Having thus given the characteristics and condition of the "legal", or honourable trade, I next turn my inquiry to the state of the labouring men, women, and children employed by the slop-masters, who are distinguished from the "wages" (or legal) shops by the terms *"illegal"*, *"scab"*, or *"slaughter-shop"* keepers. I have reason to believe that the disclosures I shall make of the patiently-endured privations of numbers of the poor people working for these masters, and of the oppressions practised on them, will probably surpass the narratives of misery, and consequent dirt and disease, which I have made public concerning the tailors.

Relative, then, to the branch of the business with which I have next to deal, I give the following communications from a shoemaker, a working man, of whose intelligence I received sufficient proofs, and whose character assures me that every reliance may be placed upon his statement—to say nothing of the corroboration I received incidentally in the course of my present enquiry. In my next letter I shall give evidence on this subject. My correspondent says :

"I put together in the best way I can, a few matters of fact on the subject of which you are treating. I first give you information belonging to the branch called '*men's men*', and I will endeavour to put down in order all that I know of what directly injures the once honourable trade of boot and shoe makers, leaving all supposition and indirect means of injury out of the question for the present. First, in Northampton, the greatest boot and shoe manufacturing town in the world, the work is made after the manner of the East-end women's work—sewers, stitchers, women, boys, girls, families all labour together. I will show you, sir, how this and other systems operate against the honourable trade. There are several hundred shops in London known by the names of Emporium, Magazine, Depot, &c., which receive most of the thousands of pairs of boots daily made in Northampton. These houses are kept going by such men as undermentioned, which is only a sample : each person has several shops in different parts, and not one in ten knows anything of the trade previous to commencing business : W., has 6 shops, and he was originally a milkman; D., 6, formerly a carver and gilder; D., 6, an old painter and glazier; D., 4, once a lawyer's clerk; S., 6, a pawnbroker's man; H., 7, a huckster; H., 3, a linendraper; F.H.R., 3; O., 5; P., 5; S., 3; D., 4; B., 5; B., 6; M., 2; K., 4. In all 75 shops among 16 persons. These men are a curse to the bespoke trade, in the men's department, and refuges for the destitute for the chamber master, in the women's trade. The smaller shopkeepers in the slop, or Northampton trade, are allowed 10 per cent for cash, if they go to 'Hampton for their goods. The manufacturers at 'Hampton have many agents in town and country. In a store in Hatton-garden may be seen, any day, from 300,000 to 400,000 pairs of boots and shoes, and these agents are empowered to give, upon recommendation, one month's credit and 5 per cent. In St. John-street-road, City, &c., there are many private houses for disposing of the better or best sort of Northampton work. These private houses sell wholesale and export, but will sell a single pair at the wholesale price. Their wholesale price for best work, Wellingtons, is 13s. 6d. per pair. They are supplied from 'Hampton, at 10s. per pair, so they get a profit of 3s. 6d. per pair. The shopkeeper who sends them home to his customer as bespoke, charges £1 1s.; sometimes more. This is one tremendous blow to the honourable trade.

"The Northampton of London is the East-end. It can be proved that 10,000 pairs of boots and shoes are manufactured daily in the three principal districts, Bethnal-green, Whitechapel, and Spital-fields. When I first thought I would place the state of the East-end trade before you, it did not enter into my mind to conceive what an important task I had undertaken. I have waded through many difficulties to obtain the truthful information which I now bring under your notice. I have got together information from all parts of London, and will endeavour to show the principal bad influences which have brought the once honourable trade of boot and shoe making to what it is. Thousands of ladies' French shoes, that never saw France, are made at this end of the town, and worn by the first ladies in the land. There are shopkeepers in all parts of London who have lasts and patterns of a French shape, who find their own material, send them to the East-end, and have them made at a very low rate of wages. The material and wages cost under 2s. per pair, and they are sold for goods imported from France at 4s. 6d. and 5s. 6d. One instance will show the way in which goods are, what we call, 'got up', and will exhibit the working of the whole system. I will take Mr. —— an exporter, of ——, for example, who serves many shops in town and country, besides having a large export trade. Some years since, town and country shops cut their own work, and employed men to make it, and paid a fair rate of wages, besides employing a clicker; but now they can buy their work by the gross or dozen of Mr. —— making as much or more profit by purchasing than they can by cutting it themselves. Mr. —— supplies his customers in the following manner. A.B., of the West-end, or country, sends a letter to Mr. ——, after this form :

"Mr. ——

"Sir—Please to send me a half-gross of sew-rounds, as quick as possible. Pairs—6, 5, 12, 24, 12, 12. Sizes—1, 2, 3, 4, 5, 6. Yours,
&c. A.B."

The order may be for any sort of work, such as I have mentioned. A, in Bethnal-green, makes sew-rounds; B manufactures springs; C manufactures welts; D manufactures channels; E manufactures common boots; F manufactures best boots.

"Mr. A, please to send me by such a time—pairs, 6, 6, 12, 24, 12, 12; sizes, 1, 2, 3, 4, 5, 6. You will oblige——."

"The same plan is adopted for getting up orders for exportation. Sew-rounds are made for 3d., 4d., and 5d. per pair. A man must be quick at his work to make six pairs a day, 2s. 6d.—that is, in the summer season. There are between 300 and 400 boys at the East-end, known by the name of sewers. Some of these boys can sew 18 pairs a day. The man uses the knife, &c.; the boy sews for him; and the man and boy between them complete the work of three men, the boy having 5s., 6s., or 7s., a week, according to agreement. Sometimes the boy is paid 1d. a pair. Again, A, manufacturing sew-rounds, keeps a private house : say, in the summer he employs thirty hands out of doors, and five to work and lodge in the house;

PLATE XV.   Family Work by Cruikshank

PLATE XVI. Seamen Demonstrating Against the Repeal of the Navigation Acts, 1848

in the winter A will discharge his hands, or, if he has capital, he will employ, say ten single men to work and lodge in his house. All work and sleep in one large room—there are some exceptions. Their employer charges 2s. 6d. a week for lodging and sitting room—£1 5s. per week for the ten. The work which he paid 5s. a dozen for making in summer he reduces to 4s. a dozen in winter; so, if the men make six pairs each day, A makes out of their labour 5s. per day. He keeps his work neatly packed in a dry room until the spring of the year, and then he makes a pretty penny. These kind of barracks abound at the East-end. Most of the splendid ladies' work shown in shop windows is made in these winter barracks, where, in Spitalfields, several men work in a room, with only one coat among them, and rarely see a clean shirt. Some masters serve their in-door workmen with tea, coffee, bread, tobacco, coals : some keep Tom-and-Jerry shops, and the poor wretches rarely have 6d. to take on Saturday night. There are also many families who make work, and hawk it about from house to house.

"This system which has, I believe, the worst effect on the woman's trade throughout England, is *chamber-mastering*. There are between 300 and 400 chamber-masters. Commonly the man has a wife and three or four children, ten years old or upwards. The wife cuts out the work for the binders, the husband does the knife-work; the children sew with uncommon rapidity. The husband, when the work is finished at night, goes out with it, though wet and cold, and perhaps hungry—his wife and children waiting his return. He returns sometimes, having sold his work at cost price, or not cleared 1s. 6d. for the day's labour of himself and family. In the winter, by this means, the shopkeepers and warehouses can take advantage of the chamber-master, buying the work at their own price. . . .

"It is impossible to ascertain accurately how many men are employed on this business. It is according to the state of the trade for export or home use; but in the brisk season (summer) it is, as near as I can ascertain, as undermentioned."

### Numbers employed in the slop trade

My correspondent here gives a list of 58 masters, employing, as nearly as he can ascertain, 1,173 men, and paying them at the rate of 3s., 3s. 6d., 4s., 4s. 6d., and 5s. 6d. *per dozen* pairs for wages. Of these the greatest number (120) are employed by a person in Hounsditch; the next in order (as regards the number of poor men employed) is a house in Cheapside (100). My correspondent then continues :

"There are many other private warehouses in the City. Kings-

I

land, Hackney, Somers-town, Petticoat-lane, abound with them. At the back of Shoreditch there are a great many chamber-masters who employ from four to five persons to work and lodge in the house, herding together in dirt and filth—scenes which must be seen to be understood. Commencing from Farringdon-street, and embracing the City, Islington, Somers-town, Bethnal-green, Hackney, Kingsland, Shoreditch, Whitechapel, Spitalfields, Moorfields, Tower Hamlets, Mile-end, Haggerstone, and the adjacent neighbourhoods of these shoe manufacturing districts, there are :

| | |
|---|---:|
| Women's and children's makers | 2,000 |
| Sewing boys, upwards of | 400 |
| Engaged for bespoke and shopwork, not slops | 500 |
| Sewing girls and women, boot and shoe binders | 1,500 |
| Chamber-masters (not including wives and children) upwards of | 400 |
| Persons of all ages and sexes—makers, binders, sewers | 4,800 |

I do not suppose that my calculations are free from error, but I can say with certainty that they are considerably *under* the mark, for in no instance have I overrated; indeed, I believe, if, instead of 4,800, I reversed it to 8,400 it would not be much above the truth. . . ."

## LETTER XXXV—14 FEBRUARY 1850

I now come to the Cheap and Slop Shoe Trade. It will be seen that the lowness of prices is maintained by the same iniquitous means as in the tailors' trade. Every meanness and petty cheat is practised upon the working man to reduce his wages, and to increase the gains of the slop capitalist for whom he labours. Not a trade have I investigated where the cheap prices have been maintained by the ordinary operation of the laws of commerce.

For the present the shoemakers shall speak for themselves. One fact, however, the reader will not fail to perceive—that the distress of the workmen at the East-end is in no way referable to the importation of French boots into this country. The evil can be ascribed to nothing else than the insatiable greed of those who employ them. The slop shoemakers are, if possible, in a worse state than the slop tailors.

*They speak for themselves: a shoebinder*

As an exponent of the horrors of this system, let me first give the narrative of a poor shoe-binder—a widow woman—a struggling, industrious, honest creature, to whom I was directed as a fair specimen of the class. It will be seen that I found the poor creature literally starving—and that, after toiling night and day to support herself. She was without a home, and was indebted to the sympathy of friends—as poor as herself—for her share of the wretched abode where I visited her. I never yet saw so much patience under so much suffering, nor such benevolence amid such privation :

"I have got no home, sir," she said. "My work wouldn't allow me to pay rent—no, that it wouldn't at the price we have now. I live with this good woman and her husband. The rent is half-a-crown a week, and they allow me to live with them rent free. We all live in this one room together—there are five of us, four sleep in one bed; that is the man and the wife and the two children, and I lie on the floor. If it wasn't for them I must go to the workhouse; out of what little I earn I couldn't possibly pay rent.

"I bind shoes, or boots generally; but boot work is not to be had at this time of the year. I do the same for the shoe as the boot-closer does for the boot—that is, I prepare the upper for the maker to sew the sole to. . . . In a week I can make 3s. 1½d. by sitting close to my work—getting only up to my meals, and not being long over them. The way in which I take my meals generally is what I call worrying the victuals. I get regular employment. I have been twenty-two years at the business. When I first began I could earn 2s. a day, or 12s. a week, easily, by myself, and do for my family as well. To sit the hours that I do now I could earn 14s. a week well then. These slippers that used to be 3½d. a pair binding, are now come to 1¼d.; the shoes that used to be 4d. a pair are 1½d. The boots that we were paid 1s. for binding have come down to 5d., and extra work put into them as well—the closer's work is put upon the binder's work now—that is to say, the binder has now to stab the leather goloshe on to 'the uppers' of the women's boots. Formerly this was done by the closer. The binder at that time had merely to stitch the uppers together, and after that they were given out to the closer to stab on the leather goloshe. Fourteen or fifteen years ago this was altered, and the binders had to learn the stabbing and buy the tools to do it with, without any increase in the price. Before that I could have bound a pair of boots in three hours; but afterwards it took me nearly double the time to finish them. I never heard the cause of the alteration, but I know it took place immediately after a great strike among the women's men. The working men were forced to give in, and the employers immediately reduced the wages.

"The first reduction that took place with me was about 17 years ago, and since that time wages have been regularly going down.

The employers always take advantage of the winter to cut something off our pay, saying they don't want the goods till the spring.
The excuse is always that the trade is slack in the winter months and
they tell us, if we don't like to do it, we may leave it. There's plenty,
they say, that wants employment. I never knew the wages to rise
in the spring when business is brisk—never once in the whole of
the 22 years that I have been connected with the trade—that is the
policy of the employers. When I first began the business there were
but very few slop shoe warehouses. We mostly worked for the shops
direct; this, indeed, was the practice for the first fourteen years
that I was at the trade. After that time the slop shoe warehouses
kept increasing very fast, and they supplied the shops instead of
ourselves. The shopkeepers said they couldn't make them up as
cheap as they could buy them off the warehouses; and so the manufacture passed from the shopkeepers to the warehouses. . . . If there
is any increase of hands it has arisen from the low prices paid to
the shoemakers, for now they are obliged to put all their family to
work at some branch or other of their trade.

"My husband was a post-boy at a large posting-yard in Whitechapel. He has been dead five years this month. His business was
cut up by the railways, and his earnings before he died were half
what he used to get in better times. When he was alive, and doing
well, we had a comfortable home. Our joint earnings were, upon
an average, £3 a week, for a great many years after we were
married. Our wages kept coming down every twelvemonth from
about ten years back. However, I struggled on until he died. My
husband was fond of drink, and had saved nothing in his better
times. When he died I was left with my only daughter, and nothing
but my trade to keep me and her. My girl was ill with a rheumatic
fever and had lost the use of her limbs. She is dead. After my
husband's death, I could earn at shoebinding from 6s. to 7s. a week.
I paid 1s. 6d. a week rent, and I had 5s. left to keep the two of us.
I did manage to make a shift with this somehow, and appear a little
respectable, but it was indeed a hard struggle. We never knew what
a bit of butter was, nor yet sugar, for six months round; but still,
so long as I had my child, I went on happily and contentedly. At
last it pleased God to take my only comfort from me. Then I went
to service for a twelvemonth. . . . I went to service at 1s., and had
my board and lodging found me, of course. But my health had been
so cut up by the little nourishment I could get while working at
my trade that I couldn't do the work of my place—so I was forced
to leave it and take to shoebinding again. Since that time I have
been laid up with erysipelas, and then I was forced to part with
everything I had in the world to keep body and soul together. All

the little furniture I had got together except my bed, is gone; and
if it was not for the good friends I am with now I should be in the
workhouse.

"The husband of the good woman here is a painter by trade.
He has had no constant employment for this five years past.
Occasionally he gets an odd job when out with his frame in the
street." "Sometimes he brings me home sixpence," said his wife.
Here the man took one of the children on his knee, and the poor
little thing began asking for something to eat. I happened to hear
this, and on inquiring, I found that they had none to give it.
"I was obliged to sell a dish this morning, sir," said the woman, "to
get the only meal of bread we have had to-day, and how we are
to get another loaf I do not know." She told me she was within a
week of her confinement, and not a rag of baby linen in the house.
Indeed the poor things were literally starving, the whole of them.
"I give them and the little ones what I earn," said the poor shoe-
binder, "and we all starve together as contentedly as we can."
"I went down to the workhouse a few days ago (said the wife), to
ask them to take me in to be confined, and they told me to come
before the board on Friday night, but then I asked what can I
do with my husband and children. They must go in too, was the
answer; and so we must break up even the poor little home we
have; but then you know, sir, it *is* a home; and once broken up
we should never be able to get it together again. We are all under
the doctor's hands. My husband is suffering from determination of
blood to the head, and has been ill for this month past."

*A shoemaker kept from starvation*

The following narrative, which I had from the lips of a man
whom I have known for some few months, and whose family have
been kept from starvation during the winter by the funds placed
at the disposal of the *Morning Chronicle*, is a statement which
forms a fit sequel to the foregoing. I can vouch for the integrity
and industry of the man, for he has been long employed in making
boots and shoes for the poor people who applied for relief at the
office of this Journal; and a more hard-working and sober man I
have seldom met with.

"I have lived at the East-end nearly two years. Some months
back, I took a shop in Great Saffron-hill, Holborn; being a low
neighbourhood, and having a good stock to start with, I thought
in such a place we might do. I bought and sold old clothes, mended
old boots, &c, for sale; but all my efforts were useless. I lived there
four months; and as fast as I sold my property the money was spent

to support my family. Not being able to obtain employment, we began here to feel the pinching of poverty, and got in arrear for rent. The folks we lived with were Jews; they was kind to an extreme, knowing our circumstances.

"I had an acquaintance in Bethnal-green, —— street, poor, but honest people, who very kindly offered an asylum for us in their house till things should mend with us. We accepted the kind offer. I in vain endeavoured to get work in my own line, a man's man. Then I turned my attention to women's work; it was a great struggle to get a crust for six of us. I worked in the top room with my dear friend and his family, and their privations often made my heart ache. We were too poor to assist each other. It was common for us to have breakfast about twelve, and dinner, tea, and supper last thing at night. Our two families numbered fifteen persons. When I became better acquainted with women's work, and longing to return to my own domestic privacy, my friend agreed that we should have the kitchen at 1s. 3d. per week. We lived there eleven months, but out of my scanty earnings we were not able to pay much of the rent. My friend never asked us for it. The kitchen we lived in was damp, dark, and dirty. The ceiling was six feet only from the floor. The health of myself, wife, and children suffered much here, with the bad quality of food we were obliged to eat, bad ventilation, and many hours of toil. My wife was kind and affectionate, and loved her children with that kind of affection which a mother only can feel. We used to look on those little beings with hearts ready to break. We saw them waste day after day, almost forgetting to notice the havoc that mental anxiety and the attendant miseries of poverty made upon ourselves.

"I was at this time making cloth button boots, that were said to be women's, but which were as large as men's; the foreparts must not be less than half an inch thick, stitched with a square French blade, military heels, and top pieces, braided on with copper sprigs; the price for making 1s. 5d. per pair. I was obliged to work from five or six in the morning till twelve at night. At this work, bad as the pay was, we could, by long hours, get bread and coffee, and school-money for two children—meat we could not get. I could not get Sunday's dinner. My children had, with myself and wife, been used, in our better days (formerly we kept a shop), to have a comfortable dinner, and it was months before they got used to do without. We felt much hurt when the children told other children that they had had no dinner. But at last we got them used to it. We would reserve 2d. on Saturday night to buy pudding for them on Sunday; we thought that if they told their playmates they had pudding for dinner that would do. They, with ourselves, are now

so used to do without, that Sunday's dinner, and other little comforts connected with a working man's Sunday, are looked upon as
things that were. I thought things could not be worse than they were
at this time, but experience has taught me the contrary. I was next
obliged to take slop work, women's lasting springs at 6½d. a pair—
the commoner the work the more difficult and bad the stuff is to
use. Common as the work was, should the bottom 'thumb soft', or
should there be the least foulness in the lasting, we must either pay
for the boots or alter the work. With this miserable work, I was
obliged to set my poor wife down to sew, while bread we could not
buy much of. We lived upon boiled rice and hard biscuits, sold at
2d. per pound at the East-end.

"About this time we thought we would emigrate, if we could get
the means. I calculated the time it would take to save £20, and we
resolved to prolong the hours of labour, and cut short a meal a-day,
and save 1s. or more each day. We commenced with a resolution to
better our condition by emigration, and to obtain the means in the
way described. At the end of three weeks we abandoned the idea.
Our strength was spent; we were ill through over exertion, and the
want of proper nourishment to keep up physical strength. Knowing
that I was a sober man, and that none of my difficulties were brought
on by my improvidence, I resolved to lay my condition before some
of the noblemen of the country, feeling certain in my own mind
that if the beggar and imposter could obtain money, I with truth on
my side, would be sure to find friends among them in my sad situation. I made known my past and present condition to several noblemen, in order, if possible, to obtain the means to emigrate. I have
letters in my possession, which I received from some of them, but in
no solitary instance did I obtain one penny. Once I had a promise
from Lord —— of £1 if I could obtain the rest. My heart sickened
within me; despair seemed to lay hold of me. I knew not how to turn.

"I next obtained work at making women's leather shoes for a retail
shop, 8d. a pair; patent shoes, 9d. I took a room better ventilated,
though I did not know how to pay the rent. Hope still kept me alive.
I had 100 circulars printed. I wandered through wet and cold, leaving one at any house wherein I thought dwelt hearts who had a
care for suffering humanity. I went from house to house like a thief,
my natural independence was gone. I felt as if my heart would break,
as door after door, as well as the hearts within, were shut against
every appeal I made. I did not obtain one halfpenny. I had many
things which I had purchased, which I was wont to look upon
with pleasure, and felt a deep regret to part with them. My dear
little ones wanted; so day after day we sold and pawned, till we
became a perfect wreck.

"I was next advised by a friend to seek workhouse relief. My friend gave me reasons for wishing me to apply to a workhouse. After many hard struggles to screw my courage to the sticking place, I *did* go. My business being a useful one, they wished myself and family to go into the house, and would not relieve us out. I would sooner have died in the street than consented to part from my family in such a way. I returned home, and cursed in my heart such a country as England, which seemed to deny me the only privilege that I felt that I wanted—labour sufficiently remunerative to support my children without becoming a pauper. Thus, sir, every effort on my part failed, and I was obliged to settle down to do as best I could. I am waiting the will of God, and he who has so often saved me and my family from starvation, will assuredly help me out of my present difficulties. . . ."

## The family system

The only means of escape from the inevitable poverty which sooner or later overwhelms those in connection with the cheap shoe trade is, by the employment of the whole family of children as soon as they are able to be put to the trade. I give the statement of such a man residing in the suburbs of London, and working with three girls to help him :

"I have known the business," he said, "many years, but was not brought up to it. I took it up because my wife's father was in the trade, and taught me. I was a weaver originally, but it is a bad business, and I have been in this trade seventeen years. Then I had only my wife and myself able to work. At that time my wife and I by hard work, could earn £1 a week; on the same work we could not now earn 12s. a week. As soon as the children grew old enough the falling off in the wages compelled us to put them to work one by one—as soon as a child could make threads. One began to do that between eight and nine. I have had a large family, and with very hard work too. We have had to lie on straw oft enough. Now three daughters, my wife, and myself work together, in chamber-mastering; the whole of us may earn, one week with another, 28s. a week, and out of that I have eight to support. Out of that 28s. I have to pay for grindery and candles, which cost me 1s. a week the year through. I now make children's shoes for the wholesale houses and anybody.

"About two years ago I travelled from Thomas-street, Bethnal-green, to Oxford-street, 'on the hawk'. I then positively had nothing in my inside, and in Holborn I had to lean against a house through weakness from hunger. I was compelled, as I could sell nothing at that end of the town, to walk down to Whitechapel at ten at night. I went into a shop near Mile-end turnpike, and the same articles (children's patent leather shoes), that I received 8s. a dozen for from the wholesale houses, I was compelled to sell to the shopkeeper for 6s. 6d. This is a very frequent case—very frequent, with persons circumstanced as I am, and so trade is injured and only some hard man gains by it. From people being obliged to work twice the hours they once *did* work, or that in reason they *ought* to work, a glut of hands was the consequence, and the masters were led to make reductions in the wages. They took advantage of our poverty and lowered the wages, so as to undersell each other, and command business.

"My daughters have to work fifteen hours a day that we may make the sum I've told you. They seem to have no spirit and no animation in them; in fact, such very hard work takes the youth out of them. They have no time to enjoy their youth, and, with all their work, they can't present the respectable appearance they ought." "I" (interposed my informant's wife) "often feel a faintness and oppression from my hard work, as if my blood did not circulate. I sit and work on the seat, and was once told by an eminent physician that I suffered from my sedentary employment, and that I ought to go, now and then, to a dance. He might as well have advised me to go to court." "Indeed," resumed the husband, "if we wished to get to the Literary and Scientific Institution Lectures, or to a dance, then we had to work on a Sunday to do it. . . ."

*The apprentice system*

The family system of working is one of the means by which the cheap system is maintained. The party pursuing it, though forced to resort to it for the maintenance of his wife and children, whom his own unaided labour is incapable of supporting, is enabled to produce the goods at so cheap a rate that it is impossible for a single-handed artisan to do the work at the same price, and live. Another means by which the cheap prices are maintained is the *apprentice system*, concerning which I received the following statements :

"My employer had seven apprentices when I was with him; of these, two were parish apprentices (I was one), and the other five from the Refuge for the Destitute at Hoxton. With each Refuge boy he got £5, and three suits of clothing and a kit (tools). With the parish boys of Covent-garden and St. Andrew's, Holborn, he got £5 and two suits of clothes, reckoning what the boy wore as one. My employer was a journeyman, and by having all us boys he was able to get up work very cheap, though he received good wages for it. We boys had no allowance in money—only board, lodging, and clothing. The board was middling, the lodging was too, and there was nothing to complain about in the clothing. He was severe in the way of flogging. I ran away six times myself, but was forced to go back again, as I had no money and no friend in the world. When I first ran away I complained to Mr. —— the magistrate, and he was going to give me six weeks. He said it would do me good; but Mr. —— interfered, and I was let go. I don't know what he was going to give me six weeks for, unless it was for having a black eye that my master had given me with the stirrup. Of the seven only one served his time out. He let me off two years before my time was up, as we couldn't agree.

"The mischief of taking so many apprentices is this: The master gets money with them from the parish, and can feed them much as he likes as to quality and quantity; and if they run away soon, the master's none the worse, for he's got the money, and can get another boy and more money; and so boys are sent out to turn vagrants when they run away, as such boys have no friends. Of us seven boys (at the wages our employer got) one could earn 19s., another 15s., another 12s., another 10s., and the rest not less than 8s. each, for all worked sixteen hours a-day—that's £4 8s. a week for the seven, or £225 10s. a year. You must recollect I reckon this on nearly the best wages in the women's trade. My employer you may call a sweater, and he made money fast, though he drank a good deal. We seldom saw him when he was drunk; but he *did* pitch into us when he was getting sober. Look how easily such a man with apprentices can undersell others when he wants to work as cheap as possible for the great slop warehouses. They serve haberdashers so cheap that oft enough it's starvation wages for the men who work for the same shops."

*Child hiring*

Akin to the system of using a large number of apprentices, is that of employing boys and girls to displace the work of men, at the less laborious parts of the trade. To such a pitch is this carried, that there is a market in Bethnal-green, where children stand twice a week to be hired as binders and sewers. Hence it will be easily understood that it is impossible for the skilled and grown artisan to compete with the labour of mere children, who are thus literally brought into the market to undersell him.[11]

To show the sort of labour supplied by such boys as are to be met

[11] One account of the Bethnal Green market (here cut) was reprinted in *L.L. & L.P.*, 1861, II, 313.

with at the market I have described, and the way in which it is remunerated, I give the statement of a sharp little fellow not yet 13, and little even for that tender age :

"My parents are living," he said; "my father being a shoe-man— a man's-man. He works in a bulk (stall); but work is very bad with him. My mother makes hat-boxes for the shops at 1s. 6d. per dozen, finding the stuff—it gives her 6d. profit, and takes a day to make them. I wanted a few halfpence for myself, but most of all I wanted clothes. If I hadn't been at work this week I shouldn't have had this jacket out of pawn. I knew a boy who took me to where he worked, and I got a job there. I gave three months' work for being taught. The general thing is to give 10s. and three months' work, but my father was too poor to pay the 10s. It's about a year ago since I began to learn the trade. I can now sew a dozen pairs of slippers a day. Slippers they call them, that's the right name of them, but you would call them women's boots or pumps. The work is made ready for me, and I stitch the sole to the upper. I get three-farthings a pair, that's 9d. a day. I work six days in the week when my master has work, but sometimes he turns lazy after he's been drinking and lies in bed all day. He's kind to me, and I ain't got no missus. There are a great many boys like me, employed the same way. Some boys can make three dozen a day. There's plenty of boys can sew faster than men. Men get no more at such work than we do. I give the money I earn to my mother; she's very poor, and it's a help to her. I have had seven masters, but was never badly used. I sometimes work from six in the morning to ten at night. I can neither read nor write—I wish I could. Do you know of any school, sir, where I could learn on a Sunday?"[12]

## The chamber-master system

Another of the evils of the cheap shoe trade is the chamber-master system, as it is termed. The chamber-master is a petty tradesman, who employs a number of the worst and cheapest hands to manufacture the goods on his premises. He has no shop, but is either employed directly by the warehouses, or else he makes up a large quantity on speculation at the lowest possible rate, and then hawks them round to the trade.

The following is a statement of a journeyman slipper maker, concerning different evils to the *men working under a chamber-master* :

"I have only been at the trade four years. I know there is a great amount of misery existing among married hands; being a single

[12] The statement of a girl followed.

man, and having a comfortable home with my father and mother, I have not as yet felt any of the miseries consequent on competition. I have only worked in one of the slipper-making barracks, Mr. ——, of —— street; his house is private, and has a respectable exterior. In one large room at the top of the house, in which were two beds, eight men worked. One had boys to sew. One man had two sewers; the quickest man at work I ever saw. With his two sewers he could make thirty-one pairs a day (sew-round). The dirt and filth of the room were almost incredible; weeks would elapse, and the room not be swept. We sat up to our knees in shreds (leather cuttings). Fleas were in abundance; and a dirtier set of creatures could not be imagined. Some would not wash themselves once a week. The pan in which we wet our leather was used for indecent purposes, and not emptied for a week or two. The place stank. The man I worked for was once a journeyman; started for himself, with a loan, by cutting down the wages of makers and binders. He has got on well, and has forgot he once worked on the seat himself. I left him because he *would* charge 6d. a week to sit to work in his house. Whether the men work there or not, they must pay 6d. a week. The man I mentioned as being a quick workman has left him, and set up chamber-master in opposition to his late employer, and is endeavouring to cut him out of the warehouses by underselling him. I work for this one. This 'ready' man was a costermonger a few years since, and learnt to sew. . . ."

## The lodging-house system

The lodging-house system which is resorted to by the chamber-master in order to eke out his petty profits is equivalent to the worst forms of "sweating" under the cheap tailors.[13] Concerning the "strong" trade, as carried on in a "slaughter" house in Westminster, I give the statement of a man now employed by a firm in—— :

"I have been in the trade about 16 years. At that time I could earn 15s. a week, take the year through. The treatment of the men was always what it is now, both as to earnings and the accommodation and treatment of myself and the other men employed with me. The house where we work, generally twelve of us—there were eleven to-day—was formerly a pork butcher's. The room where we sleep is rather smaller than where we work. The length is 20 feet, the width 15 feet, height 7 feet. The window width is 1 ft. 10 in., and its length 1 ft. 2 in. The room is very seldom washed; the walls are damp, and there is always a dreadful stench, made up of all sorts

[13] The testimony of a shoemaker lodging with a chamber-master has been cut.

of bad smells; it's not one of them, but a lot of stinks together. No wonder I look pale. This very sleeping-room was Mr. ———'s slaughter-house, where he killed his pigs, and where human pigs are kept now. In this room, the dimensions of which I have given you, are four beds—and in them sleep eight men, two in each. There has been three in a bed. There is no ventilation, as the window will not open. From the stench I cannot, often enough, get to sleep until two or three in the morning, let me be as tired as I may.

"I and my mates are compelled to have from the employer what is called tea and coffee. I can't tell what the tea is, but it is curious tasting; it is indeed, sir; and the coffee is so bad that burnt beans, not good enough for horses, would make better. We call it 'slosh', but that's too good a name. We find our own dinner, but can cook nothing on the premises, unless with the leave of the mistress, who makes it a great compliment to grant a favour, such as the loan of a gridiron. If you become too troublesome, there's a discharge ticket for you; but we haven't so very much to cook. Half-a-pound of steak between two—it costs $2\frac{1}{2}$d.—is the usual thing; we call that sort of steak 'block ornaments'—what the butchers dress their blocks with—it's reckoned a luxury with us. Tea is like breakfast, only tea (as it's called) instead of coffee (as it's called), and for each meal we have to allow $1\frac{1}{2}$d., finding our own bread and butter—that is when we can afford butter. The payment for the coffee and tea is exacted in this way; we are paid every night for the work we do in the day, and out of the payment due, the master every Monday stops 1s. for lodging, tea and coffee, and 6d. every night after for lodging, tea and coffee; so that there can be no arrears from the man, and that pays him 3s. 6d. a week, Sunday included.

"Whether I am there or not I have to pay for my tea and coffee. I must pay for it if I am miles off, if I'm employed there. If a man be off on a visit to his friends, as I know has happened, for five days, he must pay for it, though neither tea nor coffee has been made for him. Every man must lodge on the premises, and if a man employed be a married man, he must have a room for his wife and himself; but I have known a married man who had to pay for his lodgings with this master at another shop (for he has three) though he didn't lodge there; all circumstanced that way must pay or lose their work. That's the master's system. We work on those considera-tions. The men feel they are in a state of slavery. My master has the false measurement in his size-stick. We often feel languid; but shoemakers, particularly the strong men, mustn't complain when they're ill, unless they're ready for the hospital. I average, take the year through, about 9s. a week. I feel degraded by the way I'm employed, and we all do, but how are we to get out of it? It's just degradation or starvation, and I'm not quite ready for starvation."

Another man, connected with the same trade, gave this statement :

"I am a married man, with a wife and family at D——. I 'occasioned' Mr. D—— in —— ——. He offered me work if I would lodge in the house as a single man. I was obliged to accept his offer through necessity. The first work I got was the lowest priced, and I had to buy all my grindery of him, for that truck system flourishes with him; for a ball of hemp I had to pay 2½d, the regular price being 1½d., and other things in proportion. The room I work in is washed once a year at the Whitsun holidays. My master has the false-size stick, and pays some men 1s. 8d. a pair for what, with true measure, I receive 2s., which is the lowest rate. The men humbugged with the 1s. 8d. curse him, but not to his face—they *must* put up with the pinch of the corn."

My informant then repeated the fact that a man who did not lodge in the house, being employed there, must pay 2s. a week for his lodgings all the same. "I have often heard my employer say, in the summer, when men have left, trying to better themselves, 'Ah, they soon will come back to my Refuge for the Destitute, d——n 'em, when they want to warm their hands in cold weather, and I shall say, No, d—— you, go where the sun shined all the summer; but stop,' he'll say again, 'I have a bed empty—you can go to that.' And the man says, 'I've a family.' The master says, 'You may go to h—— unless you take my lodgings.' That's the way he talks. There is no truck system except in grindery with this master, and there is no accommodation for common decency. As for cooking, there is one frying-pan among fifteen men, and that won't hold half-pound o' steak. The lodgings *are* dens, God knows. I earn 10s. a week on the average, and the grindery costs me 1s. 3d. out of that, and my lodgings 2s."

Another man in the same employ said : "Please to let this be made public. In the rooms where we work we sleep, making our own beds—middling flock beds, but very filthy and dirty. I saw a troop of 'Scotch Greys' creeping about the quilt the other day; Scotch Greys are the regular household troops there; it's a sort of headquarters for them in that there Refuge for the Destitute. You understand, sir, what Scotch Greys are—the vulgar call them lice, sir. Two rooms with five beds bring my employer in 21s. a week (he may pay 5s. rent for them). One of the men has a boy of 14, but very little, and though he sleeps with his father, he is charged 1s. a week. About fifteen years ago I was a country lad, and had two choices—to starve, or go in a place like G——'s (a similar concern). At that time I preferred water to beer or spirits; but I had no home, the refuge was no home. I could not read by any fireside, for there was no fire-side and no chair to sit on. By degrees I made a sort of home in a tap-room; and it grew and grew until I was fond of beer, and found myself a fuddler. That's a certain evil of the system. Men must find an hour of comfort, and it can only be found in the public-house. It creates drunkenness and ruins health. At P——'s, nine men out of ten had the itch at one time, master and missus and all. Men at these places have to violate decency in a way I cannot describe to you. . . ."

## LETTER XXXVI—18 FEBRUARY 1850

My investigations into the condition of the men working at the Slop Boot and Shoe trade are now drawing to a close. I have already given illustrations of the different systems by which the slop articles are produced at a far lower rate than those of the regular and honourable part of the trade. The principal of these appears to be the employment of what is called by the workmen "compound labour"—that is to say, by the use of boys, girls, apprentices, or unskilled journeymen, as helps to some skilled or superior workman. Again, it has been shown that the same system which is called "sweating" in the slop-trade of the tailors is carried on among the slop boot and shoemakers, but under the more euphonious, but less forcible title of "chamber-mastering". The object of each and all of these different practices is to bring an inferior and consequently cheaper, labour into competition with that of the skilled artisan, and to be able to undersell others in the market. . . .

*Tendency of the slop-trade to destroy the fair trade: testimony of a tradesman*

As a further corroboration of the tendency of the cheap slop-trade to destroy not only the able artisan, but the honourable tradesman, and to substitute for employer and employed, cheats, children and criminals, I subjoin the statement of a lady's shoemaker—a trades-man of the highest respectability, at the west end of the town, who gave me the following account concerning the way in which a fair trade is injured by the slop system, with its starvation wages :

"I remember," he said, "when there was no shoe slop-seller in London, except B——. I speak of the West-end some thirty years ago. At that time Mr. Taylor, in Bond-street, Mr. Sutton, Mr. Sly, and other first-class tradesmen (all now dead) used to carry on very extensive businesses, getting everything made by their own men, employed directly by themselves, without the intervention of any middleman system. They also gave their journeymen and binders fair and liberal wages. As it is, I pay 3s. 5d., and not at all extravagant wages, for what —— and —— pay 1s. 4d. Of course, mine is an infinitely superior article; but the 'firm', as they parade themselves, actually puff off their wares as equal to the best.

"I first felt the low-priced system tell upon me when the chamber-masters became numerous, and indulged in keen competition. These chamber-masters will now come to my shop and offer to sell me goods at the price I pay for wages alone. The low-priced goods affected my profits gradually. My books show this; first my profits fell 10 per cent, then 15, and now I reckon my profits 20 per cent less than they were 30 years ago. I have been obliged to reduce my prices and consequently the wages; I still pay the highest wages and this last week I looked carefully through my books to ascertain the earnings of my men. The first two weeks in February, by an arrangement I introduced into the trade some years ago, is the period for adjusting any change in wages, or in the trade generally, so as to obviate the necessity of strikes. I looked, as I have said, through my books, and as an honest man I felt that I could not reduce any one man's wages a half-penny.

"Businesses like mine are kept together by connection—by a principle of respect between tradesman and customer, because the customer knows and perhaps has long known the tradesman's integrity. But no business like mine could be started now with any prospect of success. All the money at present embarked in the shoe trade, or nearly all, is on the low-priced system. I fear that if no check be interposed to the Northampton and slop-system, matters will get worse. The underpaid and inferior workman will drag down the able well-conducted artisan to his level. First-rate workmen become scarcer and scarcer. The trade is falling into the hands of an inferior craft—it's becoming slop-work, not the fine workmanship of skilled labour—of a nice handicraft. That's another evil to all who look to ulterior consequences. *Bad workmen have little self-respect.* We can beat the French—it's the slop-system that is so vile. Fashion is so strong, however, that a lady bought a pair of shoes of me, thinking they were made in Paris. In the course of the conversation I told her they were made by my own men in London, and she has never had such a shoe from me since—much as she admired them."

*Statement from an East-end employer*

As a fitting sequel to the above, I annex the statement that I received from one of the *East-end employers*. His account is the more valuable, because it comes from a man who has himself resorted to some of the most reprehensible practices of the cheap trade.

"I recollect the trade before there were any chamber-masters. In 1819, I only knew one chamber-master in London, and the number gradually spread through this; Masters were oft tyrannical, and kept men waiting, and humbugged them all sorts of ways, and so the men made a few sets of shoes, and sold them at a penny a pair profit. To drapers' shops and such like; and that went on for a while, until some wide-awake gentlefolks, that had their wits about them, like ——, and ——. Bless you, they've their country houses now, and are worth thousands—thought there was a chance to turn a penny—I mean a pound, and they opened great warehouses and bought of the chamber-masters and of anybody in the trade. These chamber-masters are often, or were often precious rogues. They'd owe money to the tallyman, and the chandler, and the baker, and the butcher (if they could spring tick), and then 'made a death' in Whitechapel, and 'rose again in the Borough'. That's what we call their leaving a place which gets too hot for them, and leaving them that they're in debt to to whistle for chamber-masters and their money. The chamber-masters were always sure of a market if they could stand screwing, and didn't care for a turn at hunger now and then, and so they kept up 'deaths' here, and 'resurrections' throughout London, for a rare spin. Of course, it's nothing to the wholesale man that the chamber-master has a large circle of weeping tradesmen belonging to his acquaintance. The more he 'does' people what wants honest money of him, the cheaper he can live and the cheaper he can sell. It's a system that ought to be exposed. And so you see, things is made so very cheap that it's wonderful the *perfection* trade's brought to. . . ."

## Importation of foreign labour

As regards the *foreign labour*, I was anxious to discover, if possible, whether the same systematic importation of cheap workmen from the continent was carried on in the cheap boot and shoe trade, as I had found out was pursued in connection with the slop-trade among the tailors. After considerable trouble, I was able to track out the same annual immigration. This was principally confined to the Germans. Formerly the Frenchmen were brought over to England by their countrymen who had settled in business, and who made periodic trips to Paris, in order to introduce French workmen into London before the duty was reduced on the French boots, and when there was a great demand for the article. The wages in this country have, however, declined so rapidly within the last nine years, that the number of French workmen have already decreased one-half; for now the prices paid to the workmen by some of our best shops are lower than those in France. The Germans, however, continue to be brought over annually, and are kept in such subjection by their masters, that they are afraid to make the least disclosure. The following narrative I give in the man's own broken English:

"I am a native of Chermany. I come apout six miles dis site of Frankfort; de down is named Butzbach—yes, dat is quite right. I have peen in dis country nine year. I vent over py my own account. A man had been over here, and he come over to my country and he told me as I could earn plenty money coming over here." "Yes, it is plenty money," said the wife with a derisive laugh. "Aye, a starvation life," joined in the shoebinder, who was at work upon some red morocco slippers—"I know *I* find it so." "Yes, I did vork at dis drade in my country," continued the German. "I had been apprentice to it in Chermany dree year and a half. Oh de wages is very low in Chermany, because you gets everyting a man gets—his lodging and everyting—and he get pesites apout 5s. a week, just as a man can vork. Vot ve gets by our vork in Chermany goes farder dere dan vot you gets here vid a pount. I call dat a very goot wages dare, only de money we gets don't look so much as it does here.

"Ven I came over here I vent to sew at one of my own countrymens, and I have mostly been vorking for my own countrymens ever since. Most of the Chermans I have vorked for have peen vot you call sveaters in dis country, because dey do make a man sveat. The vorst of de lot I ever vorked for vas von I tell you of." "Ah, he ought to have peen sent out of dis country long ago" (chimed in the wife). "He spoilt de slipper drade, he did—he was a Cherman, living down here in ——. He has a cas-light in every room. He go out vith his cold rings on his finkers, and his cold vatch in his pocket, and de poor man vot gets em for him sitting in de kitchin. He's cot a clock vot plays de music in his trawing-room dat cost him dirty pounds. I should like for you to step insite dat toor to see dat place and de poor man at vork for him. He von't let a poor man stay vid him vitout he vork for him on a Suntay morning while his crand musical clock is a playing. He say you von't be no goot to me. You can't get a loaf of pred." "I tell you," cried the wife, "my huspant vorked for him and never see de outsite of de tore for dree veeks."

"He had elefen at vork for him. They most all lived in his house. He cot von room where he cot your peds in it. Dere was dree married men—de rest dey vas single men. He let out his rooms, you know; de married men had dem, and de upstairs he had de peds in for de single men. Dere vas eight men sleeped in dat room vid de vour peds. I had a pedroom. He charge me half-a-grown." "It vas dree pair of stairs high," cried the wife. "De room I had vas not vurnished. I pought a pedstead and seferal dings of him. Oh yes, he always sell to de men—he puy of a old proker, and de men must give him so much provit." "Oh, it's very ill," said the wife, of a poor little infant that lay moaning in her lap. "I puried one not long ago, and ah dat gets any von pack. You got to vork and slave all de year round, and ven trouble come you can't pay your vay at all." "I say de room I had of him," continued the man, "vasn't worth no more dan eightpence a week. De vurniture perhaps I could have cot for nine shilling, and he charge me vour and twenty shilling.

"I done all sorts of vork for him. I done some of dem poots vot is used for de Italian Opera. Sometimes de poots was de puckskin vons vot dey use in de playhouses—pig vons up apove de knees; and he pay me only von shilling for dem vid touble soles. Any sort of vork I made—slippers, springs, vot he got from de shop—anyting. I vorked from morning five o'clock till night elefen, dwelve o'clock; yes, very near every tay I done dat in de summer. Oh! I could not make no more dan vourteen shillings in de veek, Suntay and all. Den I had to pay out of dat de money for de rent, dat was half-a-grown, and half-a-grown for de tings and vurniture vot I pought of him : dat vos vive shilling. Den I used to pay for de pred and de peer. Ve had a pint every night. He always vished us to have our pred and peer of him. He vas very angry if you vent outsite. Not to force you, certainly; he couldn't have done dat; put if ve hadn't done it he vould have turned us avay—yes, dat he vould, for he did give me dree or vour times notice 'cause I fetched a pint of peer outsite. . . .

"Oh, he is de ruin of de slipper trade, because he go to every shop and say I do de vork for such and such a price. He do it a shilling a tozen less dan any von else, so dats vot cuts all de poor people out from a varehouse, because he goes in de varehouse vit a cold vatch in his pocket and dree or vour cold rings on his finkers—dat make him look a respectable man, and dey tink dey can drust him. Now, if de oder poor man comes in de shop, dey say dey vont give none—dey must have de secoority down—and pecause he takes all de vork from de varehouse, dat is de reason a poor man can't get no vork to do—so de poor man must go vork for him. He can made de slippers so much sheeper dan me, pecause he gives de poor man so much less, and gets de provit out of de lodgings and food of de men in his houze. He gets vive shilling a tozen, and gives de men dree-and-zixpence and zometimes dree shilling—dat is de vay he can get his cold vatch in his pocket, and his dirty-pound musical clock in his trawing-room. Most of de Chermans vot take out de slippers to made do de zame as dis man. Dere is von I know vot pays de men vour shilling a dozen pair vor batent leather slippers. Yes, I know dey do send for hands from Chermany ven de hands here are slack in de summer. He can't do vell you see vit dose he has had pefore; dey vont come pack again so he always looks for vot you call de creen hand from de country. I have knowed him send for vour at a dime. Most of my countrymen is prought over here by such men as he. I know myself a goot many of my vriends, vot have been teceived by him. You see Chermany, since de revolutions, has had so many vot are clad to come over, dat men like dis von can vell get dare cold vatches out of dem. . . ."[14]

## Slop trade in men's boots and shoes

I turned my attention also to the workmen employed in *men's boots and shoes for the slop shops*, to see if the abuses under which they suffered were similar in character and degree to those I have described in the case of the women's-men. I found these workmen generally pale, sickly-looking men, but for the most part intelligent also, and with a manliness in their words and notions. Nearly all were indignant at the privations which they and their wives and families had to endure from the wretched wages they received. Several spoke of their employers with bitterness. One quiet-looking elderly man—I met very few elderly men, be it observed, among these slop-workers,—said.

"There was Mr. —— here, the other day, a very good man, and he laid it down how we ought to respect our masters, and how the middle class, such as the masters belong to, are the wealth and strength of the country. As for the wealth of the country, they may have a good deal among them, but as you have been among us workmen for Mr. ——, and Mr. ——, you can judge what respect *we* can have for our masters."

The average of the earnings of the men's-men employed by the slop-masters was given to me at 12s. and 13s. a week, when the workman is in full work—but to get that much he must work six days, and a great portion of six nights. The average wages of the men partially employed I cannot give, as I met with men whose earnings last week were 3s., 3s. 6d., and so up to 9s. 6d. Some of the men's wives and children were wretchedly clad and lodged, and showed by their looks as well as words that they were as wretchedly

[14] Next appeared an interview with a French shoemaker, then a general account of the women's trade from a shoemaker who "had made the calling his particular study", finally a list of the principal slop-traders, the prices they give and the number of men they are "supposed to employ".

fed. "Beer," said one of these men to me, "hasn't been in my room these ten months, and I've never tasted it away from home but when I've been treated. What matters it, though, about *beer*? That little fellow there (pointing to a boy of five or six) doesn't yet know the taste of *beef*." The married men of this class generally work in their own rooms, but it is common enough for single men to work four or five in one room, as the rent is thereby lightened, and there is a saving in candle, since one of their thick candles gives light sufficient (at least what they accept as sufficient) for the whole. The practice of chamber-masters prevails among the slopmen's-men, but not nearly to the same extent as among the women's-men. The abuses and degradation are such as I have already described as existing among the women's-men, so that I need not enumerate them. . . .

*The system of translating*

To show the system of *translating*, as it is called, I give the following narrative :

"Translation, as I understand it (said my informant) is this—to take a worn old pair of shoes or boots, and by repairing them make them appear as if left off with hardly any wear—as if they were only soiled. I'll tell you the way they manage in Monmouth-street. There are in the trade 'horses' heads'—a horse's head is the foot of a boot with sole and heel, and part of a front—the back and the remainder of the front having been used for re-footing the boots. There are also 'stand bottoms' and 'lick-ups'. A 'stand-bottom' is where the shoe appears only soiled, and a 'lick-up' is merely a boot or shoe re-lasted to take the wrinkles out, the edges of the soles rasped and squared, and so blacked up to hide blemishes, the bottom being covered with a 'smother', which I will describe. There is another article called 'a flyer', that is, soling a shoe without welting it. In Monmouth-street a 'horse's head' is generally retailed at 2s. 6d., but some fetch 4s. 6d.—that's the extreme price. The old feet cost the translator from 1s. a dozen pair to 8s., but those at 8s. are good feet, and are used for the making up of Wellington boots. Some feet—such as are cut off that the pair may be re-footed on account of old fashion or a misfit when hardly worn—fetch 2s. 6d. a pair, and they are made up as new-footed boots, and sell from 10s. to 15s. The average price of feet (for the horse's head, as we call it) is then 4d., for a pair of backs say 2d.; the back is attached loosely by chair stitching, as it is called, to the heel, instead of being stitched to the insole, as in a new boot. The wages for all this is 1s. 4d. in Monmouth-street (in Union-street, Borough, 1s. 6d.); but I was told by a master that he had got the work done, in Gray's-inn-lane, at 9d.

Put it, however, at 1s. 4d. wages—that, with 4d. and 2d. for the feet and back, gives 1s. 10d. outlay (the workman finds his own grindery), and 8d. profit on each pair sold at no higher a rate than 2s. 6d. Some masters will sell from 70 to 80 pairs per week, that's under the mark; and that's in horse's heads alone. . . .

"I believe that all these tradesmen in Monmouth-street have lodgers. I was one before I married a little while ago, and I know the system to be the same now, unless, indeed, it be altered for the worse. To show how disgusting these lodgings must be, I will state this : I knew a Roman Catholic, who was attentive to his religious duties, but when pronounced on the point of death, and believing firmly that he was dying, he would not have his priest administer extreme unction, for the room was in such a filthy and revolting state he would not have the priest see it. Five men worked and slept in that room, and they were working and sleeping there in the man's illness—all the time that his life was despaired of. He was ill nine weeks. Unless a man lodged there he would not be employed. Each man pays 2s. a week. I was there once, but I couldn't sleep in such a den; and five nights out of seven I slept at my mother's, but my lodging had to be paid all the same. These men (myself excepted) were all Irish, and all teetotallers, as was the master." "How often was the room cleaned out do you say?" "Never, sir, never. The refuse of the men's labour was generally burnt, smudged away in the grate, smelling terribly. It would stifle you, though it didn't me, because I got used to it. . . . There was no chair in the Monmouth-street room that I have spoken of, the men having only their seats used at work; but when the beds were let down for the night, the seats had to be placed in the fire-place because there was no space for them in the room. In many houses in Monmouth-street there is a system of sub-letting among the journeymen. In one room lodged a man and his wife (a laundress worked there), four children, and two single young men. The wife was actually delivered in this room whilst the men kept at their work—they never lost an hour's work; nor is this an unusual case—it's not an isolated case at all. I could instance ten or twelve cases of two or three married people living in one room in that street. The rats have scampered over the beds that lay huddled together in the kitchen. The husband of the wife, confined as I have described, paid 4s. a week, and the two single men paid him 2s. a week each, so the master was rent free; and he receives from each man 1s. 6d. a week for tea (without sugar), and no bread and butter, and 2d. a day for potatoes—that's the regular charge.

"To show the villanous way the stand-bottoms are got up, I will tell you this. You have seen a broken upper-leather. Well, we place

a piece of leather, waxed, underneath the broken part, on which
we set a few stitches through and through. When dry and finished,
we take what is called 'soft hell-ball' and 'smother' it over, so that it
sometimes would deceive a currier, as it appears like upper-leather.
With regard to the bottoms, the worn parts of the sole is opened
from the edge, a piece of leather is made to fit exactly into the hole
or worn part, it is then nailed and filed until level. Paste is then
applied, and what we call 'smothered' over the part, and that imitates
the dust of the road. This 'smother' is obtained from the dust of
the room. It is placed in a silk stocking, tied at both ends and then
shook through, just like a powder-puff, only we shake at both ends.
It is powdered out into our leather apron, and mixed with a certain
preparation which I will describe to you (he did so), but I would
rather not have it published in the *Morning Chronicle,* as it would
lead others to practise similar deceptions. I believe there are about
2,000 translators, so you may judge of the extent of the trade; and
translators are more constantly employed than any other branch of
the business. Many make a great deal of money. A journeyman translator can earn from 3s. to 4s. a day. You can give my average at
20s. a week, as the wages are good. . . ."[15]

[15] Mayhew concluded the letter with an account of numbers and earnings in
the London trade and calculated the average weekly wage of London shoemakers to be 12s. 1¾d.

# THE TOY-MAKERS

## LETTER XXXVII—21 FEBRUARY 1850

I shall, in this and the following letter, seek to give as comprehensive a view as possible of the condition and earnings of the London manufacturer of toys. First, however, let me endeavour to impress the reader with some faint idea as to the variety of arts and sciences which are brought into operation in the construction of the playthings of the young. . . .

### Sciences and arts in toy-making

The sciences which are laid under contribution in the construction of toys are almost as multifarious as the arts which are employed in the manufacture of them. Optics gives its burning glass, its microscope, its magic lantern, its stereoscope, its thaumatrope, its phantasmascope, and a variety of others; electricity, its Leyden jars, galvanic batteries, electrotypes, etc.; chemistry, its balloons, fireworks, and crackers; mechanics, its clock-work mice—its steam and other carriages, pneumatics contributes its kites and windmills; acoustics, its Jew-harps, musical-glasses, accordions, and all the long train of musical instruments; astronomy lends its orreries; in fine, there is scarcely a branch of knowledge which is not made to pay tribute to the amusement of the young. Nor are the arts and artists that are called into play in the manufacture of toys less numerous. There is the turner, to turn the handles of the skipping-ropes, the ninepins, the peg, the humming, and the whipping tops, the hoop-sticks; the basket-worker, to make dolls' cradles, and babies' rattles, and the wicker-work carts and carriages; the tinman, to manufacture tin swords and shields, pea-shooters and carts, money-boxes, and miniature candlesticks; and the pewterer to cast the metal soldiers, and dolls' cups, and saucers, and fire-irons, and knives and forks, plates and dishes, chairs and tables, and all the leaden furniture of the baby-house; the modeller, to make the skin and composition animals; the glassblower, to make the dolls' eyes; the wigmaker, to manufacture the dolls' curls; the tallowchandler, to mould miniature candles for the dolls' houses; the potter to produce dolls' cups and saucers. Then there are image-men, conjurors, cutlers, cardmakers, opticians, cabinet-makers, firework-makers, and, indeed, almost every description of artisan—for there is scarcely a species of manufacture or handicraft that does not contribute something to the amusement of the young. . . .

## Classes of toy-makers

According to the Occupation Abstract, there were in the metropolis, in 1841, 407 toy-makers, and 146 toy-merchants and dealers. The number of toy-makers and dealers in Great Britain was 1,866.[1]

The London toy-makers are divided into several classes—such as the toy-turner, the Bristol or green wood toy-maker, the white wood toy-maker, the fancy toy-maker or modeller, and the doll-maker—of which there are two grand branches, viz., the makers of the wooden and of the sewed dolls. Then there are the tin toy-maker, the lead and pewter toy-maker, the basket toy-maker, the detonating firework maker, the drum and tambourine maker, the kite maker, and an infinity of others. The principal division, however, is into the toy-makers for the rich, and those for the poor. I shall deal in the present article with those who principally supply the children of the working classes with toys. These are not sold in the arcades and bazaars, but are chiefly vended in the street markets, from barrows and stalls. One toy stall keeper, I am told, clears 30s. a week by the sale of the cheap penny toys. Occasionally they are sold in the chandlers' and sweetmeat shops in the suburbs and the country, but the principal marts are the fairs and street markets. The toys sold by these people consist of either white or green wood—the latter being called Bristol toys.[2]

## Supplying the children of the poor: A Bristol toy-maker

*A worker in green wood* is termed a "Bristol toy-maker". The quality and nature of the *Bristol toys* are detailed in the following narrative given to me by one of the makers of those articles. In the room where I conversed with him two boys were at work, making the wheels of scratch-backs—toys used by frolicsome people at fairs, the fun consisting in suddenly "scratching" any one's back with the toy, which gives a sudden, whirring sound. One boy was an apprentice, a well-grown lad; the other was a little fellow, who had run

[1] A "rough estimate" of toy-makers' earnings and information about the import of foreign toys followed and was reprinted in Mayhew's *London Characters*, 1874 edition in the chapter "The Natural History of Toys."

[2] The next interview with a crippled toy-maker appeared in *L.L. & L.P.*, 1861, III, 21–24 and in *London Characters*. Also cut are the statements of a white-wood toy-maker and a toy-turner which ended the letter.

away from a City institution at Norwood, to whom the toy-maker had given employment, having known his mother. It was curious enough, and somewhat melancholy, to observe the boy working at that which constitutes other boys' play. Toys were piled all over the workshop. It was not very easy for a stranger to stir without the risk of upsetting a long line of omnibuses, or wrecking a perfect fleet of steam-boats. My informant, while giving his statement, was interrupted now and then by the delivery of orders, given, of course, in the usual way and tone of business, but sounding very grandiloquent—"A dozen large steamers", "Two dozen waggons"; and then a customer had room left in his sack for "half-a-dozen omnibuses with two horses". My informant said :

"The Bristol toys are the common toys made for the children of the poor, and generally retailed at a penny. They were first made in Bristol, but they have been manufactured in London for the last 50 years. I believe there is still one maker in Bristol. Bristol toys are carts, horses, omnibuses, chaises, steamers, and such like—nearly all wheel-toys. We make scratch-backs too—that has a wheel in it. To make the toys we boil the wood—green and soft, though sometimes dry; alder, willow, birch, poplar, or ash are used. When the wood has been boiled, the toy is cut with a knife, and fixed together with glue, then painted. Trade is very bad at present, for when the labouring people are out of employ I feel it in my business. They cannot then buy toys for the children; unless they have decent earnings, children must go without—poor things! As all my goods go to the poor, and are a sort of luxury to the children, I can tell what's up with working and poor people by the state of my trade—a curious test, isn't it? but a sure one. When weaving is bad, Bristol toy-making is very bad. (He lived in the neighbourhood of Spitalfields).

"When things are not so bad in Ireland, it's a rare time for my trade; they are so fond of them there. No cheap toys, at least in my way, are made in Ireland. When the big horses, the spotted fellows on wheels, that you must have seen, went out of fashion, it was a blow to my business. Steamers which have come up rather lately—though they have grand names painted on them, you perceive, Fire Flies and Dash Alongs, and such like—don't go off as the old horses did. Every child has seen a horse, but there's numbers never see a steamboat, and so care nothing about them; how can they? The men employed at journey work in the Bristol Toy trade can earn 3s. and 3s. 6d. a day. But when work is slack, they just earn what happens to turn in in the way of work."

## LETTER XXXVIII—25 FEBRUARY 1850

I continue my inquiries among the Toy-makers. In my last Letter I dealt chiefly with the makers of playthings for the children of the poor. In the present one I purpose dealing with those who manufacture the superior description of articles, such as are seen principally in the arcades and bazaars.

### *The celebrated publisher of penny theatrical characters*

One among those whom I visited was a celebrated publisher of penny theatrical characters and maker of toy theatres. He is the person to whom the children of the present generation are indebted for the invention. I found him confined to his room with asthma. He sat in a huge armchair, embedded in blankets, with a white nightcap on his head. He evidently was very proud of having been the original inventor of the toy theatres, and he would insist upon presenting me with the earliest prints in connection with the mimic stage. He was a little spare man whose clothes hung loose about him.

"I am a maker of children's theatres, and a theatrical print publisher. I have been in the line ever since 1811. The first time I began to publish anything of the kind was when the pantomime of Mother Goose was performing. I was the first in the line. I think I had the business all to myself for two years. Mrs. J ——, who lived in Duke's court, Bow-street, took to it after that. She sold my prints at first, and then she began to print and publish for herself. Now, I think, there's about six in the line. I was originally in the circulating library and haberdashery line. My mother was in the haberdashery way, and I continued it. We had a glass case of toys as well, and among the toys we sold children's halfpenny lottery prints—common things that were done in those days, sir. Well, you see, my parents used to be at Covent-garden Theatre, and I took it in my head to have a print done of *Mother Goose*, I can show you the old original print by me. You shall see, sir, the first theatrical print ever published. (He here produced a bundle of impressions.) Here's the third cheap theatrical print ever published. It's numbered up here, you see—but I brought 'em out so fast after that I left off numbering them very soon. I brought out one a day for three years. The print consisted of eight characters in as many separate compartments. The first was the elder Grimaldi as Clown, the second Bologna as Harlequin, the third was the Columbine of that day. Oh dear," said the publisher, "what was her name?—she was a very excellent Columbine at Covent-garden

Theatre." The other compartments were filled with other characters in the piece. "You'll see, sir," continued the old man, "there's a line of foolish poetry under each of the characters. I made it myself to please the children. It runs :

'The Clown, Joe Grim,
John Bologna, the Harlequin;
Gay and merry Columbine,
With her lover, Spaniard fine;
Demon of Interest, fiend of gold,
Don Alvero very old;
A poor Chinese man,
And Mr. Raymond, as Magician.'

The first theatrical print published was not very different from the third in the character of its art or poetical descriptions. There was, however, a spirit and freedom of touch about the execution that was far superior to what might have been expected.

The lines under the eight distinct characters were as follows :

"The golden egg and Mother Goose—
Prime, bang-up, and no abuse.
Here's Harlequin as feather light,
And Zany's antics to please you with delight;
Here's Mr. Punch you plainly see,
And Joan, his wife, both full of glee.
In woman's habits does Harlequin
Deceive the clown, by name Joe Grim."

"I brought out this print, you'll understand, to please the children. The lottery things was so bad, and sold so well, that the idea struck me that something theatrical would sell. And so it did—went like wildfire among the young folks. Shopkeepers came to me far and near for 'em. Bad as the drawing of these here is, I can assure you it was a great advance on the children's halfpenny lotteries. These two figures here in the corner, you see, a'n't so bad, but they're nothing to what we do now. This plate was done by a 'prentice of the name of Green, who worked at Mr. Simkins', an engraver in Denmark-court. He used to do them in his overtime. He was obliged to have something to look at to copy. He was no draughtsman himself, you know. This here picture of *Mother Goose* he took from a large print of Mr. Simmonds in that there character published by Ackerman, and sold in Covent-garden at 2s. 6d. plain, and 5s. coloured; the others was all copied from large prints of the day. I dare say I sold right off as many as 5,000. It was printed many times over, and every edition I know was a thousand. We don't do so many now. It was sold at a penny plain, and twopence coloured. You had better take that there impression with you. It's a curiosity, and a bit of the history of one's country—yes, that it is, sir. Why it's 39 years ago. I think I must have been about 24 when it was published—I'm 63 in June. The success of the theatrical prints was so great, I was obliged to get three presses to print them fast enough. I brought out a new one every day, as I told you before. We only did the characters in the pantomime at Christmas time. The small ones wasn't likenesses—they was merely characters to give the costumes. We didn't make likenesses till very late. The wardrobe people at the minor theatres and masquerade people used to buy a great many to make their dresses from. Young Green only did me two plates. He was such a bad draughtsman he couldn't do anything without a copy, and I was forced to get permission of the better printsellers for all he did. I gave Green 30s. or £2 for each plate he did for me. He was very dear, 'cause he was so slow over the engravings. Well, I think I had done about seven prints—they were bad-uns—only copies, and badly done too—all by apprentices, when Mr. Hashley, of the Hamphitheayter, sent young —— with a drawing to show me. It was uncommon well done; oh, such a beautiful picture! he got on to be one of the first-rate artists after-wards, and drawed half-crown caricatures; he did all the battle-pieces of them times—all Bonaparte's battles and Nelson's shipping. Well I gave him an order directly for the whole of the characters in the *Blood Red Knight*, wot Hashley was performing at that time. I can show you the print on it—you must see it, for it was a great advance in my purfession, sir. I should like you to look at it, sir, cause I considers it as a matter of history like." He here brought out another brown parcel of prints. "Look here, sir," he said, as he turned over the impressions—"here's one of the stage fronts we do now—it's only part of it, you'll understand. It's done by a real architectural designer—but *he's* dead too : I suppose I shall go next. . . .

"At first, you see, we didn't do any but the principal characters in a piece, 'cause we didn't think of making theayters then, and went on as we begun for two years. After that we was asked by the customers for theayters to put the characters in, so I got up the print of a stage front, thinking that the customers would get the wood-work done themselves. But after the stage front they wanted the theaytres themselves of me more than ever, so that I was obliged to keep three carpenters to make 'em for me. One was a horgan builder and could make anything in machinery. I turned out the first toy theayter for children as ever was got up for sale, and that was in the year 1813. You see my father was the under property-man at

Covent Garden Theatre, and I had a sister a dancer there, and another sister belonging to the fruit-office in the boxes—so we was all theatrical; and when I was about seven years old, I got my father's 'prentice in the shop to make me a wooden theayter—he was uncommon clever at carpenter work, and the printers and carpenters of Covent Garden used to come and see it when we exhibited in our one-pair back three times a week. We used to charge 2d. a piece. It was thought a great thing in those days; and so many people used to come to see it, that father and mother wouldn't allow it after a time; so it was put up as a raffle, and it was won by a young man, who took it with him to Scotland.

"It was that as gave me the hidea of making toy theayters for sale. After I made a few I was hobligated to make scenery, and to do the sets of characters complete. Nobody but me made toy theayters for a long while; nor did they do the scenery. One man used to do me three dozen theayters a week; and another man did me a dozen more of the small. The larger theayters took longer time, and I don't think I made more than a dozen of them in a year. I used to make, I think, about fifty toy theayters a week. I always had a room full of them upstairs, except at Christmas, when we couldn't turn them out fast enough. I think I must have sold about 2,500 every year of 'em. Some theayters I made came to as much as £20 a piece. I have made about four of them, I think, in my life time. They was fitted up with very handsome fronts—generally 'liptic harch fronts, built all out of wood, with ornaments all over it—and they had machinery to move the side wings on and off; lamps in front, to rise and fall with machinery, and side lamps to turn on and off to darken the stage, and trick sliders to work the characters on and change the pantomime tricks; then there was machinery to make the borders rise and fall as well, and cut traps to open for the scenery to go up and down through the stage.

" 'The Miller and His Men' has sold better than any other play I ever published. I wore out a whole set of copper plates of that there. I must have sold at least five thousand of that play, all complete. It's the last scene, with the grand explosion of the mill, as pleases the young 'uns, uncommon. Some on 'em greases the last scene with butter—that gives a werry good effect with a light behind; but warnish is best, I can't abear butter. Some of them explosions we has made in wood work, and so arranged that the mill can fly to pieces; they comes to about 4s. 6d. a piece. The next most taking play out of my shop has been 'Blue Beard'. That the boys like for the purcession over the mountains—a coming to take *Fatima* away—and then there's the blue champer with the skelingtons in it—that's werry good too—and has an uncommon pretty effect with a little blue fire, though it in general sets all the haudience a sneezing. The next best after that was the 'Forty Thieves'—they likes that there, for the fairy grotto and the scenery is werry pretty throughout. Then again, the story pleases the children uncommon—it's a werry good one I call it.

"I'll give you the date of the first likeness as ever I did; I've got it here handy, and I should like you to see it, and have it all correct, 'cause you see, as I said before, it's a matter of history, like. Here's all my large portraits—there's 111 of them. This here's one of ——. It's Liston, as *Moll Flaggon*, you see. That there one is done by Mr. ——, the royal academician. It's Mr. H. Johnston as *Glaffier*. I think the part was in a tragedy called the 'Hillusion'. That was the werry first portrait as I published. Here's one by ——, done about the same time. That's Mrs. Egerton, as Hellen Macgregor. The portraits I have just been showing you are 2d. plain, and 4d. coloured—but they don't sell now, the penny has quite knocked them up . . . I haven't published a new set of characters for this seven year. You see they began to make halfpenny plates—they used to copy my penny ones and sell 'em at half-price, so I thought it high time to give over. I had come down in my large portraits from 2d. to 1d., and I wasn't going to reduce to halfpenny—not I. It seemed like lowering the purfession to me—besides, the theaytres themselves couldn't make a do of it, so I gave over publishing. The decline of the drama is hawful, and it's just the same with the toy theaytres as it is with the real ones." (He then showed me his books. They were all indexed alphabetically. First came the small characters under A—"Aladdin;" then came those in B—"Blue Beard," "Battle of Waterloo" (of this nearly 10,000 had been printed), and "Bottle Imp;" under C were "Comus" and "Corio-lanus;" under F was the "Forty Thieves;" under H "Harlequin Brilliant;" under I came "Ivanhoe;" under M the "Miller and his Men," "Maid and the Magpie," "Montrose," and "Midsummer Night's Dream;" under O was the "Old Oak Chest" and "Olympic Revels;" under R, "Robinson Crusoe" and "Rob Roy;" and under T, "Timour the Tartar." Then came the index of the scenes in the same plays, arranged in a similar manner, with the number of impressions attached.

I remarked that he had printed a great many portraits of Mr. Bradley? He said that gentleman was such a great favourite with the children—he made himself up so murderous looking—and then he was such a fine swordsman with T. P. Cooke, you'd think they were going to kill one another. It was quite beautiful to see 'em—people used to go on purpose. He told me he had printed more por-traits of Huntley, Bradley, and Blanchard, than of any other members of the theatrical profession—with the exception of Kean in Richard. . . .

## A fancy toy-maker

The statement I now publish is that of a man whose room presented an accumulation of materials—paper, paste, wires, gilding, wood, pasteboard, leather, and other things, mixed up with instruments for nice admeasurement. The *fancy toy-maker's* appearance was that of a hearty, jovial man, and I was referred to him as being a workman alike humorous, trustworthy, and intelligent. He said :—

"I am a fancy toy-maker. Fancy toys are mechanical and moving toys. To describe the whole would tire you. I invent them, all that I made, even to the casting line. I can go from the clay of the model to the perfect toy. I made the model. I model the toy myself. These are all my own models." (My informant showed me several. They were remarkable for their nice art and ingenuity). "I was out on the world" (he continued) "young, and brought up to no business—and so, having confidence in my ingenuity, I took to the toy trade, and have carried it on for 35 years on my own account, working in the warehouses. My toys, though well known in the trade for their ingenuity, are not of great cost, but are chiefly within the reach of the middle classes. They include animals of all descriptions—donkeys, horses, cows, cats, elephants, lions, tigers (I could make giraffes, but they're not in demand), dogs and pigs. Here is a boat. These model men fix on here. By movements which I have contrived, they row the boat. I forget many of my inventions; the inventions in my calling are generally made in a slack time, when we have leisure to devote to the subject. It's slack now. Any man going into my trade must have great readiness as well as ingenuity—be quick as well as inventive. A man who hadn't those qualities would have as good a chance of succeeding in my trade, as a man who wrote badly and spelt worse would have in yours, sir. We are all working men, sir—you'll not be offended by my saying that.

"I started the figures on the donkeys, and the donkeys had a good run for a good while, and I hope they'll not leave off running for a good while longer, especially if they've good masters on their backs—I mean employers like Mr. G——. The boats with the men rowing in them had as good a run as the donkeys. The donkeys beat, though. There are very curious phrases in my trade. A boy who looked in at my workshop window, said, 'I'm blessed if I know what trade they are, but I heard them talk about cutting off three dozen donkey's heads.' Donkey's heads, you see, are made of papier-maché (I was shown a very good specimen), and the head is affixed

so as to move—so are the ears, and the tail too, if demanded. I
invented that donkey. The ass is made entire, and then the head is
cut off to be refitted, with the faculty of moving. Here's an elephant
—he moves his tail as well as his trunk. If I think of inventing a
new toy, I often can't sleep from thinking of it. I assure you I have
actually *dreamed* the completion of a new toy—of one that required
great thought. I went to bed with the plan working in my brain
and that led to the dream. I talk about it in my sleep. I consider
that I am not at all well paid for my labour. No toy-maker is *well*
paid for his mere labour, let alone his ingenuity. I can't state my
average earnings, there is such a casualty about the work; it is
often a speculation. I have to pay for so many things for my
experiments, and for colours and varnishes, that my earnings are
really very low. Two pound a week, do you ask if I make? Not one,
sir, though I'm the top of the trade. . . ."

## The "world's shop" for copper toys

A statement was given to me by a man whose workshop, as he
explained, had one peculiar characteristic; *for copper toys of the
better sort*—or perhaps, he added, of any sort—it was the workshop
of the world. He bears an excellent character, and the appearance
of his wife and children was highly creditable to an artisan of his
limited means. He worked in a small room on a ground floor,
devoted to the purposes of his trade. He said :

"I have known the trade in copper and brass toys since I was
a child. I am only 23, but when I was four or five years old, my
father, who was in the trade, and indeed invented it, set me to
work to clean the toys off, or punch holes, or do anything I could.
We knew nothing but industry, and so were never driven to the
streets; but my father might have made a fortune with steadiness.
At present I make chiefly copper tea-kettles, coffee-pots, coal-
skuttles, warming-pans, and brass scales (toy scales); these are the
most run on, but I make besides brass and copper hammers, saucepans, fish kettles, stewpans, and other things. I am now, you see,
making copper tea-kettles and saucepans. There are sixteen pieces
in one copper tea-kettle—first the handle, which has three pieces,
seven pieces in the top and cover (lid), one piece for the side, two
in the spout, one for the bottom, and two rivets to fix the handle,
in all sixteen. That's the portion of the trade requiring the most
art. Copper toys are the hardest work, I consider, or any toy-work.
The copper is this dull sheet copper here, eight square feet in a
sheet of it. I use generally a four-pound sheet, costing 13d. a
pound. I make six dozen tea-kettles out of one sheet. The copper

K

you see must be 'planished', that is, polished by hammering it with a steel-faced hammer on a steel-faced 'head', four inches square to make it bright.

"I make, on the average for the year, eight dozen tea-kettles every week; that is 4,992 a year. I make all that are made in London, yes, in the world. Here's the world's shop, sir, this little place, for copper toys. My father and I (when he worked at the trade) had it all to ourselves; now *I* have, for my father is on other work. He is now helping to fit up a ship for California, belonging to a gentleman who is going to send out his son to settle there as a bottled-porter merchant. An uncle of mine once *did* make a few. I make as many scuttles in a week as I do tea-kettles, for I'm always at it, and as many coffee-pots; altogether, that's 13,976 teas, scuttles, and coffees. Of the other sorts, I make, I know, as many as I do of teas, coffee-pots, and saucepans. They're all fit to boil water in, cook anything you like—every one of them. You can make broth in them. They are made on exactly the same principles as the large kettles, except that *they* are brazed together, and mine are soft-soldered. Altogether, then, I make 27,952 of copper toys in a year. I sell my copper toys—all sorts, take one thing with another—at 36s. a gross. All my toys are retailed at 6d. each.

"I think I can earn 20s. a week, if my wife and I work early and late, which we do when we've call, there's so much work in those things. Sometimes we earn only 10s. I calculate it as an average of 15s. the year through. That's but little to keep a wife and two children on—one only just born a month ago last Monday, and another is only just buried. It's little to earn for making all the copper toys, as far as I know, in the world. I think I could do well in New York, where my trade is not known at all. I have all the art of the trade to myself. It was very good once, but now it's come down very bad in this country, and I should like to try another. People here haven't got money for toys; besides, mine last too long; they ought to break quicker. What my father once had 20s. for, I now get 5s. When these toys first came up, an Irishman cleared £1,400 in five years by selling them in the streets. That's twenty years ago; and he's now thriving in America." "If my husband wasn't steady, good, and careful," said the wife who was present, "my children and I might see the inside of the 'large house.' " "Things get worse," resumed the husband. "Almost every time I go to the warehouses they say, you must work cheaper; but it's not possible if a man must live, and see his family living."[3]

[3] Interviews with a maker of rocking horses, a pewter toymaker, a basket toy-maker, a kite maker and a woman in the fancy dress ball business have been cut.

*The only maker of papier-maché toys clothed with fur*

I had the following statement from a Frenchman, who took no little pride in his art. He is the only person who carries on the making of *papier-maché toys* (as they have been called), which are covered—or, more properly, and that was my informant's word, *clothed*—with fur or hair. These toys display great taste and ingenuity. Some rabbits were as large as life—he brought different specimens to show me—and they looked natural enough, the body of the animal being made of paper formed by an art and a process (according to his own account) peculiar to my informant. A French accent was perceptible throughout the entire conversation, but was only very remarkable in rapid speech or in a dash of excitement. He said :

"Papier-maché was made before my father was born, or before my father's grandmother, but improvements took place twenty-five years ago. I can make you, if you please, the biggest animal in the world, waterproof, and that nothing can never break, of paper, or papier-maché. Anything may be done with the paper, but I now use a composition as well—it is my secret of what he is made. I make only animals. I make them both way, for the ornament of the chimney and the amusement of the children. I make every domestic. There is none but I manufacture him with natural hair and wool. French poodle dogs have the call; rabbits is good; lambs go very well; goats is middling. All the world can be supplied, from 3d. up to £5, with the French poodles. I do not make the lions, nor the tigers, nor those creatures—I make only domestic animals, but I *could* make the lions and the tigers as well. I make forty dozen domestic animals a week. Why you come here to ask? Lately my trade has been bad.

"I employ women and girls only, at so much on the dozen. I do not like to tell at what. It cannot be necessary. I cannot tell what relates to my secret. I will not. The skins for the poodles stink. The cost—oh, I will not tell, they cost too much. I have been here for twenty-one years. I get the stink-lambs for skins. Last year I used 4,800 lamb skins, and 5,000 some year. I employ eight English women. The dogs is all lamb skins—their outsides. I use nearly as many rabbit skins. I do not ever admit persons into my work-room. It is a very artful ingenuity. I can beat the French—indeed, I have beat my countrymen at home, for I have exportation to Paris; but the Germans come in cheap, cheap, and ruin the trade. This is a barking dog. I have made him, his bark and all—you see; yes, and barks can you expect for a penny? There's no get fat about him at 9d. This rabbit, you see, has a different skin to this other—the skin is the great cost with me. He have, too—the spring in his ears and tail, so that he lift them when the wheels go round.

"The earnings of my women? Oh! never mind; but I am not ashamed to tell. They earn 7s., and 9s., and 11s. a week, and never not less than 4s. My late wife could earn twenty and two shilling a week in this trade; but then she had the talent. Oh, no, none can now earn like that—they have not the talent—they have not the art in it—the nature—the interest. The work can only be done best by a relative of the master, one that has the interest in the making. The toys are not exactly papier-maché, which is fluid for mouldings, they are paper, common paper, in a solid form. The *how* is my secret. None other persons are in my trade. I cannot open the secret any further. Pardon my reserve, for which I have account to you. How you say, sir, four dozen domestic animals a week, that's quite reasonable as to the arithmetic of it, and he makes 22,960 domestics a year. Yes, that at least and my women do not work hard. They might work harder. They work hard if they want new dresses for the Sundays. What will the twenty thousand and odd toys bring in in money? The price vary, you comprehend, according to sizes and qualities, and arts and beauties. Yes, you can say 1s. each. How much, £1,148 in a year for all the domestics. Yes; but I will not tell prices or secrets."

## LETTER XXXIX—28 FEBRUARY 1850[4]

*A gun toy-maker*

*A gun toy-maker*, whom I found at work, his wife assisting him, gave me this statement:

"I was born to the business of toy, gun, and pistol, as well as of tin toys, which consist of mugs and trumpets; but the foreigner have got all the trumpet trade now, what we got 30s. a gross for we now get only 7s. The other tin toys—such as horses and carts got up by machinery for a penny—are made in Birmingham. None are made in that way in London; they're but *slop toys*. The tin toy trade at Birmingham is the factory system with children; think of children working hard at toys—poor little things to whom a toy is a horror! A gun is made in this manner. The wooden part, the stock, is made ready for the gunmaker's use by any carpenter; it is of pine. The next process is the making of the wire spring, then the barrel (tin). These different parts are then put to the stock

---

[4] This letter began with information and interviews about the branche of doll-making.

the lock is made by ourselves; they are of solder, and cast. The spring is placed inside the barrel, a ring is placed at the end by which it is drawn out, fastened to the pin (like the nipple of one of your deadly guns), and the weapon is ready for discharge. I make the week through three gross, which is 22,464. There is one other toy gunmaker in London, and he may make as many as I do, which will be 44,928 made in London. Reckon a third retailed to the public at 4d. (called pistols), and reckon those retailed at 6d. in the proportion of 6 to 4 in number with those retailed at 1s. and you have the sum of £1,238 4s. . . .

"In war time, bless you, that was the time for my business—there *was* a demand for guns then I can tell you! I sold eight, then, to one that I sell now, though the population's increased so. These pistols, which I get 1s. 6d. a dozen for now, I had 3s. 6d. a dozen for then. I remember the first botched-up peace in 1802. I can just recollect the illumination. My father (I heard him say so) thought the peace would do no good to him, but it didn't last very long, and the toy-gun trade went on steadily for years—with a bit of a fillip, now and then, after news of a victory; but the grand thing for the trade was the constant report that Bonaparte was coming—there was to be an invasion, and then every child was a soldier. Guns *did* go off briskly at that period—anything in the shape of a gun found a customer in those days. Working people could then buy plenty of toys for their children, and did buy them too. The men in the trade earn 12s. a week. The warehouses send out quantities of my guns and pistols to the colonies, especially to Australia—the duty keeps them out of the United States. The slop toy trade goes down here now."

*The detonating cracker business*

An Italian gave me the following account of the *detonating cracker business*. His parlour, as well as the window of his workshop, presented an admixture sufficiently curious. Old foreign paintings, religious, mythological, or incomprehensible, were in close connection with unmistakeable Hogarth prints. Barometers (for these also were "made and repaired"), showed that it was "set fair", and alongside them were grosses of detonating crackers. Of frames and mouldings there was a profusion, and in all stages, from the first rough outline to the polished gilding. He said, in pretty good English with a strong Italian accent :

"Yes. I make the detonating crackers, and am de only man in England skilful to make dem. It is a grand secret, mine art. It live in my breast alone—de full, entire secret. I will show you de pulling

crackers. Dey go in wid de pastry-cook's things at de parties of
de rich. A gentleman say to a lady, so I have heard, in de pleasant-
ness of de party, 'please to pull'. Yes, indeed, as they write above de
bells. And so de pretty lady pull, and de cracker goes bang—a
sudden bang—and de lady goes 'Ah-h-h!' quite sudden too, of
course, dough she must have known before dat de crack was to
come. Ah! sir, dey seldom tink of de Italian artist who make de
pulling cracker dat has brought out her nice 'Ah-h-h!' for 3½d. de
gross—dat is all we gets for de dozen dozen. I dare say de rich
fashionable pastry-cook get a great deal for dem. I don't know how
much. Dey are sold at de retail shops, dat are not high shops, at a
halfpenny a dozen. Den de detonatings—them what are trone down
on de stones, and go bang, and make de people passing go start.
Do dey cause many accidents do I tink? Bah, nonsense. It is de
play of de boys : it keep dem out of mischief. I sell fifty gross, one
week with another. I can make, if required, wid my boy, eighteen
gross a day. All last year I sold, as near as I can tell, fifty of de
pulling, and fifty gross of de detonating. Dat is—yes, no doubt—
14,400 a week, or 748,800 a year. How curious!—More dan seven
hundred dousand bang-bangs made in dis little place. Dere is
danger, perhaps in de make to some, but not to de right artist. At
a halfpenny a dozen, dat is £260 paid by de public—dat is only
part of my business; but den de pastry-cook charges may make de
amount double, and double again, and more dan double dat again."


*A camera obscura maker*

A very ingenious man, who resided in two spacious rooms at the
top of a high house, gave the following statement concerning camera
obscura making. I may here remark that I have always found the
intelligent artisan—who could easily be made to understand the
purport of my inquiries—ready to give me the necessary information,
not only without reluctance, but with evident pleasure. Among the
less informed class I am often delayed by meeting with objections
and hesitations; these, however, are always obviated by having
recourse to a more intelligent person. My present informant said :
    "I have known the camera obscura business for twenty-five years
or so; but I can turn my hand to clock-making, or anything. My
father was an optician, employing many men, and was burnt out;
but the introduction of steam machinery has materially affected
the optical glass grinder—which was my trade at first. In a steam-
mill in Sheffield, one man and two boys can now do the work that
kept sixty men going. I make bagatelle boards—there's no great
demand for them—and targets—they go off very fair. The only

improvement I remember in the making of the common cameras is this : Formerly the object glass was a fixture in the wood of the box, and immovable, and of course could only take an object at a certain distance, whereas by applying a movable brass tube, with the glass in it, you can command objects at any distance, adjusting it precisely on the principle of a telescope. Too much light obliterates your object, and too little light won't define it. Last year I think I made three gross. Here is the stuff of the box-body, cedar; all blacked in the inside, so as to exclude any false light. The bottom is deal, and the natural colour of that or of the cedar would obliterate an object by giving false lights. The small cameras are 2s. 6d. (retail), the next size is 5s., and so by half-crowns, generally up to 20s. or 21s. I make more than one half 2s. 6d. ones; they sell well in the summer season. I don't get more than 6d. a piece out of the 2s. 6d. ones. Perhaps I make two gross smaller, and the other sizes, of the third gross, in about equal proportions; altogether £126 19s. There is no other maker for the toy-shops in the camera obscura trade, to my knowledge, beyond myself. In making my cameras I test them from this door to objects at a distance. It gives every line of those tiles, every shape of those chimney pots, and every tumble of those tumbler pigeons. So I detect any error in the focus, and regulate it. I must test them at a good height, with a good light. A fog gives you only a fog—no defined object. The perfect adjustment of the focus, and, indeed, of every portion, is the nice art of my trade."

*Account of magic lanterns*

A very ingenious and intelligent man to whom I was referred, as the best in his trade, gave me the following account of magic lanterns. His parlour behind the shop—for he had risen to be a shopkeeper in some kinds of toys and other articles, known as the "fancy trade", was well furnished, and in a way that often distinguishes the better class of prosperous artisans. A fondness for paintings and for animals was manifested. On a sofa lay two very handsome King Charles's spaniels. On a chair were a fine cat and kitten. Outside his parlour window was a pigeon colony, peopled with fine large birds, a cross between those known as a "carrier" and a "horseman". Books, of no common class, were abundant enough, and his periodical was not wanting. He said :

"I have known the business of magic lantern making thirty-five years. It was then no better than the common galantee shows in the streets, Punch and Judy, or any peepshow or common thing. There was no science and no art about it. It went on so for some time—

just grotesque things for children, as 'Pull devil and pull baker'. This is the old style, you see, but better done." (He showed me one in which, to all appearance (for it was rather obscurely expressed), a cat was busy at the wash-tub, with handkerchiefs hanging on her tail to dry; Judy, with a glass in her hand, was in company with a nondescript sort of devil, smoking a pipe, and a horse was driving a man, who carried the horse's panniers.) "Bluebeards were fashionable then—uncommon blue their beards were, to be sure; and Robin Hoods—and Robinson Crusoes with Fridays and the goats, and the parrot, and the man's footmark on the sand—and Little Red Riding Hoods, as red as the Blue Beards were blue. I don't remember Ali Babas and Forty Thieves, there were too many of the thieves for a magic lantern—too many characters; we couldn't very well have managed forty thieves—it's too many. There were things called 'comic changes' in vogue at that period. As the glasses moved backwards and forwards, fitted into a small frame like that of a boy's slate, a beggar was shown as if taking his hat off, and Jim Crow turning about and wheeling about, and a blacksmith hammering—moving his hammer. There were no theatrical scenes beyond Harlequins and Clowns.

"About thirty years ago the diagrams for astronomy were introduced. These were made to show the eclipses of the sun and moon, the different constellations, the planets with their satellites, the phases of the moon, the rotundity of the earth, and the comets with good long tails. What a tail 1811 had! and similar things that way. This I consider an important step in the improvement of my art. Next, moving diagrams were introduced. I really forget, or never knew, who first introduced those improvements. The opticians then had the trade to themselves, and prices were very high. The moving diagrams were so made that they showed the motion of the earth and its rotundity, by the course of a ship painted on the lantern—and the tides, the neap and spring, as influenced by the sun and moon. Then there was the earth going round the sun, and, as she passed along, the different phases were shown, day here and night there. Then there were the planets going round the sun, with their satellites going round them. How wonderful are the works of the Creator! The comets, too; that of 1811, however, with a famous tail, as he deserved. His regular course—if you may call it regular—was shown. I saw him when a schoolboy in Wiltshire then. There has not been a comet worth calling a comet since. The zodiac made very pretty slides—twelve of them, each a sign. These things greatly advanced the art and the demand for magic lanterns increased, but not much for some years, until the dissolving views were introduced, about eighteen years ago, I think it was. But I should tell you that

Dollond, before that, made improvements in the magic lantern; they called the new instrument the phantasmagoria. Mr. Henry, who conjured at the Adelphi Theatre some eighteen years ago, was one of the first—indeed I may say *the* first—who introduced dissolving views at a place of public amusement. Then these views were shown by the oil light only, so that the effect was not near so good as by gas, but even that created a great impression. From that period I date what I may call the popularity of magic lanterns. Henry used two lanterns for his views; but using them with oil, and not on so large a scale, they would be thought very poor things now.

"Then the Careys introduced the gas microscope, up in Bond Street. The gas microscope (the hydro-oxygen it's sometimes called) is the magic lantern, and on the principle of the magic lantern, only better glazed, showing the water lions and other things in a drop of stagnant water. Thames water may do. I now introduce insects and butterflies' wings in my lanterns—real insects and real wings of insects on the slides. I make such as fleas, bugs, pig-lice (an extraordinary thing, with claws like a crab, sir), and so up to butterflies— all between glasses, and air tight—they'll last for ever if necessary. Here's the sting, tongue and wing of a bee. Here you see flowers. Those leaves of the fern are really beautiful—of course they are, for they are from the fern itself. This is one great improvement of the art, which I have given in a more simple form than used to be the fashion. You can magnify them to any size, and it's still nature— no disproportion and no distortion. Butterflies may be made as big as the wall of this room, through one of my magic lanterns with microscope power attached—but the larger the object represented, the less the power of the light. Gas, in some degree, obviates that fault. No oil can be made to give a light like gas. After this the question arose as to introducing views with the lime light, but the paintings in the lanterns were then too coarse, for the light brought them out in all their coarseness. Every defect was shown up, glaringly, you may say. That brought in better paintings—of course at a greater cost. The Polytechnic has brought the lime-light for this purpose to great perfection. For the oil-lights the paintings are bold, for the lime-light fine and delicate. Next the chromatrope was introduced, revolving stars chiefly—the hint being taken from Chinese fireworks. Mount Vesuvius was made to explode and such like. That's the present state of the art in London. The trade is five or six fold what I once knew it. Landscapes, Fingal's caves, cathedrals, sea views, are most popular now. In the landscapes we give the changes from summer to winter—from a bright sun in July to the snow seen actually falling in January.

"I make between 500 and 600 a year, say 550; I think I make one half of those made. The lowest price of a well-made lantern is 7s. 6d., and so on up to £20, dissolving and double lanterns. About a third of the lowest price are made, but people often go on from that to a superior article. I sold last year about 100 of the best of single lanterns, retailed at £10. Calculate a third at 7s. 6d., and 100 at £10, and the intermediate prices in—I think we may say—equal proportions—and you have the amount. Average the middle lot at 30s., suppose—that is £1,469 14s. I think that the other magic lanterns made, though they may be double my quantity, will not realize more, as so many lower-priced lanterns are made; so double the amount, and we have £2,939 8s. for London-made magic lanterns. I think I can, and shall, introduce further improvements. There are slop magic lanterns; they are slops, made, I believe, but I am not sure, in French Flanders; and I believe more of them are sold than of our own. What is worse than slop art, sir? These slop lanterns are generally retailed at 1s. 6d. each, with 12 slides. The tin part is neatly made; but altogether, it is sad rubbish. I have been told by persons who bought them—and I have been often told it—that they could make nothing of them. The only good that they can do is, that they may tempt people to buy better ones—which is something. The admission of foreign toys at a low rate of duty has not injured the magic lantern business, but has rather increased it."

# THE MERCHANT SEAMEN

## LETTER XL—7 MARCH 1850[1]

*Number of seamen*

According to the census of 1841, the number of seamen in the metropolis was as follows :

| | |
|---|---:|
| Merchant Seamen | 7,002 |
| Navy | 1,092 |
| | 8,094 |

This, I am informed, may be said to represent the number of seamen in London in the month of June of each year; in the spring and autumn, however, I am assured that the number of sailors in the metropolis is decreased nearly one-half. . . .

*Legislation*

The reckless and improvident character of sailors, and the peculiar nature of their service, coupled with a consideration of their vast importance to our national welfare, have long induced both the Legislature and Courts of Justice to treat them differently from other labourers, to dictate the form of their contracts, and to construe those contracts in a peculiar manner. . . .

In 1835 an act was passed, by which all the previous acts were replaced and consolidated, forming in fact a code for merchant seamen. The principal features were—the establishment of a registration of seamen—the regulation of articles, not only by requiring the insertion of an accurate statement of the wages, the voyage, and the scale of provisions, but by forbidding certain inequitable stipulations, and compelling the use of certain given forms, which it was supposed would render evasion impossible—the infliction of forfeiture of wages and other penalties, for desertion and misconduct—the affording means for recovering wages by summary proceedings before a Justice—stringent regulations to

[1] The letter began with a long statistical section which included tables to show the strength of British Maritime resources compared with France and the U.S., the growth of the British Merchant marine and its various foreign trades and the value of imports and exports "intrusted to the merchant marine mainly" for 1839–1848.

prevent men from being abandoned abroad—provisions for compelling all ships to be provided with medicines, and large ships with surgeons—regulations for binding apprentices—and provisions for obtaining full returns of all casualties happening on the voyage. This act was repealed in 1844, by 7 and 8 Victoria, 112 (the act now in force), which re-enacts in substance the important provisions of the former act, with additional means for effecting them. . . .

The Mercantile Marine Bill now before the House of Commons provides an office in every seaport, in which hands may be engaged and discharged, in the same way as by the establishment of the Coalwhippers' office. The act proposes to give to the superintendent, among other things, power to recover the wages of deceased seamen, and to pay them over to their families, without the tedious and expensive process of procuring letters of administration. The bill also contains means for enforcing sanitary regulations on board. Additional means are provided for enforcing discipline. Another feature in the measure is the requiring all future masters and mates to pass examinations, and the giving powers to cashier those who are convicted of incompetence, drunkenness, or tyranny. There are, however, no express provisions for the education of officers or men.

I have thus cited the principal provisions of the bill now before Parliament. It is my object at present to inquire into the state of the merchant seamen, with the view of ascertaining, among other matters, the opinions of the men mainly interested, as to the necessity for, or the benefits likely to accrue from, the proposed measure. . . .

### The boatswain of an emigrant ship

The Merchant Service afloat is divisible into the *foreign* and *coasting* trade. The foreign trade, again, has many distinct branches, such as the East India and China trade—the Baltic—the Mediterranean—the Greenland—the South Sea—the United States—the British North American—the Austrian—the African—and other trades. In the present letter I have space only for an exposition of the state of the seamen on board the Australian ships. Upon this subject a man who was much more than bronzed—as he was actually red in the face and neck—gave me the following statement. He had free and jovial manners, but sometimes evinced much feeling, especially when speaking of the emigrant ships. He wore three shirts—a clean one over two which were not perfectly clean— for he could not bear, he said, to show dirty linen. This happened only, however, he told me, when he was "out on the spree", for then he was in the habit of buying a clean white shirt as soon as he wanted "a change", and putting it on over his soiled one, in order to obviate the necessity of carrying his dirty linen about with him; so that by the stratification of his shirts he could always compute the duration of "the lark". He wore only a jacket, and felt inconvenience, when on the spree, in having a dirty shirt to carry about; and to obviate this he adopted the plan I have mentioned :

"I was *boatswain of an emigrant ship* last voyage. They were Government emigrants we had on board. The ship was 380 tons according to the new mode of measurement, and 500 tons according to the old mode. She had eight able men before the mast, four apprentices, a second mate, steward, cook, first mate, and captain. In addition to these, there were eight supernumeraries. You see, sir, all the Government emigrant and convict ships are obliged to take out four men and a boy to each 100 tons. We were near upon 400 tons burden; so we were obligated to have 16 able seamen and four boys; but, as I told you before, we had only eight able seamen. To make up the deficiency, we shipped eight supernumeraries. These supernumeraries were no sailors at all—not able to go aloft— couldn't put their foot above the shearpole. They were mostly men that the Government had refused to assist to emigrate. The shipping masters had put them on blue jackets, and told them the names of ships to say they had served in, so as to get them a berth. The shipping masters will get them a register, ticket and all; and these are the men who are taken in preference to us, because they go upon nominal wages of a shilling a month. I tell you what it is, sir. I saw to-day half a dozen of these fellows taken instead of six good able-bodied seamen, who were left to walk the streets : that's the candid fact, sir.

"It's a shameful thing to see the way we are treated. We are not treated like men at all; and what's more, there's no dependence to be placed on us now. If a war was to break out with America, there's thousands of us would go over to the other country. We're worse than the black slaves; they are taken care of, and we are not. On board ship they can do anything with us they think proper. If in case you are a spirited man, and speaks a word against an officer that tyrannicalises over you, he will put you in irons, and stop your money—six days for one : for every day you're in irons he stops six days' pay, and may be forfeits your whole wages. . . . The navy is just as much dissatisfied as the merchant seamen. If a war was to come with France, we might turn out against them— for we owe them a grudge for old times past. For myself, I can't abear the hair of a Frenchman's head. It would never do not to stand by the little island again the Mounseers; but, again America, I'd

never fire a shot! They have got feeling for a seaman there. There's
no people running after you there to rob you. The pay's a great
deal better, too, and the food twice as good as in the English ships.
There's no stint of anything; but in this country they do everything
they can to rob a seaman. . . .

"I was out Christmas-eve twelvemonth, and I arrived in London
the 8th of February last; and what do you think I got, sir, for
the whole of my service—for risking my life, for working all hours,
in all weathers—what do you think I got, sir? Why, I had £10 2s.
—that's it, sir—for thirteen months and a half. I ought to have
received about £32. My wages as boatswain were £2 10s. a month.
I have had £4 and £3 10s. for the same duty. But the little petty
owners is cutting down the wages as low as they can, till they're
almost starving us and our families. The rest of the money that was
due to me was stopped, because I spoke out for my rights, and five
of the other hands was served in the same manner. . . . The reason
why the owners stopped our pay was because we spoke out when
the ship was short of hands. There was only four able men in her,
and there should have been eight; so we had to do double work all
of us, night and day. We complained to the captain that the ship
was short-handed. But, you see, the wages for able seamen is more
in foreign countries than in England; so, to keep the ship's
expenses down, the captains object to take on fresh hands in foreign
ports. Well, the captain promised us to get some new men at
Sydney, but he went to sea short-handed as we were. So we axed
him again to get fresh hands, as the ship was leaky, and we wanted
our full complement of men; but he refused to do so, because the
wages at the next port was nearly double the pay in London; and
then we told him we wouldn't do any more work. This he called
a mutiny, and our wages was stopped to near upon £20 a man.
The usual rate of pay in an emigrant ship for an able seaman is £2
a month.

"The tonnage varies from 200 to 1,000. Ships of 200 are not safe
to go as far as Sidney or New Zealand; but that the owners don't
trouble heads about, so long as they can get their ship full of
emigrants. The greater number of emigrant ships are about 500 tons.
To understand how many emigrants can be comfortably accom-
modated in a ship, I should first tell you that in the best ships the
emigrants are divided—that is, the single people are separated from
the married; the single men are for'ard, the married people are
'midships, and the single women are aft. In a vessel of such an
arrangement not more than sixty emigrants to every 100 tons can
be taken out with comfort. I have known near upon 100 emigrants
taken out to each 100 tons—that is to say, I have known a ship of

380 tons have as many as 380 emigrants on board." (A carpenter, who had made his two last voyages in emigrant ships, here said "That is too often the case, I am sorry to say.")

"I have often seen," the carpenter said, "the poor people, in some of the worst ships, stowed away for'ard so close that you might have said they were 'in bulk'. There were thirty people in thirty feet space. I know, as a carpenter, that many of the emigrant ships are not fit to bring home a cargo; though, as the owners say, they are quite fit to take emigrants out. I have seen right through the top sides (the timbers above the copper-sheating) of many of them— the planks have warped with the heat of the sun. A man has often to carry an emigrant ship in his arms, from one port to another, for the hands are always at the pumps. It may astonish the public that so many emigrants are lost, but we ships'-carpenters are only astonished that there are so few."

The boatswain here continued : "The carpenter has told you nothing but the truth. In the worst class ships there is scarcely any separation of the sexes. A partition is certainly run up between the sleeping-berths; but as these do not reach the top, any one can make it convenient to get over, or look over, the partition into the next berth. There is scarcely a young single woman who emigrates that keeps her character on board o' ship, and after that she mostly makes her appearance on the town in Sidney. I'm speaking of those who go out unprotected; and what else can be expected, sir, among a parcel of sailors? The captains and doctors often set the example, and the mates and the sailors, of course, imitate their superior officers. There has been no chaplain on board the emigrant ships that I have been in. Some captains read prayers once on a Sunday, but many don't; and I have often known a ship go right away from London to Sidney, without divine service ever being performed.

"The Government emigrants, I believe, usually pay about £7 per head, and those who are not sent out by the Government pay from £18 to £20 for the passage. For this sum they are found in provisions. There is a certain scale of provisions allowed; but this is almost nominal, for the greater number of emigrant ships carry false weights, and the allowance served out is generally short, by at least a quarter." (I could hardly credit that the spirit of commercial trickery had reached even the high seas, and that shipowners had taken to false weights as a means of enabling them to undersell their brother merchants. On inquiring, however, I was assured that the practice was becoming *common*.) "Again, the quality of the food is of the worst kind. There are regular Government surveyors to overhaul the provisions of such ships; but, Lord love you! they are easily got to windward of. The captain, under the direction of the owners, puts some prime stuff among the top casks, and all the rest is old condemned stores—rotten beef and pork, that's positively green with putrefaction—and the biscuits are all weevily; indeed they're so full of maggots, that the sailors say they're as rich as Welsh rabbits, when toasted. The poor things who emigrate have no money to lay in their own private stock of food, and so they're wholly dependent on the ship's stores; and often they run so short that they're half-starved, and will come and beg a mouthful of the sailors. They're not allowed above one-third of what the sailors have. *We* have one pound and a half of meat, and they don't get above half a pound, and that's several ounces short from false weights. They have three quarts of water served out to them every day, and that very often of the filthiest description. It's frequently rotten and stinking; but, bad as it is, it's not enough for the poor people to cook with, and make their tea and coffee morning and evening. I have seen plenty of the emigrants hard put to with thirst—they would give anything for a drop to wet their lips with.

"From all I have seen of the emigrant ships, I believe it's a system of robbery from beginning to end. There are gentlemen shipowners who treat their men and the passengers justly and fairly. These are mostly the owners of the largest ships; but of late years a class of petty owners has sprung up—people who were clerks of the large owners a few years back—and they take every opportunity of tricking all in their pay. . . ."

## LETTER XLI—11 MARCH 1850[2]

*Narrative concerning the South American trade*

I had the following narrative concerning the *South American trade* from a sedate and intelligent man, who had all his "papers" with him, his watch, and was well-dressed, and with every appearance of what is called a "substantial" man. . . .

"In my last voyage from Port Phillip to Callao, and then to London, I had £3 10s. a month as able seaman. I consider that I ought to have had £4 for going round the Horn on a homeward voyage only. From London to Callao and back £3 a month would be fair. In my last voyage we had very good provisions, and a fair proportion of them. In my voyage out the provisions were very bad. We had, last voyage, neither false weight, nor any imposition of that

[2] Starting with a calculation of the capital employed in shipping, the letter went on to detail the principal foreign trade routes (conditions and wages) from the port of London.

sort, but I know that such things are common. They do so try to cheat the seaman that way, that it oft causes great disturbances. We had a good captain, but a strict man in regard of duty. He had worked his way from the 'hawse-pipes aft,' and knew every branch. He was a seaman, every inch of him. But I have met with many an officer not fit to be trusted with either life or property at sea. In my last ship there was really nothing for a reasonable man to complain of, except in the berths, which were both too small and too large, as some were meant for double berths. We shipped a sea off the Horn, and the forecastle was drenched, and we had to sleep on wet beds three or four nights. The captain offered to give us a sail, and let us sleep on the guano that we had on board. In the small berths we were scrouged up like pigs in a stye—hardly room to move.

"We brought home a cargo of guano from the Chinqua Islands. We first got sufficient guano to ballast the ship, and for that we discharged our old ballast. The way the guano is put on board is this. The guano is in cliffs—we call it 'the mountain'—it runs to a certain depth, and it's all stone at the bottom. From the sea it looks like a rocky mountain; there's nothing green about it—it's the colour of stone there. They say it's the ordure of birds, but I have my doubts about that, as there could never be birds, I fancy, to make that quantity. Why, I have seen as much guano on the Chinqua Islands— they're about two degrees south of Callao, on the coast of Peru— as would take thousands of ships twenty years to bring away. There are great flocks of birds about the guano places now, chiefly small web-footed birds. Some burrow in the ground like a rabbit. Among the larger birds are pelicans, plenty of them. A flock of them has a curious appearance. I have seen hundreds of them together. There is plenty of penguins, too, and plenty of seals, but the British ships are not allowed to capture them. I believe the Peruvian Government prevents it. A Peruvian man-of-war, a schooner, lies there.

"The guano is put on board this way: We have two 'shoots'. A shot is made of canvas, equally square on all sides. The diggers bring the guano a quarter of a mile, to the shore. A place is prepared on the side of the guano mountain, by the sea, railed off for security with what you would call a hurdle, but it's very strong bamboo cane. There the diggers empty their bags, through an open place into the shoot which is spread below, and held by ropes. The shoot is then lowered down from the guano mountain by the diggers, and the seamen who hold the ropes to regulate it must keep the lines a moving, to keep the guano from choking (going foul) in the shoots. We must regulate it by the pitch of the ship. The ship is moved alongside, and so the shoot is emptied down the hatchways at a favourable moment. There is a very strong smell about the guano mountain. It oft makes people's noses bleed. The diggers on shore and trimmers in the ship have to keep handkerchiefs round their noses, with oakum inside the handkerchiefs. It affects the eyes, too; no trimmer can work more than fifteen or twenty minutes at a time. . . ."

## The African Trade

A seaman, who was recommended to me as a trusty and well-conducted man, gave me the following statement as to the *African Trade* . . .

"Ours was a ship of the best sort as regards its management and accommodation—no false weights and no humbug about fines or such like, to cheat the men and please the owners; but there's a great deal of it about. Messrs ——— are good men to have to do with, and the owners in the African trade are good men generally. It's your cheap owners mostly in other trades that pluck every feather out of a seaman if they can, and they always can somehow. Provisions were good and plenty in my last ship; grog at the master's option. Very few ships now give it as an allowance.

"When we reached the Gold Coast we put ourselves in communication with a consignee. We took out a general cargo, and brought back ground-nuts, ivory, gold dust, and palm oil. The great thing is palm oil. The consignee trades with the natives, giving them cowries—they're shells that are the money there—cloth, beads, cotton, iron pots, and other things, in exchange for the cargo home. We very seldom went on shore on the west coast of Africa, on account of the surf. It's very few places where you can land with a boat. I have known that coast for five years, and I have been on shore. The place was green enough, but was very sickly. The natives come on board in their canoes; as they are all naked, they get through the surf in their canoes well enough, and if the canoe be capsized they swim ashore, for they are like fish in the water. They come to sell yams, or birds, or anything they have, and some of them are good hands, rather, at a bargain. No women come with them, and the seamen are not allowed to visit the women on shore. If a man be ashore a day or two he generally has the fever when he gets on board again. Masters go off the quickest, as they are most ashore. I don't think they drink. There were some fine strong fellows among the natives; some had a few words of English; all that knew any English could swear; they soon pick that up; it's like their ABC among sailors.

"I never was up any of the rivers. We generally leave the cargoes at different places along the west coast. There is no regular harbour on the Gold Coast, not, I believe, until you get down to the Bight of Benin. We may lie a week or ten days where we discharge most cargo, and then the men can't get ashore; plenty would if they could, but I think it's not worth the risk. We often had talk on board about African Travellers, such as Mungo Park. Sailors are more intelligent than they used to be. It's a dull coast. It seems mountainous in some parts, and with valleys in others, but all looks dull and dead. Indeed, you can't see much of the coast, for you see it chiefly at the forts. The mortality there is great; the white people die the quickest. I heard a captain say that out of twenty-one clerks he had taken out there seventeen had died. It must be a very profitable trade to those on shore who can stand the climate, or they wouldn't stay there, leading such dull lives. Many a seaman won't go there.

"The great dissatisfaction of seamen generally, is the lowness of their wages. Look how the Americans are paid, and then look at this. In the African trade, and other trades, a man may be employed nine months out of the twelve, and if he average £2 2s. a month, which is a liberal reckoning, why he has £18 18s. a year, and perhaps a wife and family to keep. What's £18 18s.? I would never go to that African coast again, only I make a pound or two in birds. We buy parrots—grey parrots chiefly—of the natives, who come aboard in their canoes. We sometimes pay 6s. or 7s. in Africa for a fine bird. I have known 200 parrots on board; they made a precious noise; but half the birds die before they get to England. Some captains won't allow parrots. There's very little desertion on the African coast. Seamen won't land to desert and wait ashore there for another ship. It's more than their life is worth."

## The West India Trade

A very fine looking fellow, as red as a hot climate could make him, with bright eyes, black curly hair, and a good expression of countenance, next gave me the following information concerning the *West India trade* :

"I have been at sea," he said, "nearly eleven years, and my last voyage was to the West Indies—to Kingston, Jamaica. The vessel was a barque of 240 tons. We had a crew of fourteen, being five able seamen, one ordinary seaman, two boys, cook, carpenter, steward, chief and second mates, and captain. The wages of the able seamen were £2 5s. a month. £2 5s. is now the general rate for a voyage to the West Indies, but I think it isn't sufficient; indeed I'm sure of it. I have had £2 10s. and £2 15s. for the West Indies from the Clyde. In the Scotch ports and Liverpool, it's never less than £2 10s. I reckon that London is the worst paid port in the country. I account for it, because there are so many men here, and some of them scamps enough to take anything; and then the foreigners that want to go back will go for anything. I have often sailed with foreign seamen, but never with a Jew seaman in my life. I see *them* only in the bum-boats in England. The steward had £2 10s., the cook the same, the carpenter £4, the chief mate £4, the second mate £2 15s., the ordinary seaman £1 15s. The boys were apprentices. The crew were all foreigners, or from British colonies, except myself, the ordinary seaman, the captain, and the boys. Two of the foreigners were very good seamen. They spoke very little English.

"We agreed very bad—not the foreigners and us—but the captain and us. When we left the Downs, we had very bad weather in the Channel, and two men were laid up sick, and sometimes three. The captain, because he couldn't get the ship worked to his liking, kept calling all hands a 'parcel of d——d soldiers'. She worked very hard with too few hands, such as the complement we had, and dreadful hard when three were laid up. The captain swore terribly. He didn't read prayers—swearing captains do though oft enough—by way of a set-off they say. Nobody can respect prayers from such people. I do from good men. I am a Scotchman. My last captain was a good seaman, though not much of a navigator. He pretty well ran the ship ashore in coming into the English Channel off the Scilly Islands. He nearly ran ashore, too, on the French coast, and with a fair wind right up the Channel. From the ignorance I have seen in officers, I am certain it is wrong to let anybody command a ship without his being examined as to his fitness. Young fellows often get the command through favour; they're relations of the owner, or something of that kind, and so they are trusted with men's lives. Our second mate was appointed by the owners, and hardly knew how to knot a yarn.

"At Kingston the men could go ashore every night, but no women were allowed on board. We took out a general cargo, and brought back a cargo of logwood, fustic, and black ebony. Me and a darky stowed it all. The men that were slaves in Kingston are starving. Those that were working on board our ship had only 2s. a day, and for such work 3s. 6d. is paid in England. It is all stuff that they won't work. They'll work hard enough if anybody will employ them. I have seen 100 of them come down to our ship the last voyage, a few weeks back, and beg for a crust. Me and my mates gave them half our grub to get rid of them, and because we couldn't bear to see them starving. I have heard hundreds of them say, and many a hundred times—for I've been four voyages to the West Indies—

that they were far better off when they were slaves, but I never heard them say they wished they were slaves again. There are thousands of blacks in Kingston seeking for work and can't get it. They work pretty hard when at work, but not like an European. No man in the world works harder than an European. There seems no trade in Jamaica now, and all the people is ruined.

"In my last ship our fare was very bad. We had pork and beef— the regular mahogany, you see—$1\frac{1}{4}$ lb. of each, and $\frac{3}{4}$ lb. of bread each—for the bread was allowanced—but $\frac{3}{4}$ lb. of bread is too little. We had also rice and flour, but not enough. Grog was at the captain's option. There was no splicing the mainbrace; a glass of grog now and then, when we reefed the topsails, and sometimes not then. I'm sure grog does a man good on board ship, especially in hard weather. To show what things sometimes go on in merchant ships, I will tell you this—a man daren't speak a word for his rights on board ship, or all the officers are down upon him. The pay gets worse, and the accommodation worse still. To show you what may go on in merchant ships, I'll tell you what I know.

"We were once, and lately too, off the Chinqua Islands, round the Horn, laying for a cargo of guano, just astern of a Bristol full-rigged ship. On a Saturday, as is the usual thing with merchant ships, we sent there for a 'Saturday night's bottle' to drink 'Sweethearts and Wives', and the skipper said he'd be d——d if he'd give it. His own men persevered in asking him for the bottle, and he went below and came up with a brace of pistols. He fired at one man, and the ball grazed his forehead, and took a bit off the top of his ear; that was the first pistol fired. He was not drunk. He then fired the other pistol, and shot a man dead through the breast. That man took no part at all. The man that was shot never spoke after. We heard the two shots on board our ship. There was then a cry of 'mutiny', from all the ships in the harbour—about a dozen—a cry of 'mutiny on board the *Eleanor*', and the captains sent off their officers and crews, with arms, to make peace. Afterwards the captains went aboard and held a council of war, and the two men who had threatened to take the Bristol captain's life for shooting their shipmate were chained to the mizen topsail sheets—I saw the men there myself. Our boat and another ship's boat, next day took those two men to the man-of-war schooner on the station, and what was done in the matter I never heard; but the Peruvian man-of-war and the Bristol ship came together to Callao when we were there, and there we left them.

"The best way, sir—aye, and the only way, too—to stop desertion, is better usage and better pay, and more to eat, and then never a man would grumble, and there'd be no bad language either—unless when allowable. You may register and register, and go nibbling on, but I tell you its the only way. In my last ship I had no berth; there was no room in the forecastle to hang up hammocks except for four. The cook slept there every night; he couldn't be disturbed; and the rest took their turns, turn in and turn out, but I never turned in at all, because others had the turn before me. I slept all the time on a water-cask. In the West India trade I have worked 13, and 14, and 16 hours a day, though from six to six is the law of England, and there was no necessity for longer hours, only it was the captain's whim, that was all. A quick voyage was wanted, but good seamanship and good usage—and they often go together—are enough to do that without distressing the men, who are neither so well paid, or so well treated, or so well fed, as to care about the interests of the owner. What's the owner to me? He doesn't care for me, or very seldom; if he did, I'd care for him."

## The whale fishery in the South Seas

A ship carpenter, a fine-looking man, in plain clothes, well and even handsomely dressed, gave me the following account of *the whale fishery in the South Seas*:

"I have returned from a South Sea voyage in a whaler. It is the custom of whalers in the South Seas to go 'on the lay'. In Greenland the men go partly by wages and partly by the lay; but I never was in Greenland. The system known as 'the lay' is this: the seaman is entitled (as a general rule) to the 190th share of the money obtained by the sale of the oil. There are from 30 to 36 hands generally. The officers are paid according to rank. The boat-steerer (the same officer as the harpooner in the Greenland trade) has a 140th share; so has the cook; the chief mate a 40th; the carpenter (myself) a 90th; the steward a 130th; the captain a 12th.

"The process of catching the sperm whale is this: They go in schools (shoals), and I have seen as many as 40 in a school. Sometimes I have seen a stray whale, and then it is generally a large one. Well, the man at the mast-head sings out, 'There she blows—a whale in sight!' If it's a school, they lower all the boats; if a stray whale, two boats are lowered. In each boat are three harpoons and two drags; the drag is to secure a whale until he can be got at, if the men are busy with another whale, and killed with the harpoon. The boat steerer, who rows first oar of the boat, drives his harpoon into a sperm whale. When struck, the whale will often seize a boat with his teeth, and upset it with his flux (tail). The sperm whale is much fiercer than the Greenland whale. No boat is lowered after sundown, because it is unsafe; the danger is great at all times. When one of a school is struck, the whole seem to know. A few spring out of the water at the moment a whale is struck. I have seen one four miles off spring out. A cow (she whale) will miss her calf (young whale) in an instant; the men drive at the calf, and so can generally make sure of the cow. A bull (he whale) generally does not show such affection, but a cow won't go far from her calf. At 'gendering' time the cow is struck first, if possible, to make sure of the bull. While the harpooning is going on, the whole school is in commotion; blood and white water is flung about on the waves, and the moment blood flows sharks appear, though one wasn't seen previously. If a man fall overboard the shark won't touch him as long as the shark has a chance to prey on the carcase of the whale. I have seen a man and a shark swim alongside one another. One of the crew must go overboard, when cutting-in the whale; that is, cutting the blubber off the carcase when the whale is brought alongside the ship. A boat steerer generally does it and though there are thousands of sharks about, he's never injured. I have known the sharks devour the carcase of a calf as it hung all night hooked to the ship. The carcase must first be cut, or the shark can't get hold of it with his teeth; he must have one place to fix on first. A whale dies without noise, but 'flurries'; that's the death motion. In those vast solitudes in the Pacific the feeling is often overwhelming to any thinking man. I have been for four months without seeing even a sail. Nothing but the fish and the waters, and often very few of the fish. The common seamen are terribly oppressed by the long, long solitudes.

"The regulations on board the whalers are not what they ought to be. Provisions are not what they should be. Of beef, $\frac{3}{4}$ lb. is allowed a day, and of pork the same, on alternate days; but they are generally of bad quality. A few casks of good provisions are put forward to the surveyor's inspection, and the bad is kept in the background. Out at sea the good is kept for the cabin. The peas, flour, and bread, sometimes kept for four years—about the term of a whaling voyage—are bad, because no care is taken to preserve them. Grog is at the captain's option; it is generally allowed when the men are 'trying out';—that is, boiling the blubber for oil. The captain on leaving England has £300, £400 or £500 worth of slops on board ship for the use of the crew. Slops are clothing from the slop-shops—any rubbish he can pick up cheap in the Minories, or anywhere. These as a favour he serves out at about 150 per cent profit. . . .

"In the whaling voyage I am describing we went out for four years, and lost our captain at two years' end; he died of fever off Copang, a Dutch settlement, an island in Torres Straits. There was no person to take charge of the ship. The mate, as his duty, read the articles to the crew, and the crew were surprised to find that instead of the 160th, they were only entitled to the 180th lay. They were deceived. In most whalers the articles are not made out before the seaman is called upon to sign them. . . . In England I was told by the ship-owners—merchant princes, sir—that the ship had brought home little or no oil, and I was entitled to no money. I knew the contrary. I inquired, as if I were a stranger, of the wharfinger at the London Docks, where the ship was discharged, and he told me that she turned fifty-one tons of oil worth £80 a ton; that's £4,080. I was entitled to £30, in addition to my advances. By the articles the men on the lay are not allowed to employ their own gauger, and are often cheated by the owners. . . . The crews of English whalers are Spaniards—and coloured men, when they can get them—ignorant fellows, easily imposed upon; and nearly all the American whalers are manned by Spaniards and coloured men. All the men were dissatisfied. They didn't care one jot for their country. Fight against America if a war broke out! Not they. Would I? No. They don't impose on sailors in America. . . ."

*A Scotsman in the American Service*

A short man, but evidently of very great strength, brawny and muscular, and with a very good frank expression of countenance, gave me the following account as to the treatment on board the *American ships*:

"I am a *Scotchman* born, but am now *in the American service*, and on board a transit (merchant) ship trading from New York; not a liner, which runs only to one place. I have been in the English service, and was brought up in it. . . . I have been off and on, in the American service these last five years. It's a far better service than the English—better wages, better meat, and better ships. No half-pounds of meat short there; eat when you're hungry, and the best of grub. What goes into an English ship's cabin goes into an American ship's forecastle. The Americans are fast getting the pick of the English navy. I have now 15 dollars a month, or £3 2s. 6d. . . . For the same sort of service in an English merchant ship I might get £2, or £2 5s., and starving all the time, unless I chance on a good employer, but they are scarce. The sleeping berths are far better in the forecastles of the American than the English ships— more room, and better fitted up. Why, of course, the English seamen flock into the American service as fast as they can, petty officers and all. . . . There's very little else but English seamen in the American ships. Our crew is nineteen, and only four are American born; fourteen are British subjects. If a war broke out—I could answer for myself and for hundreds besides—I wouldn't fight for England against America, but for America against England. I'll not fight for a country that starves and cheats you. I'll never fight for short weights and stinting in everything, not I. I left an English ship at Quebec, which is the greatest place in British America for sailors deserting. The living is so bad that men won't put up with it. They can easily hide in Quebec, and so go overland into the States. Nothing will check desertion in the English Service but better wages, better treatment, and better food. The discipline is much the same on board the American as on board the English ships. An English seaman is very little thought of in his own country, but he's well thought of in America. He's a man there."

## The View of an American Seaman

A very stalwart, fine-looking fellow, dressed in a drab-coloured jacket, of a texture resembling fur, with long boots, under blue trowsers, turned high up the leg, gave me the following account of the same service. He had a florid look, a quantity of long brown hair, and large whiskers, with a free off-hand manner, and was, judging from his appearance, about 35 :

"I'm an American born," he said—"a New York man, and now in the American service, but I have served under the English flag as well, and I have had good living under it and bad living; but bad living has it. In one of —— ——'s ships there was the horridest living I ever knew. She was from Bombay to London. The very horridest living I have known for 37 years, as man and boy. I'm 47 now— at least my mother says so. I don't dislike the English flag, and wouldn't fight against it if I could help it. I'd go into the backwoods, or take a farm, or something of that kind, rather than fight my brothers. I'm a man of peace—an Elihu Burritt man. The American-born seamen, as far as I know, have all friendly feelings to this country. When English and American sailors get drinking together, they hardly ever quarrel. What have they to quarrel about? . . .

"In America it's customary in a seaman's boarding-house to take a friend in to dinner with you, and his dinner's not charged to you. I was once invited by a friend to dine at a seaman's home here; but he didn't know the ways of the place. The waiter, I guess you call him, says 'Who are you?' I told him who I came with, and he took the plate away—'you can't dine here, or any fellow might come out of the streets and dine.' If it had been America I'd have knocked him down. It's a land of freedom in America, certainly; but there's a deal of humbug about all that. I'm just as free here. I never was insulted in the streets of London in my life. The living is so good in

American boarding-houses, and so different to what English seamen have on board ship, that it's one thing to tempt them to desert. In an American boarding-house for seamen, they will have for dinner, on different days, fish, beef, mutton, boiled ham, fowls (perhaps every day), and a dessert after dinner—always a pudding or a pie, with apples and other fruit. The rum being so cheap is another reason, and not a little one. Another reason to tempt to desertion is—but I don't reckon that it influences them so much as the better meat and drink—a tumbler of rum in a decanter at the bar in New York for three-halfpence, take what you like—a tumbler full if you will, though the landlord looks at you if you fill the tumbler—none of your wine-glasses there. Another reason is, their lower wages in England. In long voyages I believe it's the cruelty, along with the bad wages and bad accommodation, that makes English seamen desert. The discipline is the same in the two services.

"In America the people are kinder to a seaman, I reckon. Here they seem to keep a sort of distance like; I don't understand it. In a New York boarding-house a landlord will give you two or three or more dollars the first night, because he's sure of his money; and he'll keep you three or four weeks, for the shipping-master will pay him when the man signs articles, and it's deducted from the man's wages at the finish of the voyage. An English seaman can get from Quebec to the States for a couple of dollars. In America they can buy 'a protection' for 50 cents, or two English shillings. The landlords have plenty of protections to sell. By a protection ticket an English seaman can pass as an American in any British port in North America. I see plenty of English seamen hard up here. They come down to our ship and say they've got the key of the street, and have no other place to go to, and some beg of you. Such a thing's never known in America. People don't enjoy themselves here, I think, as they do in America; they're distant, like, and haven't that feeling for a working-man that there is across the water."

## LETTER XLII—14 MARCH 1850[3]

*The East India trade: Mr. Green's company*

I had the next statement from a seaman in the employ of Mr. Green, the eminent shipowner. High as the man speaks in praise of his master, I am happy to have it in my power to state, that all I have heard fully bears out this most honourable eulogium. . . .

[3] The letter began with an account of an East Indian voyage aboard a bad ship.

"I have been to sea about four or five and thirty years, I expect. I was apprenticed in the West India Trade, in 1814 or 1815. I remained in the West India trade for ten or twelve years. Then I went to Sydney for three or four years. After that I was sailing in small craft from St. Thomas's to different ports in South America and to different islands in the West Indies, till 1840. Since that time I have been sailing out of London to the East Indies in Mr. Green's employ. When I first joined Mr. Green, in 1840, his Home, for the sailors in his employ, was not open, but on my return from Calcutta it was. Before that time I had been in the habit of living in the Home in Well-Street. This was opened about 1832 or '33, I can't recollect exactly which. I know I shipped out of it in 1840 to join Mr. Green's company. I had £2 a month on first joining Mr. Green's ship. In other ships I had £2 5s.; but I had heard that Mr. Green gave better employ and better usage, at £2 a month than others at £2 5s., and so I thought I'd be one of his men. . . .

"Of all owners I have ever shipped with I have found Mr. Green to be the best. Why, sir, in the first place, when a man comes back there is a place for him to go—a home, sir. I call it a real home, sir; and there is no other shipowner that I know of that cares so much for his men. I am a single man. I have been ten years in Mr. Green's service, and I can conscientiously state that a better master to his men I never knew." (I endeavoured to impress upon the man that, if he had anything private to communicate, his name could never transpire, nor would he be in any way injured, and he again assured me that Mr. Green was a gentleman who had invariably shown a disposition to benefit his men, and that the men had the same feeling towards their master as he had towards them; they would do all they could to serve him.)

"My last voyage was made in the *Northumberland*, from London to Madras, and from Madras to Calcutta. She was about 800 tons. . . . We had full weight of provisions, always good, and plenty. We had sufficient of good water—well filtered and sweet. We had salt beef and plums and flour one day, and pork and peas the next —as much as we could eat. We had plenty of room on board Mr. Green's ship, and plenty of air. The midshipmen's berth had a porthole and scuttle, and was a very large and airy cabin; so, indeed, were all the berths. . . .

"I think that if all owners were like Mr. Green there would be fewer men to leave the merchant service of this country. What the merchant seamen generally require is to be well treated, and then they would be sure to be good men. Mr. Green has a school for the children of sailors. It will hold more than 300 I have heard, and I know the sailors love him for his regard to their little ones, and so indeed does all Poplar. I have been in ships that are as badly found and the men as little cared for as those of Mr. Green's are well provisioned and the men truly regarded; and I can conscientiously say that if all owners were like Mr. Green, our merchant service would be the envy of the world. The masters lay the blame upon the men, but from what I have seen I can declare that it is not the men's fault, but the captains or the owners, as to how the men behave themselves. I never knew any act of insubordination to occur on board of Mr. Green's ship, and I attribute this solely to the good treatment of the men. What man can speak again a master like that? There is a good home and a good bed always to go to, and I only wish such masters were more general, and then the country would be safer I can tell you."[4]

## Voyages to Quebec

A man, who had been a seaman for eleven years, gave me the following account as to the *Quebec trade* :

"My last voyages were to Quebec and the River de Loup, in the port of Quebec. I last sailed in a barque of about 400 tons. We went out in ballast, and brought back deals. We had 17 in crew— 7 able seamen, 2 ordinaries (one fell overboard from the maintopsailyard, and was drowned), cook, carpenter, steward, first and second mates, captain, and two apprentices. I had £2 10s. a month. It's not enough, as no sailors see more hardships than those that go to North America. It ought not to be less than £3. The provisions were good and plentiful, but the accommodation, in the forecastle, was very bad and very leaky. I had to heave my bed over-board when we returned, as it wasn't worth bringing on shore; it was rotten from the wet. I have heard many men say they would never fight for England; but I would fight for England—that is, if I saw occasion—to be sure I would.

"The seamen put the deals on board through the port-holes. They are brought down, to the ship in lighters, which they call 'bateaux'. The deals are cut ready in mills up the country, but I never saw one. In the River de Loup they slide the deals down a shoot (a sort of spout), into the river; the shore is high. French Canadians—they're not very active—pick them out of the river, put them on their bateaux, and take them to a pier-head, where they pile them ready for the loading of the ship. The forests there look very black. Along the Gulf of St. Lawrence they have a cold, miserable look—the wind's always blowing, and you don't see a sign of life about the

---

[4] A statement about the Baltic trade has been cut.

forest (we were close in shore too) except a few birds. The noise of the wind among the trees there is very outlandish.

"Desertions are very common in Quebec; the reason is, that men can hide better there than in smaller places, and so get away to the States, perhaps, and have far better pay, and far better food. But some seamen are never satisfied. Plenty go to British North America on purpose to desert. I never ran away from a ship in my life. But men are sure to desert until you give them better wages and better living; and a glass of grog comes very handy at sea. I like a glass of grog at sea now and then myself; but I don't care for liquor on shore.

"The captain drank very hard aboard, and was mad from it. He was so mad that we ran back 700 miles, to bring the ship to England. Within twenty-four hours of Plymouth, he came to his senses, and persuaded us to take the ship back to North America. He was eleven days below, ill. When he did come on deck, he looked very fierce about the eyes. He drank hard in America, and was unshipped when we got to England. Men's lives weren't safe with him, but the mate was a good seaman. When we left England we were bound for Quebec; if it hadn't been for the captain's drunken management, in the gales of wind, we should have made Portugal in forty-eight hours. We kept standing away to the southward by his orders. It was a mercy we got home at all. Off Dungeness the captain was that mad after liquor, that he gave £1 for a gallon of spirit to a pilot cutter. There was three and a half gallons of brandy on board when we left America. The captain drank it nearly all himself, and there was no liquor on board for nine days before we got to Dungeness. The steward told me the captain would drink vitriol, to keep his spirits up, when there was no brandy left. I was sorry for the captain, for he wasn't a tyrant, with all his drinking."[5]

## The Hudson's Bay ships

I had a statement from a middle-aged and, as I was assured on the best authority, a very trusty man, concerning the *Hudson's Bay Ships*. He stated as follows:

"My last voyage was in the Hudson's Bay Company's service. I have been 24 years at sea in various services. I have been out as boatswain, mate, and able seaman. In the Hudson's Bay Company's service there is really nothing to complain of. I have been in that service for, say 20 years. Before that I was in the employ of good shipowners. When men complain, they generally have not been

---

[5] Accounts of the Brazilian, Mediterranean and Portuguese trades appeared here.

kindly treated, or have been underpaid. Underpaid men are never good men—never good seamen. My last voyage, as I have said, was in the Hudson's Bay Company's service in the fur trade. In my last voyage I was boatswain, and I was formerly able seaman. Last time I went to Mouse River for furs.

"The half-breeds—the descendants of an Englishman and an Indian woman—are the principal people that the company deals with. The men who bring the skins to the factories are Indians, and they have a strong sense of religion. They do nothing on a Sunday. I don't understand much about their religious feelings on a Sunday, but they're very clean and won't work then. They are copper-coloured, and with long hair hanging loose about the neck, all black. They had a good expression—that they had. If I met one of them I should feel confident he would conduct me safe wherever I wanted to go. Some of them were fine-looking fellows. The old men are pensioned (as you would say) by the Hudson's Bay Company. I don't know at how much. Money is nothing there; but these natives have provisions served out to them to keep them. They really love the company. I'm certain of it; they would go through fire and water for it; they would give their lives for it—certainly they would.

"When I first went to the Mouse River I felt no great sense of novelty, I can tell you. The country was flat—plains, you see—what may be called the bush. Our principal trade was in beaver skins. The beaver is shot as well as trapped; it is a very ingenious creature, and is trapped and shot as it builds its house in the marshes, or by the brook or river's side. There's not such a demand for beavers as there was, as far as I know; there's slop hats instead of beaver hats. Beaver is really good eating. The skins go to the company, and the flesh is eaten. It's very like beef, and fat beef too—tasty, uncommon. I have tasted it in the Indian's huts; it's generally roasted before a wood fire. Its flesh never comes to the factories to be served out to the people; the Indians take care of that. They carry quantities of wild geese and ducks to the factories. It's all barter. The barter is regulated by the price of beaver skins. Powder and shot was for a long time exchanged for beaver skins, and is indeed still; so is bread, flour, tobacco, tea, and sugar; the Indians there like tea four or five times a day. . . .

"Before I went to Hudson's Bay, I was in the Greenland whale fishery, and the ice I met with in that fishery wasn't to compare with what I saw in Hudson's Straits (which leads into Hudson's Bay), and in Hudson's Bay itself. I have been fifty days in Hudson's Bay, and the ship has only made twelve miles one way or other in those fifty days, as she was bound up in the ice, and couldn't move for a fortnight together. In Hudson's Straits we saw—for they were counted—35 icebergs in an evening, when we were outward bound; there are more counted homeward bound. The first I saw was above 200 feet high; the ship's mast head might be 100 feet. I have some-times seen them topple over; the top parts are melted by the sun, and run down as they thaw in channels, and so the iceberg capsizes. The first I saw was like the Tower of London moving on the water, only the real Tower here was a fool to it in size. I have seen ice-bergs a tremendous size, and looking as if one church steeple was piled upon another. A high iceberg looks as if it carries clouds on its top; and in going along in a dark night it makes a clear atmosphere about it. A mile, or a mile and a half off, it shows itself like a white mountain of light. The great care is to avoid icebergs; for small pieces of ice we don't care if we run again them. I have known an iceberg 200 fathoms (1,200 feet) under the water, and the compu-tation is that it is one-third above the water. In the sunlight you can see an iceberg twenty miles off glittering, just the same as you see windows lighted up here by the sun. An able seaman's wages are £3 3s. a month in the Hudson's Bay service. I consider that fair pay. If the seamen in other trades were paid in the same proportion there would be no grumbling and no dissatisfaction."[6]

## LETTER XLVI—3 APRIL 1850[7]

*Two experienced men on board steamers*

I now give the statements of two long-experienced men on board *steamers belonging to the foreign trade of the Port of London*—one in the engine-room, the other on deck as a general seaman. The fire-man was very well-informed, and produced his papers, when neces-sary, to vouch for the truth of what he stated. His appearance was not that of a strong man, and his narrative accounts for it. . . .

"Twenty years ago I served in a steamer which plied between London and Boulogne. I had 30s. a week, finding my own provisions. Now, if I were in the same trade, with twenty years' experience at my back, I should have 24s., instead of 30s. The engineer twenty years ago had £3 a week in that trade, finding his own provisions; now he has from 38s. to 44s.; the last is the very highest. My last voyage was to Marseilles, and I had then at the rate of 20s. a week, as fireman, for taking the vessel out, but provisions were found to us.

[6] The letter closed with statistics about the number of steamers and their yearly rate of increase since first introduced.

[7] Ragged Schools were the subject of letters XLIII–XLV. The opening of the present letter included statistics about the number and tonnage of steamers engaged in foreign trade.

The first engineer had, I believe, £20 a month, and the second £16. I greatly prefer finding my own provisions (but that can only be done in short voyages)—for those found us by the masters are often very bad and very salt, and eating that stuff with constant fire and steam about one is terribly trying. . . .

"The iron boats are the worst for accommodation. The iron is always wet and cold, and the cold is always in the berths, and into them such as me have to go from the heat of the engine-room. A man to stand it should have the constitution of a negro by day, and an Esquimaux by night, especially in bad weather. The water keeps always working its way between the iron plates of the vessel, and so into the forecastle. I have been drenched so in bad weather that it has brought on four weeks' rheumatics. In our berths there is (as a general rule) no ventilation, except by the very hatch that you come into the place by. A lamp is generally there night and day, however, or there would be no light. I can't complain of having been so much cramped for sleeping-room in steamers; the berths are mostly 6 ft. 2 in. by 2 ft. Some of the engine-men, in some steamers, have to sleep in the engine-room, and there we cannot sleep from the heat, and from the damp caused by the steam. There are mostly swarms of bugs too, helping the heat and the damp to keep one awake. I hardly knew what bugs were, in comparison, on shore, but their head-quarters are in the engine-rooms of steamers (I don't say of all steamers).

"There is another thing I must tell you of. When new machinery is put into a steam-boat, the engineer of the factory puts his own man on board the steamer as engineer, to manage the machinery, which the makers generally warrant for twelve months. The captain of the vessel has nothing to do with the appointment of the men in the engine-room (except in the Oriental and Peninsular Company), and the engineer selects his own men. The engineer from the factory, ten to one, has never been to sea before, and is very often sea-sick too, and laid up, and the vessel may take her chance. I have known the seamen sent down from the deck to do the work of the engineer's people below. A bad system prevails as regards boys. An engineer, or a captain, will employ boys in the place of men, who must stand idle while boys are underselling them, and the boy is registered as a fireman, and the registrar can't help it if the captain applies.

"The way the work on board a steamer is carried on by us in the engine-room is this: The engineer has the charge of the engines, and is to attend to the commands of the captain and the pilot, as to 'stop her', and any such order; he is looked upon as the responsible man. The business of a fireman, or stoker, is to keep up the supply of steam, by regulating the water pumped into the boilers, and by

PLATE XVII. Sawyers: Topman and Pitman at Work

PLATE XVIII.   The Honourable Carpenter

keeping the fires up to the required height. A great deal of responsibility as to the safety of a ship depends upon the fireman. In voyages of more than twenty-four hours' duration, there are two engineers generally, and firemen according to the length of the voyage and the power of the boat. I have worked in a West India boat with twenty-eight firemen, seven coal-trimmers, and five engineers. The engineers relieve each other every four hours; only the head engineer in a West India boat keeps no regular watch, and the others may relieve each other oftener if they choose; the firemen keep their regular four hours the same. The work is very exhausting. We must have something to drink, and ought really to have lime-juice, for it gives an appetite. In the Gravesend and Richmond boats there is no relief; one engineer and one stoker does the work; but they are not considered in our class at all. In the above-bridge boats there is generally nothing but a parcel of boys, had cheap.

"The stokers are not at all satisfied. I have served on board an American steamer, and know what good reason we have to be dissatisfied. None of us, I believe, if a war broke out, would fight against America. In the American steamer I was in we were all Englishmen, captain and all, but three. We were 136 or near that, in crew. I wish I was in the American service again. Better pay, and better provisions, and better accommodation. They know how to behave to a man, in America, and I would never have left them but for family matters. . . ."

*A Seaman on board a steamer* gave me the following account : . . .

"The steamers in the Continental trade are well manned, and have good men. The wages of the able seamen are £1 per week, of the firemen 24s.; the first engineer gets £2 4s., and the second £1 15s. per week, the first mate has £1 15s., the second £1 6s., and the captain has generally £2 11s. a week, or £140 a year. The apprentices are bound for five years, and have about £120 for the whole of their servitude. The foreign and continental steam trade with this country is now very considerable. . . . I don't remember the first steamer out of the port of London, but I recollect very well coming up the Pool, in a fog, in 1814, in a fishing smack, and hearing the noise of the first steam-vessel I ever saw. We were all of us plaguey frightened on board. The noise of the steam blowing off, and the beat of the paddles, produced a very terrible effect in the darkness. The first steamer I saw after the one that I heard, I thought a very comical affair, and for years after that I used to swear I'd never go to sea in one. Now I think they are the safest and best vessels of all.

L

"The accommodation for the seamen on board steamers is very small and very bad. Every usable part of the vessel is sacrificed for passengers and for cargo. I have often represented to the managing director of the steam company that I belong to, that the men had not fit places to live and sleep in. The answer was that they would see that it was remedied, but no alteration ever took place. In the men's berths there is little or no ventilation, and scarcely any room. The men always find themselves in provisions in the Continental trade, and they are glad to do so. I think the men have nothing to complain of, with the exception of their accommodation. The wages are fair, and the treatment good. I was in one vessel nine years, and several of the hands had been longer than I had; so I leave you to judge we are not very discontented in the steam service. The men are not allowed any grog. I think the owners of the steam vessels should be compelled to give better accommodation to the seamen— the men should be thought of *a little*. . . ."[8]

[8] The remaining statistics and interviews about the coasting trade have been cut.

# THE WOODWORKERS: SAWYERS

## LETTER LIX—4 JULY 1850[1]

The London Sawyers, though not a numerous body, still require full consideration, as belonging to a trade which has been extensively superseded by machinery.

### Number of sawyers

According to the last census the number of sawyers in Great Britain in 1841 was 29,593; of these 23,360 resided in England, 4,500 in Scotland, 1,508 in Wales, and the remaining 175 in the British Isles. About one-tenth part of the whole of the sawyers in Great Britain were then located in the metropolis, the number in London being 2,978, of whom only 186 were under twenty years of age. Strange to say, one of the sawyers above twenty was a *female*! At the time of taking the previous census the number of the Metropolitan Sawyers above twenty years of age was 2,180; so that, from 1831 to 1841, the London trade had increased 612. Since then, however, I am informed that the number has declined nearly one half. The number of steam saw-mills in the metropolis, in 1841, was 15; at the present moment, they are 68, including those for cutting veneers as well as timber and deals. . . .

### Four kinds of sawyers and their work

Of sawyers there are four kinds—viz., the hardwood and timber sawyers, the cooper's stave, and the shipwright sawyers. The hardwood sawyers are generally employed in cutting mahogany, rosewood, and all kinds of foreign fancy woods. This work demands the greatest skill in sawing. It requires special nicety in cutting, because the timber is more valuable, and a "bungler" might be the cause of great loss to his employer. A hardwood sawyer can generally turn his hand to timber sawing, but the timber sawyers are seldom able to accomplish the cutting of hard woods. Timber sawyers are mostly engaged in cutting for carpenters and builders.

---

[1] After treating the seamen ashore, Mayhew studied street entertainers. Using his "scientific" classification of labour, based on the raw material worked, he next turned to workers in wood. Letters LVII and LVIII covered the volume of the wood trade and workers at the timber docks.

The work of the cooper's stave sawyers consists principally in cutting "doublets" out of the foreign wood. The shipwright sawyers cut the "futtocks" and planks for ships.

*Timber Sawing*, by manual labour, has been unchanged within the recollection of the oldest man in the trade. One elderly man assured me that his grandfather, a sawyer, had told him that the work was always the same in his day. Two men work in a pit, which is generally 6 feet deep, and 4 feet 6 inches wide. These two men are termed the topman and pitman, according as they work *above* or *in* the pit. The pits are of two kinds, "scaffold" and "sunk" pits; the scaffold pit being raised from the ground, and almost always constructed of timber, while the sunk pit is dug into the earth. . . . The process observed by the shipwrights' or coopers' sawyers is the same as that of the timber and hardwood sawyers; it is all carried on in pits.

### Decline of the trade due to machinery

These four classes of the trades, with the exception of the cooper's stave sawyers, are greatly reduced in numbers. It is generally considered in the trade that there are not half as many sawyers at present as there were five and twenty years ago. Formerly there used to be a great many shipwright sawyers along the banks of the Thames, but now, I am informed, the greater part of the yards are shut up, and many of the sawyers and shipwrights have emigrated to America. The year after the strike in 1833 there were 1,500 sawyers on the books of the union, exclusive of the cooper, staves, and shipwright sawyers; and now there are not more than 320 members belonging to the three district societies. The great decrease in the numbers of the trade is owing to the introduction of machinery. The first steam saw-mill set up in the neighbourhood of London was established at Battersea, about the year 1806 or 1807. It was erected principally for the cutting of veneers, and the trade, though aware that it could not fail to take the work from them, still believed that it never could do so to the extent that it has. "We knew," says my informant, "that the mills could cut the veneers better and thinner than what we could, and more in an inch, which is a great object of course, in valuable woods, but still we never expected that steam power would be applied to the cutting of timber and deals. Since that time the mills have gone on increasing gradually, year after year, until now there are twenty regularly at work between Stangate and London-bridge, and no less than sixty-eight altogether, scattered throughout the metropolis."

## The trade society of sawyers

The trade society of sawyers is divided into six districts. The first of these is the West London which extends from Back-hill, near Hatton-garden, to Brentford; the second, or City District, reaches from Back-hill to St. George's-in-the-East; while the third, or Surrey District, runs from Dock-head, Bermondsey, to Westminister. These three belong to the general or timber and hardwood sawyers. The fourth district is in connection with the coopers' staves sawyers, and extends from Southwark-bridge to the Commercial Docks on the one side of the river, and to Limehouse on the other. The districts frequented by the shipwright-sawyers are Limehouse and Rother-hithe. Each class (excepting the shipwright-sawyers) has a trade society; and the following table shows the number of members belonging to each society, as well as the "non-society men" in each district, together with the total number and the aggregate total of the London operative sawyers generally :

| | Society Men | Non Society Men | Total Society and Non-Society men in each District |
|---|---|---|---|
| West London District | 60 | 140 | 200 |
| City District | 150 | 275 | 425 |
| Surrey District | 20 | 300 | 320 |
| | | | |
| Total General Sawyers | 230 | 715 | 945 |
| Southwark, or Cooper's Stave Sawyers | 60 | 40 | 100 |
| Limehouse | — | 450 | 450 |
| Rotherhithe | — | 100 | 100 |
| | | | |
| Total Shipwright Sawyers | — | 590 | 550 |
| | | | |
| Aggregate Total of Society and Non-society Men | 290 | 1,305 | 1,595 |

The houses of call at which the different societies meet have nothing whatever to do with the obtaining of employment for the men (as in the tailors' trade), but are simply places of meeting to discuss the affairs of the trade. The mode adopted by men wishing to obtain employment is making inquiry at the different yards. Concerning "benefits", or sums given in cases of affliction or distress, there are a few such provisions in connection with the trade societies, though they have no *provident funds*, such as the superannuation and vocation funds of other trades. The way in which assistance is rendered to the sick, and to the widow of a member of the trade

societies, is by voluntary subscriptions, obtained either by petition
or raffle—from 30s. to £3 being the sum usually collected in this
manner, while, in the case of death, £5 is sometimes obtained in the
city.

The shipwright sawyers have a benefit society, called "The Good
Samaritan", to render assistance to each other, in case of accident
or death. Here the weekly contributions are 3d., and the "benefits"
received from £1 to £10. The weekly contributions paid by the
members of the trade societies, are 2d. in the West London and
City districts, and 3d. in the Surrey and Southwark. The chief part
of the money thus obtained is devoted to "trade purposes", and the
remainder to philanthropic objects. These "trade purposes" consist
principally of means adopted to uphold the wages of the trade—
and the philanthropic objects, in the payment of small sums to the
aged and infirm members, as well as those suffering from accidents.
The tramps belonging to country societies are relieved by some of
the London bodies. They are usually furnished with a card of the
society to which they belong, and duplicates of these cards are kept
at one or other of the London district houses. The operative sawyers of the metropolis are in correspondence with almost all the
societies throughout the country, and the country societies are likewise in correspondence with each other, especially those in the north
of England, where the greatest number of sawyers are located.

A tramp, upon arriving in town and producing the card of his
society at one of the London houses of call, receives from the metropolitan society the sum of 5s. The country societies usually give
from 1s. to 2s. to tramps, and in some cases a supper and a bed.
The object of this relief to tramps is to assist a man in getting employment in another town, and the donations are given only to those
parties who subscribe to some recognized society throughout the
kingdom. Once a year an account of the money thus dispensed to
tramps is taken; the delegates of the different country societies
meeting annually in the north of England for that purpose. In the
case of London, however, the districts meet in "central committee",
and then make out a statement of the sum which has been disbursed
by them throughout the year; this they forward to the different
societies in the country.

Of late years the London operative sawyers, I am informed, have
been greatly opposed to any active resistance to their employers.
The last strike among them took place in the years 1833 and 1834,
and since that time they have generally sought to remedy any
difference between them and their masters by more conciliatory
measures. As an instance of this, I was furnished with copies of some
circulars that had been sent round to the leading timber merchants

on the occasion of the last disagreement. The tone of these was courteous and manly—neither cringing nor insulting—and spoke volumes for the intellectual and moral advance of the class since the days when Richardson's mill was destroyed by them.

## Social habits of the sawyers

The majority of the London sawyers, I am informed by some of the most intelligent and experienced members of the trade, are countrymen. They are generally sons of village carpenters or wheel-wrights, though some have been "bred and born" in the trade, as they say. As a body of men they are essentially unpolitical. I could not hear of one Chartist among them; and, although suffering greatly from machinery, I found few with what may be called violent or even strong opinions upon the subject. They spoke of the destruction of Richardson's Saw-mill as one of the follies and barbarisms of past days, and were quite alive to the importance of machinery as a means of producing wealth in a community. They also felt satisfied that it was quite out of their power to stop the progress of it. As a body of men I found them especially peaceable, and apparently of very simple and kindly dispositions. They are not what can be called an educated class, but those whom I saw were certainly distinguished for their natural good sense.

They are usually believed to be of intemperate habits, and I am informed that in the palmy days of the trade there was good reason for the belief. But since then work has declined, and they have become much more sober. There are many teetotallers now among them; it is supposed that about one in ten has taken the pledge, and one in twenty kept it. The cause of the intemperance of the sawyers, say my informants, was their extremely hard labour, and the thirst produced by their great exertion. Moreover, it was the custom of their employers, until within the last 15 years, to pay the men in public-houses. Since then, however, the sawyers have received their wages at the counting-houses of the timber merchants; and this, in connection with the general advance of intelligence among the body, has gone far to diminish the intemperance of the trade. The coffee-shops, again, I am assured, have added greatly to the sobriety of the operative sawyers.

The large reduction which has taken place in the earnings of the sawyers has not been attended with any serious alteration in their habits. As a general rule, neither their wives nor their children "go out to work"; and since the decline of their trade no marked change in this respect has occurred. The majority of the men are certainly beyond the middle age—many that I saw were between sixty and seventy years. Cooper's stave-sawyers, however, are younger men. This is accounted for by the fact that since the decline of the trade of the "general sawyers", very few fresh hands have been brought into the trade, while many of the younger men have emigrated or sought some other employment—whereas the old men have been not only loath to leave the country, but unable to turn their hand to a new business. The coopers' stave-sawyers, however, have considerably increased in number, owing to the difficulty of machinery to effect their work; hence, many of the other sawyers have taken to this branch. A large number of the general sawyers have been compelled to seek parish relief. Within the Lambeth workhouse alone, I am informed, there are as many as sixteen sawyers, besides others, in the receipt of out-door relief. . . .

From all I can gather, it appears that the general sawyers have declined in numbers at least two-fifths, and that only one-third of those now remaining can obtain full employment; another third have about three or four days' work in the week, and the other third but one day or two, and often none at all. The slack season with the general and coopers' stave-sawyers commences about a month before, and continues till a month after, Christmas. With the shipwright sawyers, however, the winter is the busiest time.[2]

### The history of steam mills

The first steam-mill for the sawing of planks was established (as is mentioned in the statement of a sawyer previously given) about thirty-six years ago, by Mr. Smart, near Westminster-bridge. For perhaps twenty years before that period horses had been employed to supersede men's labour. The principle on which these horse-mills were constructed was not dissimilar to that now in use in the steam saw-mills. The horses then did the work of the engine now—working nine saws at once, but with perhaps only half the motive power of steam as regards velocity. About forty-five years ago a party of sawyers one night walked abruptly into the largest of these horse saw-mills—that of Mr. Richardson, of Limehouse—and with sledge-hammers and crow-bars utterly demolished the whole apparatus, which was the work of but a few minutes. The men did not carry a single fragment away with them after the work of demolition had been done, and they studiously abstained from any other act of violence, and even from any act or words of insult. Their plea was, that these horse-mills would bring them and their families to the

[2] Testimonies followed from a pair of deal sawyers, a ship-timber sawyer and two cooper's stave sawyers.

parish, by making beasts do the work of men, and that they had a right to protect themselves the best way they could, as no man, they said, merely for his own profit, had any right to inflict ruin upon a large body. So I was assured, and such feelings were at that period not uncommon among the ruder class of labourers. These horse-mills were but little remunerative, and Mr. Richardson did not think it worth his while to replace his machinery. It lay scattered about his yard until within 20 or 30 years ago. Another horse-mill, that of Mr. Lett, was demolished in the same way, not long after, by a party of sawyers; and the other proprietors of such places—there were perhaps about six in all—either discontinued the use of horses through fear, or the working of their mills became less remunerative, and they were gradually done away with. I had these particulars from a very intelligent man, now engaged in the sawing business. They were beyond his own recollection; but he had often heard his father, who passed a long life in the capacity of a sawyer, relate the circumstances. My informant was not altogether positive as to dates—he gave them to the best of his recollection. . . .

Steam saw-mills continued to be gradually established throughout the metropolis until they now number 68—six at least of the proprietors being also timber merchants. These mills average three "frames" each, a frame holding nine saws. In case all the means of these mills were called into operation at one time, 1,755 saws would be at work. . . . A gentleman, himself the conductor of a steam saw-mill—and I have to thank him also for other valuable and curious information—took pains, at my request, to calculate the number of sawyers superseded by the application of steam power. These, from the best data, he gives as 750 "pairs", or 1,500 men.

*Visit to a steam mill—the words of a foreman*

In the course of my inquiries I visited a steam saw-mill. It is situate close upon the river, being indeed, a wharf as well as a mill. Overhead is a lofty roof of thin light-coloured timber, through which the light came with a pleasant yellow hue. A timber front-age, in some parts of the nature of a casement, looks on the river. When the machinery was not at work all was pleasant and quiet, but when eighteen saws were in full operation—that number being employed on my visit—there was anything but quiet. The usual noise of a steam-engine had the addition of the grinding sound of the saws, jumping, as it would seem to any one ignorant of the agency employed, up and down most rapidly—while at intervals, through all this combination of sounds, was heard the ripple of the Thames dashing close up to the river front of the mill, for it was then high water, and a strong breeze was blowing. The steam-engine occupies one corner of the premises, and is partly detached. The wheels and machinery by which the mill is worked are beneath the timber flooring of the yard, the main shaft occupying the centre. The frame is simply nine upright saws, each four feet in length, moving up and down as the timber is sawn, and at a distance from each other, according to the substance the plank is to be sawn. When the machinery is set a-going, the plank by means familiar to engineers, is made to adjust itself to the action of the saws, being gradually advanced as each cut has been executed. A frame-worker attends to the due adjustment of the timber, however, as well as to the renewal of the saws when the teeth have become blunted by the rapid and severe friction. The machinery, when viewed at work under the flooring through the trap-doors, presents a very curious appearance. The imperfect light throws many of the wheels into the gloom, the brighter parts flashing to the eye, while the reverberation conveys the notion of extended space and far multiplied machinery.

Two engines, each of 10-horse power—and fewer are never fixed in any mill—cost from £650 to £800; about £700 being perhaps the most usual expense. These engines consume a ton of coals in a day of twelve hours, and a quart of machine oil.

Some further particulars concerning *steam saw-mills* I give in the words of a well-informed and observant man long familiar with their working:

"I have been several years—I can't say precisely how many—acquainted with all the parts of the labour required in a steam saw-mill. I am now a foreman. For the management of two engines, each of 10-horse power, or one of 20, there are, besides the foreman, who overlooks the business generally, five men employed—an engine-driver, a saw-sharpener, two frame-workers, and a labourer. The business of the engine-driver and the saw-sharpener everybody can understand; the frame-worker attends to the frames, replacing the saws when it's necessary, and looking to the deals being in a proper position, and all connected with the frames; and the labourer piles the deals when sawn, and does all the 'odd jobs'. He is paid from 3s. to 4s. a day, and the others from 5s. to 6s.

"The steam-mill saws go from 8 to 10 'runs'—9 inches a run—through 12 feet spruce deals, before they require sharpening; through some deals the saw will go more runs. The best and quickest sharpeners, by far, are men who have been used to work as top-men in sawpits; they are better than cutlers. The men's saws, in the pits, require sharpening rather oftener than steam-mill saws. . . . In our steam-mills we can't cut staves for coopers; that is, we can cut them straight, of course, but not in doublets, which is the main trade. We can't so well cut elm, oak, or ash, as the sawyers. Indeed, we can only outdo the sawyers altogether in deals; but they're more used for general purposes than all other woods put together—far more. Timber merchants who have their own steam-mill have, for some things, to employ sawyers still. We cut deals at 2s. 6d. a dozen, which, by men's labour, costs 3s. 6d. A twenty-horse power engine will do the work of thirty 'pairs' of sawyers—that's sixty men—in a day, in sawing deals, but only deal. . . . A pair of sawyers would most likely beat one saw worked by steam. Our saw would go twice as quick as theirs, but their cuts would be twice as far as ours. . . .

"Very few saw-mills, if any, can be said to be paying. But there's the capital sunk in the machinery, and a small return is better than its standing idle. The work is irregular, and many take long credit. Small orders, too, though they must be done, are anything but a profit. A frame makes ten cuts as easy as one. A circular saw, worked by steam, performs 1,800 revolutions in a minute. Take the usual diameter of 18 inches, and, of course, the saw describes a circumference of 54 inches, or one yard and a half, and does it 1,800 times. So that in a minute one mile and a half is done, with 60 yards to spare; and, not reckoning the 60 yards at all, but supposing there was no stop in the working, 90 miles an hour, which at no more than 10 hours in a day, is 900 miles. The straight saws perform 160 revolutions, each of 4 feet, in a minute, which gives 213 yards a minute, or within 15 yards of $7\frac{1}{4}$ miles an hour. Reckon 1,000 of these saws going just now, and that's performing a distance (not minding the fifteen yards) of 7,250 miles an hour. Or, if all the saws were going (1,755), of $12,223\frac{3}{4}$ miles an hour. Of course, that's supposing there is no stop. The penetration through the timber under these circumstances would be between 22 and 23 miles, at an eighth of an inch each cut."

*Two experienced sawyers discuss the effect of steam mills on working men*

Concerning the operation of the steam saw-mills upon the working men, I had the following statement from two picked men : they were general sawyers. One, who was 55 years old, had been 40 years in the trade; and the other, who was 49, had had 35 years' experience in it. "I can recollect," said the younger, "when I could save more money in a week than I can now earn in the same time. Ah ! then, if a man was a goodish sawyer, and out of work, he would have twenty or thirty people after him. Often, when I've been going

along London streets, with my saw on my back, a timber-merchant
or a cabinet maker would hail me, and cry, 'Halloa, ho. do you want
any work, my man?' and often they gave a sum of money for a
good sawyer to come and work for them."

The elder man said, "My father was a sawyer, and often I've
heard him say that the trade was better in his younger days than
even it was in mine. He used to speak of what it was seventy year
ago; the wages weren't better in his younger days than they were in
mine, but the work was—there was fewer hands, you see. I have
heard him say that him and his mate earned one pound a day. He
became a timber merchant afterwards, and he's told me that he'd
paid a pair of sawyers that he had in his employ £24 in the month.
They were veneer sawyers, and that was the finest and best paid
work in the trade—now that's *all* gone from us. There an't one
regular veneer sawyer left in the trade. All veneers are cut at present
by machinery. . . .

"In the year '26 it was about as good a time for sawyers as ever
it was—there was a good demand for men, and good wages." "I
can remember it better," said the oldest of the two; "but, never
mind, that's the last time that the trade's been what you may call
good. It began to decline between '26 and '27—just about Fault-
leroy's bankruptcy. I remember the saw mills began to get more
general from that period. I can't recollect when the horse saw-mills
was fust put up. Several cabinet-makers used to have hand-mills of
their own, which consisted of circular saws in a bench, and worked
by a couple of labourers. One of the horse-mills—I remember it
was over about Pedler's-acre—was said to kill a horse a day. The
first steam-mill that was set up was at Battersea. It was a Frenchman (Brunel) that took out the patent for cutting veneers by steam—
that's above forty years ago. The steam-mill had been up two or three
years when I first came to London, and that was in 1810. I recollect
seeing some shortly after I got to town. They was cut more true
than any sawyer could do them, but not half as well as they are done
now. The first that was done was eight in the inch, and now they
can cut 14, as thin as a wafer, and that's impossible for the best
sawyer in the world to do. I have cut as many as eight in the inch
myself, but then the wood was very shallow—eight or nine inches
deep. The general run of veneers cut by hand was about six in the
inch. It wasn't until some five or six years after the first steam saw-
mill for veneers was set up that one was erected for deals, and some
time after that they were used to cut timber. About 1827, they began
to get general, and as fast as the saw-mills have been starting up so
we have been going down. We only have the rough work, and
what the saw-mills can't or won't do. We get chiefly 'one cuts'

to do, because the saw-mills can't do that kind of work so well as we can.

"A sawyer formerly took apprentices." "I was an apprentice for seven years," said the younger man. "And I worked along with my father," said the other. "It was a rule in our trade that the eldest son was entitled to his father's business. Now I don't see a sawyer in London who has an apprentice. Formerly we would allow no man to work at our trade unless he had been apprenticed or articled for three years; now it's open to any man, and yet none that I know of come into it. Many that I am acquainted with have left it, and many more would be glad to get away from it. I was one of the enumerators at the taking of the last census in the district in which I now live, and now I think there are not more than half as many sawyers as what there were then; the old hands die off, and no young ones fill up their places. Some few sawyers perhaps put their boys to the trade because they haven't the means to apprentice them to anything else, and the boy, you see, by working with his father, will bring in something at the end of the week. All that the two earns then goes to one home. I know many sawyers that have emigrated, and among them have been some of the best workmen, and some of the most intelligent.

"The trade, we think, will keep dwindling and dwindling every year; but machinery, we think, will never be able to take it all from us. I haven't been at work not a day this week. Sometimes we are worked to death, and sometimes we are picking our fingers. At the beginning of the week we are often obligated to have extra hands, and at the end of the week we are standing still, may be. There may be some few in large firms who may have constant work; but the most of our trade is idle more than half their time. It puzzles me how they live, some of them. Twenty-six years ago, my average wages was 35s. a week all the year round. Now I should say that this last year my wages hasn't been above 18s. a week all the year through. I don't think the average wages of our trade, take the good with the bad, are above £1, and formerly it was full double that. Why, twenty years ago we used to have a trade dinner every year, somewhere out of town, and to go up to the tavern—wherever it was—in grand purcession, with bands of music and flags flying (we had a union jack that cost forty odd pound then), and the dinner for the whole of the districts used to come to near upon 50 guineas.

"After all this I leaves you to judge what our opinion is about machinery. Of course we looks upon it as a curse. We have no chance to compete with a machine; it isn't taxed, you see, as we are. I look upon machinery as an injury to society generally, because if it drives the hands out of our trade they must go into some other, so that working men is continually pressing one upon another. If machinery can cut the wood cheaper than we can, it's a gain to the timber merchant, he is enabled to reduce the price, and so some part of society may be a gainer by it, but we think society loses more than it gets. Supposing a machine do the work of 100 pair of sawyers, then of course it throws 200 men out of employ; and these 200 men have families, and they are all benefited by the employment of working man's labour. But in the case of machinery only one man is benefited." (This I found to be the common opinion of the operatives); "the money all goes to him and the others are left to starve, or else for society to support, either as paupers or felons, so that society, in the present state of things, after all, loses more than it gains. We see that as science advances the comfort of the working man declines. We believe machinery to be a blessing if rightly managed. It only works for one class at present but the time *will* come when it *will* work for all parties. . . . Let machinery go on increasing as it does, and there will come a time when the labour of the many will be entirely done away with; and then what will society gain when it has to keep the whole of the labouring classes? We can see machinery improving every day, so that there is less work for the people and more paupers. Our bread is being taken out of our mouths, and our children left to starve. I am quite satisfied that those who have nothing but their labour to depend upon get up every morning less independent than they went to bed. The many long heads that are scheming how to deprive men of their work is quite sufficient to bring that about.

"It's no use emigrating either. Let a working man go where he will, machinery pursues him. In America it's worse for sawyers, if possible, than here. There the sawing is all done by water-mills, and wood is so plentiful and so cheap that if they spoil a bit, it aint no matter. Working-men is much disheartened at the increase of machinery, when they're a standing at the corner of the streets idle and starving and see carts coming out of the yard filled with planks that they ought to have had. You see, sir, when some are injured by any alteration, they gets compensation; but here is our trade cut up altogether, and what compensation do we get? We are left to starve without the least care. I have paid 1s. 10d. for a quartern loaf before now, and I could get it much easier than I can now. When I get up in the morning, I don't know whether I shall be able to earn 6d. before nightfall. I have been at work ever since I was eight years old, and I'm a pretty good example of what the working man has to look for; and what's the good of it all? Even the machines, some of them, can't hardly raise the price of the coals to get their fire up.

When they first set up they had 6d. a foot for cutting veneers, and now they have only 1d. Machinery's very powerful, sir, but competition is much stronger."

# THE WOODWORKERS:
# CARPENTERS AND JOINERS

## LETTER LX—11 JULY 1850

*Number of Carpenters*

It is with the carpenters and joiners of the metropolis that I have especially to deal. . . .

To arrive at a correct estimate as to the number of operatives in the metropolis we must take the number of London carpenters who are in business for themselves (and these, according to the "Post-office Directory", are 1,239), and deducting them from the 18,321 individuals cited in the census, we shall come to the conclusion that there were somewhere about 17,000 operative carpenters resident in the metropolis nine years ago; and, presuming the trade to have increased since that period at the same rate as it did in the ten years previous, it follows that there are at this present time upwards of 20,000 operative carpenters in London.

Numerically considered then, the carpenters rank amongst the most important of the working classes of the metropolis. The domestic servants, the labourers, the boot and shoe makers, the tailors, the dressmakers, and the clerks, alone take precedence of them in this respect.

*Causes of overpopulation in the London trade*

About three-fourths or four-fifths of the carpenters working in the metropolis, I am informed, are from the country; for it is only within the last fifteen or twenty years that the London masters have taken apprentices. Before that time apprentices were taken—with but a few exceptions—only in the City, and those who served their time there did so solely with the view of "taking up their freedom" afterwards. Large masters in London would not then be troubled with lads, though small jobbing masters generally took one or two. Now, however, there is scarcely a master in London but what has some youths in his employ, and many of the large builders have as many lads and "improvers" as they have men, while some of them have even more. All these are used as a means of reducing the cost of men's labour. "When I first came to town, twenty years ago" (said one of the carpenters whom I saw), "I never knew a lad to be employed in any of the large firms in which I worked." As a proof of this, he told me, he never worked at that time but with one "Cockney", that is to say with a person who had been regularly brought up to the carpenter's business in London.

Twenty years ago it was usual for country carpenters to come up to London immediately after having served their apprenticeship; some did this to better their condition, the wages in town being double what they were in the west of England, and some came up to improve themselves in the business and then to return. At that time one-third at least of the number that came to London would go back into the country to settle after two or three years' practice in town. At the present time, however, it is estimated that not one in twelve who come to town from the country ever return. A great number of country carpenters are still attracted to London under the belief that the wages here maintain their former rate. When they arrive in the metropolis they find out to their cost that they can obtain employment only among the speculative builders and petty masters, where but two-thirds of the regular wages of the trade are given; and when once they take to this kind of work, it becomes impossible for them, unless very prudent indeed, ever to get away from it.

This, I am informed, is one of the principal reasons of the over population of the London trade—for the work in the metropolis is now sufficient to give employment only to two-thirds of the hands. Another cause of the trade being over stocked is the reduction of wages that has taken place among those working for the speculative builders and petty masters, for I have before shown that the necessary consequences of under-pay is over-work—that is to say, if the wages of the "non-society" carpenters and joiners have been reduced one-third, then each man will endeavour to do one-third more work in his struggle to obtain the same amount of income as he previously did. Again, it will be found that a new race of employers has sprung up in the metropolis of late years, who are known among the trade as "strapping masters", from the fact of their forcing the men to do double as much work in a day as was formerly expected of them. Hence it is clear, that though the London carpenters have increased 4 per cent less than the general population of the metropolis, still each of the operatives has been compelled of late years, either by the strapping masters, or a reduction of wages, to get through twice or three times as much work as formerly, and thus the trade has become

as overstocked by each hand doing double work, as it would have
been if the hands themselves had been doubled.

*Social condition of the carpenters and joiners*

The carpenters and joiners that work for the low speculating
builders are, generally speaking, quite a different class of men to
those who are in "society". As a rule, to which, of course, there are
many exceptions, they are men of dissipated habits. What little they
get I am assured is spent in beer or gin, and they have seldom a
second suit to their backs. They are generally to be seen on a Sunday lounging about the suburbs of London with their working
clothes on, and their rules sticking from their side pockets—the only
difference in their attire being, perhaps, that they have a clean shirt
and a clean pair of shoes.

The great majority of the hands that work for the speculating
builders are young men who have come up from the country, hoping
to better their condition. About one-fourth of those who work for
the speculative builders are, it is said, men of depraved and intemperate habits, and have scarcely a tool amongst them. The better
class of workmen would rather part with the clothes off their backs
and the beds from under them, than make away with their tools;
so that it is only in cases of the most abject distress that a skilful
joiner seeks to raise money upon the implements of his trade. When
this is the case, I am told, it is usual for the operatives in "society"
to club together, and lend a person so circumstanced, some one tool
and some another, until a sufficient "kit" is raised for him to go to
work with.

The majority of carpenters who are settled in London are married
men with families, and mostly live in lodgings; many of the working
men, however, are householders, paying as much as £70 per year
rent, and letting off apartments, so as to be wholly or nearly rent
free. In London there are several of what may be termed colonies
of working carpenters. A great many reside in Lambeth, a large
number in Marylebone, in the vicinity of Lissongrove, and a considerable proportion are to be found in Westminster. This is to be
accounted for by the fact that several of the principal firms are
established in these quarters. The carpenters who live in lodgings
mostly occupy a floor unfurnished, and pay from five to seven shillings rent; but men with large families generally contrive to be householders, from the fact that children are usually objected to in
respectable lodgings, so that they must either live in some low
neighbourhood or else pay an exorbitant rent for their residences
in a better district.

The more respectable portion of the carpenters and joiners "will not allow" their wives to do any other work than attend to their domestic and family duties, though some few of the wives of the better class of workmen take in washing or keep small "general shops". The children of the carpenters are mostly well brought up, the fathers educating them to the best of their ability. They are generally sent to day schools. The cause of the carpenters being so anxious about the education of their children lies in the fact that they themselves find the necessity of a knowledge of arithmetic, geometry, and drawing in the different branches of their business. Many of the more skilful carpenters, I am informed, are excellent draughtsmen, and well versed in the higher branches of mathematics. A working carpenter seldom sees his children except on a Sunday, for on the week day he leaves home early in the morning, before they are up, and returns from his work after they are in bed.

Carpenters often work miles away from their homes, and seldom or never take a meal in their own houses, except on a Sunday. Either they carry their provisions with them to the shop, or else they resort to the coffee-shops, public-houses, and eating houses for their meals. In the more respectable firms where they are employed, a "labourer" is kept to boil water for them, and fetch them any necessaries they may require, and the meals are generally taken at the "bench end", under which a cupboard is fitted up for them to keep their provisions in. . . . Before the men leave their work in the large shops, it is usual for them to change their working clothes for others which they keep in a little cupboard under their bench. Their appearance in the street is as respectable as that of any tradesman.

Such is an account of the social condition of the London carpenters and joiners, gleaned from my own investigation, as well as from information supplied to me by the most intelligent and truthful of the operatives. I shall give a description of the several branches of the trade.

*The several branches of the trade*

The term carpenter, I am told, is applicable to any one who cuts, fashions, and joins timber for building. Those who do the work of houses are house carpenters, while those who build ships are ship carpenters. Correctly speaking, however, the framer of a building is the *carpenter* and the finisher the *Joiner*: nor, as I learn from the most intelligent of the workmen, can there be an interchange of the labour of these two branches without an inferior degree of skill in the execution of the work being the consequence. "In my opinion," said one experienced carpenter to me, "to have the trade right well done carpenters should never be put to joiners' work, nor joiners to carpenters'. When a man's been long at carpentering, if he's put to joinering he's often too rough and rapid; and a joiner, in the same way, is too fine and finicking-like for carpenters' work. Some men will tell you that they can do one kind of work as well as another; and so they may if they're only middling hands; but the best carpenter is always cleverest and quickest at his own branch, and the best joiner at his. . . ." The joiner is generally termed—in contradistinction to the carpenter, who mostly works at the building, and seldom uses a plane—a "shop-hand" or "benchman", from the fact of most of his work being prepared in the shop, and executed at the bench. Should the carpenter require to smooth the surface of a piece of timber, he rigs up a bench on the premises, on two barrels, as he best can. This, however, is by no means an ordinary occurrence, the rule in the trade being that all which the plane passes over is joiners' work. Joinery is, consequently, of a more finished description, and more subdivided than mere carpentry, though the spirit of competition is fast trenching upon these subdivisions, and thereby upon that peculiar fineness of skill which the confining men to one class of work secures. In large establishments, where the division of labour is still maintained, different hands are employed on the staircases, the window-frames and sashes, the doors, the shutters, the flooring and skirting (for which inferior workmen are usually employed); while the other portions, such as the cupboards, are disposed of in any way most convenient to the master. . . .

*"Honourable" and "dishonourable"*

The trade, commercially speaking, divides itself, like all others of the present day, into two distinct branches, viz., the "honourable" and "dishonourable" masters—that is to say, those who have a regard for the welfare and comforts of their men, and those who care only for themselves and seek to grow rich by underselling their fellow-tradesmen, as well as by under-paying the workmen in their employ. As regards skill, these two branches of course divide themselves again into the substantial and the slop trade. The men belonging to the "honourable" part of the trade are mostly paid by the day—the wages being 5s. for ten hours' work (or sixpence per hour), from six to six, with the allowance of an hour for dinner, and half--an-hour each for breakfast and tea. Sometimes the better class of workmen are paid by the piece, and then the prices are regulated by some trade book, as Skyring's, Carpenter's, and others. Generally the operatives object to piece work. Such a mode of payment, they say, induces a man to "scamp" his work; that is, to devote less time and labour to the skilful execution of it than he would were he paid by the day. Again, they urge, that when a man is paid by the piece there is no necessity for the work being done under the eye of the master or his foreman. So long as it is completed to the satisfaction of employer, it is no matter where or by whom it is executed. Hence the journeyman is at liberty to hire whoever he pleases to help him with it, or even to do it for him, and as this assistance is sure to be paid for by him at a less rate than he himself receives, the system of piece-work thus becomes one of the prime causes of the reduction of wages, while the operative is ultimately transformed by it into the middleman or "sweater", living on the toil and degradation of his fellow working men. The evil effects of this system have been already fully set forth in these letters while treating of the operative tailors of London; and it will be seen, when I come to treat of the speculative builders, that the same system among the carpenters and joiners seems to be attended with the same pernicious results. There it will be found that all the regulations which are observed to ensure skilled labour are utterly disregarded; the work is scamped and the operative is underpaid, and he not only loses thereby his self-respect and self-reliance, but sinks into drunkenness and demoralization. The workman is, moreover, made the means of carrying out the system which results in his own degragation. The houses of "building Lawyers" or "speculating builders" are let go to a general contractor; he sub-lets the work, mostly by the piece, to others, who are usually journeymen, and these sub-contracting journeymen sub-let again to others even lower than themselves. By this process men gradually become mere machines, and lose all the moral and intellectual characteristics which distinguish the skilled artisan. . . .

### Trades societies

Of the carpenters and joiners now in London 1,770, or about one-tenth of the entire number, are "in society". Their houses of call are almost invariably held in public-houses. The objects of these societies are twofold—the upholding of the wages of their trade, and rendering assistance to the aged, disabled, or unemployed or their own body. The members meet periodically at their respective houses of call and contribute such a sum per week (varying from 1½d. to 4d.) as is deemed necessary under the circumstances of the trade and the society. Some of the societies are managed by a check steward and three committee men; others have two auditors instead; others again have a president, secretary, steward, check steward, and committee men.

The officers are all paid from the funds of the society. As regards the initiation of a new member, he is proposed at one meeting and, if considered eligible, he is admitted on the following meeting night. The expulsion of a member from society is for the following offences: If he works under the standard rate of wages; if he goes into the country to work for his employer without having his expenses paid; and (where the society is opposed to the short-hour system) if he works short hours.

The houses of call at which these "societies" are held constitute the labour market (so to speak) of the trade. Each house of call is provided with a book, in which the unemployed members' names are inscribed in rotation, and the secretary attends twice a day to call over the names of those enrolled, and to receive notice from any other member who may be out of work. If a master wants a hand he sends to the house of call, and the first in rotation has the right of engagement. If he do not accept it his name is placed last on the list, and the next in rotation has the opportunity in like manner to accept or refuse the engagement. Now, however, it has become almost a general rule for men to call upon the masters or their foremen to solicit work.

Besides what may be called the commercial objects of the society, such as upholding a fair rate of wages, there are others of a philanthropic and provident nature. In some cases they have vacation or winter funds, and in others mutual loan funds and building societies. For loss of tools by fire, security is given, from £5 to the whole amount, and by theft to half those sums. Where they have a winter fund, the unemployed members receive from 10s. to 12s. per week, but these winter funds are now giving way to loan societies and mutual building societies among the working men. Some of these loan societies charge 5 per cent for moneys advanced upon personal security; others, lend it out without the payment of interest, to be refunded by instalments when the borrower gets into employment again. The mutual building societies afford partial employment to members out of work, averaging from three days to a week, according to the number of applicants. These three last mentioned arrangements are provided for from the overplus money of the society, and require no extra contribution. There is one society, which has connected with it a Joint Stock Building Company, and is registered according to Act of Parliament—the whole of the members being connected with it. They contribute 1s. per month, for £5 shares, with the privilege of working out the whole amount of their share. Their unemployed members are "taken on" for a week, at £1 per week, in rotation, until the whole of those who are out of work get their turn, and then "go out and in" in rotation. If a man do not pay his contribution to his trade society for four months, he receives notice from the Secretary, and if he neglects payment for two months after such notice he is liable to be expelled, but extreme rigour is seldom exercised on this head.

"Tramps" have not been relieved from the society's funds since the great union in 1834. The men are now generally opposed to strikes. The only thing approximating thereunto is "the short hour system". When trade is falling off, a master, not wishing to discharge his hands, proposes to the men to work so many hours less. In some societies this is not allowed, and their members, under such circumstances, are requested to "come out", and on doing so they receive from 12s. to 15s. a week till other work be obtained. Other societies permit the short-hour system. There are no superannuation funds.[3]

### A carpenter working for the best prices

I shall now proceed to give the statements of the men employed at the several branches of the "honourable" trade, reserving for my next letter a description of the causes and effects of the cheap or slop trade in connection with the carpenters' business. The following information I received from a highly respectable journeyman carpenter working for the best shops at the best prices :

"I have known the London trade between twenty and thirty years. I came up from Lancashire, where I served an apprenticeship. I have worked all that time entirely at carpentering. No doubt I am a pure carpenter, as you call it, never having worked at anything else. Before I got married, eighteen years ago, I tried to make some odds and ends of furniture for myself, but I couldn't manage them at all to please myself, except in the frame of a bedstead, so I got a cabinet maker to finish my chairs and tables for me." (My informant then described the nature of the carpenter's work, and expressed an opinion that to have it executed in the first style a workman should do nothing else.) "I have always had 5s. a day, and in busy times and long days have made 33s. and 35s. a week, by working overtime. I have always been able to keep my family, my wife and two children, comfortably, and without my wife's having to do anything but the house-work and washing. One of my children is now a nurse-maid in a gentleman's family, and the other is about old enough to go and learn some trade. Certainly, I shan't put him to my own trade, for, though I get on well enough in it, it's different for new hands, for scamping masters get more hold every day. There's very few masters in my line will take apprentices;

[3] Next came a statement about the socially beneficial role of trades unions from "one of the most intelligent working men that I have ever met".

but I could set him on as the son of a journeyman. If I'd come to London now, instead of when I did, I might have got work quite as readily perhaps—for I didn't get it within a month when I did come; but then I was among friends; but I should have had to work for inferior wages, and scamping spoils a man's craft. He's not much fit for first-rate work after that. I am better off now than ever I was, because I earn the same, and all my expenses, except rent, are lower. I have a trifle in the savings bank. But then, you'll understand, sir, I'm a sort of exception, because I've had regular work, twelve months in the year, for these ten or twelve years, and never less than nine months before that. I know several men who have been forced to scamp it—good hands, too—but driven to it to keep their families. What can a man do? 21s. a week is better than nothing. I am a society man, and always have been.

"I consider mine skilled labour, no doubt of it. To put together, and fit, and adjust, and then fix, the roof of a mansion so that it cannot warp or shrink—for if it does the rain's sure to come in through the slates—must be skilled labour, or I don't know what is. Sometimes we make the roof, or rather the parts of it, in the shop, and cart it to the buliding to fix. We principally work at the building, however. There's no rule; it all depends upon the weather and convenience. The foremen generally know on what work to put the men so as best to suit, but in no shop I've been in has there been a fixed and regular division of the carpenters into one set as roofers, and another for the other work. Our work is more dangerous than the joiners, as we have to work more on scaffolding, and to mount ladders; but I can't say that accidents are frequent among us. If there's an accident at a building by a fall, it's mostly labourers. I'm satisfied that the carpenters on the best sort of work are as well conducted and as intelligent as any class of mechanics. . . ."[4]

### A joiner 21 years in the trade

From a joiner, to whom I was referred as one of the most intelligent men in the trade, I had the following statement :

"I have known the London trade for twenty-one years. When I first knew the trade wages were the same as they are now, 5s. a day. . . . Twenty-one years ago it wasn't so easy or so cheap to get to London as it is now, and men came then really for improvement, and went back to their own country places; now they come here and stick here longer than they used to do, especially the west of England men. Wages are lower in Somersetshire, Devon, and Dorset,

[4] A testimony about the best description of joiner's work followed.

than in any other part of England. As you go north wages are better.
The joiners wages in those three counties are only 14s. or 15s. a
week—it's an extraordinary man who gets 16s. there. They're handy
men, many of them, when they come to London. There are so many
apprentices taken in those counties, who, when out of their time,
*must* find another market for their labour. When they come to
London they don't undersell, unless occasionally, the regular hands,
and respectable masters don't expect it. . . .

"It's within the last ten years that the great falling off in our
trade has occurred, and it gets worse and worse. This is owing, I am
convinced, to the increase of population, and of workmen, and to
the decrease of men's labour, through greater use of machinery.
Building now is generally a matter of speculation more than a matter
of fair and regular trade, and so men seek to get it done in the
cheapest instead of the best way. Our book of prices, Skyring's, and
he's low enough for doors, gives 10s. 6d. for making a two-inch
double-moulded door, but some 'scamping masters', as we call the
slop-masters, give only 5s., so that a man to make his 5s. a day at
those prices must do double work, and for longer hours, at a rate
that's killing him, or make the door in a very inferior way. I have
known men work hard from six in the morning to nine at night,
and in winter find their own candles, and not make 5s., or only 5s.,
then. That's the case now at Notting-hill, but that part is not the
worst. Haverstock-hill and by the Brecknock Arms, Camden-town, is
now amongst the worst parts of London. St. John's-wood was very
bad, but building there's about over now. Some of those houses fetch
low prices if they have to be sold a *second time*, the skirtings and
doors and other work being so shrunk; but that's an after consideration, for at the time they're run up, the men who build them only
look to sell them *once*.

"Machinery was first brought into competition with us in flooring boards. At first they were only planed by machinery, and the
edges cut. I first heard of this planing 21 years ago. The next step
was to grove (groove) and tongue the flooring. Formerly, grooves
and tongues were made by hand. The joiners thought nothing at
first of the planing of these boards by machinery, as only a certain
class were put upon sash planing—it was beneath their dignity
generally, and I have known men leave a shop rather than do it.
Joiners' work is noisy, and they can't talk when carrying it on, and
that may account for joiners not being such politicians or thinkers
as shoe-makers or tailors. The next introduction of machinery, as
regards our trade, was the preparation of mouldings for doors,
architraves, cornices, and base mouldings; base mouldings are the
ornamental tops of the plinth or skirting. . . . As the matter is at

present carried on, at least one-sixth of the labour of working joiners through London is superseded in this way. It's not the mills that do all this mischief, for in Mr. ———'s, the great builder's, premises one-half of the labour is performed by his own machinery. It's not certain, however, that in our business machinery is so very profitable to the master as in a cotton factory. Machinery, besides, never does such work as moulding so perfectly as we can do it. We often have to trim and refit such mouldings."[5]

### LETTER LXI—18 JULY 1850

In my last communication I said that the carpenter's trade divided itself, like many others of the present day, into two distinct branches, viz., the "honourable" and the "dishonourable" masters—that is to say, those who have a regard for the welfare and comforts of their men, and those who care only for themselves, and seek to grow rich by underpaying the workmen in their employ.

I then treated at some length of the "honourable" part of the trade, and I now come in due order to set forth the condition and earnings of the operatives belonging to the "dishonourable" portion of it.

The journeymen in connection with the "honourable" trade amount, as I before stated, to 1,770, so that by far the greater number, or no less than 18,230 of the working carpenters and joiners in the metropolis belong to what is called the "dishonourable" class—that is to say, nearly 2,000 of the London journeymen are "society men", and object to work for less than the recognized wages of the trade, while upwards of 18,000 are unconnected with any of the trade societies, and the majority of them labour for little more than half the regular rate of pay.

### The dishonourable trade: how it is maintained

The "dishonourable" portion of the trade includes many varieties of workmen. In the first place, there are the class called "improvers", or inexperienced hands, who, having learnt their business in the country, come up to town to perfect themselves in the higher branches of the trade, and, while they are so improving themselves, consent to take less wages than the more experienced and skilful operative. These, it will be seen, now constitute a considerable portion of the London trade, and are largely employed by those

---

[5] The remaining testimonies about greenhouse work and sashmaking have been cut.

"enterprising" firms who seek to extend their business merely by underselling their neighbours. Secondly, there are the countrymen, who without any especial view to improvement in their craft, flock to London, from the badly paid parts of the country, in the hope of obtaining higher wages in the metropolis, and who, on their arrival in town, willingly accept a less rate of pay than the superior handicraftsmen. Thirdly, there are what are called the "strapping-shops"—that is to say, establishments where an undue quantity of work is expected from a journeyman in the course of the day. Such shops, though not directly making use of cheap labour (for the wages paid in them are generally of the highest rate), still, by exacting more work, may of course be said, in strictness, to encourage the system now becoming general, of less pay and inferior skill. These strapping establishments sometimes go by the name of "scamping shops", on account of the time allowed for the manufacture of the different articles not being sufficient to admit of good workmenship.

These appear to be the three principal means by which several even of the more honourable firms are now seeking to reduce the "standard rate of wages". The means employed by the dishonourable tradesmen are the contract and sub-contract system, adopted by what are called the "speculative builders". It is this contract work, it will be seen, that constitutes the great evil of the carpenters' trade, as well as of many other trades at the present time; and as in those crafts, so in this, we find that the lower wages are reduced the greater becomes the number of trading operatives or middlemen. For it is when workmen find the difficulty of living by their labour increased that they take to scheming and trading upon the labour of their fellow-operatives. In the slop trade, where the pay is the worst, these creatures abound the most; and so in the carpenters' trade, where the wages are the lowest—as among the speculative builders—there the system of contracting and sub-contracting is found in full force. I shall now proceed to set forth the effects of each of these several causes of low wages *seriatim*—beginning with the means used by the more honourable masters and concluding with an account of the practices pursued by the speculative builders.

*Extraordinary account of the "strapping system"*

First, of the *"strapping"* system. Concerning this I received the following extraordinary account from a man after his heavy day's labour; and never in all my experience have I seen so sad an instance of over-work. The poor fellow was so fatigued that he could hardly rest in his seat. As he spoke he sighed deeply and heavily, and appeared almost spirit-broken with excessive labour :

"I work at what is called a strapping shop," he said, "and have worked at nothing else for these many years past in London. I call 'strapping,' doing as much work as a human being or a horse possibly can in a day, and that without any hanging upon the collar, but with the foreman's eyes constantly fixed upon you, from six o'clock in the morning to six o'clock at night. The shop in which I work is for all the world like a prison—the silent system is as strictly carried out there as in a model gaol. If a man was to ask any common question of his neighbour, except it was connected with his trade, he would be discharged there and then. If a journeyman makes the least mistake, he is packed off just the same. A man working at such places is almost always in fear; for the most trifling things he's thrown out of work in an instant. And then the quantity of work that one is forced to get through is positively awful; if he can't do a plenty of it, he don't stop long where I am. No one would think it possible to get so much out of blood and bones. No slaves work like we do. At some of the strapping shops the foreman keeps continually walking about with his eyes on all the men at once. At others the foreman is perched high up, so that he can have the whole of the men under his eye together.

"I suppose since I knew the trade that a man does four times the work that he did formerly. I know a man that's done four pairs of sashes in a day, and one is considered to be a good day's labour. What's worse than all, the men are everyone striving one against the other. Each is trying to get through the work quicker than his neighbours. Four or five men are set the same job so that they may be all pitted against one another, and then away they go every one striving his hardest for fear that the others should get finished first. They are all tearing along from the first thing in the morning to the last at night, as hard as they can go, and when the time comes to knock off they are ready to drop. I was hours after I got home last night before I could get a wink of sleep; the soles of my feet were on fire, and my arms ached to that degree that I could hardly lift my hand to my head. Often, too, when we get up of a morning, we are more tired than we went to bed, for we can't sleep many a night; but we mustn't let our employers know it, or else they'd be certain we couldn't do enough for them, and we'd get the sack. So, tired as we may be, we are obliged to look lively somehow or other at the shop of a morning. If we're not beside our bench the very moment the bell's done ringing, our time's docked—they won't give us a single minute out of the hour. If I was working for a fair master, I should do nearly one-third less work than I am now forced to get through, and sometimes a half less; and even to manage that much, I shouldn't be idle a second of my time.

"It's quite a mystery to me how they do contrive to get so much work out of the men. But they are very clever people. They know how to have the most out of a man, better than any one in the world. They are all picked men in the shop—regular "strappers", and no mistake. The most of them are five foot ten, and fine broad shouldered, strong backed fellows too—if they weren't they would not have them. Bless you, they make no words with the men, they sack them if they're not strong enough to do all they want; and they can pretty soon tell, the very first shaving a man strikes in the shop, what a chap is made of. Some men are done up at such work— quite old men and gray with spectacles on, by the time they are forty. I have seen fine strong men, of six-and-thirty, come in there and be bent double in two or three years. They are most all country-men at the strapping shops. If they see a great strapping fellow who they think has got some stuff about him that will come out, they will give him a job directly. We are used for all the world like cab or omnibus horses. Directly they've had all the work out of us we are turned off, and I am sure after my day's work is over, my feelings must be very much the same as one of the London cab horses. As for Sunday, it is *literally* a day of rest with us, for the greater part of us lays a bed all day, and even that will hardly take the aches and pains out of our bones and muscles. When I'm done and flung by, of course I must starve."

## The treatment of elderly workmen

After this the reader can readily imagine that "the old hands" have but little chance of employment in a trade where the strapping system is coming into vogue. Concerning the treatment of the elderly workmen, a well-looking man, cleanly, but poorly dressed, gave me the following account :

"I served my apprenticeship in the country as a carpenter, but have been 49 years in London this July. I am now 79. I have worked all the 49 years in London, except six months. Of course, I can't work now as well as I could. I was obliged about five years ago to wear spectacles, as my eyesight wasn't as good. I could do the rougher work of carpentering as well as some years before, but then I can't lift heavy weights up aloft as I could. In most shops the moment a man puts the glasses on it's over with him. It wasn't so when I first knew London. Masters then said, 'Let me have an old man, one who knows something.' Now it's, 'Let me have a young man, I must have a strong fellow, an old one won't do.' One master discharged two men when he saw them at work in glasses, though the foreman told him they worked as well with them, and as well every way as ever they did, but it was all no use; they went. I used to wear glasses in one employ, and others did the same, and the foreman was a good man to the men as well as to the master; and if the master was coming, he used to sing out 'Take those sashes out of the way,' and so we had time to whip off our glasses, and the master didn't know we were forced to use them; but when he did find out, by coming into the shop unawares, he discharged two men. I now work at jobbing and repairing in buildings. It's no use my going to ask for work of any master, for if I hadn't my glasses on he'd see from my appearance I was old, and must wear them, and wouldn't hear of giving an old man a job. One master said to me, 'Pooh, you won't do—you were born too soon.' The fact is, they want strong young fellows from the country, that they can sweat plenty of work out of, and these country hands will go to work for 21s. a week, so that the master has a double pull—more work out of him and less to pay for it. The work's inferior, but they don't look much after the quality of the work now.

"The old men have only the workhouse left. Few of us have saved money. We can't, with families to bring up, on 30s. a week. I know many old men that were in their day good workmen, now in the workhouse. I know six that's now in Marylebone workhouse that I've worked along with myself. I belong to a benefit club, or there would be nothing but the workhouse for me if I lost my jobbing. Old age coming on men in my way is a very great affliction. We try to hide our want of great strength, and good sight as long as we can. I did it for two or three years, but it was found out at last, and I had to go. I average about 12s. a week at jobbing; work's so uncertain, or I could make more. . . ."

*Cheap contract work: opinions of honourable masters*

I now come to treat of the system pursued by the speculating builders of the metropolis. Of all the slop-trades that I have yet examined there appear to be greater evils connected with cheap building than with any other. . . . Of the 18,000 men working for the dishonourable portion of the building trade, it should be remembered that not one belongs to a society, and consequently they have no resource but the parish in case of sickness, accident, or old age. Consequently, as one of the more intelligent journeymen said to me, it is the master alone who, by reducing the wages of the workmen, is benefited, for though the house is built cheaper, the public have not only to pay the same rent, but to support the workmen out of the poor-rates. Moreover, it is by means of this system that the better, the more skilful, and more provident portion of the trade are being dragged down to the same wretched abasement as the un-skilful and improvident workmen.

In order, however, that I might not be misled by the journeymen, I thought it my duty to call upon some master-builders of the "hon-ourable trade"—gentlemen of high character—as well as upon architects of equally high standing. I found the same opinion enter-tained by them all as to the ruinous effects of the kind of compe-tition existing in their trade to a master who strives to be just to his customers, and fair to his men. This competition, I was assured, was the worst in the contracts for building churches, chapels, and public institutions generally. "Honesty is now almost impossible among us," said one master-builder. "It *is* impossible in cheap con-tract work, for the competition puts all honourable trade out of the field; high character, and good material, and the best workman-ship are of no avail. Capitalists can command any low-priced work, by letting and subletting and all by the piece. Most of these specu-lating and contracting people think only how to make money; or they must raise money to stop a gap (a bill perhaps to be met), and they grasp at any offer of an advance of money on account of a building to be erected. Their proceedings are an encouragament to every kind of dishonesty. They fail continually, and they drag good men down with them."

Strong as these opinions are, I heard them fully confirmed by men who could not be mistaken in the matter. "Advertise for con-tract work," said another gentleman, "and you will soon have a dozen applicants at all sorts of prices; and all tradesmen like myself, who calculate for a contract at a rate to pay the regular wages, and not to leave either the timber-merchant or anybody else in the lurch, and to yield us the smallest possible percentage for our risk and out-lay, are regarded as a pack of extortionate men."

The system of contract-work was known forty years ago, or earlier, among the tradesmen employed in the erection of houses of the best class; but it was known as an exception rather than as an established system. It was long before that, however, not unfrequent as regards the erection of public buildings. A customer would then obtain "estimates" of the probable cost from well-known firms, and so ascertain the lowest price at which a private house could be erected. Thirty years back this system had gained a strong hold on all building capitalists, and it has gone on increasing within these last ten or twelve, or more years. No mansion is built otherwise than by contract, except in the rare instance of an old connection of an old firm. The introduction of stuccos, cements, etc., within these 25 years, has further encouraged the contract system, by supplying a low-priced exterior for our houses—while the introduction of cheap paper, and of cheaper wood-work, by means of machinery, supplied the materials of a cheap interior; and a tradesman of little skill or probity can speculate in a building where he is not called upon to make heavy outlays for superior stone or timber, and can employ under-paid labour. . . .

## Statement of a foreman

Such are the opinions of the honourable masters in connection with the building trade, as to the ruinous effects of the slop or contract system. I shall now subjoin the statements, first, of the foremen, and lastly, of the workmen in connection with this part of the trade :

"I am a foreman to a speculating builder. . . . The way in which the work is done is mostly by letting and sub-letting. The masters usually prefer to let work, because it takes all the trouble off their hands. They know what they are to get for the job, and of course, they let it as much under that figure as they possibly can, all of which is clear gain without the least trouble. How the work is done, or by whom, it's no matter to them, so long as they can make what they want out of the job, and have no bother about it. Some of our largest builders are taking to this plan, and a party who used to have one of the largest shops in London has within the last three years discharged all the men in his employ (he had 200 at least), and has now merely an office, and none but clerks and accountants in his pay. He has taken to letting his work out instead of doing it at home.

"The parties to whom the work is let by the speculating builders are generally working men, and these men in their turn look out for other working men, who will take the job cheaper than they will, and so I leave you, sir, and the public to judge what the party who really executes the work gets for his labour, and what is the quality of work that he is likely to put into it. The speculating builder generally employs an over-looker to see that the work is done sufficiently well to pass the surveyor. That's all he cares about. Whether it's done by thieves, or drunkards, or boys, it's no matter to him. The overlooker, of course, sees after the first party to whom the work is let, and this party in his turn looks after the several hands that he has sub-let it to. The first man who agrees to the job takes it in the lump, and he again lets it to others in the piece. I have known instances of its having been let again a third time, but this is not usual. The party who takes the job in the lump from the speculator usually employs a foreman, whose duty it is to give out the materials, and to make working drawings. The men to whom it is sub-let only find labour, while the 'lumper', or first contractor, agrees for both labour and materials.

"It is usual in contract work, for the first party who takes the job to be bound in a large sum for the due and faithful performance of his contract. He then in his turn finds out a sub-contractor, who is mostly a small builder, who will also bind himself that the work shall be properly executed, and there the binding ceases—those parties to whom the job is afterwards let, or sub-let, employing fore-men or overlookers to see that their contract is carried out. The first contractor has scarcely any trouble whatsoever; he merely engages a gentleman, who rides about in a gig, to see that what is done is likely to pass muster. The sub-contractor has a little more trouble; and so it goes on as it gets down and down. Of course who does the *least* of all gets the *most* of all; while the poor wretch of a working man, who positively executes the job, is obliged to slave away every hour night after night to get a bare living out of it; and this is the contract system.

"The public are fleeced by it to an extent that builders alone can know. Work is scamped in such a way that the houses are not safe to live in. Our name for them in the trade is 'bird cages', and really nine-tenths of the houses built now-a-days are very little stronger. Again, the houses built by the speculators are almost all damp. There is no concrete ever placed at the foundation to make them dry and prevent them from sinking. Further, they are all badly drained. Many of the walls of the houses built by the speculators are much less in thickness that the Building Act requires. I'll tell you how this is done. In a third-rate house the wall should be, according to the Act, two bricks thick at least, and in a second-rate house, two bricks and a half. The speculators build up the third-rates a brick and-a-half thick, and the second-rates only two bricks, and behind this they run up another half brick, so that they can throw that part down immediately after the surveyor has inspected it. Many of the chimney breasts too, are filled up with rubbish instead of being solid brickwork. The surveyor is frequently hand in hand with the speculator, and can't for the life of him discover any of these defects—but you know there's none so blind as those that *won't* see.

"And yet, notwithstanding all this trickery and swindling, and starving of the workmen, rents in the suburbs do not come down. Who, then, are the gainers by it all? Certainly not the public, for all they get are damp, ill-drained, and unsafe houses, at the same prices as they formerly paid for sound, wholesome, and dry ones. And most certainly the working men gain nothing by it. And what is even worse than all is that the better class of masters are obliged

LONDON *going out of Town* — or — *The March of Bricks & Mortar*. —

PLATE XIX.   Cruikshank's Vision of Suburban Development

PLATE XX.   The Cabinet Makers Society, Leadenhall Street & Aldgate (etched 1830)

PLATE XXI. Frontispiece of the *London Cabinet Book of Prices*, 1811. Agreed "by a Committee of Masters and Journeymen" and sold at £1 7s. a copy

PLATE XXII.   A Garret Master Hawking his Work to the Warehouse

to compete with the worse, and to resort to the same means to keep up with the times, so that if things go on much longer the better class of mechanics must pass away altogether."

## Concerning ground rents

Concerning ground rents, I had the following account from one well acquainted with the tricks of the speculators :

"The party for whom I am foreman has just taken a large estate, and he contemplates making some thousands of pounds by means of the improved ground rents alone. There are several with him in the speculation, and this is the way in which such affairs are generally managed. A large plot of ground (six or seven meadows, may be) somewhere in the suburbs is selected by the speculators as likely to be an eligible spot for building—that is to say, they think that a few squares, villas, and terraces about that part would be likely to be let as soon as run up. Then the speculators go to the free-holder or his solicitor, and offer to take the ground of him on a ninety-nine years' lease at a rent of about £50 a-year per acre, and may be they take as many as fifty acres at this rate. At the same time they make a proviso that the rent shall not commence until either so many houses are built, or perhaps before a twelvemonth has elapsed. If they didn't do this the enormous rent most likely would swallow them up before they had half got through their job.

"Well, may be, they erect half or two-thirds of the number of houses that they have stipulated to do before paying rent. These are what we term 'call-birds', and are done to decoy others to build on the ground. For this purpose a street is frequently cut, the ground turned up on each side, just to show the plan, and the corner house, and three others, perhaps, are built just to let the public see the style of thing that it's going to be. Occasionally a church is begun, for this is found to be a great attraction in a new neighbourhood. Well, when things are sufficiently ripe this way, and the field has been well mapped out into plots, a board is stuck up, advertising 'THIS GROUND TO BE LET, ON BUILDING LEASES.' Several small builders then apply to take a portion of it, sufficient for two or three houses, may be, for which they agree to pay about five guineas a year (they generally make it *guineas* these gentlemen) for the ground-rent of each house. And when the parties who originally took the meadows on lease have got a sufficient number of these plots let off, and the small builders have run up a few of the carcases, they advertise that 'a sale of well-secured rents will take place at the Mart on such a day'.

"Ground-rents, you must know, are considered to be one of the

M

safest of all investments now-a-days; for if they are not paid, the ground landlord, you see, has the power of seizing the houses; so gentlemen with money are glad to lay it out this way, and there's a more ready sale for ground-rents than for anything else in the building line. There's sure to be a strong competition for them, let the sale be whenever it will. Well, let us see now how the case stands. There are fifty acres taken on lease at £50 an acre a year, and that is £2,500 per annum. Upon each of these fifty acres fifty houses can be erected (including villas and streets, taking one with the other upon an average). The ground-rent of each of these houses is (at the least) £5, and this gives for the 2,500 houses that are built upon the whole of the fifty acres £12,500 per annum. Hence you see there is a clear net profit of £10,000 a year made by the transaction. This is not at all an extraordinary case in building speculations."[6]

## Account of the letting and sub-letting system

The next point to be noticed is the system of letting and sub-letting the work. From an experienced carpenter and his son, also an experienced man in his trade, I had the following account:

"I may say," said the father, "I have been seventy-five years in the carpentering trade, for that's my age, and I was born in the business. I worked nearly fifty years in Somersetshire, chiefly as a journeyman. . . . I came to London five years ago to join my family, who were settled here. My family were then at work on a contract for a lawyer." "I knew nothing of the lawyer," said the son of my first informant, "but I saw a notice up that the carcases of six houses were to be finished, and made fit for inhabitants, and tenders were to be sent in; the lowest bidder of course to be accepted. The solicitor, that my brother and I had the contract from, was the agent of the ground landlord, who was anxious to have buildings erected on his property. The ground landlord had advertised that the land would be let on building leases, and that advances would be made, according to the usual dodge—for dodge it is, sir. A builder was soon found, one with little or no money, for money in such cases is no matter—that's an every-day affair. He agreed to erect six houses, and £250 was to be advanced for each house, something more than half as much as would be required to complete each of them. The builder got the carcases up, and then the agent put the stopper on him, and seized the houses for the ground landlord. Each house, in the manner it was left by the builder, when he was stopped, had full £300

[6] Testimonies about speculators' tricks and the use of "improvers" followed.

expended on it of *somebody's* money, and materials. For this the builder became bankrupt and he was sent to prison. The houses were then advertised for sale and sold, the agent buying them, and just for the amount advanced—£1,500. So that after full £1,800 had been expended on the houses the agent got them for £300 less. . . . The agent I've been speaking of stuck boards up over the neighbourhood stating that the finishing of the carcases, as I've said, was to be let to the lowest bidder, on certain terms; advances were to be made on the surveyor's report, among other conditions. I knew, if a low figure wasn't sent in, it was no use trying for the job, so my brother and I bid for the work at the lowest possible sum. We reckoned on our own labour being serviceable, as we could do so much among ourselves, and save the expense of a foreman and such like. We hoped to make something too, out of the extras, that is for extra work not included in the specification, for the specification is never correct. Men now bid very low in hopes of making their profit in this way.

"My father, my brother, and myself, didn't realize more than 4s. a day, working on an average 13 hours. If we'd been employed by a contractor, who took it at the rate we did, our wages couldn't have been more than 3s. a day, and that was the reason of our bidding for it. The journeymen in that neighbourhood now get 3s. a day, all the work being let and sub-let. A journeyman will undertake work to pay himself 4s. a day, and will hire men under him at 3s.—or even less—14s. or 15s. a week. One man takes the windows, another the skirtings, another the doors, another the dwarf and high cupboards, another the stairs, another the mouldings, another the boxing shutters for the windows, and another the floors. The average price for labour in contract work windows is 6s. an opening for 25 feet, and according to Skyring's prices (which are low) the charge would be 10s. Doors, double moulded, are paid 2s. 6d. on an average, and they ought to be 5s.; of course, they must be scamped. On this work I must make two doors a day, while one properly made is a good long day's job. Some of these doors don't last above ten years. . . . These prices are what I know of by my own experience; but when there's a further sub-letting by a journeyman contracting under the contractor, and so getting hands at the lowest possible rates, they are even less than I have specified. Contracting altogether is a bad system; it's carried on for the benefit of a few at the cost of the working men, and out of their sweat, and at the cost too of respectable tradesmen many a time. . . ."[7]

[7] The statement of an old man doing sub-contract work ended the letter.

## LETTER LXII—25 JULY 1850

*The difficulty of obtaining work: a destitute carpenter*

That the difficulty of obtaining work has increased among the carpenters considerably of late years, all whom I have seen, both masters and men, agree. This is attributed by many to the increase of machinery, and by many to the introduction of the "strapping" system described in my last letter, by which each man is now compelled to do four times the work that he was once expected to execute; and that this must necessarily tend greatly to overstock the trade with hands there cannot be the least doubt. However, be the cause what it may, the following statement is given as an instance of the difficulty the men find in obtaining employment.

"I am a jobbing carpenter, and in very great distress. All my tools are gone—sold or pawned. I have no means of living but by parish relief, and picking up what I can in little odd jobs along the water side. Sometimes I get a job at painting, glazing or white-washing, now that I have lost my own work; sometimes I get a day's work at the London or St. Katharine's Docks—anywhere I can get anything to do. And when I can't find any other employment I go to the workhouse yard and get a job there at wheeling the barrows and breaking stones. Sometimes I go to the yard four days in the week, sometimes only one day, and sometimes the whole of the week, according as I can get work. At the workhouse yard I get 1s. 6d. when I'm paid by the day; and when I'm at work on the stones I get 2d. a bushel for all I break, and the most I can do is six bushel in a day. Some men does 9 and 10 bushel, but then they're stronger men than me. I have got a wife and three children to keep out of my earnings, such as they are. My wife does nothing. She has a young child six months old to take care on, so it all lays on my hands. My eldest is a boy of 13 years. He got a place at a glass polisher's, and gets 5s. a week. He lives with his uncle. I've only the two others to look to. On Saturday my wife has a loaf and a shilling given to her from the parish, and that, with the shilling I earn at the yard, is all we has to keep and pay rent for the four of us, from Saturday till Monday. We can't go to work at the yard till Tuesday morning, for on Mondays we has the day to look after a job at some other place.

"Taking one week with another, I reckon I get, with parish allowance and all, from 5s. to 6s., and out of that I pays 1s. 6d. a week rent for one room—a first floor back, in an alley. It's my own things that's in it, and I'm obliged to scrape up 2d. and 3d. at a time to raise the rent, and give it 'em at the end of the week. . . . My wife

does the washing at home, and the things is dried in the room we live
and sleep in. In the winter we all of us goes into the house (the
union), because we can't afford to pay for firing outside. I leaves
my things, such as they are, with my brother-in-law. To people like
myself the cheapening of food has been the greatest of good. I don't
know who brought it about, but I'm sure whoever it was, he has
blessings for it. It was said that the bread was to be brought down
to 4d. a loaf, but it's never been less than 5d. round about us. It's
mostly bread that keeps us alive. . . . This is the way I reckon that
our money goes every week :

|  | s. | d. |  |
|---|---|---|---|
| Rent | 1 | 6 | per week |
| Half–quartern loaf a day | 1 | 3 | per week |
| Half a quartern of butter a day | 0 | 8¾ | per week |
| Pennyworth of coffee or tea a day | 0 | 7 | per week |
| One quartern of fourpenny sugar a day | 0 | 7 | per week |
| One halfpenny candle a night | 0 | 3½ | per week |
| Half–pound of soap a week | 0 | 2 | per week |
| Fourteen pounds of coal twice a week | 0 | 4 | per week |
| Four halfpenny bundles of wood a week | 0 | 2 | per week |
|  | 5 | 7¼ |  |

Yes, that's just about what it costs me, and if I manages to get a
few pence more, why we buys a Dutch plaice (if they're in), and
fries it for dinner, or else two or three fresh herrings, or maybe, as a
great treat, a pound of bits for the Sunday. I dare say there's
hundreds in London lives like us, but I'm sure there's no one lives
harder. There isn't much room for extravagance in five and sixpence a week among three and an infant—is there?

"The reason of my being in the state that I am is because I never
belonged to no society, nor no clubs nor nothing. I never could have
belonged to our regular trade society, because I never was brought
up regular to the business. My father was a carpenter, and I used
to work for him. He never apprenticed me, nor gave me no education, nor didn't teach me how to do the better kind of joiner's work.
I can do the rough work, but sashes and frames is beyond me. When
father was alive I had plenty of employment. He was a journeyman.
I can't exactly call him a small master. He used mostly to take
contracts on his own hands, to finish small houses and shop fronts,
and then him and me used to do them together. Sometimes, may
be, we'd have another hand on with us, that is, if the job was in a
hurry. Father was a Yorkshireman, and I was born in Yorkshire
too. He came to London with me and mother and settled here when
I was six years old. I did very well till father's death. He used to

keep me and give me 10s. a week. He's been dead now 12 years or better. I was 36 when he died.

"After his death I did pretty tidy for a short time. I got married about twelve months after that. I used to get a good bit of jobbing then from my father's connection. I took contracts, too, but somehow I used to lose a good deal by them, I was obliged to take so cheap. I seldom got above £1 and often 15s. a week for my labour. After that I went to work for the speculating builders about the suburbs, and then I used to pick up £1 a week as long it lasted. . . . I was seized with the cholera in the hot weather last year. In course as I didn't belong to any benefit club why I couldn't get no allowance, so I parted with my things one by one, and last of all with my tools, and when I got well I couldn't find nothing for me to do. I went about and about till I pretty well wore the shoes off my feet, looking for work and trying to keep out of the workhouse as long as I could, but when the winter came, I was forced to get an order to go in—I couldn't hold out no longer. We had made away with everything—blankets off the bed, shirts and petticoats off our backs, and, last of all, the brokers was put in for eight or nine weeks' rent that I owed, and so we made the best of our way to 'the house', and stopped in it about five months. I've striven every way to work for my living, but all to no good. . . ."[8]


# THE WOODWORKERS: CABINET MAKERS

## LETTER LXIII—1 AUGUST 1850

Having now set forth the earnings and condition of the Woodworkers who are engaged in the constructions of our houses, I shall treat of those who are engaged in the furnishing of them.

### The branches of cabinet-making

Cabinet-making is the one generic term applied to the manufacture of every description of furniture. Upholstery is, however, a distinct art of handicraft, dealing with different materials. The cabinet-maker is a pure wood-worker; and that perhaps of the very

[8] The letter also consisted of visits to moulding, planing and veneering mills, the testimony of a carpenter with views on machinery similar to the sawyers, and statistics of the criminality of the London carpenters compared with other trades.

highest order. Being generally engaged upon the most expensive woods, his work is required to be of the most finished and tasty description. The art is constantly calling forth a very high exercise of skill, ingenuity, and invention. It is a trade which perhaps, more intimately than any other, is mixed up with the fine arts. Marqueterie is mosaic work in wood; as wood-carving, in its higher branches, is sculpture in wood. The upholsterers, who confine themselves to their own proper branch, are the fitters-up of curtains and their hangings, either for beds or windows; they are also the stuffers of the chair and sofa cushions, and the makers of carpets and of beds; that is to say, they are the tradesmen who, in the language of the craft, "do the soft work"—or in other words, all connected with the cabinet-maker's art in which woven materials are the staple.

The cabinet-maker's trade of the best class, where society-men are employed, is now divided into the *General* and *Fancy* Cabinetmakers. There are also the Chair-makers and the Bedstead-makers. The General Cabinet hand makes every description of furniture apart from chairs or bedsteads. "A general hand," I was told by an intelligent workman, "must be able to make everything, from the smallest comb-tray to the largest bookcase. If he can't do whatever he's put to, he must go." He is usually kept, however, to the manufacture of the larger articles of furniture—as tables, drawers, chiffoniers, sideboards, wardrobes, and the like.

The Fancy Cabinet-maker, on the other hand, manufactures all the lighter or more portable articles of the trade, and such as scarcely come under the head of furniture. In the language of the craft he is a "small worker," and makes ladies work-boxes and tables, tea-caddies, portable desks, dressing cases, card, glove, gun, and pistol cases, cribbage-boards, and such like.

The Chairmaker constructs every description of chairs and sofas, but only the frame-work : the finishing, when stuffed backs or cushions, or stuffing of any kind, is required, is the department of the upholsterer.

The Bedstead-maker is employed in the making of bedsteads; but his work is considered less skilled than that of the other branches, as the woodcarver or the turner's art is that called upon for the formation of the handsome pillars of a bedstead of the best order.

*Numerical strength of the cabinet-makers*

To estimate the numerical strength of the cabinet-makers as a distinct body is impossible, for unfortunately the census of 1841 lumps them with the upholsterers (who are a totally different class of workmen, operating upon different materials) because their arts happen to be *locally* associated. . . .

The number of cabinet-makers and upholsterers located in the metropolis at the time of taking the last census was 6,956. The London chair-makers were 1,325, and the bedstead-makers 296 : making altogether as many as 8,577 belonging to the different branches of the London trade. According to the "Post-office Directory" no less than 1,008 of these were masters in business for themselves, so that it may be said that in 1841 the London operative cabinet-makers amounted to 7,500 and odd. Such are the Government returns of 1841; and on comparing them with those of 1831 . . . the decrease was 1 per cent—whilst the population, above 20 years, increased as much as 32 per cent, making a decline in the numbers of this class (in comparison with the rest of the population) to the amount of 33 per cent. . . .

### Does the law of supply and demand apply?

According to the law of supply and demand, the decrease of workmen should have given rise to a proportionate increase in the wages, provided there was no corresponding diminution in the quantity of work to be done. . . . With a view, therefore, of obtaining the best information on this point, I applied to the Cabinet-makers' Society for an account of the number of their unemployed members for a series of years, as well as the number of days they had been out of employment, and the sum the society had paid them during that time. The committee immediately gave directions that I should be furnished with all the information I needed, and the secretary devoted himself for several days to the compilation of a tabular statement, in which the wished-for facts were given for every quarter of a year since 1834. This table, however, being much too long to print here, I have taken the average of the four quarters of each year, and the following is the result :

| | Number of Members | Number of Unemployed | Days Unemployed | Paid to Unemployed £ s. d. | | |
|---|---|---|---|---|---|---|
| 1831 | 342 | — | — | — | | |
| 1832 | 290 | — | — | — | | |
| 1833 | 318 | — | — | — | | |
| 1834 | 371 | 40 | 632 | 60 | 18 | 8½ |
| 1835 | 435 | 41 | 748 | 67 | 7 | 8¾ |
| 1836 | 506 | 40 | 566 | 53 | 10 | 1¾ |
| 1837 | 527 | 90 | 1,675 | 156 | 6 | 10½ |
| 1838 | 513 | 82 | 2,025 | 185 | 13 | 3 |

|  | Number of Members | Number of Unemployed | Days Unemployed | Paid to Unemployed | | |
|---|---|---|---|---|---|---|
|  |  |  |  | £ | s. | d. |
| 1839 | 518 | 61 | 1,321 | 120 | 13 | 11½ |
| 1840 | 504 | 77 | 1,873 | 170 | 15 | 7 |
| Average from |  —  |  —  |  —  |  |  |  |
| 1834–40 | 482 | 62 | 1,368 | £125 | 14 | 7 |
| 1841 | 516 | 102 | 2,958 | 278 | 3 | 7¾ |
| 1842 | 464 | 110 | 3,482 | 367 | 10 | 10¾ |
| 1843 | 412 | 85 | 2,066 | 216 | 19 | 11¼ |
| 1844 | 419 | 43 | 934 | 84 | 17 | 5½ |
| 1845 | 460 | 26 | 383 | 35 | 12 | 9½ |
| 1846 | 546 | 47 | 878 | 86 | 18 | 6¼ |
| 1847 | 506 | 98 | 2,901 | 256 | 14 | 8 |
| 1848 | 413 | 125 | 4,201 | 387 | 13 | 4½ |
| 1849 | 340 | 98 | 2,204 | 204 | 13 | 5½ |
| Average from |  —  |  —  |  —  |  |  |  |
| 1840–49 | 452 | 81 | 1,158 | £213 | 4 | 11½ |

A superficial glance at this account will not enable us to come to any conclusion with regard to the state of the trade of the cabinet-makers in the different years above mentioned. In order to do this, we must find out the ratio of the employment to the non-employment of the members of the society; for the number of the unemployed is of no value *per se*. Nor is the number of members out of work alone sufficient for this purpose, for, unless we know the number of days that they were collectively unoccupied in each quarter, the true ratio of the employment to the non-employment cannot be obtained. Again, the sum paid to the unemployed members during any particular quarter is no criterion, unless we ascertain the amount that the employed members would collectively earn in the same time. It is the ratio between these several facts that will alone enable us to arrive at any definite result with regard to the state of the trade. To show the reader at a glance, therefore, the proportion that these facts bear to each other, I have in the first column of the following table given the percentage of the ratio of the days unemployed to those employed. This has been arrived at by finding first the number of days that the whole of the members in the society would have worked in the quarter, provided they had had full employment, and then calculating the proportion between that amount and the aggregate number of days unemployed. In the second column of the same table, I have likewise shown the ratio of the loss to the society by the non-employment of some of its members in comparison with its gains by the employment of the others. This I have ascertained by estimating the value of the unemployed days at the regular wages of the trade, and adding this sum to the amount paid to the members out of work, and then finding

the proportion that this sum bears to the amount that the whole of
the members would have earned had they been fully employed.

| | Ratio of days un-employed to those employed | Ratio of loss by non-employment to gains by employment |
|---|---|---|
| 1834 | 2·1 per cent | 2·9 per cent |
| 1835 | 2·2 per cent | 2·9 per cent |
| 1836 | 1·4 per cent | 1·9 per cent |
| 1837 | 4·0 per cent | 5·5 per cent |
| 1838 | 5·0 per cent | 6·8 per cent |
| 1839 | 3·2 per cent | 4·3 per cent |
| 1840 | 4·7 per cent | 6·3 per cent |
| 1841 | 7·1 per cent | 9·9 per cent |
| 1842 | 9·4 per cent | 13·2 per cent |
| 1843 | 6·4 per cent | 8·9 per cent |
| 1844 | 2·8 per cent | 3·8 per cent |
| 1845 | 1·0 per cent | 1·4 per cent |
| 1846 | 2·0 per cent | 2·8 per cent |
| 1847 | 7·3 per cent | 9·7 per cent |
| 1848 | 13·4 per cent | 17·5 per cent |
| 1849 | 8·3 per cent | 11·2 per cent |

A glance at the above table will show us that the ratio of loss by
non-employment rises and falls in the same manner, though not
precisely to the same extent, as the ratio of days employed.

We are now in a position to ascertain in what proportion the
wages of a trade rise and fall, according as the hands and the work
decrease or increase. . . . We can, then, by comparing the ratio of
the loss to the society by non-employment to its gains by employment
at one period with that existing at another, obtain an accurate
account of the increase or decrease in the earnings of the trade at
any given time. By doing the same with the ratio of the unemployed
days to those employed, we can likewise ascertain the increase or
decrease of work for the same period—while a comparison of the
number of workmen belonging to the society in different years will
further give us the increase or decrease of the workmen. We have
thus a means of demonstrating whether the wages of a trade really
depend on the quantity of work to be done and the number of hands
to do it.

| | Increase or decrease of hands | Increase or decrease of work | Increase or decrease of wages |
|---|---|---|---|
| 1835 | + 17·2 per cent | − 0·1 per cent | 0·0 per cent |
| 1836 | + 16·3 per cent | + 0·8 per cent | + 1·0 per cent |
| 1837 | + 4·1 per cent | − 2·6 per cent | − 3·6 per cent |
| 1838 | − 2·6 per cent | − 1·0 per cent | − 1·3 per cent |
| 1839 | + ·9 per cent | + 1·8 per cent | + 2·5 per cent |

|      | Increase or de-crease of hands | Increase or de-crease of work | Increase or de-crease of wages |
| ---- | ------------ | ------------ | ------------ |
| 1840 | − 2·7 per cent | − 1·5 per cent | − 2·0 per cent |
| 1841 | + 2·3 per cent | − 2·4 per cent | − 3·6 per cent |
| 1842 | − 10·0 per cent | − 2·3 per cent | − 3·3 per cent |
| 1843 | − 11·2 per cent | + 3·0 per cent | + 4·3 per cent |
| 1844 | + 1·7 per cent | + 3·6 per cent | + 5·1 per cent |
| 1845 | + 9·7 per cent | + 1·8 per cent | + 2·4 per cent |
| 1846 | + 18·6 per cent | − 1·0 per cent | − 1·4 per cent |
| 1847 | − 7·3 per cent | − 5·3 per cent | − 6·9 per cent |
| 1848 | − 18·3 per cent | − 6·1 per cent | − 7·8 per cent |
| 1849 | − 17·6 per cent | + 5·1 per cent | + 6·3 per cent |

By the above table we perceive that in the year 1835 there were 17 per cent more hands, and one-tenth per cent less work than in 1834, and yet the earnings remained the same in that year as in the previous one. In 1836 the hands increased 16 per cent, and the work only 8-10ths per cent, but still the gains rose 1 per cent. In 1842 the hands decreased 10·0 per cent, and the work only 2 per cent, and yet the earnings fell 3 per cent. In 1849, however, the number of workmen declined no less than 17½ per cent, while the quantity of work rose 5 per cent; the consequence was, that the gains of the members were upwards of 6 per cent more than they were in the year before.

Such facts as these show us that the principle of supply and demand, though undeniably true in general, still is not sufficient to account for all the fluctuations of wages. This will be even more evident when I come to treat of the Slop Cabinet Trade, for then I shall show that notwithstanding the number of cabinet-makers in the metropolis, compared with the rest of the population, decreased no less than 32 *per cent*! between 1831 and 1841, still the wages of the non-society men (whose earnings are regulated solely by competition) have fallen as much as 400 per cent—and this while the amount of work done has increased rather than decreased. The cause of this extraordinary decline will be found to be due chiefly to the rapid spread of what are called "Garret Masters"—a class of petty "trade-working-masters", who are precisely equivalent to the Chamber Masters among the boot and shoe makers, and to whom we found the decline of the wages in that trade were mainly attributable. This, indeed, appears to be the great evil likewise of the turner's trade, where, while hands have decreased, and work increased, wages have also fallen almost to the same extent as in the cabinet trade, and that from precisely the same reason, viz.—the increase of the "Small Masters", who are continually underselling each other.

In the present Letter, however, I purpose confining myself to the "honourable" part of the general cabinet-makers' trade. I shall first give a description of the work executed by the cabinet-makers, and then state the regulations of the trade. After which I propose speaking of the social condition of the men generally employed in it, and concluding with the statements of some of the best-informed members of the craft.

## The work executed

The general Cabinet hands make the following articles, on which they are principally employed : *Pembroke Tables*, which are square-cornered, with a wide "bed" (surface), and two small flaps. They are generally of solid mahogany. *Loo Tables*, which are generally round, though a few are oblong. The making of these tables in the best style is accounted one of the highest branches of the cabinet-maker's art. The carving alone of one of the most beautiful ever made, for the Army and Navy Club, cost, I am assured, £40. Loo Tables are generally veneered; rosewood, maple, and mahogany being the most frequent materials. The *Dining Table* has a narrow bed, with two long "flaps". The "extensible" dining table has telescope slides. Dining tables are all solid. The *Card Table* turns on a frame, and folds over into half the space. There are also "library", "sofa", "occasional", and other tables, which I need not describe. For the furniture of drawing-rooms oak is now a fashionable wood : the small tables in recesses, or for the display of any bust or ornament, are now often made of this material. Fine English oak for such a purpose is far costlier than mahogany.

*Chairs* are the most changeable in their fashion of all the furniture formed by the cabinet-maker. The Louis Quatorze style has now come again into fashion—a style which I am informed is always alternating, for, after some very opposite mode in style and form has been established for a limited period, "it works round again to the Louis Quatorze". Nearly all chairs are "worked solid", except that the "splat", or top of the back, is sometimes veneered. Of dining-room chairs I need not speak. Drawing-room chairs are of rosewood, maple, or walnut, and are, in the present fashion (of which alone I speak), covered with rich silk tabaret, or elaborate needlework. The bedroom chairs are of polished or stained birch; sometimes they are japanned, with cane-work or osier bottoms. The chairmaker is, moreover, the artisan employed in the making of sofas. These are known as cabriole, couch, and tête-à-tête. The tête-à-tête is the form of the letter S, and is adapted for two persons only, who occupy the respective bends.

*Sideboards* are most frequently made of mahogany, solid or veneered, but in most cases solid. Oak, however, is now the fashionable material for a sideboard, and is elaborately carved. *Cabinets* also are now made, as in the old times, of oak and walnut. For a lady's apartment rosewood is often the material used for a cabinet. *Cheffoniers* are of rosewood or mahogany, solid or veneered. *Drawers* and *Wardrobes* are of the wood which is considered most *en suite* with the other furniture, and with the general decoration of the chamber. *Book-case* making of the best quality is accounted a highly skilled portion of the cabinet-maker's productions. One at the Carlton Club, for its beauty of proportion, and strength as well as delicacy of workmanship, is pronounced by the trade, I heard in several quarters, a perfect masterpiece. It extends 90 feet. The surface is mahogany, veneered; the interior is the finest deal.

In most large establishments the work is begun and completed on the premises; general cabinet-makers, chair-makers, bedstead-makers, upholsterers, wood carvers, French polishers, and sawyers, all being employed there.

The mode of workmanship pursued by cabinet-makers is very remarkable, as showing a dependence on the skill of the individual workman unknown, perhaps, in any other trade. The best workman among the tailors in a large establishment has but to exert his skill to put together the materials which have been cut to the nicest proportions before they are placed in his hands. So it is with the bootmaker. With the cabinet-maker, however, it is different. The foreman gives him a sketch of the article he has to make, and points out the materials in the yard or the ware-room which is to be used in its construction. The journeyman then measures, saws, and cuts the wood to the shape required, and is expected to do so with the greatest economy of stuff, and so to cut it that the best portion of the wood shall occupy the most prominent part of the furniture, and any defective part be placed where it is least visible, or, in the language of the trade, "he must put the best side to London". The journeyman cuts out every portion; not only the front of the article, but every shelf required for the interior, and the minutest partitions or drawers. He then takes the material to his bench in the workshop, and puts it together without any subdivision of labour. The journeymen will assist one another in any elaborate article which is being made by piecework, but this is an arrangement merely among themselves. . . .

The cabinet-makers find all their own tools, a complete set of which is worth from £30 to £40. They all work on the master's premises, which, in establishments where many men are employed, are, with a few exceptions, spacious and well-ventilated rooms, open to the skylighted roof. Valuable timber is generally placed along the joists of the workshop, and there it remains a due time for "seasoning". When the men are at work there is seldom much conversation, as each man's attention is given to his own especial task, while the noise of the saw, the plane, or the hammer, is another impediment to conversation. Politics, beyond the mere news of the day, are, I am assured by experienced parties, little discussed in these workshops. I am told, also, that the cabinet-makers, as a body, care little about such matters.

## Social condition of the cabinet-makers

The operative cabinet-makers of the best class are, to speak generally, men possessed of a very high degree of intelligence. I must be understood to be here speaking of the best paid. Of the poor artisans of the East-end I have a different tale to tell. I was told by a cabinet-maker—and, judging by my own observations, with perfect correctness—that of all classes of mechanics the cabinet-makers have the most comfortable abodes. The same thing may be said also, if in a less degree, of the joiners and carpenters; and the reason is obvious—a steady workman occupies his leisure in making articles for his own use. Perhaps there are not many stronger contrasts than one I have remarked in the course of my present inquiry—that between the abode of the workman in a good West-end establishment, and the garret or cellar of the toiler for a "slaughter-house" at the East-end. In the one you have the warm, red glow of polished mahogany furniture; a clean carpet covers the floor; a few engravings in neat frames hang against the papered wall; and book-shelves or a bookcase have their appropriate furniture. Very white and bright-coloured pot ornaments, with sometimes a few roses in a small vase, are reflected in the mirror over the mantelshelf. The East-end cabinet-maker's room has *one* piece of furniture, which is generally the principal—the workman's bench. The walls are bare, and sometimes the half-black plaster is crumbling from them; all is dark and dingy, and of furniture there is very little, and that, it must be borne in mind, when the occupant is a furniture-maker. A drawer-maker whom I saw in Bethnal-green had never been able to afford a chest of drawers for his own use; "besides," he added, "what do I want with drawers? I've nothing to put in them".

What is meant by a "slaughter-house" will be seen in my account of the non-society cabinet-makers in Spitalfields and the adjacent districts. The same establishments in the West-end are generally described as "linendrapers"; they are indeed the drapers who sell every description of furniture and upholstery, but the workmen from whom they receive their goods are the "East-enders". These "linendrapers", and indeed all masters who employ non-society men, are known in the trade as "black" masters. "He's nothing but a black," is a sentence expressive of supreme contempt in a cabinet-maker's mouth.

"Within my recollection," said an intelligent cabinet-maker, "there was much drinking, very much drinking, among cabinet-makers. This was fifteen years back. Now I'm satisfied that at least seven-eighths of all who are in society are sober and temperate men. Indeed, good masters won't have tipplers now-a-days." According to the Metropolitan Police returns, the cabinet-makers and the turners are two of the least criminal of all the artisans; I speak not of any one year, but from an average taken for the last ten.

The great majority of the cabinet-makers are married men, and were described to me by the best informed parties as generally domestic men, living, whenever it was possible, near their workshops, and going home to every meal. They are not much of play-goers, a Christmas pantomime or any holiday spectacle being exceptions, especially where there is a family. "I don't know a card-player," said a man who had every means of knowing, "amongst us. I think you'll find more cabinet-makers than any other trade members of mechanics' institutes and literary institutions, and attenders at lectures." Some journeymen cabinet-makers have saved money, and I found them all speak highly of the advantages they, as well as their masters, derive from their trade society. The majority of the cabinet-makers in London are countrymen. There are some very good workmen from Scotland. One who has been an apprentice to a good London master is, however, considered to rank with the very highest as a skilled workman. . . .

The cabinet-maker's trade is generally learned by apprenticeship, and the apprentices to superior masters are often the sons of tradesmen, and are well-educated lads. There is no limit to the number a master may take, but the great firms in the honourable trade will, I am informed, take very many (one has eleven), and even put runaway apprentices to work. "They go for one thing, sir," a cabinet-maker said to me, "to get things done for half-price; it's little matter how." A journeyman can have his own son apprenticed to him, but only one at a time.

*Payment and trades societies*

The payment of the journeyman cabinet-maker is, both by the piece and by the week, 32s. a week, being the minimum allowed by the rules of the society as the remuneration for a week's labour, or six days of ten hours each. The prices by piece are regulated by a book, which is really a remarkable production. It is a thick quarto volume, containing some 600 pages. Under the respective heads the piece-work price of every article of furniture is specified; and immediately after what is called the "start" price, or the price for the plain article, follows an elaborate enumeration of extras, according as the article may be ordered to be ornamented in any particular manner. There are also engravings of all the principal articles in the trade, which further facilitate the clear understanding of all the regulations contained in the work. The date of this book of prices is 1811, and the wages of the society men have been unchanged since then. The preparation of this ample and minute statement of prices occupied a committee of masters and of journeymen between two and three years. The committee were paid for their loss of time from the masters' and the journeymen's funds respectively; and what with these payments, what with the expense of attending the meetings and consultations, the making and remaking of models, the cost of printing and engravings, the cabinet-makers' book of prices was not compiled, I am assured, at a less cost than from £4,000 to £5,000.

The trade societies in connection with this branch of art, are those of the cabinet, chair, and bedstead makers. They are divided into three districts, viz., West-end, Middle, and East-end. These districts contain five societies—one at the West-end another in the centre of the metropolis, and the others at the East-end. Three of these societies are in connection with the cabinet-makers' trade; the remaining two belong to the bedstead-makers and the chair-makers. The following table shows the number of men in connection with each society, together with the non-society men appertaining to each branch:

|  | Society Men | Non-Society Men | Total of Society and non-Society |
|---|---|---|---|
| West-end General Cabinet-makers | 300 | 1,400 | 1,700 |
| East-end ditto | 140 | 1,000 | 1,140 |
| Fancy Cabinet-makers | 47 | 500 | 547 |
| Chair-makers | 130 | 1,428 | 1,558 |
| Bedstead-makers | 25 | 238 | 263 |
|  | 642 | 4,566 | 5,208 |

Thus we perceive that the society men constitute not quite one-seventh part of the trade, from which it should be remembered that the upholsterers are here excluded.

These several societies, as is usually the case, have for their object the upholding of the standard rate of wages, and providing such assistance to their members as has been found to best suit the peculiar circumstances in which the workman is placed. They are mostly officered by a secretary, president, and committee, who are differently paid, according to the importance of the body and the nature of the duties required, while the payments of the members partake of the same variable character. The West-end cabinet-makers meet weekly, and pay 6d. per week as their regular trade contribution, and the members who are unemployed obtain for a given time 10s. per week from the funds, and when on strike 16s. There is also a payment for the insurance of tools, for which 1s. 6d. is paid every quarter. The West-end General Cabinet-Makers' Society have paid no less than £11,000 to the unemployed members within the last sixteen years, which is at the rate of very nearly £700 a year. They have also expended in the insurance of tools, since 1836, £1,758 and have received during that time £708 for loss of them by fire.

The members of the East-end body differ from those at the West-end in their rate of pay. They receive 30s. instead of 32s. per week, and when on piece-work they are paid by the job, or in the "lump"; that is to say, a given labour-value is put upon the entire article, whereas the West-end workman receives an additional price for everything which can be considered as coming under the denomination of an "extra". In the East-end, the members likewise meet weekly, but pay the less contribution of 4d. The unemployed members get 8s. per week, and when on strike 15s. The tools of the members are also insured by the society, but at a less rate than in the West-end.

The contributions of the fancy cabinet-makers are lower than in either of the foregoing instances, being but 3d. per week. They in like manner meet weekly. The assistance received by the unemployed, however, is mainly dependent on the state of the society's funds, 2s. per week being the lowest amount to be granted and 6s. the highest. They also have a legitimate weekly wage of 30s.; but this at present is very rarely to be obtained. The generality of this class work in their own homes, and take out the work in the "lump", the custom of paying for extras in the fancy cabinet trade being virtually extinct.

The chair-makers weekly contribution is 6d., the same as that of the West-end cabinet-maker; he gets, also, 10s. a week when unemployed; while, in cases of strike, the pay is as high as £1 per week for four weeks, and 16s. for another four weeks. Their standard wages are 32s. per week, while their piece work is regulated by their book of prices, with every description of extra or additional work carefully specified. Like the general cabinet-makers, they prefer this mode of employment to being paid by the week. An insurance is also taken out by this society for the tools of the members.

The bedstead-makers only meet once a month, and pay their

contributions by the month, which is 1s. 4d. When employed by the week they get 32s.; but they receive 5s. 6d. per day when sent out to a gentleman's house, to do such repairing (including cleaning) as may be required in their line of trade. This society also insures the tools of members, at the optional values of £12, £18, or £25, the latter sum being the highest. No payments have been made by this body either to the unemployed, or to parties on strike, for so long a time now that the custom in these cases has fallen into total disuse.

As a general rule the members of all the above societies are opposed to strikes, preferring the system of arbitration.

There is no superannuation or sick fund in connection with any of these societies. When the societies of cabinet-makers first commenced, the houses of call were established upon the same principle as the tailors'—that is to say, as the labour market of the trade; but now it is oftener the case that a man calls upon the master or his foreman, instead of receiving a call from the society house. Sometimes a man gets recommended to a master or foreman by a brother workman, and so obtains employment. The non-society men call upon the masters and ask for work.

Tramps are not encouraged, as these societies have no correspondence with the country societies. If, perchance, a tramp should call at a shop, he may get a few halfpence, but that is all. The brisk season continues during the spring and summer, and the autumn and winter months are the slack period of the trade. The following table shows the average ratio of non-employment at different seasons from 1834 to 1849. It will here be seen that the periods of greatest slackness are the first and last quarters, and the period of the greatest briskness the second quarter of the year :

TABLE SHOWING THE AVERAGE RATIO OF DAYS UNEMPLOYED TO THOSE EMPLOYED IN EACH QUARTER OF THE UNDERMENTIONED YEARS

|  | August 1st Quarter | August 2nd Quarter | August 3rd Quarter | August 4th Quarter |
|---|---|---|---|---|
| 1834–40 | 4·5 per cent | 3·0 per cent | 3·9 per cent | 3·8 per cent |
| 1840–49 | 8·3 per cent | 4·6 per cent | 6·0 per cent | 6·2 per cent |
| 1834–49 | 6·9 per cent | 3·9 per cent | 5·1 per cent | 5·1 per cent |

## The experience of a Scotsman

A good-looking man, who spoke with a hardly perceptible Scotch accent, gave me the following account of his experience as a *general cabinet-maker* of the best class. His room was one of the sort I have described in my preliminary remarks :

"I am a native of ——, in Scotland," he said, "and have been in London a dozen years or so. My mother was left a widow when I was very young, and supported herself and me as a laundress. She got me the very best schooling she could, and a cabinet-maker without some education is a very poor creature. I got to be apprenticed to Mr. ——, who took me because he knew my father. I got on very well with him, and lived at home with my mother. When I had been five years or so at the business I went with my master to Lord ——'s, a few miles off, to do some work, and among other things we had to unpack some furniture that had come from London, and see that it wasn't injured. My lord came in when we had unpacked a beautiful rosewood loo table, and said to my master, 'you can't make a table like that.' 'I think I can, my lord,' said my master, and he got an order for one, and set me to make it as I had seen the London table, but he overlooked me, and it gave great satisfaction, and that first made me think of coming to London, as it gave me confidence in my work.

"I had only occasional employment from my master when I was out of my time, and as my mother was then dead I started off for London before I got through my bit of money. I walked to Carlisle and was getting very tired of the road, and very footsore. What a lot of thoughts pass through a countryman's mind when he's first walking up to London! At Carlisle I had about a month's work, or better, as an order had just come in to Mr. —— from a gentleman who was going to be married, and the furniture was wanted in a hurry. I gave satisfaction there and that encouraged me. I walked to London all the way, coming by Leeds and Sheffield, and Leicester, and the great towns, where I thought there was the best chance for a job. I didn't get one, though. In my opinion, sir, there ought to be a sort of lodging-house for mechanics and poor people travelling on their honest business. You must either go to a little public-house to sleep, and it's very seldom you can get a bed there under 6d., and many places ask 9d. and 1s.—or you may go to a common lodging-house for travellers, as they call it, and it would sicken a dog. Then in a public-house, you can't sit by the fire on a wet or cold night without drinking something, whether you require or can afford it or not.

"I knew nobody in London except two or three seafaring people, and them I couldn't find. I went from place to place for three weeks, asking for work. I wasn't a society man then. At last I called at Mr. ——'s and met with the master himself. He asked where I'd worked last, and I said at Mr. ——'s, of ——, and Mr. ——'s, of Carlisle. 'Very respectable men,' said he, 'I haven't a doubt of it, but I never heard their names before.' And he then asked me some more questions, and called his foreman and said, 'R——, we want hands; I think you might put on this young man; just try him.' So I was put on, and was there four or five years. I had many little things to learn in London ways, to enable a man to get on a little faster with his work, and I will say that I've asked many a good London hand for his opinion, and have had it given to me as a man should give it. I do the same myself now. A good workman needn't be afraid : he won't be hurt. I work by the piece. I have been very fortunate, never having been out of work more than a month or six weeks at a time—but that's great good fortune. These are my earnings for the last eight weeks. I've only lately begun to keep accounts, all at piece-work, and a busy time : 32s. 2d., 41s. 3d., 40s. 1d., 36s., 29s. 6d., 28s., 35s. 10d., 35s. 9d. An average of near 35s. is it? Well, no doubt I make that all the year round. I can keep a wife and child comfortably. I wouldn't hear of my wife working for a slop tailor. I'd rather live on bread and water myself than see it. Slop means slavery. . . .[9]

## LETTER LXIV—8 AUGUST 1850

*Society and non-society men*

In almost all trades there are two broadly distinguished classes of workmen, known as "society" and "non-society" men; that is to say, a certain portion (usually about one-tenth of the whole) of the operatives belong to a "society" for upholding the standard rate of wages, as well as supporting their unemployed members. These society-men constitute what may be termed the aristocracy of the trade. They are not only for the most part the more intelligent and respectable of the craft, but by far the more skilful workmen. They are upholders of their order, and the sturdiest of sticklers for what they believe to be their rights. To give them their due, however, if they will not allow their employers to wrong any of their body, they also will not permit any of their body to wrong their employers. In the general cabinet-makers' trade, for instance, if a society man overdraws his account with his master, the members make a point of seeing the extra money refunded; so, in the tailors' societies, the members are answerable for the due execution of the work by any of their association. The wages, moreover, which they are bound to uphold, have generally been agreed upon by a committee composed of an equal number of operatives and employers, and in some cases

[9] Testimonies from a chair-maker, a bedstead-maker and the second oldest trade union member ended the letter.

the price-book in which the rate of pay for the making of the different articles belonging to the trade is fixed, has been got up at an expense of several thousand pounds. Further, the sums which they contribute to the support of their members out of work amount to many hundreds in the course of the year.

The wages of "society men", therefore, are regulated by *custom*; those of the non-society men, however, are determined solely by competition. It is the competitive men who are invariably the cheap workers, and the prey of the slop-sellers of every trade. Of the latter class belonging to the cabinet-making trade I shall speak in my next communication. For the present I purpose confining my remarks to the condition and earnings of the society-men employed at the fancy branch of the business. . . .

*Division of labour and social habits in the fancy branch*

Contrary to what I have remarked of the "general" trade, the employers of the fancy cabinet-makers require the operatives to confine themselves as much as possible to one especial branch that is to say, the desk-maker is expected to make only desks—the dressing-case only dressing-cases—and so through all the divisions. I was told that the "scamping", or low-priced, masters encouraged this close division of labour, as they thought it made the men more dependent. A man employed on low terms at desk-making was, for instance, unwilling to leave that for dressing-case making, at which, perhaps, his hand "was out"; and so, to avoid a change, he would submit to reduction upon reduction in his wages. All concurred in asserting, that fancy cabinet work is becoming more and more "scampish" every year—the exception of "honourable" employers in it being one in forty. . . .

The fancy cabinet-makers are, I am informed, far less political than they used to be. The working singly, and in their own rooms, as is nearly universal with them now, has rendered them more unsocial then they were, and less disposed for the interchange of good offices with their fellow workmen, as well as less regardful of their position and their rights as skilled labourers. "Politics, sir," said one man, in answer to my inquiry, "what's politics to me, compared to getting my dinner—and what's getting my dinner compared to getting food for my children?"

The amusements of the cabinet-makers, I was told by one of the older workmen, used to be principally the play. Some were very fond of going to the Polytechnic Institution. "Now however," he said, "few comparatively can afford the 1s., or 6d. that's wanted, and they go to penny concerts, and get to think that 'Sam Hall', or some nigger thing is very prime indeed. In my own case I've seen Liston play *Paul Pry*, and Farren play the *Colonel*, and Mrs. Glover the *Housekeeper*. I think that was the cast at the start, but I'm not quite sure. I went to see it, sir, at least eight times at my own expense. Latterly I've been to the play only once these three years, and then I had an order." Card-playing, dominoes, and games that are carried on without bodily exertion, seem now to be the chief recreations of the fancy-cabinet-makers. The fancy cabinet trade has of late years almost entirely sunk into low prices and inferior workmanship. . . .

A complete set of fancy cabinet-maker's tools, which they find themselves, is worth £10. The tools of the pine-workers and fitters-up are worth from 40s. to 50s.

## Statement of an elderly desk-maker

Before proceeding to give the subjoined statement of a desk-maker, I premise that "solid" desks are made out of a plank of mahogany, as it comes from the sawyer, or of whatever wood is the material required. This plank the desk-maker has to plane and to cut to his purpose. He has generally the material for twelve desks given to him at once. If the manufacture be "veneers" the same rule is observed, and the journeyman then receives a quantity of deal commensurate to the veneer. The journeyman executes the ink range, or the portion devoted to holding ink bottles, pens, pencils, wafers, etc., and indeed every portion of the work in a desk, excepting the "lining" or covering of the "flaps", or sloping portion prepared for writing. This "lining" is done by females, and their average payment is 15d. a dozen. Desks now are generally "lap-dovetailed"; that is, the side edges of the wood are made to lap over the adjoining portion of the desk.

The person from whom I received the following narrative was an elderly man, and a workman of great intelligence. He resided in a poor and crowded neighbourhood. His wife was a laundress, and there was a comfortable air of cleanliness in their rooms. I give this man's statement fully, as it contains much that has been repeated to me by others in different branches :

"I've known the London fancy cabinet trade," he said, "for forty-five years, as that's the time when I was apprenticed in London. My father was a button-maker in Birmingham, and gave a premium of fifty guineas with me. But he failed, and came to London, and was for some time a clerk with Rundell and Bridge, the great jewellers. My master was a tyrannical master; but he certainly made a workman of me and of all his apprentices. I don't recollect how

many he had. I think that now even a little master treats his apprentices middling well; for if he don't they turn sulky, and he can
hardly afford their being sulky, as he depends on them for work
and profit, such as it is.

"I got work in a good shop immediately after I was out of my
time. No good hand need, then, be a week out of work. Masters
clamoured for a good man. I have made £3 3s. a week, and one
week I made £3 15s. For twenty years after that I didn't know what
it was to want a job. I once during that time had three letters altogether in my pocket from Mr. Middleton, the great fancy cabinet-
maker—you may have heard of Middleton's pencils, for he was the
first in that line too—pressing an engagement upon me. Then I
prided myself (and so did my mates) that I was a fancy cabinet-
maker. I felt myself a gentleman, and we all held up our heads like
gentlemen. I was very fond at that time of reading all that Charles
Lamb wrote, and all that Leigh Hunt wrote. As to reading now,
why if we have a quarter of cheese or butter, I get hold of the paper
it's brought in, and read it every word. I can't afford a taste for
reading if it's to be paid for. I got married twenty-five years ago,
and could live very comfortably then without my wife having to
work to help me. We had two houses towards the West-end, and
let them out furnished.

"But twenty years ago, or less, I resisted reductions in our wages,
and fought against them. I fought against them for $3\frac{3}{4}$ years, and
things went wrong—uncommon wrong—I had to sacrifice everything
to meet arrears of rent and taxes, and I was seized at last; for it
wanted a weekly lift through a man's earnings to keep all prosperous.
I've done all sorts of work in my time, but I'm now making desks—
'ladies', 'school', or 'writing'—of mahogany, rosewood, and satin-
wood. Those are the principal; though every now and then another
fancy wood is used. Walnut sawn solid makes a beautiful desk or
box. I think walnut's coming into fashion again for that work.
Twenty years ago I made 35s. at the least a week the year through.
My family then, and for five, six, or seven, or more years after that
time, had the treat of smelling a real good tasty Sunday dinner of
beef, or pork, or mutton, as it came hot from the baker's, steaming
over the potatoes. And after smelling it we had the treat of eating it,
with a drop of beer to wash it down. On week days, too, we had the
same pretty regular. I've had six children. Now we have still the
smell and the taste of a Sunday meat dinner, but there it stops. We
have no such dinners for weekdays, I'm forced now-a-days to work
on Sundays too, and almost every Sunday. People may talk as they
like about Sunday labour; I know all about it; but an empty cupboard is stronger than everything. If I have the chance I may make

15s. a week at present prices. I work, as we mainly do at my own bench, in my own place, and find my own tools, glue, glass-paper, candles, and et ceteras; so that my 15s. a week sometimes fall down to 12s. clear. I work for masters, but not always, that find their own materials; but a great many of us have to find material and all. . . ."[10]

## LETTER LXV—15 AUGUST 1850

*Social advantages of society men*

The Cabinet-Makers, socially as well as commercially considered, consist, like all other operatives, of two distinct classes; that is to say, of "society" and "non-society men", or, in the language of political economy, of those whose wages are regulated by *custom*, and those whose earnings are determined by *competition*. The former class numbers between six and seven hundred of the trade, and the latter between four and five thousand. As a general rule, I may remark that I find the "society men" of every trade comprise about one-tenth of the whole. Hence it follows, that if the non-society men are neither so skilful nor so well conducted as the others, at least they are quite as important a body, from the fact that they constitute the main portion of the trade. The transition from the one class to the other is, however, in most cases, of a very disheartening character. The difference between the tailor at the West-end, working for the better shops at the better prices, and the poor wretch slaving at "starvation wages" for the sweaters and slop-shops at the East-end, has already been pointed out. The same marked contrast was also shown to exist between the society and non-society boot and shoe-makers. The Carpenters and Joiners told the same story. There we found society men renting houses of their own—some paying as much as £70 a year—and the non-society men overworked and underpaid, so that a few weeks' sickness reduced them to absolute pauperism. Nor, I regret to say, can any other tale be told of the Cabinet-Makers—except it be that the competitive men in this trade are even in a worse position than in any other. I have already portrayed to the reader the difference between the homes of the two classes—the comfort and well-furnished abodes of the one, and the squalor and bare walls of the other.

But those who wish to be impressed with the social advantages of a fairly-paid class of mechanics should attend a meeting of the Wood-carvers' Society. On the first floor of a small private house in

[10] The remaining accounts of fancy cabinet work, marqueterie workers, buhl cutters and wood carvers have been cut.

Tottenham-street, Tottenham-court-road, is, so to speak, the museum of the working men belonging to this branch of the Cabinet-Makers. The walls of the back room are hung round with plaster casts of some of the choicest specimens of the arts, and in the front room the table is strewn with volumes of valuable prints and drawings in connection with the craft. Round this table are ranged the members of the society—some forty or fifty were there on the night of my attendance, discussing the affairs of the trade. Among the collection of books may be found *The Architectural Ornaments and Decorations of Cottingham, The Gothic Ornaments of Pugin, Tatham's Greek Relics, Raphael's Pilaster Ornaments of the Vatican, Le Pautre's Designs* and *Baptiste's Collection of Flowers* (large size)—while among the casts are articles of the same choice description. The objects of this society are, in the words of the preface to the printed catalogue, "To enable wood-carvers to co-operate for the advancement of their art, and by forming a collection of books, prints, and drawings, to afford them facilities for self-improvement, also by the diffusion of information among its members, to assist in the exercise of their art, as well as to enable them to obtain employment." The society does not interfere in the regulation of wages in any other way than by the diffusion of information on the subject, so that "both employers and employed may, by becoming members, promote their own and each other's interests". . . . .

## The truth about trades unions

The public generally are deplorably misinformed as to the character and purpose of Trade Societies. The common impression is that they are combinations of working men, instituted and maintained solely with the view of exacting an exorbitant rate of wages from their employers, and that they are necessarily connected with "strikes", and with sundry other savage and silly means of attaining this object. It is my duty, however, to make known that the rate of wages which such societies are instituted to uphold has, with but few exceptions, been agreed upon at a conference of both masters and men, and that in almost every case I find the members as strongly opposed to "strikes", as a means of upholding them, as the public themselves. But at all events the maintenance of the standard rate of wages is not the *sole* object of such societies—the majority of them being organized as much for the support of the sick and aged as for the regulation of the price of labour; and even in those societies whose efforts are confined to the latter purpose alone, a considerable sum is subscribed annually for the subsistence of their members when out of work. The General Cabinet-Makers, I have already shown, have contributed towards this object as much as £1,000 per annum for many years past. It is not generally known how largely the community is indebted to the Trade and Friendly Societies of the working classes dispersed throughout the kingdom, or how much expense the public is saved by such means in the matter of poor-rates alone.

According to the last Government Returns, there are at present in England, Scotland, and Ireland, upwards of 33,000 such societies, 14,000 of which are enrolled, and 8,000 unenrolled—the remaining 11,000 being secret associations such as the Odd-Fellows, Foresters, Druids, Old Friends, and Rechabites. The number of members belonging to these 33,000 societies is more than three millions; the gross annual income of the entire associations is £4,980,000; and their accumulated capital—£11,360,000. The working people of this country, and, I believe, of this country alone, contribute therefore to the support of their own poor nearly five millions of money every year, which is some thousands of pounds more than was dispensed in parochial relief throughout England and Wales in 1848. Hence it may be truly said that the benefits conferred by the Trade and Friendly Societies of the working classes are not limited to the individuals receiving them, but are participated by every ratepayer in the kingdom; for, were there no such institutions, the poor-rates must necessarily be doubled.

I have been thus explicit on the subject of Trade Societies in general, because I know there exists in the public mind a strong prejudice against such institutions, and because it is the fact of belonging to some such society which invariably distinguishes the better class of workmen from the worse. The competitive men, or cheap workers, seldom or never are members of any association, either "enrolled" or "unenrolled"; the consequence is, that, when out of work, or disabled from sickness or old age, they are left to the parish to support. It is the slop-workers of the different trades—the cheap men, or non-society hands—who constitute the great mass of paupers in this country. And here lies the main social distinction between the workmen who belong to society, and those who do not—the one maintain their own poor, the others are left to the mercy of the parish. The wages of the competitive men are cut down to a bare subsistence, so that, being unable to save anything from their earnings, a few days' incapacity from labour drives them to the workhouse for relief. In the matter of machinery, not only is the cost of working the engine but the wear and tear of the machine considered as a necessary part of the expense of production. With the human machine, however, it is different—slop wages being sufficient to defray only the cost of keeping it at work, but not to compen-

sate for the wear and tear of it. Under the allowance system of the
old poor-law, wages, it is well known, were reduced far below subsistence point, and the workmen were left to seek parish relief for the
remainder; and so, in the slop part of every trade, the under-paid
workmen, when sick or aged, are handed over to the State to support.

As an instance of the truth of the above remarks, I subjoin the
following statement which has been furnished to me by the Chair-
makers' Society concerning their outgoings :

AVERAGE NUMBER OF MEMBERS, 110

| | £ | s. | d. |
|---|---|---|---|
| Paid to unemployed members from 1841–1850 | 1,256 | 10 | 0 |
| Ditto for insurance of tools | 211 | 10 | 0 |
| Ditto loss of time by fire | 19 | 2 | 8 |
| Ditto funerals of members | 210 | 15 | 0 |
| Ditto collections for sick | 60 | 4 | 0 |

"The objects which the London chair-makers have in view by
associating in a Trade Society," says the written statement from
which the above account is extracted, "is to insure, as near as
possible, one uniform price for the work they execute, so that the
employer shall have a guarantee in making his calculations that he
will not be charged more or less than his neighbours, who employ
the same class of men; to assist their members in obtaining employment, and a just remuneration for the work they perform; to insure their tools against fire; to provide for their funerals in the
event of death; and to relieve their members when unemployed or in
sickness—the latter being effected by paying persons to collect voluntary subscriptions for invalid members (such subscriptions producing on an average £5 in each case). The members have, moreover,
other modes of assisting each other when in difficulties."

*The change suffered by the chair-makers*

I may as well here subjoin the statement I have received from
this society, concerning the circumstances affecting their business :
"Our trade," say they, in a written communication to me, "has
suffered very materially from a change which took place about
thirty years ago in the system of work. We were at that time chiefly
employed by what we term : 'Trade-working masters,' who supplied
the upholsterers with the frames of chairs and sofas; but since then
we have obtained our work directly from the sellers. At first the
change was rather beneficial than otherwise. The employer and his
salesman, however, have now, in the greater number of instances,

no knowledge of the manufacturing part of the business, and this is very detrimental to our interest, owing to their being unacquainted with the value of the labour part of the articles we make. Moreover the salesman sends all the orders he can out of doors to be made by the middleman, though the customer is led to believe that the work is executed on the premises; whereas only a portion of it is made at home, and that chiefly the odd and out of the way work, because the sending of such work out of doors would not answer the end of cheapness. The middleman, who executes the work away from the premises, subdivides the labour to such an extent that he is enabled to get the articles made much cheaper, as well as to employ both unskilful workmen and apprentices. Placed in the position where the employer gets the credit of paying us the legitimate price for our labour, it would appear that we have no cause of complaint, but owing to the system of things before stated, as well as to the number of linendrapers, carpet-makers, and others who have recently entered the trade, without having any practical knowledge of the business, together with the casualty of our employment, our social position has become scarcely any better, or so good, as that of the unskilful or the dissipated workmen; while from the many demands of our fellow-operatives upon us in the shape of pecuniary assistance, we have a severe struggle to maintain anything like a respectable footing in the community. The principal source of regret with us is, that the public have no knowledge of the quality of the articles they buy. The sellers, too, from their want of practical acquaintance with the manufacturing part of the business, have likewise an injurious effect upon our interests, instead of seconding our efforts to keep up a creditable position in society.

"The subjoined is the amount of capital of our society at the present time :

|  | £ |
|---|---|
| Property in the Funds | 300 |
| Out at use | 175 |
| Other available property in the shape of Price-books, &c.[10a] | 200 |
|  | £675 |

*How to explain a 300 per cent decrease in wages*

Such, then, is the state of the society men belonging to the Cabinet-Makers' trade. These, as I before said, constitute that portion of the

[10a] "The Price-books are our exclusive right as well as copyright, we selling them to masters, journeymen, and the trade, and deriving a profit therefrom."

workmen whose wages are regulated by custom, and it now only remains for me to set forth the state of those whose earnings are determined by competition. Here we shall find that the wages of a few years since were from three to four hundred per cent better than they are at present—20s. having formerly been the price paid for making that for which the operatives now receive only 5s., and this notwithstanding that the number of hands in the London trade from 1831 to 1841 declined 33 per cent relatively to the rest of the population. Nor can it be said that this extraordinary depreciation in the value of the cabinet-maker's labour has arisen from any proportionate decrease in the quantity of work to be done. The number of houses built in the metropolis has of late been considerably on the increase. Since 1839 there have been 200 miles of new streets formed in London—no less than 6,405 new dwellings having been erected annually since that time; and as it is but fair to assume that the majority of these new houses must have required new furniture, it is clear that it is impossible to account for the decline in the wages of the trade in question upon the assumption of an equal decline in the quantity of work. How, then, are we to explain the fact that while the hands have decreased 33 per cent and work increased at a considerable rate, wages a few years ago were 300 per cent better than they are at present?

The solution of the problem will be found in the extraordinary increase that has taken place within the last twenty years of what are called "garret masters" in the cabinet trade. These garret masters are a class of small "trade-working-masters", supplying both capital and labour. They are in manufacture what "the peasant proprietors" are in agriculture—their own employers and their own workmen. There is, however, this one marked distinction between the two classes—the garret master cannot, like the peasant proprietor, *eat* what he produces; the consequence is that he is obliged to convert each article into food immediately he manufactures it, no matter what the state of the market may be. The capital of the garret master being generally sufficient to find him in materials for the manufacture of only one article at a time, and his savings being but barely enough for his subsistence while he is engaged in putting those materials together, he is compelled, the moment the work is completed, to part with it for whatever he can get. He cannot afford to keep it even a day, for to do so is generally to remain a day unfed. Hence, if the market be at all slack, he has to force a sale by offering his goods at the lowest possible price. What wonder, then, that the necessities of such a class of individuals should have created a special race of employers, known by the significant name of "slaughter-house men"—or that these, being aware of the inability of the "garret masters" to hold out against any offer, no matter how slight a remuneration it affords for their labour, should continually lower and lower their prices until the entire body of the competitive portion of the cabinet trade is sunk in utter destitution and misery. . . .[11]

### Garret masters and slaughter-houses

There is among the East-end cabinet-makers no society, no benefit or sick fund, and very little communion between the different classes. The chair-maker knows nothing of the table-maker next door, and cannot tell whether others in his calling thrive better or worse than he does. These men have no time for social inter-communication. The struggle to live absorbs all their energies, and confines all their aspirations to that one endeavour. Their labour is devoted, with the rarest exceptions, to the "slaughter-houses", "linen-drapers". "'polsterers", or "warehouses". By all these names I heard the shopkeepers who deal in furniture of all kinds, as well as drapery-goods, designated. These shopkeepers pay the lowest possible prices, and in order to insure a bare livelihood under them, the cabinet-makers must work very rapidly. This necessity has led the men to labour only at one branch, at which an artisan becomes expert; but he can do little or nothing else, and that again makes him more dependent on the warehouses. . . .

These men work in their own rooms in Spitalfields and Bethnal-green, and sometimes two or three men in different branches occupy one apartment and work together there. They are a sober class of men, but seem so perfectly subdued by circumstances that they cannot, or do not, struggle against the system, which several of them told me they knew was undoing them.

This remarkable monopoly and subdivision of labour was brought about gradually. The warehouses I have described began to flourish about twenty years since, and fifteen years ago they increased, and have increased rapidly since. The proprietors of these places purchased ready-made furniture of any one, and in large or small quantities; and men out of work eagerly seized the opportunity to employ their time in making goods for them, and so the system grew gradually to what it is now. "There's another thing, sir," said a man to me; "many a man didn't like the master or the foreman, and to work on his own account was the very thing that pleased him, so such a one would try his hand for the slaughter-houses. They've found it out since, that they have. . . ."

[11] The items cut here may largely be found in *L.L. & L.P.*, 1861, III, 222–6, where the letter was reprinted in slightly condensed form.

*A garret master with forty years' experience*

An elderly man, with a heavy careworn look, whom I found at work with his wife and family, gave me the following information concerning his occupation as a *little master*. He was then engaged in making tea-caddies, his wife and daughter being engaged in "lining" work-boxes for the husband's next employment. They resided in a large room, a few steps underground, in a poor part of Spitalfields. It was very light, from large windows both back and front, and was very clean. A large bed stood in the centre, and what few tables and chairs there were were old and mean, while the highly-polished rosewood tea-caddies, which were placed on a bare deal table, showed in startling contrast with all the worn furniture around. The wife was well-spoken and well-looking; and the daughter, who was also well-looking, had that almost painful look of precocity which characterises those whose childhood is one of toil :

"I have been upwards of 40 years a fancy cabinet-maker," the man said, "making tea-caddies and everything in that line. When I first worked on my own account I could earn £3 a week. I worked for the trade then, for men in the toy, or small furniture, or cabinet line only. There was no slaughter-shops in those days. And good times continued till about 21 years ago, or not so much. I can't tell exactly, but it was when the slaughter-houses came up. Before that, on a Saturday night, I could bring home, after getting my money, a new dress for my wife, for I was just married then, and something new for the children when they came, and a good joint for Sunday. Such a thing as a mechanic's wife doing needlework for any but her own family wasn't heard of then, as far as I know. There was no slop needle-women in the wives of my trade. It's different now. They must work some way or other. Me and my father before me, for he brought me up to the business, used to supply honourable tradesmen at a fair price, finding our own material; all the family of us is in the trade, but there was good times then. This part didn't then swarm with slaughter-houses, as it does now. I think there's fifty at this end of the town. I have to work harder than ever. Sometimes I don't know how to lie down of a night to rest best, from tiredness. The slaughtermen give less and less. My wife and family help me, or I couldn't live. I have only one daughter now at home, and she and my wife line the work-boxes as you see. I have to carry out my goods now, and have for 15 years or more hawked to the slaughter-houses. I carried them out on a sort of certainty, or to order, before that. I carry them out complete, or I needn't carry them out at all. I've now been on tea-caddies, 12-inch, with raised tops. The materials—rosewood veneers, deal, locks, hinges, glue, and polish—cost me £1 for a dozen. I must work hard and very long hours, 13 or more a day, to make two dozen a week, and for them I only get at the warehouse 28s. a dozen if I can sell them there. That's 16s. a week for labour. Sometimes I'm forced to take 25s.—that's 10s. a week for labour. Sometimes I bring them back unsold. Workboxes is no better pay, though my wife and daughter line them. If I get an order—and that's very seldom, not once a year—for a number of tea-caddies, I must take them in at a certain time, because they're mostly for shipping, and so I must have some help. But I can't get a journeyman to help me unless I can show him he'll make 15s. a week, because he knows I just want him for a turn, and can't do without him, and so the profit goes off. Old men can't work quick enough. They may be employed when there's no particular hurry. If I'm not to time with a shipping order, it's thrown on my hands. . . . No man on my earnings, which is 15s. some weeks, and 10s. others, and less sometimes, can bring up a family as a family ought to be brought up. Many a time I've had to pawn goods that I couldn't sell on a Saturday night to rise a Sunday's dinner." "Yes, indeed," interposed the wife, "look you here, sir; here's forty or fifty duplicates (producing them) of goods in pawn. If ever we shall get them out, Lord above knows. . . ."

## LETTER LXVI—22 AUGUST 1850[12]

*Over-work makes under-pay*

In the cabinet Trade, then, we find a collocation of circumstances at variance with the law of supply and demand by which many suppose that the rate of wages is invariably determined. "Wages," it is said, "depend upon the demand and supply of labour," and it is commonly assumed that they cannot be affected by anything else. That they *are*, however, subject to other influences, the history of the cabinet trade for the last twenty years is a most convincing proof; for there we find that, while the quantity of work, or, in other words, the demand for labour has increased, and the supply decreased, wages—instead of rising—have suffered a heavy decline. By what means, then, is this reduction in the price of labour to be explained? What other circumstance is there, affecting the remuneration for work, of which economists have usually omitted to take cognizance?

The answer is, that wages depend as much on the distribution of

[12] The letter was incorporated in condensed form in *L.L. & L.P.*, 1861, III, 226–31, where some of our cuts can be found.

PLATE XXIII.    Cruikshank's "Advice to 'those about to Marry'—Buy Cheap Furniture," 1852

PLATE XXIV.  The "Concordia" with her Carved Figurehead, by
Doré

PLATE XXV.  The Cooper at Work

PLATE XXVI.  Doré's Impression of the Interior of a Brewery

labour as on the demand and supply of it. Assuming a certain quantity of work to be done, the amount of remuneration coming to each of the workmen engaged must, of course, be regulated, not only by the number of hands, but by the proportion of labour done by them respectively; that is to say, if there be work enough to employ the whole of the operatives for sixty hours a week, and if two-thirds of the hands are supplied with sufficient to occupy them for ninety hours in the same space of time, then one-third of the trade must be thrown wholly out of employment; thus proving that there may be surplus labour without any increase of the population. It may therefore be safely asserted that any system of labour which tends to make the members of a craft produce a greater quantity of work than usual, tends at the same time to overpopulate the trade as certainly as an increase of workmen. This law may be summed up briefly in the expression that *over-work makes under-pay*.

## Means to increase the productiveness of labour

Hence the next point in the inquiry is as to the means by which the productiveness of operatives is capable of being extended. There are many modes of effecting this; some of these have been long known to students of political economy, while others have been made public for the first time in these letters. Under the former class are included the division and co-operation of labour, as well as the "large system of production"; and to the latter belongs the "strapping system", by which men are made to get through four times as much work as usual, and which I described in Letter LXI. But the more effectual means of increasing the productiveness of labourers is found to consist, not in any system of supervision, however cogent—nor in any limitation of the operations performed by the workpeople to the smallest possible number—nor in the apportionment of the different parts of the work to the different capabilities of the operatives; but in connecting the workman's interest directly with his labour, that is to say, by making the amount of his earnings depend upon the quantity of work done by him. This is ordinarily effected in manufacture by means of what is called piece-work. "Almost all who work by the day, or for a fixed salary, that is to say, those who labour for the gain of others, not for their own, have," it has been well remarked, "no interest in doing more than the smallest quantity of work that will pass as a fulfilment of the mere terms of their engagement. Owing to the insufficient interest which day labourers have in the result of their labour, there is a natural tendency in such labour to be extremely inefficient—a tendency only to be overcome by vigilant superintendence (such as is carried on

N

under the strapping system among the joiners) on the part of the persons who *are* interested in the result. The 'master's eye' is notoriously the only security to be relied on. But superintend them as you will, day labourers are so much inferior to those who work by the piece, that, as was before said, the latter system is practised in all industrial occupations where the work admits of being put out in definite portions, without involving the necessity of too troublesome a surveillance to guard against inferiority (or scamping) in the execution."

But if the labourer at piece-work is made to produce a greater quantity than at day work, and this solely by connecting his own interest with that of his employer, how much more largely must the productiveness of workmen be increased when labouring wholly on their own account. Accordingly it has been invariably found that whenever the operative unites in himself the double function of capitalist and labourer, making up his own materials or working on his own property, his productiveness, single-handed, is considerably greater than can be attained even under the large system of production where all the arts and appliances of which extensive capital can avail itself are brought into operation.

Of the industry of working masters or trading operatives in manufactures there are as yet no authentic accounts; we have, however, ample records concerning the indefatigability of their agricultural counterparts—the peasant proprietors of Tuscany, Switzerland, Germany, and other countries where the labourers are the owners of the soil they cultivate. . . . "The industry of the small proprietors," says Arthur Young, in his *Travels in France*, "was so conspicuous and so meritorious, that no commendation would be too great for it. It was sufficient to prove that property in land is of all others the most active instigator to severe and incessant labour." If then this principle of working for oneself has been found to increase the industry, and consequently the productiveness, of labourers to such an extent in agriculture, it is but natural that it should be attended with the same results in manufactures, and that we should find the "small masters", like the "peasant proprietors", toiling longer and working quicker than labourers serving others rather than themselves. But there is an important distinction to be drawn between the produce of the "peasant proprietor" and that of the "small master". Toil as diligently as the little farmer may, since he cultivates the soil not for profit, but as a means of subsistence, and his produce contributes *directly* to his support, it follows that his comforts must be increased by his extra production, or, in other wards, that the more he labours the more food he obtains. The small master, however, producing what he cannot eat, must carry his goods to market and exchange them for articles of consumption; hence, by overtoil, he lowers the market against himself, that is to say, the more *he* labours the *less* food he ultimately obtains. . . .

## Under-pay makes over-work

But not only is it true that over-work makes under-pay, but the converse of the proposition is equally true, that under-pay makes over-work—that is to say, it is true of those trades where the system of piece-work or small mastership admits of the operative doing the utmost amount of work that he is able to accomplish; for the workman in such cases seldom or never thinks of reducing his expenditure to his income, but rather of increasing his labour, so as still to bring his income, by extra production, up to his expenditure. This brings us to another important distinction which it is necessary to make between the peasant proprietor and the small master. The little farmer cannot increase his produce by devoting a less amount of labour to each of the articles—that is to say, he cannot scamp his work without diminishing his future stock. . . . In manufactures, however, the result is very different. There, one of the principal means of increasing the productions of a particular trade, and of the cabinet trade especially, is by decreasing the amount of work in each article; indeed, it is one of the necessary consequences of all *interested* labour, such as piece-work and small mastership, where the operative's earnings depend upon the quantity of articles made by him rather than the time he has been employed upon them, that it necessarily leads to "scamp work"—that is to say, to the omission of all such details as can be left out without the inferiority of the workmanship being detected. Hence, in such cases all kinds of schemes and impositions are resorted to to make the unskilled labour appear equal to the skilled, and thus the market is glutted with slop productions till the honourable part of the trade, both workmen and employers, are ultimately obliged to resort to the same tricks as the rest.

We find that, as the wages of a trade descend, so do the labourers extend their hours of work to the utmost possible limits—they not only toil earlier and later than before, but the Sunday becomes a work-day like the rest (amongst the sweaters of the tailoring trade Sunday labour, as I have shown, is almost universal); and when the hours of work are carried to the extreme of human industry, then more is sought to be done in a given space of time, either by the employment of the members of their own family, or apprentices, upon the inferior portion of the work, or else by "scamping it". "My employer," I was told by a journeyman tailor working for a large West-end show shop, "reduces my wages one-third, and the consequence is, I put in two stitches where I used to give three." "I must work from six to eight and later," said a Pembroke table-maker to me, "to get 18s. now for my labour where I used to get 54s. a week—that's just a third. I could in the old times give my children good schooling and good meals. Now children have to be put to work very young. I have four sons working for me at present." Not only, therefore, does any stimulus to extra producton make over-work, and over-work make under-pay, but under-pay, by becoming an additional provocative to increased industry, again gives rise in its turn to over-work—so that, the wages of a trade once reduced, there appears to be no means of predicting to what point they shall ultimately descend.

Let us now seek to apply these principles to the reduction of prices which has lately obtained among the competitive portion of the cabinet trade. . . . I purpose, therefore, inquiring more minutely than I have yet done into the history of this order of operatives— the motives for their passing from the state of *employés* into that of "masters", as well as the facilities for their so doing—their usual time of labour, together with the quantity of work they do, and the quality of it—the nature of the "helps" they employ when they require extra hands—their dependence in sickness and old age— the time lost in finding purchasers for their goods—and lastly, the effect they have had, and are likely still to have, upon the more honourable part of the trade.

### The history of garret masters

First, then, as to the history of "small", or, as they are frequently called, "garret masters" in the cabinet trade.

Little masters, both in the general and fancy cabinet trade, are now, strictly speaking, the men who purchase the material of the articles they manufacture, and who avail themselves of their own labour, that of their families, not unfrequently that of apprentices, and, very rarely, that of journeymen. In fact, they unite in their own persons the two functions of employer and employed, as they provide their own materials, set themselves to work, and execute the work by their own exertions, with the occasional aids I have men-tioned. They work on speculation, carrying their goods, when made, to the "slaughter-houses" for sale. This mode of business was hardly known until about twenty years ago. Prior to that time a little master was a man of limited means, having a front shop for the display of his goods, and a contiguous workshop for their manu-facture. He worked usually "to order", and was an employer; but

in most cases he worked himself along with those he employed, and
in all cases prepared or "cut out" the stuff which his journeymen
made into furniture, on his own premises. He employed from two
to five journeymen, having the greater number when trade was
brisk. These journeymen were non-society men, but they were paid
tolerable wages, and always, as now, by the piece, earning from
20s. to 35s. a week; the wages were generally 15 per cent lower than
those of society men. Inferior work was not then the common
practice of the little masters. They sold their goods from 15 to 25
per cent lower than the great houses. There are still some of these
little masters in the cabinet trade, but since the establishment of
the warehouses some fifteen years back they have dwindled away
to one-fiftieth of their number. Some of them, when business fell off,
"worked journeywork" for the better houses; some of the younger
men among them emigrated, and some are now working for the
"slaughter-houses".

There were also, twenty years ago, a numerous body of tradesmen,
who were employers, though not salesmen to the general public,
known as *"Trade Working Masters"*. These men, of whom there
are still a few, confined their business solely to "supplying the trade".
They supplied the greater establishments, where there were "show
rooms", with a cheaper article than the proprietors of those greater
establishments might be able to have had manufactured on their
own premises. They worked not on speculation, but to "order", and
were themselves employers; some employed at a busy time from
twenty to forty hands, all working on their premises, which were
merely adapted for making, and not for selling or "showing" furniture. There are still such "trade working masters", the extent of
their business not being a quarter what it was; neither do they now
generally adhere to the practice of having men to work on their
premises, but they give out the material, which the journeymen make
up at their own abodes.

A trade working master, now carrying on that business in the
fancy cabinet line, told me that he was about withdrawing himself
from it. He worked to order, and always kept a supply of goods for
"stock", from which either town or country tradesmen could select
whatever they required. Now, however, he assures me that it is
impossible to compete with the warehousemen, who purchase of the
garret or little masters, and avail themselves of those poor men's
necessities. And so my informant is relinquishing the business, as he
says it is "not fit for honest men—it is now only fit for scamps and
scamping masters". . . .

*The motives for becoming small masters*

Such, then, is the history of this class of workmen in the Cabinet
Trade. Concerning the motives for men to become small masters,
I had the following statement from one of the most intelligent work-
men belonging to the craft :

"One of the inducements," he said, "for men to take to making
up for themselves is to get a living when thrown out of work until
they can hear of something better. If they could get into regular
journeywork there a'n't one man as wouldn't prefer it—it would
pay them a deal better. Another of the reasons for the men turning
small masters is the little capital that it requires for them to start
themselves. If a man has got his tools he can begin as a master-man
with a couple of shillings. If he goes in for making large tables, then
from 30s. to 35s. will do him, and it's the small bit of money it takes
to start with in our line that brings many into the trade, who
wouldn't be there if more tin was wanted to begin upon. Many
works for themselves, because nobody won't employ them, their
work is so bad. Many weavers has took to our business of late. That's
quite common now—their own's so bad; and some that used to
hawk hearthstones about is turned Pembroke table-makers. The
slaughterers don't care what kind of work it is, so long as it's cheap.
A table's a table, they say, and that's all we want. Another reason
for men turning little masters is because employment's more certain
like that way; a man can't be turned off easily, you see, when he
works for himself. Again, some men may prefer being small masters
because they are more independent like; when they're working for
themselves, they can begin working when they please, and knock
off whenever they like. But the principal reason is, because there
an't enough work at the regular shops to employ them all. The
slaughterers have cut down their prices so low that there ain't no
work to be had at the better houses, so men must go on making up
for the 'butchers' (slaughterers) or starve. Those masters as really
would assist the men couldn't do it, because they're dead beat out
of the field by the slaughter-houses. . . ."

*The capital required to become a garret master*

I now come to the amount of capital required for an operative
Cabinet-maker to begin business on his own account.

To show the readiness with which any youth "out of his time", as
it is called, can start in trade as a garret cabinet-master, I have
learned the following particulars : The lad, when not living with his
friends, usually occupies a garret, and in this he constructs a rude

bench out of old materials, which may cost him 2s. If he be penniless when he ceases to be an apprentice, and can get no work as a journeyman, which is nearly always the case for reasons I have before stated, he assists another garret master to make a bedstead perhaps, and the established garret master carries two bedsteads instead of one to the slaughter-house. The lad's share of the proceeds may be about 5s., and out of that, if his needs will permit him, he buys the materials for a small clothes-horse, or any trifling article, and so proceeds by degrees. Many men, to "start themselves", as it is called, have endured, I am informed, something very like starvation most patiently. The tools are generally collected by degrees, and often in the last year of apprenticeship, out of the boy's earnings. They are seldom bought "first hand", but at the marine store shops, or at the New Cut. The purchaser grinds and sharpens them up at any friendly workman's, where he can meet with the loan of a grindstone, and puts new handles to them himself, out of pieces of waste wood; 10s., or even 5s., thus invested has started a man with tools; while 20s. has accomplished it in what was considered "good style". Old chisels may be bought from 1d., 1½d., 2d., to 5d.; planing irons from 1d. or 1½d. to 3d.; hammer heads from 1d. to 3d.; saws, from 1s. to 2s. 6d., and rules and the other tools equally low. In some cases the friends of the boy, if they are not poverty-stricken, advance him 40s. to 50s. to begin with, and he must then shift for himself. When a bench and tools have been attained, the young master buys such material as his means afford, and sets himself to work. If he has a few shillings to spare, he makes himself a sort of bedstead and buys a rug and a sheet or a little bedding. If he has not the means to do so, he sleeps on shavings stuffed into an old sack. In some few cases, he hires a bench alongside some other garret-master, but the arrangement of two or three men occupying one room for their labour is more frequent when the garrets where the men sleep are required for their wives' labour in any distinct business, or when the articles the men make are too cumbrous like wardrobes, to be carried easily down the narrow stairs.

A timber-merchant, part of whose business consists in selling material to little masters, gave me two instances, within his own knowledge of journeymen "beginning to manufacture on their own account".

A fancy cabinet-maker had 3s. 6d. at his command. With this he purchased material for a desk as follows :

|  | s. | d. |
| --- | --- | --- |
| 3 ft. of solid five-eighths mahogany | 1 | 0 |
| 2 ft. of solid three-eighths cedar, for bottom &c. |  | 6 |
| Mahogany top |  | 3 |

|  | s. | d. |
|---|---|---|
| Bead cedar, for interior |  | 6 |
| Lining |  | 4 |
| Lock and key (no wards to lock) |  | 2 |
| Hinges |  | 1 |
| Glue and sprigs |  | 1½ |
| Lining |  | 4 |
|  | 3 | 3½ |

The making of the desk occupied four hours, as the man bestowed extra pains upon it, and he sold it to a slaughterer for 3s. 6d.
He then broke his fast on bread and water, bought material for a
second desk, and went to work again, and so he proceeds now;
toiling and half-starving, and struggling to get 20s. a head of the
world to buy more wood at one time, and not pause so often in his
work. "Perhaps," said my informant, "he'll marry, as the most of the
small masters do, some foolish servant of all-work who has saved
£3 or £4, and that will be his capital."

Another general cabinet-maker commenced business on 30s., a
part of which he thus expended in the material for a 4-foot chest of
drawers :

|  | s. | d. |
|---|---|---|
| Three feet six inches of cedar for ends | 4 | 0 |
| Sets of mahogny veneers for three big and two little drawers | 2 | 4 |
| Drawer sweep (deal to veneer the front upon) | 2 | 6 |
| Veener for top | 1 | 3 |
| Extras (any cheap wood) for inside of drawers, partitioning, etc | 5 | 0 |
| Five locks | 1 | 8 |
| Eight knobs, 1s., glue, sprigs, etc. | 1 | 4 |
| Set of four turned feet, beech stained | 1 | 6 |
|  | 19 | 7 |

For the article, when completed, he received 25s., toiling at it
for 27 or 28 hours. The tradesman from whom I derived this information, and who was familiar with every branch of the trade,
calculated that three-fifths of the working cabinet-makers of London
make for the warehouses—in other words, that there are three
thousand small masters in the trade. The most moderate computa-
tion was that the number so employed exceed one half of the entire
body of the five thousand metropolitan journeymen. . . .

## Hours of Work

The labour of the men who depend entirely on the slaughter-
houses for the purchase of their articles, with all the disadvantages

that I described in a former letter, is usually seven days a week the year through. That is, seven days—for Sunday work is all but universal—each of 13 hours, or 91 hours in all; while the established hours of labour in the "honourable trade" are six days of the week, each of 10 hours, or 60 hours in all. Thus 50 per cent is added to the extent of the production of low-priced cabinet work merely from "over-hours" but in some cases I heard of 15 hours for seven days in the week, or 105 hours in all. The exceptions to this continuous toil are from one hour to three hours once or twice in the week, when the workman is engaged in purchasing his material of a timber merchant, who sells it in small quantities, and from six to eight hours when he is employed in conveying his goods to a warehouse, or from warehouse to warehouse, for sale. . . .

*Scamping*

This excessive toil, however, is but one element of over-production, "scamping" adds at least 200 per cent, to the production of the cabinet-maker's trade. I have ascertained several cases of this over-work from scamping, and adduce two. A very quick hand, a little master, working, as he called it, "at a slaughtering pace", for a warehouse, made 60 plain writing-desks in a week of 90 hours, while a first-rate workman, also a quick hand, made 18 in a week of 70 hours. The scamping hand said he must work at the rate he did to make 14s. a week from a slaughter-house; and so used to such style of work had he become, that, though a few years back he did West-end work in the best style, he could not now make eighteen desks in a week, if compelled to finish them in the style of excellence displayed in the work of the journeyman employed for the honourable trade. Perhaps, he added, he couldn't make them in that style at all. The frequent use of rosewood veneers in the fancy cabinet, and their occasional use in the general cabinet trade gives, I was told, great facilities for scamping. If in his haste the scamping hand injure the veneer, or if it has been originally faulty, he takes a mixture of gum shellac and "colour" (colour being a composition of Venetian red and lamp black), which he has ready by him, rubs it over the damaged part, smooths it with a lightly-heated iron, and so blends it with the colour of the rosewood that the warehouseman does not detect the flaw. Indeed, I was told that very few warehouse-men are "judges" of the furniture they bought, and they only require it to look well enough for sale to the public, who knew even less than themselves. In the general cabinet trade I found the same ratio of "scamping", compared with the products of skilled labour in the honourable trade. A good workman made a four-foot mahogany chest of drawers in five days, working the regular hours, and receiving at piece-work price 35s. A scamping hand made five of the same size in a week, and had time to carry them for sale to the warehouses, wait for their purchase or refusal, and buy material. But for the necessity of doing this the scamping hand could have made seven in the 91 hours of his week, of course in a very inferior manner. "They would hold together for a time," I was assured, "and that was all; but the slaughterer cared only to have them viewly and cheap." These two cases exceed the average, and I have cited them to show what *can* be done under the scamping system.

### The use of apprentices for scamping work

I now come to show how this "scamp work" is executed—that is to say, by what helps or assistants, when such are employed. As in all trades where lowness of wages is the rule, the apprentice system prevails among the cheap cabinet workers. It prevails, however, among the garret masters, by very many of them having one, two, three, or four apprentices, and so the number of boys thus employed through the whole trade is considerable. This refers principally to the general cabinet trade. In the fancy trade the number is greater, as the boys' labour is more readily available; but in this trade the greatest number of apprentices is employed by such warehousemen as are manufacturers, as some at the East-end are—or rather by the men that they constantly keep at work. Of these men, one has now eight and another fourteen boys in his service—some apprenticed, some merely "engaged" and dischargeable at pleasure. A sharp boy, thus apprenticed, in six or eight months becomes "handy"; but four out of five of the workmen thus brought up can do nothing well but their own particular branch, and that only well as far as celerity in production is considered.

In some cases the master takes boys without a fee, and the boy then lives with his parents or friends. For the first two years such an apprentice receives nothing; he is merely instructed. After that he receives half what he earns at piece-work prices. It is these boys who are put to make, or as a master of the better class distinguished it to me, not to *make* but to put together, ladies' work-boxes at 5d. a piece, the boy receiving 2½d. a box. "Such boxes," said another workman, "are nailed together; there's no dove-tailing, nothing of what I call *work* or workmanship, as you say about them, but the deal's nailed together, and the veneer's dabbed on, and if the deal's covered, why the thing passes. The worst of it is that people don't understand either good work or good wood. Polish them up and they look well. Besides, and that's another bad thing—for it encourages bad work—there's no stress on a lady's work-box, as on a chair or a sofa, and so bad work lasts far too long, though not half so long as good; in solids especially, if not in veneers."

*Members of the family are the usual assistants*

But the usual assistants of the small masters are their own children. Upon this subject I received the following extraordinary statement:

"The most on us has got large families. We put the children to work as soon as we can. My little girl began about six, but about eight or nine is the usual age." "Ah, poor little things," said the wife, "they are obliged to begin the very minute they can use their fingers at all. The most of the cabinet-makers of the East-end have from five to six in family, and they are generally all at work for them. The small masters mostly marry when they are turned of twenty. You see our trade's come to such a pass that unless a man has children to help him he can't live at all. . . .

"Just look at her," he continued, producing a rosewood tea caddy. It was French polished, lined with tinfoil, and with lock and key. "Now, what do you think we got for that, materials, labour, and all? Why, 16d.; and out of that there's only 4d. for the labour. My wife and daughter polishes and lines them, and I make them, and all we get is fourpence, and we have to walk perhaps miles to sell them for that."

"Why I stood at this bench," said the wife, "with my child, only 10 years of age, from four o'clock on Friday morning till ten minutes past seven in the evening, without a bit to eat or drink. I never sat down a minute from the time I began till I finished my work, and then I went out to sell what I had done. I walked all the way from here (Shoreditch) down to the Lowther Arcade, to get rid of the articles." Here she burst out in a violent flood of tears, saying, "Oh, sir, it is hard to be obliged to labour from morning till night as we do—all of us, little ones and all—and yet not to be able to live by it either." "Why, there's Mr. ——, the warehouseman, in ——," the husband went on, "offered me £6 a gross for the making of these very caddies, as I showed just now, and that would have left me only 1½d. a dozen for my labour. Why, such men won't let poor people remain honest.

"And you see, the worst of it is this here—children's labour is of such value now in our trade that there's more brought into the business every year, so that it's really for all the world like breeding slaves. Without my children I don't know how we should be able to get along. There's that little thing," said the man, pointing to the girl of ten years of age before alluded to, as she sat at the edge of the bed, "Why, she works regularly every day from six in the morning till ten at night. She never goes to school; we can't spare her. There's schools enough here for a penny a week, but we could not afford to keep her without working. If I'd ten more children I should be obligated to employ them all the same way. . . . Of the two thousand five hundred small masters in the cabinet line, you may safely say that two thousand of them, at the very least, has from five to six in family, and that's upwards of 12,000 children that's been put to the trade since the prices has come down. Twenty years ago I don't think there was a young child at work in our business, and I'm sure there isn't now a small master whose whole family doesn't assist him. But what I want to know is, what's to become of the 12,000 children when they're grow'd up, and come regular into the trade? Here are all my young ones growing up without being taught anything but a business that I know they must starve at."

In answer to my inquiry as to what dependence he had in case of sickness? "Oh, bless you," he said, "there's nothing but the parish for us. I did belong to a benefit society about four years ago, but I couldn't keep up my payments any longer. I was in the society above five-and-twenty years, and then was obliged to leave it after all. I don't know of one as belongs to any friendly society, and I don't think there is a man as can afford it in our trade now. They must all go to the workhouse when they're sick or old."

### The budget of a garret master's family

From a man who, with his wife and young child, occupied rather a decent room in Spitalfields, I had the following statement as to his mode of living. He was a fancy cabinet-maker :

"I get up always at six, summer and winter. I wake natural at that hour, if I'm ever so tired when I go to bed and sleep ever so dead. If it's summer I go to work in the daylight at six; if it's winter by candle-light. My wife gets up an hour after me. Indeed she can't well sleep in the room I'm working in. (We've only one room.) She makes the fire and boils the kettle, and gets breakfast ready at eight. It's coffee and bread and butter. I may take ten minutes to it, sometimes only five. She has dinner ready at one, and that's coffee and bread and butter three days at least in the week, and that's finished in ten minutes too. Then I've tea, not coffee, for a change about five, and I go to bed at ten without any supper—except on Sundays— after sixteen hours' labour, just with a few breaks, as I've told you. Most people in my way, who are as badly off as I am, work on Sundays. All that I know do, but I don't. I haven't strength for it after sixteen hours' work a day for six days, and so I rest on Sunday, and stay in bed till twelve or after. When we haven't coffee for dinner we have a bit of cheap fish—mackerel at 1½d. or 1d. a piece, or soles at 2d. a pair, and a potato with it. Sometimes they're almost as cheap as coffee for dinner. For breakfast for me, my wife, and a child five years old, coffee, half an ounce, costs ½d.; bread and butter 3½d.—1d. butter, and 2½d. bread. Dinner the same, but an ounce of coffee instead of half an ounce as at breakfast; so that's 4½d., and about the same if it's fish, or 1d. or 1½d. more, but there isn't as much fish as we could eat. Tea's ½d. more than breakfast. No supper, and to bed at ten. On Sundays we have mostly half a bullock's head, which costs 10d. to 1s. We have it boiled, with an onion and a potato to it; or when we're hard up we have it without either for dinner, and warm it for supper. There's none left for Monday sometimes, and never much. I don't taste beer above once a month, if that. In winter, fire and candlelight cost me 3s. to 4s. a week for some weeks, or 4s. 6d. a week when there's a fog, for my place isn't very light, and I'm forced to burn candles all day long then, and I must have a bit of fire all times for my glue-pot. There have been times—but things are cheaper now, though work's not so brisk—when we've had no butter to our bread, and hardly a crumb of sugar to our coffee. My rent is 1s. 10d. a week, and my own sticks. It costs at least 7s. to keep us, and that's 8s. 10d. altogether. I don't earn more than 12s. a week the year through, so that the extra fire and candle in the winter takes it every farthing, and more; and then we're forced to go without butter. There's 3s. 2d., say, left in summer time for clothing, and all that; but I haven't bought a new thing that way since I got married seven years back. My wife earns, perhaps, 2s. a week at charing, but her health's bad. I work for a slaughterer; not one in particular, but one is my principal customer. I began as a little master when I'd been a fortnight out of my time. My mother lent me 20s. She's middling off, and in service. I'd picked up tools before. Then my wife had saved on to £5 in service, which furnished the room, with what I made myself. I think most of us marry servants that have saved a trifle. A good many have, I know. My little girl's too young to do anything now, but she must work at lining with her mother when she's old enough. Children soon grow to be useful, that's one good thing. She goes to a Sunday school at present, and is learning to read."

*Time "lost" in carrying goods to the warehouse*

To show the time consumed—or, as the men universally call it, "lost"—in the conveyance of the goods to the warehouses, I am able to give the following particulars. There can be no doubt, as I have stated, that more than one-half of the working cabinet-makers in London work for the supply of the warehouses; but that I may not over-estimate the number, I will say one-half. The least duration of time expanded by these men in their commerce with the "slaughter-houses" is an average of eight hours weekly per man. But this is not all. At least one-fourth of their number expend 2s. 6d. each in the hire of carts and trucks for the conveyance of the heavier articles to the warehouses. Sometimes, when the bulk of the articles admits of it, trucks or barrows are used, the charge for which is 2d. an hour. But lighter articles of furniture are carried on the shoulder. "Why, sir," said one man to me, "I have sometimes carried as much as three-quarters of a hundredweight on my shoulder, and have taken that weight as far as Knightsbridge and Pimlico and back again, and then not sold it. I have then been obliged to take it out again the next day in a different direction, as far as Woolwich, and have took what I could get for it, or else go without victuals. I find about Thursday to be the best day, and the most profitable, as I can generally get more on a Thursday for an article than on a Saturday or Monday, because if you call on Saturday they think you are hard up for rent, and so they play upon you, and, besides, they think you couldn't get rid of it on Saturday. The usual rounds we take for the sale of our articles are Moorfields, Tottenham-court-road, Oxford-Street, Edgeware-road, Knightsbridge, Pimlico, and other parts of the West-end." Another party informed me that he has had to call no less than seven or eight times for his money after he had "sold his goods to a butcher", and then only get about half of what was coming to him. At these slaughter-houses, I was informed, "the butchers occasionally pay part cash and part by check, due in two months. But when we get outside, their clerks meet us to know if we have any checks to cash, for which they charge 3d. in the pound. . . ."

*The effect of slop business upon the honourable trade*

I shall now conclude this letter with the following statement as to the effects produced by the slop cabinet business upon the honourable part of the trade. I derived my information from Mr. ——, one of the principal masters at the West-end, and who has the highest character for consideration for his men. Since the establishment of slaughter-houses—"and aptly, indeed," said my informant, "from my knowledge of their effects upon the workmen, have they been named— the demand for articles of the best cabinet work, in the manufacture of which the costliest woods and the most skilled labour London can supply are required, has diminished upwards of 25 per cent. The demand, moreover, continues still to diminish gradually. The result is obvious. Only three men are now employed in this trade, in lieu of four, as formerly, and the men displaced may swell the lists of the underpaid, and even of the slop workers. The expense incurred by some of the leading masters in the honourable trade is considerable, and for objects the designs of which inferior masters pirate from us. The designs for new styles of furniture add from five to ten per cent to the cost of the more elaborate articles that we manufacture. The first time any of these novel designs comes to the hammer by the 'sale of a gentleman's effects', they are certain of piracy, and so the pattern descends to the slaughter-houses. These great houses are frequently offered prices, and by very wealthy persons, which are an insult to a tradesman anxious to pay a fair price to his workmen. For instance for an 8 ft, mahogany bookcase, after a new design, and made in the very best style of art, the material being the choicest, and everything about it in admirable keeping, the price is 50 guineas. 'O, dear,' some rich customer will say, 'Fifty guineas! I'll give you twenty, or, indeed, I'll give you twenty-five!' " (I afterwards heard from a journeyman that this would be the cost of the labour alone.) The gentleman I saw spoke highly of the intelligence and good conduct of the men employed, only society men being at work on his premises. He feared that the slop trade, if not checked, would more and more swamp the honourable trade.

# THE WOODWORKERS: SHIP AND BOAT BUILDERS

## LETTER LXVIII—5 SEPTEMBER 1850[12]

*Number of ship-builders*

According to the last census the number of "Ship-builders, Carpenters, and Wrights" (terms between which it is not easy to distinguish, the builder, carpenter, and wright being, according to my informants, one and the same individual), were in 1841 20,424 throughout Great Britain. Of these 17,498 were resident in England and Wales, and 2,926 in Scotland. The number located in the Metropolis—with whom I have more particularly to deal—was then 2,309. Since that period the number appears to have increased nearly one-fifth, for, according to the best-informed persons in connection with the trade, the following may be taken as a correct

[12] Letter LXVII treated the Wood-turners.

estimate of the hands belonging to the different branches of the business at the present time :

|  | Society Men | Non-society Men | Total number of Society and Non-society Men |
|---|---|---|---|
| Shipwrights | 1,500 | 500 | 2,000 |
| Shipwrights, Joiners | 110 | 230 | 340 |
| Mast and block makers | 110 | 140 | 250 |
| Boat-builders | 30 | 80 | 110 |
| Barge-builders | — | 150 | 150 |
|  | 1,750 | 1,100 | 2,850 |

The building of a ship may be not inaptly compared to that of a house, as I have described it in my former Letters. The modeller executes the plans of the architect. The shipwright is the carpenter. The ship-joiner's department of the work is not very dissimilar in its character to that of his namesake ashore; while the labour of the mast and block makers, of the boat-builders, and the sail-makers, may roughly typify that of the cabinet-makers and upholsterers, and other furnishers and finishers of our dwellings.

### Divisions of the trade shown by the work process

It is not my intention fully to describe the whole process of the important art of shipbuilding, nor would the limits of a newspaper admit of such description. To show the divisions of the trade, however, and so to render the statements I give more clear and intelligible, I will very briefly explain the process as it was described to me by working men, to whom I was referred as being the most skilful and intelligent. Three classes of workmen are employed in the construction of a vessel, before it is "ready for rigging". These are the *shipwrights*, the *ship-joiners*, and the *caulkers*. The work (as regards the mechanical labour employed) commences with the shipwright; and he and the ship-joiner make the whole "carcass" from "keel to gunal" (gunwale); the joiner's work being confined principally to the formation of the cabins. Drafts and plans are given out by the foreman for the guidance of all the operatives. The shipwright begins with the keel, which is always made of elm—sometimes American, but chiefly English, timber being used.

They then "put in the floors", which are the timbers that constitute the bottom of the vessel and float upon the water. These "floors" consist of first, second, and third "futtocks" (fuddocks), the form of which I described in my letter on ship-timber sawing, and they are made so as to give, when put together by the skill of the workman, the form, the bend and sweep of the hull. The perfect construction of this portion of the vessel is the high art of the shipwright. "Top-timber" is then placed above the floors for the purpose of binding and strengthening them by an interior as well as an exterior connection, and when that is done—English oak being used as the material—the ship is said to be "in frame". She—for I found the feminine appellative applied, no matter in what stage the vessel might be—is then "ribanded"; that is, pieces of timber, five and six inches square, are affixed fore and aft, as a temporary hold or binding to the timbers, so that they may "set" properly, for which a month is sometimes allowed. After this the ship is in a state to be "skinned", or planked, the wrights commencing with "the wale", or continuation of the bottom; and thus they work on to the completion of the "top sides" which surmount the upper deck.

Thus far outside work alone has been spoken of. After this the inside portion is begun; but sometimes the outside and inside works are carried out simultaneously. The inside work is generally commenced at the lower deck clamp—the clamp being the part which holds and supports the beam. The lower deck beams are "crossed", or adjusted, in a way not unlike the adjustment of the girders and joists of a house; and the same labour is completed as regards the middle and upper decks (supposing the vessel to be 1,000 tons), but the planking is "left to the last to give the ship air". If a smaller vessel be built, the same method is practised. The next stage is to form "the poop", which comprises the outer portion, or carcass, of the captain's, officers', and passengers' apartments; and then that of the forecastles, or sleeping places of the crew. The beams, of English or African oak—English oak and sometimes teak having been used for all the previous portions—are then laid across, to form the quarter-deck, and the decks are afterwards "planked". The planks are of Dantzic fir, and are laid in a way very similar to that practised in flooring a room, but the shipwright must lay his planks with a nice adjustment to the curved and sweeping outline of the ship; while the outline to which the house joiner has to work in the floors is generally straight.

The ship-joiner, when the work is advanced as I have detailed, is required to ply *his* avocation. He makes and fits up the whole of the interior accommodation of the ship, such as the cabins for the officers and passengers, and the forecastles. Deal, which is afterwards painted, is the wood generally used for the cabins of merchant vessels; but when the fitting up is in a superior style, handsome mahogany or maple gives a richness and elegance of appearance to the interior of the ship. I was told by an experienced person that the costly furniture and fitting-up of a cabin greatly reassured any timid passenger to whom sea voyaging was new, and who felt nervous and apprehensive before the hour of sailing. Such a passenger—a lady especially—I was assured, seemed to feel, and had not unfrequently expressed an opinion, that the owners of the ship were confident there was no danger of its being wrecked, or they would not have expended so large a sum in mere adornment. The saloon of a

Fig. 6   Caulking.

steamer, or the equivalent "cuddy" of a passengers sailing vessel of the first class, is often fitted up with mirrors, sofas, and expensive wainscotting, in a style that is known as the "gorgeous". The ship-joiner makes also the sideboards, the sofas, and every article of furniture which is fixed or stationary in the vessel, and so he must be able to work as a cabinet-maker as well as a joiner. On the very rare occasions on which the ship-joiner is required to work by the day, his wages are 5s. 6d.; on piece-work, however, he earns somewhat more.

The caulkers are employed solely in "caulking" the vessel, the process required to ensure her proper floating. They drive a caulk-ing-iron (not unlike a blunt square chisel) into the ship's seams, and then "horse it up"; that is, fill the interstice with oakum, driven in as close and tight as possible with a tool called "a horse". The surface is then pitched over, and the pitch is afterwards scraped and painted. But "caulkers", according to the divisions of artisans which I have here adopted, belong to a different class, and cannot be included among the workers in wood.

## Conditions of work and social habits

In the principal, and, indeed in nearly all the ship-building yards, the men work by contract—a system which has been pursued for the last fifty years, at the least. A shipwright contracts to do all the wright's work, or a portion of it, and employs men under him. In these cases no day-work is performed; all is done by the piece. In some yards, however, there is occasional day-work, and the pay-ment for it is 6s. and 7s. a day. I am assured, moreover, that on piece-work, in a good establishment, good workmen earn an equiva-lent amount at least, as the proprietors will not allow them to be ground down to swell the profits of the contractors. Nor, in the best yards of which I am now writing, are there any middlemen (be-yond the contractor), or any sub-letting. The same system is pursued in the departments of the joiner and the caulker. . . . The ship-wrights and all the mechanics employed in ship-building find their own tools. The wright's tools are not costly. The principal are the axe, adze, maul, mallet, saw and chisel. A complete set is not worth more than 50s., and some work with tools of the value of 25s., carry-ing them all in a bag. The joiner's tools, which are similar to those of his brother operative on shore, are worth, in their fullest complete-ness, £20. I heard of one ship-joiner whose tools, along with the handsome mahogany chests in which they were contained, were worth £80; £10 may be the average value of the tools that a ship-joiner possesses. A caulker's tools, however, cost only a few shillings.

The hours of labour are from six in the morning in summer, and from daylight in winter, until six at night, or until dusk. Out of this term of labour half an hour is allowed for breakfast, half an hour for luncheon, an hour for dinner, and half an hour for tea; so that the entire term of labour is at the utmost nine hours and a half. . . .

The work of the ship-builders is very hard, and demands not merely the customary skill and quickness of the handicraftsman, but great manual strength; they must either carry heavy beams or woodwork from the workshops to the ship, or else they must convey ponderous timbers complete to the workshop for affixing in the ship, and with these they must ascend and descend the ladders. In the course of my inquiry the weather was very sultry, and the men suffered greatly by having to work in the broiling sun; for in many parts of the labour on the ship itself they could have no shelter. The work is always carried on in the "dry dock", where the vessel is being built, or in the workshops adjacent, where everything is made (such as doors, furniture, etc.) that is susceptible of admeasurement, and then taken to the ship to be "fitted". In the winter the men suffer much from exposure to the cold. In rainy weather they are employed as much as possible in the workshops, or under cover.

The caulkers' work is especially hard, so much so that they do not toil later than three in the afternoon. The greater fatigue of the caulkers is attributable to their having to caulk in all positions of the body—recumbent or half-recumbent. When the bottom of the ship, for instance, is caulked, the men have hardly room to stand. Accidents are not infrequent among shipwrights, who work on "stages" (equivalent to the scaffolding of a house) lashed to the ships' sides. A short time before my visit to one of the yards, one of the chains of a stage holding four men broke, and they all were suddenly precipitated some twenty feet to the ground; all were hurt—one seriously—though no lives were lost. A fall of this kind is the more dangerous as the men work with sharp tools.

In point of intelligence, the ship-builders must be ranked high— quite as high as their fellow-labourers of the best class (I now allude to none other) ashore. One shipwright, however, thought that many of his fellows did not avail themselves so freely as they might of the munificent means for the education of children which an eminent ship-builder has so generously provided—I allude to Mr. Green. I was assured, notwithstanding, that every ship-builder, not an "emigration" or "a lath and plaster man", or a "boiler-maker"—terms that I shall presently explain—could, at the very least, read and write.

The ship-builders are, I found, great politicians. It is customary, during their half hours' luncheon at eleven o'clock, for one man to read the newspaper aloud in the public-house parlour; a discussion almost invariably follows, and is often enough resumed in the evening. The men for the most part go home to their dinners. The earnings of the shipwrights of the best class are, while at work, from 40s. to 50s. a week; and those of the joiners and caulkers from 10 to 15 per cent less; but it must be borne in mind that the average employment of the general body does not exceed nine months in the year. The majority of the ship-builders are married men with families, residing chiefly in Poplar and the adjacent parts. Some whom I called upon had very comfortable homes, and in their apartments there was no lack of books—a very fair test, it may be said, of the intelligence and prudence of a working man. Not a few of the ship-builders have brought up their sons to their own calling, or to some other branch of ship-building, or else to a sea-faring life. Within these twenty years the ship-builders generally were hard drinkers—now, I am assured, there are 50 steady men to 1 tippler.

In some yards the workmen are paid once a fortnight, the money being disbursed to them out of the counting-house on Friday evening, the payment being for all that was due up to the previous Tuesday night. In other yards they are paid at 4 p.m. on Saturday. I was informed that it is common enough for a ship-builder, with his wife and children, to enjoy his Saturday evening in some suburban excursion. Payment in public-houses, or anything approximating to the truck system, is unknown....

In the course of my inquiries, I heard the better class of ship-builders speak of a description of work known in the trade by the very expressive title of "emigration work"—by which was meant the building of a vessel "just for a passage out". The men thus employed were either unskilful, or not respectable, but the demand for such vessels has now almost ceased—old vessels alone being fitted up for emigrants. "There's Mr. ——," I was told, "picks out old ships and prepares them, and sends them out. He supplies emigration companies." Another class of ships I heard described as "lath and plaster" ships. "They are thrown together," I was told—another informant said "blown together—in the north of England; made cheap, of Quebec oak and inferior stuff, and inferior work; the timber ain't squared, its sided together, with the sap in it, and so it'll shrink and warp." I was told, however, that some ships are built in a northern port, almost equal to those built in London.

The ship-builders in London are—as regards the majority—natives of the metropolis. The others are principally Scotchmen, and west of England men, with a small proportion of north countrymen, and a very small proportion of Irishmen. In one large yard there was but one Irishman. All whom I saw, no matter from what part of the country, spoke of the London-built ships, in the good yards, as being the best in the world.

There are two other classes of operatives connected with ship-building, to whom I need only allude, as my present inquiry is confined to the workers in wood—viz., the workers in iron. These are the ship's smiths (called blacksmiths in the trade), who make the bolts, knees, and other iron work of the ship, and who are a highly respectable class; as well as the iron shipwrights, or men employed in constructing the iron steam-boats. Between these last-mentioned workers in ship iron and the workers in ship wood, there is no cordiality. The iron workers are called "boiler-makers" by the regular shipwrights, who describe them as an inferior class to themselves, made up from all descriptions of workers in iron, and including many boys and unskilled labourers.[13]

### Testimony of a ship-joiner

A *ship-joiner*, whom I found in a very comfortable room with his wife and family, gave me the following account :

"My father was in the business, and I was brought up to it by a friend of his. That's often reckoned a better way, as fathers are too severe or too indulgent. I was regularly apprenticed, and have never worked anywhere but in London, except once. I have always worked under the contractors, and have made my 33s., 36s., and 38s. a week when at work, according to the piece-work—it's all piece-work—that I get through. There is no fixed price—so much for the job, whatever it may be—and I've done all parts, I think. There's an understanding as to the pay. We know that we can make our living out of it. I may work rather more than nine months in the year altogether. In a good yard, after a ship is finished, there may be a slack of two or three months before we are wanted on a new ship. We are not kept going regularly at any one yard—only as long as a ship's in hand. We look out at all the yards. I'm a society man, and wish everybody was. I earn as much now as I did twelve or thirteen years back, when I first worked as a journeyman or I could not give my children—there's three of them—good schooling as I do. I don't know that I can do better than bring up my boy—the others are girls—to my own trade, if he grows up sharp and strong; it's no use without. I know of no grievances that we have. I worked, not long since, in the joinering of an iron ship. There's more joinering in them than in wood ships, as there's a lining of wood to back the iron work. I don't mix with the 'boiler-makers'. I seldom stir out of a night, as I'm generally well tired after my day's work. I live near my work, and take every meal at home, except my luncheon, and that's a draught of beer, and sometimes a crust with it and a crumb of cheese, that I now and then put in my pocket."

### The carving of figure-heads

The *carving of figure-heads* of vessels is a distinct branch of the business of ship-building. In some yards this carving, as at present pursued, partakes more and more of the characteristics of a fine

---

[13] Information about ship modelling appeared next.

art, and in all it is less rude than it was. The monstrosities, the
merely grim and grotesque, which delighted the seamen of the past
age, are now almost entirely things of the past. In the figure-heads
of the meanest vessels now built, some observance of truth and
nature is displayed. The figure-head is ordered of the carver for the
general trade (the greater builders usually comprising that department as well as others in their own establishments). Sometimes he
works from a drawing—rarely from a model. A carver upon whom
I called, had a spacious workshop in the corner of a large garden,
immediately behind his dwelling-house, which was near the Thames.
Ranged alongside the wall, at the top of the garden, were a row of
colossal and semi-colossal figure-heads, exceedingly grim and sultry,
and seeming singularly out of place, for they loomed down, with
their unmistakable sea-faring look, upon the white and orange lilies,
the many-tinted sweet peas and carnations, and the red and white
roses. The figures were all of elm, and each had a preliminary coat
of paint of a dull brick colour, to prevent the wood from cracking, so
that their uniformity of hue added to the curious effect that they presented. It was easy enough to recognize the features, or rather the
approximation to the features, of the Queen, Prince Albert, and the
Duke of Wellington; though there were several countenances which
looked familiar enough, and yet puzzled the memory as to whose
effigy was represented. Some figure-heads were robed, and starred,
and coronetted, and some had the plain coats of the present day.
With these were mingled female forms, some with braided hair,
others with very rigid ringlets, carved out of the solid wood. . . .

Along the wall of the workshop were the same array of effigies,
while in one corner, amidst heaped up timber, was a covered figure
in a sitting position, which was much more elaborately worked than
the others. A cornucopia rested on its left arm, while the right hand
grasped a snake, the head of which had been broken off, and lay close
by. The carving of the thick curly hair, was minute, and showed
great painstaking. This, I found, was at one time a choice ornament
of the Lord Mayor's state barge, and represented "Africa". An
opposite figure, allegorical of another quarter of the world, I was
told, became rotten and had to be removed from the barge, and
"Africa" was removed at the same time, or she would have appeared
isolated. When deposited in its present place the figure was gilt, but
a great part of the gilding having been rubbed or fallen off, its new
owner had it painted all over to resemble the others. . . .

A muscular, hearty, and hale-looking young man, whom I found
at work in a shop, presenting many of the characteristics of the one
I have more particularly described, but not the same, gave me the
following information :

"I was apprenticed to Mr. ——, and have never left London. My father was connected with ship-building, and so put me to this branch. I'm unmarried, and live with my friends. I have nothing to complain of in the way of business, as I have pretty good employment. We all drink beer—some of us, perhaps, too much, but nothing compared to other trades. Our's is hard work, but we don't drink much at work. Look you here, sir, this log of ellum, with just the sides taken off by the sawyers to make it square, has to be made into a 'head'—into a foreign nobleman or prince,—I don't remember his name, but it's a queer one. To do that is heavy lifting and hard work. None of these fellows here (pointing to the figures), is the proper size, hardly big enough, or I could easily gouge this one now into a lord. We first axe the log into a rough shape, a sort of outline, and then finish it with chisels and gouges. I sometimes work from a drawing, but mostly out of my own head, and direct myself by my eye. We have nothing to do with painting or gilding the heads. They're sent home in their own woods just with a coat of paint over them, to save them from cracking. Yes, you're right, sir, that head will do for the Queen; but if a Queen isn't wanted, and it's the proper size, I can soon make her into any other female. Or she might do for a 'Mary Anne', without altering; certainly she might. The way the hair's carved is the Queen's style, and has been in fashion these eight or ten years. Ringlets ain't easy; particularly cork-screw ringlets, as they're called. The watch-chain and seals to a gentleman ain't easy, as you have to bring out that part and cut away from it. The same with buttons and stars. Perhaps we aren't as good at legs as at other carving. We generally carve only to the knee. The shipwrights place our work on the ship's knee caps. We have no slop-workers among us; but there are two men who keeps a look out at the docks for broken heads, or heads damaged any way, and offer to repair them cheap. They're not workers themselves, but they get hold of any drunken carpenter, or any ship carver that happens to be hard up and out of work, and put them to the job at low prices. But the thing don't satisfy, and they do very little; still, it's a break in upon us. I make from 24s. to 30s. a week the year through, oftener nearer 30s. than 24s. I make 36s. at full work. . . ."

## The boat-builders

The London boat-builders are not now a numerous class—numbering only about 120, independently of the builders of wherries, who are not more than 35. Three-fourths of these operatives are London men; the majority of the others being from Deal and the

north of England, especially from Whitby. They are a sober and far
from ignorant class. "I really don't know one drunkard among us,"
said one of them to me, "and I think we can all read and write; but
we are a downcast lot to what we were once." Another man, whose
information I found corroborated, said, "I think the men in my
trade are steady and domestic. Most of us have wives and families. I
don't know a gambler among us, and there's only a few youngsters
that care for a hand at cards. Generally of a Saturday night, if we've
had a middling week in the yard, we pay 6d. a piece, and enjoy
ourselves quietly over our beer or ale, or whatever we like, and our
pipes, and our talk, and when the money's out we go away."

The boat-builders work by contract and by day; the contract or
piece-work system greatly predominating. The payment by day, of
ten hours' labour, is 5s. 6d. An operative contracts with a master to
build a boat complete, which he does by his unassisted labour, or if
it be a large-sized boat, or demanded in a hurry, two men undertake
it. The employer finds all the material, and the work is carried on
in his "yard", as the boat-building establishments are always called.
The operatives engaged in this business have a list of prices agreed
upon in concurrence with their masters in 1824, but now little regarded. The boat-builders have a society, but it is only for providing
members' funerals, and for relief during sickness. They have no
provisions for the regulation of wages, so that, according to the
"honourable" or "screwing" character of the employer, there is a
difference in the rate paid of 6d., 9d., and even 1s. a foot. . . .

The boat-builders are not affected by the introduction of unskilled labour. Want of regular employment and uncertainty of
remuneration are their principal grievances. The average work of
those best employed is for about nine months in the year, realizing
33s. a week during that time, or 22s. a week for the twelve. This
uncertainty or irregularity of employment is a great evil to the
working-men. "If we lives casual," said one man to me, "we grows
careless. . . ."

*A boat-builder discusses the depression in the trade*

I now give two statements from working boat-builders. The first
is that of a highly intelligent man who has had great experience,
and has observed many changes in his trade. For these changes he
gave what he considered the causes, expressing himself with terse-
ness and propriety. . . . .

"My trade," he said, "is greatly depressed to what it was. When
I was out of my apprenticeship, thirty-three years ago, there was
twice the employment for boat-builders that there is now. At that

time I think boat-builders were doubly as numerous as at present, as well as having double the employment. I consider the change owing to the many railways and steamboats now in operation. When the Scotch steamers came up, between twenty and thirty years ago, the Scotch smacks plying to London and back were soon run off that coast, and the same with other coasts. These smacks were always knocking their boats to pieces, and wanting new ones, or wanting repairs. They had to get their boats out to get alongside the wharfs, but now the steamer goes right up alongside, and hardly ever wants boats, and can hang them up as in a parlour. Then the jetties and piers do away with the use of boats. At Ryde, now, and in many a foreign part, the steamer goes right up to the pier, and the boats come home without a scratch. Before the piers came up, passengers, and luggage, and cargo, used to be landed in boats. Of course there's fewer wanted at present.

"I could and did earn 50s. a week the year through, thirty years back. At that time boat-builders were far better situated in having comfortable homes, and in being able to educate and provide for old age, or for families, than at present. There are more and cheaper schools now, certainly, but look at the difference of 50s. a week the year through, and 22s. or 23s., which I take to be the present average for those in the best work. I'm satisfied that boat-builders are an intelligent set now, but I think there was more intelligence among us in my young days. There's not much drinking among us at present, and there was less then. Indeed, the less a man earns, the more he's out of work, the more he's tempted to drink. He's driven to drink by poverty and oppression. He's often afraid to face his home.

"We were far better treated, too, by our employers formerly. Now, we're bullied and sworn at by many a master, 'till a man's blood boils. We're exposed to degrading words, that lower a man. Not that all masters are such; for there's Mr. F——, I worked for him a few months back, and there's no under-working or under-paying there; it's a good yard, I wish to God there were plenty such; and there's your money early on a Saturday evening, and all proper treatment. With the cutting masters, however, a poor man has no check. If he says anything he gets abused. And now I'll tell you, sir, of a crying evil, and if it was necessary I'd get, in two hours from this time and place, twenty honest men's signatures to prove that I state nothing but the fact.

"It's a crying evil that captains and owners will go up and down the river and buy old rotten boats, and have them painted up to look viewy. Emigrant's ships are surveyed, to be sure, but the survey of the boats is often nominal. Why, how often do we read of an emigrant ship having been in distress in a storm, and how her long-boat was launched and was stove in no time, and how numbers of poor fellows' lives were lost? And why was the boat stove so soon? Just because she was 'nail-sick'. What do I mean by nail-sick, sir? Why, it's our word when the nails have rusted asunder in the old rotten wood, and so when there's a stress on the boat, and she gets a hard blow, why, she goes slap to pieces. She was all rottenness, paint, and putty, at start. There ought to be an officer to survey every boat, and attend to nothing else, and who wouldn't be hum-bugged with paint. Owners and captains won't give anything like a fair price for necessary repairs. If a man asks £1, though that may be only a reasonable price, they'll say, 'A pound, pooh! The ship's carpenter shall do it;' and then perhaps, and very frequently too, it's not done at all. When the act of Parliament, three or four years ago, required every ship to carry a life-boat, it caused good work for us, because shipowners did provide life-boats at that time. Now, when they're wanted, owners and captains go up and down the river, and pick up any old rubbishing thing, and fit it for one. When it's trimmed up it looks very well. But, if any one were to go on board a ship that didn't belong to a good owner—some little shifty owner's ship—and if he would just try with a small knife under the bilge of the boat, why many's the time it'll go through it as if it was through a wafer. Or they'll find, perhaps, six or seven coats of paint, after a little scraping, for the paint holds the streaks together until there's stress and danger; so that when there is, down she goes with, may be, many a fine fellow in her."

## A boat-builder's budget

Another boat-builder, employed at present in the building of ships' boats, gave me the following statement. He resided in a crowded neighbourhood, not far from the river-side. His room was small and dark, but fully furnished, and a few numbers of a cheap periodical lay on the table. He was a grave good-looking man :

"I have been a boat-builder fourteen or fifteen years," he said, "and served an apprenticeship in London. My father was a water-man, and I wish he had brought me up to some better business; but they say no businesses are as good as they were once. He's been dead some years. There's no reduction in the wages paid me since I was out of my time, but I must do more work for less money." (He then made a statement as to streaks, etc., similar to what I have given.) "I lived with my mother until she died, four or five years back, and all I'd saved went to bury her. I don't think I could very well afford to keep a wife, though it's very lonesome having nobody to care about one. No doubt I could get a wife, but to keep her is another thing. I shouldn't like two to be in poverty instead of one, and I wouldn't like any decent girl I might marry to have to do work for the sweaters, to help us to make both ends meet when work's scarce. Some have to do it, though, to my knowing; and don't the girls

Fig. 7   Making ready for the fastenings.

find out the difference between that and being in good service, as some of them have been!

"I'm not employed—and very few of us are—three-quarters of my time; and, take the year through, I don't earn more than a guinea a week. I may be hard at work this month and have nothing to do for the next fortnight, but go from yard to yard and be told I'm not wanted. Now, suppose I've 21s. a week, and I'm a single man. I pay 2s. a week for the room, with a recess there for my bed. They're my own sticks. Then say 8d. a week for my washing, as I can't bear to be dirty. Well, then, I often work a good way off, and must live out. I can potter on cheaper at home. My breakfast, at the very lowest, is 3½d., and that's only 1½d. for half a pint of coffee, penny loaf, and penny butter. Properly, for a working man, it should be 7d.—pint of coffee, 3d., penny loaf, and penny butter, and 2d. for a rasher; but say 3½d. When one's hard at work one requires some refreshment before dinner time, and you can't have anything cheaper than half a pint of beer—a pint's not too much; the half pint's a penny. Then for dinner, half a pound of steak is 3½d.; if you get it cheaper it's tough and grisly, and no good. I get it cooked for nothing at a public-house if I take a pint of beer with it, and that's 2d., and a penny for potatoes, and a halfpenny for bread; altogether the lowest for a decent dinner, anything like satisfying is 7d. Tea is a halfpenny more than breakfast; for it's tea instead of coffee, you see, sir. Then there's a pint of beer, and a penn'orth of cheese and a penn'orth of bread for supper, that's 4d. I know there's plenty of working men who go without supper; but I'm hearty myself, and feel I want it. That is 1s. 7½d. for a day's keep, and a boat-builder's is hard work, and we require good support. Seven times 1s. 7½d.—and indeed Sunday should be reckoned more, for if I have a good dinner off a joint with my landlord and his family, as I have every now and then, I pay him 1s.—but, say 7 times 1s. 7½d. that's how much?—11s. 4½d.

"Well, then, there is my club money, and I pay 3d. a week for papers; and I go to chapel on a Sunday pretty regular, and there's often a collection, and I can't pass the plate without my 3d., and, indeed, I oughtn't; and I sometimes get a letter from a brother, a mason, I have in Australia, and I sometimes write to him : and besides there's 4d. a week for tobacco, at the very least, as a pipe's a sort of company to a lone man; and for such like things we can't say less than 2s. a week; indeed not less than 2s. 6d. Now, sir, what's that altogether?" (I told him 16s. 6½d.) "Then there's 4s. 6d. a week", he continued, "left for clothes, and for any new tool I may want, and for everything else; and I couldn't keep a wife, let alone a family, on that." (He seemed to enter with great zest into these explanations.) "Besides, this is the most favourable way to put it; for when I have a good week's work, and make 33s. or 34s., or as much as 36s., I want more support, and my living costs me more, though I keep it as square as I can for a rainy day or a slack time. . . ."[14]

---

[14] A short discussion of oar and scull making ended the letter.

# THE WOODWORKERS: COOPERS

## LETTER LXIX—12 SEPTEMBER 1850

*Number of coopers*

The number of London coopers at the time of taking the last census was as follows : Twenty years of age and upwards—males, 3,098; females, 22. And under twenty years of age—males, 369; making together a total of 3,489. Considering the trade to have increased since that period at the same rate as formerly, there must be very nearly 4,000 coopers at present located in London. Of this number about 300 may be said to be employers (the "Post-office Directory" gives the names of 291 coopers in business for themselves), so that it would appear that the Metropolitan Operative Coopers amount to somewhere about 3,700.

*Wet, dry and white work*

The trade of the cooper is divided into wet, dry, white, and general coopers. The wet (or tight) cooper makes every kind of vessel used for the reception of liquids—such as wines, spirits, beer, vinegar, oil, and water. The dry cooper, on the other hand, makes the casks used to contain dry goods—such as sugar, bottled wines, cement, linens, biscuits, and for dry packages generally. The white cooper forms tubs, pails, churns, and similar articles; while the block or general cooper, is practised in all of these branches. . . .

The wet cooper's work is very laborious, and requires practice and a quick and accurate eye; for it is by the eye that the cooper chiefly works. His eye, indeed, may be said to be his sole guide; he derives no help from the rule or the square, measurement being only resorted to for obtaining the due lengths of the staves prior to a commencement. The first process observed in making a wet or tight cask is to "list" the staves as they come from the saw yard or the pile. To "list" is to shape the staves with the axe, so as to render them suitable for "jointing", the ends being made somewhat narrower than the middle. "Backing" is next performed; that is, the stave is more minutely and carefully formed to the shape required by means of a two-handled "drawing knife", which the cooper holds with both hands, and "backs" or draws towards him so as to cut the stave rapidly, guided by a skilled and practised eye. "Jointing" is the next, and nicest stage, constituting, so to speak, the "high art" of this very nice craft. To joint is to prepare the sides of the staves in such a manner that they shall not only fit closely, but be adapted to ensure the perfect form of the cask, both as regards bouge and curvature. One stave is adjusted to another simply by fitting, that is to say, by the nicest adjustment, as there is no groove nor any such means of connecting the staves one with another. Nor is this all. The cask, when completed, must not only prevent the oozing of a single drop of the subject fluid, but must be made to contain a certain quantity; it must hold so many gallons and no more; and when we find that, to effect this, the artificer's eye is the chief guide and surety, the cooper's art—or, as it is called in ancient records, the "mystery"—certainly appears to partake far more of skilled labour than is usually supposed.

The staves being thus "jointed" or prepared, are fitted one to another round a block; a "head hoop" afterwards encircling them, and holding them all in one round. "Truss hoops" are then applied, which are strong wooden hoops, holding the staves firmly together until the iron hoops can be affixed. Before affixing the iron hoops, however, a fire made of chips and shavings lighted in a cresset, or small iron grate, is placed within the staves, so as to make them tough by warming the sap, and thus get them to bend without cracking. To this "firing" the closest attention must be given, for if it be prolonged beyond the exact time, the staves are rendered brittle instead of tough. As soon as the cask is sufficiently fired, an "over-runner" is put round the staves; this overrunner is a very strong wooden hoop, and is driven down by the cooper's "trussing adze", the upper part of the cask being first bent close together. The lower ends of the staves distend through the action of the heat, but the overrunner is driven gradually down to the "bouge"; to effect this in large and strong work the cooper calls out, "Truss, oh!" and immediately two or three of his fellows come to his aid, and drive the overrunner down so as to compress the staves sufficiently and reduce the distention. The cask is then prepared with tools called "chimes", used for "sloping" the ends of the staves, and grooves are made for fitting in the heads; this being done, the hoops are affixed, and the cask is then complete. All "wet" casks are made in the same way, and are iron-bound as a rule; vinegar casks, how-ever, are an exception, for they are bound with "twigged hoops", that is to say with hoops twisted round with twigs, the hoops being of hazel, and the twigs, or overlapping part, of willow.

Regarding the skill displayed in cooperage, Mr. Cox says: "Some few coopers there are who are exceedingly ingenious and skilful in giving a high degree of finish to their work when making model casks. One especially we may mention, whose name is Shaw, now an aged man, formerly employed for many years in the docks as a wine cooper, who is known to the whole trade as a most exquisite workman. His model casks are made of mahogany, and hooped with silver and cane hoops, the latter bound with silver wire. Two of such casks have recently been presented by Mr. Capel, of Tower-street, to the Coopers' Company, and are intended to ornament their hall. No cabinet work can be more highly finished than these casks; and when it is remembered that these beautifully-formed and finished models have been, in common with all other casks, made entirely by the accuracy of eye and by the perfect judgment of the workman, without measurement, square, or model to work by, they certainly present a striking illustration of what may be done by patience, care, and a diligent cultivation of the natural faculties of man."

Some of the technical terms of the trade are curious enough. To smooth the head of a barrel is called "smuggling"; and it creates no little surprise for a person to hear, on his first visit to a cooper's yard, directions given to the workmen to be "careful about that smuggling". If a cask when finished does not stand perfectly firm, that is to say, if it be at all lop-sided or top-heavy, it is called "a lord".

The dry cooper's work is carried on in the same way as that of the wet; but it is a less nice art, as so perfect an exactitude of adjustment is not required. . . .

## Coopers at the docks

At the St. Katherine's Dock there are employed about twenty "permanent" with a usual addition of from thirty to forty "preferable" hands, and all of them must be experienced coopers. Those employed at dry work are paid by the day, receiving 4s. 2d. per diem; while the wet coopers work by the piece, and average about 4s. 8d. a day. In the summer season, which is the busiest, about fifty more hands are employed; but in the slack season, only two or three extra hands are taken on. The additional men are known as "ticket men", in contradistinction to the "permanent" men. They have tickets duly numbered, and among them are the distinctions of "preferable" and "extra" men. They are employed by rotation (the preferable having the first turns) and if a vacancy occur among the "permanent" men, a preferable man is appointed to fill it, and an "extra" man thus becomes a preferable. The "extras" are appointed by the head of the department, and the men so appointed must be good workmen and of good character. This, however, is the system adopted concerning all the labourers at these admirably conducted docks. The labour of the coopers at the docks depends upon the

PLATE XXVII. Brewer's Men, including Coopers, by Doré

PLATE XXVIII.    "Drama" in a Dressmaker's Workroom

consignment of goods, and they average, according to the nature of
the year's business, from six to nine months labour in the year, the
"extra" men obtaining, of course, the lower amount, the "preferable"
the higher, and the "permanent" men being employed the year
through.

Among the permanent men are the "bond" coopers. They have
the charge of all the casks of wine, or spirits, or whatever the wet
casks may contain bonded in the dock. The bond cooper must report
any deficiency he may find in the contents of a cask. It is common
enough, I am assured, for sailors to "tap" a wine or spirit cask
during the voyage, but all such pilfering is made good before the
cask is deposited in the vault of a dock. The deficiency then occur-
ing is through leakage or the bursting of a hoop. The acid of the
wine not unfrequently rots the hoop; "it eats right through, sir,"
I was told. There are four bond coopers at each of the three wine
vaults, and at this dock "preferable" hands do the same work as the
permanent bond coopers when the state of dock business requires it.
It is also in the department of the bond cooper to draw samples
of wines and to wait upon and supply those who have orders for
"tasting". "I have seen," said a highly respectable dock cooper to
me, "very temperate gentlemen—aye, and ladies, too—very queer
indeed after tasting wines at our dock. In the atmosphere of the
vault the wine goes down so mildly; but it is served in very big wine
glasses, so that when the 'tasters' get into the open air, their heads
go round like whirligigs." The permanent men in the wet department
have all 28s. a week. The dry coopers have 25s. The casual hands,
or the ticket men, are paid by the piece as regards the wines, as a
rule, and earn from 3s. to 4s. 10d. a day, according to the demand
for their services, averaging on the week something near the payment of the dry cooper. . . . The most efficient hands at coopering on
piece-work who are at the St. Katherine's Dock, limit their earnings,
by an understanding among themselves, to a certain sum a day, to
enable them to assist older and slower hands to a better day's earnings. "In my opinion," said a gentleman familiar with the matter to
me, "this very praiseworthy arrangement does away with much of
the inequality, and therefore the mischief of piece-work."

The dock cooper is the repairer, re-adjuster, or re-fitter of the full
casks unshipped at the dock. This labour requires no little practice
and no little skill. The re-adjustment of the "wet" goods seldom
extends beyond the refitting and renewing of the hoops, but with
"dry" goods it is different. After a stormy voyage, sugar casks, for
instance, are landed in all possible shapes. Some have been compared to an old hat which had just been subjected to the operation
known as "bonneting"; they are crushed into irregular flatness. Some

are rudely triangular, others are as rudely quadrangular; indeed, they present every shape except their original rotundity. Yet these "crippled nondescripts", as Mr. Cox calls them, are restored to a proper form by the dry cooper, and without loss of the sugar. This is done by the renewing or re-adjusting of the hoops, and by inserting new staves in the room of those that are bent or broken. The dock coopers, then, are principally employed in the charge and repairs of the casks. But some of the good and experienced hands selected from the body of dock coopers do occasionally make casks, and that chiefly by reducing larger casks that have been damaged into smaller dimensions.

I had the pleasure of hearing very high commendations of the management of the St. Katharine's Docks from all the coopers I saw; and the most respectful and even in some instances grateful mention of Sir John Hall and Mr. Tomlins, for their attention to the well-being of the working men generally. I wish I could say the same for the superintendents of the London Docks. The St. Katharine's Dock coopers have no superannuation or burial funds. They have what is called "the gift", to which it is optional to belong. This "gift" has generally from 20 to 30 members, and each contributes 6d. a week to a sick member. The dock coopers are, on the whole, intelligent men—sober men they must be, as drunkenness is certain dismissal. Their hours of labour are from eight to four, only a quarter of an hour being allowed for luncheon, which is of course the men's dinner. At that meal a pint of beer is allowed to each working cooper, and that is all he can drink during his work at the dock, for each man is searched upon entering and is not allowed to leave the dock until the regular hour. I heard also many acknowledgments (from the working men) of the system of gradation and advancement—as respects the "permanent", and "preferable", and "ticket" men—working well, and being an incentive to good conduct.

In the London Docks, there are 50 working coopers permanently employed at day-work, for which they receive 28s. a week, and generally 20 first-class and 150 second-class recommended men, who earn at piece-work about 27s. a week. Here the coopers' work is done chiefly by contract; and such has been the practice for a considerable time. But the coopers were not materially injured by it until about twelve months ago. The contractors are men who have been well recommended to the company, and are, therefore, equivalent to the preferable workmen of the most respectable docks. The contractors usually consist of a gang of seven or eight men, who work together, without any foreman over them, and share all alike. They contract with the company to make all the casks in a particular ship, sound, and fit for housing. . . . This contract system, I am assured on excellent authority, makes the men so contracting hurry recklessly through their work, careless of what property is destroyed, so that they can complete their undertaking and hurry to another job, as they get the same remuneration whether the ship be "worked out" in a week or in two days. "No one who hasn't seen it would credit the destruction of property," said an experienced London Dock man to me. "I have seen it and have been sometimes a party, and forced to be a party, to the destruction. Both the merchant's property and the Company's material, such as hoops, staves, and nails, are consumed needlessly in the hurry of the contract work. The worst lot of coopers generally go to this work; many of them are men that have been turned out of the other docks. I'm sure of that. Much as I hate an Union house, I would rather be in one than work on such contracts at the London Docks." This refers only to dry goods. The wine-cooper's trade used also to be done by contract at this dock, but it is now done by piece-work. The employment of the wine-coopers is left to the discretion of the principal wine-cooper, who, I am assured, exercises a wise and honourable discretion in this particular. There are at the London Docks no such regulations as at the St. Katharine's Docks as regards "permanent" men, etc. The wet coopers are paid for this piece-work less than at the St. Katharine's Docks; on brandy pieces a farthing an end less, and other work in proportion. The established men working at the London Docks, of whatever calling, are enrolled in a benefit society under the direction of the company.

When a cooper is employed permanently by the company, from 4d. to 6d. a week (according to his age) is stopped out of his wages, and when he reaches sixty years of age he is superannuated, and receives 10s. a week for the remainder of his life. If, however, the man be guilty of the least misdemeanour, he is immediately discharged, whereupon all the money he has previously paid in to the superannuation fund is forfeited. One man, who has been in the company's service upwards of twelve years, was found intoxicated, and he was instantly cashiered. The consequence was that he lost all the money he had contributed to the superannuation fund during that time, or upwards of £40. I am told that many instances of this kind occur. "Indeed" (said my informant) "such circumstances are a pleasure to the company, as they are benefited thereby. . . ."

## Coopers in the general trade

The journeymen coopers in the general trade are paid almost entirely by the piece. The distinctions of work which I have noticed are becoming less and less regarded; general hands, or men practised, however superficially, in all branches, are more sought after than they were. The work for the brewers is still, however, kept distinct. At a great brewery, inferior cooperage is detected in a moment. In the very best shops—which, however, are now exceptional establishments—the men can earn, by working long hours, £2 a week. The average earnings in the honourable trade are from 26s. to 30s. the year through, when fully employed, at twelve hours a day deducting two hours for meals; and the majority are so employed nine months in the year, and perhaps one-tenth of the whole body are so employed for twelve months. The summer is the brisk and the winter the slack season, and in winter very many are out of employment. There is nothing to class precisely as slop work in the cooper's trade, for every "wet" cooper's work is tested. The cask is "quarter filled" with boiling water; this generates a powerful steam which will ooze through any slight flaw in the work (which the journeyman must then make good), or even through a worm hole, or any petty defect in the timber. Thus slop work is not so easy among coopers as in some trades. "Our work, sir," said a man to me, using a professional joke, "*must* hold water." Even in the lowest priced yards the foreman closely tests and examines both the wet and dry work, and nothing bad passes, lest it should be sent back from the purchaser. There is not among them even a technical term for under-paying or slop employers. In all shops, wages have been reduced. Twenty years ago a cooper on the best work could earn £3 where he now earns £2, and the fall in inferior work is greater still. The society men's prices are regulated by themselves, and printed. A rum puncheon made of "single imported" staves, is now 3s. 6d.; and within ten years was 3s. 10d. and 4s., and yet that is the article which has declined the least. Oil butts have fallen from 15 to 20 per cent in journeymen's wages in the last seven years, and all other goods in proportion. The coopers find their own tools, a kit for a general workman being worth £12. These tools are the axe, adze, backing, heading, hollow and drawing knives, jiggers, crows, and saws. The wear and tear of his tools costs the workman 1s. a week. . . .

*Social condition of the coopers*

As a body the coopers are an intelligent class of mechanics. I met among them some superior men, and heard of several who had saved a little money. Hard drinking, I regret to say, though not drunkenness, prevails among the majority of the men employed in large cooperages. "I seldom see them drunk," said one cooper to me, "and I think it's not in the drink to intoxicate some of the seasoned hands. This addiction to continuous drinking, rather than to drunkenness—and the coopers drink principally beer—was accounted for to me by their work being very laborious, while the heat is often so great that they acquire a distaste for solids during the hours of labour, and stay the cravings of the appetite with draughts of beer. In a shop where "large work" is made, and where the timber is the stoutest and the fire the hottest, a moderate drinking cooper, as he is accounted, drinks two pots of beer a day; some will drink three pots and upwards, but in such circumstances two pots is the average drinking. The most moderate coopers, I am told, expend not less, on the average, than 4s. a week on beer. The coopers become prematurely old, suffering greatly from pains in the chest, and across the back, attributable to their bending over their hot work. "A cooper at large work is an old man, sir, at forty," said one of them to me; "his physical energies then are nearly exhausted."

Coopers are generally fond of manly exercises, such as cricket. There are very few skittle-players among them. Cards are played sometimes in the public-house on Saturday night, but not generally. "Had the coopers a taste for cards, it would be very easy to introduce them into the workshops," said one of them to me, "by making a card table on a barrel head. Often for days together a master never enters a shop, and the foreman, when he has given a man the stuff, leaves him almost entirely to himself." The theatre and the public gardens, I am told, are, however, the principal recreations of the coopers.

The coopers are mostly married men, living in unfurnished lodgings (generally two rooms), at about 4s. a week rent. They usually reside as near to their work as possible; consequently the majority are to be found in Whitechapel, where the largest sugar-houses are situate; whilst some of the men, for the same reason, are located in St. George-in-the-East. A few have houses at £25 a year rent, letting off part of them, but this is the exception rather than the rule. The operatives have generally from two to five or six in family, and only some of the children are put to school. "I don't consider," said an intelligent member of the trade to me, "that coopers' children are properly looked after, or that they are as well educated as they ought to be. I believe that it is owing to the drinking habits of our trade that the men's families are neglected as they are; perhaps another reason for this is, because during the slack season it takes all the men can earn to procure even food for their families. Upon an average in the slack season, which lasts about four months in the year, I think the coopers' earnings are not above 10s. a week. In the brisk, however, they make about 30s. a week; and I have no doubt

it is this great fluctuation in their income that makes the men less
provident and less attentive to their homes than they otherwise
would be. I think the majority of the operative coopers' wives take
in slop-work, and many of their daughters do so. This has been the
custom as long as I can remember. Some of the wives were formerly
employed in winding silk for the Spitalfields weavers; but now that's
all knocked on the head. The cause of the coopers' wives taking to
slop-work is partly owing to the slackness of the trade at certain
times and partly to their living in the neighbourhood of the slop-
sellers. . . .

The usual time of labour among the coopers is from six in the
morning till eight o'clock at night (fourteen hours a day). This is
generally considered in the trade to be two hours too much, and is
looked upon as a great evil, it being considered one of the principal
reasons why so many are out of employment. The hours of labour,
however, have always been the same. The coopers are not very
partial to piece-work, though this is their usual mode of payment.
They consider it makes men do more work than they ought, and
thus deprives others of their fair share of employment. They are
never employed at day work in the shops, but I am assured that
they would prefer this mode of working to all others. Most of the
coopers are London men, having served their time in the metropolis.
About half, I am told, are the sons of former workmen.

The coopers in large establishments work in lofty brick sheds,
with large open frontages; these are usually well ventilated, which,
indeed is indispensible, on account of the fires, where there is the
slightest regard for the health and comfort of the workmen. They
work singly, each man being engaged on his own cask. When it is
finished, it is rolled into an adjacent yard, and there awaits the
testing or inspection of the foreman or master.

Nearly all the working coopers can read and write, and some are
educated men. Their normal standard is quite equal to that of the
generality of trades. They were described to me as rough but manly.
Some years ago, "strikes" were common among the coopers, and
tended to promote idleness and foster the love for drink; but within
the last twenty years strikes have been few and partial, and the men
are now opposed to them as to a bad policy.

If any disagreement arises between master and men, the president of one of the societies to be presently mentioned, waits upon
the master in a friendly manner, nor in one solitary instance has
there been a failure, the grievance being always amicably settled.

The trade of a cooper is usually acquired by an apprenticeship of
seven years. The little masters take very many apprentices, and take
them for the fees, but they have very few from the parishes. Some

of them get a premium with their apprentices of from £10 to £20, and in some instances keep the boy, finding him board and lodging for one or two years, allowing him one-third of the regular wages when he has completed a piece of work, which he is seldom able to do in less than three years' training. For the last two years of his apprenticeship, he has two-thirds of the regular wages of the trade. This system unquestionably tends to increase the number of hands willing to work for inferior wages, and so to perpetuate inferior handicraftsmen.

*Trades societies*

The Coopers have four societies in connection with their trade. One is the Parent Society and the other three are Branches. The branch societies are called the "Local Trade Societies". The Parent Society is termed the "Philanthropic", and is held at the Tower Shades, Tower-hill. The local trade societies are designated the "Hand-in-Hand"—the "Brewhouse Coopers" and the "Runlett Coopers". The first of these is held at the Old Commodore, Montague-street, Whitechapel; the second at the Queen's Head, Blackfriars; and the last at the Eight Bells, Bermondsey.

The White Coopers have no trade society, but many of them are connected with Friendly Benefit Societies of various kinds.

The following table will show the number of society men and non-society men in the Cooper's trade, exclusive of the white and the dock coopers:

|  | In Society | Out of Society | Total of Society and Non-Society men in each Branch |
|---|---|---|---|
| Philanthropic Coopers | 460 |  | 460 |
| Hand-in-Hand Coopers | 100 | 70 | 170 |
| Brewhouse Coopers | 70 | 70 | 140 |
| Runlett Coopers | 60 | 40 | 100 |
|  | 690 | 180 | 870 |

The objects of the trades societies in connection with the coopers are twofold—first, for the purposes of trade; secondly, for philanthropic objects.

The trade purposes consist of the upholding of such prices as the operatives consider a just remuneration for their work, and of the maintenance of their members when out of employ; while the philanthropic objects are the support of their aged and helpless members, and the allowance of a certain sum at the death of a member or a member's wife. These objects are carried out by assembling at their society houses weekly, monthly, and half-yearly, and contributing a portion of their weekly earnings in aid of the funds. The affairs of each society are placed in the hands of a president, secretary, two auditors, four stewards, and six committee-men. If an individual wishes to become a member, he is proposed at one of the monthly meeting nights, and admitted by a show of hands on the following night of meeting.

The society houses are not houses of call, but simply "trade societies". However, when any of the members are out of work, they make it known to the president, who, being acquainted with the trade generally, can tell whether there are any fresh hands wanted; and, if there be an opening, the president sends such individuals as are qualified to undertake the job. The non-society men call at the various cooperages and solicit employment.

The amount of contribution varies with the "society". The members of the parent society contribute a per centage of their earnings—one-forty-eighth part, or a farthing in every shilling they obtain by their labour; those belonging to the branch societies pay 1s. per month. The "benefits" of the societies are 6s. per week to the unemployed members during the season of slackness, £5 at the death of a member, and £3 at the death of a member's wife. There is a superannuation fund in connection with the parent society, from which an aged or infirm member is allowed 3s. per week. There are at present seven members in receipt of this fund. The wages of the white coopers have been reduced full two-thirds within the last twelve years, and this, I am informed is mainly owing to the Irish underworking the rest of the trade. Machinery has not in the least affected the coopers' art, as at present, to use the words of the operatives, "it cannot touch it". The coopers having no connection with country societies, they entirely discountenance all relief of tramps; they are firmly persuaded, they say, that it merely fosters idleness and vagabondism.

The coopers' trade, like other trades, ebbs and flows. Their brisk season continues generally from May to Christmas, and is then slack from Christmas to May. During the slack time the unemployed coopers repair to the different docks, where they generally obtain two or three days' work during the week. As to the cause of these fluctuations in trade, the coopers cannot assign any particular reason. The present season has been the best that they have realized for many years past, there having been a great quantity of new work required.[15]

---

[15] Testimonies from wet and dry coopers followed here.

## The "slop" part of the trade

"The "slop" part of the coopering trade consists in what are called "cutting shops", and the "small trade-working masters". But these are confined solely to the "dry and white work". The cutting shops usually employ non-society men, with a number of apprentices, and are enabled to undersell the more honourable tradesmen by this cheaper labour. Many of these cutting masters are engaged in the manufacture of one article alone, and I was informed of one such master who had a number of hands continually engaged in converting old American flour barrels into bottled-porter casks, at 1d. a piece. One of the small employers whom I visited, lived at the corner of a low, dirty street. His premises were entered by means of what was literally a hole in the wooden wall, on which swung a small door. In the interior of his shop were heaped hoops, staves, and all the requirements of the coopers' trade. In an inner room, four men were at work. "I make only colour kegs," he said, "and have been in the trade many years. My men work by the piece, and the best and quickest hands make from 32s. to 33s. a week. Inferior hands get from 22s. to 25s. I used to employ fourteen hands, where I now employ half that number. Nearly all colour kegs, more than nineteen-twentieths of those made, are for exportation. For the home trade, a colourman will make the same casks go backwards and forwards fifty times. There used to be 800 hands employed in the wood keg trade for colourmen; now there is not half that quantity. The falling off is owing to the demand for sheet iron kegs, made under Brown's patent by steam machinery. They now make from 300,000 to 400,000 iron kegs every year, and have done so for five or six years past. They are much neater casks than the wooden to look at. I don't know about their durability, but that's little looked to in the export trade. . . ."

The small employers in the neighbourhood of St. George's-in-the-East now number about thirty or forty, whereas a few years back I am credibly informed there were from 100 to 120 located in that neighbourhood. The little trade-working masters consist principally of the casual hands working as coopers at the docks. There appear to be two or three reasons for the dock coopers taking to make up small articles on their own account. One is, the early hour at which their labour at the docks ceases, so that a man, if in any way industrious, on returning home in the early part of the evening usually sets to work for himself, and makes up in his over-time tubs, pails, or kegs, which he either sells to the country hawkers, or his wife carries them round town for sale to the houses or shops. Another reason why the journeymen coopers become small trade-working masters, is owing to the uncertainty of all kinds of dock labour. . . . The "extra coopers", therefore when not wanted at the docks, employ their spare time in manufacturing small articles on speculation, for which, as in the cabinet trade, they are obliged to find a market as soon as made, whether there be a demand for them or not. The third and principal reason is the small capital required for journeymen coopers to begin labouring for themselves in the white branch of the trade, as well as upon the smaller articles appertaining to dry work.

### Interview with an Irish small master

The majority of the small masters are Irishmen, living in the neighbourhood of the docks; one of these, whom I saw, resided in a court at the back of Rosemary-lane. In the centre of this place stood clothes-props supporting lines laden with yellow-looking shirts and brown blankets, which swung backwards and forwards in the wind. Seated on the stones outside of each of the doors, were small groups of fuzzy-haired Irishwomen, all engaged in chopping wood and talking to one another across the court. The working cooper himself was a good-looking intelligent man, with the handsome grey eye and long sweeping lash peculiar to the natives of the Emerald Isle. He was very proud of the neatness of his sitting-room, and took me upstairs expressly to show it to me. It was decorated with portraits of Mitchell, Meagher, and Father Moore, together with a picture of the Siege of Limerick dedicated to the women of Ireland. Downstairs, amid the shavings, lay a copy of the *Nation* newspaper, in which my informant told me there was "some sublime poethry".

"I am a small master," he said, "though I don't know exactly that you can call me so rightly—I don't employ anyone. You can put me down a manufacturer, if you please. I make up things on my own account. I have been at coopering now I dare say 26 years. I was about 14 when I first went to it. It was in Ireland I learnt the trade. I used to be engaged in my own unfortunate counthry making provision casks, but now that trade's entirely done away with. I came over here—let me see— fourteen years last May. Then I got my name on at the West India Dock as an extra cooper, and I have worked there in succession every year since. I got a number, and have kept at it all along. After working in the docks, if I don't feel too much fatigued, I do a bit of work for myself when I get home at night; or if I have an order for my customers that requires speed, then I stop here and work at it altogether. You see I am not obligated to go to work at the docks unless I please. I should say that, take it the year through, I am employed at the docks about three months out of the twelve. After October, the season is looked upon to be over, and it begins again about April. I don't always go to work after coming from the docks; but the most of the small masters works after their dock labour.

"When I work at home, I begin about seven and keep on till about nine at night, that's fourteen hours. One small master I know begins often at four or five in the morning. You see it all depends upon the industrial habits of men. If you're at work for an employer, you must leave off at a certain hour, but if you're your own master, you can work all night, if you've a fancy. I've often worked all night myself. I feel more pleasure doing a bit for myself here by candle-light than if I was wandering about the streets. I sell the goods I make to hawkers, and they make a living of it by hawking them to the public and to shops. I am in the habit of making oval tubs of different sizes—that's the principal branch that I'm employed in. Other small masters are engaged in making flour kegs, colour kegs, oyster barrels, mustard kegs—but that's all dry work. The small masters never do any large work. Some of the small masters will take round a sample of their work to a colour or mustard factory, or to a merchant, and so get an order; and many make up goods on speculation, and then take them round to sell. As simple a trade as oyster barrels is, still there's hundreds made up on speculation, and taken round to be sold. I've made them up myself. A man does this because he can't get other employment. May be there'll be a slack-age at the docks, and a man will rather do that than be idle and starve. . . ."

# THE DRESSMAKERS AND MILLINERS

## LETTER LXXV—24 OCTOBER 1850[1]

*Number of dressmakers and milliners*

The working *dressmakers* and *milliners* of London are, as a body, composed of a more mixed class of the community than are the members of any other calling. Among them are the daughters of clergymen, of military and naval officers, and of surgeons, farmers, and tradesmen of every description. The great majority of these dressmakers—fully three-fourths of them—have been reared in the country. The number of dressmakers and milliners in London, at the time of taking the last census (1841), was 20,780. Of this number 17,183 were female of twenty years of age and upwards, and 3,480 under that age. The remaining 117 were males, 10 of whom were below twenty years of age.

*Division of labour*

The business of dressmaking is carried on by two classes—the dressmaker and the milliner. The dressmaker's work is confined to the making of ladies' dresses, including every kind of outwardly-worn gown or robe. The milliner's work is confined to making caps, bonnets, scarfs, and all outward attire worn by ladies other than the gown; the bonnets, however, which tax the skill of the milliner, are what are best known as "made bonnets"—such as are constructed of velvet, satin, silk, muslin, or any other textile fabric. Straw bonnet-making is carried on by a distinct class, and in separate establishments. The milliner, however, often *trims* a straw bonnet, affixing the ribbons, flowers, or other adornments. When the business is sufficiently large, one or more millinery hands are commonly kept solely to bonnet-making, those best skilled in that art being of course selected; but every efficient milliner so employed is expected to be expert also at cap-making, and at all the other branches of the trade. The milliner is accounted a more skilled labourer than the dressmaker.

Of milliners and dressmakers there are, as in most other trades of the present day, two distinct classes—viz., the adequately and

---

[1] Letters LXX–LXXIV treated the transport workers.

the poorly paid, or, in other words, those belonging to the "honourable", and those belonging to the "dishonourable" or "slop" part of the trade. I shall confine my present letter to an exposition of the earnings and conditions of the former class.

The division of labour which I have pointed out is closely observed in all large establishments, though in some only millinery work is done, and in others only dressmaking; but in the majority of the London houses the two branches are carried on together. The workers employed consist of apprentices, improvers, assistants (including day workers), third hands, second hands, and first hands. Each department has a *first hand*, whose business it is to wait upon the customers, receive orders, take measures, cut out the material (unless a second hand or another first hand be so employed in a very large establishment), and give it out to the work-women to be made. . . . Each department has also a *second hand* or *superintendent*, who works along with the others, directs or superintends their labour, and instructs the improvers and apprentices. She is responsible for the proper execution of the work, and for the due exertion of industry on the part of all employed. A *third hand* is employed in a similar way.

The *assistants* are hired workwomen, employed on the premises in some cases, and when so employed sleeping there, and in most cases boarding with their employers. Some are engaged by the month, or the quarter, or the year; others by the week or the season. Their "busy time" is during the fashionable season, or about six months out of the twelve, from February to July. A week or two before and after Christmas is also a busy time in many houses, and in others six weeks before Christmas for the winter fashions, and three or four weeks after it.

The *improvers* are a very numerous class. When a girl has completed her apprenticeship or other term of engagement in a country town, or even in Edinburgh, or Dublin, she comes to London *to improve*. If she has an intention of establishing herself in business in the town where her parents and friends reside, she and they feel that it would be hopeless to attain the "patronage" of the neighbouring ladies unless she have the *prestige* of having been trained to the perfect exercise of London taste and skill—a *prestige* which must be duly maintained, when in business, by at least one annual visit to London "for the fashions", The improver is engaged for a given period (generally for two years) and is almost always boarded in the house of her employer, who, not unfrequently, receives a premium with her, while the improver receives no remuneration for her labour. She is there not to be paid, but to be improved. The premiums with improvers vary from £10 to £50.

The *apprentice* is the young girl placed with a dressmaker to be instructed in all the "art and mystery" of the calling. If she be lodged and boarded in the house, as is frequently the case, a premium is paid with her. If she remain with her friends, lodging with them, and going home also to her meals, no premium is given, while her labour is considered merely equivalent to her tuition, and she consequently receives no payment for what she does. The term of apprenticeship is from two to five years, and the premium from £10 to £50; sometimes, however, but rarely, it is even higher. In addition to these varieties of workwomen, but connected more particularly with dressmakers, are the *day-workers*—a class of assistants hired, as their name expresses, by the day, in contradistinction to those who are engaged by the month or year.[2]

## A first-rate establishment in the West-end

I now subjoin the account given by a lady concerning the internal economy of some of the first-rate milliners' establishments at the West-end. I give it as it was furnished to me in writing:

"A first-rate house of business, conducted by a dressmaker and milliner of the highest fashion, is always a very large house, more like a mansion for a nobleman than a milliner's establishment. In some there is nothing to indicate that they are places of business, except a plate on the door with the names of the proprietors engraved thereon; while others have two or three splendid plate-glass windows—each window consisting of one pane—with a brass bar outside, across which a lace vest or an embroidered collar or handkerchief is hung, to show the business carried on within. These large houses are not only milliners and dressmakers, but they supply every kind of ladies' wearing apparel, with the exception of shoes. A lady goes to order perhaps her wedding *trousseau*, or a train for the Queen's Drawing-room, or her morning and evening dresses. She alights from her carriage. The hall-door is opened by the footman of the establishment, who bows her into what is called the 'premier magazin', or 'first show-room'. Then comes a French lady, dressed in a silk dress, with short sleeves, and a very small lace cap, with long streamers of ribbon that fall over her shoulders down to her feet. She walks before the lady to a counter, and places a chair for her. These French ladies are styled 'magazinières', or 'showroom-women'. There are generally five or six of these showroom-women kept in a first-rate establishment. The first showroom is about 130 feet long, and 60 feet wide. In every other panel there is a looking-glass from

[2] Information about conditions in first-rate houses and the morals of the girls followed.

the floor to the ceiling, set in a handsome carved gilt frame. The floor is covered with a very expensive carpet of a rich pattern, sometimes of a violet and amber colour. The window-curtains are of rich dark green velvet. In different parts of the room there are counters of polished ebony, elegantly ornamented with gilding. The lady customer is then shown an assortment of magnificent silks and velvets. She looks them all over, tries the shades in different lights, asks the Frenchwoman which is most becoming by daylight, and which most becoming by candlelight. After a considerable deliberation, she selects one or two dresses of whatever colour she may want. . . . When the lady visitor has been bowed out to her carriage, and has driven off from the establishment, the showroom-woman measures off a certain quantity of silk or velvet (whichever it may be), sends for the first hand dressmaker, and gives her the order to make the dress. After this, as soon as convenient to the lady, the first hand goes to take her measure. For this purpose a one-horse Brougham, with a servant in livery, is brought to the door, and the first hand goes in it to measure the lady for her dress. When she returns she gives it out to another first hand, who takes it up into the work-room and cuts it out.

"The work-room is nearly as large as the first show-room, with a fireplace at each end. Three large deal tables run down the middle, with a gas-pipe over them, and there are as many chairs as the room will hold, all filled with young ladies working at the tables. These young ladies are generally short. If there is a tall one amongst them she is usually an 'improver', and has grown up before she learned her business. Very few of them can be called pretty, for if their features are well formed, they are so thin and pale-looking that their appearance is not very prepossessing. The first hand comes in with the dress, and throws it down on the first table she comes to. The young ladies look up to see what is the matter. At last one ventures to ask, 'Who is it for?' 'Oh,' the first hand answers, 'it's for Lady or Mrs. So-and-so, and she wants it to-morrow morning.' 'To-morrow morning,' cry half-a-dozen voices, 'how is it possible, when we have so many other dresses to do? Why, she has kept us up three nights this week already.' 'Well, it's of no use,' replies the first hand, 'she must have it; so we must all sit up to-night again.'

"Shortly afterwards one of the porters comes to the door, and says, 'Please Miss —— have you got any skirts? Mrs. ——'s boy has called to know if you have any.' 'Yes, wait a minute, I have one,' and gives him the skirt of the dress. He takes it down, and in an obscure corner of the hall stands Mrs. ——'s boy, a ragged dirty little creature, about seven years old. 'Here,' says the porter, 'take this to your mother, and tell her if she doesn't get it done by nine o'clock to-morrow morning she will get no more work from this house.' 'I shall be sure to tell her, sir,' the boy replies, taking the skirt. He goes his way with the magnificent Genoa velvet under his arm, and walks slowly along until he comes to a dirty narrow street, in the neighbourhood of Carnaby Market, Golden-square. He stops at a house, pushes open the door, for it has no fastening, and mounts to the top of the house. On the landing-place there are washing-tubs and slop-pails full of dirty water, saucepans, frying-pans, and old stumps of brooms. He makes his way through these with the 'velvet skirt', and enters a room to the left; there being four families living on this story. The garret he enters is a sort of triangular-shaped room, about twelve feet square; the window is near the ceiling. In one corner of the apartment there is a small skeleton stove; in the opposite corner stands an old broken bedstead, and in one an old rickety chair. In the middle of the room is the deal table and around this are seated seven women, dirty, thinly clad, with pale and hollow countenances, weak red-looking eyes, and lean emaciated frames. The one working at the head of the table is Mrs. ——, the boy's mother. Her husband is dead; she is about middle age. She rises and takes the skirt from the boy and demands of him what is wanted. He answers that it is to go in at nine. 'Nine in the morning!' she exclaims. 'Why I have got six from the City to go home at eight.' 'How do you know,' inquires one of the workpeople, 'that it is the lady's fault? I dare say the lady who this dress is for knows nothing about how it is made. She pays a very high price to the French people whom you have it from.'

"I must now return to the work-room at the dressmaker's where the bodies and sleeves of the lady's dresses are made. A few minutes after the porter goes away with the skirt a bell rings, on hearing which the first hand gets up to go down to tea, and all the others follow her. All who are employed in the house take their meals together. In the class of houses I speak of there is a superintendent at the head of the table, and in others the mistress of the establishment serves at the meals. When there is a superintendent, the mistress does not appear. The tea consists of bread and butter and tea of very good quality, and all can have as much as they wish. After tea they go up to work again until ten o'clock, when they go down to supper, and partake of cold meat, cheese, and table ale. They then go up to work again, and work probably until four the next morning. Perhaps one of them may faint, and ask if she may leave off and go to bed, as she feels too ill to continue working. The first hand says that it is quite impossible, as, if she did allow her to go to bed, the work could not be done. So the poor creature sits down to work again. At four in the morning they leave off, and retire to rest.

The first hand has a small room to herself, very nicely furnished. The room in which the young ladies sleep is at the top of the house—about fifty feet long and forty wide, but no carpet on the floor, and neither drawers nor wardrobes. The young people keep their things in the boxes they bring with them. There are two or three dressing-tables with looking-glasses and a few chairs. There are eight beds in it, and two sleep in each bed. At half past seven the young ladies are obliged to assemble to breakfast. They have tea and bread and butter of very good quality, and as much as they wish to eat. They go up to the workroom at eight; and at ten the lady's dress is finished. The first hand tries it on one of the young ladies, and looks it well all over to see that there is no fault. It is then packed up in a wicker basket lined with oilskin, and one of the porters (of whom there are generally four or five kept in the large houses) is called up, and the dress is given to him to take home. . . .

"In a large house they keep five or six showroom-women, six or seven first hands, and from fifteen to twenty young people as second and third hands. The first hands have from £40 to £100 a-year, and the others from £12 to £20, and their board and lodging. Besides these, they employ in the season from sixty to eighty day-workers. These large and very fashionable houses seldom take more than four apprentices and two or three improvers, as they do not take them for the sake of the premium, like others. In some of the large houses there are eight or ten domestic servants. . . ."

*Statement from a first hand*

From a first hand in one of the best houses I had the following statement :

"I have been five or six years a first hand in dressmaking in different houses. In my recollection there has been an improvement in the treatment of young women in the superior houses. I cannot say that the sleeping rooms are better ventilated than they were, but they are less crowded. Where there might be eight, there are now six. I attribute this improvement a good deal to the Association. I have nothing to do with it myself, so I speak impartially. In a bad case, the manager will call on the proprietor and expostulate, or, perhaps, some member of the committee will call, and that has a great effect. The prices and profits of the business are not what they were. I have known great shabbiness practised by great people, even on a wedding occasion; and yet they wanted everything in the best style. I have waited upon very many ladies, and have generally, but not always, been politely treated; but some ladies, both young and old and middle-aged, are so very hard to please about dress, that it is very trying to the temper. I had £35, board and lodging, the first year I was a first hand, and £40 the second. I have never had less than £40. Many working dressmakers, and more milliners with good earnings, might save money than do so. I can hardly tell how some spend it, when they are so little out."[3]

### A young day-worker

One young woman, a day-worker, who lived with her mother, a poor widow, told me that she earned 7s. a week eight or nine months of the year, and not 1s. 6d. a week the three or four months she was not at her usual work. "There are," she said, "several respectable tradesmen who get day-work for their daughters, and who like that way of employing them better than in situations as assistants, because their girls then sleep at home, and earn nice pocket-money or dress-money by day-work. That, again, is a disadvantage to a young person like me who depends on her needle for her living. The most of our day-workers are from twenty to thirty, some from fifteen to twenty, and a few between thirty and forty; but I know of no old woman who is a day-worker in the superior trade. You must be quick and have good sight. You never, or very seldom, see a milliner or dressmaker wear glasses, unless she's quite young and does it to preserve her sight, or because she thinks she looks better in them, or unless she's a first hand and is independent and doesn't care. I have gone from my work to my mother's at all hours of the night, as I always endeavour to work overhours if I can, and I never was insulted in the streets. I have heard, and a very good thing it is, that if any young person is insulted by any bad drunken fellow in the street, the police-inspectors, if she tells them she is a dressmaker going home from her work, and they are satisfied she is so, are instructed to call a cab and send her home in it, and the Association pays the expense."—(I ascertained that this was the case).[4]

### The Dressmakers' and Milliners' Association

Day-workers were unknown as a systematic part of the business of dressmaking until the latter part of the year 1844. As this mode of employment was called into existence by the exertions of the "Association for the Aid and Benefit of Dressmakers and Milliners", before alluded to, it is necessary that I should give an account of the institution.

[3] A short section dealing with a second-hand, an improver and an apprentice followed.

[4] Next came testimonies about hours of work and diet in the best houses.

In 1841, Parliament instituted the "Children's Employment Commission", for which a mass of evidence, showing the then state of the "London dressmakers and milliners", was collected by Mr. R. D. Grainger. The evils of long hours, insufficient food, and ill-ventilated working and sleeping apartments, which were then exposed, called public attention to the matter, and the society in question was established in March 1843, chiefly through the exertions of a committee of ladies. The objects of the Association are :

"1. To induce the principals of dressmaking and millinery establishments to limit the hours of actual work to 12 per diem, and to abolish working on Sundays. 2. To promote improved ventilation. 3. to aid in obviating the evils connected with the present system, by inducing ladies to allow sufficient time for the execution of orders. 4. To afford pecuniary assistance to deserving young persons in temporary distress. 5. To afford to such young persons as require it early and effective medical advice, change of air, and other assistance in sickness."

The report for the year ending March 25, 1850, says :

"When the effort to reduce the inordinate hours of work formerly prevailing in the dressmaking and millinery business was first made by this Association, it was immediately perceived that the only effectual method of securing this object, without injuriously interfering with the occupation itself, would be to introduce a system of registration, by means of which it was confidently anticipated that any presumed necessity for overtaxing the powers of the young women, especially during the busy season of the year, would be entirely obviated, inasmuch as the principals, by applying at the office, might, without delay, be provided with any number of extra assistants, according to the emergency. That this expectation was well founded has been amply confirmed by the experience of several years. The number of young persons registered in the books of the Association has, until last year, steadily continued to increase. . . ."

## LETTER LXXVI—31 OCTOBER 1850

*Honourable and dishonourable*

Of the twenty thousand "young ladies" working as Milliners and Dressmakers in the metropolis it is difficult to say how many belong to the "honourable" part of the trade—that is to say, to the better paid and better fed portion of it. The only means of arriving at any conclusion on this point is by consulting the registry of that most admirable institution, the Dressmakers' and Milliners' Association.

There are upwards of 7,500 names entered on the books of that establishment; of these, 1,500, I am informed, are employed in the country, the remaining 6,000 being engaged by the better class of milliners and dressmakers in London. As the Association supplies "hands" only to the more respectable houses, we may assume that there are upwards of ten thousand young women working for the "dishonourable", or slop part of the trade.

The Milliners and Dressmakers constitute a peculiar class of workpeople—a part of the remuneration for their labour being paid in kind rather than money. Those who are engaged by the year, like domestic servants, not only receive wages, but are generally boarded and lodged in the houses of their employers; while the day-workers, or those who receive a daily salary, are supplied with their tea. Hence it is evident that those establishments which seek to undersell or compete with their neighbours by reducing the price of the labour of their workpeople, may do so as well by supplying them with a less quantity or inferior quality of food, or by providing them with worse lodging than is usual in the trade, as by diminishing the amount of their salary. Moreover they may attain the same end by extending the ordinary hours of labour, and so making a small number of hands do the work of many. Such, I find, are the common expedients resorted to for reducing the ordinary remuneration of the operative milliners and dressmakers. . . .

*More classes of houses*

The employers of the operative dressmakers are divisible into two distinct classes—according as they have or have not the skirts of the dresses made on the premises. The more fashionable houses always put out the skirts, and of these houses there are again two kinds—"first" and "second" rates, as they are usually termed in the trade. A first-rate house is one where Court dresses are made and which works for the ladies of the nobility rather than the gentry In a second-rate house, Court dresses are but seldom furnished, the customers belonging to the middle rather than the upper classes Those houses where the skirts are made at home seldom work for "gentlefolks", but are supported by the wives of tradesmen and mechanics. These are termed third- and fourth-rate houses, and they are distinguished from one another by the circumstance that in a third-rate "establishment" more silk dresses than cotton ones are made, whereas in the fourth-rate houses it is the reverse.

But these constitute what are called the private milliners, where no show is made. Besides these there are the shops in which the goods are displayed and ticketed in the windows. These are divided

into the West- and East-end "show-shops". The first-class of these
establishments is at the West-end, in Regent-street; the second-class
in Oxford-street, Edgware and Tottenham-court Roads; and the
third-class in Cranbourne-street. At the East-end, the first-class
milliner shops are situate on Ludgate-hill and St. Paul's-church-
yard; and the second-class in Whitechapel and the Commercial-
road. . . . The first-rate shops all put out their skirts and mantles,
whereas the second-rate, like the inferior private establishments, do
a great quantity of this work on the premises. Further there are
the cap and drawn-bonnet warehouses, where the articles are produced wholesale, there being now a large export trade carried on
in drawn bonnets, a considerable number of which are sent off every
year to Canada, Australia, and the British settlements. Then, again,
there are the skirt and mantle-makers, or rather middlemen, who
take them out by hundreds from the linendrapers; and, lastly, the
wardrobe shops, where ladies' old dresses are purchased, and either
re-made, or mended, as may be needed.[5]

*A third-rate house in the suburbs*

I had the following account of a third-rate house in one of the
best parts of the suburbs :

"Mrs. —— was in another way of business, but connected with
ladies' dress. Her husband was a humble man working at his business, but Mrs. —— had lofty ideas, and what was earned was not
sufficient to keep up her gentility; so she thought she would com-
bine the dressmaking with her former business, and she advertised
in the newspapers for apprentices and improvers, stating the extraordinary comforts they would have at her house. Although she had
then only a small parlour, her advertisement was answered by people
in a distant part of the country, who were tempted by the lowness of
her terms, and she got four apprentices at £20 premium each, and
three improvers at £10; so that she received £110, and with that she
took the other part of the house, and furnished it. She then had
home the apprentices and improvers. There were but four rooms
in the house, and she made the most of them. The parlour in which
she had been accustomed to live she made the dining-room, and a
small room over that, at the back of the house, was converted into
the work-room; and over that was the bedroom, in which the young
people were to sleep. Mrs. —— had a large family, and in this room
slept her six daughters—the four apprentices, the three improvers,
and the first-hand, who has to teach them—Mrs. —— and none of
her family knowing anything of the business. The other room was

[5] An account of a second-rate house has been cut.

that of Mr. and Mrs. ——. She engaged a person as first-hand, and
got a very good business. As the apprentices and improvers leave her
she gets others, and makes quite a living by the premiums she gets;
and if their parents complain that they have not learnt anything,
she says that it was owing to their stupidity. The first-hand she had
died not very long ago, and she sent to the Association for one, and
she was referred to a young lady who was going to leave the situation
she was in. I had better let her tell the story herself, as I heard it.

"Mrs. —— came to Mrs. —— where I was living, and I agreed
to go for £18 a year. Mrs. —— went upstairs to give her my reference, and Mrs. —— said, 'I am quite satisfied, but I am afraid she
does not look strong, and I am pestered out of my life by all my
young people going home ill.' Mrs. —— said I could but try, and I
did try. I promised to go the following Monday. I arrived there
about nine in the evening. I had been occupied all day, and had had
nothing to eat since breakfast. Mrs. —— met me at the door of
her shop, and took me upstairs to the work-room. 'Do you want any
supper?' she said, 'we have all done.' It was asked in such a tone
that it was impossible to say yes—so I went faint and weary to bed
that night. I never saw such a desolate-looking place. There was
not the sign of a smile on one of their countenances. The bed-room
was deplorable. Six or seven old ricketty bedsteads, and one wash-
stand, with two dirty broken basins. When we got up in the morning there was such pulling and dragging of one another to get at
the basins; and at last it came to a fight.

"Mrs. —— and the Misses —— (her daughters), and the Masters
—— and Mr. ——, all had a secret breakfast, and then she rang
for us. When we went in they were all seated, as if they had not
had anything. The breakfast was deplorable. The tea was scarcely
coloured, and was sweetened with a small portion of the coarsest
brown sugar, without milk. The bread was as hard as if it had been
a week old; it was all cut ready for us with the least scrape of
rancid butter on it. I could not eat the bread, and felt quite ill from
want. I had to go out to try on a lady's dress after breakfast; so I
bought myself a bun, or I should have been starved. At dinner there
was a joint of meat and a plain pudding. Mr. —— carved, and he
cut two bits of meat as thin as a wafer, and put them on each plate;
and if any of us asked for more, Mrs. —— would say to one of her
daughters, 'Do you want any more, love?' 'Oh no, mama,' would
be the certain answer, 'I have had quite sufficient!' After this anybody was, of course, afraid to ask for a fresh supply. We then each
had a piece of pudding. They never allowed bread at dinner, and
the potatoes were of the worst kind. At five we had tea, the same
as breakfast; and supper at half-past nine—a very small piece of

Dutch cheese about an inch square, and a quarter of a round of bread.

"I did not go into work after supper, but went to the door to see if I could get a breath of air; when I heard Mrs. ——'s voice like a fury all over the house calling my name. I went to her, and she said, 'Why have you not gone to work again? this is no time to leave off.' I said, 'That I thought as it was not in the season, I need not work late.' 'And do you suppose,' she answered, 'that I am going to keep you and pay you for nothing?' We worked every night until twelve or one. The ladies were pleased with the things made for them, and told Mrs. —— so; and consequently she was very anxious for me to stay, and let me into the secret of her private dinners and breakfasts, and said I might join them if I would stay, and keep the secret from the others. But I could not stay. I never was so wretched in my life. The apprentices could not complain to their friends, as they were all from a long way off in the country."

This account applies equally well to many a third-rate house in town.[6]

[6] The rest of the letter dealt with mantle-makers working for warehouses, dressmakers in private houses, and the milliners of the East-end.

# THE HATTERS

## LETTER LXXVII—7 NOVEMBER 1850

*Geography of the trade*

The hat manufactories of London are to be found in the district to the left of the Blackfriars road (as the bridge is crossed from the Middlesex side), stretching towards and beyond the Southwark-bridge-road towards to the High-street, Borough, and to Tooley-street. There are, moreover, no inconsiderable number of hat factories in Bermondsey. Hat making is almost entirely confined to the Surrey side of the Thames, and until within the last twenty years, or thereabouts, it was carried on chiefly in Bermondsey. In Bermondsey, however, there are still many large "hatteries"; one of them, the property of a wealthy Quaker firm, ranks among the largest in London, rarely employing, in the slackest season, fewer than 90 or 100 men, and sometimes as many as 300, with, of course, a proportionate number of the women who are employed in the trade. Although hat-making has experienced a migration, the trades-men who supply the hatters with the materials of manufacture are still more thickly congregated in Bermondsey than elsewhere. These tradesmen comprise wool-staplers, hat-furriers, hat-curriers, hat-block makers, hat-druggists, hat-dyers, hat-lining makers, hat-bow-string makers, hat-trimming and buckle makers, hat calico makers, hat-box makers, hat-silk shag makers, and hat-brush makers. These several appellations indicate the character of the business carried on; only two of them require any explanation here.

*Hat furriers and curriers*

The hat *furriery* business, as regards beaver skins, is now little more than a twentieth of what it was twelve years ago. The hat furriers remove the fur of the beaver, the hare, or the rabbit from the skin—which, when thus denuded, is called a pelt—and they prepare this fur for the uses of the hatter. An intelligent man calcu-lated that from fifteen to twenty years ago, and for some years preceding, four millions of beavers were killed annually for the supply of the hat-makers of the United Kingdom. . . . The trappers and hunters had more and more difficulty to keep up the supply of beaver skins—those animals being pursued so hotly and continu-ously that they were exterminated in many of their most accustomed

haunts, or retreated before their pursuers further into the interior
of the American forests; and as the importation fell off the introduction of a new material became imperative.

The *Hat Currier* prepares the leather lining, which is made of
sheep or well-grown lamb's skin. After the wool is removed the pelt
is slit into two portions. The surface (to which the wool was attached)
is called a skiver, and is dressed for the hat lining; the other division
is usually curried as a "chamois", the common wash-leather used in
cleaning plate, windows, etc., and is largely hawked.

### The manufacture of silk hats, now the staple of the trade

The first process in the manufacture of silk or velvet hats—for
they are identical—is "body-making". Silk and velvet hats are now
the great staple of the trade. Calico, made for the purpose of silk hat
body-making, is steeped in a solution of gum shellac, and wrung
whilst wet, after being thoroughly saturated; it is then dried on a
frame. The part to form the brim and the "tip" (or crown) is subjected to the same process, the brims and tip being afterwards sewn
to the body by women. When thoroughly dried, the body, &c., is put
round a block, the desired shape of the hat, the ends being nicely fitted
to adhere together by the application of the admixture just described;
and the calico thus prepared is "ironed to make it firm". In an
inferior silk hat the sewing together of the ends soon becomes apparent. The heated irons used to weigh twelve and fourteen lb. The
application of spirits of wine, or of naphtha, and after that of an
oil varnish to the body, completes the "bodymaker's" work—and the
hat, in its so far advanced state, then comes into the hands of the
*finisher*. The master, or foreman, gives the finisher the quantity of
"silk" required. This material is a silk plush, made for the purpose,
the surface being that shown in the "nap" of the hat. This silk is
cut "on the bias", as that "puts it on the stretch, and it sticks better."
It is damped on the under side, and so readily adheres to the prepared body—the adjoining parts of the silk, alike in the body and
the brim, being "closed", in a good hat, with the utmost nicety. Any
"bump", even the slightest, at this adjoinment, is bad workmanship,
and the finisher may be twitted with being "fit for the fowls", or best
suited to work for the slop-trade.

After this comes the *shaper's* art. He is considered the most accomplished workman, and, in the language of the trade, "puts the curl
in". He forms the brim, to make it assume and retain a graceful
curve, by ironing it on blocks, and adjusting it, by his eye, to the
shape required. This is the last process, as far as the men's labour
is concerned. The irons used by the finishers and shapers weigh

about 8 lbs.; they are provided by the employer, and cost about 2d. or 3d. per lb. The women's work is then again called into exercise to affix the linings. These are of silk, of muslin, or of glazed calico, as regards the body or upper part of the hat—and of light or dark coloured, or black patent (glazed) leather attached above the interior of the brim, and coming immediately upon the head of the wearer. . . The making of the stuff or beaver hats, which were the staple of the trade until 12 years ago, is by another process, and one in some respects so different that old hands, when they could not get employment in "stuff", had almost to re-learn their craft on "silk". This they called being "whimsied".[1]

*Number of hatters*

The hatters and hat manufacturers of the metropolis in 1841 were 3,506 in number, of whom 2,600 were males of twenty years of age and upwards, the other 900 being composed of nearly 600 women, and upwards of 300 children. The Government returns do not admit of any comparison being made between these numbers and those of the previous census; for, in the Occupation Abstract of 1831, the hatters are mixed up with the hosiers—the workmen employed in those two trades being lumped together, and computed at 2,662 individuals. . . .

*Conditions in the "fair" and "foul" trades*

The hatters work by the piece, and have done so beyond the memory of the oldest members of the trade. The scale of prices I am enabled to give, through the courtesy of Mr. Holland, the secretary of the Hatters' Society. Their present average earnings are shown in the statements I have collected.

WAGES GIVEN FOR MAKING AND REPAIRING DIFFERENT KINDS OF HATS IN THE METROPOLIS DURING THE UNDER-MENTIONED YEARS

| Years | For finishing French or English short-nap, per doz. | For making gossamer bodies, per doz. | For repairing stuff bodies, per doz. |
|---|---|---|---|
| 1824–26 | None | None | 18s. |
| 1834–36 | 8s., 10s., and 14s. | 9s. and 10s. | 15s. and 18s. |
| 1844–46 | 9s., 11s., and 13s. | 8s. and 9s. | 8s. |

The above statement represents the wages paid to society-men only, whose regulations I now subjoin :

[1] The process of making stuff hats was here detailed, followed by census figures for hatters in Great Britain, as usual broken down by county.

RESOLUTIONS OF THE JOINT COMMITTEE OF THE STUFF-HATTERS' SOCIETY AND THE SILK-HATTERS' PROTECTIVE UNION, AS SANCTIONED BY A GENERAL CONGRESS OF EACH BODY.

"September, 1846.

"1st. We mutually agree not to work in any shop where the prices are below 9s., 11s., and 13s. per doz. for French or English short-nap silk finishing; 8s. and 9s. per doz. gossamer body-making; and 8s. per doz. for preparing stuff bodies.

"2nd. We mutually agree that in case of a strike by the members of one society, no man belonging to the other shall be allowed to go in, except when the object sought for by the men so striking would be positively injurious to the interest of the members of the other society.

"3rd. We mutually agree by every means in our power to suppress the system of out-door work, believing it to be pregnant with ruin to ourselves, and ultimately to our employers.

"4th. We mutually agree that if any man wishes to be asked for in any shop where there are none of the society employed to which he belongs, and the men of the shop refuse to ask for him, he shall get a man from the nearest shop where his own society men are employed to do so. But such man shall call down the regular short turn of the shop, who may, if he pleases, hear the man asked for, and see that nothing unfair takes place. In shops where both sides are working, each shall ask for their own men.

"5th. We mutually agree not to stand by more than two apprentices, either in silk or stuff, who shall serve seven years.

"6th. We mutually agree to stand by each other's caulkers for contributions and other trade business.

"7th. We mutually agree not to take any important step affecting the general interests of the trade without first communicating with each other.

"8th. And in order to prevent any serious misunderstanding, and to avoid as much as possible the existence of any ill-feeling between the members of the two societies, we earnestly recommend the members of each not to give credence to idle rumours, but in all cases to apply to the committee, who will give correct information, and see that justice be done if an injury has been sustained.

Printed by order of the joint committee.

"January, 1846."

The secretary of the Hatters' Society, in a written communication to me, says: "The prices above-named would no doubt have been maintained if it had not been for the slop-workers, who will work at any price sooner than lose the job; as it is, we have been obliged to give way, particularly in the lower qualities."

These workmen carry on their trade in large rooms, generally well ventilated and commodious, but in some employs dirty, dark and confined. Each workman has his own "plank", or "bench", as it is called in other trades, for certain stages of his work; but the men, when engaged in working their "proofs", stand round a large tub, or open vat, the "liquor" in it steaming freely. In summer the heat is often excessive, as in so many stages of the manufacture the workmen require fires. The men work in trowsers, flannel shirts, and slippers, or wooden clogs, their arms being bared above the elbows. Notwithstanding the exposure to heat, I am assured that the hatters is not an unhealthy calling, as their lives are of an average duration, and men of 65 are now working efficiently in the business.

These operatives used to drink great quantities of beer when at work—two pots, or even ten pints, a day being a frequent consumption by a man not accounted a "fuddler". There is now a great change in this respect, few drinking more than a pot a day whilst at work. In the larger shops, however, it is still the practice for a new comer to pay his "footing", which in this trade is called "garnish". A workman refusing to join in this conviviality is stigmatized as a "straight stick". A first-rate workman informed me that 18 or 19 years ago he regularly spent 18s. a week in drink, but at that time he earned as much as £4 in a week, and very frequently £3. The same workman told me that at the Wheatsheaf, a public-house near the Borough-market, 20 years back, the hatters used to be "dancing and footing it, and drinking, of course," all the week long, but that now there is nothing of the kind.

In the London houses from 12 to 20 journeymen are more frequently employed in the "fair" trade than any larger or smaller number. The majority of these journeymen, perhaps three-fourths of them, are countrymen, chiefly from Cornwall, Gloucestershire, and Lancashire, with a few Scotchmen, and a very few Irishmen. A great number of hats, principally of the cheaper sorts, used to be sent from the country to London until eleven or twelve years ago, when the substitution of silk hats for stuff put an end to the trade, or nearly so, as the country hat-makers were not sufficiently skilled in the new manufacture. Winterbourne and Hollands Common in Gloucestershire, and Oldham and its neighbouring villages in Lancashire, were places in which were many large hat factories, the trade being now in those localities only a tenth of what it was. "The stuff hands," I was told by a hatter, himself acquainted with the Gloucestershire factories, "went into silk, such as could work on silk and could get work; some emigrated, and some got navvy's work on the railways."

The demand for Paris hats, of which I have spoken, caused a

number of hatters—one man said between 200 and 300—to come from France to England; but coarse silk hats were introduced twenty years ago. These men soon became on good terms with the English workmen, and readily instructed them in the Parisian mode of workmanship. There are now about 20 Frenchmen to every 500 Englishmen in the "fair" trade, the Frenchmen being members of "society". I heard of no foreigners in the slop or "foul" trade. The best silk plush is still imported from France; it is manufactured in Paris and Lyons. The "slop", or underpaid hat-makers are known as the "foul" trade, in contradistinction to the "fair" or "honourable" trade.

The way in which a hat-maker acquires a knowledge of his craft is by apprenticeship. In the strictest branch of the "fair" trade no man is admitted as a member of "society" who has not served a seven years apprenticeship; and no master, employing society men, can have more than two apprentices at one time besides the members of his own family whom he may choose "to put to the trade", and they must be regularly "bound". The number of apprentices is not influenced, as in the printers' and some other businesses, by the number of journeymen employed. Whether a master hatter employ one journeyman or 100, he is alike limited to two apprentices. Small as this number of apprenticeships may appear, it ensures a full supply of skilled labourers.

In the "foul" or slop trade, no regulations of the kind I have described exist. The workers in this trade are men who have served no apprenticeship, or who, from drunkenness or other causes, have not kept up their payments to the society, and have ceased to be members of it—or who have left other callings, such as that of weaving, to work as hatters; a course which is facilitated by the silk hat manufacture being a much easier or less skilled process than that of the stuff hat. I was told, indeed, that sweeps and coster-mongers had "turned foul hatters". These men are somewhat equivalent to the garret masters in the cabinet-making business; but with this distinction, that the hatters do not *complete* the articles of their manufacture as does the slop cabinet-maker for the "slaughter-houses"; the "foul" hatter makes only "bodies". They are to be found about Brick-lane, Whitechapel, in Spitalfields, and in Lock's-fields, Walworth. They work in their own rooms—which the operatives in the fair trade never do—and have to find their own irons and material. They are thus "little masters", as they nearly all work on their own account. . . .

The bodies when completed are hawked to the trade, and the inferior workman, or "little master" as he may more properly be called, is of course exposed to the evils, delays, and hindrances which

I have so often pointed out as inseparable from this mode of business. These bodies are sold to the master hatters, especially the "cutting-shops", who furnish the low-priced hats, best known as the "four-and-nines". They are sometimes finished, by workmen on the premises of the purchaser, such workmen receiving a much lower remuneration than is given in the "fair" trade. Some of the bodies produced by this slop labour are, I am assured, "finished for superior work", and sold at good prices.

The "foul" hatters are many of them young men, with a smaller proportion of married men among them than is common, perhaps, among handicraftsmen. When they are married, the wives have usually some slop employment. . . . I heard the number of these little masters (who were unknown in the trade ten years ago) computed at 1,000 at the present time, and their earnings at from 10s. to 12s. a week, taking the year's average. Previously to ten years back the little masters in the trade supplied the general public, or worked to order, as "out-door hands", for the greater houses. A man "taking up the trade" has generally to pay for instruction about £2, and to supply three weeks' or a month's labour gratuitously to his instructor. A working hatter told me that in a fortnight's time he could teach a quick lad how to make calico bodies for common silk hats well enough for the slop trade.

The working hatters in the honourable trade generally take some interest in politics, and are for the most part Protectionists, as they think protection would have "kept out the French hats". Indeed, I did not meet with one Free-trader. I did not hear of their being more inclined to one particular amusement than to another, but a game at cards is common with them in the public-house when the day's work is over. They are generally married men, and reside in the neighbourhoods of the hatteries. Some of their wives are employed as hat binders and liners, but none, I am informed, work at slop-work. Among the hatters I found many intelligent men, but as a body they are certainly less advanced in education than some other classes of handicraftsmen. Some of them have saved money. . . .

## A stuff body maker

From a *stuff body maker* I had the following account :

"My father was a hatter," he said, "and I was put as an errand boy to a hat dyer, and then I learned that business; but when I was twenty, I got myself apprenticed to a hatmaker whom I knew, and who paid me the journeymen's wages, by agreement, with a small deduction for himself. I did very well at this, as I had known the business pretty well before. I did so well, indeed, that I got married during my apprenticeship. This was in the country, but near London, and I have worked in London 13 years. I am now a stuff body maker, but can make silk bodies as well. I found it necessary to learn that, since the Paris hats came in, or I might have been out of work oft enough, there are so few beaver hats made now. I now earn 30s. and 32s. a week during the busy time, and not less than 20s. in the slack. The busy time is for six or seven months; but when there's a slack my employer divides the work among us in preference to discharging hands. We like that plan better than a smaller number being kept on at full work. I have two children, and do pretty well on my earnings. If ladies' beavers came into fashion again it would be a great thing for the trade, as, after the gentlemen's summer trade was over, they would come in. I wish they would become fashionable, and in my opinion a handsome lady looks handsomest in a beaver. When beaver bonnets were last in they were so frightfully big that I'm afraid ladies got to dislike them, but the fashion may come round again."

Another stuff body maker, in better employ, averaged 36s. a week; he did average 55s. to 60s. twenty years back.

*Statement from a shaper*

The earnings of the *finishers* and *shapers* are higher than those of the body-makers, in the proportion of 40s. to 30s., or thereabouts; so that a clever body-maker generally aims at following one or other of those branches. From a shaper I had the following statement:

"I served my apprenticeship in London, and have been a journeyman, off and on, in town, for twenty-two years. I could earn three guineas a week twenty years ago, and seldom earned less than £2. I saved money then, and might have saved more, but I am well satisfied as it is, and needn't have much fear when a rainy day comes. The trade is not what it was, but I make from 35s. to 40s. still in a busy time, and from 20s. to 25s. or 28s. in a slack. Hatters are an independent set of men still, but they were more so. If a master said a word that wasn't deserved, when I first knew the trade, a journeyman would put on his coat and walk out, and perhaps get work at the next shop. It's different now. The 'fouls' have become more numerous, and we are afraid of letting them into good shops, though I don't know why we should be afraid, for few of them can work well enough. None indeed can work well enough on the best stuff. There used to be far more drinking among hatters when I was a lad. I have known some of them be steady and industrious for the week, and on a Saturday night order 'a bottle of wine in a white bottle' (decanter), just for themselves. A man was almost forced to drink a lot of beer at that time in a workshop, or he would be counted a sneak. Now we do just as we like in that way. . . ."[2]

## A weaver turned little master

The most numerous class of little masters I have already described. From one of the class I received the following account. He was a pale, weak-eyed looking man, with a stoop, as if contracted by leaning over his work. When I saw him he was busy at work in the garret of an old and apparently frail house, the narrow stairs seeming to bend under the tread. The walls of his room had been recently white-washed. A penny sheet almanac was pinned over the fire-place, and was almost illegible from the smoke it was exposed to, "when the wind was in the north", the man said. The furniture was a small bed, covered by a thin but clean rug, on a heavy old frame, a table, two chairs, a stool, a hatter's plank, fitted below the small window, a kettle, a gridiron, and a few pots and pans.

"I was a weaver in the north," he said; "never mind where. I left home in a bit of a scrape, but for nothing dishonest, and so we'll say nothing about that. I was a fool, and that's a fact. I had £9 or £10 to call my own, fairly, and I came to London, as fools often do. I found I could as soon have got work at being a lawyer as at my own trade—so, as I had an acquaintance a hatter, he said to me, 'learn hatting.' I bargained with him, and wish I hadn't. I paid my friend for learning me a bad trade, two guineas; he wanted £3 and then 50s. It's between three and four years ago, and I worked for him a month for nothing, finding myself. Before my month was up my money ran taper, and I was afeard I shouldn't have enough left to start me, but I had.

"I took this very room as you see me in, and gave 30s. for the sticks, just as an old cobbler, that died in that very bed, had left them. The landlady took his traps for burying him. She's really a good soul. That was £2 2s. gone; and two hat irons, one 14 lb, and the other 10 lb., cost me 2s. 9d. at a sale. They are old things. Here they are still. But they cost 3d. a pound now. I got twelve blocks at 1s. a-piece second-hand. They cost 4s. to 5s. a piece new, and they would have been about as cheap new, for they wasn't just in the fashion; two of them in particular, and I paid 2s. a-piece to get them 'turned down' again, and put into the fashionable shape, for you must work fashionable. A plank and a table cost me 4s. 9d., second-hand of course. I paid 5s. for the calico and gums to make

[2] Next appeared testimonies from two women who did binding and lining and from one type of small master who employed several hands in the brisk season and worked alone during the "slack".

PLATE XXIX.   A.   The Hat Battery

## *My Hat's from the Borough!*

*Air.—" My Heart's in the Highlands."*

My Hat's from the Borough, my Hat was not *dear*,
My Hat's from the Borough, where *good* Hats appear :
Napped like the raven, black as the sloe,
My Hat's from the Borough, wherever I'll go!
     My Hat's from the Borough, &c.

All hail to the Borough, all hail to the place,
The *Hat Mart of cheapness*, of beauty and grace ;
Wherever I wander, I very well know.
To the *Foot of the Bridge, in the Borough I'll go*.
     My Hat's from the Borough, &c.

Farewell to the shops, where I've sported my ' tin,'
Farewell to the Hats which let ' *heavy wet* ' in ;
Adieu to the *sharpers* that proved me a *flat*.
To the Boro' I'll go and I'll buy me a hat.

From *thee*, not a moment, loved Borough, I'll stray ;
You have *felt* what I *feel* it my duty to say ;
That I hail the glad time when thy *Hatting Renown*,
Gave thy *blocks* for my *head*, and my head for thy *crown !*
     My Hat's from the Borough, &c.

B.   An Advertising Handbill

PLATE XXX.  A Last Resort: The Male Ward of the Field Lane Refuge for the
Destitute, 1859.

my first twelve bodies to begin with, and I set to work. The bigger fool for it. It took me a day and a half, or 19 hours to make the dozen—I can do it in 13 or 14 hours now—and I took them to Mr. —— for sale. I asked him 8s. 6d., as I thought he would reckon that low, and it would recommend me, for my friend got 10s. Mr. —— said, 'Pooh, I can get better at 7s.,' but I got 7s. 6d. for them; and if I had asked him 7s., he'd have said 'I can get better at 6s.' I carry on this way still.

"I had a bit of a demand the autumn before last for bodies, and I got a man to help me, and I made 18s. a week for four weeks, and 16s. for the next week, and the next week to that only 4s. I can't tell what made the brisk, exactly; but I thought I was doing rarely, and I took an apprentice; his parents is poor people, close by. I gave him nothing. I was to teach him his trade—there's no indenture or anything of that sort—for two months, and then he was to have half of what he brought me in; but he and his father and mother cut away after I'd had him three weeks, and I've never seen him since. I've gone on this way all along, living from hand to mouth very often. I'm not treated like a Christian by some of the shops I take my bodies to. Last winter I was often starving. I've gone out with half-a-dozen bodies in a morning, and have brought them back at night, without a farthing in my pocket; of course I couldn't break my fast. I've gone to bed to try and sleep off the hunger—gone there at four o'clock, as I had neither fire nor candle, and have kept waking every hour, a dreaming that I was eating and drinking. I suppose it was the gnawing at my stomach that caused the dream. I was three weeks in arrear for rent, too, at 18d. a week, but my landlady's very good.

"I hardly know what I make a week, take the year through; perhaps 6s. to 7s. a week; some weeks only 4s., some weeks 10s. or 12s., or more. I've been rather in luck these three or four last weeks as I haven't made—that is, I haven't cleared—less than 10s. 6d. a week. But if I do make 10s. at this time (October), what is it? Fire costs me 5d. a day—say for six days. I'm out the rest of the week, when I'm busiest. That's 2s. 6d.; candles is 1s. for the time I'm at work; rent's 1s. 6d., and 3d. extra to rub off the arrear that's out this week. How much is that?" 5s. 3d. "Then there's 5s. 3d. left to live on. I live mostly on coffee, three times a day, with bread and butter. If I can't afford butter, I toast the bread. I gave ½d. for this old fork to do it with. It's better that way than dry. Sometimes I have one or two, or three, fresh or salt herrings for dinner, that cost 1½d. to 2d., or sometimes only 1d.; or ½lb. of beef sausages, that cost 2d. common, or 2½d. better; but what's ½ lb. sausages for a man like me, that, when it's wanted, gets out of his bed at daylight, and goes

P

to his plank? That sort of living costs 7d. or 8d., or 9d. a day. Beer I very seldom taste. Tobacco 2d. for three days; it puts off the hunger. . . ."

## "Going on tramp" years ago

From an elderly man I had the following account of his "going on tramp" 22 years ago. I give it to show what the system then was; there is comparatively little of it at present :

"There's no doubt," he said, "that many a hatter went on tramp, and got to like the life, when he needn't have gone, if he'd looked out fairly for work. When I started from London, I needn't have gone if I hadn't liked it, if I'd exerted myself; but I wanted a change. I made for Lancashire. I had 1½d. a mile allowed then, and a bed at every 'lawful town'. Sometimes, if the society's house, which was always a public-house, was small, and full, I had half a bed— for other societies used the house, and I have slept with tailors, and curriers, and other trades on tramp. Sometimes the landlord bedded me out. It was a pleasant life enough. You saw something new every day, and the fresh air and exercise made a man as strong as a horse. I know plenty of men in different trades that wouldn't thank you for work—they liked tramping better. I got good work at Oldham, and after that came to London, or I might have become one of that sort myself. When I went to work at first, after tramping, I didn't feel quite settled for a week or so. I've seen some queer doings among tramps. One was regularly joined by a woman as soon as he left a town, and she quitted him just before he went into one, if it was a small place, though a 'lawful town', or she might be noticed with him. She sold laces, and was no better than she should be, so tramp money went to help to keep her. A tramp's was a jolly life enough, but it's different now. But I reckon I should be very sorry to see the allowance to tramps done away with, for I think it helps to keep a man more independent, and prevents many a hand from having to work at under wages as he might be driven to do otherwise."

The result of my inquiries is certainly not favourable to the tramping system. Habits of vagabondism appear to be generally induced by it, and the civilized artisan is gradually transformed into the predatory (because non-producing) nomade. That in every well-regulated trade there should be some means of passing the surplus of indigent labourers from one town to another, no one can doubt; still I am convinced that the tramping system is not the best mode of attaining this end.

# THE TANNERS AND CURRIERS

## LETTER LXXVIII—15 NOVEMBER 1850

*The importance of Bermondsey*

"The leather manufacture of Great Britain," says Mr. M'Culloch, "is of very great importance, and ranks either third or fourth on the list, being inferior only in point of value and extent to those of cotton, wool, and iron—if it be not superior to the latter." As regards the metropolis, the tanned material required for this great manufacture is prepared almost exclusively in Bermondsey. A walk through the streets and roads of that district is sufficient to convince three of the senses—the sight, the smell, and the hearing—how extensive is this branch of industry. On every side are seen announcements of the carrying on of the leather trade; the peculiar smell of raw hides and skins, and of tan pits, prevades the atmosphere; and the monotonous click of the steam engines used in grinding bark assails the ear.

A cursory glance even at the signboards of Bermondsey shows that the commerce and manufacture of the district are mainly derived from the uses to which hides and skins, with their coverings of hair and wool, and their appendages of horns and hoofs, are subjected. The signboards announce, in thick profusion, dealers in bark, tanners, curriers, French tanners and curriers, leather-dressers, morocco and roan manufacturers, leather-warehousemen, leather factors, leather dyers, leather enamellers, leather sellers and cutters, hide salesmen, skin salesmen, fellmongers, tawers, parchment makers, wool factors, wool-staplers, wool warehousemen, wool dealers, wool dyers, hair and flock manufacturers, dealers in horns and hoofs, workers in horn, glue makers, size makers, and neat's-foot oil makers. To this list must be added the tradesmen who supply the different implements used by the workmen in the industrial occupations I have enumerated. Occasionally, too, is seen an announcement, not very common in London manufactures, "tan given away".

What may be styled the *architecture* of the district is that rendered necessary by the demands of its chief commerce. Long, and sometimes high, and always black wooden structures, without glass windows, but with boards that can be closed or opened to admit air at pleasure, irregularly surround a series of closely-adjacent pits, filled to the brink with a dark, chocolate-coloured, thick liquid. Running alongside the pits, or in any convenient part of the premises, are low sheds, with red-tiled roofs, but blackened with age, often covering other pits; while, high above all, towers a tall narrow chimney, throwing out thick columns of black smoke. Stacks of new bark, or of bark "spent" in the pits, and ready to be carted away for manure or other purposes—such as to spread over the street pavement that no noise may disturb the rich invalid—occupy corners of the tan "yards". In other corners is spread what appears refuse, but is really the parings, the "odds and ends", of the leather, such as are used by the glue-makers. Elsewhere are heaped horns to be disposed of to comb-makers, knife-handle makers, etc. These places are the tanneries. As regards the wooden structures of the tanneries, where leather is hung "to dry" in what may be called a series of galleries, the curriers' and leather dressers' premises present a rather close resemblance, but there is an absence of similar pits of tan. The fellmonger's trade is carried on in large "yards", partly in the open air and partly in sheds. The wool warehouses are lofty stone buildings, some of them with considerable architectural pretensions. Where, in other edifices, is seen the window, is a large door, which can be "let down" level with the floor, and through which huge bales of wool are craned to and from any of the floors. What windows there are, are small and dusty.

To the right and left of some of the principal thoroughfares, such as Bermondsey-street, run series of small streets of small houses. A few of these off-streets or alleys are trim and new; but many of them are dirty and ruinous-looking, showing broken and uncleaned windows, and with water standing on the black unpaven ground. These are the residences of working people, according as their character, habits, or means, induce a tidy or a squalid dwelling-place. The names of some streets, such as Abbey-street and Crucifix-lane, tell of the existence of an age when Bermondsey presented very different characteristics—when it was chiefly remarkable for conventual magnificence, wealth, and hospitality.

The early establishment of the tanning trade in the locality was no doubt owing to the number of tidal streams or ditches that intersect it, and supply the abundant water necessary for trade purposes. Perhaps there was formerly but one tidal stream—the Neckinger. At the present time this and its associate streams are far less the medium of water supply to the tanners than was the case ten or twelve years ago. The proprietors of many tanneries have made the fine springs with which Bermondsey abounds more available for their business purposes, and some have expended considerable sums in the sinking of Artesian wells.[1]

## Number and social habits of tanners

The number of tanners in the metropolis in 1841 amounted to 901; of these, 819 were males of twenty years of age and upwards, 7 adult females, and 75 boys. . . .

The several workers in the preparation of leather—the curriers being an exception—are not an educated class. There need be no stronger proof of this than the fact, as I was informed by an intelligent workman from his own knowledge, that in their societies not one man in three can write his name legibly, or spell it correctly. I found a working tanner, to whom I was directed, in a public-house, reading to two of his trade, who regretted their inability to read an account of a prize fight. Among tanners, I was told, there was still a strong "hankering after a prize fight", and that some noted boxers had sprung from them—among others "Ned Turner", who was brought up as a tanner, but was afterwards a *frizer*, or a man who divided the grain of a sheep-skin for hat linings and other purposes from the flesh, to be manufactured into "chamois". The operation is now done unerringly by machinery, and the frizer's occupation is extinct.

The workmen in this trade are generally married men. They reside in Bermondsey or its immediate vicinity, occupying one room at about 1s. 6d., or sometimes two rooms (according to their means) at from 2s. 6d. to 3s. a week. There is still a good deal of drinking prevalent among them, and little inclination for working on Mondays, but in both these respects there has been within 12 years a decided improvement. The workers not *in* but *on* leather, now rarely drink more than a pot of beer a day when at work; from twelve to twenty years ago they consumed twice that quantity. On Father Mathew's visit to Bermondsey, six or seven years ago, a great number of the men in this trade took the pledge, but, with the exception of about one in 20 or 25, they have all broken it. "I took the pledge, sir," said a tanner to me, "and kept it rather more than two years. I was often teased by my mates to drink, but they got tired of that. I used to say when I walked past Simon the Tanner, 'Simon you'll get no more tanners out of me;' but I found, or fancied, though I don't think it was fancy, that I couldn't work so well without a reasonable allowance of beer, so I gave up teetotalling." I may

---

[1] Information followed on changes in the duty on skins and hides, the articles made from these materials, the number and distribution of tanners nationally, the markets and volume of the London leather trade.

explain that "Simon the Tanner" is the sign of a house of call, much frequented by the fraternity, and that a "tanner", in slang language, is sixpence.

One custom still prevails—but very partially, indeed to only one-tenth, if so much, of its former prevalence—which is now known in very few trades, viz. the payment of men in public-houses. These public-houses are called "garrison" houses. The foreman makes him-self responsible to the innkeeper for all the liquor drunk on the premises of the employer when the men are at work, and he deducts the amount from their wages on the Saturday night. The journey-men shrewdly suspect that there is an understanding between the foreman and the publican, and that the beer, which is 4d. a pot to the workmen, is but 3½d. to the foreman. On inquiring of a man who gave me information on this subject, if the masters approved of such a mode of payment, I was told that the master was perhaps a rich man, having his country house at some distance, and that, provided his returns were satisfactory, he left all such matters entirely to his foreman. The system seems dying out, however, and is com-mended by no one, not even by those workmen who are addicted to drinking. . . .

### The process of tanning

The divisions in the tanning trade, in large establishments, are into the beam-men, yard (or job) men, and shed-men. The beam-man is the first hand employed on a hide, which, I will suppose, is to be tanned for soling leather. He removes the horns from the head, and in the country he removes the tail, which, however, is removed by the London butchers. In country tanneries, I may mention, the tail, with the flesh attached to it or to any part of the hide, is the perquisite of the working tanner. This perquisite is called "rumps and birrs", and in some weeks suffices to maintain a family independ-ently of other sources; sometimes it can be sold to advantage, but only in the larger towns. In London, the tail, for which 1s. is an average price, is sold by the butcher for the making of oxtail soup. The beam-man next "sleeks" the hair off the hide, using lime to facilitate the process. He next pulls the hide out to its utmost extent, pares away any jagged particles hanging loosely to it, and puts it into a pit of pigeon's dung, which is of a very acrid nature. In this dung, it remains on an average five days. The operative next "fleshes" the hide, removing all excrescences, shaving it where necessary, and preparing it in every way for the pit of oak bark tan.

It is then consigned to the yardman. Under the direction of the foreman, the yardman places the hide in the tan pit. As the name imports (for I heard him also called the jobman), he is not a skilled, but he is a laborious worker. He places the hides in the pit, carries the bark in a basket, and deposits it in the pit; pumps the water in or out; "draws" the hides, using a long hooked pole, out for inspection, that it may be ascertained when they have been pitted a sufficient time. A hide weighing 70 lbs. remains in the pit for a twelvemonth. The yardman also fulfils other functions, often understood as those pertaining to an "odd man".

When the hide—then, indeed, the "crop"—is ultimately drawn from the pit, it comes to the hands of the shed-man, and is "sammed". For this purpose it is hung up on an iron beam, in a drying shed, that it may drip; and, to facilitate the dripping, it is struck at intervals with a kind of stave; any protuberant part being struck, so that the leather, whilst wet, may be made as level as possible. The hanging etc., continues two days, and then the finishing work commences. The shed-man "rolls" it. The rolling is done by means of a brass roller, on which is a frame containing from seven to ten cwt.; nine cwt. being a usual weight for larger hides. This rolling levels the hide, expresses the wet from it, and so prepares it for market. Rolling is only resorted to for soling leather. The crop is not, however, fit for sale until it has been for three or four days hung in the sun, or in a heated apartment.

There are no working tanners—except perhaps some yardmen—but what are masters of all branches of the business; nor does any branch tax their ingenuity or skill very severely. It is only in some larger establishments, that the workmen are confined with strictness to the branches I have described. The payment of the tanner is both by day and by piece. The beam work averages 21s. a week, the yard work 18s. a week, and the shed work 21s. to 25s. a week; but the shed work alone, the most skilled portion of the tanner's labour, is paid by the piece, and that only in some yards. Piece prices or day prices realize about the same to the workman.

In one of the principal tanneries, the regular hours of labour—which are from six to seven in summer, and from daylight to dark in winter—have been extended an hour, gas being now used. This increase of labour has not, however, been accompanied with any increase of remuneration; so that it is a virtual decrease of wages, to the extent of more than half a day's work in a week, or of six hours. The cause assigned is the cheapness of provisions enabling men to live at less cost; but the house in question, rather than reduce the actual amount of payment, has added to the hours of work. The men resisted at first, but gave way rather than lose their employment. Another large firm has just proposed a similar measure, but the matter is as yet unsettled.

## A shed-man comfortably off

From a shedman, a strong, fresh-coloured man, I had the following statement :

"I learned all parts of the tanning trade, and was apprenticed to my father, who had the management of a business in the country. I've known the London trade for twenty years, or thereabouts. I work in the shed now, and have for a long time. I don't remember how long. I work by the piece at present, and have from 1s. to 1s. 9d. a hide, according to size. My work's constant now, and I make about 24s. a week. I live as comfortably as a working man can, and support a wife and two children on that. I have a sort of double room, and pay 2s. 3d. a week for it, unfurnished. I could read a little once, but I've been out of practice so long that I've forgot it; but I'm very fond of hearing my wife read the paper on Sundays, as I smoke my pipe. It was capital reading about Manning and his wife, as they lived just by us, you see. My children both go to school. The work in tanning's the same, whether the hide goes into clean oak bark or terra japonica. The terra tans the offal well, but the prime parts not so well. I have no grievances to complain of in my yard, none at all; and I hope bread won't be any dearer this winter, as some say it will. It's a great good to a man like me that it's so cheap, as well as fish and meat, for I'm a hearty eater. I go home to all my meals."

Some working tanners complained that the use in tanning of terra japonica etc., which they called "chemicals", was a serious injury in diminishing the amount of work, and consequently the number of workmen. I found, moreover, that the men all represented "chemical" tanning as producing a very inferior article to that produced by the use of bark.

## An Irish yard-man

The majority of the yard-men are Irishmen, and are paid by the day. Their work is laborious, and they are paid 2s. 6d. and 3s. a day. One of them told me that he was very grateful for the good earnings of 18s. a week; he had learned the tanning trade in Ireland, his master being both a farmer and tanner; and on his master's failure he could obtain no employment, and with his wife and one child came to Liverpool, and tramped to London, eight or ten years ago. "We had to live on 5d. a day, sir," he continued, "and nothing for Sundays, when we got to London, for I had odd jobs that brought me 2s. 6d. a week, for three weeks; when I was lucky enough to get work thro' a friend—and have kept it pretty regular ever since. How we lived on 2s. 6d. a week—I have now 18s.—I can hardly tell, but the poor helps the poor." This man told me he had saved a little money, and that he drank a pot of beer a day, and had to "slave", as he called it, very hard indeed. He resided in a small but not bare, and certainly not clean room, which smelt strong of fried fish, on which, he said, he lived a good deal, and never touched meat on any fast day, as they were Catholics. His wife sometimes made 1s. or 1s. 6d. by washing for a neighbour, the child being then left in the care of another neighbour at 3d. a day. There are now many tanners out of work. I saw one strong young man who had been out of work for seven months, and had tramped half the time. He was in no society, and lived principally on the little help he got from his former mates; but that was chiefly in giving him beer, or in sharing their bread and cheese with him. He was very anxious to emigrate, as he had heard that tanners were wanted in Sydney. "But there's no way out of England for me," he said, alluding to his want of means.

## Working dress of the tanners.

The working dress of the tanners is most commonly a pair of thick corduroy or yellow canvas trowsers, dyed a deeper yellow with bark at the ends, leather leggings, a striped shirt of strong calico, a jacket of corduroy or coarse flannel, wooden clogs, a leather or flannel apron, and a paper cap. I was informed that, notwithstanding the constant dabbling in wet by the working tanners, rheumatism and colds were almost unknown among them. "Use," said one of my informants, "is second nature."

## The tanners union

The London tanners have a society with three branches—the Old Union with 172 members, the Tramp Union with 50, and a branch of the Old Union, and consisting chiefly of elderly men, numbering also 50; in all 272. There are moreover, now in London between 600 and 700 working tanners not belonging to any society. Tramps continue to be relieved by the United Tanners, or the Old Union. If the funds are under £50 a tramp is paid 10d. a day, and if accompanied by his wife, 1s. 3d.; when the funds are over £50 and under £100, 1s. a day for a single man, and 1s. 6d. for a married couple; when over £100, 1s. 2d. and 1s. 9d. a day respectively. The tramping is to average twenty miles a day, no tramping being allowed on Sundays; but what is called a "Sunday benefit", regulated as the day allowance is by the state of the funds, is granted instead. Any member tramping with a woman to whom he is not married is expelled the society. The payments by the members to support the fund are 3d. each entrance money, and 1s. 3d. per month.

Apprenticeship used to be the regular mode of acquiring a knowledge of the tanner's business, but it is now much less so—the reason given to me being that so few would now pay any premium. The apprentices are now generally the sons of the operative tanners.

The payment to the three branches generally is 3d. a week per member. The allowance to a member out of work is 6s. a week, regulated in great measure, as I was afterwards told, by the curriers, whose rules are full and clear. All the tanners' societies, except the one I have described, discourage tramping, and withhold any allowance to men on tramp in the country.

## Currying

In *currying*, the men work both by the day and by the piece, but far more frequently by the piece. An operative currier is expected to know every branch of the trade, but in London his labour is generally confined to one department—viz., to shoe curriers', saddlers' curriers', or coach curriers' work.

In shoe currying, the production of fine "cordovan" demands the highest skill of any article in the trade, and a nice judgement; for no precise rule can be laid down, as to the oil, etc., to be applied, as the horse-hide varies in the fineness of the "grain", the part from which the hair has been removed, and in the substance and softness or toughness of the *"flesh"*, or underside of the leather; and so the application of oil, "dubbing", etc., must be duly apportioned. In the currying of calf-skins and of kips there is a material difference when compared with that of cordovan, for the calf and kip skins are "coloured" (blacked) on the flesh side, instead of the grain. The "uppers" of gentlemen's shoes and the "fronts" of their boots are unlined, and therefore the cleanest (or grain) part of the leather is made to come into contact with the stocking, which otherwise would be sooner soiled. The grain side, too, "cracks" sooner than the flesh.

In saddlers' work, the most difficult articles to curry for the tradesmen who require the very best and best-coloured leather are bridle hides, which must be at once strong and flexible. In the currying of a harness hide, which is the same process as that in currying the other leathers used in saddlery, and does not much differ from that observed by the shoe currier, the first process is to "strike out" the "hide", as the tanned leather continues to be called. To effect this, it is steeped in water, spread on a table, and "sleeked" with a "sleeker"—a wooden instrument like a flattened rolling-pin. It is thus sleeked to its utmost extent of dilation, until the water is pressed out of it. When so stretched it is affixed to iron hooks, each side being so held, and left to dry. It is then put on a "beam" and "fleshed". The beam is a sloping and upright wooden frame, of some hard firm wood such as beech or ash; and the "flesher" is a long two-handled, somewhat blunt, knife—one edge being sharper than the other—made of fine steel. The currier thus removes whatever portions of the flesh are protuberant; and when a "thin" hide is required, the fleshing is carried on—a sharp flesher being then used—so nicely and gradually that some of the "shavings" are as thin as writing paper. "Scouring" is the next process; the grain and flesh being rubbed rapidly with pumice or other stone, so that it is "raised" on both sides, and the better adapted for the next stage, which is the application of the "dubbing", or, as it is indifferently called, "stuffing". The dubbing is an admixture of oil and tallow, which is spread alike upon the grain and flesh, to "mellow" the leather. The dubbing remains on the leather for two days, and is then "sleeked" off by the process I have described. After that the surface is "coloured", according to the purpose required; the hide is dried, and is then complete for the market. Boot-top colouring is often very difficult. "The fashion has changed in them, sir," said an old currier to me, "from a deep yellow, or yellowish brown, to a sick white, and now it's a white with a yellowish bloom to it."

A currier who had worked about eight years in London, a man of about thirty-five, gave me an account of his earnings, which, as he had been fortunate in obtaining good work, ranged from 30s. to 42s. a-week. His earnings however, are those of the very best, the readiest (the usual word in most trades for a quick workman), and the most skilful workmen. . . . The great grievance of the superior workmen in currying is the employment, at inferior wages, of non-society men, who, in all branches of the leather trade, are called "blacks".

*Social condition of the curriers*

The curriers in society, and working for good shops, are the most intelligent of the operatives engaged in the trade I am treating of. One currier knew of none but what could read and write, and some of them were very well informed and took an interest in politics, there being as many Freetraders as Protectionists, or nearly as many among them. The abodes of the curriers are in different parts of the metropolis and of the suburbs, as the trade is not so exclusively confined to Bermondsey as that of the tanners, though Bermondsey is its headquarters. They are principally married men, occupying one or two comfortable rooms. The non-society men, on the other hand, are driven to the usual shifts of slop workmen.

The working dress of the curriers is generally very thick blue flannel trowsers and jacket, strong coarse shirts, and blue flannel aprons. As is common enough with working men of the better class whose trade necessitates the wearing of coarse and inexpensive clothing and linen all day, the curriers are rather remarkable for being well dressed and with superior linen on Sundays, or when they "dress to go out on an evening". Their boots are often of the very best.

### The Curriers' Society

The wages of the operative curriers were settled by agreement with their masters in 1812, and have continued unchanged. The list of prices may be called even an elaborate production—it contains such ample specifications, and descends to such minutiae. To give anything but a condensed account of it is not possible in my limits. Under the very first head, "calf skins", there are divisions into "English", and "Foreign", and into "russet", and "black", the prices being regulated by the weight of the skins consigned to the workmen to be curried. I give a specimen :

|  | English | | Foreign | |
|  | Russet | Black | Russet | Black |
|  | s.  d. | s.  d. | s.  d. | s.  d. |
| Skins under 20 lbs., per doz. | 4  0 | 4  6 | 4  3 | 4  6 |
| And so the scale proceeds to additional weights of 10 lbs. per doz. to, | | | | |
| Skins 90 lbs, to 100 lbs., per doz. | 8  6 | 9  6 | 9  6 | 10  6 |

"and to advance 1s. for every 10 lb. (the advance on the lighter weight being 6d. per dozen). All skins shaved on the butt with a currier's knife, 1s. per dozen. Skins rounded before tanned, under 60 lbs. per dozen, to be allowed 4 lbs, and upwards, to add 7 lb. per dozen. Skins dressed with two cheeks 6d. per dozen." Equally precise are the specifications of the journeymen's charges under the heads, "kips, English and foreign", "calf butts", "kip butts", "boot legs", "seal skins", "goat skins", "French fronts", "shoe hides", "horse hides", "extra work at the option of the master", and "water-scouring". The longest enumeration of prices relates, however, to the diversified articles of leather required for the uses of the saddler, the harness maker, the army accoutrement maker, and the coachbuilder; of these prices there are 85.

The Curriers' Society also publishes a "list of employers", of all

who are recognized in the "honourable", or "fair" trade. Of these
there are in the City division, 33; in the Westminster inner division,
14; in the Westminster outer division, 28; in the Borough division,
46.

I have heard working men in other callings point to the curriers
as a very compact and well regulated trade society, and I was assured
that, so far from their employers having been injured by the opera-

Fig. 8.   A Tanner Fleshing.

tions of the society, they ranked as wealthy tradesmen, with any
other class, and much higher than many other classes, and that
both in town and country; while the "black" masters, or those
employing non-society men, were far less prosperous, and were indeed
often needy. This account was confirmed to me by a master currier
of the honourable class; but his profits, he said, had fallen off from
five to ten per cent these last four or five years, owing to the demand
for French leather by the first-rate bootmakers having diminished
the demand for the "best (English) calf butts and legs", which formed

a considerable part of his business. My informant spoke favourably of the independent spirit of his men; but what he called independence, he said, other masters might perhaps call sauciness.

The articles of the London society provide that a house suitable for the reception of the unemployed country members shall be appointed, and that "the landlord shall furnish a sufficient number of good and clean beds for their accommodation, together with a separate room or rooms for those who have wives or families with them". For this the landlord receives £31 10s. yearly. The secretary receives £1 weekly. The contribution of the members is 1s. per week, and 20 weeks must be paid before a currier is entitled to the benefits of the society. One of those benefits is the "home allowance". This is 8s. a week for thirteen weeks, to a free member, and 4s. a week for the next thirteen weeks, "and not to receive any more for thirteen weeks; after which, if still out of work, he may receive 4s. per week for thirteen weeks longer, and then cease. Should he be a married man, and goes upon tramp, his wife may receive the home allowance; and if single, he may have it remitted to him at any place he may appoint." This home allowance is not paid a second time, unless a member has been working and paying for twenty weeks before he claims it. Men on tramp in the country are allowed 8s. per week, with 2s. additional for a wife, and 1s. for each child under fourteen, with beds for six nights.

The instruction of the currier in his ancient art and mystery is by apprenticeship. In the "fair" or "honourable" trade an employer has, if he chooses, two apprentices and one turnover, or two turnovers and one apprentice. Among the rules regarding apprentices I find : "N.B. No foreigner can be admitted."

The "arms" of the journeymen curriers, as they appear on the title-pages of their articles, show the appropriate supporters of a horse and an ox rampant; the shield is set off with curriers' tools, and the motto is, "United to support, but not combined to injure". The non-society hands outnumber the others. The curriers have instituted a pension or superannuation fund in connection with their society. As soon as a sum of £500 has been funded, pensions or superannuations (all life annuities) will be granted to the members considered best entitled to them.[2]

[2] The letter ended with short accounts of the leather dressers, the Skinners, the morocco and roan trade and the oil and white leather finishers.

# CONCLUSION

## LOW WAGES[1]

*Subsistence Wages*

*We now come to consider what is the standard of sufficiency of remuneration, as the determining principle of good and bad wages.* By sufficiency, I mean such remuneration as is absolutely required by the labourer for the continuance of his own existence, as well as of that of those who are naturally dependent upon him. When the rate of remuneration rises above this point of absolute necessity, I call the wages good; even as when they fall below it, I consider them bad wages. The point of sufficiency, as regards remuneration for labour, includes three things :

1. The subsistence of the labourer during his work.
2. The subsistence of him, when incapacitated for further work.
3. The present and future subsistence of his family, and education of his children.

It is evident that the *minimum* value of all labour must be regulated by the subsistence of the labourers, since in order to work, the workmen must live. In an over-populated country, where the wages depend upon supply and demand, the cost of production must in all over-stocked trades determine not only what economists call the natural value, but the market value of the labour in connection with such trades. (Ricardo, p. 90.) The cost of producing so much work can only be governed by the quantity of food required to be consumed during the performance of it. Food is to the human machine what coals are to the steam engine—the motive power. With all muscular action there is destruction of muscular tissue, and if that be not reproduced, the labourer must live on his capital of accumulated strength; and this, if continued, must, of course, end in that physical bankruptcy which is commonly called starvation. The use of food to the labourer is to replace the stock of muscular power which he expends in his labour, and all that he receives over and above what

---

[1] The following extracts are selected from Parts One and Two of the publication, *Low Wages, Their Causes, Consequences and Remedies* (November/December 1851), for which see p. 42. Mayhew commenced by distinguishing between "high" and "low" wages, "good" and "bad" wages, and "fair" and "unfair" wages.

he so expends may be considered as his gain. Hence it is evident
that where there is an overplus of workpeople, and wages are regulated by the principle of demand and supply, the *mimimum value*
of all labour *must* be regulated by the cost of the food consumed
during the work. This is the lowest point to which wages can be
driven down; and to this, when there are too many labourers, they
*must* by the mere force of competition ultimately descend.

But this refers only to the *present* subsistence of the labourer;
and a man who has nothing but his labour to depend upon, requires,
in order to be self-supporting and avoid becoming a "burden" to the
parish, something more than bare subsistence-money in remuneration for his industry—and yet this is generally the mode by which
we test the *sufficiency of wages.* "A man can live very comfortably
upon that!" is the exclamation of those who have seldom thought
upon what constitutes the *minimum* of self-support in this country.

It is, however, not only necessary that a workman should subsist
during his work, and that his wages should consequently be sufficient
to keep him while labouring, but he must get enough by his labour
when in health to support him during sickness, and, when young,
to maintain him in old age. If he be unable to do this, and his wages
be only just sufficient to maintain him for the time being, it follows,
that, when incapacitated for labour either by illness or infirmity, he
must declare on the State for his support. Moreover, if his wages
be so limited that he is unable, when in work, to lay by out of them
anything as a store for his subsistence when out of work, or to make
the earnings of the "brisk season" in his trade contribute towards
his maintenance in the "slack"; then, in both these cases, as in the
others, he must either be supported by the community, or die from
starvation.

Hence we see that a man's wages, to prevent pauperism,
should include, besides present subsistence, what Dr. Chalmers has
called "his secondaries"; viz., a sufficiency to pay for his maintenance : 1st, during the slack season; 2nd, when out of employment;
3rd, when ill; 4th, when old. If insufficient to do this, it is evident
that the man at such times must seek parochial relief for these items.
The cost of the production of human labour, indeed, is precisely
the same as the cost of the production of steam labour; viz., the
market value of the substances required to produce it—together
with the expense of the wear and tear of the machine, and interest
for the capital sunk in it. Reduce any of these items, and the labour
can and will (provided there be a glut of the article) be correspond-
ingly cheapened. What coals are to the engine, food is to the man—
the source of power; what the wear and tear is to the thing of brass
and iron, so is sickness and accident to the creature of flesh and

blood; and what the capital sunk in its *con*struction is to the machine, so is the time and money expended in *in*struction to the workman. For each and all of these an equivalent should be given as the lowest compensation to the producer; and, in the case of the steam-engine, such an equivalent is generally yielded to the capitalist (for if not, he withdraws his capital, and leaves off producing); but in the case of the human engine, when wages are driven down to their ultimatum—as in hand-loom weaving, shirt-making, slop-work, ballast-heaving, making of soldiers' clothing, fancy cabinet-work, and the like—there is seldom any allowance made to the labourer for the wear and tear of the machinery of his frame; nor do his wages include any return for the capital and labour sunk in learning his business. The consequence is, that the burden of the wear and tear of the human machine is thrown upon the parish in the time of sickness or accident, and "the Guardians" are left to remedy it as best they can and will. Moreover, as the manufacturer in the price he receives for the labour of his engine when *in* work, is paid for the interest of his capital when *out* of work, even so should the wages of the employed labourer be sufficient to keep him when unemployed; for otherwise, unless he be starved to death, the rateplayers will have to make up the difference in *charity* to him.

The same may be said as to the subsistence of the labourer's family. If the remuneration for his work be not sufficient for the present and future maintenance of his wife, as well as the keep and education of his children, one of two results is self-evident— either the wife must toil, to the neglect of her young ones, and they be allowed to run wild and pick their morals and education, out of the gutter, or else the whole family must be transferred to the care of the parish.

The test, then, for bare sufficiency of wages is, such a rate of remuneration as will maintain not only the labourer himself while working and also when unable to work, but support his family, and admit of the care and education of his children; and as those wages may be termed good which admit of more than this being done, even so are they bad which admit of less.[2]

*Wages and work-load*[3]

Now, from the above, it follows that it is, in all matters concerning wages, of the first importance that the rate or ratio of the labour

[2] There followed a long footnote taking issue with W. T. Thornton, *Over-Population* (1846).
[3] We have cut sections on "fair" and "unfair" wages, and on "the rate of wages".

to the remuneration should be accurately ascertained and stated; for if we deal solely with the amount of pay, without reference to the amount of work given or exacted in exchange for it, then it is clear that we may be treating of two very different things, under a dunderhead impression that they are one and the same. For it is manifest that if a carpenter, paid by the day, is made at a "strapping shop" to get through double the amount of work to what is usual in other shops, and is nevertheless paid only the same amount of remuneration, then his wages are virtually reduced one-half; or, in other words, the ratio of his remuneration to the labour performed by him is diminished to that extent. The same result may be brought about at piece-work. The quantity of work in each piece may be increased, while the sum paid for it remains the same; in which case the ratio of the remuneration to the labour being changed, the rate of wages must, of course, be changed likewise. Hence we see that wages may be reduced without any diminution being made in the amount of money which the employer *engages* to pay, but simply by an increase in the quantity of work undertaken by the labourer. This point is invariably lost sight of by Economists, who cite a carpenter's, or mason's, or shoemaker's wages, at so much per week, without dreaming that it is necessary to state the quantity of work given in exchange for the money. The absolute amount of wage tells us only what the employer has to give the workmen; whereas the amount of labour tells us what the workmen has to give the employer : and the one is quite as necessary as the other for the just understanding of the matter. The sacrifice in such matters—it should be remembered—is not made by the employer *solely*. . . .

Of absolute as of relative wages, then, there are several kinds. In the first place the nominal wages of operatives are, in many cases, widely different (owing either to additions by way of perquisites, etc., or deductions by way of fine, etc., but oftener the latter) from the *actual* wages received. Again; the average wages, or gross yearly income of the *casually-employed* men, are very different from those of the *constant* hands, and so the gains of a *particular individual* are often no criterion of the *general* or average earnings of the trade. Indeed, I find that the several kinds of absolute wages may be arranged as follows :

1. *Nominal and Actual Wages*—or those which refer to the real and supposed *weekly* income of the workman.
2. *Casual and Constant Wages*—or those which refer to the regular and average weekly income of the workman throughout the *year*.
3. *Individual and General Wages*—or those which refer to the incomes of different members of the same trade.

## Nominal and Actual Wages

*First, of the nominal and actual wages.* Nominal wages are of course those which the employer *engages* to pay; but these are often widely different from those which he *really does* pay. Frequently, indeed, the *nominal* wages of a trade are merely a blind to the public and the workmen, being in some cases as much as 50 and even 75 per cent more than the actual wages, or the sum positively received by the operatives. The popular mode of proceeding among "cutting employers", at present, is not to reduce wages directly, but indirectly; that is to say, not to *engage* to pay the men less, but *really* to pay them less than they engage to do, by laying some extra charge upon them—that is to say, to decrease the gains of the workmen by a kind of *indirect* taxation. Hence it behoves us to set forth most particularly what are the *deductions* from the nominal wages, or those engaged to be paid.

Now wages being remuneration for work, the *rate* of remuneration depends, as has been shown, upon the *ratio between the amount of pay and the quantity of labour*; and hence, in order to understand what the *rate* of wages may be, it is necessary that we should know how much labour is given or exacted for the stated amount of remuneration. If the workmen be paid by the day, they may, by extra supervision, be made to do daily double the amount of work usual in the trade, when, of course, the *rate* of wages is virtually reduced one-half. (Such is the case in the "strapping shops" of the carpenters' trade.) Or the men may be worked over hours, as by the "scurf employers" in the scavengers' trade; in which case the rate of wages will be lessened in a direct proportion to the over-work. If, on the other hand, the men are paid by the piece, it is essential that we should ascertain the precise quantity of work required for the stated amount of pay; for a common mode of reducing wages among employers now-a-days, is not to engage to pay less for the piece, but to make the workmen engage to put a greater quantity of labour into "the piece". This was the trick resorted to by Sir Elkanah Armitage, the slop-mayor of Manchester, who sought to reduce his men's wages by increasing the length of the "cut", rather than decreasing the price paid for it.

But the actual rate of wages can be altered by other means than changing the ratio of the work to the remuneration. The nominal wages may be diminished either by deductions, in the form of fines, etc., or increased by means of additions, in the shape of perquisites, etc.; both of which circumstances must necessarily tend again to make the nominal wages of a workman differ widely from his actual wages.

*Deductions from Wages*

The *deductions from wages*, I find, by experience, to be of two opposite kinds, viz., *direct* and *indirect*. Direct deductions from a man's wages are such as tend *immediately* to diminish the amount engaged to be given to him, the deductions being stopped, or paid directly out of his earnings.

Now these *direct deductions* experience has taught me to be mainly as follows :

1. Fines or stoppages for positive or assumed breach of arbitrary regulations.

2. Rent or charges for the use of tools or implements of trade, as in the system of "pence" among the sawyers, and the "frame rents" among the stockingers.

3. Cost of such appurtenances as the workman is made to find; as trimmings, in the cheap tailors' trade.

4. Charges for gas or candles.

5. Rent for the shop, or charges for "standing", as with the shawl-weavers of Paisley, who pay a certain sum per week for the use of the place where they work. This mode of deduction is occasionally practised among piece-workers as a fine for absence from work, on the plea that "the rent is going on all the same".

6. Bonus paid to the foreman in order to obtain work.

7. "Commission" paid to the middleman from whom the work is obtained.

8. Charges for taking in and out of the work; as in the stocking trade, where the middleman deducts from the earnings of the operative the assumed cost of time in going backwards and forwards for work to the employers.

9. Stoppages for benefit or provident fund, to which the workman loses all claim in case of being discharged. This is not at all an unusual practice among employers. Several of the large brewers, and some of the principal railway carriers, do this; fourpence a week is the sum stopped, in some cases; and to the fund thus created, by the men's money, the employers consider the workmen to have no claim on quitting their establishment.

10. If the work be done at home we must deduct all the necessary expenses in connection with it, which are thus forced on the workman. These are : (a) Such candles and firing as are used expressly for the work. (b) Rent where the work is carried on in a distinct place. The Messrs. Nicoll are said—by themselves—to save "several thousands" by these means—or rather to decrease, to that

extent, the wages of the work-people in their employ by making the men do the work at their own homes.

But the foregoing constitute merely the direct deductions from wages. The *indirect deductions*, or those which are *not* stopped or paid *immediately* out of the wages, I find to be as follows :

1. Reducing the quality of the provisions among those who board and lodge with their employers, as milliners, servants, sweeps, etc.

2. Forcing or expecting the men to deal with the employer for their provisions, and charging them an undue price for the same, as in the truck,[5] or "tommy" system.

3. Forcing or expecting the men either to take lodgings of their employers which they do not use, or for which they are charged an undue price, or to rent houses of them on the same terms. This system of providing homes for the work-people by employers is largely on the increase : it is, however, very dangerous to the freedom of working men, and admits of being used as the means of great tyranny on the part of the employer, seeing that he then has the power of depriving those who will not submit to whatsoever he may propose of house and home, as well as work.

4. Forcing or expecting the men to have their drink of their employer, and favouring those who expend the most of their earnings in this manner, as with the "lumpers" and "ballast-heavers".

5. Forcing the hands to find security for the work they take out, and thus to pay an undue price for their food or drink to those bakers, butchers, or publicans, who make a trade of "standing security" for the poorer work-people. This is very common in the slop shirt and stay trade at the East-end of London.

## Additions to Wages

But the *additions*, or as they are sometimes called *"aids to wages"*, are quite as necessary to be ascertained as even the *deductions* or *drawbacks*, in order to distinguish accurately between nominal and actual wages. These aids are, like the drawbacks, of two kinds, consisting of either direct or indirect additions made to the earnings of the workmen.

The *Direct* Additions to Wages consist of :

1. Perquisites or gratuities obtained by the workmen from various sources; as with dustmen, waiters, box-keepers, pew-openers, drivers and guards of stage-coaches, etc.

2. Allowance for beer or other articles connected with the work.

This was, and is still, usual in many trades; among the coopers, for instance a certain sum of money is allowed weekly, while in other trades the men have so much beer per head.

3. Tribute money, or a certain portion of the proceeds of the work, given to the workmen over and above their regular wages; as the fourth penny to the Irish weavers, etc.

4. Premiums given to those operatives, or assistants, who do better than others; as the douceurs allowed to the shopmen in the linen-draper's trade, for "introducing" and obtaining a customer for ordinarily unsaleable articles.

5. Profits derived by the workmen from the employment of other labourers to assist them; as is the case with "sweaters", "piece-masters", "lumpers", and the like.

6. Family workers, or those who avail themselves of the assistance of their wives and children; as the Spitalfield weavers, the fancy cabinet-makers, etc.

The *Indirect* Additions to Wages, on the other hand, include all extraneous sources of income, or such gains as are *not* derived *immediately* from the work. These appear to be :

1. Pensions.

2. Allowances from Provident or Charitable Societies.

3. Other work done in over-time.

4. Allotments of land.

5. Parish relief.

6. Subsistence derived from other sources than the work itself; as with women, children, "improvers", amateurs, and all those who do not labour for their living, but merely as a means of adding a little to the comforts already provided for them.

Nominal wages then, we perceive, are those which are engaged to be paid in a trade; while actual wages are those *really* received by the workmen, and which are equal to the nominal wages, *plus* the additions to, or *minus* the deductions from, them.

### Casual and Constant Wages

*We now come to the casual and constant forms of wages*; for even when all the above-mentioned additions and deductions are made, we arrive at, solely, the actual wages *occasionally* paid to workmen, and these afford us no means of estimating the amount of their actual *constant* wages, or absolute yearly income. To ascertain this point, we must set forth the quantity of employment obtained by each operative throughout the year; and this is a matter of the

highest importance in forming a just estimate of the condition of
the labourers, especially belonging to those callings which depend
on the seasons, or on the fashion of the time. To frame a correct
notion of the income of any workman, we must not only cite his
actual weekly earnings when employed, but we must set forth the
number of weeks he is employed throughout the year, and then see
how much his gross annual receipts will afford him for a constant
weekly income. If he have been constantly employed, then, of course,
his actual wages every week will have been his actual constant
wages throughout the year. But if he have been employed occasionally rather than regularly, and had only six months' work out of
the twelve, then his actual constant wages will have been exactly
one-half of his actual casual earnings.

Constant employment, and consequently constant wages, are
gradually passing into casual labour, and therefore casual earnings;
for the economy of labour is daily teaching capitalists to employ
their labourers only when they are wanted, and to get rid of them
immediately the business in any way declines; and as most trades
are "brisk" and "slack" at various periods of the year, a large number
of workmen are employed only in the busy, and discharged in the
dull times. Most assuredly, therefore, it would not be fair to quote
the weekly gains of the hop-pickers, for instance, for the few weeks
of their employment in the course of the year, as an example of
their *ordinary* earnings; nor to set forth the wages of the "preference men" at the docks (omitting all mention of the "casual hands")
as a type of the *regular* income of the dock labourers.

Casual wages, then, are the actual gains of the men who are only
*temporarily* employed.

Constant wages are the average of all the actual casual gains
obtained throughout the year by such as are either *temporarily* or
*permanently* employed. The rule to ascertain the constant or regular
wages of the men in any trade, is to take the sum of all the actual
casual gains in the course of the twelve months, and divide by the
number of weeks in the year; so that, if a tailor, working at the
better-paid trade, earned 36s. a week for twenty-six weeks in the
year, then 36s. would be his actual casual wages, while his actual
constant wages, would be only half that sum. Hence we perceive
that casual and constant wages are as different as light and darkness. Yet such is the loose and ignorant way in which statements
of wages are generally given by Economists, that the *nominal* weekly
wages of a few *constantly-employed* men are cited as examples of the
average actual wages of the whole class—the fully employed as well
as the partially-employed—throughout the year; though the two
things are as different as *gross* and *net* profits.

*Individual and General Wages*

*The next important distinction to be made lies between individual and general wages*; that is to say, between the earnings of different persons, with different abilities, working at the same part of a trade, or, with the same abilities, working at different parts of the same trade. A "quick hand", for instance, may work twice as fast as a slow one, and hence the gains of a particular individual are no criterion as to the earnings of the ordinary hands in a trade. The same may be said of those domestic workers who are more industrious than the generality of the trade, and who continue longer every day at their labour.

But these matters refer more particularly to workmen of different abilities, employed at the same part of a trade and doing work paid for at the same rate. There are, however, in almost all trades of the present day, two distinct kinds of employers; viz., those paying good and those paying bad wages; or, in other words, all handicrafts may be divided, in the phraseology of the workmen themselves, into the "honourable" and "dishonourable" parts of the trades. Hence it becomes most important in speaking of wages, and in citing individual earnings, to state the portion of the trade for which the man is working, or else egregious blunders and confusion, and injustice, may be the result. For instance, a political economist asserts that the wages of a working tailor are 36s. a week, and instantly the public conclude that the operatives in that trade have little to complain of. But in receiving this statement, we have, of course, to inquire first whether the operative earning this amount of money belongs to the better or worse paid class of workmen; and, secondly, whether the wages cited are his constant or casual earnings; and if the latter, how many weeks' work he obtains in the course of the year.

To ascertain the *general* rate of wages in a trade, we must take the *actual constant* wages of all the *individuals*—the quick and the slow hands, the industrious and the comparatively idle, the better paid and the worse paid men; and adding these together, divide the sum by the number of hands; this will give us the *actual, constant,* and *general* rate of wages in that particular business—matters that are widely different from the *nominal, casual,* and *individual* scale of remuneration.

Individual wages, then, are the actual and constant earnings of particular hands, whether belonging to the honourable or dishonourable part of the trade, whether working long or short hours, and whether partially or fully employed.

General wages, on the other hand, are the actual and constant wages of the whole trade, constant and casual, fully and partially employed, honourable and dishonourable, long and short-hour men, etc., etc., made into one sum, and divided by the gross number of operatives, and the mean taken of the whole.

We have now finished with the several forms of wages, relative as well as absolute; we have seen how high wages differ from low, good from bad, fair from unfair; we have also established certain standards of moderation, sufficiency, and equity, as regards wages, by which to judge of their several relations : while in the matter of absolute wages, we have discovered how widely the actual rate of remuneration may differ from the nominal, the constant gains of a workman from his casual, and the individual from the general earnings of a trade—points which though essential for the right understanding of the subject, and often varying to a considerable extent, have been overlooked and confounded by every Economist who has written upon the wage question.

## Conclusion

*There is now but one other preliminary to be settled—viz., Is there a uniform set of circumstances regulating wages;* or are the matters affecting the rate of remuneration accruing to the labourer so many, so complex, and so arbitrary, that it is beyond human ability to shape them into distinct and regular laws? At first sight it must be admitted that the latter assumption appears to be the nearer to the truth; but such is the case with the objects of every science until reduced to order, and consequently brought within the compass of the comprehension. What task would seem so hopeless to one unacquainted with astronomy as to attempt to number and classify the stars?—who would think that the infinite variety of plants and flowers that plume and spangle the earth could be reduced to anything like "system"? or that the tiny insects which crowd the air and fields and even the animalcules that are invisible to the human eye, and of whom whole families inhabit a single drop of water— who would fancy, I say, that these could be methodically arranged, and that we should make sciences, and group into *genera* and *species* things of which there was almost a distinct world in each little particle of the earth? The same apparent impossibility of generalizing and systematizing is forced upon us, if we run over in our minds the many things that may tend to decrease or increase the labourer's rate of pay—the quantity of wealth there is in the country—the speculative spirit of the capitalists—the number of labourers—the skill, industry, and honesty of the men—the greed and ambition of the employers—the necessities of the employed—the firmness or weakness of the work-people—the price of food—the sum spent in materials—the hours of labour—the quantity of articles imported from abroad—the amount of the taxes—the number of non-producers—the extension of the markets—the profits of trade—the limitation of the suffrage—the invention of machinery—the alteration of the mode of working—the large system of production—the division of labour—the employment by middle-men—the introduction of the contract system—the prevalence of piece-work—the extent of the term of hiring—the state of the law for the relief of the poor—these, and a thousand-and-one other circumstances, each and all tending either to raise or depress the ordinary rate of wages—produce in the mind a sense of bewilderment rather than comprehension on contemplating the multiplicity and complexity of the details.

It is evident, however, on reflection, that wages must be regulated by *something*—either by some one circumstance, or some **series of** circumstances. If the workman be badly paid, if the remuneration he obtain for his labour be *insufficient* for the satisfaction of the wants and requirements of himself and those who are dependent on him for their bread, there must be *some* cause for such a state of things—some "reason why" he receives so little—the discovery of which must necessarily be the first step to his obtaining more. If his wages were higher formerly than they are now, then, how came they to be so high in times past; and what circumstances have led to their being so low at present? To know these things is to know what is required to induce a return to the same high rate of remuneration as formerly, even as to know the circumstances which have brought about the depression is to be able to control, and perhaps to remedy them. Again : if the remuneration for labour be really less than is due to the labourer—if the workman be unfairly deprived of the proper reward of his work—then *what* is his proper reward, and *how* comes it he *is* deprived of it? In a word, what *should* regulate wages, and what *does* at present regulate them? To comprehend these matters is to be able not only to test what *is* paid by what *ought* to be paid, but to enlist in behalf of the sufferers the sympathies at least of all those who desire to see justice prevail between man and man.

This is all that is wished by the writer of the present volume. He has learnt, by personal investigation into the condition and earnings of the humble classes of the Metropolis, how many are defrauded of what he believes to be their *due*; he has found the labourer cheated, by an infinity of petty tricks, out of even the pittance that was *engaged* to be paid him; he has discovered whole families too poor to purchase candles by which to work, toiling from the earliest dawn to the last gleam of twilight, and yet unable to subsist after all their long toiling; he has seen men entrapped into the taverns of their employers, to drink away the earnings that should have gone to feed their starving wives and children; he has heard women tell how they were forced to prostitute their bodies for the bread they could not earn by their labour; he has found employers, who had palaces for shops, compelling their ragged workpeople to deposit money with them, lest their necessities should force them to steal the work they could not live by; he has learnt how the late Sheriff of our City amassed no less than £80,000 in a few years, by reducing the wages of the thousand operatives in his employ 10s. a week each; he has met with men who were forced to rent of their employers rooms they could not occupy, to subscribe to provident funds they lost all claim upon immediately they were discharged;—these and a thousand like iniquities has he discovered to be perpetrated by those whom he believes had *engagements* to fulfil towards their labourers as well as their labourers had towards them; and when he sought, in the works of such as profess to teach the rights of labour as well as of capital, a remedy for the wrongs he witnessed, he found there doctrines only which made the impoverishment and fraud of the labourer part of the necessities and expediencies, if not glories, of the times.

# APPENDIX I

*THE MORNING CHRONICLE* Letters and *LONDON LABOUR AND THE LONDON POOR*, 1851 and 1861

Mayhew's various London investigations are most usefully seen as parts of one developing and unfinished project. The *Morning Chronicle* letters ended with a study of the markets of London; *London Labour and the London Poor* began with an expanded study of the costermongers, the section of the poor that hawked the commodities from the markets. When Mayhew left the *Morning Chronicle* and set up his own office to continue the survey, the weekly and monthly numbers he published became the 1851 edition of *London Labour* (usually bound without the fascinating "Answers to Correspondents" column on the original weekly covers).

From early prospectuses, it is clear that Mayhew had enlarged the scope of the project, along lines already laid down in the *Morning Chronicle* letters. *London Labour* aimed to be nothing less than a complete "cyclopaedia" of those that will work, cannot work and will not work. Starting with the street folk, Mayhew then planned to consider the producers (artisans and labourers), carriers, distributors, protectors and servants. He used early "To Correspondents" columns to solicit specific information from employers, operatives and especially trades societies about the condition of the various metropolitan trades (Nos. 6 & 7). He evidently intended to classify the producers according to the "scientific" principles developed in Letter LII, May 16, 1850, grouping them around the materials they worked upon. Starting with "Workers in Silk, Cotton, Wool, Worsted, Hair, Flax, Hempen," he would then move to "Workers in Skin, Gut and Feathers" ("To Correspondents" and Back Cover, No. 5).

Mayhew never reached his target. The examination of the street folk, scheduled to take six months and occupy only one volume, spilled over into a second. Apologies were offered on the grounds that more time was needed to collect information about the artisans (Cover, vol. II, pt. I). But Mayhew never managed a full consideration of the trades of London. He did, however, add some new material on the workers involved in cleaning the streets to complete volume II of the 1851 edition. While treating the rubbish carters, he took the opportunity to examine the mechanisms which created casual labour and caused low wages, using illustrative material from his *Morning Chronicle* work on the tailors, shoemakers and cabinet-makers. But it is clear, even as late as October 18, 1850, that he still aimed to do more comprehensive work on the London trades ("Answers to Correspondents", No. 45).

On August 23, 1850, he began to examine prostitutes, as part of a series on those that will not work. This material, including his classification of workers and non-workers as well as his comparative study of prostitution in different societies, formed the third volume of the 1851 edition, only 192 pages long. Asked by a correspondent how long the whole survey would continue, Mayhew replied, "it is believed some years—probably five or six". He spoke too optimistically. The *London Labour* numbers seem to have ended abruptly on February 21, 1852; *Low Wages* had already stopped on December 20, 1851. Both closed down probably owing to a legal dispute with the printer (see above, p. 42).

Griffin, Bohn and Company published the 1861 edition of *London Labour and the London Poor*. It would seem that Mayhew expanded this edition in a quick and sloppy way to fill the standard three volume format. A new third volume was created, with new material on exterminators of rodents and vermin, expanded work on street performers and finally a "sample" of letters from the *Morning Chronicle,* including those on the slop cabinet-makers, dock-labourers, transit workers and vagrancy. A striking example of his carelessness, Mayhew made no attempt to delete transitions which made perfect sense in the *Morning Chronicle,* but seem puzzling here, such as the paragraph explaining the move from Spitalfields to the docks (1861 ed., vol. III, p. 300). In 1862, a fourth volume was added, dealing with those that will not work. Mayhew's earlier work on prostitution was supplemented by new material on thieves, swindlers and beggars which had been collected by other investigators. (The [1865] edition, brought out by Charles Griffin and Company, was virtually a reprint of the first three volumes of 1861, with different pagination. The British Museum gives the date as [1865], the *English Catalogue of Books* as 1866.) Thus the 1861 edition, which is usually read in isolation and treated as the total of Mayhew's London researches, is, perhaps, the most unsatisfactory remnant of an unfinished venture.

The table below shows how much of the *Morning Chronicle* material was incorporated into *London Labour and the London Poor,* 1851 and 1861 editions. An "X" indicates that material does not appear.

E.Y.

| MORNING CHRONICLE | | | LONDON LABOUR AND THE LONDON POOR | |
| --- | --- | --- | --- | --- |
| Letter | Dates | Subject | 1851 | 1861 |
| 1 | Oct. 19, 1849 | Introduction with notion "poverty line" | X | X |
| 2 | Oct. 23, 1849 | Spitalfields silk weavers (Nearly all reprinted in *London Characters*, 1874 ed., in chapter "And ye shall walk in Silk Attire") | X | X |
| 3–5 | Oct. 26, 30, Nov. 2, 1849 | Casual labour at the docks and low lodging houses | X | III, 300–318 |
| 6–11 | Nov. 6, 9, 13, 16, 20, 23, 1849 | Slop-workers and needlewomen | X | X |
| 12–15 | Nov. 27, 30, Dec. 4, 7, 1849 | "Hucksters" or costermongers | Most of the material appears in vol. I, but is entirely rearranged in sections about social habits or about the items sold. | X |
| 16–18 | Dec. 11, 14, 18, 1849 (Bits were worked up into the chapter "In the Sweat of Thy Face, Shalt Thou Eat Bread" in *London Characters*, 1874) | Tailors—honourable and slop | X | Except illustrative material, II, 314–315, 316, 328–329. |
| 19–24 | Dec. 21, 25, 28, 1849, Jan. 1, 4, 1850 | Dockers, including those who handle coal and ballast; study of drinking habits in hard manual jobs | X | material appears slightly condensed and rearranged, III, 233–291. |
| 25–31 | Jan. 11, 15, 18, 22, 25, 29, 31, 1850 | Vagrancy and provision for the homeless | X except I, 408–423. | material in slightly different order III, 368–427, I, 408–423. |
| 32–36 | Feb. 4, 7, 11, 14, 18, 1850 | Boot and Shoemakers—honourable and dishonourable | X | Except illustrative material, II, 34–35, 302, 312, 313–314. |

| Letter | Dates | Subject | 1851 | 1861 |
|---|---|---|---|---|
| 37–39 | Feb. 21, 25, 28, 1850 | Toymakers (37 largely reprinted in *London Characters*, 1874, as "Natural History of Toys") | X | X except for statements Penny Mousetrap and Doll's Eye Makers, III, 21–24, 231–233. |
| 40–42 | Mar. 7, 11, 14, 1850 | Merchant seamen in foreign trade | X | X |
| 43–45 | Mar. 19, 25, 29, 1850 | Ragged Schools | X | X |
| 46–48 | Apr. 3, 11, 19, 1850 | Seamen in steam and coasting trade; seamen ashore and the better boarding houses | X | X |
| 49 | Apr. 25, 1850 | Reply to the Secretary of the Ragged School Union (letter from the Secretary appeared April 22) | X | X |
| 50–51 | May 2, 9, 1850 | Seamen ashore, the worst boarding houses, charitable institutions for sailors | X | X |
| 52–56 | May 16, 25, 30, June 6, 13, 1850 | Street performers (prefaced by attempt to develop a "scientific" classification of labour) | X | scattered in III, but largely between 161–220. |
| 57 | June 20, 1850 | Volume of trade in wood | X | X |
| 58 | June 27, 1850 | Labourers at timber docks | X | III, 292–300 |
| 59–62 | July 4, 6, 11, 18, 25, 1850 | Sawyers; Carpenters and Joiners—honourable and dishonourable; Moulding, Planing and Veneering Mills | X  Illustrations in II, 304–305, 330. | X |
| 63–66 | Aug. 1, 8, 15, 22, 1850 | Cabinet-makers, honourable and dishonourable | X | only condensed version dishonourable section of trade III, 221–231. Illustrative material II, 302, 303, 312, 314. |

| Letter | Dates | Subject | 1851 | 1861 |
|---|---|---|---|---|
| 67 | Aug. 29, 1850 | Turners | X | X |
| 68 | Sept. 5, 1850 | Ship and Boat Builders | X | X |
| 69 | Sept. 12, 1850 | Coopers | X | X |
| 70–74 | Sept. 19, 26, Oct. 3, 10, 17, 1850 | Transit workers: omnibus crews, Hackney coach and cabmen, carmen and porters, watermen, lightermen and steamboatmen | X | X material slightly rearranged III, 318–336. |
| 75–76 | Oct. 24, 31, 1850 | Dressmakers and milliners—honourable and slop | X | X |
| 77 | Nov. 7, 1850 | Hatters | X | X |
| 78 | Nov. 15, 1850 | Tanners and Curriers | X | X |
| 79–82 | Nov. 21, 28, Dec. 5, 12, 1850 | London markets—live, meat, green and fish | Some of the material incorporated into enlarged sections on street selling in vol. I. | |

PLATE XXXI. Scripture Reader in a Night Refuge by Doré

PLATE XXXII.   Coffee in the Morning on the Way to Work, by Doré

# APPENDIX II

## COST OF LIVING

Mayhew found it to be easier to obtain accurate accounts of earnings than of expenditure, and, while he presents abundant evidence from which patterns of expenditure can be reconstructed, he does not present many detailed budgets. "I keeps no account," a scavenger told him : "money comes and it goes, and it often goes a damned sight faster than it comes."

Frequently in these pages—especially when dealing with dishonourable or slop labour—Mayhew offers evidence as to a serious decline in money earnings over the years. It is sometimes suggested that over the same years the prices of many goods had declined sufficiently to offset the apparent decline in earnings. Although there have been careful attempts to present real wages (or price movements) in statistical form, these have generally been based upon wholesale prices, or upon a "basket of goods" consumed by a prosperous artisan, rather than those consumed by the semi-skilled and the poor (see note 1).

The problem can be considered in two parts. It is supposed that there was a decline (with many intervening fluctuations) between a date shortly after the end of the Napoleonic Wars (say, 1820) and 1845. We have not found evidence that this decline had any significant effect on the goods bought by the London poor. There was, however, a sharper decline, perhaps associated with the reduction of duties on sugar and coffee (see note 2) and with the reduction in the price of wheat (which may or may not have been influenced by the repeal of the Corn Laws in 1846). This fall was not apparent in the budgets of the poor until well into 1848, since in 1847 the price of wheat soared to its highest point since 1839 (and, with that exception, 1819). It then plummeted until in 1851 it reached the lowest point until then recorded in the 19th century, a point not to be improved upon until 1884.

Thus Mayhew's investigation commenced when his informants were still looking anxiously over their shoulders to 1847, when bread had reached the mountainous price of 11½d. a quartern (4lb. 5oz.) loaf. Towards its conclusion, in 1851, when he collected among the street-scavengers his most systematic budgets, prices—according to one of the best indices—had reached their lowest point between

1793 and 1886, and the quartern loaf was now selling at 6d., 5d., or even less.

We have made an attempt to list prices over a number of years, taking as a basis the budget for a family with three children (1841), with a weekly consumption of five quartern loaves, 5lb. of meat, 1lb. of sugar, 1lb. of butter, 3oz. of tea, about half a pound each of candles and soap, and 7 pints of beer (note 2) :

|  | 1825 | 1831 | 1841 | 1845 | 1851 |
|---|---|---|---|---|---|
| Bread | 3s. 6d. | 3s. 9d. | 3s. 6½d. | 2s. 11d. | 2s. 6d. |
| Butter | 7½d. | 10d. | 9d. | 10d. | 10d. |
| Sugar | 6d. | 7d. | 7d. | 6d. | 4d. |
| Tea | 11½d. | 9d. | 11d. | 1s. 0d. | 1s. 0d. |
| Meat | 2s. 1d. | 2s. 6d. | 2s. 1d. | 2s. 6d. | 2s. 1d. |
| Candles & Soap | 10½d. | 8d. | 6½d. | 6d. | 6d. |
| Beer | 7d. | 7d. | 1s. 2d. | 1s. 2d. | 1s. 2d. |
|  | 9s. 1½d. | 9s. 8d. | 9s. 7d. | 9s. 5d. | 8s. 5d. |

It is probably unwise to set down these budgets, since tables on a page have a way of seeming more factual than qualifications beneath them. The budgets may be influenced by accidental factors, such as the time of year in which they were taken, and the quality of meat selected. If a different series of years were taken, different results might appear : 1835, with a 6d. loaf, might show about 8s. 8d., and 1847, with the loaf at 11½d., might show 11s. 3d. ! The budgets also conceal a rise in the quality of one item—from table ale or home-brewed beer (in the first two) to the richer porter (in the last three). But, in doing so, the budgets probably follow the pattern of what poorer London workers actually consumed.

The budgets also do not show a number of other items of weekly expenditure, the most commonly listed being rent, coals, and washing : and potatoes, milk, coffee, and fish. London rents were rising over this period, but the poor were probably more affected by over-crowding and deteriorating environment than by money increases. Mayhew suggested that some rents had been raised by slum landlords after the introduction of income tax in 1843 (see *L.L. & L.P.*\* II, 258), but his own figures seem to show rents as moving between 1s. 6d. and 2s. 6d. for the single man, 2s. 6d. to 4s. for a family (according to size and circumstances)—much as they had been twenty years before. Coal, on the other hand, showed a distinct fall in price over these years. Of the other items, milk (1d. a pint, 1850) appears in few budgets of the poor. The price of cheap fish was falling between 1845 and 1851, but, over the period as a whole, it does not appear as an important item in the English Londoners'

* All references in this appendix are to the 1865 edition of *L.L. & L.P.*

budget (for the Irish Londoner, who consumed less bread and meat, but much more potatoes and fish, a different series of budgets would have to be constructed). Coffee, however, was important, as many testimonies in this book make clear. The high duty maintained throughout the 1840's upon tea had led to its replacement in many poorer households by coffee. Tea, during Mayhew's investigation, stood at 4d. an ounce. whereas coffee was 2d. (and cheaper varieties as low as 1d.) an ounce.

The budgets give some indication as to what poor families might have consumed when they could afford it. Perhaps these families consumed less bread and beer and more meat than might be expected (note 1). But even by the end of the 18th century London workers were noted for their preference for a bread, meat, and beer diet. As the price of bread rose, the poor would move across to cheaper foods : from bread to oatmeal or potatoes, or to rice and broken biscuits : from butter to dripping or lard : from tea to coffee : from meat to herrings or tripe. The selection of the quality of meat could make a large difference to a weekly budget. Thus the budget for 1845 shows meat at 6d. a pound; but in this year mutton rose to 7½d. a pound, while the poor could buy instead pickled Australian beef at 3d. a pound (although people "couldn't eat the stringy stuff, for it was like pickled ropes"). More commonly they would buy offal or fagots—one hot fagot cost 1d., a fagot being 6 ounces of "chopped liver and lights, mixed with gravy, and wrapped in pieces of pig's caul." (*L.L. & L.P.* II, pp. 255, 257).

If the poor could save here and there by moving to cheaper foods, they probably lost what they gained through buying poor quality and adulterated goods, through having to redeem, at a usurous rate of interest, their goods in pawn, and through recourse to small packets of goods (penny loaves, penny papers of tea or sugar) and to expensive credit at the local shop. (note 3).

Two general conclusions can be offered from these figures. First, for the London poor there was no significant fall between 1825 and 1845 in the cost of living; hence, where those of Mayhew's informants with long memories show a decline in earnings over the previous two decades, this indicates (except perhaps for the years of low wheat prices, 1834–6) a decline in real wages. Second, there was a significant fall in the cost of bread, sugar, meat, and fish between 1848 and 1851 (as the boot-closer, on p. 240 above, told Mayhew : "there is no fault to be found with the present price of provisions"). A basket of goods which cost 10s. in the first year might cost only 9s., or even 8s. 6d., in the second. The reader should make his allowances accordingly.

*          *          *

Q*

We might leave the matter there. But Mayhew took a sardonic view of those who attempt to construct viable budgets for the poor, and our eye has fallen on one such comment, very probably from his pen, during his editorship of *Figaro in London* (1 April 1837). The writer was discussing the Poor Law Commissioners : "It appears that the Commissioners receive one guinea a day, as a just compensation for their trouble in estimating how much, or rather how *little*, a poor man can live upon . . . By good fortune we have picked up the estimate of a Commissioner for the keep of an able-bodied man, and we take the liberty of contrasting it with the bill for the Commissioner's keep at an hotel for one day, including (to use his own words) nothing more than absolute necessaries :

### *Estimate for an able-bodied man*

|                       | £ | s. | d. |
|-----------------------|---|----|----|
| Half a loaf per day   | 0 | 0  | 4  |
| Half a pound of cheese| 0 | 0  | 4  |
| Tea and sugar         | 0 | 0  | 2  |
| Milk                  | 0 | 0  | 1  |
|                       | 0 | 0  | 11 |

"It appears from this calculation," the writer continued, "that there will remain for the poor fellow—

|                   | £ | s. | d. |
|-------------------|---|----|----|
| Meat              | 0 | 0  | 0  |
| Rent              | 0 | 0  | 0  |
| Candles           | 0 | 0  | 0  |
| Soap              | 0 | 0  | 0  |
| Clothes           | 0 | 0  | 0  |
| Washing           | 0 | 0  | 0  |
| Coals             | 0 | 0  | 0  |
| Potatoes          | 0 | 0  | 0  |
| Anything          | 0 | 0  | 0  |
| Making a total of | 0 | 0  | 0  |

"We now give the—

### *Day's Bill at an Inn for a Poor Law Commissioner*

|                                                              | £ | s. | d. |
|--------------------------------------------------------------|---|----|----|
| Breakfast (including eggs, ham, cold meat, toast and coffee) | 0 | 2  | 0  |
| Luncheon (including cold meat and bottled ale)               | 0 | 1  | 6  |

| Dinner (including the usual course) | 0 | 3 | 0 |
|---|---|---|---|
| Bottle of Wine | 0 | 3 | 6 |
| Tea, cold meat, and eggs | 0 | 1 | 9 |
| Supper | 0 | 2 | 0 |
| Grog | 0 | 2 | 3 |
| | 0 | 16 | 0." |

## NOTES

1  *Indices.* For a discussion of some problems, see John Burnett, *A History of the Cost of Living* (1969), pp. 197–202. T. S. Ashton criticized the Silberling, Tucker, and the Gayer-Rostow-Schwartz indices in "The Standard of Living", *Jour. Econ. Hist.*, IX, 1949, Supplement, pp. 31 *et seq.* and in "Economic Fluctuations, 1790–1850", *Econ. Hist. Rev.*, VII, 1954–5, pp. 379–80. Since these criticisms a new index has been prepared by E. H. Phelps Brown and S. Hopkins (in *Economica*, new series, XXIII, 92 1956), but the authors warn that "our prices are not those at which the craftsman's wage was spent with the butcher, the baker, the candlestick maker" (p. 304). Their weighting (which gives more weight to meat and fish than to bread) does not correspond with the expenditure which we have noted among the London poor; but it is closer to that found in the budgets of better-paid workers—e.g. a well-paid scavenger (1851), *L.L. & L.P.*, II, pp. 261–2; a skilled London cutler (1851), F. Le Play, *Les Ouvriers Européens* (Tour, 1877), III, pp. 292–3; and a well-paid London tailor—a "society man"—in "Answers to Correspondents", 6 December 1851. For such men the Tucker and the Phelps Brown indices are helpful. Our budgets show bread well ahead of meat until the fall in the price of wheat at the end of the 1840s. They show a per capita bread consumption of 4·4 lb. per week, which appears to be low when set beside a pauper dietary of the 1830s which suggests 8·4 lb.; estimates for Lancashire factory workers and their families in 1841 which suggests 5·4 lb.; and a survey of 1862–3 which shows a range between 6·4 lb. and 5·5 lb. (for these see R. S. Neale, "The Standard of Living", *Econ. Hist. Rev.*, XIX, 3, 1966, p. 598; T. C. Barker, J. C. McKenzie and J. Yudkin (Eds.), *Our Changing Fare* (1966), pp. 70–1; D. J. Oddy, "Working-Class Diets in late Nineteenth Century Britain", *Econ. Hist. Rev.*, XXIII, 2, 1970, pp. 317–8.) But the relative weighting of items in our budgets seems to be confirmed by a questionnaire to 67 scavengers in 1851 (reported by Mayhew, *L.L. & L.P.* II, pp. 300–301), in which bread topped the great majority of budgets, followed closely by meat, then by tea and sugar, and then by butter. The majority of those questioned did not buy any bacon or potatoes, although a good many bought about 6d. worth of fish a week.

2  *Sources and Cautions.* The basic budget is taken from S. R. Bosanquet, *The Rights of the Poor and Christian Almsgiving Vindicated* (1841), p. 98 (Bosanquet, who was a barrister, offers a number of budgets (pp. 87–104): some part of his book had been previously published in the *British Critic*, XXVIII, July 1840, and the budgets may perhaps refer to that year.) Budgets for other years have been adjusted to make up the same quantities, but are based upon: 1825, Anon. [Mrs. Rundle?], *A New*

*System of Practical Domestic Economy* (new edition, 1825), pp. 397–401, 410; 1831, *Plain Statement of the Case of the Labourer* (1831), pp. 4 and 21; 1845 and 1851, Mayhew's enquiry into the effects of Free Trade upon the scavengers. *L.L. & L.P.* (1865), II, pp. 255–62 (supplemented by other evidence from Mayhew). One or two corrections have been made to the budgets in the light of information in the same source. All are London budgets with the possible exception of that for 1831, which is addressed to labourers in the Winchester area although it seems to quote London prices; in this budget we have adjusted the price from bacon to meat. Certain comments and cautions must still be offered: *Bread*—the budgets generally follow the movement of bread prices shown by B. R. Mitchell and P. Deane, *Abstract of British Historical Statistics* (Cambridge, 1962), p. 498, but are always at least 1d. a loaf beneath these. Bread varied in price from one district to another of London, and according to quality (not counting "seconds" and stale bread, which was cheaper again: *L.L. & L.P.*, II, p. 391). Taking Mayhew's informants, one finds the quartern loaf cited at 5d. or 4½d. in December 1849 (above, p. 209); at 5d. in July 1850 (above, p. 357); and at either 6d. or 5½d. in 1851 (*L.L. & L.P.*, II, pp. 255, 257, 333.) The tables in Mitchell and Deane show the average price of London bread in these years as 1849, 7d.; 1850, 6¾d.; 1851, 6¾d. *Meat*—the variation here could be much greater, and it presents problems. In Mrs. Rundle's budgets for 1825 she shows meat in her cheapest budget at 4½d. a pound, in her next budget at 6d., and thence ascending. We have compromised at 5d.; 6d. is the price quoted for "common joints"; but she notes elsewhere that on a Saturday night butchers will sometimes sell off veal or lamb at 3d. or 4d. a pound which had been worth in the morning 7d. or 8d. (*Mrs. Rundle's Young Housekeeper's Pocket Account Book* (1843), p. 163). It is not possible to adjust the budgets according to quality: it is more probable that the poor adjusted the quality according to their earnings. With high earnings, nothing was more prized than a large joint of good beef: a teetotal coal-whipper told Mayhew that he and his children clubbed their earnings each Sunday for a joint of 16 or 17 lb.! (*L.L. & L.P.*, III, p. 260). For the Londoners' meat diet see E. J. Hobsbawm, *Labouring Men* (1964), pp. 96–7; and for offal, fagots, &c., see Dorothy Davis, *A History of Shopping* (1966), p. 223; *L.L. & L.P.*, II, pp. 255, 257; T. C. Barker *et al*, op. cit. p. 20. *Beer*—Our budgets show ale at 7d. in 1825 and 1831, and porter thereafter at 1s. 2d. Porter was the thick, black, bitter beer to which Londoners had become habituated by the end of the 18th century (see P. Mathias, *The Brewing Industry in England, 1700–1830* (Cambridge, 1959), pp. vii, 15) and which was still their "favourite beverage" in the 1850s (J. R. McCulloch, *A Descriptive and Statistical Account of the British Empire* (4th edition, 1854), I, p. 757). As Mathias shows, the brewers held the price up by artificial means; after the ending of beer duties in 1830, the price settled down to a standard 4d. a quart pot, although Mayhew occasionally quotes a lower price (e.g. 3d., 1850, *L.L. & L.P.* III, p. 287). Mrs. Rundle in her 1825 budgets, clearly regarded porter as too expensive for the lower-paid workers, and substituted table ale; but other labourers' budgets show porter (e.g. *Labourer's Friend and Handicraftsman's Chronicle*, new series, IX, November 1822), so that we should perhaps correct the first two budgets: 1825, 7 pints of porter at 5½d. a quart (Mathias, op. cit. p. 546) = 1s. 7d.; 1831, 7 pints at 4d. a quart = 1s. 2d. Budget for 1825

10s. 1½d. Budget for 1831: 10s. 3d. *Fish*—Of 62 scavengers who replied to the 1851 questionnaire (*L.L. & L.P.* II, pp. 300–301) 3 spent 1s. a week on fish, 5 spent 8d., 23 spent 6d., 8 spent 4d. and 23 spent nothing. The destitute carpenter (above p. 357) who had no meat in his regular budget would buy fish if his earnings exceeded 5s. 7¼d. per week. A garret master (above p. 397) spoke of fish as an alternative to coffee for dinner ("sometimes they're almost as cheap"). The "slop" hatter (above, p. 449) alternated between herrings and sausage. Mayhew was informed by two butchers that cheap fish "was the great thing for the Irish and the poor needlewomen and the like, who were never at any time meat eaters"; among the rubbish-carters the Irish were "the principal consumers of cheap fish" (*L.L. & L.P.* II, pp. 257, 381). Mayhew estimated (ibid., II, p. 257) that the same quantity of fish that cost 6d. in 1845 will have only cost 4d. in 1851. *Taxes*—The budgets show clearly the effect of the following reductions: candles, excise repealed in 1831: soap, duties reduced in 1833: sugar, duties reduced in 1845, 1848, and 1850; coal, duty abolished in 1831: tea, no reduction, and a slight *increase* in duties after 1840. See J. Burnett, *Plenty and Want* (1966), pp. 8–11; G. R. Porter, *Progress of the Nation* (1843), Section V, Chapter 4 & 5; McCulloch, op. cit., I, p. 764. *Coal*—Tables in Mitchell and Deane, op. cit., p. 482 show the fall in the price of best London coal per chaldron (or ton). Our budgets shows a corresponding—or greater— fall, but estimates are difficult. The prices for 1825 and 1831 are taken by dry measure, which could vary greatly in weight according to size and quality of coal. Prices will have varied not only according to quality but according to season and according to the quantity bought: Mayhew's figures suggest that in 1850–1 coal will have been 1s. 4d. for a hundred-weight if bought in 14 lb. lots (above p. 357), 1s. 2d. if bought in 28 lb. lots (*L.L. & L.P.*, II, p. 214); and 1s. if bought in one lot (ibid., II, p. 96). The quantity necessary varied greatly according to such circumstances as whether fire was required (summer as well as winter) for any industrial process (like the cabinet-maker, above p. 397, who needed heat for his glue-pot, or the poor hatter, above p. 449, who spent 5d. a day (2s. 6d. a week) on fuel), and whether the family washing was sent out or done at home (Mayhew made careful estimates of this, *L.L. & L.P.* II, pp. 213–15). With these reservations we estimate as follows, taking 1¼ bushels for the first two dates and ½cwt. for the last three:

| | 1825 | | 1831 | | 1841 | | 1845 | | 1851 | |
|---|---|---|---|---|---|---|---|---|---|---|
| | s. | d. | s. | d. | s. | d. | s. | d. | s. | d. |
| Coal | 1 | 9 | 1 | 5½ | | 9½ | | 9 | | 8 |
| Budget | 9 | 1½ | 9 | 8 | 9 | 7 | 9 | 5 | 8 | 5 |
| Revised Total | 10 | 10½ | 11 | 1½ | 10 | 4½ | 10 | 2 | 9 | 1 |

It must again be emphasized that these totals take no account of rent, washing, boots and clothing; nor of milk, cheese, potatoes, vegetables, fish, salt and pepper, starch and blue, and other common necessaries; nor of tobacco, furniture, schooling, or amusements.

3  *Unseen Liabilities: Pawn*—for Mayhew's figures as to the value of goods in pawn see above p. 180 (needlewomen) and p. 206 (tailors), and *L.L. & L.P.* III, p. 251 (coal-whippers). *Petty purchases and "tick"*—see, among others, the docker who told Mayhew: "I had this afternoon a

quarter of an ounce of tea and a pennyworth of sugar"; purchases of 7 lb.
of coals; and the coal-whipper who estimated that he paid 1s. 8d. a
week extra for credit to the baker, butcher, and grocer: ibid., III., p.
317, II, p. 94, III, p. 251. *Adulteration*—this is discussed by J. Burnett,
*Plenty and Want*, Chapter 5. The trade in second-hand tea-leaves was
investigated by Mayhew: *L.L. & L.P.*, II, pp. 149–51. In view of the
widespread shift from tea to cheap coffee evidenced by Mayhew's informants it is interesting to note the comments of "A Ceylon Proprietor"
in 1851 : coffee was extensively mixed, not only with excessive quantities
of chicory, but with all kinds of "loathsome trash"—"beans, peas,
damaged corn, potatoes, acorns, horse-chestnuts, lupin seed, earth, brick-
dust, sawdust, dog-biscuits, tan . . ."; "in some pounds of coffee, the
actual quantity of that ingredient is two ounces." Anon. [A Ceylon
Proprietor], *A Statement of the Present Position of the Coffee Trade*
(1851), pp. 12–14.

E. P. T.

# SOURCES OF ILLUSTRATIONS

Cruikshank cartoons : Plate II.A from *Our Own Times* (1842); Plates XIII and XXIII from the *Comic Almanack*, edited by Cruikshank and the Mayhew brothers; Plates XV (1828) and XIX (1829) from *Scraps and Sketches*.

Plates VII, XXIV, XXVI, XXVII, XXXI, XXXII from G. Doré and B. Jerrold, *London. A Pilgrimage*, 1872.

Plates I and XXII from *London Labour and the London Poor*, 1851 and 1861.

Plates II.B., XX, XXX, and Fig. 1 from the Guildhall Library Prints Collection. We would like to thank Mr. Hyde, the prints librarian, for his great assistance.

Plates V and VI from *A Visit to Regent Street London* in the Guildhall Library.

Plate VIII from George Godwin, *London Shadows. A Glance at the Homes of the Thousands*, 1854.

Plates XI, XIV, XVIII, XXVIII from the *British Workman and Friend of the Sons of Toil*.

Plates XII (a composite of two sides of an advertising card), XXIX.B., and Figs. 2, 3, 4, and 5 from E. Witherstone (a scrapbook of) Advertising Broadsheets (1835–55) in the Victoria and Albert Museum Library.

Plate XVI from the *Illustrated London News*.

Plates XVII and XXV from *The Book of English Trades and Library of Useful Arts*, 8th ed., 1846.

Plate XXI : several editions of *The London Cabinet Book of Prices* are in the Library of the Victoria and Albert Museum.

Plate XXIX.A., Figs. 7 and 8 from G. Dodd, *Days at the Factories. Series I., London*, 1843.

We should like to thank Mr. David Rumsey for help with photographs.